Professional
Ajax
2nd Edition

Nicholas C. Zakas

Jeremy McPeak

Joe Fawcett

Wiley Publishing, Inc.

Professional Ajax, 2nd Edition

Published by
Wiley Publishing, Inc.
10475 Crosspoint Boulevard
Indianapolis, IN 46256
www.wiley.com

Published simultaneously in Canada

ISBN: 978-0-470-10949-6

Manufactured in the United States of America

10 9 8 7 6 5 4 3

Library of Congress Cataloging-in-Publication Data:
Zakas, Nicholas C.
  Professional Ajax / Nicholas C. Zakas, Jeremy McPeak, Joe Fawcett. -- 2nd ed.
     p. cm.
  Includes index.
  ISBN-13: 978-0-470-10949-6 (paper/website)
  ISBN-10: 0-470-10949-1 (paper/website)
  1. Ajax (Web site development technology) 2. Web sites--Design--Computer programs. 3. JavaScript (Computer program language) 4. Asynchronous transfer mode. 5. World Wide Web. I. McPeak, Jeremy, 1979- II. Fawcett, Joe, 1962- III. Title.
  TK5105.8885.A52Z35 2007
  005.13'3--dc22
                            2006103094

For general information on our other products and services please contact our Customer Care Department within the United States at (800) 762-2974, outside the United States at (317) 572-3993 or fax (317) 572-4002.

Wiley also publishes its books in a variety of electronic formats. Some content that appears in print may not be available in electronic books.

To mom, dad, Greg, Yiayia, and the rest of my family and friends who have supported me throughout my cross-country move.

—Nicholas C. Zakas

To the love of my life, Starla. Thank you for your love, patience, and encouragement.

—Jeremy McPeak

To my parents, Sheila and William, who instilled in me a love of reading. Thank you!

—Joe Fawcett

About the Authors

Nicholas C. Zakas has a BS in Computer Science from Merrimack College and an MBA from Endicott College. He is the author of *Professional JavaScript for Web Developers* (Wiley 2005) as well as several online articles. Nicholas works for Yahoo! as a frontend engineer and has worked in web development for more than 6 years, during which time he has helped develop web solutions in use at some of the largest companies in the world. Nicholas can be reached through his web site at www.nczonline.net.

Jeremy McPeak began tinkering with web development as a hobby in 1998. Currently working in the IT department of a school district, Jeremy has experience developing web solutions with JavaScript, PHP, and C#. He has written several online articles covering topics such as XSLT, WebForms, and C#. He is also co-author of *Beginning JavaScript, 3rd Edition* (Wiley 2007). Jeremy can be reached through his web site at www.wdonline.com.

Joe Fawcett started programming in the 1970s and briefly worked in IT upon leaving full-time education. He then pursued a more checkered career before returning to software development in 1994. In 2003 he was awarded the title of Microsoft Most Valuable Professional in XML for community contributions and technical expertise. He currently works in London as a developer for FTC Kaplan, a leading international provider of accountancy and business training, where he specializes in systems integration.

Credits

Senior Acquisitions Editor
Jim Minatel

Senior Development Editor
Kevin Kent

Technical Editor
Alexei Gorkov

Production Editor
Angela Smith

Copy Editor
Jeri Freedman

Editorial Manager
Mary Beth Wakefield

Production Manager
Tim Tate

Vice President and Executive Group Publisher
Richard Swadley

Vice President and Executive Publisher
Joseph B. Wikert

Graphics and Production Specialists
Sean Decker
Jennifer Mayberry
Amanda Spagnuolo
Alicia B. South

Quality Control Technician
Rob Springer

Project Coordinator
Bill Ramsey

Proofreading
Christopher Jones

Indexing
Johnna VanHoose Dinse

Anniversary Logo Design
Richard Pacifico

Acknowledgments

It takes many people to create a book such as this, and as such, we'd like to thank some people for their contributions to this work.

First and foremost, thanks to everyone at Wiley for their support: to Jim Minatel for starting the process once again, and Kevin Kent for putting up with all of the last-minute changes and course diversions throughout the process. Also, a thanks to our technical editor, Alexei Gorkov, for doing a fantastic job keeping us honest.

Last, a big thanks to those who provided feedback pre-publication including Peter Frueh, Adam Moore, Jenny Han, Matt Sweeney, Tyson Guskiken, Steve Carlson, and especially Hedger Wang, who suggested adding the chapter on request management.

Contents

Contents

Contents

Contents

Contents

Contents

Introduction

With recent advances in JavaScript, web developers have been able to create an unprecedented user experience in web applications. Breaking free of the "click and wait" paradigm that has dominated the web since its inception, developers can now bring features formerly reserved for desktop applications onto the web using a technique called Ajax.

Ajax is an all-encompassing term surrounding the use of asynchronous HTTP requests initiated by JavaScript for the purpose of retrieving information from the server without unloading the page. These requests may be executed in any number of ways and using any number of different data transmission formats. Combining this remote data retrieval with the interactivity of the Document Object Model (DOM) has bred a new generation of web applications that seem to defy all the traditional rules of what can happen on the web. Big companies such as Google, Yahoo!, and Microsoft have devoted resources specifically towards the goal of creating web applications that look and behave like desktop applications.

This book covers the various aspects of Ajax, including the different ways you can initiate HTTP requests to the server and the different formats that can be used to carry data back and forth. You will learn different Ajax techniques and patterns for executing client-server communication on your web site and in web applications.

Who This Book Is For

This book is aimed at two groups of readers:

❑ Web application developers looking to enhance the usability of their web sites and web applications.

❑ Intermediate JavaScript developers looking to further understand the language.

In addition, familiarity with the following related technologies is a strong indicator that this book is for you:

❑ XML

❑ XSLT

❑ Web Services

❑ PHP

❑ C#

❑ HTML

❑ CSS

This book is not aimed at beginners without a basic understanding of the aforementioned technologies. Also, a good understanding of JavaScript is vitally important to understanding this book. Those readers without such knowledge should instead refer to books such as *Beginning JavaScript, Second Edition* (Wiley 2004) and *Professional JavaScript for Web Developers* (Wiley Publishing, Inc., 2005).

What This Book Covers

Professional Ajax provides a developer-level tutorial of Ajax techniques, patterns, and use cases.

The book begins by exploring the roots of Ajax, covering how the evolution of the web and new technologies directly led to the development of Ajax techniques. A detailed discussion of how frames, JavaScript, cookies, XML, and XMLHttp requests (XHR) related to Ajax is included.

After this introduction, the book moves on to cover the implementation of specific Ajax techniques. Request brokers such as hidden frames, dynamic iframes, and XHR are compared and contrasted, explaining when one method should be used over another. To make this discussion clearer, a brief overview of HTTP requests and responses is included.

Once a basic understanding of the various request types is discussed, the book moves on to provide in-depth examples of how and when to use Ajax in a web site or web application. Different data transmission formats, including plain text, HTML, XML, and JSON are discussed for their advantages and disadvantages. Also included is a discussion on web services and how they may be used to perform Ajax techniques.

Next, more complex topics are covered. A chapter introducing a request management framework explores how to manage all of the requests inside of an Ajax application. Ajax debugging techniques are also discussed, including the popular FireBug and Fiddler utilities.

The last part of the book walks through the creation of two full-fledged Ajax web applications. The first, FooReader.NET, is an Ajax-powered RSS reader. The second, called AjaxMail, is an Ajax-enabled email system. Both of these applications incorporate many of the techniques discussed throughout the book.

How This Book Is Structured

This book begins by providing background about the origins of Ajax before moving into actual implementation. Next, the various ways to accomplish client-server communication are discussed, setting the stage for the rest of the book. It is recommended that you read the book straight through, as each chapter builds on information in the previous chapters.

The chapter-level breakdown is as follows:

1. **What Is Ajax?** Explains the origins of Ajax, the technologies involved, and where the term originated. Describes how Ajax developed as the web developed and who, if anyone, can claim ownership of the term and techniques.

2. **Ajax Basics.** Introduces the various ways to accomplish Ajax communication, including the hidden frame technique and XHR. The advantages and disadvantages of each approach are discussed, as well as guidelines as to when each should be used.

3. **Ajax Patterns.** Focuses on design patterns using Ajax. There are a variety of ways to incorporate Ajax into web sites and web applications; these have been organized into a handful of design patterns that describe best practices for Ajax incorporation.

4. **Ajax Libraries.** Explores three popular Ajax libraries: the Yahoo! Connection Manager, Prototype, and jQuery. The different approaches of these libraries are compared and contrasted, as well as recreating previous examples using the libraries.

5. **Request Management.** Discusses the management of XHR requests for an Ajax application, keeping in mind browser limitations. A methodology for creating a prioritization system is discussed, tying in aspects of the Ajax patterns discussed in Chapter 3.

6. **XML, XPath, and XSLT.** Introduces XML, XPath, and XSLT as complementary technologies to Ajax. The discussion centers on using XML as a data transmission format and using XPath/XSLT to access and display information.

7. **Syndication with RSS and Atom.** Deals with using Ajax together with the data syndication formats RSS and Atom to create a news-based widgets. Techniques from previous chapters are used heavily.

8. **JSON.** Introduces JavaScript Object Notation (JSON) as an alternate data transmission format for Ajax communications. Advantages and disadvantages over using XML and plain text are discussed.

9. **Comet.** Discusses the emergence of the server-push architecture called Comet. Several different techniques are discussed for implementing Comet depending upon browser capabilities.

10. **Maps and Mashups.** Explores two of the APIs available for Ajax maps: the Google Maps API and the Yahoo! Maps API. Each of the APIs is explored for their capabilities and limitations as well as their use of geocoding.

11. **Ajax Debugging Tools.** Discusses various methods of debugging Ajax requests. The FireBug extension for Firefox and the Fiddler tool for Internet Explorer are introduced as a way to debug HTTP requests.

12. **Web Site Widgets.** Brings the techniques from the previous chapters into focus by creating Ajax widgets that can be included in your web site.

13. **Ajax Frameworks.** Covers three Ajax frameworks: JPSPAN for PHP, DWR for Java/JSP, and Ajax.NET for the .NET framework. Each of these frameworks attempts to automate some part of the Ajax development process.

14. **ASP.NET AJAX Extensions (Atlas).** Introduces ASP.NET AJAX Extensions (formerly called Atlas) and how they can simplify the creation of Ajax applications. Assumes usage of .NET 2.0 for server-side code.

15. **Case Study: FooReader.NET.** Explores the creation of an RSS news aggregator. This application illustrates the use of server-side proxies, as well as the use of XML in JavaScript.

16. **Case Study: AjaxMail.** Walks through the development of a complete web application. This application, called AjaxMail, is an Ajax-based email system that uses many of the techniques described earlier in the book.

What You Need to Use This Book

To run the samples in the book, you will need the following:

❑ Windows 2000, Windows Server 2003, Windows XP, or Mac OS X

❑ Internet Explorer 5.5 or higher (Windows), Firefox 1.5 or higher (all platforms), Opera 9.0 or higher (all platforms), or Safari 2.0 or higher (Mac OS X).

The complete source code for the samples is available for download from our web site at www.wrox.com.

Conventions

To help you get the most from the text and keep track of what's happening, we've used a number of conventions throughout the book.

> **Boxes like this one hold important, not-to-be forgotten information that is directly relevant to the surrounding text.**

Tips, hints, tricks, and asides to the current discussion are offset and placed in italics like this.

As for styles in the text:

❑ We *highlight* new terms and important words when we introduce them.

❑ We show keyboard strokes like this: Ctrl+A.

❑ We show file names, URLs, and code within the text like so: persistence.properties.

❑ We present code in two different ways:

```
In code examples we highlight new and important code with a gray background.

The gray highlighting is not used for code that's less important in the present
context, or has been shown before.
```

Source Code

As you work through the examples in this book, you may choose either to type in all the code manually or to use the source code files that accompany the book. All of the source code used in this book is available for download at http://www.wrox.com. Once at the site, simply locate the book's title (either by using the Search box or by using one of the title lists) and click the Download Code link on the book's detail page to obtain all the source code for the book.

Because many books have similar titles, you may find it easiest to search by ISBN; this book's ISBN is 978-0-471-0949-6.

Once you download the code, just decompress it with your favorite compression tool. Alternately, you can go to the main Wrox code download page at `http://www.wrox.com/dynamic/books/download.aspx` to see the code available for this book and all other Wrox books.

See Appendix A for more information about what's included with the code download for this book.

Errata

We make every effort to ensure that there are no errors in the text or in the code. However, no one is perfect, and mistakes do occur. If you find an error in one of our books, like a spelling mistake or faulty piece of code, we would be very grateful for your feedback. By sending in errata you may save another reader hours of frustration and at the same time you will be helping us provide even higher quality information.

To find the errata page for this book, go to `http://www.wrox.com` and locate the title using the Search box or one of the title lists. Then, on the book details page, click the Book Errata link. On this page you can view all errata that has been submitted for this book and posted by Wrox editors. A complete book list including links to each book's errata is also available at `www.wrox.com/misc-pages/booklist.shtml`.

If you don't spot "your" error on the Book Errata page, go to `www.wrox.com/contact/techsupport.shtml` and complete the form there to send us the error you have found. We'll check the information and, if appropriate, post a message to the book's errata page and fix the problem in subsequent editions of the book.

p2p.wrox.com

For author and peer discussion, join the P2P forums at `p2p.wrox.com`. The forums are a Web-based system for you to post messages relating to Wrox books and related technologies and interact with other readers and technology users. The forums offer a subscription feature to e-mail you topics of interest of your choosing when new posts are made to the forums. Wrox authors, editors, other industry experts, and your fellow readers are present on these forums.

At `http://p2p.wrox.com` you will find a number of different forums that will help you not only as you read this book, but also as you develop your own applications. To join the forums, just follow these steps:

1. Go to `p2p.wrox.com` and click the Register link.
2. Read the terms of use and click Agree.

3. Complete the required information to join as well as any optional information you wish to provide and click Submit.

4. You will receive an e-mail with information describing how to verify your account and complete the joining process.

You can read messages in the forums without joining P2P but in order to post your own messages, you must join.

Once you join, you can post new messages and respond to messages other users post. You can read messages at any time on the Web. If you would like to have new messages from a particular forum e-mailed to you, click the Subscribe to this Forum icon by the forum name in the forum listing.

For more information about how to use the Wrox P2P, be sure to read the P2P FAQs for answers to questions about how the forum software works as well as many common questions specific to P2P and Wrox books. To read the FAQs, click the FAQ link on any P2P page.

1

What Is Ajax?

From 2001 to 2005, the World Wide Web went through a tremendous growth spurt in terms of the technologies and methodologies being used to bring this once-static medium to life. Online brochures and catalogs no longer dominated the Internet as web applications began to emerge as a significant portion of online destinations. Web applications differed from their web site ancestors in that they provided an instant service to their users, not just information. Whether for business process management or personal interests, developers were forced to create new interaction paradigms as users came to expect richer functionality.

Spurred on by little-known and lesser-used technologies that had been included in web browsers for some time, the Web took a bold step forward, shattering the traditional usage model that required a full page load every time new data or a new part of the application's logic was accessed. Companies began to experiment with dynamic reloading of portions of web pages, transmitting only a small amount of data to the client, resulting in a faster, and arguably better, user experience.

At the forefront of this movement was Google. After the search giant went public, new experiments conducted by Google engineers began popping up through a special part of the site called Google Labs (labs.google.com). Many of the projects at Google Labs, such as Google Suggest and Google Maps, involved only a single web page that was never unloaded but was constantly updated nevertheless. These innovations, which began to bring the affordances of desktop software interfaces into the confines of the browser, were praised around the Web as ushering in a new age in web development. And indeed they did.

Numerous open source and commercial products began development to take advantage of this new web application model. These projects explained their technology using a variety of terms such as JavaScript remoting, web remote procedure calls, and dynamic updating. Soon, however, a new term would emerge.

Ajax Is Born

In February 2005, Jesse James Garrett of Adaptive Path, LLC published an online article entitled, "Ajax: A New Approach to Web Applications" (still available at `www.adaptivepath.com/publications/essays/archives/000385.php`). In this essay, Garrett explained how he believed web applications were closing the gap between the Web and traditional desktop applications. He cited new technologies and several of the Google projects as examples of how traditionally desktop-based user interaction models were now being used on the Web. Then came the two sentences that would ignite a firestorm of interest, excitement, and controversy:

> *Google Suggest and Google Maps are two examples of a new approach to web applications that we at Adaptive Path have been calling Ajax. The name is shorthand for Asynchronous JavaScript + XML, and it represents a fundamental shift in what's possible on the Web.*

From that point forward, a tidal wave of Ajax articles, code samples, and debates began popping up all over the Web. Developers blogged about it, technology magazines wrote about it, and companies began hitching their products to it. But to understand what Ajax is, you first must understand how the evolution of several web technologies led to its development.

The Evolution of the Web

When Tim Berners-Lee crafted the first proposal for the World Wide Web in 1990, the idea was fairly simple: to create a "web" of interconnected information using hypertext and Uniform Resource Identifiers (URIs). The ability to link disparate documents from all around the world held huge potential for scholarly endeavors, where people would be able to access referenced material almost instantly. Indeed, the first version of the HyperText Markup Language (HTML) featured little more than formatting and linking commands, a platform not for building rich interactive software but rather for sharing the kinds of textual and illustrative information that dominated the late age of print. It was from these static web pages that the Web grew.

As the Web evolved, businesses saw potential in the ability to distribute information about products and services to the masses. The next generation of the Web saw an increased ability to format and display information as HTML also evolved to meet the needs and match the expectations of these new media-savvy users. But a small company called Netscape would soon be ready to push the evolution of the Web forward at a much faster pace.

JavaScript

Netscape Navigator was the first successful mainstream web browser, and as such, moved web technologies along quickly. However, Netscape often was ridiculed by standards organizations for implementing new technologies and extensions to existing technologies before the standards were in place (much as Microsoft is being chastised today for ignoring existing standards in its development of Internet Explorer). One such technology was JavaScript.

Originally named LiveScript, JavaScript was created by Brendan Eich of Netscape and included in version 2.0 of the browser (released in 1995). For the first time, developers were able to affect how a web page could interact with the user. Instead of making constant trips to the server and back for simple tasks such as data validation, it became possible to transfer this small bit of processing to the browser. This ability was very important at a time when most Internet users were connected through a 28.8 Kbps modem, turning every request to the server into a waiting game. Minimizing the number of times that the user had to wait for a response was the first major step toward the Ajax approach.

Frames

The original version of HTML intended for every document to be standalone, and it wasn't until HTML 4.0 that frames were officially introduced. The idea that the display of a web page could be split up into several documents was a radical one, and controversy brewed as Netscape chose to implement the feature before the HTML 4.0 standard was completed. Netscape Navigator 2.0 was the first browser to support frames and JavaScript together. This turned out to be a major step in the evolution of Ajax.

When the browser wars of the late 1990s began between Microsoft and Netscape, both JavaScript and frames became formalized. As more features were added to both technologies, creative developers began experimenting using the two together. Because a frame represented a completely separate request to the server, the ability to control a frame and its contents with JavaScript opened the door to some exciting possibilities.

The Hidden Frame Technique

As developers began to understand how to manipulate frames, a new technique emerged to facilitate client-server communication. The hidden frame technique involved setting up a frameset where one frame was set to a width or height of 0 pixels, its sole purpose being to initiate communication with the server. The hidden frame would contain an HTML form with specific form fields that could be dynamically filled out by JavaScript and submitted back to the server. When the frame returned, it would call another JavaScript function to notify the calling page that data had been returned. The hidden frame technique represented the first asynchronous request/response model for web applications.

While this was the first Ajax communication model, another technological advance was just around the corner.

Dynamic HTML and the DOM

In 1996, the Web was still mainly a static world. Although JavaScript and the hidden frame technique livened up the user interaction, there was still no way to change the display of a page without reloading it, aside from changing the values contained within form fields. Then came Internet Explorer 4.0.

At this point, Internet Explorer had caught up with the technology of market leader Netscape Navigator and even one-upped it in one important respect through the introduction of Dynamic HTML (DHTML). Although still in the development phase, DHTML represented a significant step forward from the days of static web pages, enabling developers to alter any part of a loaded page by using JavaScript. Along with the emergence of Cascading Style Sheets (CSS), DHTML reinvigorated web development, despite deep disparities between the paths Microsoft and Netscape followed during the early years of each discipline. Excitement in the developer community was justified, however, because combining DHTML with the hidden frame technique meant that any part of a page could be refreshed with server information at any time. This was a genuine paradigm shift for the Web.

DHTML never made it to a standards body, although Microsoft's influence would be felt strongly with the introduction of the Document Object Model (DOM) as the centerpiece of the standards effort. Unlike DHTML, which sought only to modify sections of a web page, the DOM had a more ambitious purpose: to provide a structure for an entire web page. The manipulation of that structure would then allow DHTML-like modifications to the page. This was the next step towards Ajax.

Iframes

Although the hidden frame technique became incredibly popular, it had a downside — one had to plan ahead of time and write a frameset anticipating the usage of hidden frames. When the `<iframe/>` element was introduced as an official part HTML 4.0 in 1997, it represented another significant step in the evolution of the Web.

Instead of defining framesets, developers could place iframes anywhere on a page. This enabled developers to forego framesets altogether and simply place invisible iframes (through the use of CSS) on a page to enable client-server communication. And when the DOM was finally implemented in Internet Explorer 5 and Netscape 6, it introduced the ability to dynamically create iframes on the fly, meaning that a JavaScript function could be used to create an iframe, make a request, and get the response — all without including any additional HTML in a page. This led to the next generation of the hidden frame technique: the hidden iframe technique.

XMLHttp

The browser developers at Microsoft must have realized the popularity of the hidden frame technique and the newer hidden iframe technique, because they decided to provide developers with a better tool for client-server interaction. That tool came in the form of an ActiveX object called XMLHttp, introduced in 2001.

One of the Microsoft extensions to JavaScript allowed the creation of ActiveX controls, Microsoft's proprietary programming objects. When Microsoft began supporting XML through a library called MSXML, the XMLHttp object was included. Although it carried the XML name, this object was more than just another way of manipulating XML data. Indeed, it was more like an ad hoc HTTP request that could be controlled from JavaScript. Developers had access to HTTP status codes and headers, as well as any data returned from the server. That data might be structured XML, pre-formatted swaths of HTML, serialized JavaScript objects, or data in any other format desired by the developer. Instead of using hidden frames or iframes, it was now possible to access the server programmatically using pure JavaScript, independent of the page load/reload cycle. The XMLHttp object became a tremendous hit for Internet Explorer developers.

With popularity mounting, developers at the open source Mozilla project began their own port of XMLHttp. Instead of allowing access to ActiveX, the Mozilla developers replicated the object's principal methods and properties in a native browser object, `XMLHttpRequest`. With both of the major browsers supporting some form of XMLHttp, the development of Ajax-type interfaces really took off and forced the fringe browsers, Opera and Safari, to support some form of XMLHttp as well (both chose to do so natively with an `XMLHttpRequest` object, mimicking Mozilla). Ironically enough, the popularity of this XMLHttp clone reached back to Microsoft, which introduced the native `XMLHttpRequest` object in Internet Explorer 7.

The Real Ajax

Despite the frequently asked questions attached to the end of Garrett's essay, some confusion still exists as to what Ajax really is. Put simply, Ajax is nothing more than an approach to web interaction. This approach involves transmitting only a small amount of information to and from the server in order to give the user the most responsive experience possible.

Instead of the traditional web application model where the browser itself is responsible for initiating requests to, and processing requests from, the web server, the Ajax model provides an intermediate layer—what Garrett calls an *Ajax engine*—to handle this communication. An Ajax engine is really just a JavaScript object or function that is called whenever information needs to be requested from the server. Instead of the traditional model of providing a link to another resource (such as another web page), each link makes a call to the Ajax engine, which schedules and executes the request. The request is done asynchronously, meaning that code execution doesn't wait for a response before continuing.

The server—which traditionally would serve up HTML, images, CSS, or JavaScript—is configured to return data that the Ajax engine can use. This data can be plain text, XML, or any other data format that you may need. The only requirement is that the Ajax engine can understand and interpret the data

When the Ajax engine receives the server response, it goes into action, often parsing the data and making several changes to the user interface based on the information it was provided. Because this process involves transferring less information than the traditional web application model, user interface updates are faster, and the user is able to do his or her work more quickly. Figure 1-1 is an adaptation of the figure in Garrett's article, displaying the difference between the traditional and Ajax web application models.

Traditional Web Application Model

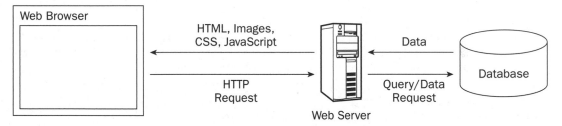

Ajax Web Application Model

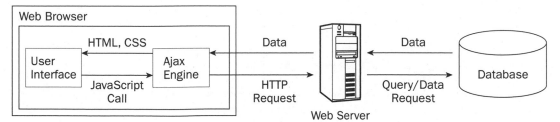

Figure 1-1

Ajax Principles

As a new web application model, Ajax is still in its infancy. However, several web developers have taken this new development as a challenge. The challenge is to define what makes a good Ajax web application versus what makes a bad or mediocre one. Michael Mahemoff (www.mahemoff.com), a software developer and usability expert, identified several key principles of good Ajax applications that are worth repeating:

❑ **Minimal traffic:** Ajax applications should send and receive as little information as possible to and from the server. In short, Ajax can minimize the amount of traffic between the client and the server. Making sure that your Ajax application doesn't send and receive unnecessary information adds to its robustness.

❑ **No surprises:** Ajax applications typically introduce different user interaction models than traditional web applications. As opposed to the web standard of click-and-wait, some Ajax applications use other user interface paradigms such as drag-and-drop or double-clicking. No matter what user interaction model you choose, be consistent so that the user knows what to do next.

❑ **Established conventions:** Don't waste time inventing new user interaction models that your users will be unfamiliar with. Borrow heavily from traditional web applications and desktop applications, so there is a minimal learning curve.

❑ **No distractions:** Avoid unnecessary and distracting page elements such as looping animations and blinking page sections. Such gimmicks distract the user from what he or she is trying to accomplish.

❑ **Accessibility:** Consider who your primary and secondary users will be and how they most likely will access your Ajax application. Don't program yourself into a corner so that an unexpected new audience will be completely locked out. Will your users be using older browsers or special software? Make sure you know ahead of time and plan for it.

❑ **Avoid entire page downloads:** All server communication after the initial page download should be managed by the Ajax engine. Don't ruin the user experience by downloading small amounts of data in one place but reloading the entire page in others.

❑ **User first:** Design the Ajax application with the users in mind before anything else. Try to make the common use cases easy to accomplish and don't be caught up with how you're going to fit in advertising or cool effects.

The common thread in all these principles is usability. Ajax is, primarily, about enhancing the web experience for your users; the technology behind it is merely a means to that end. By adhering to the preceding principles, you can be reasonably assured that your Ajax application will be useful and usable.

Technologies behind Ajax

Garrett's article mentions several technologies that he sees as parts of an Ajax solution. These are:

❑ **HTML/XHTML:** Primary content representation languages

❑ **CSS:** Provides stylistic formatting to XHTML

❑   **DOM:** Dynamic updating of a loaded page

❑   **XML:** Data exchange format

❑   **XSLT:** Transforms XML into XHTML (styled by CSS)

❑   **XMLHttp:** Primary communication broker

❑   **JavaScript:** Scripting language used to program an Ajax engine

In reality, all these technologies are available to be used in Ajax solutions, but only three are required: HTML/XHTML, DOM, and JavaScript. XHTML is obviously necessary for the displaying of information, while the DOM is necessary to change portions of an XHTML page without reloading it. The last part, JavaScript, is necessary to initiate the client-server communication and manipulate the DOM to update the web page. The other technologies in the list are helpful in fine-tuning an Ajax solution, but they aren't necessary.

There is one major component that Garrett neglected to mention in his article: the necessity of server-side processing. All of the previously listed technologies relate directly to the client-side Ajax engine, but there is no Ajax without a stable, responsive server waiting to send content to the engine. For this purpose, you can use the application server of your choice. Whether you choose to write your server-side components as PHP pages, Java servlets, or .NET components, you need only ensure that the correct data format is being sent back to the Ajax engine.

> *The examples in this book make use of as many server-side technologies as possible to give you enough information to set up Ajax communication systems on a variety of servers. Most of the examples covered in the book are available in PHP, JSP, and ASP.NET versions at* www.wrox.com.

Who Is Using Ajax?

A number of commercial web sites use Ajax techniques to improve their user experience. These sites are really more like web applications than traditional brochureware web sites that just display information because you visit it to accomplish a specific goal. The following are some of the more well-known and well-executed web applications that use Ajax.

Google Suggest

One of the first examples that developers cite when talking about Ajax is Google Suggest (www.google.com/webhp?complete=1). The interface is simply a clone of the main Google interface, which prominently features a text box to enter search terms. Everything appears to be the same until you start typing in the textbox. As you type, Google Suggest requests suggestions from the server, showing you a drop-down list of search terms that you may be interested in. Each suggestion is displayed with a number of results available for the given term to help you decide (see Figure 1-2).

This simple client-server interaction is very powerful and effective without being obtrusive to the user. The interface is responsive beyond what you may have learned to expect from a web application; it updates no matter how quickly you type and, as with autocomplete features in desktop software, you can use the up and down arrows to highlight and select each item in the suggestions list. Although still in beta, expect to see this approach make its way into the main Google page eventually.

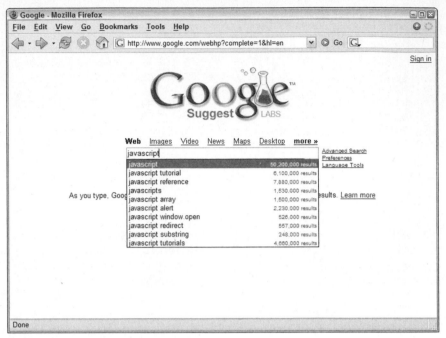

Figure 1-2

Gmail

Gmail, Google's free e-mail service, has been raved about as a marvel of client-server interaction in the age of Ajax. When you first log in to Gmail, a user interface engine is loaded into one of the few iframes the application uses. All further requests back to the server occur through this user interface engine through an XMLHttp object. The data being transferred back and forth is JavaScript code, which makes for fast execution once downloaded by the browser. These requests serve as instructions to the user interface engine as to what should be updated on the screen.

Additionally, the Gmail application uses several frames and iframes to manage and cache big user interface changes. The extremely complicated use of frames enables Gmail to function properly with the Back and Forward buttons, which is one of the advantages of using frames or iframes instead of or in conjunction with XMLHttp (discussed later in the book).

The biggest win for Gmail is its usability. The user interface, as shown in Figure 1-3, is simple and uncluttered. Interaction with the user and communication with the server is all seamless. Once again, Google used Ajax to improve on an already simple concept to provide an exceptional user experience.

Figure 1-3

Google Maps

Another part of Google's dominant Ajax web applications is Google Maps (maps.google.com). Designed to compete with well-established mapping sites, Google Maps uses Ajax to avoid reloading its main page at all (see Figure 1-4).

Unlike other mapping web applications, Google Maps enables you to drag the map to move it in various directions. The dragging code is nothing new to JavaScript developers, but the tiling of the map and seemingly endless scrolling effect are another story. The map is broken up into a series of images that are tiled together to make the appearance of a contiguous image. The number of images used to display the map is finite, as creating new images every time the user moves the map would quickly lead to memory problems. Instead, the same images are used over and over to display different segments of the map.

The client-server communication is done through a hidden iframe. Whenever you do a search or ask for new directions, this information is submitted and returned within that iframe. The data returned is in XML format and is passed to a JavaScript function (the Ajax engine) to handle. This XML is then used in a variety of different ways: some is used to call the correct map images, and some is transformed using XSLT into HTML and displayed in the main window. The bottom line is that this complex Ajax application is, as of late 2006, the number two destination for mapping on the Web.

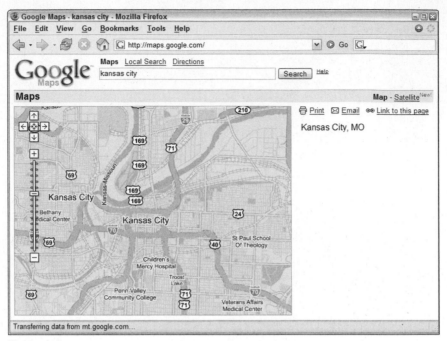

Figure 1-4

A9

Amazon.com is world famous for being an online marketplace for just about anything, but when it released a search engine, it did so with little fanfare and attention. The introduction of A9 (www.a9.com) showed off enhanced searching, enabling you to search different types of information simultaneously. For web and image searches it uses MSN to fetch results. It performs searches of books on Amazon.com and movies on IMDb (Internet Movie Database). Searches for Yellow Pages, Wikipedia, and Answers.com debuted in mid-2005.

What makes A9 unique is how its user interface works. When you perform a search, the different types of results are displayed in different areas of the page (see Figure 1-5).

On the search results page, you have the option of selecting other searches to perform using the same criteria. When you select a check box corresponding to a type of search, the search is performed behind the scenes using a combination of hidden iframes and XMLHttp. The user interface shifts to allow room for the extra search results, which are loaded as soon as they are received from the server. The result is a more responsive search results page that doesn't need to be reloaded when you want to search on different types of information.

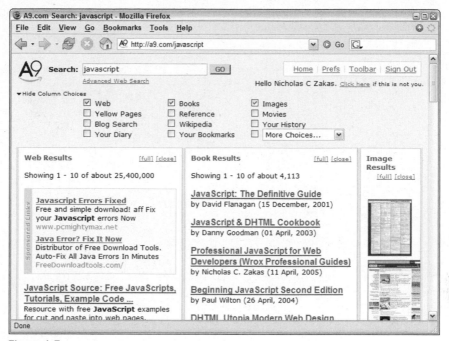

Figure 1-5

Yahoo! News

Also introduced in 2005 was a new design for the Yahoo! News site (news.yahoo.com). The new design features an interesting enhancement: when you move your mouse over a particular headline, a small box pops up with a summary and, optionally, a photo associated with that story (see Figure 1-6).

The photo information and summary are retrieved from the server using XMLHttp and inserted into the page dynamically. This is a perfect example of how Ajax can be used to enhance a web page. Rather than making Ajax the primary usage mode, the Yahoo! News site is completely usable without Ajax; the Ajax functionality is used only to add a more responsive user experience in browsers that support it. Underneath is a semantically correct HTML page that is laid out logically even without CSS formatting.

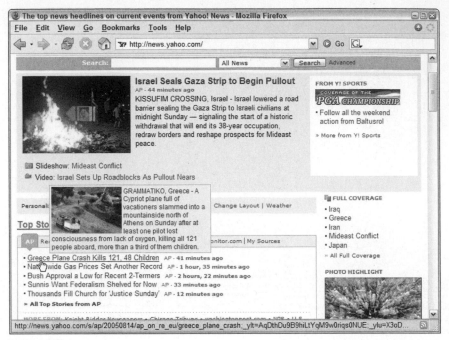

Figure 1-6

Bitflux Blog

Another great example of using Ajax only as an enhancement is Bitflux Blog (`blog.bitflux.ch`), which features a technology called LiveSearch. LiveSearch works in conjunction with the search box on the site. As you type into the box, a list of possible search results is displayed immediately below (see Figure 1-7).

The search results are retrieved using XMLHttp as an HTML string that is then inserted into the page. You can search the site the old-fashioned way as well: by filling in the text box and pressing Enter. The LiveSearch Ajax functionality is just an enhancement to the overall site and isn't required to search.

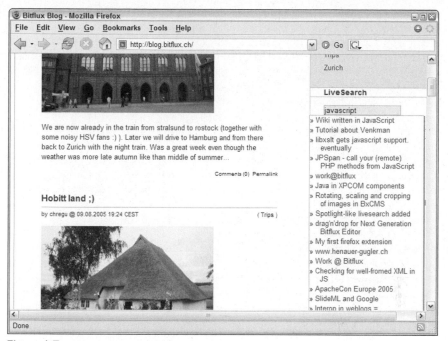

Figure 1-7

Confusion and Controversy

Despite the popularity of the term *Ajax*, it has been met with its fair share of dissenters and controversy. Some believe that Ajax is an aberration of what the Web was moving toward before Ajax entered the picture. The proponents of semantic HTML design, accessibility, and the separation of content and presentation were gaining ground and acceptance among web developers, and some believe that the popularity of Ajax has pushed that movement into the background. The belief of these detractors is that Ajax promotes creating presentation within JavaScript, thus turning it into a messy mix similar to the early days of server-side scripting. Many believe that accessibility will suffer if more developers turn to Ajax solutions.

Others have spent a significant amount of time dissecting Garrett's article and disproving several assumptions that he makes. For instance, the article mentions using XML and XMLHttp repeatedly as being the core of the Ajax model, but many of the examples he lists don't use them. Gmail and Google Maps use these technologies sparingly; Google Suggest uses only XMLHttp and uses JavaScript arrays instead of XML for data exchange. Critics also point out that the technical explanation of Ajax in the article is completely misleading, citing several technologies that are not only unnecessary (such as XML and XMLHttp) but unlikely to be used in many cases (such as XSLT).

Another big argument surrounding Ajax and Garrett's Adaptive Path article is that it's merely a new name for a technique that has already been used for some time. Although this type of data retrieval could be enacted in Netscape Navigator 2.0, it really became more prominent in 2001–2002, especially with the publication of an article on Apple's Developer Connection site entitled, "Remote Scripting With IFRAME" (available at `http://developer.apple.com/internet/webcontent/iframe.html`). This article is widely believed to be the first mainstream article published on Ajax-like methodologies. The term *remote scripting* never caught on with quite the staying power as Ajax.

Still others scoff at the term *Ajax* and Garrett's article, believing that its creation was little more than a marketing gimmick for Garrett's company, Adaptive Path, LLC. Some believe that creating a name for a technique that already existed is disingenuous and a clear sign of ill intent. Regardless of this and other controversies surrounding Ajax, the approach now has a name that developers are quickly becoming familiar with, and with that comes a need for a deeper understanding and explanation so that it may be used in the best possible ways.

Ajax and Web 2.0

Shortly after the term *Ajax* was coined, another term began popping up. Web 2.0 was originally the name of a conference held by O'Reilly Media and CMP Media in late 2005. After that, the term *Web 2.0* took on a life of its own and began popping up all over the Internet in descriptions of how the Web had changed. To try to rein in the term before it got out of control, Tim O'Reilly (founder and CEO of O'Reilly) wrote an article entitled, "What is Web 2.0" (available online at `www.oreillynet.com/pub/a/oreilly/tim/news/2005/09/30/what-is-web-20.html`), describing the concepts that he believes Web 2.0 represents. These concepts include:

❑   The Web as services, not software

❑   The group mentality of the Web — users encouraged to participate (as with tagging, blogging, networking, and so on)

❑   Separation of data and presentation – data can be represented in any number of ways and combined with any other data sources (called *mashups*)

❑   Richer, more responsive user experience

Ajax is tied to the last point, creating a richer experience for the user. To be clear, Ajax is not synonymous with Web 2.0, and Web 2.0 doesn't speak just of Ajax; Web 2.0 is about a shift in the very character of the Web. While Ajax is an important part of creating the next generation user experience that Web 2.0 signifies, it is just a one piece of a much larger puzzle.

Summary

This chapter introduced you to the basic premise of Ajax. Short for Asynchronous JavaScript + XML, the term *Ajax* was coined by Jesse James Garrett in an article posted on the Adaptive Path, LLC web site. The article introduced Ajax as a new user interaction model for web applications in which full page loads are no longer necessary.

This chapter also explored the evolution of the Web in relation to the development of technologies that enable Ajax to be a reality today. Ajax owes its existence to the introduction of both JavaScript and frames into web browsers, which made asynchronous data retrieval using JavaScript theoretically possible in Netscape Navigator 2.0. Throughout the evolution of new web technologies, Ajax methodologies such as the hidden frame technique developed. The introduction of iframes and XMLHttp really pushed Ajax development forward.

Although Ajax can be used to accomplish many things, it is best used to enhance the user experience rather than providing cool effects. This chapter discussed several Ajax principles, all circling back to the requirements of the user being paramount to anything else in web application development.

Several of the most popular Ajax applications were also discussed, including Google Suggest, Gmail, Google Maps, Yahoo! News, and the Bitflux Blog.

Finally, the chapter covered the controversy surrounding Ajax, Garrett's article, and Ajax's place on the Web. Some feel that the popularization of Ajax will lead to an overall lack of accessibility, whereas others question Garrett's motive for writing the now-famous article. As with all approaches, Ajax is at its best when used in a logical enhancement to a well-designed web application.

2

Ajax Basics

The driving force behind Ajax is the interaction between the client (web browser) and the server. Previously, the understanding of this communication was limited to those who developed purely on the server-side using languages such as Perl and C. Newer technologies such as ASP.NET, PHP, and JSP encouraged more of a mix of client- and server-side techniques for software engineers interested in creating web applications, but they often lacked a full understanding of all client-side technologies (such as JavaScript). Now the pendulum has swung in the other direction, and client-side developers need to understand more about server-side technology in order to create Ajax solutions.

HTTP Primer

Central to a good grasp of Ajax techniques is hypertext transmission protocol (HTTP), the protocol to transmit web pages, images, and other types of files over the Internet to your web browser and back. Whenever you type a URL into the browser, an "http://" is prepended to the address, indicating that you will be using HTTP to access the information at the given location. (Most browsers support a number of different protocols as well, most notably FTP.)

Note that this section covers only those aspects of HTTP that are of interest to Ajax developers. It does not constitute an HTTP reference guide or tutorial.

HTTP consists of two parts: a request and a response. When you type a URL in a web browser, the browser creates and sends a request on your behalf. This request contains the URL that you typed in as well as some information about the browser itself. The server receives this request and sends back a response. The response contains information about the request as well as the data located at the URL (if any). It's up to the browser to interpret the response and display the web page (or other resource).

HTTP Requests

The format of an HTTP request is:

```
<request-line>
<headers>
<blank line>
[<request-body>]
```

In an HTTP request, the first line must be a request line indicating the type of request, the resource to access, and the version of HTTP being used. Next, a section of headers indicate additional information that may be of use to the server. After the headers is a blank line, which can optionally be followed by additional data (called the *body*).

There are a large number of request types defined in HTTP, but the two of interest to Ajax developers are GET and POST. Anytime you type a URL in a web browser, the browser sends a GET request to the server for that URL, which basically tells the server to get the resource and send it back. Here's what a GET request for www.wrox.com might look like:

```
GET / HTTP/1.1
Host: www.wrox.com
User-Agent: Mozilla/5.0 (Windows; U; Windows NT 5.1; en-US; rv:1.7.6)
          Gecko/20050225 Firefox/1.0.1
Connection: Keep-Alive
```

The first part of the request line specifies this as a GET request. The second part of that line is a forward slash (/), indicating that the request is for the root of the domain. The last part of the request line specifies to use HTTP version 1.1 (the alternative is 1.0). And where is the request sent? That's where the second line comes in.

The second line is the first header in the request, Host. The Host header indicates the target of the request. Combining Host with the forward slash from the first line tells the server that the request is for www.wrox.com/. (The Host header is a requirement of HTTP 1.1; the older version 1.0 didn't require it.) The third line contains the User-Agent header, which is accessible to both server- and client-side scripts and is the cornerstone of most browser-detection logic. This information is defined by the browser that you are using (in this example, Firefox 1.0.1) and is automatically sent on every request. The last line is the Connection header, which is typically set to Keep-Alive for browser operations (it can also be set to other values, but that's beyond the scope of this book). Note that there is a single blank line after this last header. Even though there is no request body, the blank line is required.

If you were to request a page under the www.wrox.com domain, such as http://www.wrox.com/books, the request would look like this:

```
GET /books/ HTTP/1.1
Host: www.wrox.com
User-Agent: Mozilla/5.0 (Windows; U; Windows NT 5.1; en-US; rv:1.7.6)
          Gecko/20050225 Firefox/1.0.1
Connection: Keep-Alive
```

Note that only the first line changed, and it contains only the part that comes after www.wrox.com in the URL.

Sending parameters for a GET request requires that the extra information be appended to the URL itself. The format looks like this:

```
URL?name1=value1&name2=value2&..&nameN=valueN
```

This information, called a *query string*, is duplicated in the request line of the HTTP request, as follows:

```
GET /books/?name=Professional%20Ajax HTTP/1.1
Host: www.wrox.com
User-Agent: Mozilla/5.0 (Windows; U; Windows NT 5.1; en-US; rv:1.7.6)
            Gecko/20050225 Firefox/1.0.1
Connection: Keep-Alive
```

Note that the text "Professional Ajax" had to be encoded, replacing the space with %20, in order to send it as a parameter to the URL. This is called *URL encoding* and is used in many parts of HTTP. (JavaScript has built-in functions to handle URL encoding and decoding; these are discussed later in the chapter). The name-value pairs are separated with an ampersand. Most server-side technologies will decode the request body automatically and provide access to these values in some sort of logical manner. Of course, it is up to the server to decide what to do with this data.

> **Browsers often send many more headers than the ones discussed in this section. The examples here have been kept short for simplicity.**

The POST request, on the other hand, provides additional information to the server in the request body. Typically, when you fill out an online form and submit it, that data is being sent through a POST request.

Here's what a typical POST request looks like:

```
POST / HTTP/1.1
Host: www.wrox.com
User-Agent: Mozilla/5.0 (Windows; U; Windows NT 5.1; en-US; rv:1.7.6)
            Gecko/20050225 Firefox/1.0.1
Content-Type: application/x-www-form-urlencoded
Content-Length: 40
Connection: Keep-Alive
```

```
name=Professional%20Ajax&publisher=Wiley
```

You should note a few differences between a POST request and a GET request. First, the request line begins with "POST" instead of "GET," indicating the type of request. You'll notice that the Host and User-Agent headers are still there, along with two new ones. The Content-Type header indicates how the request body is encoded. Browsers always encode post data as application/x-www-form-urlencoded, which is the MIME type for simple URL encoding. The Content-Length header indicates the byte length of the request body. After the Connection header and the blank line is the request body.

As with most browser POST requests, this is made up of simple name-value pairs, where name is Professional Ajax and publisher is Wiley. You may recognize that this format is the same as that of query string parameters on URLs.

As mentioned previously, there are other HTTP request types, but they follow the same basic format as GET and POST. The next step is to take a look at what the server sends back in response to an HTTP request.

For security purposes, GET requests should be used to retrieve information only. If data needs to be added, updated, or deleted, a POST request should be used.

HTTP Responses

The format of an HTTP response, which is very similar to that of a request, is:

```
<status-line>
<headers>
<blank line>
[<response-body>]
```

As you can see, the only real difference in a response is that the first line contains status information instead of request information. The status line tells you about the requested resource by providing a status code. Here's a sample HTTP response:

```
HTTP/1.1 200 OK
Date: Sat, 31 Dec 2005 23:59:59 GMT
Content-Type: text/html;charset=ISO-8859-1
Content-Length: 122

<html>
    <head>
        <title>Wrox Homepage</title>
    </head>
    <body>
        <!-- body goes here -->
    </body>
</html>
```

In this example, the status line gives an HTTP status code of 200 and a message of OK. The status line always contains the status code and the corresponding short message so that there isn't any confusion. The most common status codes are:

❑   **200 (OK):** The resource was found and all is well.

❑   **304 (NOT MODIFIED):** The resource has not been modified since the last request. This is used most often for browser cache mechanisms.

❑   **401 (UNAUTHORIZED):** The client is not authorized to access the resource. Often, this will cause the browser to ask for a user name and password to log in to the server.

❑ **403 (FORBIDDEN):** The client failed to gain authorization. This typically happens if you fail to log in with a correct user name and password after a 401.

❑ **404 (NOT FOUND):** The resource does not exist at the given location.

Following the status line are some headers. Typically, the server will return a `Date` header indicating the date and time that the response was generated. (Servers typically also return some information about themselves, although this is not required.) The next two headers should look familiar as well, as they are the same `Content-Type` and `Content-Length` headers used in POST requests. In this case, the `Content-Type` header specifies the MIME type for HTML (text/html) with an encoding of ISO-8859-1 (which is standard for the United States English resources). The body of the response simply contains the HTML source of the requested resource (although it could also contain plain text or binary data for other types of resources). It is this data that the browser displays to the user.

Note that there is no indication as to the type of request that asked for this response; however, this is of no consequence to the server. It is up to the client to know what type of data should be sent back for each type of request and to decide how that data should be used.

Ajax Communication Techniques

Now that you understand the basics of how HTTP communication works, it's time to look into enacting such communication from within a web page. As you know, there are a lot of requests going back and forth between the browser and server while you are surfing the Web. Initially, all these requests happened because the user made an overt action that required such a step. Ajax techniques free developers from waiting for the user to make such an action, allowing you to create a call to the server at any time.

As discussed in Chapter 1, Ajax communication supports a number of different techniques. Each of these techniques has advantages and disadvantages, so it's important to understand which one to use in which situation.

The Hidden Frame Technique

With the introduction of HTML frames, the hidden frame technique was born. The basic idea behind this technique is to create a frameset that has a hidden frame that is used for client-server communication. You can hide a frame by setting its width or height to 0 pixels, effectively removing it from the display. Although some early browsers (such as Netscape 4) couldn't fully hide frames, often leaving thick borders, this technique still gained popularity among developers.

The Pattern

The hidden frame technique follows a very specific, four-step pattern (see Figure 2-1). The first step always begins with the visible frame, where the user is interacting with a web page. Naturally, the user is unaware that there is a hidden frame (in modern browsers, it is not rendered) and goes about interacting with the page as one typically would. At some point, the user performs an action that requires additional data from the server. When this happens, the first step in the process occurs: a JavaScript function call is made to the hidden frame. This call can be as simple as redirecting the hidden frame to another page or as complicated as posting form data. Regardless of the intricacy of the function, the result is the second step in the process: a request made to the server.

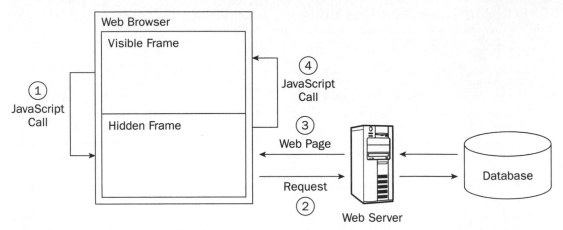

Figure 2-1

The third step in the pattern is a response received from the server. Because you are dealing with frames, this response must be another web page. This web page must contain the data requested from the server as well as some JavaScript to transfer that data to the visible frame. Typically, this is done by assigning an `onload` event handler in the returned web page that calls a function in the visible frame after it has been fully loaded (this is the fourth step). With the data now in the visible frame, it is up to that frame to decide what to do with the data.

Hidden Frame GET Requests

Now that the hidden frame technique has been explained, it's time to learn more about it. As with any new technique, the best way to learn is to work through an example. For this example, you'll be creating a simple lookup page where a customer service representative can look up information about a customer. Since this is the first example in the book, it is very simple: The user will enter a customer ID and receive in return information about the customer. Since this type of functionality will most often be used with a database, it is necessary to do some server-side programming as well. This example uses PHP, an excellent open source server-side language, and MySQL (available at www.mysql.org), an open source database that ties together very well with PHP.

> **In PHP 5, MySQL support is disabled by default. For information on enabling MySQL support in PHP 5, visit** www.php.net/mysql/.

First, before customer data can be looked up, you must have a table to contain it. You can create the customer table by using the following SQL script:

```sql
CREATE TABLE `Customers` (
  `CustomerId` int(11) NOT NULL auto_increment,
  `Name` varchar(255) NOT NULL default '',
  `Address` varchar(255) NOT NULL default '',
  `City` varchar(255) NOT NULL default '',
  `State` varchar(255) NOT NULL default '',
  `Zip` varchar(255) NOT NULL default '',
  `Phone` varchar(255) NOT NULL default '',
```

```
    `Email` varchar(255) NOT NULL default '',
    PRIMARY KEY  (`CustomerId`)
) TYPE=MyISAM COMMENT='Sample Customer Data';
```

The most important field in this table is `CustomerId`, which is what you will use to look up the customer information.

You can download this script, along with some sample data, from www.wrox.com.

With the database table all set up, it's time to move on to the HTML code. To use the hidden frame technique, you must start with an HTML frameset, such as this:

```
<!DOCTYPE html PUBLIC "-//W3C//DTD XHTML 1.0 Frameset//EN"
"http://www.w3.org/TR/xhtml1/DTD/xhtml1-frameset.dtd">
<html>
  <head>
    <title>Hidden Frame GET Example</title>
  </head>
  <frameset rows="100%,0" style="border: 0px">
    <frame name="displayFrame" src="DataDisplay.php" noresize="noresize" />
    <frame name="hiddenFrame" src="about:blank" noresize="noresize" />
  </frameset>
</html>
```

The important part of this code is the `rows` attribute of the `<frameset/>` element. By setting it to `100%,0`, browsers know not to display the body of the second frame, whose name is `hiddenFrame`. Next, the `style` attribute is used to set the border to 0, ensuring that there isn't a visible border around each frame. The final important step in the frameset declaration is to set the `noresize` attributes on each frame so that the user can't inadvertently resize the frames and see what's in the hidden one; the contents of the hidden frame are never meant to be part of the visible interface.

Next up is the page to request and display the customer data (`DataDisplay.php`). This is a relatively simple page, consisting of a textbox to enter the customer ID, a button to execute the request, and a `<div/>` element to display the retrieved customer information:

```
<p>Enter customer ID number to retrieve information:</p>
<p>Customer ID: <input type="text" id="txtCustomerId" value="" /></p>
<p><input type="button" value="Get Customer Info"
          onclick="requestCustomerInfo()" /></p>
<div id="divCustomerInfo"></div>
```

You'll notice that the button calls a function named `requestCustomerInfo()`, which interacts with the hidden frame to retrieve information. It simply takes the value in the textbox and adds it to the query string of `GetCustomerData.php`, creating a URL in the form of `GetCustomerData.php?id=23`. This URL is then assigned to the hidden frame. Here's the function:

```
function requestCustomerInfo() {
    var sId = document.getElementById("txtCustomerId").value;
    top.frames["hiddenFrame"].location = "GetCustomerData.php?id=" + sId;
}
```

The first step in this function is to retrieve the customer identification number from the textbox. To do so, `document.getElementById()` is called with the textbox ID, `"txtCustomerId"`, and the `value` property is retrieved. (The `value` property holds the text that is inside the textbox.) Then, this ID is added to the string `"GetCustomerData.php?id="` to create the full URL. The second line creates the URL and assigns it to the hidden frame. To get a reference to the hidden frame, you first need to access the topmost window of the browser using the `top` object. That object has a `frames` array, within which you can find the hidden frame. Since each frame is just another window object, you can set its `location` to the desired URL.

That's all it takes to request the information. Note that because the request is a GET (passing information in the query string), it makes the request very easy. (You'll see how to execute a POST request using the hidden frame technique shortly.)

In addition to the `requestCustomerInfo()` function, you'll need another function to display the customer information after it is received. This function, `displayCustomerInfo()`, will be called by the hidden frame when it returns with data. The sole argument is a string containing the customer data to be displayed:

```
function displayCustomerInfo(sText) {
    var divCustomerInfo = document.getElementById("divCustomerInfo");
    divCustomerInfo.innerHTML = sText;
}
```

In this function, the first line retrieves a reference to the `<div/>` element that will display the data. In the second line, the customer info string (`sText`) is assigned into the `innerHTML` property of the `<div/>` element. Using `innerHTML` makes it possible to embed HTML into the string for formatting purposes. This completes the code for the main display page. Now it's time to create the server-side logic.

The basic code for `GetCustomerData.php` is a very basic HTML page with PHP code in two places:

```
<!DOCTYPE html PUBLIC "-//W3C//DTD XHTML 1.0 Transitional//EN"
"http://www.w3.org/TR/xhtml1/DTD/xhtml1-transitional.dtd">
<html xmlns="http://www.w3.org/1999/xhtml" >
    <head>
        <title>Get Customer Data</title>
<?php

    //php code

?>
    </head>
    <body>
        <div id="divInfoToReturn"><?php echo $sInfo ?></div>
    </body>
</html>
```

In this page, the first PHP block will contain the logic to retrieve customer data (which is discussed shortly). The second PHP block outputs the variable `$sInfo`, containing customer data, into a `<div/>`. It is from this `<div/>` that the data is read and sent to the display frame. To do so, create a JavaScript function that is called when the page has loaded completely:

```
window.onload = function () {
    var divInfoToReturn = document.getElementById("divInfoToReturn");
    top.frames["displayFrame"].displayCustomerInfo(divInfoToReturn.innerHTML);
};
```

This function is assigned directly to the `window.onload` event handler. It first retrieves a reference to the `<div/>` that contains the customer information. Then, it accesses the display frame using the `top.frames` array and calls the `displayCustomerInfo()` function defined earlier, passing in the `innerHTML` of the `<div/>`. That's all the JavaScript it takes to send the information where it belongs. But how does the information get there in the first place? Some PHP code is needed to pull it out of the database.

The first step in the PHP code is to define all of the pieces of data you'll need. In this example, those pieces of data are the customer ID to look up, the `$sInfo` variable to return the information, and the information necessary to access the database (the database server, the database name, a user name, a password, and the SQL query string):

```php
<?php

    $sID = $_GET["id"];
    $sInfo = "";

    $sDBServer = "your.databaser.server";
    $sDBName = "your_db_name";
    $sDBUsername = "your_db_username";
    $sDBPassword = "your_db_password";
    $sQuery = "Select * from Customers where CustomerId=".$sID;


    //More here
?>
```

This code begins with retrieving the `id` argument from the query string. PHP organizes all query string arguments into the `$_GET` array for easy retrieval. This `id` is stored in `$sID` and is used to create the SQL query string stored in `$sQuery`. The `$sInfo` variable is also created here and set to be an empty string. All the other variables in this code block contain information specific to your particular database configuration; you'll have to replace these with the correct values for your implementation.

Having captured the user's input and set up the foundation for the connection to the database, the next step is to invoke that database connection, execute the query, and return the results. If there is a customer with the given ID, `$sInfo` is filled with an HTML string containing all the data, including the creation of a link for the e-mail address. If the customer ID is invalid, `$sInfo` is filled with an error message that will be passed back to the display frame:

```php
<?php

    $sID = $_GET["id"];
    $sInfo = "";

    $sDBServer = "your.databaser.server";
    $sDBName = "your_db_name";
    $sDBUsername = "your_db_username";
    $sDBPassword = "your_db_password";
```

```
        $sQuery = "Select * from Customers where CustomerId=".$sID;

        $oLink = mysql_connect($sDBServer,$sDBUsername,$sDBPassword);
        @mysql_select_db($sDBName) or $sInfo="Unable to open database";


        if ($sInfo == "") {
            if($oResult = mysql_query($sQuery) and mysql_num_rows($oResult) > 0) {
                $aValues = mysql_fetch_array($oResult,MYSQL_ASSOC);
                $sInfo = $aValues['Name']."<br />".$aValues['Address']."<br />".
                        $aValues['City']."<br />".$aValues['State']."<br />".
                        $aValues['Zip']."<br /><br />Phone: ".$aValues['Phone']."<br
/>".

                        "<a      href=\"mailto:".$aValues['Email']."\">".
                        $aValues['Email']."</a>";
                mysql_free_result($oResult);
            } else {
                $sInfo = "Customer with ID $sID doesn't exist.";
            }
        }

        mysql_close($oLink);
    ?>
```

The first two lines in the highlighted section contain the calls to connect to a MySQL database from PHP. Following that, the `mysql_query()` function is called to execute the SQL query. If that function returns a result and the result has at least one row, then the code continues to get the information and store it in `$sInfo`; otherwise, `$sInfo` is filled with an error message. The last line cleans up the database connection.

> *It's beyond the scope of this book to explain the intricacies of PHP and MySQL programming. If you'd like to learn more, consider picking up these other Wrox titles: Beginning PHP, Apache, MySQL Web Development (Wiley 2004) or Beginning PHP5, Apache, MySQL Web Development (Wiley 2005).*

One final step is necessary before moving on. The preceding code, though functional, has a major security flaw. Because the customer ID is being passed in on the query string, it is not safe to take that value and add it directly into a SQL query. What if the user passed in some additional SQL that was inserted at that point? This is what is called a *SQL injection attack* and is very dangerous to have in a production environment. The fix for this is simple: just make sure that customer ID is actually a number and nothing more. To do this, the PHP `is_numeric()` function is very useful, as it determines if a string (or any other value) represents a number:

```
    <?php

        $sID = $_GET["id"];
        $sInfo = "";

        if (is_numeric($sID)) {
            $sDBServer = "your.databaser.server";
            $sDBName = "your_db_name";
            $sDBUsername = "your_db_username";
            $sDBPassword = "your_db_password";
            $sQuery = "Select * from Customers where CustomerId=".$sID;

            $oLink = mysql_connect($sDBServer,$sDBUsername,$sDBPassword);
```

```
    @mysql_select_db($sDBName) or $sInfo="Unable to open database";

    if ($sInfo == "") {
        if($oResult = mysql_query($sQuery) and mysql_num_rows($oResult) > 0) {
            $aValues = mysql_fetch_array($oResult,MYSQL_ASSOC);
            $sInfo = $aValues['Name']."<br />".$aValues['Address']."<br />".
                $aValues['City']."<br />".$aValues['State']."<br />".
                $aValues['Zip']."<br /><br />Phone: ".$aValues['Phone']."<br
/>".
                "<a href=\"mailto:".$aValues['Email']."\">".
                $aValues['Email']."</a>";
            mysql_free_result($oResult);
        } else {
            $sInfo = "Customer with ID $sID doesn't exist.";
        }
    }
} else {
    $sInfo = "Invalid customer ID.";
}

    mysql_close($oLink);
?>
```

Adding this very simple data check avoids possible SQL injection attacks by returning an error message instead of database information.

Now when $sInfo is output into the <div/>, it will contain the appropriate information. The onload event handler reads that data out and sends it back up to the display frame. If the customer was found, the information will be displayed, as shown in Figure 2-2.

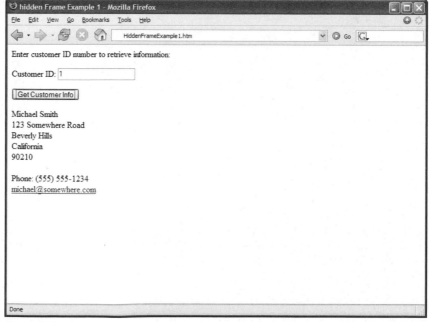

Figure 2-2

If, on the other hand, the customer doesn't exist or the ID isn't a number, an error message will be displayed in that same location on the screen. Either way, the customer service representative will have a nice user experience. This completes your first Ajax example.

This example and all of the examples in the book are also available in ASP.NET and JSP in the code download for this book, available at www.wrox.com.

Hidden Frame POST Requests

The previous example used a GET request to retrieve information from a database. This was fairly simple because the customer ID could just be appended to the URL in a query string and sent on its way. But what if you need to send a POST request? This, too, is possible using the hidden frame technique, although it takes a little extra work.

A POST request is typically sent when data needs to be sent to the server as opposed to a GET, which merely requests data from the server. Although GET requests can send extra data through the query string, some browsers can handle only up to 512KB of query string information. A POST request, on the other hand, can send up to 2GB of information, making it ideal for most uses.

Traditionally, the only way to send POST requests was to use a form with its `method` attribute set to `post`. Then, the data contained in the form was sent in a POST request to the URL specified in the `action` attribute. Further complicating matters was the fact that a typical form submission navigates the page to the new URL. This completely defeats the purpose of Ajax. Thankfully, there is a very easy workaround in the form of a little-known attribute called `target`.

The `target` attribute of the `<form/>` element is used in a similar manner to the `target` attribute of the `<a/>` element: it specifies where the navigation should occur. By setting the `target` attribute on a form, you effectively tell the form page to remain behind while the result of the form submission is displayed in another frame or window (in this case, a hidden frame).

To begin, define another frameset. The only difference from the previous example is that the visible frame contains an entry form for customer data:

```
<!DOCTYPE html PUBLIC "-//W3C//DTD XHTML 1.0 Frameset//EN"
"http://www.w3.org/TR/xhtml1/DTD/xhtml1-frameset.dtd">
<html>
  <head>
    <title>Hidden Frame POST Example</title>
  </head>
  <frameset rows="100%,0" style="border: 0px">
    <frame name="displayFrame" src="DataEntry.php" noresize="noresize" />
    <frame name="hiddenFrame" src="about:blank" noresize="noresize" />
  </frameset>
</html>
```

The body of the entry form is contained within a `<form/>` element and has textboxes for each of the fields stored in the database (aside from customer ID, which will be autogenerated). There is also a `<div/>` that is used for status messages relating to the client-server communication:

```
<form method="post" action="SaveCustomer.php" target="hiddenFrame">
    <p>Enter customer information to be saved:</p>
    <p>Customer Name: <input type="text" name="txtName" value="" /><br />
```

```
       Address: <input type="text" name="txtAddress" value="" /><br />
       City: <input type="text" name="txtCity" value="" /><br />
       State: <input type="text" name="txtState" value="" /><br />
       Zip Code: <input type="text" name="txtZipCode" value="" /><br />
       Phone: <input type="text" name="txtPhone" value="" /><br />
       E-mail: <input type="text" name="txtEmail" value="" /></p>
       <p><input type="submit" value="Save Customer Info" /></p>
   </form>
   <div id="divStatus"></div>
```

Note also that the `target` of the `<form/>` element is set to `hiddenFrame` so that when the user clicks the button, the submission goes to the hidden frame.

In this example, only one JavaScript function is necessary in the main page: `saveResult()`. This function will be called when the hidden frame returns from saving the customer data:

```
function saveResult(sMessage) {
    var divStatus = document.getElementById("divStatus");
    divStatus.innerHTML = "Request completed: " + sMessage;
}
```

It's the responsibility of the hidden frame to pass a message to this function that will be displayed to the user. This will either be a confirmation that the information was saved or an error message explaining why it wasn't.

Next is `SaveCustomer.php`, the file that handles the POST request. As in the previous example, this page is set up as a simple HTML page with a combination of PHP and JavaScript code. The PHP code is used to gather the information from the request and store it in the database. Since this is a POST request, the `$_POST` array contains all the information that was submitted:

```
<?php
    $sName = mysql_real_escape_string($_POST["txtName"]);
    $sAddress = mysql_real_escape_string($_POST["txtAddress"]);
    $sCity = mysql_real_escape_string($_POST["txtCity"]);
    $sState = mysql_real_escape_string($_POST["txtState"]);
    $sZipCode = mysql_real_escape_string($_POST["txtZipCode"]);
    $sPhone = mysql_real_escape_string($_POST["txtPhone"]);
    $sEmail = mysql_real_escape_string($_POST["txtEmail"]);

    $sStatus = "";

    $sDBServer = "your.database.server";
    $sDBName = "your_db_name";
    $sDBUsername = "your_db_username";
    $sDBPassword = "your_db_password";

    $sSQL = "Insert into Customers(Name,Address,City,State,Zip,Phone,`Email`) ".
            " values ('$sName','$sAddress','$sCity','$sState', '$sZipCode'".
            ", '$sPhone', '$sEmail')";

    //more here
?>
```

29

This code snippet retrieves all the POST information about the customer; moreover, it defines a status message ($sStatus) and the required database information (same as in the previous example). The SQL statement this time is an INSERT, adding in all the retrieved information.

To protect against SQL injection attacks, each of the datum retrieved from the $_POST array is escaped using mysql_real_escape_string(), a function that inserts the necessary escape sequences to ensure a string is wholly contained as a string (for example, all apostrophes are escaped so that data containing an apostrophe doesn't break the query).

The code to execute the SQL statement is very similar to that of the previous example:

```php
<?php
    $sName = mysql_real_escape_string($_POST["txtName"]);
    $sAddress = mysql_real_escape_string($_POST["txtAddress"]);
    $sCity = mysql_real_escape_string($_POST["txtCity"]);
    $sState = mysql_real_escape_string($_POST["txtState"]);
    $sZipCode = mysql_real_escape_string($_POST["txtZipCode"]);
    $sPhone = mysql_real_escape_string($_POST["txtPhone"]);
    $sEmail = mysql_real_escape_string($_POST["txtEmail"]);

    $sStatus = "";

    $sDBServer = "your.database.server";
    $sDBName = "your_db_name";
    $sDBUsername = "your_db_username";
    $sDBPassword = "your_db_password";

    $sSQL = "Insert into Customers(Name,Address,City,State,Zip,Phone,`Email`) ".
            " values ('$sName','$sAddress','$sCity','$sState', '$sZipCode'".
            ", '$sPhone', '$sEmail')";


    $oLink = mysql_connect($sDBServer,$sDBUsername,$sDBPassword);
    @mysql_select_db($sDBName) or $sStatus = "Unable to open database";

    if ($sStatus == "") {
        if(mysql_query($sSQL)) {
            $sStatus = "Added customer; customer ID is ".mysql_insert_id();
        } else {
            $sStatus = "An error occurred while inserting; customer not saved.";
        }
    }

    mysql_close($oLink);
?>
```

Here, the result of the mysql_query() function is simply an indicator that the statement was executed successfully. In that case, the $sStatus variable is filled with a message indicating that the save was successful and the customer ID assigned to the data. The mysql_insert_id() function always returns the last auto-incremented value of the most recent INSERT statement. If for some reason the statement didn't execute successfully, the $sStatus variable is filled with an error message.

The $sStatus variable is output into a JavaScript function that is run when the window loads:

```
<script type="text/javascript">

    window.onload = function () {
        top.frames["displayFrame"].saveResult("<?php echo $sStatus ?>");
    }

</script>
```

This code calls the saveResult() function defined in the display frame, passing in the value of the PHP variable $sStatus. Because this variable contains a string, you must enclose the PHP echo statement in quotation marks. When this function executes, assuming that the customer data was saved, the entry form page resembles the one shown in Figure 2-3.

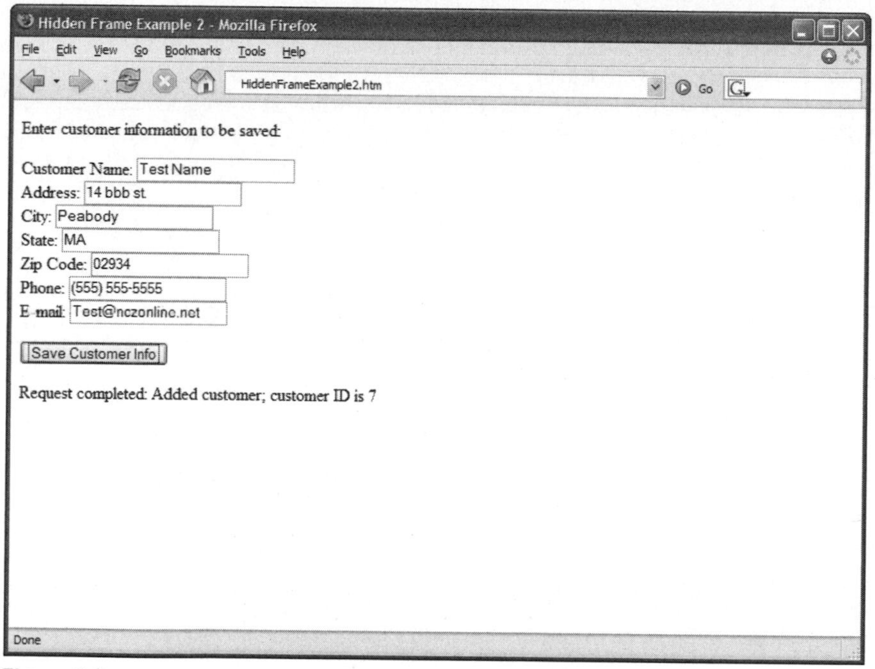

Figure 2-3

After this code has executed, you are free to add more customers to the database using the same form because it never disappeared.

Hidden iFrames

The next generation of behind-the-scenes client-server communication was to make use of iframes (short for inline frames), which were introduced in HTML 4.0. Basically, an iframe is the same as a frame with the exception that it can be placed inside of a non-frameset HTML page, effectively allowing any part of a page to become a frame. The iframe technique can be applied to pages not originally created as a frameset, making it much better suited to the incremental addition of functionality; an iframe can even be created on the fly in JavaScript, allowing for simple, semantic HTML to be supplied to the browser with the enhanced Ajax functionality serving as a progressive enhancement (this is discussed shortly). Because iframes can be used and accessed in the same way as regular frames, they are ideal for Ajax communication.

There are two ways to take advantage of iframes. The easiest way is to simply embed an iframe inside of your page and use that as the hidden frame to make requests. Doing this would change the first example display page to:

```
<p>Enter customer ID number to retrieve information:</p>
<p>Customer ID: <input type="text" id="txtCustomerId" value="" /></p>
<p><input type="button" value="Get Customer Info"
          onclick="requestCustomerInfo()" /></p>
<div id="divCustomerInfo"></div>
<iframe src="about:blank" name="hiddenFrame" style="display: none"></iframe>
```

Note that the iframe has its `style` attribute set to `"display:none"`; this effectively hides it from view. Since the name of the iframe is `hiddenFrame`, all the JavaScript code in this page will continue to work as before. There is, however, one small change that is necessary to the `GetCustomerData.php` page. The JavaScript function in that page previously looked for the `displayCustomerInfo()` function in the frame named `displayFrame`. If you use this technique, there is no frame with that name, so you must update the code to use `parent` instead:

```
window.onload = function () {
    var divInfoToReturn = document.getElementById("divInfoToReturn");
    parent.displayCustomerInfo(divInfoToReturn.innerHTML);
};
```

When accessed inside of an iframe, the `parent` object points to the window (or frame) in which the iframe resides. Now this example will work just as the first example in this chapter did.

The second way to use hidden iframes is to create them dynamically using JavaScript. This can get a little bit tricky because not all browsers implement iframes in the same way, so it helps to simply go step by step in creating a hidden iframe.

The first step is easy; you create the iframe using the `document.createElement()` method and assign the necessary attributes:

```
function createIFrame() {
    var oIFrameElement = document.createElement("iframe");
    oIFrameElement.style.display = "none";
    oIFrameElement.name = "hiddenFrame";
    oIFrameElement.id = "hiddenFrame";
    document.body.appendChild(oIFrameElement);

    //more code
}
```

The last line of this code is very important because it adds the iframe to the document structure; an iframe that isn't added to the document can't perform requests. Also note that both the `name` and `id` attributes are set to `hiddenFrame`. This is necessary because some browsers access the new frame by its `name` and some by its `id` attribute.

Next, define a global variable to hold a reference to the frame object. Note that the frame object for an iframe element isn't what is returned from `createElement()`. In order to get this object, you must look into the frames collection. This is what will be stored in the global variable:

```
var oIFrame = null;

function createIFrame() {
    var oIFrameElement = document.createElement("iframe");
    oIFrameElement.style.display = "none";
    oIFrameElement.name = "hiddenFrame";
    oIFrameElement.id = "hiddenFrame";
    document.body.appendChild(oIFrameElement);

    oIFrame = frames["hiddenFrame"];
}
```

If you place this code into the previous iframe example, you can then make the following modifications to `requestCustomerInfo()`:

```
function requestCustomerInfo() {
    if (!oIFrame) {
        createIFrame();
        setTimeout(requestCustomerInfo, 10);
        return;
    }

    var sId = document.getElementById("txtCustomerId").value;
    oIFrame.location = "GetCustomerData.php?id=" + sId;
}
```

With these changes, the function now checks to see if `oIFrame` is `null` or not. If it is, it calls `createIFrame()` and then sets a timeout to run the function again in 10 milliseconds. This is necessary because only Internet Explorer recognizes the inserted iframe immediately; most other browsers take a couple of milliseconds to recognize it and allow requests to be sent. When the function executes again, it will go on to the rest of the code, where the last line has been changed to reference the `oIFrame` object.

Although this technique works fairly easily with GET requests, POST requests are a different story. Only some browsers will enable you to set the `target` of a form to a dynamically created iframe; IE is not one of them. So, to use the hidden iframe technique with a POST request requires a bit of trickery for cross-browser compatibility.

Hidden iFrame POST Requests

To accomplish a POST request using hidden iframes, the basic approach is to load a page that contains a form into the hidden frame, populate that form with data, and then submit the form. When the visible form (the one you are actually typing into) is submitted, you need to cancel that submission and forward the information to the hidden frame. To do so, you'll need to define a function that handles the creation of the iframe and the loading of the hidden form:

```
function checkIFrame() {
    if (!oIFrame) {
        createIFrame();
```

```
    }
    setTimeout(function () {
        oIFrame.location = "ProxyForm.php";
    }, 10);
}
```

This function, `checkIFrame()`, first checks to see if the hidden iframe has been created. If not, `create IFrame()` is called. Then, a timeout is set before setting the location of the iframe to `ProxyForm.php`, which is the hidden form page. Because this function may be called several times, it's important that this page be loaded each time the form is submitted.

The `ProxyForm.php` file is very simple. It contains only a small bit of JavaScript to notify the main page that it has been loaded:

```
<!DOCTYPE html PUBLIC "-//W3C//DTD XHTML 1.0 Transitional//EN"
"http://www.w3.org/TR/xhtml1/DTD/xhtml1-transitional.dtd">
<html xmlns="http://www.w3.org/1999/xhtml" >
<head>
    <title>Proxy Form</title>
    <script type="text/javascript">
    //<![CDATA[

        window.onload = function () {
            parent.formReady();
        }

    //]]>
    </script>
</head>
<body>
    <form method="post" action="#">
    </form>
</body>
</html>
```

As you can see, the body of this page contains only an empty form and the head contains only an `onload` event handler. When the page is loaded, it calls `parent.formReady()` to let the main page know that it is ready to accept a request. The `formReady()` function is contained in the main page itself and looks like this:

```
function formReady() {
  var oForm = document.forms[0];
  var oHiddenForm = oIFrame.document.forms[0];

  for (var i=0 ; i < oForm.elements.length; i++) {
    var oField = oForm.elements[i];

    switch (oField.type) {

      //ignore buttons
      case "button":
      case "submit":
      case "reset":
```

```
            break;

        //checkboxes/radio buttons - only return the value if the control is checked.
        case "checkbox":
        case "radio":
          if (!oField.checked) {
            break;
          }

        //text/hidden/password all return the value
        case "text":
        case "hidden":
        case "password":
          createInputField(oHiddenForm, oField.name, oField.value);
          break;

        default:
          switch(oField.tagName.toLowerCase()) {
            case "select":
              createInputField(oHiddenForm, oField.name,
                               oField.options[oField.selectedIndex].value);
              break;
            default:
              createInputField(oHiddenForm, oField.name, oField.value);
          }
      }
    }

    oHiddenForm.action = oForm.action;
    oHiddenForm.submit();
};
```

The first step in this function is to get a reference to the form in the hidden iframe, which you can do by accessing the document.forms collection of that frame. Because there is only one form on the page, you can safely get the first form in the collection (at index 0); this is stored in oHiddenForm. Following that, a reference to the form on the main page is saved into oForm. Next, a for loop iterates through the form elements on the main page (using the elements collection). For each form element, a new hidden input element is created in the hidden frame using the createInputField() function (defined in a moment). Since there can be many different types of form elements, this code takes into account the different ways that values are stored. Buttons are ignored, since their values are usually unimportant; checkboxes and radio buttons are included only if they are checked; textboxes are always included; select boxes are given the correct value for the selected option. The function to create the fields is defined as follows:

```
function createInputField(oHiddenForm, sName, sValue) {
    oHidden = oIFrame.document.createElement("input");
    oHidden.type = "hidden";
    oHidden.name = sName;
    oHidden.value = sValue;
    oHiddenForm.appendChild(oHidden);
}
```

This function accepts three arguments: the hidden form, the name of the input field, and the value of the input field. Then, an <input /> element is created and added into the hidden form.

After each form element has been added, the hidden form is assigned the same `action` as the main page form. By reading the `action` out of the form instead of hard-coding it, you can use `formReady()` on any number of pages. The last step in the function is to submit the hidden form.

The only thing left to do is to make sure the main page form doesn't submit itself in the normal way. To do this, assign an `onsubmit` event handler that calls `checkIFrame()` and returns `false`:

```
<form method="post" action="SaveCustomer.php"
      onsubmit="checkIFrame();return false">
    <p>Enter customer information to be saved:</p>
    <p>Customer Name: <input type="text" name="txtName" value="" /><br />
    Address: <input type="text" name="txtAddress" value="" /><br />
    City: <input type="text" name="txtCity" value="" /><br />
    State: <input type="text" name="txtState" value="" /><br />
    Zip Code: <input type="text" name="txtZipCode" value="" /><br />
    Phone: <input type="text" name="txtPhone" value="" /><br />
    E-mail: <input type="text" name="txtEmail" value="" /></p>
    <p><input type="submit" value="Save Customer Info" /></p>
</form>
<div id="divStatus"></div>
```

By returning `false` in this way, you are preventing the default behavior of the form (to submit itself to the server). Instead, the `checkIFrame()` method is called and the process of submitting to the hidden iframe begins.

With this complete, you can now use this example the same way as the hidden frame POST example; the `SaveCustomer.php` page handles the data and calls `saveResult()` in the main page when completed.

> Note that the examples in this section have been simplified in order to focus on the Ajax techniques involved. If you were to use these in a real web application, you would need to provide more user feedback, such as disabling the form while a request is being made.

Advantages and Disadvantages of Hidden Frames

Now that you have seen the powerful things that you can do using hidden frames, it's time to discuss the practicality of using them. As mentioned previously, this technique has been around for many years and is still used in many Ajax applications.

One of the biggest arguments for using hidden frames is that you can maintain the browser history and thus enable users to still use the Back and Forward buttons in the browser. Because the browser doesn't know that a hidden frame is, in fact, hidden, it keeps track of all the requests made through it. Whereas the main page of an Ajax application may not change, the changes in the hidden frame mean that the Back and Forward buttons will move through the history of that frame instead of the main page. This technique is used in both Gmail and Google Maps for this very reason.

> Be careful, because iframes don't always store browser history. Whereas IE always stores the history of iframes, Firefox does so only if the iframe was defined using HTML (that is, not created dynamically using JavaScript). Safari never stores browser history for iframes, regardless of how they are included in the page.

Hidden frames do have some disadvantages. For one, you cannot make requests outside of your own domain. Due to security restrictions in browsers, JavaScript can only interact with frames that are from the same domain. Even a page from a subdomain (such as p2p.wrox.com instead of www.wrox.com) can't be accessed.

Another downside of hidden frames is that there is very little information about what's going on behind the scenes. You are completely reliant on the proper page being returned. The examples in this section all had the same problem: If the hidden frame page fails to load, there is no notification to the user that a problem has occurred; the main page will continue to wait until the appropriate JavaScript function is called. You may be able to provide some comfort to a user by setting a timeout for a long period of time, maybe five minutes, and displaying a message if the page hasn't loaded by then, but that's just a workaround. The main problem is that you don't have enough information about the HTTP request that is happening behind the scenes. Fortunately, there is another option.

XMLHttp Requests (XHR)

When Microsoft Internet Explorer 5.0 introduced a rudimentary level of XML support, an ActiveX library called MSXML was also introduced (discussed at length in Chapter 6). One of the objects provided in this library quickly became very popular: XMLHttp.

The XMLHttp object was created to enable developers to initiate HTTP requests from anywhere in an application. These requests were intended to return XML, so the XMLHttp object provided an easy way to access this information in the form of an XML document. Since it was an ActiveX control, XMLHttp could be used not only in web pages but also in any Windows-based desktop application; however, its popularity on the Web has far outpaced its popularity for desktop applications.

Picking up on that popularity, Mozilla duplicated the XMLHttp functionality for use in its browsers, such as Firefox. They created a native JavaScript object, XMLHttpRequest, which closely mimicked the behavior of Microsoft's XMLHttp object. Shortly thereafter, both the Safari (as of version 1.2) and Opera (version 7.6) browsers duplicated Mozilla's implementation. Microsoft even went back and created their own native XMLHttpRequest object for Internet Explorer 7. Today, all four browsers support a native XMLHttpRequest object, commonly referred to as XHR.

Creating an XHR Object

The first step to using an XHR object is, obviously, to create one. Because Microsoft's implementation prior to Internet Explorer 7 is an ActiveX control, you must use the proprietary ActiveXObject class in JavaScript, passing in the XHR control's signature:

```
var oXHR = new ActiveXObject("Microsoft.XMLHttp");
```

This line creates the first version of the XHR object (the one shipped with IE 5.0). The problem is that there have been several new versions released with each subsequent release of the MSXML library. Each release brings with it better stability and speed, so you want to make sure that you are always using the most recent version available on the user's machine. The signatures are:

- ❏ Microsoft.XMLHttp
- ❏ MSXML2.XMLHttp
- ❏ MSXML2.XMLHttp.3.0
- ❏ MSXML2.XMLHttp.4.0
- ❏ MSXML2.XMLHttp.5.0
- ❏ MSXML2.XMLHttp.6.0

Windows Vista ships with version 6.0, which is the preferable version to use if able. However, those running other versions of Windows won't have this available, so Microsoft recommends using the 3.0 signature as a fallback. All other versions aren't recommended for use due to varying issues with security, stability, and availability.

Unfortunately, the only way to determine which version to use is to try to create each one. Because this is an ActiveX control, any failure to create an object will throw an error, which means that you must enclose each attempt within a try...catch block. The end result is a function such as this:

```
function createXHR() {
    var aVersions = [ "MSXML2.XMLHttp.6.0", "MSXML2.XMLHttp.3.0"];

    for (var i = 0; i < aVersions.length; i++) {
        try {
            var oXHR = new ActiveXObject(aVersions[i]);
            return oXHR;
        } catch (oError) {
            //Do nothing
        }
    }
    throw new Error("MSXML is not installed.");
}
```

The createXHR() function stores an array of valid XHR signatures, with the most recent one first. It iterates through this array and tries to create an XHR object with each signature. If the creation fails, the catch statement prevents a JavaScript error from stopping execution; then the next signature is attempted. When an object is created, it is returned. If the function completes without creating an XHR object, an error is thrown indicating that the creation failed.

Fortunately, creating an XHR object is much easier in other browsers. Mozilla Firefox, Safari, Opera, and Internet Explorer 7 all use the same code:

```
var oXHR = new XMLHttpRequest();
```

Naturally, it helps to have a cross-browser way of creating XHR objects. You can create such a function by altering the createXHR() function defined previously:

```
function createXHR() {

    if (typeof XMLHttpRequest != "undefined") {
        return new XMLHttpRequest();
    } else if (window.ActiveXObject) {
        var aVersions = [ "MSXML2.XMLHttp.6.0", "MSXML2.XMLHttp.3.0"];

        for (var i = 0; i < aVersions.length; i++) {
            try {
                var oXHR = new ActiveXObject(aVersions[i]);
                return oXHR;
            } catch (oError) {
                //Do nothing
            }
        }

    }
    throw new Error("XMLHttp object could not be created.");
}
```

Now this function first checks to see if an XMLHttpRequest class is defined (by using the typeof opera-tor). If XMLHttpRequest is present, it is used to create the XHR object; otherwise, it checks to see if the ActiveXObject class is present and, if so, goes through the same process of creating an XHR object for IE 6 and below. If both of these tests fail, an error is thrown.

The other option for creating cross-browser XHR objects is to use a library that already has cross-browser code written. The zXml library, written by two of your authors, is one such library and is available for download at www.nczonline.net/downloads/. This library defines a single function for the creation of XHR objects:

```
var oXHR = zXmlHttp.createRequest();
```

The createRequest() function, and the zXml library itself, will be used throughout this book to aid in cross-browser handling of Ajax technologies.

Using XHR

After you have created an XHR object, you are ready to start making HTTP requests from JavaScript. The first step is to call the open() method, which initializes the object. This method accepts the following three arguments:

❑ **Request Type:** A string indicating the request type to be made — typically, GET or POST (these are the only ones currently supported by all browsers)

❑ **URL:** A string indicating the URL to send the request to

❑ **Async:** A Boolean value indicating whether the request should be made asynchronously

The last argument, async, is very important because it controls how JavaScript executes the request. When set to true, the request is sent asynchronously, and JavaScript code execution continues without waiting for the response; you must use an event handler to watch for the response to the request. If async is set to false, the request is sent synchronously, and JavaScript waits for a response from the server before continuing code execution. That means if the response takes a long time, the user cannot interact with the browser until the response has completed. For this reason, best practices around the development of Ajax applications favor the use of asynchronous requests for routine data retrieval, with synchronous requests reserved for short messages sent to and from the server.

To make an asynchronous GET request to a file such as info.txt, you would start by doing this:

```
var oXHR = zXmlHttp.createRequest();
oXHR.open("get", "info.txt", true);
```

Note that the case of the first argument, the request type, is irrelevant even though technically request types are defined as all uppercase.

Next, you need to define an onreadystatechange event handler. The XHR object has a property called readyState that changes as the request goes through and the response is received. There are five possible values for readyState:

- ❑ **0 (Uninitialized):** The object has been created but the open() method hasn't been called.
- ❑ **1 (Loading):** The open() method has been called but the request hasn't been sent.
- ❑ **2 (Loaded):** The request has been sent.
- ❑ **3 (Interactive).** A partial response has been received.
- ❑ **4 (Completed):** All data has been received and the connection has been closed.

Every time the readyState property changes from one value to another, the readystatechange event fires and the onreadystatechange event handler is called.

> As a result of differences in browser implementations, the only reliable readyState value is 4. Some browsers neglect states 1 and 2 altogether, and some fire 3 multiple times until the response is complete. For these reasons, it's best to only rely on readyState 4.

The onreadystatechange event handler is typically defined as:

```
var oXHR = zXmlHttp.createRequest();
oXHR.open("get", "info.txt", true);
oXHR.onreadystatechange = function () {
    if (oXHR.readyState == 4) {
        alert("Got response.");
    }
};
```

The last step is to call the send() method, which actually sends the request. This method accepts a single argument, which is a string for the request body. If the request doesn't require a body (remember, a GET request doesn't), you must pass in null (you cannot just omit the argument):

```
var oXHR = zXmlHttp.createRequest();
oXHR.open("get", "info.txt", true);
```

```
oXHR.onreadystatechange = function () {
    if (oXHR.readyState == 4) {
        alert("Got response.");
    }
};
oXHR.send(null);
```

That's it! The request has been sent and when the response is received, an alert will be displayed. But just showing a message that the request has been received isn't very useful. The true power of XHR is that you have access to the returned data, the response status, and the response headers.

To retrieve the data returned from the request, you can use the responseText or responseXML properties. The responseText property returns a string containing the response body, whereas the responseXML property is an XML document object used only if the data returned has a content type of text/xml. (XML documents are discussed in Chapter 6.) So, to get the text contained in info.txt, the call would be as follows:

```
var sData = oXHR.responseText;
```

Note that this will return the text in info.txt only if the file was found and no errors occurred. If, for example, info.txt didn't exist, then the responseText would contain the server's 404 message. Fortunately, there is a way to determine if any errors occurred.

The status property contains the HTTP status code sent in the response, and statusText contains the text description of the status (such as "OK" or "Not Found"). Using these two properties, you can make sure that the data you've received is actually the data you want or tell the user why the data wasn't retrieved:

```
if (oXHR.status == 200) {
    alert("Data returned is: " + oXHR.responseText);
} else {
    alert("An error occurred: " + oXHR.statusText);
}
```

Generally, you should always ensure that the status of a response is 200, indicating that the request was completely successful. The readyState property is set to 4 even if a server error occurred, so just checking that is not enough. In this example, the responseText property is shown only if the status is 200; otherwise, the error message is displayed.

> The statusText **property isn't implemented in Opera and sometimes returns an inaccurate description in other browsers. You should never rely on** statusText **alone to determine if an error occurred.**

Another thing to watch out for is browser caching. You may end up with a status code of 304 on a response in IE and Opera. If you are going to be accessing data that won't be changing frequently, you may want to alter your code to also check for a 304:

```
if (oXHR.status == 200 || oXHR.status == 304) {
    alert("Data returned is: " + oXHR.responseText);
```

```
    } else {
        alert("An error occurred: " + oXHR.statusText);
    }
```

If a 304 is returned, the responseText and responseXML properties will still contain the correct data. The only difference is that data comes from the browser's cache instead of from the server. Caching issues are discussed later in the chapter.

As mentioned previously, it's also possible to access the response headers. You can retrieve a specific header value using the getResponseHeader() method and passing in the name of the header that you want to retrieve. One of the most useful response headers is Content-Type, which tells you the type of data being sent:

```
var sContentType = oXHR.getResponseHeader("Content-Type");
if (sContentType == "text/xml") {
    alert("XML content received.");
} else if (sContentType == "text/plain") {
    alert("Plain text content received.");
} else {
    alert("Unexpected content received.");
}
```

This code snippet checks the content type of the response and displays an alert indicating the type of data returned. Typically, you will receive only XML data (content type of text/xml) or plain text (content type of text/plain) from the server, because these content types are the easiest to work with using JavaScript.

If you'd prefer to see all headers returned from the server, you can use the getAllResponseHeaders() method, which simply returns a string containing all of the headers. Each header in the string is separated by either a new line character (\n) or a combination of the carriage return and new line (\r\n), so you can deal with individual headers as follows:

```
var sHeaders = oXHR.getAllResponseHeaders();
var aHeaders = sHeaders.split(/\r?\n/);

for (var i=0; i < aHeaders.length; i++) {
    alert(aHeaders[i]);
}
```

This example splits the header string into an array of headers by using the JavaScript split() method for strings and passing in a regular expression (which matches either a carriage return/new line couple or just a new line). Now you can iterate through the headers and do with them as you please. Keep in mind that each string in aHeaders is in the format *headername: headervalue*.

It's also possible to set headers on the request before it's sent out. You may want to indicate the content type of data that you'll be sending, or you may just want to send along some extra data that the server may need to deal with the request. To do so, use the setRequestHeader() method before calling send():

```
var oXHR = zXmlHttp.createRequest();
oXHR.open("get", "info.txt", true);
```

```
oXHR.onreadystatechange = function () {
    if (oXHR.readyState == 4) {
        alert("Got response.");
    }
};
oXHR.setRequestHeader("myheader", "myvalue");
oXHR.send(null);
```

In this code, a header named `myheader` is added to the request before it's sent out. The header will be added to the default headers as `myheader: myvalue`.

Synchronous Requests

Up to this point, you've been dealing with asynchronous requests, which are preferable in most situations. Sending synchronous requests means that you don't need to assign the `onreadystatechange` event handler, because the response will have been received by the time the `send()` method returns. This makes it possible to do something like this:

```
var oXHR = zXmlHttp.createRequest();
oXHR.open("get", "info.txt", false);
oXHR.send(null);

if (oXHR.status == 200) {
    alert("Data returned is: " + oXHR.responseText);
} else {
    alert("An error occurred: " + oXHR.statusText);
}
```

Sending the request synchronously (setting the third argument of `open()` to `false`) enables you to start evaluating the response immediately after the call to `send()`. This can be useful if you want the user interaction to wait for a response or if you're expecting to receive only a very small amount of data (for example, less than 1K). In the case of average or larger amounts of data, it's best to use an asynchronous call.

> There is a chance that a synchronous call will never return. For instance, if the server process is long-running, perhaps due to an infinite loop or distributed data lookup, this could lock the entire web browser (including other tabs) for a long period of time.

XHR GET Requests

It's time to revisit the hidden frame GET example to see how the process could be improved using XHR. The first change will be to `GetCustomerData.php`, which must be changed from an HTML page to simply return an HTML snippet. The entire file now becomes streamlined:

```
<?php
    header("Content-Type: text/plain");

    $sID = $_GET["id"];
    $sInfo = "";

    if (is_numeric($sID)) {
```

```php
        $sDBServer = "your.databaser.server";
        $sDBName = "your_db_name";
        $sDBUsername = "your_db_username";
        $sDBPassword = "your_db_password";
        $sQuery = "Select * from Customers where CustomerId=".$sID;

        $oLink = mysql_connect($sDBServer,$sDBUsername,$sDBPassword);
        @mysql_select_db($sDBName) or $sInfo="Unable to open database";

        if ($sInfo == "") {
            if($oResult = mysql_query($sQuery) and mysql_num_rows($oResult) > 0) {
                $aValues = mysql_fetch_array($oResult,MYSQL_ASSOC);
                $sInfo = $aValues['Name']."<br />".$aValues['Address']."<br />".
                    $aValues['City']."<br />".$aValues['State']."<br />".
                    $aValues['Zip']."<br /><br />Phone: ".$aValues['Phone']."<br
/>".
                    "<a      href=\"mailto:".$aValues['Email']."\">".
                    $aValues['Email']."</a>";
                mysql_free_result($oResult);
            } else {
                $sInfo = "Customer with ID $sID doesn't exist.";
            }
        }
    } else {
        $sInfo = "Invalid customer ID.";
    }

    mysql_close($oLink);

    echo $sInfo;
?>
```

As you can see, there are no visible HTML or JavaScript calls in the page. All the main logic remains the same, but there are two additional lines of PHP code. The first occurs at the beginning, where the header() function is used to set the content type of the page. Even though the page will return an HTML snippet, it's fine to set the content type as text/plain, because it's not a complete HTML page (and therefore wouldn't validate as HTML). You should always set the content type in any page that is sending non-HTML to the browser. The second added line is towards the bottom, where the $sInfo variable is output to the stream by using the echo command.

In the main HTML page, the basic setup is this:

```html
<p>Enter customer ID number to retrieve information:</p>
<p>Customer ID: <input type="text" id="txtCustomerId" value="" /></p>
<p><input type="button" value="Get Customer Info"
        onclick="requestCustomerInfo()" /></p>
<div id="divCustomerInfo"></div>
```

The requestCustomerInfo() function previously created a hidden iframe but now must be changed to use XHR:

```javascript
function requestCustomerInfo() {
    var sId = document.getElementById("txtCustomerId").value;
```

```
    var oXHR = zXmlHttp.createRequest();
    oXHR.open("get", "GetCustomerData.php?id=" + sId, true);
    oXHR.onreadystatechange = function () {
        if (oXHR.readyState == 4) {
            if (oXHR.status == 200 || oXHR.status == 304) {
                displayCustomerInfo(oXHR.responseText);
            } else {
                displayCustomerInfo("An error occurred: " + oXHR.statusText);
            }
        }
    };
    oXHR.send(null);
}
```

Note that the function begins the same way, by retrieving the ID the user entered. Then, an XHR object is created using the zXml library. The open() method is called, specifying an asynchronous GET request for GetCustomerData.php (which has the aforementioned ID added to its query string). Next comes the assignment of the event handler, which checks for a readyState of 4 and then checks the status of the request. If the request was successful (status of 200 or 304), the displayCustomerInfo() function is called with the response body (accessed via responseText). If there was an error (status is not 200 or 304), then the error information is passed to displayCustomerInfo().

There are several differences between this and the hidden frame/iframe example. First, no JavaScript code is required outside of the main page. This is important because any time you need to keep code in two different places there is the possibility of creating incompatibilities; in the frame-based examples, you relied on separate scripts in the display page and the hidden frames to communicate with one another. By changing GetCustomerInfo.php to return just the data you're interested in, you have eliminated potential problems with JavaScript calling between these locations. The second difference is that it's much easier to tell if there was a problem executing the request. In previous examples, there was no mechanism by which you could identify and respond to a server error in the request process. Using XHR, all server errors are revealed to you as a developer, enabling you to pass along meaningful error feedback to the user. In many ways, XHR is a more elegant solution than hidden frames for in-page HTTP requests.

XHR POST Requests

Now that you've seen how XHR can simplify GET requests, it's time to take a look at POST requests. First, you need to make the same changes to SaveCustomer.php as you did for GetCustomerInfo.php, which means you need to remove extraneous HTML and JavaScript, add the content type information, and output the text:

```php
<?php
```

```php
    header("Content-Type: text/plain");

    $sName = mysql_real_escape_string($_POST["txtName"]);
    $sAddress = mysql_real_escape_string($_POST["txtAddress"]);
    $sCity = mysql_real_escape_string($_POST["txtCity"]);
    $sState = mysql_real_escape_string($_POST["txtState"]);
    $sZipCode = mysql_real_escape_string($_POST["txtZipCode"]);
    $sPhone = mysql_real_escape_string($_POST["txtPhone"]);
```

```
    $sEmail = mysql_real_escape_string($_POST["txtEmail"]);

    $sStatus = "";

    $sDBServer = "your.database.server";
    $sDBName = "your_db_name";
    $sDBUsername = "your_db_username";
    $sDBPassword = "your_db_password";

    $sSQL = "Insert into Customers(Name,Address,City,State,Zip,Phone,`Email`) ".
            " values ('$sName','$sAddress','$sCity','$sState', '$sZipCode'".
            ", '$sPhone', '$sEmail')";


    $oLink = mysql_connect($sDBServer,$sDBUsername,$sDBPassword);
    @mysql_select_db($sDBName) or $sStatus = "Unable to open database";

    if ($sStatus == "") {
        if($oResult = mysql_query($sSQL)) {
            $sStatus = "Added customer; customer ID is ".mysql_insert_id();
    } else {
            $sStatus = "An error occurred while inserting; customer not saved.";
        }
    }

    mysql_close($oLink);

    echo $sStatus;
?>
```

This now represents the entirety of SaveCustomer.php. Note that the header() function is called to set the content type, and echo is used to output $sStatus.

In the main page, the simple form that was set up to allow entry of new customer info is the following:

```
<form method="post" action="SaveCustomer.php"
    onsubmit="sendRequest(); return false">
    <p>Enter customer information to be saved:</p>
    <p>Customer Name: <input type="text" name="txtName" value="" /><br />
    Address: <input type="text" name="txtAddress" value="" /><br />
    City: <input type="text" name="txtCity" value="" /><br />
    State: <input type="text" name="txtState" value="" /><br />
    Zip Code: <input type="text" name="txtZipCode" value="" /><br />
    Phone: <input type="text" name="txtPhone" value="" /><br />
    E-mail: <input type="text" name="txtEmail" value="" /></p>
    <p><input type="submit" value="Save Customer Info" /></p>
</form>
<div id="divStatus"></div>
```

You'll note that the onsubmit event handler has now changed to call the function sendRequest() (although the event handler still returns false to prevent actual form submission). This method first assembles the data for the POST request and then creates the XHR object to send it. The data must be sent in the format as a query string:

```
name1=value1&name2=value2&name3=value3
```

Both the name and value of each parameter must be URL-encoded in order to avoid data loss during transmission. JavaScript provides a built-in function called encodeURIComponent() that can be used to perform this encoding. To create this string, you'll need to iterate over the form fields, extracting and encoding the name and value. A helper function is used to do this encoding:

```
function encodeNameAndValue(sName, sValue) {
    var sParam = encodeURIComponent(sName);
    sParam += "=";
    sParam += encodeURIComponent(sValue);
    return sParam;
}
```

The actual iteration over the form fields takes place in the getRequestBody() function:

```
function getRequestBody(oForm) {

    //array to hold the params
    var aParams = new Array();

    //iterate over each element in the form
    for (var i=0 ; i < oForm.elements.length; i++) {

        //get reference to the field
        var oField = oForm.elements[i];

        //different behavior based on the type of field
        switch (oField.type) {

            //buttons - we don't care
            case "button":
            case "submit":
            case "reset":
                break;

            //checkboxes/radio buttons - only return the value if the control is
checked.
            case "checkbox":
            case "radio":
                if (!oField.checked) {
                    break;
                }

            //text/hidden/password all return the value
            case "text":
            case "hidden":
            case "password":
                aParams.push(encodeNameAndValue(oField.name, oField.value));
                break;

            //everything else
            default:

                switch(oField.tagName.toLowerCase()) {
```

```
                    case "select":
                        aParams.push(encodeNameAndValue(oField.name,
                                        oField.options[oField.selectedIndex].value));
                        break;
                    default:
                        aParams.push(encodeNameAndValue(oField.name,
                                            oField.value));
            }
        }
    }

    return aParams.join("&");
}
```

This function assumes that you will supply a reference to the form as an argument. An array (aParams) is created to store each individual name-value pair. Then, the elements of the form are iterated over, building up a string using encodeNameAndValue(), which is then added to the array. Doing this prevents multiple string concatenation, which can lead to slower code execution in some browsers. The last step is to call join() on the array, passing in the ampersand character. This effectively combines all the name-value pairs with ampersands, creating a single string in the correct format.

> *String concatenation in most browsers is an expensive process because strings are immutable, meaning that once created, they cannot have their values changed. Thus, concatenating two strings involves first allocating a new string and then copying the contents of the two other strings into it. Repeating this process over and over causes a severe slowdown. For this reason, it's always best to keep string concatenations at a minimum and use the array's join() method to handle longer string concatenation. Firefox actually has very efficient string concatenation, but for the purposes of cross-browser coding, it's still best to use an array and the join() method.*

The sendRequest() function calls getRequestBody() and sets up the request:

```
function sendRequest() {
    var oForm = document.forms[0];
    var sBody = getRequestBody(oForm);

    var oXHR = zXmlHttp.createRequest();
    oXHR.open("post", oForm.action, true);
    oXHR.setRequestHeader("Content-Type", "application/x-www-form-urlencoded");

    oXHR.onreadystatechange = function () {
        if (oXHR.readyState == 4) {
            if (oXHR.status == 200) {
                saveResult(oXHR.responseText);
            } else {
                saveResult("An error occurred: " + oXHR.statusText);
            }
        }
    };
    oXHR.send(sBody);
}
```

As with previous examples, the first step in this function is to get a reference to the form and store it in a variable (oForm). Then, the request body is generated and stored in sBody. Next comes the creation and setup of the XHR object. Note that the first argument of open() is now post instead of get, and the second is set to oForm.action (once again, so this script can be used on multiple pages). You'll also notice that a request header is being set. When a form is posted from the browser to a server, it sets the content type of the request as application/x-www-form-urlencoded. Most server-side languages look for this encoding in order to parse the incoming POST data properly, so it is very important for it to be set.

The onreadystatechange event handler is very similar to that of the GET example; the only change is the call to saveResult() instead of displayCustomerInfo(). The last line is very important, as the sBody string is passed to send() so that it will become part of the request body. This effectively mimics what the browser does, so all server-side logic should work as expected.

Advantages and Disadvantages of XHR

Undoubtedly, you can see the advantage of using XHR for client-server communication instead of hidden frames. The code you write is much cleaner and the intent of the code is much more apparent than using numerous callback functions with hidden frames. You have access to request and response headers as well as HTTP status codes, enabling you to determine if your request was successful.

The downside is that, unlike hidden frames, there is no browser history record of the calls that were made. The Back and Forward buttons do not tie in to XHR requests, so you have effectively cut off their use. It is for this reason that many Ajax applications use a mixture of XHR and hidden frames to make a truly usable interface.

Another disadvantage, which applies to Internet Explorer 6 and earlier only, is that you depend on ActiveX controls being enabled. If the user has your page set up in a particular security zone that doesn't allow ActiveX controls, the code cannot access the XHR object. In that case, you may have to default to using hidden frames.

It is also worth noting that XHR has the same restrictions as hidden frames when it comes to cross-domain communication. Even XMLHttp was designed for making ad hoc requests from JavaScript, it still doesn't break the cross-domain scripting rules. An XHR object is still only allowed to access resources from the same domain. If you need to access a URL located in a different origin, you must create a server-side proxy to handle the communication (see Figure 2-4).

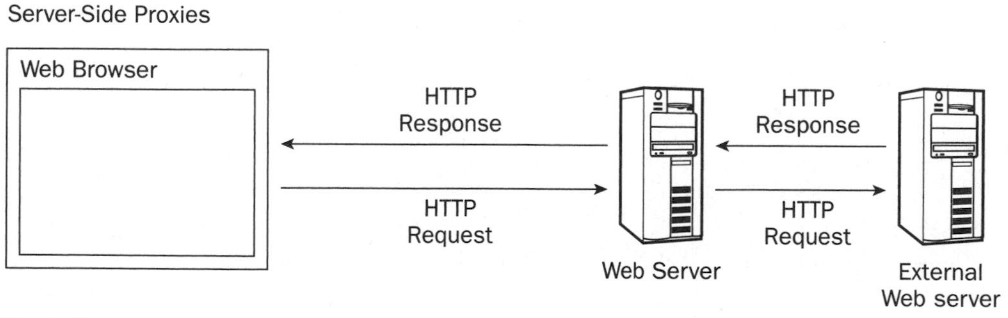

Server-Side Proxies

Figure 2-4

Using a server-side proxy, the browser makes a request to the web server. The web server then contacts another web server outside of the domain to request the appropriate information. When your web server receives the response, it is forwarded back to the browser. The result is a seamless transmission of external data. You'll be using server-side proxies later in this book.

Ajax with Images

Since Netscape Navigator 3, it has been possible to change the src attribute of an image using JavaScript. Changing this attribute actually sends a request to the server for the image, allowing an opportunity to return data to the client. Clearly, the data is sometimes simply what is stored in the image, but there is a much greater capability for client-server communication using images.

Dynamically Creating Images

The basic technique behind using images for Ajax communication is similar to preloading images. You need to create a <img/> element and then assign its src attribute. To tell when the image is loaded, assign an onload event handler:

```
var oImg = document.createElement("img");
oImg.onload = function () {
  alert("Image is ready");
}
oImg.src = "/path/to/myimage.gif";
```

The downloading of an image begins as soon as the src attribute is assigned, meaning that you don't even need to add the image to the page. In fact, you don't even need to use an <img/> element at all; you can use the Image object:

```
var oImg = new Image();
oImg.onload = function () {
  alert("Image is ready");
}
oImg.src = "/path/to/myimage.gif";
```

There is also an error event that you can use to determine when something has gone wrong. This is most often fired when something other than an image has been returned from the server (such as HTML):

```
var oImg = new Image();
oImg.onload = function () {
  alert("Image is ready");
}
oImg.onerror = function () {
  alert("ERROR!");
};
oImg.src = "/path/to/myimage.gif";
```

These two events, load and error, give enough information to be a reliable communication medium from client to server. Imagine that instead of changing the src to point to another image, you have it point to a PHP, ASP.NET, or JSP page. That page can do any amount of processing that you'd like so long as it returns an image at the end. You can easily send small bits of information on the query string of the page, such as:

```
var oImg = new Image();
oImg.onload = function () {
  alert("Image is ready");
}
oImg.onerror = function () {
  alert("ERROR!");
};
oImg.src = "/path/to/myimage.php?message=ok";
```

Once again, as long as `myimage.php` returns an image, everything will behave as expected. You can return an image in one of two ways:

❑   redirecting to an image

❑   writing an image to the output stream

Redirecting to an Image

To redirect to an image with PHP, you need to first set the appropriate content type and then use the `Location` header:

```php
<?php
    header("Content-type: image/gif");
    header("Location: pixel.gif");
?>
```

This example uses a GIF image. If you are redirecting to a JPEG image, you need to set the content type to `image/jpeg`.

In ASP.NET, you need only do a redirect:

```
<%@ Page Language="C#" %>
<script runat="server">
    private void Page_Load(object sender, System.EventArgs e)
    {
        Response.Redirect("pixel.gif");
    }
</script>
```

And in JSP:

```
<%
    response.sendRedirect("pixel.gif");
%>
```

Note that this redirect to an image, regardless of your server-side language, should be done after other processing has occurred.

Creating an Image

To output an image using PHP, you'll need to use the GD library (which is included in most PHP installations):

```php
<?php
    header("Content-type: image/jpeg");
```

```
    $image = imagecreate(1,1);
    $white = imagecolorallocate($image, 255, 255, 255);
    imagejpeg($image);
    imagedestroy($image);
?>
```

The first command outputs the content type for a JPEG image (GIF image creation/manipulation isn't supported in all version of GD, so it's best to use another image format). After that, a 1x1 image is created and has white allocated as a color on it. The imagejpeg() function outputs the image to the response stream and imagedestroy() frees up the memory it used.

To create and output an image using .NET, you'll need to use the System.Drawing and System.Drawing.Imaging namespaces:

```
<%@ Page Language="C#" ContentType="image/jpeg"%>
<%@ Import Namespace="System.Drawing" %>
<%@ Import Namespace="System.Drawing.Imaging" %>
<script runat="server">
    private void Page_Load(object sender, System.EventArgs e)
    {
        Bitmap image = new Bitmap(1, 1);
        image.Save(Response.OutputStream, System.Drawing.Imaging.ImageFormat.Jpeg);
        image.Dispose();
    }
</script>
```

This code mimics the previous PHP code, setting the content-type for a JPEG image, then creating a 1x1 image and outputting it to the response stream. Lastly, the image's memory is freed by calling the dispose() method.

Dynamically creating images is very similar in JSP:

```
<%@page contentType="image/jpeg"%>
<%@page import="java.awt.*" %>
<%@page import="java.awt.image.*" %>
<%@page import="com.sun.image.codec.jpeg.*"%>
<%
    BufferedImage image = new BufferedImage(1, 1, BufferedImage.TYPE_INT_RGB);

    Graphics2D g = (Graphics2D) image.getGraphics();
    g.setColor(Color.white);
    g.fillRect(0,0,1,1);
    g.dispose();

    ServletOutputStream output = response.getOutputStream();
    JPEGImageEncoder encoder = JPEGCodec.createJPEGEncoder(output);
    encoder.encode(image);
%>
```

Here, the Java AWT library is used with the Sun JPEG codec. First, a `BufferedImage` is created to draw upon. Next, the graphics interface is extracted, and the image is filled with white. The last step is to output the image using a `JPEGImageEncoder`.

From these examples, it's easy to see that creating images dynamically is fairly straightforward, regardless of your server-side language preference.

> *As with redirecting to an image, the creation of an image should be done after all other processing has taken place.*

Creating images dynamically or redirecting to an image provides the beginnings of Ajax communication, since both are requests that send data to the server. But this is only one part of the equation; the second part is returning data back to the client.

Images and Cookies

When people think about cookies in this age of cyber threats, most think about security concerns, spyware, and evil corporations tracking their every move. Certainly, those fears are warranted given what goes on in the world of the Web, but cookies really are just small pieces of data that can be accessed by both the client (through JavaScript) and the server. There are also several restrictions placed on cookies that you need to be aware of before using them:

❑ Each domain can store a maximum of 20 cookies on a user's machine. It's best to reuse cookies whenever possible instead of creating new ones.

❑ The total size of the cookie (including name, equals sign, and value) cannot exceed 4096 bytes (512 characters), meaning cookies are useful for storing small amounts of data only.

❑ The total number of cookies allowed on a machine is 300.

Each request to and response from the server contains cookie information, regardless of what type of resource is being requested. This means that setting the `src` attribute of an image brings back updated cookie information from the server. Assuming that an `onload` event handler has been assigned to the image, this is where you can retrieve the new cookie information. The following function can be used to access specific cookie values:

```
function getCookie(sName) {
    var sRE = "(?:; )?" + encodeURIComponent(sName) + "=([^;]*);?";
    var oRE = new RegExp(sRE);

    if (oRE.test(document.cookie)) {
      return decodeURIComponent(RegExp["$1"]);
    } else {
      return null;
    }
}
```

This function looks through the `document.cookie` property, which is a series of name-value pairs representing each cookie accessible by the page. The pairs are URL-encoded and separated by semicolons, which is why a regular expression is used to extract the appropriate value. If the cookie with the given name doesn't exist, the function returns `null`.

It is also considered a best practice to delete cookies once they are no longer used. The following function deletes a cookie with a given name:

```
function deleteCookie(sName) {
    document.cookie = encodeURIComponent(sName) + "=0; " +
        "expires=Thu, 1 Jan 1970 00:00:00 UTC; path=/";
}
```

Setting the expiration date of a cookie to some date that has already passed effectively removes the cookie from the client machine. This function uses January 1, 1970, in GMT format to delete the cookie (the JavaScript Date object has a toGMTString() method that can be used to get this format for any date). The path argument is important as well, as it ensures that the cookie is removed for every location on the domain, not just the current page.

It's possible to recreate an earlier example, pulling customer data from a database, using this technique. Since cookies are an insecure means of storing data, this example will only pull the customer's name. The GetCustomerData.php used with the XHR example must be updated slightly to this end:

```
<?php
    header("Content-Type: image/gif");

    $sID = $_GET["id"];
    $sInfo = "";

    if (is_numeric($sID)) {
        $sDBServer = "your.databaser.server";
        $sDBName = "your_db_name";
        $sDBUsername = "your_db_username";
        $sDBPassword = "your_db_password";
        $sQuery = "Select * from Customers where CustomerId=".$sID;

        $oLink = mysql_connect($sDBServer,$sDBUsername,$sDBPassword);
        @mysql_select_db($sDBName) or $sInfo="Unable to open database";

        if($oResult = mysql_query($sQuery) and mysql_num_rows($oResult) > 0) {
            $aValues = mysql_fetch_array($oResult,MYSQL_ASSOC);
            $sInfo = $aValues['Name'];
            mysql_free_result($oResult);
        } else {
            $sInfo = "Customer with ID $sID doesn't exist.";
        }
    } else {
        $sInfo = "Invalid customer ID.";
    }

    mysql_close($oLink);

    setcookie("info", $sInfo);
    header("Location: pixel.gif");
?>
```

Note that only four lines of code have changed from the XHR example. The first sets the content-type to be image/gif, so the browser knows to expect an image back from the server; the second retrieves only the person's name and stores it in $sInfo. The other two lines (highlighted in the example code) set a cookie named "info" to contain the value of $sInfo and then redirect to the image pixel.gif.

On the client side, make sure to include the getCookie() function defined earlier in this section. This function will be used to retrieve the data sent back from GetCustomerInfo.php. The function requestCustomerInfo(), which previously used XHR, now can be updated to use an image instead:

```
function requestCustomerInfo() {
    var sId = document.getElementById("txtCustomerId").value;
    var oImg = new Image();
    oImg.onload = function () {
        displayCustomerInfo(getCookie("info"));
        deleteCookie("info");
    };
    oImg.onerror = function () {
        displayCustomerInfo("An error occurred while processing the request.");
    };
    oImg.src = "GetCustomerData.php?id=" + sId;
}
```

In this code, an Image is created and its event handlers assigned. The same displayCustomerInfo() function used in the XHR example is called to display any message returned from the server or any error message. Lastly, the src of the image is set to GetCustomerData.aspx with an ID passed in. This will yield the same user experience as the XHR example without any cross-browser compatibility issues. It is important to mention, though, that this example works because there is only a small amount of data being returned to the server. The data comfortably fits inside of a cookie; any large strings would end up being concatenated.

> Be very careful about the type of data you assign to cookies. This information is not encrypted, and it is considered poor practice to create a cookie that contains personal information such as addresses, credit card numbers, and so on. Always delete cookies once you have retrieved data from them.

Using Image Size

Another way to indicate information to the client is through the size of an image. Suppose that you want to save some information into a database, but there's the possibility the insert won't be successful. You could set up an Ajax request using images so that an image of size 1x1 means success and an image of size 2x1 is a failure. Or perhaps the request simply needs to determine if someone is logged in or not, in which case a 1x1 image indicates the user is not logged in whereas a 2x1 image indicates the user is logged in. This technique is useful when you don't need to be returning text back to the client and only need to indicate some sort of server or request state.

To check the dimensions of the image, just use the width and height properties inside of the onload event handler:

```
oImg.onload = function () {
    if (this.width == 1 && this.height == 1) {
        alert("Success!");
```

```
      } else {
          alert("Error!");
      }
  };
```

Since this anonymous function is assigned to the image as an event handler, the `this` object points to the image itself. The image's `width` and `height` are then available (because the call returned successfully) and can be interrogated to see what information the server is sending back. Of course, this technique assumes that you are merely doing something simple such as updating a customer's name, because you are not receiving specific information from the server.

This next example sends a customer ID and a name to `UpdateCustomerName.php`. This information is then used to update the customer's name in the database, and an image is returned to determine if this update is successful or not. Since the user must provide a customer ID to be updated, it is entirely possible that this customer may not exist in the database, in which case an error code (specific image size) must be returned. The possible return conditions are:

❑   **Success:** 1x1 image

❑   **Invalid ID:** 2x1 image

❑   **Other error:** 3x1 image

The `UpdateCustomerName.php` file is:

```php
<?php

    header("Content-Type: image/jpeg");

    $sID = $_GET["id"];
    $sName = mysql_real_escape_string($_GET["name"]);

    if (is_numeric($sID)) {
        $iWidth = 1;

        $sDBServer = "your.database.server";
        $sDBName = "your_db_name";
        $sDBUsername = "your_db_username";
        $sDBPassword = "your_db_password";

        $sSQL = "Update Customers set `Name` = '$sName' where CustomerId=$sID";

        $oLink = mysql_connect($sDBServer,$sDBUsername,$sDBPassword);
        @mysql_select_db($sDBName) or $iWidth = 3;

        if ($iWidth == 1) {
            if (mysql_query($sSQL)) {
                $iWidth = (mysql_affected_rows() > 0) ? 1 : 2;
                mysql_close($oLink);
            } else {
                $iWidth = 3;
            }
        }
    } else {
```

```
        $iWidth = 2;
    }

    $image = imagecreate($iWidth,1);
    $white = imagecolorallocate($image, 255, 255, 255);
    imagejpeg($image);
    imagedestroy($image);
?>
```

This file runs a simple SQL UPDATE statement on the customer database. The $iWidth variable determines what the width of the created image will be. If an error occurs at any time during the execution of this page, $iWidth is set to 3 to indicate the error. If, on the other hand, the ID isn't in the database, $iWidth is set to 2. This situation can occur in two different ways:

❏ The ID isn't numeric, so the statement is never executed.

❏ The statement executes but no rows are affected.

The very last step is to create and output the image as discussed earlier.

On the client side, you need a textbox to input a customer ID, a textbox to input a name, and a button to send the request:

```html
<form method="post" action="UpdateCustomerName.php"
        onsubmit="sendRequest(); return false">
    <p>Enter the customer ID: <input type="text" name="txtID" value="" /></p>
    <p>New customer name: <input type="text" name="txtName" value="" /></p>
    <p><input type="submit" value="Update Customer Name" /></p>
</form>
<div id="divStatus"></div>
```

The sendRequest() method is responsible for sending the information and interpreting the response:

```javascript
function sendRequest() {
    var oForm = document.forms[0];
    var sQueryString = "id=" + encodeURIComponent(oForm.txtID.value)
                            + "&name=" + encodeURIComponent(oForm.txtName.value);
    var oImg = new Image();
    oImg.onload = function () {
        var divStatus = document.getElementById("divStatus");
        switch(this.width) {
            case 1:
                divStatus.innerHTML = "Customer name updated successfully.";
                break;
            case 2:
                divStatus.innerHTML = "Invalid customer ID; name not updated.";
                break;
            default:
                divStatus.innerHTML = "An error occurred.";
        }
    };

    oImg.onerror = function () {
        var divStatus = document.getElementById("divStatus");
```

```
        divStatus.innerHTML = "An error occurred.";
    };

    oImg.src = "UpdateCustomerName.php?" + sQueryString;
}
```

There's nothing very different in this function versus the earlier examples. The first step is to construct the query string for the request. Next, an image is created and event handlers are assigned to it. The onload event handler is of the most importance because it is the one that interrogates the image response to determine what message to show to the user. In this case, it makes sense to use a switch statement on the image's width so that the status message can be supplied.

It's always a good idea to assign an onerror event handler to provide as much feedback as possible to the user. For this example, the event handler just outputs a simple error message. The last step is to set the src of the image to initiate the request.

> **Although you could create different image sizes for different conditions, try to refrain from making an image too big. You don't want to affect user experience while waiting for a simple status from the server.**

Advantages and Disadvantages

As with the other techniques mentioned to this point, using images for Ajax communication is not the solution to every task. However, the image techniques discussed in this section do offer advantages:

- ❑ They are supported in all modern browsers as well as some older ones (such as Netscape Navigator 4, Internet Explorer 5, and Opera 6), offering a high level of compatibility.

- ❑ Unlike hidden frames, there is some indication as to when a request is successful and when it has failed.

- ❑ Yet another upside to using images for Ajax is that, unlike hidden frames and XHR, images are free to access images on any server, not just the one on which the containing page resides. The ability to communicate cross-domain using images has long been used by advertisers and link tracking systems to capture information; you can also use this to your advantage.

There are also disadvantages to using images for Ajax communication:

- ❑ Not the least of these disadvantages is that images can only send GET requests, so the amount of data that can be sent back to the server is limited to the length of the URL that your browser supports (2MB in most cases). When using cookies, the amount of data that can be sent back from the server is fairly limited as well (as mentioned previously, 512 characters is the maximum size of a cookie).

- ❑ There's a possibility that images are disabled on the client.

- ❑ You should also be aware that some users disable cookies, so it is important to always test for cookie support before relying on any cookie-based Ajax solutions.

Dynamic Script Loading

A little-known and little-utilized Ajax technique is called *dynamic script loading*. The concept is simple: create a new `<script/>` element and assign a JavaScript file to its `src` attribute to load JavaScript that isn't initially written into the page. The beginnings of this technique could be seen way back when Internet Explorer 4.0 and Netscape Navigator 4.0 ruled the web browser market. At that time, developers learned that they could use the `document.write()` method to write out a `<script/>` tag. The caveat was that this had to be done before the page was completely loaded. With the advent of the DOM, the concept could be taken to a completely new level.

The basic technique behind dynamic script loading is very easy, just create a `<script/>` element using the DOM `createElement()` method and add it to the page:

```
var oScript = document.createElement("script");
oScript.type = "text/javascript";
oScript.src = "/path/to/my.js";
document.body.appendChild(oScript);
```

Downloading and evaluation of the JavaScript file doesn't begin until the new `<script/>` element is actually added to the page, so it's important not to forget this step. (This is the opposite of dynamically creating an `<img/>` element or `Image` object, which automatically begins downloading once the `src` attribute is assigned.)

Once the download is complete, the browser interprets the JavaScript code contained within. Now the problem becomes a timing issue: how do you know when the code has finished being loaded and interpreted? Unlike the `<img/>` element, the `<script/>` element doesn't have an `onload` event handler, so you can't rely on the browser to tell you when the script is complete. Instead, you'll need to have a callback function that is the executed at the very end of the source file.

Simple Example

The page in this example contains a single button which, when clicked, loads a string ("Hello world!") from an external JavaScript file. This string is passed to a callback function, named `callback()` for simplicity, which displays the text in an alert. The HTML for this page is:

```
<!DOCTYPE html PUBLIC "-//W3C//DTD XHTML 1.0 Transitional//EN"
    "http://www.w3.org/TR/xhtml1/DTD/xhtml1-transitional.dtd">
<html xmlns="http://www.w3.org/1999/xhtml">
  <head>
    <title>Dynamic Script Loading Example 1</title>
    <script type="text/javascript">
//<![CDATA[
        function makeRequest() {
          var oScript = document.createElement("script");
          oScript.type = "text/javascript";
          oScript.src = "example1.js";
          document.body.appendChild(oScript);
        }

        function callback(sText) {
          alert("Loaded from file: " + sText);
```

```
        }
    //]]>
    </script>
  </head>
  <body>
    <input type="button" value="Click Me" onclick="makeRequest()" />
  </body>
</html>
```

The JavaScript file example1.js contains a single line:

```
callback("Hello world!");
```

When the button is clicked, the makeRequest() function is called, initiating the dynamic script loading. Since the newly loaded script is in context of the page, it can access and call the callback() function, which can do with the returned value as it pleases. This example works in any DOM-compliant browsers (Internet Explorer 5.0+, Safari, Firefox, and Opera 7.0+).

Dynamic Example

The previous example illustrated loading data from a static file that already exists on the server. While this may occur, it's much more likely that you'll want to load dynamic data, as with examples in the previous sections. The basic technique for this is very similar to that of using images for Ajax communication: create a dynamic page (using PHP, ASP.NET, or JSP) that accepts query string arguments and outputs JavaScript code.

Among the data being passed to the dynamic page on the server should be the name of the callback function call. This is the most optimal thing to do for maintenance purposes. Imagine what would happen if you changed the name of the function in the static page or script file and forgot to change it in the dynamic file. So, in the interest of avoiding such tight coupling and the problems that accompany it, it is much safer to pass in the name of the function that should be called.

The dynamic page then has several important jobs to do. First, it must set its content type to be text/javascript so as to identify the output as JavaScript code and not HTML or some other format. Next, the page needs to pull the callback function name from the query string and then output it, passing in any relevant data.

Suppose that the request to the dynamic page looks like this:

```
/path/to/js.php?id=25&callback=myCallbackFunc
```

The file creating the JavaScript then must look similar to this:

```php
<?php
    header("Content-type: text/javascript");
?>

var sMessage = "Hello world!";
<?php echo $_GET["callback"] ?>(sMessage);
```

The first part of this file sets the content type to text/javascript so that the browser recognizes it as JavaScript. Next, a JavaScript variable called sMessage is defined as a string, "Hello world!". The last line outputs the name of the callback function that was passed through the query string, followed by parentheses enclosing sMessage, effectively making it a function call. If all works as planned, the last line becomes:

```
myCallbackFunc(sMessage);
```

Taking all of this into account, it's possible to recreate the XHR example that retrieves data from the server about a specific customer. The only part that needs to change on the client side is the requestCustomerInfo() function:

```javascript
function requestCustomerInfo() {
    var sId = document.getElementById("txtCustomerId").value;
    var oScript = document.createElement("script");
    oScript.type = "text/javascript";
    oScript.src = "GetCustomerData.php?id=" + sId
                    + "&callback=displayCustomerInfo";
    document.body.appendChild(oScript);
}
```

Note that the same displayCustomerInfo() function will be used, so its name is passed in on the query string.

The GetCustomerData.php page also must change, though only slightly, to accommodate this technique:

```php
<?php
    header("Content-Type: text/javascript");

    $sID = $_GET["id"];
    $sCallbackFunc = $_GET["callback"];
    $sInfo = "";

    if (is_numeric($sID)) {
        $sDBServer = "your.databaser.server";
        $sDBName = "your_db_name";
        $sDBUsername = "your_db_username";
        $sDBPassword = "your_db_password";
        $sQuery = "Select * from Customers where CustomerId=".$sID;

        $oLink = mysql_connect($sDBServer,$sDBUsername,$sDBPassword);
        @mysql_select_db($sDBName) or $sInfo="Unable to open database";

        if($sInfo == "") {
            if($oResult = mysql_query($sQuery) and mysql_num_rows($oResult) > 0) {
                $aValues = mysql_fetch_array($oResult,MYSQL_ASSOC);
                $sInfo = $aValues['Name']."<br />".$aValues['Address']."<br />".
                  $aValues['City']."<br />".$aValues['State']."<br />".
                  $aValues['Zip']."<br /><br />Phone: ".$aValues['Phone']."<br />".
                  "<a href=\"mailto:".$aValues['Email']."\">".
                  $aValues['Email']."</a>";
                mysql_free_result($oResult);
```

```
            } else {
                $sInfo = "Customer with ID $sID doesn't exist.";
            }
        }
    } else {
        $sInfo = "Invalid customer ID.";
    }

    mysql_close($oLink);

    $sEncodedInfo = str_replace("\"", "\\\"", $sInfo);
    $sEncodedInfo = str_replace("\n", "\\n", $sEncodedInfo);
    echo "$sCallbackFunc(\"$sEncodedInfo\");";
?>
```

The first change to the code is setting the content type to text/javascript, which as previously mentioned is necessary to identify the type of content the page is outputting. Then, the callback function name has to be retrieved from the $_GET array and stored in $sCallbackFunc. The $sInfo variable is then encoded so it will be a proper JavaScript string. To do so, all the quotation marks and new line characters have to be escaped. The resulting string is stored in $sEncodedInfo and output on the last line as a literal being passed into the callback function. This is the only line that will be output by the page.

With these changes, this example acts just as the XHR version does, including all error messages and client-side behavior.

Advantages and Disadvantages

Though dynamic script loading is a quick and easy way to establish client-server communication, it does have some drawbacks.

❑   For one, there is no feedback as to what is going on once the communication is initiated. If, for example, the file you are accessing doesn't exist, there is no way for you to receive a 404 error from the server. Your site or application may sit, waiting, because the callback function was never called.

❑   Also, you can't send a POST request using this technique, only a GET, which limits the amount of data that you can send. This could also be a security issue: make sure that you don't send confidential information such as passwords using dynamic script loading, as this information can easily be picked up from the query string.

Dynamic script loading does offer a couple of advantages over other techniques as well.

❑   First, just like using images, it is possible to access files on other servers. This can be very powerful if you are working in a multidomain environment.

❑   Further, dynamic script loading offers the ability to execute an arbitrary amount of JavaScript as the result of server-side calculations. You aren't limited to simply one callback function; use as many as necessary to achieve the desired results.

Cache Control

Whenever you are dealing with repeated calls to the same page, you should be concerned about browser caching. For those unaware, web browsers tend to cache certain resources to improve the speed with which sites are downloaded and displayed. This can result in a tremendous speed increase on frequently visited web sites, but can also cause problems for pages that change frequently. If you are making several Ajax calls, you need to be aware that caching may cause you problems.

The best way to deal with caching is to include a header with caching information on any data being sent from the server to the browser. This can be done using the `Cache-Control` and `Expires` headers, which should be set up as follows:

```
Cache-Control: no-cache
Expires: Fri, 30 Oct 1998 14:19:41 GMT
```

This tells the browser not to cache the data coming from the specific URL. Instead, the browser always calls a new version from the server instead of a saved version from its own cache. Most browsers support the `Cache-Control` header, and almost all support the `Expires` header (which is set to a date in the past to prevent caching). Using a combination of the two headers ensures that all browsers will not cache the page.

> **It is important to note that technically the `no-cache` directive simply requires the browser to ensure that the resource in question is the most up-to-date version available. If the version in the cache is the most recent version, then the cached version is used. To force the browser never to store a copy of the resource locally, use the `no-store` directive with the `Cache Control` header.**

Summary

This chapter introduced you to several Ajax techniques for client-server communication. It began with an HTTP primer, exploring HTTP requests and responses. You learned about the format of HTTP messages and the differences between a GET request and a POST request. The concepts of headers and message bodies were introduced.

The first Ajax technique you learned was the hidden frame technique, which uses a frame with a width or height of zero, effectively hiding it from the user. This technique uses JavaScript calls to and from the hidden frame to facilitate the client-server communication. Using the hidden frame technique, you learned how to send both GET and POST requests.

Next, you learned about replacing hidden frames with hidden iframes. Because iframes can be created dynamically using JavaScript, this may be a preferable way to initiate client-server communication in modern browsers. The same techniques were used as with hidden frames, although iframes provide a bit more flexibility in the design of your pages.

The chapter also introduced the use of XHR for client-server communication. You learned that Internet Explorer, Mozilla Firefox, Safari, and Opera all support some form of XHR object, and some extra coding is necessary to detect these differences. The differences between asynchronous and synchronous requests were explained, and you learned how to make GET and POST requests using XHR. You also learned how to use request and response headers along with HTTP status codes to better handle requests.

You learned about two alternate Ajax techniques using images and dynamic script loading. It was discussed how these two techniques allow cross-domain communication, unlike XHR and hidden frames. Two different methods of using images were covered and the advantages and disadvantages of each were discussed.

The last topic covered in this chapter was cache control and its importance in Ajax. You learned to always set the cache control headers to avoid possible caching-related issues.

3

Ajax Patterns

Design patterns describe programming techniques to solve common problems. Given that programming has been around for several decades, chances are that many of the problems you face every day have already been solved by someone else. Since the mid-1990s, a lot of attention has been drawn to design patterns as a way to cut development time.

Even though the term *Ajax* has been around only since early 2005, the techniques that Ajax describes have been used since the late 1990s, giving rise to several Ajax patterns that solve specific problems. You've already seen some of these patterns in action, namely the hidden frame technique and asynchronous XHR calls. These are *communication patterns* between the client and server using JavaScript. As you may have expected, there are many more types of patterns.

Author and programmer Michael Mahemoff was the first to attempt to document Ajax design patterns at his web site, www.ajaxpatterns.org. The patterns presented in this chapter are a mixture of Mahemoff's and others that your authors have identified. Note that design patterns, whether described on a web site or in a book, can never be official, only accepted. Design patterns are not standards to be followed, but merely designs of solutions that have worked previously. It is up to the development community to generate a "collective wisdom" around specific patterns; it's up to the individual developer to decide whether to implement a given pattern in his or her own application.

Communication Control Patterns

You already know, from Chapter 2, how to communicate with the server from JavaScript. The real question is: What is the best way to initiate and continue to make requests back to the server? In some cases, it may be best to preload information from the server so that it is available immediately upon some user action. In other cases, you may want to send data to, or receive data from, the server in varying intervals. Perhaps everything shouldn't be downloaded at once, and instead should be downloaded in a particular sequence. Ajax affords you fine granularity in controlling the communication between client and server to achieve your desired behavior.

Predictive Fetch

In a traditional web solution, the application has no idea what is to come next. A page is presented with any number of links, each one leading to a different part of the site. This may be termed "fetch on demand," where the user, through his or her actions, tells the server exactly what data should be retrieved. While this paradigm has defined the Web since its inception, it has the unfortunate side effect of forcing the start-and-stop model of user interaction upon the user. With the help of Ajax, however, this is beginning to change.

The Predictive Fetch pattern is a relatively simple idea that can be somewhat difficult to implement: the Ajax application guesses what the user is going to do next and retrieves the appropriate data. In a perfect world, it would be wonderful to always know what the user is going to do and make sure that the next data is readily available when needed. In reality, however, determining future user action is just a guessing game depending on your intentions.

There are simple use cases where predicting user actions is somewhat easier. Suppose that you are reading an online article that is separated into three pages. It is logical to assume that if you are interested in reading the first page, you're also interested in reading the second and third page. So, if the first page has been loaded for a few seconds (which can easily be determined by using a timeout), it is probably safe to download the second page in the background. Likewise, if the second page has been loaded for a few seconds, it is logical to assume that the reader will continue on to the third page. As this extra data is being loaded and cached on the client, the reader continues to read and barely even notices that the next page comes up almost instantaneously after clicking the Next Page link.

Another simple use case happens during the writing of an e-mail. Most of the time, you'll be writing an e-mail to someone you know, so it's logical to assume that the person is already in your address book. To help you out, it may be wise to preload your address book in the background and offer suggestions. This approach is taken by many web-based e-mail systems, including Gmail and AOL Webmail. The key, once again, is the "logical-to-assume" criterion. By anticipating and preloading information related to the user's most likely next steps, you can make your application feel lighter and more responsive; by using Ajax to fetch information related to any possible next step, you can quickly overload your server and make the browser bog down with extra processing. As a rule of thumb, only prefetch information when you believe it's logical to assume that information will be requisite to completing the user's next request.

Page Preloading Example

As mentioned previously, one of the simplest and most logical uses of the Predictive Fetch pattern is in the preloading of pages in an online article. With the advent of weblogs, or blogs for short, everyone seems to have been bitten by the publishing bug, writing their own articles on their own web sites. Reading long articles online is very difficult on the eyes, so many sites split them into multiple pages. This is better for reading, but takes longer to load because each new page brings with it all of the formatting, menus, and ads that were on the original page. Predictive Fetch eases the load on both the client and server by loading only the text for the next page while the reader is still reading the first page.

To begin, you'll need a page that handles the server-side logic for page preloading. The file ArticleExample.php contains code for displaying an article online:

```php
<?php
    $page = 1;
    $dataOnly = false;
```

```php
        if (isset($_GET["page"])) {
            $page = (int) $_GET["page"];
        }

        if (isset($_GET["dataonly"]) && $_GET["dataonly"] == "true") {
            $dataOnly = true;
        }

        if (!$dataOnly) {
?>
<!DOCTYPE html PUBLIC "-//W3C//DTD XHTML 1.0 Transitional//EN"
    "http://www.w3.org/TR/xhtml1/DTD/xhtml1-transitional.dtd">
<html xmlns="http://www.w3.org/1999/xhtml">
    <head>
        <title>Article Example</title>
        <script type="text/javascript" src="zxml.js"></script>
        <script type="text/javascript" src="Article.js"></script>
        <link rel="stylesheet" type="text/css" href="Article.css" />
    </head>
    <body>
        <h1>Article Title</h1>
        <div id="divLoadArea" style="display:none"></div>
<?php
        $output = "<p>Page ";

        for ($i=1; $i < 4; $i++) {
            $output .= "<a href=\"ArticleExample.php?page=$i\" id=\"aPage$i\"";
            if ($i==$page) {
                $output .= "class=\"current\"";
            }
            $output .= ">$i</a> ";
        }
        echo $output;
    }

    if ($page==1) {
?>
    <div id="divPage1"><!-- contents of page 1 --></div>
<?php
    } else if ($page == 2) {
?>
    <div id="divPage2"><!-- contents of page 2 --></div>
<?php
    } else if ($page == 3) {
?>
    <div id="divPage3"><!-- contents of page 3 --></div>
<?php
    }

    if (!$dataOnly) {
?>
    </body>
</html>
<?php
    }
?>
```

By default, this file displays the first page of text for the article. If the `page` query string parameter is specified, such as `page=2`, then it shows the given page of the article. When the query string contains `dataonly=true`, the page outputs only a `<div/>` element containing the article text for the given page (not the `<html/>`, `<head/>`, or `<body/>` tags). Combining this with the `page` parameter enables you to retrieve any page of the article that you need.

> **Note that this page calls itself to get more data. When using an Ajax call, it passes in** `dataonly=true` **on the query string to ensure that it gets only the data and none of the extra markup that already exists in the page.**

The HTML in this page has a space for the article title as well as a `<div/>` element used for loading extra pages. This `<div/>` element has its display property set to `none` to ensure that its contents are not displayed accidentally. The PHP code immediately following contains logic to output a list of pages available for the article. In this example, there will be three pages of content, so there are three links output at the top (see Figure 3-1).

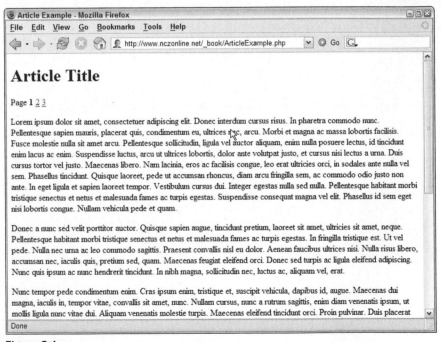

Figure 3-1

The current page is assigned a CSS class of `current` so that the user knows which page he or she is viewing. This class is defined in `Article.css` as:

```
a.current {
    color: black;
    font-weight: bold;
    text-decoration: none;
}
```

When the reader is viewing a particular page, the link for that page becomes black and bold, and is no longer underlined, providing a clear indication of the page that he or she is reading. By default, these links simply load the same page and change the page parameter of the query string; this is the way that most web sites handle multipage articles. Using Predictive Fetch, however, will improve the user's experience and the speed with which the data is available.

Several global JavaScript variables are required to implement Predictive Fetch for this example:

```
var oXHR = null;            //The XHR object
var iPageCount = 3;          //The number of pages
var iCurPage = -1;           //The currently displayed page
var iWaitBeforeLoad = 5000; //The time (in ms) before loading new page
var iNextPageToLoad = -1;    //The next page to load
```

The first variable is a global XHR object that is used to make all requests for more information. The second, iPageCount, is the number of pages used in this article. (This is hard-coded here, but in actual practice this would have to be generated.) The iCurPage variable stores the page number currently being displayed to the user. The next two variables deal directly with the preloading of data: iWaitBeforeLoad is the number of milliseconds to wait before loading the next page, and iNextPageToLoad contains the page number that should be loaded once the specified amount of time has passed. For this example, a new page is loaded behind the scenes every 5 seconds (5000 milliseconds), which should be long enough for someone to read the first few sentences of an article to determine if it's worth reading the rest. If the reader leaves before 5 seconds are up, chances are they have no intention of reading the rest of the article.

To begin the process, you'll need a function to determine the URL for retrieving a particular page. This function, getURLForPage(), accepts a single argument that specifies the page number you want to retrieve. Then, the current URL is extracted and the page parameter is appended to the end:

```
function getURLForPage(iPage) {
    var sNewUrl = location.href;
    if (location.search.length > 0) {
        sNewUrl = sNewUrl.substring(0, sNewUrl.indexOf("?"))
    }
    sNewUrl += "?page=" + iPage;
    return sNewUrl;
}
```

This function begins by extracting the URL from location.href, which gives the complete URL for the page, including the query string. Then, the URL is tested to see if there is a query string specified by determining if the length of location.search is greater than 0 (location.search returns just the query string, including the question mark, if there is one specified). If there is a query string, it is stripped off using the substring() method. The page parameter is then appended to the URL and returned. This function will come in handy in a number of different places.

The next function is called showPage(), and as you may have guessed, it is responsible for displaying the next page of the article:

```
function showPage(sPage) {

    var divPage = document.getElementById("divPage" + sPage);

    if (divPage) {
```

```
        for (var i=0; i < iPageCount; i++) {
            var iPageNum = i+1;
            var divOtherPage = document.getElementById("divPage" + iPageNum);
            var aOtherLink = document.getElementById("aPage" + iPageNum);
            if (divOtherPage && sPage != iPageNum) {
                divOtherPage.style.display = "none";
                aOtherLink.className = "";
            }
        }
        divPage.style.display = "block";
        document.getElementById("aPage" + sPage).className = "current";
    } else {
        location.href = getURLForPage(parseInt(sPage));
    }
}
```

This function first checks to see whether the given page has a `<div/>` element already loaded. The `<div/>`
element would be named `divPage` plus the page number (for example, `divPage1` for the first page,
`divPage2` for the second, and so on). If this `<div/>` element exists, the page has been prefetched already,
so you can just switch the currently visible page. This is done by iterating through the pages and hiding all
pages except the one indicated by the argument `sPage`. At the same time, the links for each page are given
an empty string for their CSS class. Then, the `<div/>` element for the current page has its `display` property set to `block` in order to show it, and the link for the page has its CSS class set to `current`.

If, on the other hand, the `<div/>` element doesn't exist, the page navigates to the next page in the article
the old-fashioned way, by getting the URL (using the `getURLForPage()` function defined previously)
and assigning it to `location.href`. This is a fallback functionality so that if the user clicks a page link
before 5 seconds are up, the experience falls back to the traditional web paradigm.

The `loadNextPage()` function is used to load each new page behind the scenes. This function is responsible for ensuring that requests are made only for valid pages and that pages are retrieved in order and
in the specified intervals:

```
function loadNextPage() {

    if (iNextPageToLoad <= iPageCount) {

        if (!oXHR) {
            oXHR = zXmlHttp.createRequest();
        } else if (oXHR.readyState != 0) {
            oXHR.abort();
        }

        oXHR.open("get", getURLForPage(iNextPageToLoad)
                                    + "&dataonly=true", true);
        oXHR.onreadystatechange = function () {

            //more code here
        };
        oXHR.send(null);
    }
}
```

The function begins by ensuring that the page number stored in iNextPageToLoad is valid by comparing it to iPageCount. Passing this test, the next step is to see if the global XHR object has been created yet. If not, it is created using the zXml library's createRequest() method. If it has already been instantiated, the readyState property is checked to ensure that it's 0. If readyState is not 0, the abort() method must be called to reset the XHR object.

Next, the open() method is called, specifying that the request will get an asynchronous GET request. The URL is retrieved by using the getURLForPage() function and then appending the string "&dataonly=true" to ensure that only the page text is returned. With all of that set, it's time to move on to the onreadystatechange event handler.

In this case, the onreadystatechange event handler is responsible for retrieving the article text as well as creating the appropriate DOM structure to represent it:

```
function loadNextPage() {

    if (iNextPageToLoad <= iPageCount) {

        if (!oXHR) {
            oXHR = zXmlHttp.createRequest();
        } else if (oXHR.readyState != 0) {
            oXHR.abort();
        }

        oXHR.open("get", getURLForPage(iNextPageToLoad)
                                    + "&dataonly=true", true);
        oXHR.onreadystatechange = function () {

            if (oXHR.readyState == 4) {
                if (oXHR.status == 200) {
                    var divLoadArea = document.getElementById("divLoadArea");
                    divLoadArea.innerHTML = oXHR.responseText;
                    var divNewPage = document.getElementById("divPage"
                                                    + iNextPageToLoad);
                    divNewPage.style.display = "none";
                    document.body.appendChild(divNewPage);
                    divLoadArea.innerHTML = "";
                    iNextPageToLoad++;
                    setTimeout(loadNextPage, iWaitBeforeLoad);
                }

            }

        };
        oXHR.send(null);
    }
}
```

As discussed in the previous chapter, the readyState property is checked to see when it is equal to 4, and the status property is checked to make sure there was no error. Once you've passed those two conditions, the real processing begins. First, a reference to the load area <div/> element is retrieved and stored in divLoadArea. Then, the responseText from the request is assigned to the load area's innerHTML property. Since the text coming back is an HTML snippet, it will be parsed and the appropriate DOM objects will be created. Next, a reference to the <div/> element that contains the next page is retrieved (you know the ID will be divPage plus iNextPageToLoad) and its display property is set to none to ensure it remains invisible when it is moved outside of the load area. The next line appends divNewPage to the document's body, putting it into the regular viewing area for usage. Then the load area's innerHTML property is set to an empty string to prepare for another page to be loaded. After that, the iNextPageToLoad variable is incremented and a new timeout is set to call this function again after the specified period of time. This function will continue to be called every 5 seconds until all pages have been loaded.

Because this page should be functional without JavaScript, all this code is attached at runtime after determining if the browser is capable of using XHR. Fortunately, the zXmlHttp object in the zXml library has a function, isSupported(), that can be used to determine this:

```
window.onload = function () {
    if (zXmlHttp.isSupported()) {
        //begin Ajax code here
    }
};
```

Inside this code block is where all the Predictive Fetch code will go, ensuring that browsers without XHR support will not have their usability adversely affected by half-functioning code.

The first step in the process of setting up Predictive Fetch for the article is to determine which page the user is currently viewing. To do so, you must look into the URL's query string to see if the page parameter is specified. If it is, you can extract the page number from there; otherwise, you can assume that the page number is 1 (the default):

```
window.onload = function () {
    if (zXmlHttp.isSupported()) {

        if (location.href.indexOf("page=") > -1) {
            var sQueryString = location.search.substring(1);
            iCurPage = parseInt(sQueryString.substring(sQueryString.indexOf("=")+1));
        } else {
            iCurPage = 1;
        }

        iNextPageToLoad = iCurPage+1;

        //more code here
    }
};
```

In this section of code, the page's URL (accessible through location.href) is tested to see if page= has been specified. If so, the query string is retrieved by using location.search (which returns only the query string, including the question mark, that the call to substring(1) strips out). The next line retrieves just the part of the query string after the equals sign (which should be the page number), converts it to an integer using parseInt(), and stores the result in iCurPage. If, on the other hand, the page parameter isn't specified in the query string, the page is assumed to be the first one, and 1 is assigned to iCurPage. The last line in this section sets the iNextPageToLoad variable to the current page plus one, ensuring that you don't end up reloading data that is already available.

The next step is to override the functionality of the page links. Remember, by default, these links reload the same page with a different query string to specify which page should be displayed. If XHR is supported, you need to override this behavior and replace it with function calls to the Ajax functionality:

```
window.onload = function () {
    if (zXmlHttp.isSupported()) {

        if (location.href.indexOf("page=") > -1) {
          var sQueryString = location.search.substring(1);
          iCurPage = parseInt(sQueryString.substring(sQueryString.indexOf("=")+1));
        } else {
          iCurPage = 1;
        }

        iNextPageToLoad = iCurPage+1;

        var colLinks = document.getElementsByTagName("a");
        for (var i=0; i < colLinks.length; i++) {
            if (colLinks[i].id.indexOf("aPage") == 0) {
                colLinks[i].onclick = function (oEvent) {
                    var sPage = this.id.substring(5);
                    showPage(sPage);

                    if (oEvent) {
                        oEvent.preventDefault();
                    } else {
                        window.event.returnValue = false;
                    }
                }
            }
        }

        setTimeout(loadNextPage, iWaitBeforeLoad);

    }
};
```

Here, a collection of links (<a/> elements) is retrieved using `getElementsByTagName()`. If the link has an ID beginning with `aPage`, it is a page link and needs to be addressed; this is determined by using `indexOf()` and checking for a value of 0, which indicates that `aPage` is the first part of the string. Next, an `onclick` event handler is assigned to the link. Within this event handler, the page number is extracted by using the ID of the link (accessible through `this.id`) and using `substring()` to return everything after `aPage`. Then, this value is passed into the `showPage()` function defined earlier in this section, which displays the appropriate page. After that point, you need only worry about canceling the default behavior of the link, which is to navigate to a new page. Because of differences in the Internet Explorer (IE) and DOM event models, an `if` statement is necessary to determine the appropriate course of action. If the `event` object was passed in to the function (the argument `oEvent`), then this is a DOM-compliant browser and the `preventDefault()` method is called to block the default behavior. If, however, `oEvent` is `null`, that means it's IE and so the `event` object is accessible as `window.event`. The `returnValue` property is then set to `false`, which is the way IE cancels default event actions.

After the links have been properly handled, a timeout is created for the initial call to `loadNextPage()`. This first call will take place after 5 seconds and will automatically load the second page at that point.

When you test this functionality yourself, try clicking the page links at different points in time. If you click it before 5 seconds have passed, you will see the page navigate to a new URL with the query string changed. The next time, wait about 10 seconds and click a page link. You should see that the text changes while the URL does not (it is also noticeably faster than navigating to a URL).

Submission Throttling

Predictive Fetch is one pattern for retrieving data from the server; the other side of an Ajax solution is the sending of data to the server. Since you want to avoid page refreshes, the question of when to send user data is important. In a traditional web site or web application, each click makes a request back to the server so that the server is always aware of what the client is doing. In the Ajax model, the user interacts with the site or application without additional requests being generated for each click.

One solution would be to send data back to the server every time a user action occurs, similar to a traditional web solution. Thus, when the user types a letter, that letter is sent to the server immediately. The process is then repeated for each letter typed. The problem with this approach is that it has the possibility to create a large number of requests in a short amount of time, which not only may cause problems for the server but also may cause the user interface to slow down as each request is being made and processed. The Submission Throttling design pattern is an alternative approach to this problematic issue.

Using Submission Throttling, you buffer the data to be sent to the server on the client and then send the data at predetermined times. The venerable Google Suggest feature does this brilliantly. It doesn't send a request after each character is typed. Instead, it waits for a certain amount of time and sends all the text currently in the textbox. The delay from typing to sending has been fine-tuned to the point that it doesn't seem like much of a delay at all. Submission Throttling, in part, gives Google Suggest its speed.

Submission Throttling typically begins either when the web site or application first loads or because of a specific user action. Then, a client-side function is called to begin the buffering of data. Every so often, the user's status is checked to see if he or she is idle (doing so prevents any interference with the user interface). If the user is still active, data continues to be collected. When the user is idle, which is to say he or she is not performing an action, it's time to decide whether to send the data. This determination varies depending on your use case; you may want to send data only when it reaches a certain size, or you may want to send it every time the user is idle. After the data is sent, the application typically continues to gather data until either a server response or some user action signals to stop the data collection. Figure 3-2 outlines this process.

> The Submission Throttling pattern should never be used for mission-critical data. If information must be posted to the server within a specific amount of time, you are better off using a traditional form to ensure the correct and timely delivery of the information.

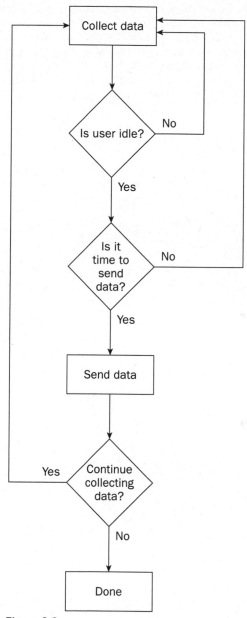

Figure 3-2

Incremental Form Validation Example

As mentioned previously, Submission Throttling can be achieved through various user interactions. When using forms, it's sometimes useful to upload data incrementally as the form is being filled out. The most common usage is to validate data as the user is filling in the form instead of waiting until the end to determine any errors. In this case, you would most likely use the onchange event handler of each form element to determine when to upload the data.

The change event fires for a <select/> element whenever a different option is selected; it fires for other controls when its value has changed and it has lost focus. For example, if you typed a couple of letters into a textbox and then clicked elsewhere on the screen (causing the textbox to lose focus), the change event fires, and the onchange event handler is called. If you click in the textbox again, and then click elsewhere (or press the Tab key), the textbox will lose focus but the change event will not fire because no changes have been made. Using this event handler for Submission Throttling can prevent extraneous requests.

Normally, the form validation is simply a precursor to submission. The form's submit button starts out disabled, becoming enabled only when all fields in the form have been validated by the server. For example, suppose you are running a web site where users must sign up to gain access to certain features. This may be a shopping site that requires sign-in to purchase items or a site that requires membership to access the message board. The items you'll want to be sure of when creating this new account are:

❑   The user name must not be taken.

❑   The e-mail address must be valid.

❑   The birthday must be a valid date.

Of course, the type of data required will differ depending on your usage, but these items provide a good starting point for most applications.

The first step in creating such interaction is to define the HTML form that will collect the data. This form should stand alone so that it can be used even if Ajax calls aren't possible:

```
<form method="post" action="Success.php">
    <table>
        <tr>
            <td><label for="txtFirstName">First Name</label></td>
            <td><input type="text" id="txtFirstName" name="txtFirstName" /></td>
        </tr>
        <tr>
            <td><label for="txtLastName">Last Name</label></td>
            <td><input type="text" id="txtLastName" name="txtLastName" /></td>
        </tr>
        <tr>
            <td><label for="txtEmail">E-mail</label></td>
            <td><input type="text" id="txtEmail" name="txtEmail" /><img
src="error.gif" alt="Error" id="imgEmailError" style="display:none" /></td>
        </tr>
        <tr>
            <td><label for="txtUsername">Username</label></td>
```

```
                <td><input type="text" id="txtUsername" name="txtUsername" /><img
src="error.gif" alt="Error" id="imgUsernameError" style="display:none" /></td>
        </tr>
        <tr>
            <td><label for="txtBirthday">Birthday</label></td>
            <td><input type="text" id="txtBirthday" name="txtBirthday" /><img
src="error.gif" alt="Error" id="imgBirthdayError" style="display:none" />
(m/d/yyyy)</td>
        </tr>
        <tr>
            <td><label for="selGender">Gender</label></td>
            <td><select id="selGender"
name="selGender"><option>Male</option><option>Female</option></select></td>
        </tr>
    </table>
    <input type="submit" id="btnSignUp" value="Sign Up!" />
</form>
```

You should note a few things about this form. First, not all fields will be validated using Ajax calls. The fields for first and last name as well as gender (represented by a combo box) don't require validation. The other fields — for e-mail, user name, and birthday — will make use of Ajax validation. Second, you'll note that these fields have a hidden image after the textbox. This image is used only in the event that there is a validation error. Initially the images are hidden, because those browsers without Ajax capabilities should never see them. There is absolutely no JavaScript on this form; all the appropriate functions and event handlers are defined in a separate file.

A single function called `validateField()` is used to validate each form field. This is possible because each field uses the same validation technique (call the server and wait for a response). The only differences are the types of data being validated and which image to show if validation is unsuccessful.

The server-side functionality is stored in a file named `ValidateForm.php`. This file expects a name-value pair to be passed in the query string. The name should be the name of the control whose value is being checked, and the value should be the value of that control. Depending on the name of the control, this page runs the appropriate validation tests on the value. Then, it outputs a simple string in the following format:

```
<true|false>||<error message>
```

The first part of this string indicates whether the value is valid (`true` if it is; `false` if not). The second part, after the double pipes (||), is an error message that is provided only when the value is invalid. Here are a couple of examples of what the returned string might look like:

```
true||
false||Invalid date.
```

The first line represents a valid value; the second represents an invalid date.

> This is a plain-text message, although later in the book you will learn about using other data formats, such as XML and JSON for this same purpose.

The code that does the validation is as follows:

```php
<?php
    $valid = "false";
    $message = "An unknown error occurred.";

    if (isset($_GET["txtUsername"])) {

        //load array of usernames
        $usernames = array();
        $usernames[] = "SuperBlue";
        $usernames[] = "Ninja123";
        $usernames[] = "Daisy1724";
        $usernames[] = "NatPack";

        //check usernames
        if (in_array($_GET["txtUsername"], $usernames)) {
            $message = "This username already exists. Please choose another.";
        } else if (strlen($_GET["txtUsername"]) < 8) {
            $message = "Username must be at least 8 characters long.";
        } else {
            $valid = "true";
            $message = "";
        }

    } else if (isset($_GET["txtBirthday"])) {

        $date = strtotime($_GET["txtBirthday"]);
        if (!is_numeric($date) or $date < 0) {
            $message = "This is not a valid date.";
        } else {
            $valid = "true";
            $message = "";
        }

    } else if (isset($_GET["txtEmail"])) {

        if(!eregi(
            "^[_a-z0-9-]+(\.[_a-z0-9-]+)*@[a-z0-9-]+(\.[a-z0-9-]+)*(\.[a-z]{2,3})$",
            $_GET["txtEmail"])) {
            $message = "This e-mail address is not valid";
        } else {
            $valid = "true";
            $message = "";
        }
    }

    echo "$valid||$message";
?>
```

In this file, the first step is to determine which field to validate. This is done using the isset() function to test the $_GET array for a value. If there is a value for a particular field, then the validation commences. For the user name, the value is checked to see if it already exists in an array of user names and then checked to ensure that it is at least eight characters long. The birthday is passed directly into PHP's built-in `strtotime()` function, which converts a date string in any number of U.S. formats into a UNIX timestamp (the number of seconds since January 1, 1970). If there is an error, this function returns −1 or false (depending on the version of PHP), indicating that the string passed in was not a valid date. The e-mail address is checked against a regular expression to ensure that it is in the correct format. This regular expression was devised by John Coggeshall in his article, "E-mail validation with PHP 4," available online at `www.zend.com/zend/spotlight/ev12apr.php`.

> Note that the user names in this example are stored in a simple array and hard-coded into the page. In an actual implementation, the user names should be stored in a database and the database should be queried to determine whether the user name already exists.

The `$valid` and `$message` variables are initialized to `false` and `"An unknown error occurred"`. This ensures that if the file is used incorrectly (passing in an unrecognized field name, for example), a negative validation will always be returned. When a positive validation occurs, however, this requires that both variables be reset to appropriate values (`true` for `$valid`, an empty string for `$message`). In the case of a negative validation, only the `$message` variable has to be set since `$valid` is already `false`. The very last step in this page is to output the response string in the format mentioned previously.

Next, the JavaScript to perform the validation must be created. A single function, `validateField()`, can be used to validate each field as long as it knows which field it should be validating. This takes a little bit of work to counteract cross-browser compatibility issues:

```
function validateField(oEvent) {
    oEvent = oEvent || window.event;
    var txtField = oEvent.target || oEvent.srcElement;

    //more code to come
}
```

The first two lines of code inside this function equalize the differences between event models in IE and DOM-compliant browsers (such as Mozilla Firefox, Opera, and Safari). DOM-compliant browsers pass in an `event` object to each event handler; the control that caused the event is stored in the `event` object's `target` property. In IE, the `event` object is a property of `window`; therefore, the first line inside the function assigns the correct value to the `oEvent` variable. Logical OR (`||`) returns a non-`null` value when used with an object and a `null` object. If you are using IE, `oEvent` will be `undefined`; thus, the value of `window.event` is assigned to `oEvent`. If you are using a DOM-compliant browser, `oEvent` will be reassigned to itself. The second line does the same operation for the control that caused the event, which is stored in the `srcElement` property in IE. At the end of these two lines, the control that caused the event is stored in the `txtField` variable. The next step is to create the HTTP request using XHR:

```
function validateField(oEvent) {
    oEvent = oEvent || window.event;
    var txtField = oEvent.target || oEvent.srcElement;
    var oXHR = zXmlHttp.createRequest();
    oXHR.open("get", "ValidateForm.php?" + txtField.name + "="
                            + encodeURIComponent(txtField.value), true);
    oXHR.onreadystatechange = function () {
        //more code to come
```

```
    };
    oXHR.send(null);
}
```

As in Chapter 2, you are using the zXml library for cross-browser XHR support. The XHR object is created and stored in oXHR. Next, the connection is initialized to a GET request using open(). Note that the query string for ValidateForm.php is created by combining the name of the field, an equals sign, and the value of the field (which is URL encoded using encodeURIComponent()). Also note that this is an asynchronous request. This is extremely important for this use case, because you don't want to interfere with the user filling out the rest of the form while you are checking the validity of a single field; remember that synchronous requests made using XHR objects freeze most aspects of the user interface (including typing and clicking) during their execution. The last part of this function is to handle the response from the server:

```
function validateField(oEvent) {
    oEvent = oEvent || window.event;
    var txtField = oEvent.target || oEvent.srcElement;
    var oXHR = zXmlHttp.createRequest();
    oXHR.open("get", "ValidateForm.php?" + txtField.name + "="
                            + encodeURIComponent(txtField.value), true);
    oXHR.onreadystatechange = function () {
        if (oXHR.readyState == 4) {
            if (oXHR.status == 200 || oXHR.status == 304) {
                var arrInfo = oXHR.responseText.split("||");
                var imgError = document.getElementById("img"
                                        + txtField.id.substring(3) + "Error");
                var btnSignUp = document.getElementById("btnSignUp");

                if (!eval(arrInfo[0])) {
                    imgError.title = arrInfo[1];
                    imgError.style.display = "";
                    txtField.valid = false;
                } else {
                    imgError.style.display = "none";
                    txtField.valid = true;
                }

                btnSignUp.disabled = !isFormValid();
            } else {
                alert("An error occurred while trying to contact the server.");
            }
        }
    };
    oXHR.send(null);
}
```

After checking for the correct readyState and status, the responseText is split into an array of strings (arrInfo) using the JavaScript split() method. The value in the first slot of arrInfo will be the value of the PHP variable $valid; the value in the second slot will be the value of the PHP variable $message. Also, a reference to the appropriate error image and the Sign Up button is returned. The error image is gained by dissecting the field name, removing the "txt" from the front (using substring()), prepending "img" and appending "Error" to the end (so for the field "txtBirthday", the error image name is constructed as "imgBirthdayError").

The value in `arrInfo[0]` must be passed into `eval()` in order to get a true Boolean value out of it. (Remember, it's a string: either `true` or `false`.) If this value is `false`, the error image's `title` property is assigned the error message from `arrInfo[1]`, the image is displayed, and the custom `valid` property of the textbox is set to `false` (this will come in handy later). When a value is invalid, the error image appears, and when the user moves the mouse over it, the error message appears (see Figure 3-3). If the value is valid, however, the error image is hidden and the custom `valid` property is set to `true`.

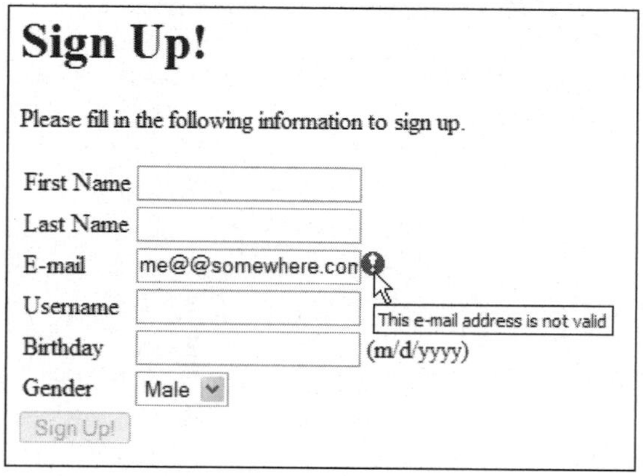

Figure 3-3

You'll also notice that the Sign Up button is used in this function. The Sign Up button should be disabled if there is any invalid data in the form. To accomplish this, a function called `isFormValid()` is called. If this function returns `false`, the Sign Up button's `disabled` property is set to `true`, disabling it. The `isFormValid()` function simply iterates through the form fields and checks the `valid` property:

```
function isFormValid() {
    var frmMain = document.forms[0];
    var blnValid = true;

    for (var i=0; i < frmMain.elements.length; i++) {
        if (typeof frmMain.elements[i].valid == "boolean") {
            blnValid = blnValid && frmMain.elements[i].valid;
        }
    }

    return blnValid;
}
```

For each element in the form, the `valid` property is first checked to see if it exists. This is done by using the `typeof` operator, which will return `boolean` if the property exists and has been given a Boolean value. Because there are fields that aren't being validated (and thus won't have the custom `valid` property), this check ensures that only validated fields are considered.

The last part of the script is to set up the event handlers for the textboxes. This should be done when the form has finished loading, but only if XHR is supported (because that is how the Ajax validation is being performed here):

```
//if Ajax is enabled, disable the submit button and assign event handlers
window.onload = function () {
```

```
        if (zXmlHttp.isSupported()) {
            var btnSignUp = document.getElementById("btnSignUp");
            var txtUsername = document.getElementById("txtUsername");
            var txtBirthday = document.getElementById("txtBirthday");
            var txtEmail = document.getElementById("txtEmail");

            btnSignUp.disabled = true;
            txtUsername.onchange = validateField;
            txtBirthday.onchange = validateField;
            txtEmail.onchange = validateField;
            txtUsername.valid = false;
            txtBirthday.valid = false;
            txtEmail.valid = false;

        }
    };
```

This `onload` event handler assigns the `onchange` event handlers for each textbox as well as initializes the custom `valid` property to `false`. Additionally, the Sign Up button is disabled from the start to prevent invalid data from being submitted. Note, however, that the button will be disabled only if XHR is supported; otherwise, the form will behave as a normal web form and the validation will have to be done when the entire form is submitted.

When you load this example, each of the three validated text fields will make a request to the server for validation whenever their values change and you move on to another field. The user experience is seamless using the Submission Throttling pattern, but the form remains functional even if JavaScript is turned off or XHR is not supported.

> Even when using this type of validation, it is essential that all the data be validated again once the entire form is submitted. Remember, if the user turns off JavaScript, you still need to be sure the data is valid before performing operations using it.

Incremental Field Validation Example

Whereas the previous example validated each field when its value changed, the other popular form of the Submission Throttling design pattern involves submitting a single field periodically as changes are made. This is the version of Submission Throttling used for both Bitflux LiveSearch and Google Suggest, where data is repeatedly sent to the server as the user types. In both of these cases, the submission activates a search on the server; however, the same method can be used to validate a single field repeatedly as the user types.

Suppose that instead of asking you to fill in a whole form, the sign-up for a given site requires you first to select a user name (maybe as step 1 of a multistep sign-up process). In this case, you'd want to ensure that only a nonexistent user name be used. Instead of waiting for the form to be submitted, you can periodically upload the data to the server for validation, making sure that the data can't be submitted until a valid user name is entered.

> Note that this example is for demonstration purposes. If you were to use the technique described in a production environment, you would have to protect against spam bots that may use this feature to harvest user names and passwords.

The form for this example is much simpler, made up of a single textbox and a Next button:

```
<form method="post" action="Success.php">
    <table>
        <tr>
            <td><label for="txtUsername">Username</label></td>
            <td><input type="text" id="txtUsername" name="txtUsername" />
                <img src="error.gif" alt="Error" id="imgUsernameError"
                    style="display:none" /></td>
        </tr>
    </table>
    <input type="submit" id="btnNext" value="Next" />
</form>
```

Note that the same basic format of the previous example has been kept, including the hidden error image. Next, the validateField() function from the previous example is used, with a few changes:

```
var oXHR = null;
var iTimeoutId = null;

function validateField(oEvent) {
    oEvent = oEvent || window.event;
    var txtField = oEvent.target || oEvent.srcElement;

    var btnNext = document.getElementById("btnNext");
    btnNext.disabled = true;

    if (iTimeoutId != null) {
        clearTimeout(iTimeoutId);
        iTimeoutId = null;
    }

    if (!oXHR) {
        oXHR = zXmlHttp.createRequest();
    } else if (oXHR.readyState != 0) {
        oXHR.abort();
    }

    oXHR.open("get", "ValidateForm.php?" + txtField.name + "="
                        + encodeURIComponent(txtField.value), true);
    oXHR.onreadystatechange = function () {

        if (oXHR.readyState == 4) {
            if (oXHR.status == 200 || oXHR.status == 304) {
                var arrInfo = oXHR.responseText.split("||");
                var imgError = document.getElementById("img"
```

```
                                                 + txtField.id.substring(3) + "Error");

                if (!eval(arrInfo[0])) {
                    imgError.title = arrInfo[1];
                    imgError.style.display = "";
                    txtField.valid = false;
                } else {
                    imgError.style.display = "none";
                    txtField.valid = true;
                }

                btnNext.disabled = !txtField.valid;
            } else {
                alert("An error occurred while trying to contact the server.");
            }
        }
    };

    iTimeoutId = setTimeout(function () {
        oXHR.send(null);
    }, 500);
};
```

The first thing to note about this updated function is the inclusion of two global variables: oXHR and iTimeoutId. The first, oXHR, holds a global reference to an XHR object that is used repeatedly (as opposed to being used just once in the previous example); the second, iTimeoutId, holds a timeout identifier used to delay sending a request. Inside the function, the first new part sets the Next button to be disabled right away. This is important because a request may not be sent out immediately following a call to this function. The next block after that clears the timeout identifier if it's not null, which prevents the sending of too many requests in succession. (If there is a pending request, this cancels it.)

Next, the global oXHR object is tested to see if it is null. If so, a new XHRobject is created and assigned to it. If an XHR object already exists, its readyState is checked to see if it's ready for a request. As mentioned in the previous chapter, the readyState changes from 0 to 1 when the open() method is called; therefore, any readyState other than 0 indicates that a request has already been started, so the abort() method must be called before attempting to send a new request. Note that the same ValidateForm.php page is used for validation purposes.

Inside of the onreadystatechange event handler, the only new line is one that changes the Next button's disabled state based on the validity of user name. Toward the end of the function, the setTimeout() function is called to delay the sending of the request by half a second (500 milliseconds). The identifier from this call is saved in iTimeoutId, so it is possible to cancel the request the next time the function is called. By using the timeout functionality of JavaScript in this way, you are ensuring that the user hasn't typed anything for at least half a second. If the user types something quickly, the timeout will repeatedly be cleared and the request aborted. It's only when there is a pause that the request will finally be sent.

The only part left now is to set up the event handler. Since this method uploads information as the user types, you can't rely on the onchange event handler alone (although it is still needed). In this case, you need to use the onkeyup event handler, which is called every time a key is pressed and then released:

```
window.onload = function () {
    if (zXmlHttp.isSupported()) {
        var btnNext = document.getElementById("btnNext");
        var txtUsername = document.getElementById("txtUsername");

        btnNext.disabled = true;
        txtUsername.onkeyup = validateField;
        txtUsername.onchange = validateField;
        txtUsername.valid = false;
    }
};
```

Once again, this is very similar to the previous example. The only changes are the name of the button (which is now btnNext) and the assignment of validateField() to the onkeyup event handler. As the user types, the user name will be checked for validity. Every time a valid user name is entered, the Next button becomes enabled. Whenever a request is being made, the button is first disabled to accommodate a specific situation. It is possible that the user will continue typing even after a valid user name has been entered. As a side effect, the extra characters may cause the user name to become invalid, and you don't want to allow invalid data to be submitted.

> **Although it's a nice feature, incremental field validation should be used sparingly because it creates a high volume of requests. Unless your server configuration is set up specifically to handle an increased volume of requests, it is best to forego this approach.**

Periodic Refresh

The Periodic Refresh design pattern describes the process of checking for new server information in specific intervals. This approach, also called *polling*, requires the browser to keep track of when another request to the server should take place.

This pattern is used in a variety of different ways on the Web:

❑ ESPN uses Periodic Refresh to update its online scoreboards automatically. For example, the NFL Scoreboard, located at http://sports.espn.go.com/nfl/scoreboard, shows up-to-the-minute scores and drive charts for every NFL game being played at the time. Using XHR objects and a little bit of Flash, the page repeatedly updates itself with new information.

❑ Gmail (http://gmail.google.com) uses Periodic Refresh to notify users when new mail has been received. As you are reading an e-mail or performing other operations, Gmail repeatedly checks the server to see if new mail has arrived. This is done without notification unless there is new mail, at which point the number of new e-mails received is displayed in parentheses next to the Inbox menu item.

❑ XHTML Live Chat (www.plasticshore.com/projects/chat) uses Periodic Refresh to implement a chat room using simple web technologies. The chat room text is updated automatically every few seconds by checking the server for new information. If there is a new message, the page is updated to reflect it, thus creating a traditional chat room experience.

❑ The Magnetic Ajax demo (www.broken-notebook.com/magnetic) re-creates online the experience of magnetic poetry (using single word magnets that can be rearranged to make sentences). The full version polls the server for new arrangements every few seconds, so if you and someone else are rearranging words at the same time, you will see the movement.

Clearly, there are many different ways that Period Refresh can increase user experience, but the basic purpose remains the same: to notify users of updated information.

New Comment Notifier Example

A feature that has been creeping into blogs across the Web since the beginning of 2005 is a New Comment Notifier. A New Comment Notifier does exactly what it says it does: it alerts the user when a new comment has been added. This can take the form of a simple text message displayed on the page or an animated message that slides in from out of view, but the basic idea is the same. In this example, Periodic Refresh is used to check a database table containing comments to see which is the newest.

Suppose that you have a simple MySQL table, defined as follows:

```
CREATE TABLE `BlogComments` (
`CommentId` INT NOT NULL AUTO_INCREMENT ,
`BlogEntryId` INT NOT NULL ,
`Name` VARCHAR( 100 ) NOT NULL ,
`Message` VARCHAR( 255 ) NOT NULL ,
`Date` DATETIME NOT NULL ,
PRIMARY KEY (`CommentId`)
) COMMENT = 'Blog Comments';
```

The SQL query to run this is:

```
select CommentId,Name,LEFT(Message, 50)
from BlogComments order by Date desc
limit 0,1
```

This query returns the comment ID (which is autogenerated), the name of the person who left the comment, and the first 50 characters of the message text (using the LEFT() function) for the most recent comment. The 50 characters are used as a preview of the actual comment (you probably don't want to get the entire message because it could be long).

The page that runs this query is called CheckComments.php, and it outputs a string in the following format:

```
<comment ID>||<name>||<message>
```

This format allows the JavaScript Array.split() method to be used in order to extract the individual pieces of information with little effort. If there are no comments or there is an error, the comment ID will be –1 and the other parts of the string will be blank. Here is the complete code listing for CheckComments.php:

```php
<?php
    header("Cache-control: No-Cache");
    header("Expires: Fri, 30 Oct 1998 14:19:41 GMT");

    //database information
```

```
$sDBServer = "your.database.server";
$sDBName = "your_db_name";
$sDBUsername = "your_db_username";
$sDBPassword = "your_db_password";

//create the SQL query string
$sSQL = "select CommentId,Name,LEFT(Message, 50) as ShortMessage from
        BlogComments order by Date desc limit 0,1";

$oLink = mysql_connect($sDBServer,$sDBUsername,$sDBPassword);
@mysql_select_db($sDBName) or die("-1|| || ");

if($oResult = mysql_query($sSQL) and mysql_num_rows($oResult) > 0) {
    $aValues = mysql_fetch_array($oResult,MYSQL_ASSOC);
    echo $aValues['CommentId']."||".$aValues['Name']."||".
        $aValues['ShortMessage'];
} else {
    echo "-1|| || ";
}

mysql_free_result($oResult);
mysql_close($oLink);
?>
```

Perhaps the most important parts of this file are the two headers included at the top. By setting Cache-control and Expires headers, you are telling the browser to always retrieve this file from the server and not from the client cache. Without this, some browsers would return the same information repeatedly, effectively nullifying this functionality altogether. The rest of this file should look very familiar, because it uses essentially the same algorithm as previous examples that make use of MySQL database calls.

> *You can also avoid caching problems by changing the query string every time a request is made to this file. This is often done by assigning a timestamp into the query string to trick the browser into getting a fresh copy from the server.*

Next comes the JavaScript that calls this file. To start, you'll need a few global variables once again:

```
var oXHR = null;            //The XHR object
var iInterval = 1000;           //The interval to check (in milliseconds)
var iLastCommentId = -1;        //The ID of the last comment received
var divNotification = null;  //The layer to display the notification
```

As usual, the first global variable is an XHR object called oXHR, which will be used for all requests. The second variable, iInterval, specifies the number of milliseconds that should occur between each check for new comments. In this case, it is set to 1000 milliseconds, or 1 second, although this can and should be customized based on your needs. Next, the iLastCommentId variable is used to store the last comment ID in the database. It is by comparing this value to the most recently retrieved comment ID that you can determine whether a new comment has been added. The last variable, divNotification, holds a reference to the <div/> element that is used to display a notification to the user about new comments.

When a new comment is detected, divNotification is filled with information about the new comment, including the name of the person making the comment, a summary of the message, and a link to view the entire comment. If the <div/> element hasn't yet been created, it must be created and assigned the appropriate style information:

```
function showNotification(sName, sMessage) {
    if (!divNotification) {
        divNotification = document.createElement("div");
        divNotification.className = "notification";
        document.body.appendChild(divNotification);
    }

    divNotification.innerHTML = "<strong>New Comment</strong><br />" + sName
            + " says: " + sMessage + "...<br /><a href=\"ViewComment.php?id="
            + iLastCommentId + "\">View</a>";
    divNotification.style.top = document.body.scrollTop + "px";
    divNotification.style.left = document.body.scrollLeft + "px";
    divNotification.style.display = "block";
    setTimeout(function () {
        divNotification.style.display = "none";
    }, 5000);
}
```

As you can see, the showNotification() function accepts two arguments: a name and a message. However, before this information is used, you must ensure that divNotification is not null. If necessary, a new <div/> element is created and its CSS class set to notification before being added to the document's body. After that, the innerHTML property is used to set the notification HTML, which says "New Comment" in bold, followed by the name, the message, and the link to view the comment. The link points to ViewComment.php and assigns a query string parameter id the value of iLastCommentId, which indicates the comment to view. Then, the position of the notification is set by using the scrollTop and scrollLeft properties of document.body. This ensures that the notification is always visible at the upper-left corner of the page regardless of the scroll position (if you have scrolled down or right). Following that, the display property is set to block to make the notification visible.

> The document.body.scrollLeft and document.body.scrollTop **properties should be used only in the quirks mode of Internet Explorer, Firefox, and Opera. If your page uses standards mode (using an XHTML doctype), you must instead use** document.documentElement.scrollLeft **and** document.documentElement.scrollTop.

The last part of this function is a timeout that hides the notification after 5 seconds (5000 milliseconds). It's not a good idea to leave the notification up unless you have a spot specifically designated for such a purpose in your design; otherwise, you could be covering up important information.

In this example, the notification CSS class is defined as follows:

```
div.notification {
    border: 1px solid red;
    padding: 10px;
    background-color: white;
    position: absolute;
    display: none;
    top: 0px;
    left: 0px;
}
```

This creates a white box with a red border around it. Of course, you'll want to style this in a manner that's appropriate for the site or application in which it is used. The important parts for this example are that position is set to absolute and display is set to none. Setting both properties ensures that when the <div/> element is added to the page, it won't interrupt the normal page flow or move any elements around. The result is a notification area, as displayed in Figure 3-4.

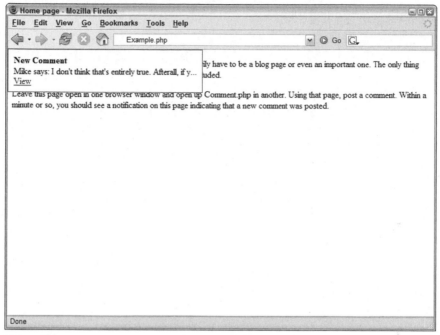

Figure 3-4

The JavaScript function that does the most work is checkComments(), which is responsible for checking the server for updates. The code is very similar to the previous examples:

```
function checkComments() {
    if (!oXHR) {
        oXHR = zXmlHttp.createRequest();
    } else if (oXHR.readyState != 0) {
        oXHR.abort();
    }

    oXHR.open("get", "CheckComments.php", true);
    oXHR.onreadystatechange = function () {

        if (oXHR.readyState == 4) {
            if (oXHR.status == 200 || oXHR.status == 304) {

                var aData = oXHR.responseText.split("||");
                if (aData[0] != iLastCommentId) {

                    iLastCommentId = aData[0];

                    if (iLastCommentId != -1) {
```

```
                                    showNotification(aData[1], aData[2]);
                        }
                }

                setTimeout(checkComments, iInterval);
        }
    }
};

oXHR.send(null);

}
```

This function creates an XHR object and calls `CheckComments.php` asynchronously. The important part of this code is highlighted (the rest is almost exactly the same as the previous examples). In this section, the `responseText` is split into an array using the `split()` method. The first value in the array, `aData[0]`, is the comment ID that was added last. If it isn't equal to the last comment ID stored, then a notification may be needed. Next, if the last comment ID is –1, no comment IDs have been retrieved and thus a notification should not be shown. If the last comment ID is not –1, at least one comment ID has been retrieved, and since it's different from the one just received from the server, the notification should be displayed. After that, the new ID is assigned to `iLastCommentId` for future use. The very last step in the event handler is to set another timeout for `checkComments()`, to continue checking for more comments.

The final step in the process is to initiate a call to `checkComments()` once the page has loaded. This will retrieve the most recent comment ID in the database but won't display a notification (because `iLastCommentId` will be equal to –1 initially). When the next call is made to `checkComments()`, the ID retrieved from the database can be checked against the one stored in `iLastCommentId` to determine if a notification must be displayed. As usual, this functionality should be initiated only if the browser supports XHR:

```
window.onload = function () {
    if (zXmlHttp.isSupported()) {
        checkComments();
    }
};
```

That's all it takes to create this Periodic Refresh solution. You need only remember to include the necessary JavaScript and CSS files in any page that you would like this functionality on.

> The files for this example are available for download at www.wrox.com. Along with those files are other pages you can use to add and view comments for the purpose of testing.

Multi-Stage Download

One of the lasting problems on the Web has been the speed at which pages download. When everyone was using 56 Kbps modems, web designers were much more aware of how much their pages "weighed" (the size of the page in total bytes). With the popularity of residential broadband Internet solutions, many sites have upgraded, including multimedia, more pictures, and more content. This approach, while giving the user more information, also leads to slower download times as everything is loaded in seemingly random order. Fortunately, there is an Ajax solution for this problem.

Multi-Stage Download is an Ajax pattern wherein only the most basic functionality is loaded into a page initially. Upon completion, the page then begins to download other components that should appear on the page. If the user should leave the page before all of the components are downloaded, it's of no consequence. If, however, the user stays on the page for an extended period of time (perhaps reading an article), the extra functionality is loaded in the background and available when the user is ready. The major advantage here is that you, as the developer, get to decide what is downloaded and at what point in time.

This is a fairly new Ajax pattern and has been popularized by Microsoft's start.com. When you first visit start.com, it is a very simple page with a search box in the middle. Behind the scenes, however, a series of requests is being fired off to fill in more content on the page. Within a few seconds, the page jumps to life as content from several different locations is pulled in and displayed.

Although nice, Multi-Stage Download does have a downside: the page must work in its simplest form for browsers that don't support Ajax technologies. This means that all the basic functionality must work without any additional downloads. The typical way of dealing with this problem is to provide *graceful degradation*, meaning that those browsers that support Ajax technologies will get the more extensive interface while other browsers get a simple, bare-bones interface. This is especially important if you are expecting search engines to crawl your site; since these bots don't support JavaScript, they rely solely on the HTML in the page to determine your site's value.

Additional Information Links Example

When reading through an article online, frequently there are Additional Information links included for further reading on the topic. The key question here is this: What is the main content? Clearly the article text is the main content on the page, so it should be downloaded when the page is initially loaded. The additional links aren't as important, so they can be loaded later. This example walks you through the creation of such a solution.

First, you'll need to lay out a page to hold the article. For this example, it's a very simple layout:

```
<!DOCTYPE html PUBLIC "-//W3C//DTD XHTML 1.0 Transitional//EN"
    "http://www.w3.org/TR/xhtml1/DTD/xhtml1-transitional.dtd">
<html xmlns="http://www.w3.org/1999/xhtml">
    <head>
        <title>Article Example</title>
        <script type="text/javascript" src="zxml.js"></script>
        <script type="text/javascript" src="Article.js"></script>
        <link rel="stylesheet" type="text/css" href="Article.css" />
    </head>
    <body>
        <h1>Article Title</h1>
        <div id="divAdditionalLinks"></div>
        <div id="divPage1">
            <!-- article content here -->
        </div>
    </body>
</html>
```

The important part of the HTML is the `<div/>` with the ID of `divAdditionalLinks`. This is the container for the additional links that will be downloaded for the article. By default, it is styled to be right aligned and invisible:

```css
#divAdditionalLinks {
    float: right;
    padding: 10px;
    border: 1px solid navy;
    background-color: #cccccc;
    display: none;
}
```

It's very important that the CSS `display` property be set to `none` so that the empty `<div/>` element doesn't take up any space in the page layout. Without this, you would see a small empty box to the right of the article.

Unlike the previous examples, the content to download is just plain text contained in a text file containing links and a header. This file, `AdditionalLinks.txt`, contains some simple HTML code:

```html
<h4>Additional Information</h4>
<ul>
    <li><a href="http://www.wrox.com">Wrox</a></li>
    <li><a href="http://www.nczonline.net">NCZOnline</a></li>
    <li><a href="http://www.wdonline.com">XWeb</a></li>
</ul>
```

This file could just as well be created dynamically using server-side logic, but for the purposes of this example, static content works just as well.

The JavaScript that makes this work is very simple and quite similar to all the previous examples in this chapter:

```javascript
function downloadLinks() {
    var oXHR = zXmlHttp.createRequest();

    oXHR.open("get", "AdditionalLinks.txt", true);
    oXHR.onreadystatechange = function () {
        if (oXHR.readyState == 4) {
            if (oXHR.status == 200 || oXHR.status == 304) {
                var divAdditionalLinks =
                                document.getElementById("divAdditionalLinks");
                divAdditionalLinks.innerHTML = oXHR.responseText;
                divAdditionalLinks.style.display = "block";
            }
        }
    }
    oXHR.send(null);
}

window.onload = function () {
    if (zXHR.isSupported()) {
        downloadLinks();
    }
};
```

The function that does the work is `downloadLinks()`, which is called only if the browser supports XHR and only once the page is completely loaded. The code inside of `downloadLinks()` is the standard XHR algorithm that you've used before. After the content from `AdditionalLinks.txt` has been retrieved, it is set into the placeholder `<div/>` using the `innerHTML` property. The last step in the process is to set the `<div/>` element's `display` property to `block` so that it can be seen. The end result is displayed in Figure 3-5.

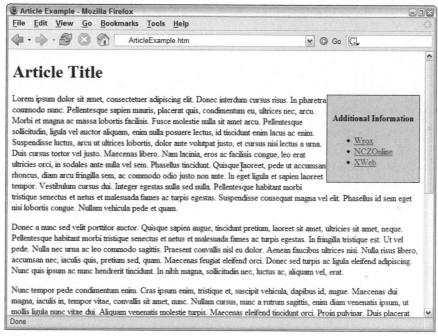

Figure 3-5

If XHR isn't supported in the browser, the block containing the additional links will never appear and so the first paragraph will stretch all the way across the top.

This technique can be done numerous times for any number of sections of a page; you certainly aren't restricted to having only one section that is loaded after the initial page is complete. You can create new XHR objects for each request and then send them off one after the other, or you can do it sequentially, waiting until a response has been received before sending off the next request. The choice is completely up to you and your desired functionality.

Fallback Patterns

The previous section dealt with when to send or receive data from the server, which presupposes that everything goes according to plan on the server side: the request is received, the necessary changes are made, and the appropriate response is sent to the client. But what happens if there's an error on the server? Or worse yet, what if the request never makes it to the server? When developing Ajax applications, it is imperative that you plan ahead for these problems and describe how your application should work if one of these should occur.

Cancel Pending Requests

If an error occurs on the server, meaning that a status of something other than 200 or 304 is returned, you need to decide what to do. Chances are that if a file is not found (404) or an internal server error occurred (302), trying again in a few minutes isn't going to help, since both of these require an administrator to fix the problem. The simplest way to deal with this situation is to simply cancel all pending requests. You can set a flag somewhere in your code that says, "don't send any more requests." This clearly has the highest impact on solutions using the Periodic Refresh pattern.

The comment notification example can be modified to take this into account. This is a case where the Ajax solution provides additional value to the user but is not the primary focus of the page. If a request fails, there is no reason to alert the user; you can simply cancel any future requests to prevent any further errors from occurring. To do so, you must add a global variable that indicates whether requests are enabled:

```
var oXHR = null;
var iInterval = 1000;
var iLastCommentId = -1;
var divNotification = null;
var blnRequestsEnabled = true;
```

Now, the `blnRequestsEnabled` variable must be checked before any request is made. This can be accomplished by wrapping the body of the `checkComments()` function inside of an `if` statement:

```
function checkComments() {

    if (blnRequestsEnabled) {
        if (!oXHR) {
            oXHR = zXmlHttp.createRequest();
        } else if (oXHR.readyState != 0) {
            oXHR.abort();
        }

        oXHR.open("get", "CheckComments.php", true);
        oXHR.onreadystatechange = function () {
            if (oXHR.readyState == 4) {
                if (oXHR.status == 200 || oXHR.status == 304) {
                    var aData = oXHR.responseText.split("||");
                    if (aData[0] != iLastCommentId) {
                        iLastCommentId = aData[0];
                        if (iLastCommentId != -1) {
                            showNotification(aData[1], aData[2]);
                        }
                    }
                    setTimeout(checkComments, iInterval);
                }
            }
        };

        oXHR.send(null);
    }
}
```

But that isn't all that must be done; you must also detect the two different types of errors that may occur: server errors that give status codes and a failure to reach the server (either the server is down or the Internet connection has been lost).

To begin, wrap everything inside of the initial if statement inside a try...catch block. Different browsers react at different times when a server can't be reached, but they all throw errors. Wrapping the entire request block in a try...catch ensures that you catch any error that is thrown, at which point you can set blnRequestsEnabled to false. Next, for server errors, you can also set blnRequestsEnabled to false whenever the status is not equal to 200 or 304. This will have the same effect as if the server couldn't be reached:

```
function checkComments() {

    if (blnRequestsEnabled) {
        try {
            if (!oXHR) {
                oXHR = zXmlHttp.createRequest();
            } else if (oXHR.readyState != 0) {
                oXHR.abort();
            }

            oXHR.open("get", "CheckComments.php", true);
            oXHR.onreadystatechange = function () {
                if (oXHR.readyState == 4) {
                    if (oXHR.status == 200 || oXHR.status == 304) {

                        var aData = oXHR.responseText.split("||");
                        if (aData[0] != iLastCommentId) {

                            if (iLastCommentId != -1) {
                                showNotification(aData[1], aData[2]);
                            }

                            iLastCommentId = aData[0];
                        }

                        setTimeout(checkComments, iInterval);
                    } else {
                        blnRequestsEnabled = false;
                    }
                }
            };

            oXHR.send(null);
        } catch (oException) {
            blnRequestsEnabled = false;
        }
    }
}
```

Now, when either of the two error types occurs, an error will be thrown (either by the browser or by you), and the blnRequestsEnabled variable will be set to false, effectively canceling any further requests if checkComments() is called again.

> You may also have noticed that a timeout for another request is created only if the status is 200 or 304, which prevents another request from occurring for any other status. That works fine for server errors, but it doesn't do anything for communication errors. It's always better to have more than one way to handle errors when they occur.

Try Again

Another option when dealing with errors is to silently keep trying for either a specified amount of time or a particular number of tries. Once again, unless the Ajax functionality is key to the user's experience, there is no need to notify him or her about the failure. It is best to handle the problem behind the scenes until it can be resolved.

To illustrate the Try Again pattern, consider the Multi-Stage Download example. In that example, extra links were downloaded and displayed alongside the article. If an error occurred during the request, an error message would pop up in most browsers. The user would have no idea what the error was or what caused it, so why bother displaying a message at all? Instead, it would make much more sense to continue trying to download the information a few times before giving up.

To track the number of failed attempts, a global variable is necessary:

```
var iFailed = 0;
```

The `iFailed` variable starts at `0` and is incremented every time a request fails. So, if `iFailed` is ever greater than a specific number, you can just cancel the request because it is clearly not going to work. If, for example, you want to try 10 times before canceling all pending requests, you can do the following:

```
function downloadLinks() {
    var oXHR = zXmlHttp.createRequest();

    if (iFailed < 10) {
        try {
            oXHR.open("get", "AdditionalLinks.txt", true);
            oXHR.onreadystatechange = function () {
                if (oXHR.readyState == 4) {
                    if (oXHR.status == 200 || oXHR.status == 304) {
                        var divAdditionalLinks =
                                    document.getElementById("divAdditionalLinks");
                        divAdditionalLinks.innerHTML = oXHR.responseText;
                        divAdditionalLinks.style.display = "block";
                    } else {
                        iFailed++;
                        downloadLinks();
                    }
                }
            }

            oXHR.send(null);
```

```
        } catch (oException) {
            iFailed++;
            downloadLinks();
        }
    }
}
```

This code is constructed similarly to the previous example. The `try...catch` block is used to catch any errors that may occur during the communication, and a custom error is thrown when the `status` isn't `200` or `304`. The main difference is that when an error is caught, the `iFailed` variable is incremented and `downloadLinks()` is called again. As long as `iFailed` is less than `10` (meaning it's failed less than 10 times), another request will be fired off to attempt the download.

In general, the Try Again pattern should be used only when the request is intended to occur only once, as in a Multi-Stage Download. If you try to use this pattern with interval-driven requests, such as Periodic Refresh, you could end up with an ever-increasing number of open requests taking up memory.

Summary

In this chapter, you learned about various design patterns for Ajax solutions. You first learned how to use Predictive Fetch to improve the user experience through preloading information that is likely to be used in the future. You created an example using Predictive Fetch to preload pages in an article after a few seconds, when it is likely that the user intends to read the entire article.

Next, you learned about Submission Throttling, which is a way of incrementally sending data to the server instead of doing it all at once. You learned how to use this pattern for data validation in a form. It's sibling pattern, Periodic Refresh, was also discussed, which periodically receives information from the server. You built an example using Periodic Refresh that displays a notification when a new comment has been posted to a blog or message board.

This chapter also introduced you to the Multi-Stage Download pattern, which is a way of continuing to download extra information after the page has loaded. You learned that this would lead to faster initial download time for pages and that you can control the frequency and sequence of requests in any way you see fit.

The last section discussed fallback patterns that are used to handle errors in client-server communication. You learned that there are two types of errors you may encounter: server errors (such as 404 not found) or communication errors (where the server cannot be contacted). Two patterns, Cancel Pending Requests and Try Again, were discussed as ways of dealing with these errors.

4

Ajax Libraries

With the popularity of Ajax applications exploding in 2005, developers and companies began looking for ways to streamline the process. As with many common programming practices, Ajax involves a lot of repetitive procedures that can be identified and simplified for common use. It wasn't long before JavaScript developers started introducing libraries to ease the redundant and sometimes quirky behavior of Ajax communication techniques. These libraries sought to break outside of the hidden frame and XHR modalities of communication and introduce their own methods (which typically are just wrappers for already accepted forms of Ajax communication). All of the libraries discussed in this chapter use interfaces that resemble but do not mimic the techniques discussed in Chapter 2. Remember, the goals of such libraries are to free the developer from worrying about cross-browser Ajax issues by hiding the details.

The Yahoo! Connection Manager

In late 2005, Yahoo! introduced its Yahoo! User Interface (YUI) library to the open source community. Available under a BSD-style license at `http://developer.yahoo.com/yui`, the YUI comprises several JavaScript libraries used within the company to aid in the rapid development of web applications such as Yahoo! Mail and Yahoo! Photos. One of these libraries is the Yahoo! Connection Manager.

With Ajax making heavy use of XHR, many developers are looking for ways to equalize the differences between browser implementations. The Yahoo! Connection Manager does this by handling all of the processing behind the scenes, exposing a simple API that frees developers from cross-browser concerns.

Setup

Before beginning, download the YUI library at `http://sourceforge.net/projects/yui`. A single ZIP file contains all of the JavaScript files necessary to use the Connection Manager. For basic Connection Manager usage, you need two required JavaScript files: `YAHOO.js`, which sets up the YAHOO namespace (this file is used by all Yahoo! JavaScript components), and connection.js, which contains the Connection Manager code. The files must be included in this order:

```
<script type="text/javascript" src="/js/YAHOO.js"></script>
<script type="text/javascript" src="/js/connection.js"></script>
```

With these files included in your page, you are now ready to begin using the Connection Manager.

Basic Requests

The Yahoo! Connection Manager uses a different interface for sending XHR requests than the default one provided by modern browsers. Instead of creating objects, the Connection Manager exposes several static methods to handle requests. The method you'll use most often is asyncRequest(), which has the following signature:

```
transaction=YAHOO.util.Connect.asyncRequest(request_type, url, callback, postdata);
```

The first argument is the type of HTTP request to make: "GET" or "POST" (these are case-sensitive). The second argument is simply the URL of the request. The third argument is a callback object containing methods to handle the response from the request. The final argument of asyncRequest() is the data to post to the server. For POST requests, this value is a string of URL-encoded values to be sent; for GET requests, this value can either be omitted or set to null.

When the call is completed, asyncRequest() returns a transaction object that can be used to monitor and interact with the currently executing request.

The Callback Object

The most important Connection Manager concept to understand is the role of the callback object. As opposed to having a simple event handler assignment, the callback object allows you to specify a number of options. In its simplest form, the callback object provides two methods: a success() method that is called when a valid response has been received and a failure() method that is called when an invalid response is received. For example:

```
var oCallback = {
    success: function (oResponse) {
        //handle a successful response
    },
    failure: function (oResponse) {
        //handle an unsuccessful request
    }
};
```

Each of the two methods is passed an object (oResponse) containing response information from the server and/or the Connection Manager itself. The response object has the following properties:

❑ argument: A developer-defined value to be returned with the response

❑ responseText: The text response from the server

❏ `responseXML`: An XML DOM containing XML from the server (if the content type is "text/xml")

❏ `status`: The HTTP status code returned from the server or an error code provided by the Connection Manager

❏ `statusText`: The HTTP status description or an error message provided by the Connection Manager

❏ `tId`: The transaction ID uniquely assigned to this request by the Connection Manager

Additionally, the response object has two methods:

❏ `getAllResponseHeaders()`: Returns a string containing all header information

❏ `getResponseHeader(name)`: Returns the value of the named HTTP header

Some of these properties and methods are direct carryovers from the XHR object.

The Connection Manager's goal is to free developers from worrying about small details, and part of that is in determining when a response was successfully received and when it was not. If the `status` of the response is between 200 and 300, the `success()` method is called; otherwise, the `failure()` method is called. Unlike using XHR directly, the developer needn't be bothered by checking the `status` property to take an appropriate action. Here's a simple example:

```
var oCallback = {
    success: function (oResponse) {
        alert("Response received successfully.");
    },

    failure: function (oResponse) {
        alert("The request failed.");
    }
};

YAHOO.util.Connect.asyncRequest("GET", "test.php", oCallback);
```

This example sends a GET request to `test.php`, passing in the callback object. When the response is received, either `success()` or `failure()` is called. A POST request can be sent in a similar fashion, just by changing the first argument of the `asyncRequest()` method and appending the post data:

```
var oCallback = {
    success: function (oResponse) {
        alert("Response received successfully.");
    },

    failure: function (oResponse) {
        alert("The request failed.");
    }
};

var sPostData = "title=Professional%20Ajax&authors=Zakas%20McPeak%20Fawcett";
YAHOO.util.Connect.asyncRequest("POST", "test.php", oCallback, sPostData);
```

Here, the post data is added as a fourth argument. Note that the post data must be URL encoded before being passed to the method. Connection Manager handles setting the appropriate content type for the request, which by default is the HTTP form submission content type of "application/x-www-form-urlencoded". It's possible to turn this header off for submission of non-form data by calling setDefaultPostHeader(false):

```
var sPostData = "raw text data";
YAHOO.util.Connect.setDefaultPostHeader(false);
YAHOO.util.Connect.asyncRequest("POST", "test.php", oCallback, sPostData);
```

The callback object isn't limited to just two methods; a few additional properties are provided for ease of use.

The argument Property

Suppose that there's some additional information necessary to process either a successful or an unsuccessful HTTP request. Using the techniques described in Chapter 2 would require some additional thought and planning. The Connection Manager makes this easy by using the argument property on the callback object. This property can be set to any value or object, and that same value or object is passed into both the success() and failure() methods as a property on the response object. For example:

```
var oCallback = {
    success: function (oResponse) {

        //retrieve the argument
        var sArg = oResponse.argument;

        alert("Request was successful: " + sArg);

    },
    failure: function (oResponse) {

        //retrieve the argument
        var sArg = oResponse.argument;

        alert("Request failed: " + sArg);

    },

    argument: "string of info"
};
```

In this code, the argument property is specified as a string on the callback object. The success() and failure() methods access the argument property on the response object and use it as part of a message displayed to the user.

> Note that the argument **property is client side only, so the server never sees the value.**

The scope Property

You may have a case when you want the success() and failure() methods to call methods on another object. To facilitate this case, the callback object offers the scope property.

Suppose you have an object that is responsible for executing server requests.

Further suppose you have an object oAjaxObject that has the methods handleSuccess() and handleFailure() that should be called for success() and failure(), respectively:

```
var oAjaxObject = {
    name : "Test Object",

    handleSuccess : function (oResponse) {
        alert(this.name + " Response received successfully.");
    },

    handleFailure : function (oResponse) {
        alert(this.name + " An error occurred.");
    }
};
```

One might think of creating a callback object such as this:

```
var oCallback = {
    success: oAjaxObject.handleSuccess,
    failure: oAjaxObject.handleFailure
};
```

This code would work if the methods didn't both reference the this object. Since this always refers to the scope of the function being called, it would evaluate to oCallback if this callback object were used. In order to execute the function in the proper scope, as a method of oAjaxObject, add the scope property to the callback object:

```
var oCallback = {
    success: oAjaxObject.handleSuccess,
    failure: oAjaxObject.handleFailure,
    scope: oAjaxObject
};
```

The scope property says, "run the success() and failure() functions as methods of this object." Since good object-oriented design requires all functions to be methods of an object, this ends up being a very common case.

The timeout Property

There is one last optional property for a callback object: timeout. The timeout property specifies how long, in milliseconds, it should take for the response to be received. If the response is not received within that time period, the request is cancelled and the failure() method is called. Only if the response is received within the specified time period will the success() method be called. For instance, if a request must return within 5 seconds to be considered successful, the following callback object may be used:

```
var oCallback = {
    success: oAjaxObject.handleSuccess,
    failure: oAjaxObject.handleFailure,
    scope: oAjaxObject,
    timeout: 5000
};
```

If the `failure()` method is called due to a timeout, the `status` property of the response object is set to –1 and the `statusText` property is set to "transaction aborted."

> **Though this property is helpful, you can create a race condition using it. Since the Connection Manager uses a timeout to periodically check the condition of requests, a response may have been received but not registered before the timeout expires. For this reason, make sure that the timeout specified is large enough to allow ample time for a response to be received and recognized.**

Monitoring and Managing Requests

One of the limitations of XHR is the lack of a built-in method to monitor and manage multiple requests. The Yahoo! Connection Manager has implemented features that allow the monitoring of multiple requests as well as the ability to abort a request that has not yet completed.

As mentioned previously, the `asyncRequest()` method returns an object representing the request transaction. This object can be used to determine if the request is still pending by passing it to the `isCallInProgress()` method, like this:

```
var oTransaction = YAHOO.util.Connect.asyncRequest("GET", "info.htm", oCallback);
alert(YAHOO.util.Connect.isCallInProgress(oTransaction)); //outputs "true"
```

The `isCallInProgress()` method returns `true` if the transaction hasn't completed yet or `false` otherwise.

You might have a case when a request was initiated but should not be allowed to complete. In this case, the Connection Manager provides an `abort()` method. The `abort()` method expects the transaction object to be passed in:

```
var oTransaction = YAHOO.util.Connect.asyncRequest("GET", "info.htm", oCallback);
if(YAHOO.util.Connect.isCallInProgress(oTransaction)) {
    YAHOO.util.Connect.abort(oTransaction);
}
```

Calling `abort()` stops the current request and frees the resources associated with it. Of course, it only makes sense to abort requests that haven't received a response yet, so it's good practice to call `isCallInProgress()` prior to calling `abort()`.

Form Interaction

It is becoming more and more common to submit form values through an Ajax request instead of using the traditional form posting technique. The Yahoo! Connection Manager makes this easy by allowing you to set a form whose data should be sent through the request. For instance, suppose that you have a form with the ID of `"frmInfo"`. A POST request to submit the data contained in the form can be created like this:

```
var oForm = document.getElementById("frmInfo");
YAHOO.util.Connect.setForm(oForm);
YAHOO.util.Connect.asyncRequest("POST", "datahandler.php", oCallback);
```

Using the `setForm()` method, the Connection Manager creates a string of data to be sent in the next request. Because of this, there is no need to specify the fourth argument for the `asyncRequest()` method, since all the data is already retrieved from the form.

> It's important to note that the data string to post is constructed when you call `setForm()`, not when `asyncRequest()` is called. The data being sent is the data at the time when `setForm()` was called, so this method should be called only right before a call to `asyncRequest()` to ensure that the data is the most recent available.

File Uploads

Unlike XHR, the Connection Manager allows file uploads through forms. Before using this feature, be sure to include the Yahoo! Event utility:

```
<script type="text/javascript" src="/js/YAHOO.js"></script>
<script type="text/javascript" src="/js/event.js"></script>
<script type="text/javascript" src="/js/connection.js"></script>
```

Next, set the second argument of `setForm()` to `true` to indicate that a file upload needs to occur:

```
var oForm = document.getElementById("frmInfo");
YAHOO.util.Connect.setForm(oForm, true);
YAHOO.util.Connect.asyncRequest("POST", "datahandler.php", oCallback);
```

When supplying this argument, the Connection Manager switches to using an iframe to send the request. This means that the URL receiving the POST (`datahandler.php` in the previous example) must output HTML code. Since the transaction takes place in an iframe, status codes aren't available for file upload operations, and thus, `success()` and `failure()` can't be used to monitor the status of the request. Instead, define an `upload()` method on the callback object:

```
var oCallback = {
    upload: function (oResponse) {
        alert(oResponse.responseText);
    }
};
```

A response object is passed into `upload()`, just as it is for `success()` and `failure()`. The `responseText` property of the response object is then filled with the text contained within the resulting page's `<body/>` element (the `status` and `statusText` properties are not available when uploading a file). If the text returned in the iframe is valid XML code, the `responseXML` property of the response object is filled with an XML document. It is, however, up to you to determine from `responseText` or `responseXML` whether the upload was successful or not.

> As with `success()` and `failure()`, you can also use the `scope` and `argument` properties to provide additional information for the `upload()` method.

As a final note, if you are uploading a file over SSL, set the third argument of `setForm()` to `true`:

```
var oForm = document.getElementById("frmInfo");
YAHOO.util.Connect.setForm(oForm, true, true);
YAHOO.util.Connect.asyncRequest("post", "datahandler.php", oCallback);
```

This is necessary due to an issue in Internet Explorer when unloading the iframe used for the transaction, but is good to use regardless of the browsers you intend to support.

GET Example

By revisiting the XHR GET example from Chapter 2, you can see how the Yahoo! Connection Manager simplifies the JavaScript code:

```
<!DOCTYPE html PUBLIC "-//W3C//DTD XHTML 1.0 Transitional//EN"
    "http://www.w3.org/TR/xhtml1/DTD/xhtml1-transitional.dtd">
<html xmlns="http://www.w3.org/1999/xhtml">
<head>
    <title>Connection Manager GET Example</title>
    <script type="text/javascript"src="yahoo.js"></script>
    <script type="text/javascript"src="connection.js"></script>
    <script type="text/javascript">
        //<![CDATA[
        function requestCustomerInfo() {
            var sId = document.getElementById("txtCustomerId").value;
            var oCallback = {
                success: function (oResponse) {
                    displayCustomerInfo(oResponse.responseText);
                },
                failure: function (oResponse) {
                    displayCustomerInfo("An error occurred: " +
                                        oResponse.statusText);
                }
            };
            YAHOO.util.Connect.asyncRequest("GET",
                            "GetCustomerData.php?id=" + sId, oCallback);
        }

        function displayCustomerInfo(sText) {
            var divCustomerInfo = document.getElementById("divCustomerInfo");
            divCustomerInfo.innerHTML = sText;
        }
        //]]>
    </script>
</head>
<body>
    <p>Enter customer ID number to retrieve information:</p>
    <p>Customer ID: <input type="text" id="txtCustomerId" value="" /></p>
    <p><input type="button" value="Get Customer Info"
            onclick="requestCustomerInfo()" /></p>
    <div id="divCustomerInfo"></div>
</body>
</html>
```

Using the same `displayCustomerInfo()` function and updating the `requestCustomerInfo()` function, the example works perfectly. The major difference is that the code doesn't have to check for a failure case; the Connection Manager handles that. Since the response object returns the same information as an XHR object, the success and error messages are handled using the `responseText` and `statusText` properties, respectively, mimicking the original example.

POST Example

When you are using the Connection Manager for POSTing information back to the server, the simplification of the JavaScript code is even more dramatic. Consider the second XHR example from Chapter 2, which involves adding a customer record to a database. In that example, code had to be written to encode the form's values, which included a large function designed specifically for that task. Since the Connection Manager handles that for you, the code becomes very simple:

```html
<!DOCTYPE html PUBLIC "-//W3C//DTD XHTML 1.0 Transitional//EN"
"http://www.w3.org/TR/xhtml1/DTD/xhtml1-transitional.dtd">
<html xmlns="http://www.w3.org/1999/xhtml">
<head>
    <title>Connection Manager POST Example</title>
    <script type="text/javascript"src="yahoo.js"></script>
    <script type="text/javascript"src="connection.js"></script>
    <script type="text/javascript">
//<![CDATA[
        function sendRequest() {
            var oForm = document.forms[0];

            var oCallback = {
                success: function (oResponse) {
                    saveResult(oResponse.responseText);
                },

                failure: function (oResponse) {
                    saveResult("An error occurred: " + oResponse.statusText);
                }
            };

            YAHOO.util.Connect.setForm(oForm);
            YAHOO.util.Connect.asyncRequest("POST", oForm.action, oCallback);
        }

        function saveResult(sMessage) {
            var divStatus = document.getElementById("divStatus");
            divStatus.innerHTML = "Request completed: " + sMessage;
        }
//]]>
    </script>
</head>
<body>
    <form method="post" action="SaveCustomer.php"
            onsubmit="sendRequest(); return false">
        <p>Enter customer information to be saved:</p>
        <p>Customer Name: <input type="text" name="txtName" value="" /><br />
```

```
        Address: <input type="text" name="txtAddress" value="" /><br />
        City: <input type="text" name="txtCity" value="" /><br />
        State: <input type="text" name="txtState" value="" /><br />
        Zip Code: <input type="text" name="txtZipCode" value="" /><br />
        Phone: <input type="text" name="txtPhone" value="" /><br />
        E-mail: <input type="text" name="txtEmail" value="" /></p>
        <p><input type="submit" value="Save Customer Info" /></p>
        </form>
        <div id="divStatus"></div>
    </body>
    </html>
```

What previously took more than 90 lines of JavaScript code using XHR now takes only 19 lines of code. Most of the savings comes with the use of setForm() to encode the form values. When completed, this example behaves exactly the same as its XHR counterpart.

Additional Features

As mentioned previously, the Connection Manager uses a polling mechanism to check the status of request transactions it initiates. If you find that the default polling interval isn't good enough for your needs, the setPollingInterval() method can be called to reset the interval as desired:

```
YAHOO.util.Connect.setPollingInterval(250);
```

This method should be called before any requests have been sent, since this new setting takes effect on all requests, both those that are in process and all those that have yet to be initiated.

Another method, initHeader(), allows specification of request headers:

```
YAHOO.util.Connect.initHeader("MyName", "Nicholas");
YAHOO.util.Connect.asyncRequest("get", "info.php", oCallback);
```

In this example, an extra header with a name of "MyName" and a value of "Nicholas" is sent to the server. Note that this header is good for only one request; all headers reset to default values after each call to asyncRequest().

Limitations

While the Yahoo! Connection Manager does make some requests easier, it does have its limitations.

❑   Currently, only asynchronous requests are supported, so you'll be stuck using old school XHR if you need to make a synchronous request. Though many argue that synchronous requests should never be used, sometimes there are practical reasons for using them.

❑   It is also worth noting that as of this writing the current version of the Connection Manager is 0.12.0 , so undoubtedly there will be some additions and changes in the future. However, for the time being, it remains one of the most compact libraries for cross-browser Ajax communication.

Prototype

One JavaScript library that has gained considerable popularity with the emergence of Ajax is Prototype, available at `http://prototype.conio.net`. Prototype is not simply an Ajax library; it is actually a complete JavaScript framework designed to ease the development of all types of JavaScript solutions.

It is beyond the scope of this book to fully explore all of Prototype's features, so the focus here is on its Ajax capabilities.

The Ajax.Request Object

Most of Prototype's low-level Ajax features are contained on the aptly named `Ajax` object. The Ajax object has several properties containing methods and constructors for useful objects. The simplest object, and the most similar to XHR, is the `Ajax.Request` object, which has the following constructor:

```
request = new Ajax.Request(url, options);
```

The first argument is the URL to send the request to. The second argument is an object containing any number of options for the request. As soon as the creation of the `Ajax.Request` object is complete, the request is sent (think of it as combining XHR's `open()` and `send()` methods in one call). For this reason, the options object is very important.

The Options Object

The options object, as used in the `Ajax.Request()` constructor, contains all of the information about the request except for the URL. In its simplest form, the options object contains the following properties:

❑ `method`: Either "get" or "post."

❑ `parameters`: The data to be sent to the URL. Typically, a URL-encoded string of name-value pairs, but can also be other data formats when `method` is "post."

❑ `onSuccess`: Function to call when the response has been successfully received. Similar to the `success()` method in the Yahoo! Connection Manager, it fires when the `status` of a response is between 200 and 300.

❑ `onFailure`: Function to call when the response has failed. Similar to the `failure()` method in the Yahoo! Connection Manager, it fires when the `status` of a response is not between 200 and 300.

Also like the Connection Manager callback object, the `Ajax.Request` options object is defined with a simple object literal, such as:

```
var oOptions = {
    method: "get",
    parameters: "first%20name=Nicholas&last%20name=Zakas",
    onSuccess: function (oXHR, oJson) {
        //your code here
    },
    onFailure: function (oXHR, oJson) {
        //your code here
    }
}
```

The onSuccess() and onFailure() methods are functions that are passed two arguments: the XHR object used to make the request and an optional JSON object with additional information about the request (JSON is discussed in Chapter 8). The second argument is used mostly in conjunction with a feature in Ruby on Rails (www.rubyonrails.org), so it won't be discussed here.

> **There is an important distinction between GET requests made using** Ajax.Request **and GET requests made with traditional XHR or with the Yahoo! Connection Manager: the** Ajax.Request **object automatically adds the** parameters **property value to the end of the URL specified in the constructor.**

When using Ajax.Request, the URL should be specified without a query string and the parameters property should be used:

```
var oOptions = {
    method: "get",
    parameters: "name=Nicholas",
    onSuccess: function (oXHR, oJson) {
        alert("Response received successfully.");
    },
    onFailure: function (oXHR, oJson) {
        alert("Request was unsuccessful.");
    }
};
var oRequest = new Ajax.Request("test.php", oOptions);
```

The combining of the URL and the parameters property is handled by Prototype behind the scenes. This same methodology can be used for POST requests by just changing the method property:

```
var oOptions = {
    method: "post",
    parameters: "name=Nicholas",
    onSuccess: function (oXHR, oJson) {
        alert("Response received successfully.");
    },
    onFailure: function (oXHR, oJson) {
        alert("Request was unsuccessful.");
    }
};
var oRequest = new Ajax.Request("test.php", oOptions);
```

In this way, Prototype simplifies Ajax requests so that the switch between a GET and a POST request is simply a one-step change. Prototype also handles setting the default POST content type on the XHR request, further simplifying things for the developer.

The requestHeaders Property

To add headers to the outgoing request, specify the requestHeaders property in the options object. This must be an array with an even number of items so that the first item is the name of a header, the second item is the value of that header, and so on. For example:

```
    var oOptions = {
        method: "get",
        parameters: "name=Nicholas",
        requestHeaders: [ "header1", "header1 value", "header2", "header2 value"],
        onSuccess: function (oXHR, oJson) {
            alert("Response received successfully.");
        },
        onFailure: function (oXHR, oJson) {
            alert("Request was unsuccessful.");
        }
    };
```

This code adds two headers to the request: `"header1"`, which has a value of `"header1 value"`, and `"header2"`, which has a value of `"header2 value"`. This is the same as calling `setRequestHeader()` on an XHR object for each header.

The asynchronous Property

By default, all requests initiated using `Ajax.Request` are sent asynchronously, meaning that the JavaScript doesn't wait for a response. If, for some reason, you need to send a request synchronously, which locks the JavaScript code execution and the user interface, it can be accomplished by setting the asynchronous property to `false`:

```
    var oOptions = {
        method: "get",
        parameters: "name=Nicholas",
        asynchronous: false
    };
```

In this case, there is no need for `onSuccess()` or `onFailure()`, because the next line of code after the request is sent can handle all conditions. After the call has been completed, the XHR object can be accessed directly via `Ajax.Request.transport`.

Remember, synchronous requests should be used sparingly and only for small amounts of data, since they lock the user interface while the request is being processed.

Other Events

The `Ajax.Request` object supports several custom events outside of the success/failure realm. Each of these events can be handled with developer-defined functions through the options object. The complete list of event handlers is as follows:

❑   `onException()`: Called when an error occurred in the JavaScript code while trying to execute the request or during a callback function call.

❑   `onLoaded()`: Called when the response has been received but not evaluated. The same as XHR ready state 2. Not recommended for use due to cross-browser differences.

❑   `onLoading()`: Called repeatedly while a request is waiting for or receiving a response.

❑   `onInteractive()`: Called when the response has been received and parsed; some information is available. The same as XHR ready state 3. Not recommended for use due to cross-browser differences.

❏ onComplete(): Called when the response has been completely received and parsed. The same as XHR ready state 4.

Each of these event handlers are passed the same two arguments as onSuccess() and onFailure(): the XHR object used to make the request and an optional second object containing response information.

In general, onException() is probably the most useful of these event handlers, since onSuccess() and onFailure() handle most of the important cases.

GET Example

Revisiting the first XHR example from Chapter 2 again, you can see that the code for the Prototype version is fairly straightforward and similar, in many respects, to the Yahoo! Connection Manager version:

```
<!DOCTYPE html PUBLIC "-//W3C//DTD XHTML 1.0 Transitional//EN"
"http://www.w3.org/TR/xhtml1/DTD/xhtml1-transitional.dtd">
<html xmlns="http://www.w3.org/1999/xhtml">
<head>
    <title>Prototype GET Example</title>
    <script type="text/javascript"src="prototype.js"></script>
    <script type="text/javascript">
        //<![CDATA[
        function requestCustomerInfo() {
            var sId = document.getElementById("txtCustomerId").value;
            var oOptions = {
                method: "get",
                parameters: "id=" + sId,
                onSuccess: function (oXHR, oJson) {
                    displayCustomerInfo(oXHR.responseText);
                },
                onFailure: function (oXHR, oJson) {
                    displayCustomerInfo("An error occurred: " +
                                                    oXHR.statusText);
                }
            };
            var oRequest = new Ajax.Request("GetCustomerData.php", oOptions);
        }

        function displayCustomerInfo(sText) {
            var divCustomerInfo = document.getElementById("divCustomerInfo");
            divCustomerInfo.innerHTML = sText;
        }
        //]]>
    </script>
</head>
<body>
    <p>Enter customer ID number to retrieve information:</p>
    <p>Customer ID: <input type="text" id="txtCustomerId" value="" /></p>
    <p><input type="button" value="Get Customer Info"
            onclick="requestCustomerInfo()" /></p>
    <div id="divCustomerInfo"></div>
</body>
</html>
```

The important thing to note here is that the query string is not appended directly to the URL, as in the previous examples.

POST Example

The XHR POST example can also be changed to use Prototype. Unfortunately, since Prototype doesn't include a method to encode the data in a form, you'll still need all the code that was in the original example. The only thing that changes is the `sendRequest()` function:

```
function sendRequest() {
    var oForm = document.forms[0];
    var sBody = getRequestBody(oForm);

    var oOptions = {
        method: "post",
        parameters: sBody,
        onSuccess: function (oXHR, oJson) {
            saveResult(oXHR.responseText);
        },
        onFailure: function (oXHR, oJson) {
            saveResult("An error occurred: " + oXHR.statusText);
        }
    };

    var oRequest = new Ajax.Request("SaveCustomer.php", oOptions);
}
```

Note that the data to POST is still passed in using the `parameters` property of the options object.

The Ajax.Updater Object

Each of the two XHR examples had something in common: they outputted a status message to an element on the page once the response had been received. This is actually a fairly common use case of Ajax calls, and Prototype has made it easy to handle this automatically using the `Ajax.Updater` object.

The `Ajax.Updater` object is created using a constructor similar to that of `Ajax.Request`:

```
request = new Ajax.Updater(element_id, url, options);
```

Behind the scenes, `Ajax.Updater` uses `Ajax.Request` to initiate a request, so it should come as no surprise that the arguments to the constructor include the ones needed for `Ajax.Request`. The only difference is the insertion of an additional argument at the beginning of the list: an HTML element's ID. When a response is received, `Ajax.Updater` takes the `responseText` from the XHR object and puts it into the HTML element with the given ID using the `innerHTML` property.

When you are using `Ajax.Updater`, it's not necessary to assign the `onSuccess()` or `onFailure()`, methods because the `responseText` is output to the HTML element either way. For example, consider how the GET example can change using `Ajax.Updater`:

```
<!DOCTYPE html PUBLIC "-//W3C//DTD XHTML 1.0 Transitional//EN"
"http://www.w3.org/TR/xhtml1/DTD/xhtml1-transitional.dtd">
<html xmlns="http://www.w3.org/1999/xhtml">
<head>
    <title>Prototype Updater Example</title>
    <script type="text/javascript"src="prototype.js"></script>
    <script type="text/javascript">
        //<![CDATA[
        function requestCustomerInfo() {
            var sId = document.getElementById("txtCustomerId").value;
            var oOptions = {
                method: "get",
                parameters: "id=" + sId
            };
            var oRequest = new Ajax.Updater("divCustomerInfo",
                                "GetCustomerData.php", oOptions);
        }

        //]]>
    </script>
</head>
<body>
    <p>Enter customer ID number to retrieve information:</p>
    <p>Customer ID: <input type="text" id="txtCustomerId" value="" /></p>
    <p><input type="button" value="Get Customer Info"
            onclick="requestCustomerInfo()" /></p>
    <div id="divCustomerInfo"></div>
</body>
</html>
```

In this code, the displayCustomerInfo() function has been completely removed since its only purpose was to display text in divCustomerInfo. Note that the ID is passed in as the first argument of the Ajax.Updater() constructor as well. That's all that is necessary to maintain the functionality of the example.

Of course, there is the possibility that a 404 or other error status may occur, and it may bring with it some ugly HTML. To handle this case, there is an alternate constructor for Ajax.Updater where the first argument is an object that can direct the output to one HTML element for a successful response and another for a failure, such as:

```
var oRequest = new Ajax.Updater({
    success: "success_element_id",
    failure: "failure_element_id"
}, url, options);
```

Realistically, however, you probably want the output to be displayed only when the request was successful. In that case, just assign the success element ID and add an onFailure() method to the options object, such as:

```
<!DOCTYPE html PUBLIC "-//W3C//DTD XHTML 1.0 Transitional//EN"
"http://www.w3.org/TR/xhtml1/DTD/xhtml1-transitional.dtd">
<html xmlns="http://www.w3.org/1999/xhtml">
<head>
```

```
<title>Prototype Updater Failure Example</title>
<script type="text/javascript"src="prototype.js"></script>
<script type="text/javascript">
    //<![CDATA[
    function requestCustomerInfo() {
        var sId = document.getElementById("txtCustomerId").value;
        var oOptions = {
            method: "get",
            parameters: "id=" + sId,
            onFailure: function (oXHR, oJson) {
                alert("An error occurred: " + oXHR.status);
            }
        };
        var oRequest = new Ajax.Updater({
            success: "divCustomerInfo"
        }, "GetCustomerData.php", oOptions);
    }
    //]]>
</script>
</head>
<body>
    <p>Enter customer ID number to retrieve information:</p>
    <p>Customer ID: <input type="text" id="txtCustomerId" value="" /></p>
    <p><input type="button" value="Get Customer Info"
onclick="requestCustomerInfo()" /></p>
    <div id="divCustomerInfo"></div>
</body>
</html>
```

In this revision of the previous example, data is displayed on the page only if the request was successful because only the success property is provided in the first argument. If a request fails, then an alert is displayed using the onFailure() method of the options object.

The Ajax.Responders Object

Suppose that you want the same action to take place each time an Ajax request takes place. Why would you want to do this? Think in terms of a generic loading message that should be displayed every time there is a request in progress (to ensure the user interface is consistent). Using other libraries or XHR directly, you'd be forced to manually call a specific function each time. Prototype makes this easy using the Ajax.Responders object.

To set up event handlers for all Ajax requests, define an options object containing onCreate() and/or onComplete() methods, such as:

```
var oGlobalOptions = {
    onCreate: function (oXHR, oJson) {
        alert("Sending request...");
    },
    onComplete: function (oXHR, oJson) {
        alert("Response received.");
    }
};
```

This options object can then be passed to the `register()` method:

```
Ajax.Responders.register(oGlobalOptions);
```

Adding this code, means there is no need to make any changes to the previously existing example JavaScript code. All that is required is the addition of an area to display request status:

```html
<!DOCTYPE html PUBLIC "-//W3C//DTD XHTML 1.0 Transitional//EN"
"http://www.w3.org/TR/xhtml1/DTD/xhtml1-transitional.dtd">
<html xmlns="http://www.w3.org/1999/xhtml">
<head>
    <title>Prototype Responders Example</title>
    <script type="text/javascript"src="prototype.js"></script>
    <script type="text/javascript">
        //<![CDATA[

        var oGlobalOptions = {
            onCreate : function (oXHR, oJson) {
                document.getElementById("divStatus").innerHTML =
                                                "Contacting the server...";
            },
            onComplete : function (oXHR, oJson) {
                document.getElementById("divStatus").innerHTML =
                                                "Response received.";
            }
        };
        Ajax.Responders.register(oGlobalOptions);

        function requestCustomerInfo() {
            var sId = document.getElementById("txtCustomerId").value;
            var oOptions = {
                method: "get",
                parameters: "id=" + sId,
                onFailure: function (oXHR, oJson) {
                    alert("An error occurred: " + oXHR.status);
                }
            };
            var oRequest = new Ajax.Updater({
                success: "divCustomerInfo"
            }, "GetCustomerData.php", oOptions);
        }

        //]]>
    </script>
</head>
<body>
    <p>Enter customer ID number to retrieve information:</p>
    <p>Customer ID: <input type="text" id="txtCustomerId" value="" /></p>
    <p><input type="button" value="Get Customer Info"
                onclick="requestCustomerInfo()" /></p>
    <div id="divStatus" style="color: blue"></div>
    <div id="divCustomerInfo"></div>
</body>
</html>
```

When the button is clicked to retrieve customer information in this example, the divStatus element is filled with status information about the request. Specifically, when the request is first sent, the status changes to "Contacting the server..." and when the response is received, the status is set to "Response received." As you can see, the Ajax.Responders object allows seamless interaction with all Ajax requests without the need to change the code that already exists.

Advantages and Disadvantages

Prototype offers a fairly straightforward approach to Ajax communication that allows both synchronous and asynchronous communication (unlike the Yahoo! Connection Manager, which supports only asynchronous requests). The Ajax.Updater object offers a clean interface for updating HTML elements, and the Ajax.Responders object allows developers to respond to all requests and responses with ease. Clearly, Prototype has some major advantages as far as ease of use and practicality.

That being said, some things are noticeably missing from the library.

❑ Unlike Yahoo! Connection Manager, Prototype lacks the ability to encode all of the values in a form, necessitating developers to write their own function to do so.

❑ Further, Prototype lacks support for non-XHR types of communication, making it impossible to upload files.

❑ And of course, Prototype is not simply an Ajax communication library, so loading the file automatically brings in many other functions, objects, etc., that you may not use. However, this is the same for all JavaScript libraries, and ultimately, it is up to your individual requirements as to whether or not Prototype is a right fit.

jQuery

The jQuery library (available at www.jquery.com) is another library that does much more than simply Ajax communication, but at its small size (15KB), the extra features can be helpful in some situations.

Unlike the previous two libraries discussed in this chapter, jQuery aims to change the way you write JavaScript. It uses a querying interface to find specific nodes in the web page. The basic expression language used by jQuery is a mix of CSS selectors (from CSS Levels 1–3) and simple XPath expressions. Using this mix, it's possible to find specific nodes or groups of nodes without manipulating the DOM directly.

Simple jQuery Expressions

Since jQuery relies to heavily on its querying system, it's important to first understand how it works. The function used to query the DOM is $(), which accepts a string argument containing an expression. The expression may match one or many nodes in the DOM document, and the return value is another jQuery object that can be used to manipulate the result set (you won't be receiving any arrays or DOM elements back from most jQuery methods). This allows you to chain together jQuery methods into long groups of actions. Here are some sample queries:

```
//get all <p> elements
$("p");

//get the <div> element with an ID of myDiv
$("div#myDiv");

//get all textboxes (all <input> elements with type attribute equal to "text")
$("input[@type=text]");
```

As mentioned previously, each of these calls returns another jQuery object that can be used to manipulate the result set. Here are the same queries with actions attached:

```
//get all <p> elements and hide them
$("p").hide();

//get the <div> element with an ID of myDiv and change its font to Arial
$("div#myDiv").css("font-family", "Arial");

//get all textboxes (all <input> elements with type attribute equal to "text")
//and set their width to 400 pixels
$("input[@type=text]").width("400px");
```

For each of these result sets, an action is now taking place. The first line hides all <p> elements on the page; the second changes the font of the <div> element with an ID of "myDiv"; the third sets the width of all textboxes to 400 pixels. Programming JavaScript in this manner takes some getting used to, but jQuery already has a pretty strong following among developers due to its simple interface.

> It's beyond the scope of this book to discuss all of the features of jQuery. Please visit www.jquery.com to learn more.

Executing GET Requests

There are several options for performing GET requests using jQuery. The simplest method is to use $.get(), which accepts a URL and a callback function as arguments. The callback function receives two arguments, the text sent back from the server and a status string ("success" or "error"), such as:

```
$.get("path/to/data.php?name=value", function (sData, sStatus) {
    alert(sStatus + ":" + sData);
});
```

It's also possible to pass in an associative array of name-value pairs to pass with the URL instead of specifically defining a query string:

```
$.get("path/to/data.php", { name: "value" }, function (sData, sStatus) {
    alert(sStatus + ":" + sData);
});
```

The properties of the associative array are encoded and added to the query string, taking this responsibility away from the developer.

There are also several specialized GET methods in jQuery, each designed for a different purpose:

❑ `$.getIfModified()`: Performs a GET request only if the resource has been modified since the last time it was requested. Same arguments as `$.get()`.

❑ `$.getJSON()`: Performs a GET request and evaluates the JSON response into a JavaScript object. Same arguments as `$.get()` except the callback function receives a JavaScript object instead of text. JSON is discussed in Chapter 8.

❑ `$.getScript()`: Performs a GET request and expects JavaScript code as a response. The code is executed upon response. Same arguments as `$.get()` except that the callback function doesn't receive any information.

Of course, it is up to your individual requirements as to which method is appropriate.

GET Example

By revisiting the first XHR example, you can see that jQuery can be used to simplify the code necessary to retrieve information from the server:

```
<!DOCTYPE html PUBLIC "-//W3C//DTD XHTML 1.0 Transitional//EN"
"http://www.w3.org/TR/xhtml1/DTD/xhtml1-transitional.dtd">
<html xmlns="http://www.w3.org/1999/xhtml">
<head>
    <title>jQuery GET Example</title>
    <script type="text/javascript"src="jquery.js"></script>
    <script type="text/javascript">
        //<![CDATA[
        function requestCustomerInfo() {
            var sId = $("input#txtCustomerId").val();
            $.get("GetCustomerData.php?id=" + sId, displayCustomerInfo);
        }

        function displayCustomerInfo(sText, sStatus) {
            if (sStatus == "success") {
                $("div#divCustomerInfo").html(sText);
            } else {
                $("div#divCustomerInfo").html("An error occurred.");
            }
        }
    //]]>
    </script>
</head>
<body>
    <p>Enter customer ID number to retrieve information:</p>
    <p>Customer ID: <input type="text" id="txtCustomerId" value="" /></p>
    <p><input type="button" value="Get Customer Info"
            onclick="requestCustomerInfo()" /></p>
    <div id="divCustomerInfo"></div>
</body>
</html>
```

All of the JavaScript code in this example has been changed to use jQuery, which drastically reduces the amount of code necessary to perform this operation. The value of the textbox is retrieved by the expression $("input#txtCustomerId").val() and stored in sId (the val() method retrieves the value of a form field). Next, the $.get() method is called, passing in displayCustomerInfo() as the callback function. Since callback functions receive only one argument, text back from the server, the displayCustomerInfo() method can be used directly as the callback. The function itself has also been changed to use jQuery in order to show the html() method, which gets or sets the HTML content of a given element or set of elements.

Using the $.get() method with an associative array of requestCustomerInfo() can be rewritten as:

```
function requestCustomerInfo() {
    var sId = $("input#txtCustomerId").val();
    $.get("GetCustomerData.php", { id : sId }, displayCustomerInfo);
}
```

This takes responsibility for properly formatting the query string out of the developer's hands, allowing jQuery to handle the encoding and formatting.

The $.post() Method

POST requests are sent in jQuery using the $.post() method. This method accepts the same arguments as $.get(): a URL, an associative array of parameters, and a callback function to receive the returned data. For example:

```
$.post("path/to/data.php", { name: "value" }, function (sData, sStatus) {
    alert(sStatus + ":" + sData);
});
```

As with GET requests, jQuery encodes the POST parameters in the associative array and sends that data as the request body.

Both the second and third arguments to $.post() are optional; however, there's no reason to send a POST without data (the second argument). It's also recommended that a callback function always be provided to monitor the status of the response.

POST Example

To illustrate using the $.post() method, recall the POST example using XHR from Chapter 2. In that example, it was necessary to serialize a form into a string. Since the $.post() method doesn't accept a string for data, the getRequestBody() function must be changed to create an associative array of data instead of a string:

```
<!DOCTYPE html PUBLIC "-//W3C//DTD XHTML 1.0 Transitional//EN"
"http://www.w3.org/TR/xhtml1/DTD/xhtml1-transitional.dtd">
<html xmlns="http://www.w3.org/1999/xhtml">
<head>
    <title>jQuery POST Example</title>
    <script type="text/javascript"src="jquery.js"></script>
    <script type="text/javascript">
```

```
//<![CDATA[
    function sendRequest() {
        var oForm = document.forms[0];
        var oBody = getRequestBody(oForm);
        $.post("SaveCustomer.php", oBody, saveResult);
    }

    function getRequestBody(oForm) {

        var oParams = {};

        for (var i=0 ; i < oForm.elements.length; i++) {
            var oField = oForm.elements[i];
            switch (oField.type) {

                case "button":
                case "submit":
                case "reset":
                    break;

                case "checkbox":
                case "radio":
                    if (!oField.checked) {
                        break;
                    }

                case "text":
                case "hidden":
                case "password":
                    oParams[oField.name] = oField.value;
                    break;

                default:

                    switch(oField.tagName.toLowerCase()) {
                        case "select":
                            oParams[oField.name] =
                                    oField.options[oField.selectedIndex].value;
                            break;
                        default:
                            oParams[oField.name] = oField.value;
                    }
            }
        }

        return oParams;
    }

    function saveResult(sMessage, sStatus) {
        if (sStatus == "success") {
            $("div#divStatus").html("Request completed: " + sMessage);
        } else {
            $("div#divStatus").html("An error occurred.");
        }
```

```
            }
        //]]>
        </script>
    </head>
    <body>
        <form method="post" action="SaveCustomer.php"
                onsubmit="sendRequest(); return false">
        <p>Enter customer information to be saved:</p>
        <p>Customer Name: <input type="text" name="txtName" value="" /><br />
        Address: <input type="text" name="txtAddress" value="" /><br />
        City: <input type="text" name="txtCity" value="" /><br />
        State: <input type="text" name="txtState" value="" /><br />
        Zip Code: <input type="text" name="txtZipCode" value="" /><br />
        Phone: <input type="text" name="txtPhone" value="" /><br />
        E-mail: <input type="text" name="txtEmail" value="" /></p>
        <p><input type="submit" value="Save Customer Info" /></p>
        </form>
        <div id="divStatus"></div>
    </body>
</html>
```

The only other changes are to saveResult(), to use jQuery to access the divStatus element. There isn't a large amount of code savings for this particular example, but there are several other ways to initiate Ajax communication using jQuery.

The load() Method

The previous two examples simply fill an HTML element with the data returned from the server, which is a common Ajax pattern. The Prototype library provided Ajax.Updater to simplify this pattern; jQuery provides the load() method for the same purpose.

The load() method can be called on any element or group of elements in jQuery and has two modes: GET and POST. To use GET mode, provide a URL (with a query string) and an optional callback function; for POST, provide a URL, an associative array of values, and an optional callback function.

Changing the GET example to use load() really simplifies the JavaScript necessary to achieve the desired effect:

```
function requestCustomerInfo() {
    var sId = $("input#txtCustomerId").val();
    $("div#divCustomerInfo").load("GetCustomerData.php?id=" + sId);
}
```

The first step in this example is to get a reference to divCustomerInfo. Once that has been completed, the load() method is called with only a URL as an argument. The callback function isn't necessary here, since the default behavior is to place the returned data into the <div/>. It's also important to note that the displayCustomerInfo() function is no longer needed, reducing the amount of code dramatically.

In the POST example, it's also possible to reduce the amount of code by updating the sendRequest() function:

```
function sendRequest() {
    var oForm = document.forms[0];
    var oBody = getRequestBody(oForm);

    $("div#divStatus").load("SaveCustomer.php", oBody);
}
```

By changing just one line, it's possible to eliminate the saveResult() function completely. This code now gets a reference to divStatus and then calls load(). Since the second argument is an associative array (oBody), the load() method assumes the request is a POST. Once again, a callback function isn't necessary.

The load() method provides a quick way to load content into an element, though you do lose the ability to handle individual cases of success or failure. There is, however, another method that allows more fine-grained control over Ajax communication.

The $.ajax() Method

All of the other methods discussed in this section are high level, hiding a lot of the communication detail from developers. These methods all have one thing in common: under the covers, they all use the $.ajax() method to initiate and handle requests. This method provides more fine-grained control over requests and responses.

The $.ajax() method accepts a single argument, which is an associative array of options, not unlike Prototype's Ajax.Request constructor. This options object is made up of the following properties:

❑　type: The type of request, either GET or POST.

❑　url: The URL to request.

❑　data: An encoded string of data. Used for POST requests only.

❑　dataType: The type of data expected as a response: "script," "xml," "html," or "json." If "script" is specified, then the returned data is loaded as JavaScript into the page.

❑　success(): A function to call when a successful response is received. A successful response is anything with a status of 2xx or 304. This function receives two arguments: the XHR object and a status string.

❑　error(): A function to call when an error occurs. Anything that isn't considered a success is considered an error. This function receives two arguments: the XHR object and a status string.

❑　complete(): A function to call when a response is received; called for both successful and unsuccessful responses. This function receives two arguments: the XHR object and a status string.

So to recreate the GET example using $.ajax(), the requestCustomerInfo() function is changed to the following:

```
function requestCustomerInfo() {

    var sId = $("input#txtCustomerId").val();

    $.ajax({
        type : "GET",
        url : "GetCustomerData.php?id=" + sId,
        success : function (oXHR, status) {
            $("div#divCustomerInfo").html(oXHR.responseText);
        },
        error : function (oXHR, status) {
            $("div#divCustomerInfo").html("An error occurred.");
        }
    });
}
```

Since this is a low-level operation in jQuery, the success() and error() functions must look at the XHR object for additional information about the request, including the returned data.

The ajaxStart() and ajaxStop() Methods

Prototype isn't the only library that has global event handlers for Ajax requests; jQuery supports similar functionality by using the ajaxStart() and ajaxStop() methods. The ajaxStart() method fires when there are no Ajax requests pending and one is started. Likewise, the ajaxStop() method is called when all Ajax requests have completed. Both methods accept a function that should be called when the event occurs.

The first step to using these methods is to retrieve a reference to an element. Then, the ajaxStart() and ajaxStop() methods can be called on that element. For instance, to use a <div/> element with an ID of divStatus, the following code can be used:

```
$("div#divStatus").ajaxStart(function () {
    $(this).html("Contacting the server...");
}).ajaxStop(function () {
    $(this).html("Response received.");
});
```

This code calls both methods on divStatus. Since the ajaxStart() and ajaxStop() methods return jQuery objects, the two can be chained together. Because it is divStatus itself that should be updated, the $(this) object is used inside the functions along with the html() method to set the status text.

Limitations

The jQuery library provides a very interesting interface not only for Ajax communication but also for JavaScript in general; this is also one of the limitations. Using jQuery means abandoning some of the more common methods of JavaScript programming, including DOM manipulation. The library makes you more dependent on itself, since many of the features are implemented only as methods of jQuery objects. Still, there are some powerful methods that can enable simple or complex Ajax communication.

Summary

In this chapter, you learned about several Ajax communication libraries. These libraries facilitate Ajax communication by wrapping XHR behind methods that handle all of the details. All of the libraries mentioned in this chapter introduce different interfaces for Ajax designed to save developers from the mundane details.

The first library introduced was the Yahoo! Connection Manager. Created by Yahoo!, this open source library allows Ajax requests with a minimal amount of additional code. The library handles the determination of success and failure based on the HTTP status of a response as well as handling scoping issues with callback functions. The Yahoo! Connection Manager is a pure Ajax library that does only Ajax communication and nothing else.

Next, you learned about Prototype, an open source JavaScript library. Prototype, unlike the Yahoo! Connection Manager, is a complete JavaScript library that isn't solely used for Ajax communication. The library has several objects that make Ajax communication and monitoring much easier for developers.

The last library discussed was jQuery. Unlike the other two libraries previously mentioned, jQuery aims to change the way you write JavaScript. It wraps common DOM methods inside its own object structure, which allows advanced querying of DOM documents. The library also introduces several convenient methods to enable Ajax communication.

Choosing to use an Ajax library is a decision that must be based on requirements. One may be more appropriate for your project than another. Make sure to do some research into any library you choose before committing to it to ensure that it can grow and evolve with your application.

5

Request Management

Ajax applications, while powerful and user-friendly, do have some issues relating to the requests sent from the client to the server and the responses received back. A major concern is the number of times that communication occurs between the client and server. If the requests are initiated frequently, the server can get bogged down trying to handle requests from multiple users. Further, the client can become unresponsive while waiting for a large number of responses from the server.

Central to this problem is part of the HTTP 1.1 specification that states a client can have no more than two simultaneous connections to a single domain name at a time. While there are ways of working around this strict limitation, such as using subdomains to handle some requests, most browsers do have a maximum number of connections that can be open at a single time. When using XHR, this limitation is handled behind the scenes: you simply initiate requests as you see fit, and the browser queues them up for sending when there's an open connection. This works fine when requests are few and far between, but when requests are being sent from various parts of an application at different times, the built-in queuing mechanism just doesn't provide enough control over when requests are sent and what requests should be sent first. Fortunately, it's not too difficult to implement a custom request manager that can handle more complex communication patterns.

Priority Queues

Whenever pieces of data need to be arranged in order of priority, the typical solution is to use a *priority queue*. A standard queue is a first-in, first-out data structure: items are added at the back of the queue, wait in line, and eventually are removed from the front of the queue. A priority queue augments that methodology by inserting new values into the queue based on a priority, so a new value with a higher priority doesn't go to the back of the queue, but rather, gets inserted into an appropriate location. In a priority queue where 0 is the highest priority and 4 is the lowest, items with a priority of 3 will always be inserted into the queue before any items with a priority of 4. Likewise, items with a priority of 2 are inserted ahead of those with a priority of 3, and so on. This is the perfect paradigm for managing multiple XHR requests. Unfortunately, JavaScript doesn't have a built-in priority queue, so it's necessary to create one.

A generic priority queue can be made with a single `Array` object, making use of the built-in `sort()` method. When values are added to this custom priority queue, they are added to the array, which is then sorted. By providing a custom comparison function to the `sort()` method, it's possible to determine the order in which the values should appear within the array, making it perfect for assigning priorities. A comparison function has the following generic form:

```
function compare(oValue1, oValue2) {
    if (oValue1 < oValue2) {
        return -1;
    } else if (oValue1 > oValue 2) {
        return 1;
    } else {
        return 0;
    }
}
```

Very simply, a comparison function returns a negative number when the first value is less than the second (when the first should come before the second), a positive number when the first value is greater than the second (when the first should come after the second), and zero if the values are equal (don't change position in the array).

The constructor for the `PriorityQueue` object is:

```
function PriorityQueue(fnCompare) {
    this._items = new Array();
    if (typeof fnCompare == "function"){
        this._compare = fnCompare;
    }
}
```

This constructor accepts a single argument, `fnCompare`, which is a comparison function to use when determining priorities. If this argument is provided, it's assigned to the `_compare` property; otherwise, the default `_compare()` method is used (the default method is defined on the prototype). There is also a single property, `items`, which holds the `Array` object used to manage the values.

> Note that the single underscore (_) prefixed to these names indicates that they are not intended to be publicly accessible.

Next, the methods for the `PriorityQueue` need to be defined. The first method is the default `_compare()` method to use when one isn't supplied. Since this method isn't intended to be publicly accessible, a `prioritize()` method is implemented to use it:

```
PriorityQueue.prototype = {

    _compare : function (oValue1, oValue2) {
        if (oValue1 < oValue2) {
            return -1;
        } else if (oValue1 > oValue2) {
            return 1;
        } else {
```

```
            return 0;
        }
    },

    //more code here

    prioritize : function () {
        this._items.sort(this._compare);
    }

    //more code here

};
```

The _compare() method is just a basic comparison function that uses the primitive values of each item to figure out which goes before which (using the less-than and greater-than operators caused a behind-the-scenes call to valueOf() on each item). When an item is added to the queue, the prioritize() method is called to ensure that items appear in the correct order. This is also important in case a value inside of the queue changes, at which point it's necessary to call prioritize() explicitly to ensure that the ordering is valid.

There are five methods that deal with the normal operation of a priority queue: get(), item(), peek(), put(), and size().

❑   The get() method retrieves the next item in the queue.

❑   item() returns an item in a given position.

❑   peek() gets the next item in the queue without actually removing it (just a preview of the next item).

❑   put() is responsible for adding a new value to the queue.

❑   size() simply returns the number of items in the queue.

These methods are all fairly simple:

```
PriorityQueue.prototype = {

    _compare : function (oValue1, oValue2) {
        if (oValue1 < oValue2) {
            return -1;
        } else if (oValue1 > oValue2) {
            return 1;
        } else {
            return 0;
        }
    },

    get : function() {
        return this._items.shift();
    },

    item : function (iPos) {
        return this._items[iPos];
```

```
    },

    peek : function () {
        return this._items[0];
    },

    prioritize : function () {
        this._items.sort(this._compare);
    },

    put : function (oValue) {
        this._items.push(oValue);
        this.prioritize();
    },

    //more code here

    size: function () {
        return this._items.length;
    }
};
```

In the preceding code, you see all five methods in action:

❑ The `get()` method uses the array's `shift()` method to remove and return the first item in the array (if the array is empty, `shift()` returns `null`).

❑ The next method, `item()`, returns an item in the specified position in the queue.

❑ `peek()` just gets the first item in the array using the 0 index, which returns the value without removing it.

❑ The `put()` method is the one that adds a value to the queue. It first adds the value to the array and then calls `prioritize()`.

❑ Last, the `size()` method simply returns the length of the array, so it's possible to tell how many items are in the queue.

The final method for the `PriorityQueue` object is `remove()`, which searches the queue for a specific value and then removes it. This can be very important if an item loses priority and no longer needs to be in the queue:

```
PriorityQueue.prototype = {

    _compare : function (oValue1, oValue2) {
        if (oValue1 < oValue2) {
            return -1;
        } else if (oValue1 > oValue2) {
            return 1;
        } else {
            return 0;
        }
    },

    get : function() {
```

```
            return this._items.shift();
        },

        peek : function () {
            return this._items[0];
        },

        prioritize : function () {
            this._items.sort(this._compare);
        },

        put : function (oValue) {
            this._items.push(oValue);
            this._items.sort(this._compare);
        },

        remove : function (oValue) {
            for (var i=0; i < this._items.length; i++) {
                if (this._items[i] === oValue) {
                    this._items.splice(i, 1);
                    return true;
                }
            }
            return false;
        },

        size : function () {
            return this._items.length;
        }

    };
```

The remove() method uses a for loop to search for a specific value in the array. The value is determined by using the identically equal operator (===) to ensure that types aren't converted when making the comparison. If the matching value is found, it is removed from the array using the splice() method and a value of true is returned; if no matching value is found, it returns false.

This PriorityQueue object is the base upon which a robust request management object can be created.

> Although this object will be used for XHR request management, the PriorityQueue is generic enough that it can be used in any application that needs prioritizes data items.

The RequestManager Object

The RequestManager object is the main object used for handling XHR requests. Its main job is to manage two simultaneous XHR requests, since no more than two can be sent on any client that obeys the HTTP 1.1 specification. This object handles the creation and destruction of all XHR objects used to make the requests, meaning that the developer never has to worry about creating an XHR object directly. Additionally, the `RequestManager` object handles the monitoring of all requests and the marshaling of results to particular event handlers.

Since requests are metered by connections that the client is making, the `RequestManager` is implemented using the singleton pattern (meaning that only one instance can be created per page). It wouldn't make sense to allow more than one instance to be created, since there's only ever two available requests for an entire page (for example, it wouldn't make sense to create three `RequestManager` objects because there are still only two requests to manage). The basic pattern used to define this object is:

```
var RequestManager = (function () {

    var oManager = {
        //properties/methods go here
    };

    //initialization goes here

    //return the object
    return oManager;

})();
```

This is one of several ways to implement a singleton pattern in JavaScript. The outermost function is anonymous and is called immediately as the code is executed, creating the object, initializing it, and returning it. In this way `RequestManager` becomes a globally available object with its own properties and methods without creating a prototype.

Before delving into the inner workings of this object, consider the information that is to be handled. All of the information about each request must be handled by `RequestManager` in order for it to be effective. However, the goal is to free developers from instantiating XHR objects directly, which is where request description objects come in.

Request Description Objects

Instead of creating XHR objects directly, developers can define an object describing the request to execute. Since there are no methods on this object, there's no reason to define a constructor; just use an object literal with the following format:

```
var oRequest = {
    priority: 1,
    type: "post",
    url: "example.htm",
    data: "post_data",
    oncancel: function () {},
    onsuccess: function () {},
    onnotmodified: function () {},
    onfailure: function () {},
    scope: oObject
}
```

This object literal contains all of the information used by the RequestManager object. First is the priority property, which should be a numeric value where the smaller the number, the higher the priority (priority 1 is higher than priority 2, for example); this property is required. Next come the type and url properties, which should be set to the type of request (typically "get" or "post") and the URL to request, respectively. If you are sending a POST request, then the data property should be assigned to the post data to be sent to the server; otherwise, it can be omitted.

Next come the event handlers. Each of these methods is called according to the HTTP status of the response from the server:

❑   oncancel() is called when a request is canceled before a response has been received.

❑   onsuccess() is called to handle a response with a status in the 200 range.

❑   onnotmodified() is called to handle a response with a status of 304.

❑   onfailure() is called to handle a response with all other statuses.

The scope property works with each of these methods, setting the scope in which the function should be called (this allows for methods on other objects to be called for any of the three methods). If the scope isn't specified, then all of the functions are run in the global (window) scope.

Request description objects are stored and used by RequestManager in the handling of Ajax communication. These are the only other objects that developers interact with, so they are passed around repeatedly.

Queuing Requests

All pending requests (represented by request description objects) in the RequestManager are stored in a priority queue. The property name _pending (a private property) is used to store the PriorityQueue object, which is created with a custom comparison function to sort the objects by priority:

```
var RequestManager = (function () {

    var oManager = {

        _pending: new PriorityQueue(function (oRequest1, oRequest2) {
            return oRequest1.priority - oRequest2.priority;
        }),

        //more code here
    };

    //initialization goes here

    //return the object
    return oManager;

})();
```

The comparison function used here simply subtracts the value of each object's priority property, which will return a negative number if oRequest1.priority is less than oRequest2.priority, a positive number if the opposite is true, and 0 if they're equal. Simply subtracting the two priorities is a much faster way of implementing this function versus creating the full if...else structure discussed previously.

With the pending request queue is set up, there needs to be a publicly accessible way for developers to add requests to the queue. The method responsible for this is called send(), which expects a request description object to be passed in:

```
var RequestManager = (function () {

    var oManager = {

        DEFAULT_PRIORITY: 10,

        _pending: new PriorityQueue(function (oRequest1, oRequest2) {
            return oRequest1.priority - oRequest2.priority;
        }),


        //more code here

        send : function (oRequest) {
            if(typeof oRequest.priority != "number"){
                oRequest.priority = this.DEFAULT_PRIORITY;
            }
            oRequest.active = false;
            this._pending.put(oRequest);
        }
    };

    //initialization goes here

    //return the object
    return oManager;

})();
```

The first step in the send() method is to check for a valid priority on the request description object. If the property isn't a number, then a default priority of 10 is defined so as not to cause an error in the priority queue (this priority is stored in the constant DEFAULT_PRIORITY). Next, the active property is set to false; this property is used to determine if the request is currently being executed. The last step is to add the object into the priority queue so that it's prioritized among other pending requests.

Sending Requests

Now that requests can be queued, there must be a way to send them. To accomplish this, several methods are necessary. The first, _createTransport(), is a private method that creates an XHR object appropriate for the browser being used. This code is essentially the same as the XHR creation code discussed in Chapter 2 (note that to save space, other properties and methods have been shortened to "..."):

```
var RequestManager = (function () {

    var oManager = {
```

```
DEFAULT_PRIORITY: 10,

//more code here

_pending: new PriorityQueue(function (oRequest1, oRequest2) {...}),

_createTransport : function (){
    if (typeof XMLHttpRequest != "undefined") {
        return new XMLHttpRequest();
    } else if (typeof ActiveXObject != "undefined") {
        var oHttp = null;
        try {
            oHttp = new ActiveXObject("MSXML2.XmlHttp.6.0");
            return oHttp;
        } catch (oEx) {
            try {
                oHttp = new ActiveXObjct("MSXML2.XmlHttp.3.0");
                return oHttp;
            } catch (oEx2) {
                throw Error("Cannot create XMLHttp object.");
            }
        }
    }
},

send : function (oRequest) {...}
};

//initialization goes here

//return the object
return oManager;

})();
```

Now that an appropriate XHR object can be created, the next pending request needs to be sent. Remember, there can be two active requests at a time, so there must be a way to track this. The active property contains a simple array of request description objects whose requests are active.

Initiating Requests

It's the job of the _sendNext() method to get the next request from the queue, assign it to the active list, and send it:

```
var RequestManager = (function () {

    var oManager = {

        DEFAULT_PRIORITY: 10,

        _active: new Array(),

        _pending: new PriorityQueue(function (oRequest1, oRequest2) {...}),

        _createTransport : function (){...},
```

```
    _sendNext : function () {
        if (this._active.length < 2) {
            var oRequest = this._pending.get();
            if (oRequest != null) {
                this._active.push(oRequest);
                oRequest.transport = this._createTransport();
                oRequest.transport.open(oRequest.type, oRequest.url, true);
                oRequest.transport.send(oRequest.data);
                oRequest.active = true;
            }
        }
    },

    send : function (oRequest) {...}
};

//initialization goes here

//return the object
return oManager;

})();
```

The sendNext() method starts by checking to see if there's an available connection. If the active array has less than two items in it, that means a connection is available and the function continues, calling get() on the priority queue to retrieve the next request. Since there may be no next request, it must be checked to ensure it's not null. If it's not null, then the request is added to the active list and an XHR object is created and stored in the transport property (this makes it easier to keep track of which XHR object is executing each request). Next, the open() and send() methods are called with the information inside the request description object. The last step is to set the active property to true, indicating that the request is currently being processed.

Monitoring Requests

It may seem odd that an XHR object is used asynchronously without an onreadystatechange event handler. This decision is intentional, since binding to the onreadystatechange event handler can cause memory issues in Internet Explorer. Instead, the RequestManager polls the status of the active requests, monitoring each XHR object every 250 milliseconds (four times a second) for changes to the readyState property. When the readyState changes to 4, then a sequence of event-handling steps takes place. This takes place in the _checkActiveRequests() method which, along with _sendNext(), is called in a function that exists outside of the RequestManager object so that it can be called via setInterval():

```
var RequestManager = (function () {

    var oManager = {

        DEFAULT_PRIORITY: 10,

        INTERVAL : 250,

        _active: new Array(),

        _pending: new PriorityQueue(function (oRequest1, oRequest2) {...}),
```

```
            _checkActiveRequests : function () {

                var oRequest = null;
                var oTransport = null;

                for (var i=this._active.length-1; i >= 0; i--) {
                    oRequest = this._active[i];
                    oTransport = oRequest.transport;
                    if (oTransport.readyState == 4) {
                        oRequest.active = false;
                        this._active.splice(i, 1);
                        var fnCallback = null;
                        if (oTransport.status >= 200 && oTransport.status < 300) {
                            if (typeof oRequest.onsuccess == "function") {
                                fnCallback = oRequest.onsuccess;
                            }
                        } else if (oTransport.status == 304) {
                            if (typeof oRequest.onnotmodified == "function") {
                                fnCallback = oRequest.onnotmodified;
                            }
                        } else {
                            if (typeof oRequest.onfailure == "function") {
                                fnCallback = oRequest.onfailure;
                            }
                        }
                        if (fnCallback != null) {
                            setTimeout((function (fnCallback, oRequest, oTransport) {
                                return function (){
                                    fnCallback.call(oRequest.scope||window, {
                                        status : oTransport.status,
                                        data : oTransport.responseText,
                                        request : oRequest});
                                }
                            })(fnCallback, oRequest, oTransport), 1);
                        }
                    }
                }
            },

        _createTransport : function (){...},

        _sendNext : function () {...},

        send : function (oRequest) {...}
    };

    //initialization
    setInterval(function () {
        RequestManager._checkActiveRequests();
        RequestManager._sendNext();
    }, oManager.INTERVAL);

    //return the object
    return oManager;

})();
```

The `checkActiveRequests()` method is the longest function, but it's also the one that does most of the work. Its job is to check the status of each active request to see if `readyState` is equal to 4. To accomplish this, a `for` loop is used to loop over each request in the `active` array (since items will be removed, the loop goes in reverse order to avoid skipping items). For convenience, the request description object is stored in `oRequest`, and the XHR object is stored in `oTransport`. Next, the `readyState` property is checked; if it's equal to 4, then some processing occurs.

The first step in processing a completed request is to set the `active` property to `false`, to indicate that it has returned and is complete. Then, the request is removed from the _active array using `splice()`. Next comes the decision as to which callback function should be executed. A variable, `fnCallback`, is created to store the callback function. This variable is assigned a value based on the status of the response and the availability of the callback function. If the status is between 200 and 299, then `fnCallback` is assigned the value of `onsuccess`; for a status of 304, `fnCallback` is set equal to `onnotmodified`; all other statuses force `fnCallback` to be assigned to `onfailure`. Each of these assignments takes place only if the given callback function is available (`typeof` is used to ensure that the function is defined).

After the assignment of `fnCallback`, the variable is checked to see if it's a valid function. If so, then a timeout is created to execute it. The timeout is important because it's possible for a callback function to take longer than 250 milliseconds to execute, which creates a race condition where the first call inside the interval may not have been completed by the time the next call begins. Delaying the execution of the callback ensures that the interval function executes completely before it is executed again.

In order to ensure proper scoping, a special time of function is created to pass into the `setTimeout()` function. This anonymous function accepts three arguments: `fnCallback`, `oRequest`, and `oTransport` (the same variables necessary to execute the callback function). These arguments are passed in immediately to the anonymous function in order to create proper copies of each variable. Inside of the anonymous function, another function is returned that actually executes the callback. It is safe to execute the callback within that scope because the variables are no longer the ones used within the `for` loop; they are copies. This technique is a bit involved, so consider the step-by-step buildup. First, the anonymous function is defined:

```
function (fnCallback, oRequest, oTransport) {
    ...
}
```

Next, the anonymous function defines and returns a function in its body:

```
function (fnCallback, oRequest, oTransport) {
    return function () {
        ...
    };
}
```

The returned function is written to execute the callback function:

```
function (fnCallback, oRequest, oTransport) {
    return function () {
        fnCallback.call(oRequest.scope||window, {
            status : oTransport.status,
            data : oTransport.responseText,
            request : oRequest});
    };
}
```

Then, the outer function is called, passing in the necessary variables:

```
(function (fnCallback, oRequest, oTransport) {
    return function () {
        fnCallback.call(oRequest.scope||window, {
            status : oTransport.status,
            data : oTransport.responseText,
            request : oRequest});
    };
})(fnCallback, oRequest, oTransport)
```

This effectively creates and returns a function to execute, so the result can be passed into `setTimeout()`:

```
setTimeout((function (fnCallback, oRequest, oTransport) {
    return function () {
        fnCallback.call(oRequest.scope||window, {
            status : oTransport.status,
            data : oTransport.responseText,
            request : oRequest});
    };
})(fnCallback, oRequest, oTransport), 1);
```

Now, the callback function will be executed with the proper variables by using `call()` and passing in the appropriate scope in which to run and a data object. The first argument is a logical OR of the `scope` property and the `window` object, which returns `scope` if it's not `null`; otherwise, it returns `window`. The second argument is an object literal with three properties: `status`, which is the HTTP status of the request; `data`, which is the response body; and `request`, which returns the request description object that was used to make the request. This function call takes place inside a timeout, which is delayed for 1 millisecond.

After `checkActiveRequests()` is called in the interval function, it's time to see if there's room to make another request. The `sendNext()` method is then called to initiate the next request (if another request is pending).

> As mentioned previously, this whole function is called using `setInterval()` every 250 milliseconds. The interval setting is stored as `INTERVAL` on the `RequestManager` object. For most uses, this rate of polling is fine, but this interval length can and should be customized according to individual needs.

Cancelling Requests

It's entirely possible that a request may need to be canceled before it's executed. The `cancel()` method handles this, accepting the request description object as an argument and ensuring that it doesn't get sent. This is accomplished by removing the object from the list of pending requests. If the request is already active (it's in the `active` array, not the priority queue), then the XHR request must be aborted and the request removed from the active list:

```
var RequestManager = (function () {

    var oManager = {
```

139

```
            DEFAULT_PRIORITY: 10,

            INTERVAL : 250,

            _active: new Array(),

            _pending: new PriorityQueue(function (oRequest1, oRequest2) {...}),

            _checkActiveRequests : function (){...},

            _createTransport : function (){...},

            _sendNext : function () {...},

            cancel : function (oRequest) {
                if (!this._pending.remove(oRequest)){

                    oRequest.transport.abort();

                    if (this._active[0] === oRequest) {
                        this._active.shift();
                    } else if (this._active[1] === oRequest) {
                        this._active.pop();
                    }

                    if (typeof oRequest.oncancel == "function") {
                        oRequest.oncancel.call(oRequest.scope||window,
                            {request : oRequest});
                    }

                }
            },

            send : function (oRequest) {...}
        };

        //initialization
        setInterval(function () {...}, 250);

        //return the object
        return oManager;

    })();
```

The `cancel()` method begins by attempting to remove the request description object from the priority queue. Remember that the priority queue's `remove()` method returns `true` if the item was found and removed, and `false` if not. So, if this call to `remove()` returns `false`, it means that the request is active. When the request is active, the first step is to call `abort()` on the XHR object being used by the request. Since there are only two possible items in the array, it's easy to check each item in `_active` to see if it's the request of interest. If the request is the first item, then `shift()` is called to remove it; if the request is the second item, `pop()` is called to remove it. The last step is to execute the `oncancel()` callback function if it's defined.

Age-Based Promotion

With priority queues, there's a danger that a low-priority item will remain at the back indefinitely. This means that, in the case of the RequestManager, there may be low priority requests that are never executed. Obviously, this is an undesirable occurrence, since even the lowest-priority requests should be executed eventually. *Age-based promotion* seeks to resolve this issue by automatically bumping up the priority of requests that have remained in the queue for a longer-than-normal time.

The actual time considered to be "longer than normal" is directly related to the functionality that your application requires. In this case, assume that the time limit is 1 minute (60,000 milliseconds). Any request that hasn't been executed for 1 minute will receive an automatic priority promotion. Doing this ensures that a request will only be in the queue for a maximum of 1 minute times its initial priority (a request with a priority of 4 will be in the queue for a maximum of 4 minutes).

To accomplish age-based promotion, the RequestManager needs to add an additional property to each request description object. The age property tracks how long the request has been at a given priority. When age reaches the maximum, the priority property is automatically decremented (remember, the lower the number, the higher the priority), and age is reset back to 0. This functionality takes place in the _agePromote() method:

```javascript
var RequestManager = (function () {

    var oManager = {

        AGE_LIMIT : 60000,

        DEFAULT_PRIORITY: 10,

        INTERVAL : 250,

        _active: new Array(),

        _pending: new PriorityQueue(function (oRequest1, oRequest2) {...}),

        _agePromote : function() {
            for (var i=0; i < this._pending.size(); i++) {
                var oRequest = this._pending.item(i);
                oRequest.age += this.INTERVAL;
                if (oRequest.age >= this.AGE_LIMIT){
                    oRequest.age = 0;
                    oRequest.priority--;
                }
            }
            this._pending.prioritize();
        },

        _checkActiveRequests : function (){...},

        _createTransport : function (){...},

        _sendNext : function () {...},

        cancel : function (oRequest) {...},

        send : function (oRequest) {
```

```
            if(typeof oRequest.priority != "number"){
                oRequest.priority = this.DEFAULT_PROPERTY;
            }
            oRequest.active = false;
            oRequest.age = 0;
            this._pending.put(oRequest);
        }
    };

    //initialization
    setInterval(function () {
        RequestManager._checkActiveRequests();
        RequestManager._sendNext();
        RequestManager._agePromote();
    }, oManager.INTERVAL);

    //return the object
    return oManager;

})();
```

This new code adds a constant, AGE_LIMIT, to define how long a request should remain at the given priority. The constant is used inside of _agePromote() to determine when a request should be promoted. Before a request can be checked, its age property must be initialized; this takes place in the send() method with one additional line. The _agePromote() method is called inside of the interval function, just after _sendNext() to ensure that all of the pending requests are in the correct order for the next interval. Inside of _agePromote(), each item in the _pending queue has its age updated by adding the INTERVAL value to its current age. If age is greater than or equal to the limit, age is reset to 0 and the priority is decremented. The last step is to call prioritize() on the queue, since this method effectively changes the priority of an item already in the queue.

Handling Ajax Patterns

Having a prioritized list of requests is very helpful in managing traffic between the client and server, but it does require the developer to determine the relative priority of each request. In some cases, this is quite simple. For example, if a user action (a mouse click, a key press, etc.) initiated a request, clearly it is very important because the user is waiting for a response, so a priority of 0 would be most appropriate. In other cases, however, it's not always clear what the priority should be. To remedy this situation, it may be necessary to provide methods that decide priorities according to the Ajax pattern being used. Recall the patterns discussed earlier in the book:

❑ **Predictive Fetch:** Guesses what the user will do next and preloads the necessary information from the server.

❑ **Submission Throttling:** Incrementally sends data to the server.

❑ **Periodic Refresh:** Also known as polling, periodically polls the server for updated information.

❑ **Multi-Stage Download:** Downloads only the most important information first and then sends subsequent requests for additional information.

Consider the relative priorities among these four patterns. None of them is as important as a user action, so that means a priority of 1 or lower.

While helpful, Predictive Fetch is far from high priority. Its intent is to improve the user experience, not to control it. In an Ajax application that is making requests using various patterns, chances are that Predictive Fetch requests are a fairly low priority. Assuming that priorities are assigned from 0 to 10, Predictive Fetch may accurately be described as a priority of 5.

Submission Throttling is more important than Predictive Fetch because it is sending user information to the server as opposed to retrieving information from the server. Once again, this is not as important as a user action, so it falls somewhere between a priority of 0 and 5, probably landing at 2.

Periodic Refresh is very similar to Predictive Fetch, though the fact that it's sent on a recurring basis indicates that it's more important. More than likely, Periodic Refresh is waiting to indicate some new information to the user as soon as it's available. Because it's receiving data from the server, however, it would be a lower priority than Submission Throttling, which sends data to the server. So, Periodic Refresh is a priority of 3.

The last pattern is Multi-Stage Download, which is actually just another form of Predictive Fetch. The only difference between the two is when the request(s) take place. For Multi-Stage Download, the requests typically take place at the initial page load, while Predictive Fetch can occur at any time, depending on user action. Really, the two patterns are too close to consider one a higher priority than the other, so Multi-Stage Download can also be considered a 5.

Now that the priorities are clear among these patterns, what can be done to make this easier for developers? The best approach is to add a method for each pattern, along with one for a user action, so that developers don't need to remember these priorities on their own. Also, by encapsulating this functionality and auto-assigning priorities, this frees you to easily change priorities later without changing code in multiple places.

Each of these methods works the same way: accept a request description object as an argument, assign the given priority, and then pass the modified object to the send() method to be queued. Since the names of the Ajax patterns are rather verbose, the method names have been shortened:

- ❑ poll(): Use for Periodic Refresh.
- ❑ prefetch(): Use for Predictive Fetch and Multi-Stage Download.
- ❑ submit(): Use for a user action.
- ❑ submitPart(): Use for Submission Throttling.

The code for each is as follows:

```
var RequestManager = (function () {

    var oManager = {

        AGE_LIMIT : 60000,

        DEFAULT_PRIORITY: 10,

        INTERVAL : 250,

        _active: new Array(),
```

```
        _pending: new PriorityQueue(function (oRequest1, oRequest2) {...}),

        _agePromote : function() {...},

        _checkActiveRequests : function (){...},

        _createTransport : function (){...},

        _sendNext : function () {...},

        cancel : function (oRequest) {...},

        poll : function (oRequest) {
            oRequest.priority = 3;
            this.send(oRequest);
        },

        prefetch : function (oRequest) {
            oRequest.priority = 5;
            this.send(oRequest);
        },

        send : function (oRequest) {...},

        submit : function (oRequest) {
            oRequest.priority = 0;
            this.send(oRequest);
        },

        submitPart : function (oRequest) {
            oRequest.priority = 2;
            this.send(oRequest);
        }

    };

    //initialization
    setInterval(function () {...}, oManager.INTERVAL);

    //return the object
    return oManager;

})();
```

These methods can be used in place of send(), such as:

```
RequestManager.poll({
    type: "get",
    url: "example.htm",
    data: "post_data",
    onsuccess: function () {},
});

RequestManager.submitPart({
    type: "post",
```

```
        url: "handler.php",
        data: "name=Nicholas",
        onsuccess: function () {},
    });
```

Note that a `priority` property isn't assigned in these request description objects, as it is not needed. If a `priority` property were assigned, however, it would be overridden by the method being called.

Using RequestManager

To try out the `RequestManager` object, it's easiest to set up a page that sends multiple requests in a row and reports back when the results have been received. In this way, the order in which the responses are received indicates the order in which the requests were sent (with a small margin of error due to different server response times per request). Consider the following simple HTML page:

```
<!DOCTYPE html PUBLIC "-//W3C//DTD XHTML 1.0 Transitional//EN"
    "http://www.w3.org/TR/xhtml1/DTD/xhtml1-transitional.dtd">
<html xmlns="http://www.w3.org/1999/xhtml">
<head>
    <title>Request Manager Example</title>
    <script type="text/javascript" src="PriorityQueue.js"></script>
    <script type="text/javascript" src="RequestManager.js"></script>
    <script type="text/javascript" src="RequestManagerExample.js"></script>
</head>
<body>
    <fieldset>
        <legend>Responses</legend>
        <div id="divResponses"></div>
    </fieldset>
</body>
</html>
```

This page includes the necessary `RequestManager` files and has a `<fieldset/>` surrounding a `<div/>` called `"divResponses"`. This `<div/>` element is responsible for outputting the results of each request so that it's obvious as to what has occurred. The `RequestManagerExample.js` file contains the JavaScript for this example, beginning with some callback functions to handle various responses:

```
function outputResult(oResponse, sColor) {
    var divResponses = document.getElementById("divResponses");
    var oRequest = oResponse.request;
    var sMessage = "<div style=\"background-color:" + sColor + "\">"
            + oResponse.status + " (" + oRequest.priority + ") "
            + oRequest.type + " " + oRequest.url + " " + oRequest.age + "</div>";
    divResponses.innerHTML += sMessage;
}

function outputSuccessResult(oResponse) {
    outputResult(oResponse, "white");
}

function outputFailureResult(oResponse) {
```

```
        outputResult(oResponse, "red");
    }

    function outputNotModifiedResult(oResponse) {
        outputResult(oResponse, "silver");
    }
```

Each of these functions handles a different case and is used as the values of onsuccess, onfailure, and onnotmodified for each request. They each output a message, including the HTTP status, the priority (in parentheses), the request type, the URL, and the age of the request. The outputSuccessResult() function prints its message with a white background, outputFailureResult() uses a red background, and outputNotModifiedResult() has a silver background. This color-coding makes it easier to differentiate which function was called. Since the color is the only thing that changes, the outputResult() function provides the basic functionality used by the other functions.

Next, there are some functions to create specific types of requests:

```
    function addPoll() {
        RequestManager.poll({
            type : "get", url : "poll.txt",
            onsuccess : outputSuccessResult,
            onfailure : outputFailureResult,
            onnotmodified : outputNotModifiedResult
        });
    }

    function addSubmit() {
        RequestManager.submit({
            type : "post", url : "post.txt", data : "name=Nicholas",
            onsuccess : outputSuccessResult,
            onfailure : outputFailureResult,
            onnotmodified : outputNotModifiedResult
        });
    }

    function addSubmitPart() {
        RequestManager.submitPart({
            type : "post", url : "post.txt", data : "name=Nicholas",
            onsuccess : outputSuccessResult,
            onfailure : outputFailureResult,
            onnotmodified : outputNotModifiedResult
        });
    }

    function addPreFetch() {
        RequestManager.prefetch({
            type : "get", url : "data.txt",
            onsuccess : outputSuccessResult,
            onfailure : outputFailureResult,
            onnotmodified : outputNotModifiedResult
        });
    }

    function addLowPriority() {
```

```
    RequestManager.send({
        priority: 10, type : "get", url : "data.txt",
        onsuccess : outputSuccessResult,
        onerror : outputFailureResult,
        onnotmodified : outputNotModifiedResult
    });
}
```

Each of these functions creates a different type of request to be placed in the queue. The addPoll() function creates a poll request to poll.txt, which doesn't exist; this should result in a 404 error. Next, the addSubmit() and addSubmitPart() functions create POST requests to a text file, post.txt, which should fail with a 405 error (most servers won't let you post data to a plain text file). The addPreFetch() function creates a GET request for data.txt, while addLowPriority() creates a very low-priority request that should be executed only after everything else has been completed.

The onload event handler is then assigned to initiate a few requests using these methods:

```
window.onload = function () {
    addPoll();
    addPoll();
    addSubmit();
    addPreFetch();
    addLowPriority();
    addSubmitPart();
    addLowPriority();
    addPreFetch();
    addPoll();
    addSubmit();
};
```

This creates a series of different requests with varying priorities. Since these requests are added in rapid succession, they effectively end up being added to the queue simultaneously, which means that the output on the page should be very similar to this:

```
405 (0)  post post.txt 0
405 (0)  post post.txt 250
405 (2)  post post.txt 500
404 (3)  get poll.txt 750
404 (3)  get poll.txt 1000
404 (3)  get poll.txt 1250
200 (5)  get data.txt 1500
200 (5)  get data.txt 1750
200 (10) get data.txt 2000
200 (10) get data.txt 2250
```

In this output, it's clear to see that the calls to submit() were executed first; they each returned a 405 error, had a priority of 0, used POST, and were 0 and 250 milliseconds old, respectively. Next up is the call created via submitPart(), which had a priority of 2. After that, the various polling requests were executed at a priority of 3, and requests created using prefetch() were executed with a priority of 5. The two low-priority requests were executed last.

It is possible to see differing results due to the differences in client machines, how long it takes to create an XHR object, and how long it takes to get a response from the server. However, most browsers should execute very similarly, producing output resembling the output reproduced in the preceding examples, with maybe one or two higher-priority requests not executing correctly (although, all other requests should still complete before the lowest-priority ones).

Summary

In this chapter, you learned about the challenges in managing Ajax requests from a single application. The two-connection HTTP 1.1 limit was discussed as it pertains to XHR objects, and a discussion of why this limitation is important followed.

Next, an alternate approach to create XHR objects was discussed, involving developer-defined prioritizations to ensure that important requests are executed before lower priority communication takes place. You were led through the creation of a priority queue data structure in JavaScript, making use of the `Array` object's built-in `sort()` method for prioritizing values in the queue. This generic `PriorityQueue` object became the basis for a request management object.

With the basic data structure created, you began creating the `RequestManager` object, which uses the priority queue to determine the requests to execute next. The `RequestManager` object expects request description objects to be provided that describe the request that should take place. It then uses this description to make the request at an appropriate time, without tying functions to XHR objects (which can cause memory leaks).

Four different callback functions were made available on each request description object, one for success (HTTP code in the 200–299 range), one for "not modified" (HTTP code 304), one for "failure" (all other codes), and one to call if the request is canceled before being sent. Each of these callback functions can be a standalone function or an object method whose scope can be provided using the `scope` property.

Last, you learned how to implement an age-based promotion system so that lower-priority requests will be ensured of execution. This works by automatically promoting requests to the next priority after they've been in the queue for a specified amount of time. By adding this to the `RequestManager` object, you now have a robust Ajax connection management object.

XML, XPath, and XSLT

As the popularity of XML grew, web developers wanted to use the technology on both the server and client side, but only the former initially offered XML functionality. Starting with Internet Explorer 5.0 and Mozilla 1.0 (predecessor to Firefox), Microsoft and Mozilla implemented JavaScript support for XML in their browsers. Opera 8 and Safari 1.2 introduced some basic XML support, and while Opera's JavaScript XML support is catching up, Safari still lags behind the pack with the least amount of implemented support. With that being said, browser makers continue to broaden the availability of XML support with new features, giving web developers powerful tools akin to those formerly found only on the server.

XML Support in Browsers

Many web browsers are available today, but few have complete support for XML and its related technologies. Internet Explorer (IE) and Mozilla Firefox lead the pack in support, followed closely by Opera (as of version 9). Apple's Safari trails significantly behind, supporting only rudimentary XML features. Despite these differences in support, all browsers implement basic XML functionality; therefore, this section covers all four major browsers.

XML DOM in IE

When Microsoft added XML support to IE 5.0, they did so by incorporating the MSXML ActiveX library, a component originally written to parse Active Channels in IE 4.0. This initial version wasn't intended for public use, but developers discovered the component and began using it. Microsoft responded with a fully upgraded version of MSXML, which was included in IE 4.01.

MSXML was primarily an IE-only component until 2001 when Microsoft released MSXML 3.0, a separate distribution available through the company's web site. Later that year, version 4.0 was released and MSXML was renamed Microsoft XML Core Services Component. Since its inception, MSXML has gone from a basic, non-validating XML parser to a full-featured component that can validate XML documents, perform XSL transformations, support namespace usage, the Simple

API for XML (SAX), and the W3C XPath and XML Schema standards, all while improving performance with each new version.

Creating an XML DOM Object

To facilitate ActiveX object creation in JavaScript, Microsoft implemented a class called `ActiveXObject`. Its constructor takes a single argument, a string containing the name and version of the ActiveX object to create; in this case, it is the version of the XML document. The first XML DOM ActiveX object was called `Microsoft.XmlDom`, and its creation looks like this:

```
var oXmlDom = new ActiveXObject("Microsoft.XmlDom");
```

The newly created XML DOM object behaves like any other DOM object, enabling you to traverse the DOM tree and manipulate DOM nodes.

At the time of this writing, there are six different versions of the MSXML DOM document; the version strings are as follows:

- ❑   Microsoft.XmlDom
- ❑   MSXML2.DOMDocument
- ❑   MSXML2.DOMDocument.3.0
- ❑   MSXML2.DOMDocument.4.0
- ❑   MSXML2.DOMDocument.5.0
- ❑   MSXML2.DOMDocument.6.0

> **MSXML is available only on Windows-based Internet Explorer. IE 5 on the Mac has no XML DOM support.**

Since there have been many improvements with each new release of MSXML, you always want to use the latest version. Microsoft recommends checking for the latest version (MSXML6 as of this writing) and to use MSXML3 as the fallback version. Therefore, it is helpful to create a function to determine which version to use. The following function, `createDocument()`, creates an MSXML6 DOM if the client machine supports it. Otherwise, a MSXML3 DOM is created:

```
function createDocument() {
    var aVersions = [
        "MSXML2.DOMDocument.6.0",
        "MSXML2.DOMDocument.3.0",
    ];

    for (var i = 0; i < aVersions.length; i++) {
        try {
            var oXmlDom = new ActiveXObject(aVersions[i]);
            return oXmlDom;
        } catch (oError) {
            //Do nothing
        }
```

```
    }
    throw new Error("MSXML is not installed.");
}
```

This function iterates through the aVersions array, which contains the version strings. It starts with the latest version, MSXML2.DOMDocument.6.0, and attempts to create the DOM document. If the object creation is successful, it is returned and createDocument() exits; if it fails, an error is thrown and then caught by the try...catch block, so the loop continues and the next version is tried. If the creation of an MSXML DOM document fails after trying the two versions, an error is thrown stating that MSXML is not installed. Call the function like this:

```
var oXmlDom = createDocument();
```

Now that you have an XML document at your disposal, it is time to load some XML data.

Loading XML Data in IE

The MSXML DOM document supports two methods of loading XML data: load() and loadXML(). The load() method accepts a single argument, which is a URL from which to download an XML file; the loadXML() method also accepts a single argument, though it is a string of XML data. Both methods have the effect of parsing XML data and creating an XML DOM structure.

The load() method behaves similar to XHR in that it can load data from an external file in two modes: asynchronous or synchronous. This is controlled by the async property. By default, async is set to true, so the load() method is asynchronous; to use synchronous mode, async must be set to false, as follows:

```
oXmlDom.async = false;
```

> Generally, it's considered poor practice to initiate requests in synchronous mode due to the possibility of freezing the user interface. Synchronous mode should be used sparingly and only when small amounts of data are being sent from the server.

When in asynchronous mode, the MSXML object exposes the readyState property, which almost has the same five states as the XHR readyState property (discussed in Chapter 2). The exception is that the MSXML object does not have the 0 (UNINITIALIZED) state. Additionally, the DOM document supports the onreadystatechange event handler, enabling you to monitor the readyState property:

```
oXmlDom.onreadystatechange = function () {
    if (oXmlDom.readyState == 4) {
        //Do something when the document is fully loaded.
    }
};

oXmlDom.load("myxml.xml");
```

In this example, the fictitious XML document named myxml.xml is loaded into an XML DOM. When readyState reaches the value of 4, the document is fully loaded and the code inside the if block will execute.

> Note that unlike XHR, there is no `status` property on the XML DOM object.

The second way to load XML data, `loadXML()`, is a bit simpler and doesn't require any HTTP requests since its data is already present on the client. The data passed in must contain well-formed XML, as in the following example:

```
var sXml = "<root><person><name>Jeremy McPeak</name></person></root>";
oXmlDom.loadXML(sXml);
```

Here, the XML data contained in the variable sXml is loaded into the oXmlDom document. There is no reason to check the `readyState` property or to set the `async` property when using `loadXML()` because it doesn't involve a server request; the data is loaded synchronously and is immediately available.

Validating XML Data While Loading

By default, an MSXML DOM object validates the XML document when it parses the data. A *valid* XML document is one that references a Document Type Definition (DTD) in a DOCTYPE declaration and conforms to that DTD.

There are times when this behavior is not desired, and instead, the document should be checked only for well-formedness. To allow this, the MSXML DOM object exposes the `validateOnParse` property. It accepts with a `true` (the default) or `false` value, and it should be set before the DOM object loads the document.

```
var oXmlDom = createDocument();
oXmlDom.async = false;
oXmlDom.validateOnParse = false;
oXmlDom.load("myxml.xml");
```

In this code, when the XML DOM object loads and parses the XML, it will be checked only to see if the document is well formed.

Preserving White Space

The MSXML DOM treats white space differently than standards-compliant DOM implementations. By default, the MSXML DOM removes white space–only nodes from the document, leaving nothing but XML and text nodes. While many consider this behavior to be a more common sense issue, the fact remains that it is not standards compliant.

The MSXML DOM, however, does offer the `preserveWhiteSpace` property that tells the parser to either throw out the white space–only nodes or to keep them. The property accepts a Boolean value, and the default is `false`. The following code loads an XML document and preserves its white space:

```
var oXmlDom = createDocument();
oXmlDom.async = false;
oXmlDom.preserveWhiteSpace = true;
oXmlDom.load("myxml.xml");
```

When `true`, this property allows an MSXML DOM object to behave like a standards-compliant DOM.

Traversing the XML DOM in IE

Navigating an XML DOM document is much like navigating an HTML DOM document; it is a hierarchical node structure. At the top of the tree is the documentElement, which contains the root element of the document. From there, you can access any element or attribute in the document using the properties listed in Table 6-1.

Table 6-1 XML DOM Properties

Property	Description
attributes	Collection of attributes for this node.
childNodes	Collection of child nodes.
firstChild	First child of the node.
lastChild	Last child of the node.
nextSibling	The node immediately following the current node.
nodeName	The qualified name of the node.
nodeType	The XML DOM node type.
nodeValue	The text associated with the node, if any.
ownerDocument	The XML DOM document of which this node is a part.
ParentNode	Parent node of the current node.
PreviousSibling	The node immediately before the current node.
Text	Returns the content of the node or the concatenated text of the current node and its descendants. This is an IE-only property.
Xml	Returns the XML string representing the current node and its children. This is an IE-only property.

Traversing and retrieving data from the DOM is a straightforward process. Consider the following XML document:

```xml
<?xml version="1.0" encoding="utf-8"?>

<books>
    <book isbn="9780470109496">Professional Ajax</book>
    <book isbn="0764579088">Professional JavaScript for Web Developers</book>
    <book isbn="0764557599">Professional C#</book>
    <book isbn="1861002025">Professional Visual Basic 6 Databases</book>
</books>
```

This simple XML document includes a root element, <books/>, with four child <book/> elements. Using this document as a reference, you can explore the DOM. The DOM tree is based on the relationships nodes have with other nodes. One node may contain other nodes, which are called child nodes (each <book/> element is a child node of the <books/> element). Another node may share the same parent as other nodes, in which case these nodes are siblings (each <book/> element is a sibling of the other <book/> elements).

Perhaps you want to retrieve the first <book/> element in the document. This is easily achieved with the firstChild property:

```
var oFirstBook = oXmlDom.documentElement.firstChild;
```

Using the firstChild property, the first <book/> element is referenced and assigned to the variable oFirstBook because it is the first child element of the root element <books/>.

You can also use the childNodes collection to achieve the same results:

```
var oFirstBook2 = oXmlDom.documentElement.childNodes[0];
```

Selecting the first item in the childNodes collection (at index 0) returns the first child of the node, just as if accessing the firstChild property. You can determine the number of children a node has by using the length property, as follows:

```
var iChildren = oXmlDom.documentElement.childNodes.length;
```

If nodes can have children, that means they can also have parents. The parentNode property returns the parent of the given node:

```
var oParent = oFirstBook.parentNode;
```

Recall that oFirstBook is the first <book/> element in the document. The parentNode property of this node refers to the <books/> element, the documentElement of the document.

The <book/> elements are siblings to each other because they share the same direct parent. Two properties, nextSibling and previousSibling, exist to access these adjacent nodes. The nextSibling property references the next occurring sibling, whereas the previousSibling property selects the preceding sibling:

```
var oSecondBook = oFirstBook.nextSibling;
```

```
var oFirstBook2 = oSecondBook.previousSibling;
```

In this code, the second <book/> element is referenced and assigned to oSecondBook. The oFirstBook2 variable is then assigned to the previous sibling of oSecondBook, resulting in oFirstBook2 containing the same value as oFirstBook. If a node has no previous or next siblings, previousSibling and nextSibling will be null.

Now that you know how to traverse through the document hierarchy, the next step is to extract from nodes in the tree. For example, to retrieve the text contained within the third <book/> element (Professional C#), you can use the text property as follows:

```
var sText = oRoot.childNodes[2].text;
```

The text property retrieves all the text contained within this node and is a Microsoft proprietary property, but it is extremely helpful. Without the text property, you would have to access the text node as follows:

```
var sText = oRoot.childNodes[2].firstChild.nodeValue;
```

This code achieves the same results as using the `text` property. Like the previous example, the third `<book/>` element is referenced using the `childNodes` collection; the text node of the `<book/>` element is then referenced with the use of `firstChild` because a text node is still a node in the DOM. The text is then retrieved by using the `nodeValue` property (which is always set to the text contents for a text node).

The results from these two examples are identical; however, the `text` property behaves in a different way than using the `nodeValue` property on a text node. The `text` property retrieves the value of all text nodes contained within the element and its children, whereas the `nodeValue` property gets only the value of the current node. The `text` property is helpful, but it has the potential to return more text than desired. For example, consider this modified XML document:

```xml
<?xml version="1.0" encoding="utf-8"?>

<books>
    <book isbn="9780470109496">
        <title>Professional Ajax</title>
        <author>Nicholas C. Zakas, Jeremy McPeak, Joe Fawcett</author>
    </book>
    <book isbn="0764579088">Professional JavaScript for Web Developers</book>
    <book isbn="0764557599">Professional C#</book>
    <book isbn="1861002025">Professional Visual Basic 6 Databases</book>
</books>
```

This new XML document adds two new children to the first `<book/>` element: the `<title/>` element, which contains the title of the book, and the `<author/>` element, which holds the author data. Once again, use the `text` property:

```
alert(oFirstBook.text);
```

There is nothing new in this code, as you have already seen it. However, look at the results, as shown in Figure 6-1.

Notice that the text nodes from the `<title/>` and `<author/>` elements are retrieved and concatenated. If `oFirstBook.nodeValue` had been used, it would have returned `null`, because `oFirstBook` is not a text node.

There are a number of methods to retrieve nodes and values from an XML node; the two most often used are `getAttribute()` and `getElementsByTagName()`.

The `getAttribute()` method takes a string argument containing the name of the attribute to retrieve. If the attribute does not exist, the value returned is `null`. Using the same XML document introduced earlier in this section, consider the following code:

```
var sAttribute = oFirstBook.getAttribute("isbn");
alert(sAttribute);
```

This code retrieves the value of the `isbn` attribute of the first `<book/>` element and assigns it to the `sAttribute` variable. This value is then displayed using `alert()`.

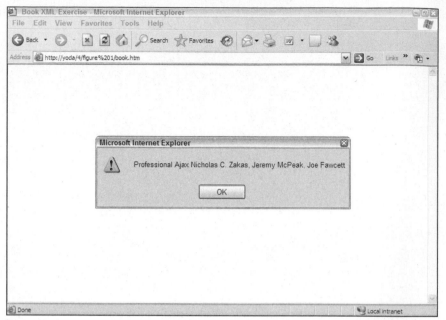

Figure 6-1

The `getElementsByTagName()` method returns a `NodeList` of child elements with the specified tag name. This method searches for elements within the given node's descendants only, so the returned `NodeList` does not include any elements that are ancestors or children of ancestors. For example:

```
var cBooks = oRoot.getElementsByTagName("book");
alert(cBooks.length);
```

This code retrieves all `<book/>` elements within the document and returns the `NodeList` to `cBooks`. With the sample XML document, an alert box displays that four `<book/>` elements were found. To retrieve all descendant elements, pass `"*"` as the parameter to `getElementsByTagName()`, as follows:

```
var cElements = oRoot.getElementsByTagName("*");
```

In this example, the `cElements` collection contains both the `<book/>` elements as well as the `<title/>` and `<author/>` elements.

Retrieving XML Data in IE

Retrieving XML data is as simple as using a property, the `xml` property. This property serializes the XML data of the current node. *Serialization* is the process of converting objects into an easily storable or transmittable format. The `xml` property converts XML into a string representation, complete with tag names, attributes, and text:

```
var sXml = oRoot.xml;
alert(sXml);
```

This code serializes the XML data starting with the document element, which is then passed to the `alert()` method. A portion of the serialized XML looks like this:

```
<books><book isbn="9780470109496">Professional Ajax</book></books>
```

You can load serialized data into another XML DOM object, send it to a server application, or pass it to another page. The serialized XML data returned by the `xml` property depends on the current node. Using the `xml` property at the `documentElement` node returns the XML data of the entire document, whereas using it on a `<book/>` element returns only the XML data contained in that `<book/>` element.

> The `xml` property is read-only. If you want to add elements to the document, you will have to use DOM methods to do so.

Manipulating the DOM in IE

To this point, you have learned how to traverse the DOM, extract information from it, and convert XML into string format. You also have the ability to add to, delete from, and replace nodes in the DOM.

Creating Nodes

You can create a variety of nodes using DOM methods, but the most often used is the `createElement()` method. This method takes one argument, a string containing the tag name of the element to create, and returns an `XMLDOMElement` reference:

```
var oNewBook = oXmlDom.createElement("book");
oXmlDom.documentElement.appendChild(oNewBook);
```

This code creates a new `<book/>` element and appends it to `documentElement` using the `appendChild()` method. The `appendChild()` method adds the new element, specified by its argument, after the last child node. This code appends an empty `<book/>` element to the document, so the element needs some text:

```
var oNewBook = oXmlDom.createElement("book");
```

```
var oNewBookText = oXmlDom.createTextNode("Professional .NET 2.0 Generics");
oNewBook.appendChild(oNewBookText);
```

```
oXmlDom.documentElement.appendChild(oNewBook);
```

This code creates a text node with the `createTextNode()` method and appends it to the newly created `<book/>` element with `appendChild()`. The `createTextNode()` method takes a string argument specifying the text contents for the text node.

At this point, you have programmatically created a new `<book/>` element, provided it a text node, and appended it to the document. One last piece of information is required to get this new element on par with its other siblings, the `isbn` attribute. Creating an attribute is as simple as using the `setAttribute()` method, which is available on every element node:

```
var oNewBook = oXmlDom.createElement("book");

var oNewBookText = oXmlDom.createTextNode("Professional .NET 2.0 Generics");
oNewBook.appendChild(oNewBookText);
oNewBook.setAttribute("isbn","0764559885");

oXmlDom.documentElement.appendChild(oNewBook);
```

The new line of code in this example creates an isbn attribute and assigns it the value of 0764559885. The setAttribute() method takes two string arguments: the first is the name of the attribute, and the second is the value to assign to the attribute. IE also provides other methods to add attributes to an element; however, they hold no real advantage over setAttribute() and require much more coding.

Removing, Replacing, and Inserting Nodes

If you can add nodes to a document, it seems only natural to be able to remove them as well; the removeChild() method does just that. This method accepts a single argument, the node to remove. To remove the first <book/> element from the document, the following code can be used:

```
var oRemovedChild = oRoot.removeChild(oRoot.firstChild);
```

The removeChild() method returns the child node that was removed, so oRemovedChild now references the removed <book/> element. With a reference to the old node, it can be placed anywhere else in the document.

Perhaps you want to replace the third <book/> element with oRemovedChild. The replaceChild() method can be used to that end:

```
var oReplacedChild = oRoot.replaceChild(oRemovedChild, oRoot.childNodes[2]);
```

The replaceChild() method accepts two arguments: the node to add and the node to replace. In this code, the node referenced by oRemovedChild replaces the third <book/> element, and the removed node is returned and stored in oReplacedChild.

Because oReplacedChild references the replaced node, you can easily insert it back into the document. You could use appendChild() to add the node to the end of the child list, or you can use the insertBefore() method to insert the node before another sibling:

```
oRoot.insertBefore(oReplacedChild, oRoot.lastChild);
```

This code inserts the previously replaced node before the last <book/> element. The insertBefore() method takes two arguments: the node to insert and the node to insert before. You'll notice the use of the lastChild property, which retrieves the last child node, effectively inserting oReplacedChild as the second-to-last child node. The insertBefore() method also returns the value of the inserted node, but it is not necessary for this example.

Error Handling in IE

When XML data is loaded, errors can occur for a variety of reasons. For example, the external XML file may not be found or the XML code may not be well formed. To handle these occasions, MSXML provides the parseError property, which contains error information.

The `parseError` object provides a number of properties to enable you to better understand an error:

❑   errorCode: The error code as a long integer

❑   filepos: A long integer specifying the position in the file where the error occurred

❑   line: The line number that contains the error as a long integer

❑   linepos: The character position in the line where the error occurred (long integer)

❑   reason: A string specifying why the error happened

❑   srcText: The text of the line where the error happened

❑   url: The URL of the XML document as a string

To check for errors, the `parseError` object exposes the `errorCode` property, which can be compared to the integer 0; if `errorCode` does not equal 0, an error has occurred. The following example is designed specifically to cause an error:

```
var sXml = "<root><person><name>Jeremy McPeak</name></root>";
var oXmlDom = createDocument();
oXmlDom.loadXML(sXml);

if (oXmlDom.parseError.errorCode != 0) {
    alert("An Error Occurred: " + oXmlDom.parseError.reason);
} else {
    //Code to do for successful load.
}
```

In the highlighted line, notice that the `<person/>` element is not closed. Since the XML being loaded is not well formed, an error occurs during the parsing process. The `errorCode` is then compared to 0; if they do not match (and they don't in this example), an alert displays the error's cause by using the `reason` property.

> The `errorCode` **property can be positive or negative; only when** `errorCode` **is** 0 **can you be sure that no error occurred.**

XML in Other Browsers

The developers of Firefox, Opera, and Safari took a more standards-centric approach when implementing XML support. Instead of an external component, these developers made it a part of the JavaScript implementation. In the case of Firefox and Opera, doing this ensured XML DOM support on all platforms in all Gecko and Opera browsers.

To create an XML DOM, the `createDocument()` method of the `document.implementation` object is called. This method takes three arguments: the first is a string containing the namespace URI for the document to use, the second is a string containing the qualified name of the document's root element, and the third is a `DocumentType` object (also called *doctype*), which is usually `null`. To create an empty DOM document, you can do this:

```
var oXmlDom = document.implementation.createDocument("", "", null);
```

By passing in an empty string for the first two arguments, and `null` for the last, you ensure a completely empty document. To create an XML DOM with a document element, specify the tag name in the second argument:

```
var oXmlDom = document.implementation.createDocument("", "books", null);
```

This code creates an XML DOM whose `documentElement` is `<books/>`. You can take it a step further and specify a namespace in the creation of the DOM by specifying the namespace URI in the first argument:

```
var oXmlDom = document.implementation.createDocument("http://www.site1.com",
        "books", null);
```

When a namespace is specified in the `createDocument()` method, the browser uses the it as the default namespace like the following XML node:

```
<books xmlns="http://www.site1.com" />
```

From here, you can populate the XML document programmatically; generally, however, you will want to load preexisting XML documents into a blank XML DOM object.

Loading XML Data

Firefox and Opera support the same `load()` method as IE. Therefore, you can use the same code to load external XML data in all three browsers:

```
oXmlDom.load("books.xml");
```

Also like IE, Firefox and Opera implement the `async` property: setting `async` to `false` forces the document to be loaded in synchronous mode; otherwise, the document is loaded asynchronously. There are, however, some differences in the implementations.

One major difference is that Firefox and Opera don't have the `readyState` property or the `onreadystatechange` event handler. Instead, they support the `load` event and the `onload` event handler. The `load` event fires after the document is completely loaded:

```
oXmlDom.onload = function () {
    //Do something when the document is fully loaded.
};
oXmlDom.load("books.xml");
```

> **Currently, Safari doesn't support the `load()` method. The only way to retrieve XML documents is to use the `XMLHttpRequest` object and retrieve the `responseXML` property.**

Firefox, Opera, and Safari do not implement the `loadXML()` method; however, it is possible to emulate this method's behavior through the `DOMParser` object. This object has a method called `parseFromString()`, which loads a string and parses it into a document:

```
var sXml = "<root><person><name>Jeremy McPeak</name></person></root>";
var oParser = new DOMParser();
var oXmlDom = oParser.parseFromString(sXml,"text/xml");
```

In this code, a string of XML is created to pass to the `DOMParser`. The two arguments for `parseFromString()` are the XML string and the content type of the data (typically set to `"text/xml"`). The `parseFromString()` method returns an XML DOM object as if it were created using `createDocument()`.

Opera 9 also supports DOM 3 Load/Save specification; however, it is beyond the scope of this book to cover these interfaces in detail.

Retrieving XML Data in the Other Browsers

Despite all of their differences, IE and the other browsers do share many properties and methods used to retrieve XML data contained in the document. As in IE, you can retrieve the root element of the document by using the `documentElement` property, as follows:

```
var oRoot = oXmlDom.documentElement;
```

The non-IE browsers also support the W3C standard properties of `attributes`, `childNodes`, `firstChild`, `lastChild`, `nextSibling`, `nodeName`, `nodeType`, `nodeValue`, `ownerDocument`, `parentNode`, and `previousSibling`. Unfortunately, these browsers do not support the Microsoft-proprietary `text` and `xml` properties, but it is possible to emulate their behavior.

As a quick recap, the `text` property returns the content of the node or the concatenated text of the current node and its descendants. Therefore, it returns not only the text of the existing node but also the text of all child nodes; this is easy enough to emulate. A simple function that takes a node as an argument can provide the same result:

```
function getText(oNode) {
    var sText = "";
    for (var i = 0; i < oNode.childNodes.length; i++) {
        if (oNode.childNodes[i].hasChildNodes()) {
            sText += getText(oNode.childNodes[i]);
        } else {
            sText += oNode.childNodes[i].nodeValue;
        }
    }
    return sText;
}
```

In `getText()`, `sText` stores every piece of text that is retrieved. As the `for` loop iterates through `oNode`'s children, each child is checked to see if it contains children. If it does, the `childNode` is passed into `getText()` and goes through the same process. If no children exist, then the `nodeValue` of the current node is added to the string (for text nodes, this is just the text string). After all children have been processed, the function returns `sText`.

The IE xml property serializes all XML contained in the current node. This can be accomplished by using an XMLSerializer object, common to Firefox, Opera, and Safari. This object has a single method called serializeToString(), which is used to serialize a DOM node:

```
function serializeXml(oNode) {
    var oSerializer = new XMLSerializer();
    return oSerializer.serializeToString(oNode);
}
```

The serializeXml() function takes an XML node as an argument. The result of this method, a string representation of the XML data, is returned to the caller.

> *IE, Firefox, Opera, and Safari share the same W3C DOM methods for manipulating nodes. Refer to the "Manipulating the DOM in IE" section earlier in this chapter for a refresher.*

Cross-Browser XML

In an Ajax application, and most JavaScript code, you always need to consider cross-browser differences. When using an XML-based solution in multiple browsers, you have two options: create your own functions that use the correct code based on the browser, or use a ready-made library. Most of the time it's easiest to use a preexisting library, such as the zXml library introduced in Chapter 2. Along with XHR support, zXml also provides common interfaces for XML operations.

For example, to create an XML DOM document, you can use zXmlDom.createDocument():

```
var oXmlDom = zXmlDom.createDocument();
```

This single line of code can be used instead of writing separate browser-dependent code each time a DOM document is needed. Additionally, zXml adds a variety of IE functionality to the standard DOM document.

One of the major things zXml does for convenience is to add support for the readyState property and the onreadystatechange event handler. Instead of needing to use the separate onload event handler in Firefox, you can write one set of code without browser detection, such as:

```
oXmlDom.onreadystatechange = function () {
    if (oXmlDom.readyState == 4) {
        //Do something when the document is fully loaded.
    }
};
```

The zXml library also adds the xml and text attributes to all nodes in Firefox. Instead of using an XMLSerializer or a standalone function to get these values, you can use them the same way as in IE:

```
var oRoot = oXmlDom.documentElement;

var sFirstChildText = oRoot.firstChild.text;

var sXml = oRoot.xml;
```

Note that these properties will only work in IE and Firefox. Opera and Safari do not currently support getters and setters; so, the `getText()` and `getXml()` methods are provided for these browsers. To get the text or XML code from a node in all browsers, the JavaScript would look like this:

```
var oRoot = oXmlDom.documentElement;
var sFirstChildText = oRoot.firstChild.text || oRoot.firstChild.getText();
var sXml = oRoot.xml || oRoot.getXml();
```

The zXml library also provides a `loadXML()` method for the non-IE browsers, eliminating the need to use a `DOMParser` object.

```
var oXmlDom2 = zXmlDom.createDocument();
oXmlDom2.loadXML(sXml);
```

Lastly, the zXml library adds a `parseError` object for non-IE browsers, which emulates the corresponding object in IE. The one major difference is the `errorCode` property, which is simply set to a non-zero number when an error occurs. Therefore, you shouldn't use this property to look for a specific error, only to see if an error has occurred. Other than that, you can use the other properties as you would in IE:

```
if (oXmlDom.parseError.errorCode != 0) {

    var str = "An error occurred!!\n" +
        "Description: " + oXmlDom.parseError.reason + "\n" +
        "File: " + oXmlDom.parseError.url + "\n" +
        "Line: " + oXmlDom.parseError.line + "\n" +
        "Line Position: " + oXmlDom.parseError.linePos + "\n" +
        "Source Code: " + oXmlDom.parseError.srcText;
    alert(str);
} else {
    //Code to do for successful load.
}
```

You certainly aren't required to use a cross-browser XML library for your solutions, but it can definitely help.

A Basic XML Example

XML is a semantic, descriptive language. Generally, the elements contained in any given XML document describe the data of that document, thus making it a decent data store for static information, or information that doesn't change often.

Imagine you run an online bookstore and have a list of Best Picks whose information is stored in an XML document, `books.xml`. This information can be displayed to the user without a server component. The following example uses the zXml library to load the XML file, parse through it, and display the information on a web page using DOM methods.

The `books.xml` file contains the following XML data:

```xml
<?xml version="1.0" encoding="utf-8"?>

<bookList>
    <book isbn="9780470109496">
        <title>Professional Ajax</title>
        <author>Nicholas C. Zakas, Jeremy McPeak, Joe Fawcett</author>
        <publisher>Wrox</publisher>
    </book>
    <book isbn="0764579088">
        <title>Professional JavaScript for Web Developers</title>
        <author>Nicholas C. Zakas</author>
        <publisher>Wrox</publisher>
    </book>
    <book isbn="0764557599">
        <title>Professional C#</title>
        <author>Simon Robinson, et al</author>
        <publisher>Wrox</publisher>
    </book>
    <book isbn="1861006314">
        <title>GDI+ Programming: Creating Custom Controls Using C#</title>
        <author>Eric White</author>
        <publisher>Wrox</publisher>
    </book>
    <book isbn="1861002025">
        <title>Professional Visual Basic 6 Databases</title>
        <author>Charles Williams</author>
        <publisher>Wrox</publisher>
    </book>
</bookList>
```

The document element `<bookList/>` contains a few `<book/>` elements, which include information about a given book.

Loading XML Data

The first step is to create an XML DOM document and load the XML data into it. Because `books.xml` will be loaded asynchronously, the `onreadystatechange` event handler must be set:

```javascript
var oXmlDom = zXmlDom.createDocument();
oXmlDom.onreadystatechange = function () {
    if (oXmlDom.readyState == 4) {

    }
};
```

When the `readystatechange` event fires and the event handler is called, the `readyState` property is checked; a value of 4 indicates that the document is completely loaded and the DOM is ready to use.

The next step is to check for errors; even though the document is loaded, it does not mean that no errors were found by the XML parser:

```
var oXmlDom = zXmlDom.createDocument();
oXmlDom.onreadystatechange = function () {
    if (oXmlDom.readyState == 4) {
        if (oXmlDom.parseError.errorCode == 0) {
            parseBookInfo(oXmlDom);
        } else {
            var str = "An error occurred!!\n" +
                "Description: " + oXmlDom.parseError.reason + "\n" +
                "File: " + oXmlDom.parseError.url + "\n" +
                "Line: " + oXmlDom.parseError.line + "\n" +
                "Line Position: " + oXmlDom.parseError.linePos + "\n" +
                "Source Code: " + oXmlDom.parseError.srcText;
            alert(str);
        }
    }
};
```

If no error occurred (`parseError` is 0), the XML DOM document is passed to `parseBookInfo()`, the function that parses the book list. If an error did occur, the error information collected in the `parseError` object is displayed in an alert box.

With the `onreadystatechange` event handler written, the `load()` method is used to load the XML data:

```
oXmlDom.load("books.xml");
```

The next step in the process is to parse the XML data.

Parsing the Book List

The `parseBookInfo()` function is in charge of parsing the DOM document. This function accepts one argument, which is the DOM document itself:

```
function parseBookInfo(oXmlDom) {
    var oRoot = oXmlDom.documentElement;
    var oFragment = document.createDocumentFragment();
```

The variable `oRoot` is set to the `documentElement` of the XML document for convenience. Next, a document fragment is created. Since the `parseBookInfo()` function generates many HTML elements and, thus, many changes to the HTML DOM loaded in the browser, this fragment is used to efficiently build up the new elements before adding them to the HTML document; adding each element to the HTML DOM individually is an expensive process in terms of the time it takes to display the changes. Instead, each element is added to the document fragment, which will be added to the document once all HTML elements are created. Doing so allows the HTML DOM to be updated only once instead of multiple times, resulting in faster rendering.

Only <book/> elements are children of the document element, so it's possible to retrieve a NodeList of <book/> elements and iterate through it:

```
var cBooks = oRoot.getElementsByTagName("book");

for (var i = 0, iLen=cBooks.length; i < iLen; i++) {
    var sIsbn = cBooks[i].getAttribute("isbn");
    var sAuthor, sTitle, sPublisher;
```

Inside the for loop, the actual parsing begins. To start, the isbn attribute of the <book/> element is retrieved with getAttribute() and stored in sIsbn. This value is used to display the book cover as well as the actual ISBN value to the user. The variables sAuthor, sTitle, and sPublisher are also declared; these variables will hold the values of the <author/>, <title/>, and <publisher/> elements, respectively.

> Note that since getElementsByTagName() returns a NodeList, it is more efficient to store the length of the list in a variable, iLen, and use it to control the for loop. Putting cBooks.length in a loop control field causes a DOM lookup every time it is checked, which is an expensive process. By storing the length of the list in a variable and comparing against that, the performance is greatly improved.

Next, the book data is retrieved, which can be done in a number of different ways. You could use the childNodes collection and loop through the children, but this example uses a different approach. The same result can be achieved using a do...while loop, which makes use of the firstChild and nextSibling properties:

```
var oCurrentChild = cBooks[i].firstChild;

do {
    switch (oCurrentChild.tagName) {
        case "title":
            sTitle = oCurrentChild.text;
            break;
        case "author":
            sAuthor = oCurrentChild.text;
            break;
        case "publisher":
            sPublisher = oCurrentChild.text;
            break;
        default:
            break;
    }
} while (oCurrentChild = oCurrentChild.nextSibling);
```

In the first line, the variable oCurrentChild is assigned the first child of the current <book/> element. (Remember, this occurs inside of the for loop.) The child's tagName is used in a switch block to determine what should be done with its data. When a match to the tagName is found, the node's text is retrieved and stored in the sTitle, sAuthor, or sPublisher variables. After that, the oCurrentChild variable is assigned the node immediately following the current node by using the nextSibling property. If a next sibling exists, the loop continues; if not, oCurrentChild is null and the loop exits.

When all data variables contain the needed data, you can start generating HTML elements to display that data. The HTML structure of the elements looks like this:

```
<div class="bookContainer">
    <img class="bookCover" alt="Professional Ajax" src="9780470109496.png" />
    <div class="bookContent">
        <h3>Professional Ajax</h3>
        Written by: Nicholas C. Zakas, Jeremy McPeak, Joe Fawcett<br />
        ISBN #9780470109496
        <div class="bookPublisher">Published by Wrox</div>
    </div>
</div>
```

To add some readability to the list, the containing <div/> elements have alternating background colors. Books that are an odd number in the list (book number 1, 3, and so on) have a grayish background color and a class name of bookContainer-odd, whereas even-numbered books (book number 0, 2, and so on) have a white background defined by the bookContainer CSS class.

Generating this HTML output through DOM methods is an easy but lengthy process. The first step is to create the containing <div/>, the <img/>, and the content <div/> elements, which is done using the createElement() DOM method once for each:

```
var divContainer = document.createElement("div");
var imgBookCover = document.createElement("img");
var divContent = document.createElement("div");

var sOdd = (i % 2)?"":"-odd";
divContainer.className = "bookContainer" + sOdd;
```

Along with the element creation, the differing class names are processed here as well. The current book is judged to be odd or even by using the modulus (%) operator. The sOdd variable is assigned the appropriate suffix, an empty string for even and "-odd" for odd, and used in the className assignment.

You can then assign the properties of the book cover image. These PNG images use the ISBN number as their file names:

```
imgBookCover.src = "images/" + sIsbn + ".png";
imgBookCover.className = "bookCover";
divContainer.appendChild(imgBookCover);
```

Here, the `src` and `className` properties are assigned and the image is appended to `divContainer`. With the image finished, the text content can be added. The first piece of information to be added is the book's title, which is a level 3 heading element (`<h3/>`). Again, this element is created with `createElement()`:

```
var h3Title = document.createElement("h3");
h3Title.appendChild(document.createTextNode(sTitle));
divContent.appendChild(h3Title);
```

To create a text node containing the title, the `createTextNode()` method is used, the result of which is appended to the `<h3/>` element. Then, the completed heading is appended to `divContent`.

The author and ISBN information are next to be added. These two pieces of information are text nodes and have no parent element other than `divContent`. There is, however, one breaking element (`<br/>`) in between the two text nodes:

```
divContent.appendChild(document.createTextNode("Written by: " + sAuthor));
divContent.appendChild(document.createElement("br"));
divContent.appendChild(document.createTextNode("ISBN: #" + sIsbn));
```

In this code, the text node containing the author information is appended to `divContent`, followed by the creation and appending of the breaking element (`<br/>`). On the third line, the text node containing the ISBN information is created and appended.

The last piece of information to add is the publisher:

```
var divPublisher = document.createElement("div");
divPublisher.className = "bookPublisher";
divPublisher.appendChild(document.createTextNode("Published by: " + sPublisher));
divContent.appendChild(divPublisher);
```

The publisher is displayed in a `<div/>` element. After its creation, the `className` "`bookPublisher`" is assigned and the text node containing the publisher's name is appended to the element. The `divPublisher` element is complete, and so can be appended to `divContent`.

At this point, all data operations are complete. However, `divContent` still lacks its class name and must be appended to `divContainer`, which in turn must be appended to the document fragment. The following three lines of code do this:

```
divContent.className = "bookContent";
divContainer.appendChild(divContent);
oFragment.appendChild(divContainer);
```

The last step is to append the document fragment to the page body after the book nodes are iterated through:

```
document.body.appendChild(oFragment);
```

This code doesn't actually append the document fragment itself; instead, it appends all the child nodes of the document fragment, making all the changes to the HTML DOM at once. With this final line of code, `parseBookInfo()` is complete.

Tying It Together

The body of this web page is generated entirely by JavaScript. Because of this, the element creation and insertion code must execute after the document is loaded. To do this, define a function called `init()` to house the XML DOM creation code:

```
function init() {
    var oXmlDom = zXmlDom.createDocument();
    oXmlDom.onreadystatechange = function () {
        if (oXmlDom.readyState == 4) {
            if (oXmlDom.parseError.errorCode == 0) {
                parseBookInfo(oXmlDom);
            } else {
                alert("An Error Occurred: " + oXmlDom.parseError.reason);
            }
        }
    };
    oXmlDom.load("books.xml");
}
```

The `init()` function handles the `window load` event. This ensures that the JavaScript-generated elements are added to the page without causing errors.

The example must be run as part of an HTML document. All that is required are two `<script/>` elements, a `<link/>` element for the CSS, and the assignment of the `onload` event handler:

```
<!DOCTYPE html PUBLIC "-//W3C//DTD XHTML 1.1//EN"
                      "http://www.w3.org/TR/xhtml11/DTD/xhtml11.dtd">

<html xmlns="http://www.w3.org/1999/xhtml" >
<head>
    <title>XML Example</title>
    <link rel="stylesheet" type="text/css" href="books.css" />
    <script type="text/javascript" src="zxml.js"></script>
    <script type="text/javascript" src="books.js"></script>
</head>
<body onload="init()">

</body>
</html>
```

When this example is run, it yields the result shown in Figure 6-2.

169

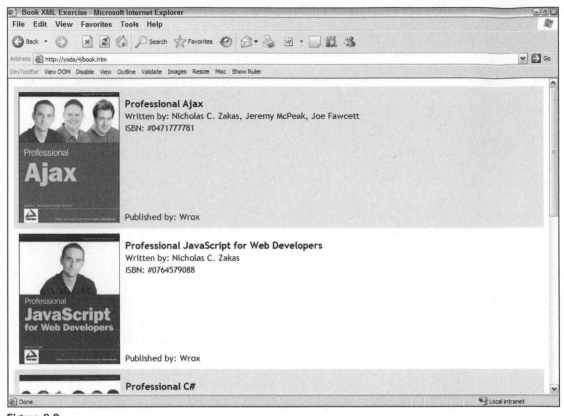

Figure 6-2

XPath Support in Browsers

As XML grew in popularity, the need to access specific pieces of data contained within large amounts of code became apparent. In July 1999, XML Path Language (XPath) was introduced in the eXtensible Stylesheet Language (XSL) specification as a means to find any node within an XML document. XPath uses a non-XML syntax that closely resembles the path syntax of a file system, allowing the construction of paths to any part of a document. The language consists of location paths and other expressions, as well as a few helpful functions to aid in retrieving specific data.

Introduction to XPath

An XPath expression consists of two parts: a context node and a selection pattern. The context node is the context from which the selection pattern begins. Referring to books.xml from the previous section, consider this XPath expression:

```
book/author
```

If this expression were executed at the root level context, all `<author/>` nodes would be returned because the `<book/>` element is a child of the document element and contains an `<author/>` element. This expression is not very specific, so all `<author/>` elements are returned.

What if you want to retrieve only the `<book/>` element that has a specific ISBN? The XPath expression would look like this:

```
book[@isbn='9780470109496']
```

The `book` part of the expression describes which element to retrieve. Inside of the square brackets is a condition that this element must match. The `@isbn` part represents the `isbn` attribute (`@` being short for attribute). So, this expression reads "find the book elements that have an `isbn` attribute of `'9780470109496'`."

XPath expressions can also be very complex. Consider the following expression:

```
book[author[contains(text(),'McPeak')]]
```

This expression reads, "find the book elements that have author elements whose text contains the string 'McPeak'." Since this is a more complicated expression, it helps to break it down, working from the outside towards the inside. Removing all conditions, you have this expression:

```
book[...]
```

First, you know that a `<book/>` element will be returned, since it is the outermost element; next come the conditions. Inside the first set of brackets is the `<author/>` element:

```
author[...]
```

So, now you now know you are looking for a book element with a child `<author/>` element. However, the children of the `<author/>` element need to be checked as well because the expression doesn't end there:

```
contains(text(),'McPeak')
```

The `contains()` function takes two arguments and returns `true` if the first string argument contains the second string argument. The `text()` function, which is an XSL function, returns a `node-set` of all descendent nodes. When passed to the `contains()` function, the `node-set` is implicitly converted to a string, essentially resulting in the text contents of the `<author/>` element being passed as the first argument in `contains()`. The second argument passed to `contains()` is the search text, in this case `'McPeak'`.

> Note that the `contains()` function, like all XPath functions, is case-sensitive.

The resulting node set is one `<book/>` element, because there is only one book with an author (or coauthor) whose name is McPeak.

As you can see, XPath is a useful language that makes finding specific nodes in XML data rather simple. It is no wonder that browser makers are implementing XPath in their browsers for client-side use.

XPath in IE

Microsoft's implementation of XPath is a part of MSXML 3.0 and later. If you are using any version of Windows XP, or have IE 6.0 or higher installed, then your browser has this capability. If not, you will need to download and install the latest MSXML package.

Before using XPath, however, it is important to set the `SelectionLanguage` property. In MSXML3, the default `SelectionLanguage` is `XSLPattern`, not `XPath`. To set this property, use the `setProperty()` method:

```
oXmlDom.setProperty("SelectionLanguage", "XPath");
```

Once `SelectionLanguage` is set, it is safe to use XPath to select nodes.

> **All MSXML versions after 3.0 have** `XPath` **as the default value of** `SelectionLanguage`**.**

Microsoft chose to implement two methods that select nodes based on XPath expressions. The first, `selectSingleNode()`, returns the first node within its context that matches the expression or `null` if there is no match. For example:

```
var oFirstAuthor = oXmlDom.documentElement.selectSingleNode("book/author");
```

This code returns the first `<author/>` element that is a child of a `<book/>` element in the context of `documentElement`. The result of this is the following node:

```
<author>Nicholas C. Zakas, Jeremy McPeak, Joe Fawcett</author>
```

The second method in Microsoft's XPath implementation is `selectNodes()`. This method returns a `NodeList`, a collection of all nodes that match the pattern in the XPath expression:

```
var cAuthors = oXmlDom.documentElement.selectNodes("book/author");
```

As you may have guessed, all `<author/>` elements with a parent of `<book/>` in the context of the document element are returned. If the pattern cannot be matched in the document, a `NodeList` is still returned, but it has a `length` of 0. It is a good idea to check the length of a returned `NodeList` before attempting to use it:

```
var cAuthors = oXmlDom.documentElement.selectNodes("book/author");

if (cAuthors.length > 0) {
    //Do something
}
```

Working with Namespaces

The *X* in XML stands for *eXtensible*. There are no predefined elements in an XML document; every element in any given XML document was created by a developer. This extensibility is part of what makes XML so popular, but it also inherently causes a problem: naming conflicts. For example, consider the following XML document:

```xml
<?xml version="1.0" encoding="utf-8"?>

<addresses>
    <address>
        <number>12345</number>
        <street>Your Street</street>
        <city>Your City</city>
        <state>Your State</state>
        <country>USA</country>
    </address>
</addresses>
```

There is nothing out of the ordinary in this document. It simply describes an address located in the USA. But what if the following lines are added?

```xml
<?xml version="1.0" encoding="utf-8"?>

<addresses>
    <address>
        <number>12345</number>
        <street>Your Street</street>
        <city>Your City</city>
        <state>Your State</state>
        <country>USA</country>
    </address>

    <address>
        <ip>127.0.0.1</ip>
        <hostname>localhost</hostname>
    </address>
</addresses>
```

This document now describes two types of addresses: a physical mailing address and a computer address. While both are legitimate addresses, handling this information requires different approaches, especially since both `<address/>` elements contain completely different child elements. This is where namespaces come into play.

Namespaces consist of two parts: a *namespace URI* and a *prefix*. The namespace URI identifies the namespace. Generally, namespace URIs are web site URLs, because they must be unique to access different web sites. The prefix is a local name in the XML document for the namespace. Every tag name in the namespace uses the namespace prefix. The syntax of namespace declarations is:

```
xmlns:namespace-prefix="namespaceURI"
```

The `xmlns` keyword tells the XML parser that a namespace declaration is taking place. The `namespace-prefix` is the local name used in the elements that fall under this namespace, and `namespaceURI` is the universal resource identifier that the prefix represents.

Namespace declarations must appear before the namespace is used in the XML document. In the example, the root element contains the namespaces declarations:

```
<?xml version="1.0" encoding="utf-8"?>

<addresses xmlns:mail="http://www.wrox.com/mail"
           xmlns:comp="http://www.wrox.com/computer">

    <mail:address>
        <mail:number>12345</mail:number>
        <mail:street>Your Street</mail:street>
        <mail:city>Your City</mail:city>
        <mail:state>Your State</mail:state>
        <mail:country>USA</mail:country>
    </mail:address>
    <comp:address>
        <comp:ip>127.0.0.1</comp:ip>
        <comp:hostname>localhost</comp:hostname>
    </comp:address>
</addresses>
```

This newly edited XML document defines two namespaces: one with the prefix `mail` to represent a mailing address, and the other with a prefix of `comp` to represent a computer address. Every element associated with a certain address type is associated with the corresponding namespace, so every element associated as a mailing address has the `mail` prefix, whereas every computer-based address has the `comp` prefix.

The use of namespaces avoids naming conflicts, and XML processors now understand the difference between the two address types.

Namespaces in XPath add a slight complication when using `selectSingleNode()` and `selectNodes()`. Consider the following modified version of `books.xml`:

```
<?xml version="1.0" encoding="utf-8"?>

<bookList xmlns="http://site1.com" xmlns:pub="http://site2.com">
    <book isbn="9780470109496">
        <title>Professional Ajax</title>
        <author>Nicholas C. Zakas, Jeremy McPeak, Joe Fawcett</author>
        <pub:name>Wrox</pub:name>
    </book>
    <book isbn="0764579088">
        <title>Professional JavaScript for Web Developers</title>
        <author>Nicholas C. Zakas</author>
        <pub:name>Wrox</pub:name>
    </book>
    <book isbn="0764557599">
        <title>Professional C#</title>
        <author>Simon Robinson, et al</author>
```

```
        <pub:name>Wrox</pub:name>
    </book>
    <book isbn="1861006314">
        <title>GDI+ Programming: Creating Custom Controls Using C#</title>
        <author>Eric White</author>
        <pub:name>Wrox</pub:name>
    </book>
    <book isbn="1861002025">
        <title>Professional Visual Basic 6 Databases</title>
        <author>Charles Williams</author>
        <pub:name>Wrox</pub:name>
    </book>
</bookList>
```

This newly revised document has two namespaces in use: the default namespace specified by `xmlns=` `"http://site1.com"`, followed by the `pub` namespace specified as `xmlns:pub="http://site2.com"`. A default namespace does not have a prefix; therefore, all non-prefixed elements in the document use the default namespace. Notice that the `<publisher/>` elements are replaced by `<pub:name/>` elements.

When dealing with an XML document that contains namespaces, these namespaces must be declared in order to use XPath expressions. The MSXML DOM document exposes a method called `setProperty()`, which is used to set second-level properties for the object. The property `"SelectionNamespaces"` should be set with an alias namespace for any default or external namespace. Aside from using the `setProperty()` method, namespace declarations are assigned just as they are in XML documents:

```
var sNameSpace = "xmlns:na='http://site1.com' xmlns:pub='http://site2.com'";
oXmlDom.setProperty("SelectionNamespaces", sNameSpace);
```

The namespaces `na` and `pub` represent the namespaces used in the XML document. Notice that the namespace prefix `na` is defined for the default namespace. MSXML will not recognize a default namespace when selecting nodes with XPath, so the declaration of an alias prefix is necessary. Now that the `SelectionNamespace` property is set, you can select nodes within the document:

```
var oRoot = oXmlDom.documentElement;
var sXPath = "na:book/pub:name";
var cPublishers = oRoot.selectNodes(sXPath);

if (cPublishers.length > 0) {
    alert(cPublishers.length + " <pub:name/> elements found with " + sXPath);
}
```

The XPath expression uses the namespaces specified in the `SelectionNamespaces` property and selects all `<pub:name/>` elements. In the case of this example, a `NodeList` consisting of five elements is returned, which you can then use.

XPath in Other Browsers

The XPath implementation in the non-IE browsers follow the DOM standard, which is quite different from the IE implementation. This different implementation allows XPath expressions to be run against HTML and XML documents alike. At the center of this are two primary objects: `XPathEvaluator` and `XPathResult`.

> At the time of this writing, Safari does not support XPath; however, the latest version of WebKit (the engine behind Safari) supports XPath to some extent. You can download the latest WebKit nightly at http://www.webkit.org.

Firefox is the only browser that allows you to explicitly create XPathEvaluator objects by calling the class' constructor. The W3C documentation, however, describes that a DOM object should implement the XPathEvaluator interface. Therefore, you do not need to create a separate XPathEvaluator object in order to use XPath.

An object implementing the XPathEvaluator interface evaluates a given XPath expression using the evaluate() method, which takes five arguments: the XPath expression to be evaluated, the context node that the expression should be run against, a namespace resolver (which is a function that handles mapping prefixes to namespaces), the result type (10 different result types are available), and an XPathResult object to contain the results (if this argument is null, then a new XPathResult object is returned).

Before moving on, it's important to understand the various result types that can be returned from evaluate(). These are:

❑ XPathResult.ANY_TYPE, which returns no specific type. The method returns the type that naturally results from the evaluation of the expression.

❑ XPathResult.ANY_UNORDERED_NODE_TYPE, which returns a node set of one node that is accessed through the singleNodeValue property; null is returned if there are no matching nodes. The returned node may or may not be the first occurring node.

❑ XPathResult.BOOLEAN_TYPE, which returns a Boolean value.

❑ XPathResult.FIRST_ORDERED_NODE_TYPE, which returns a node set consisting of one node. This node is accessed with the singleNodeValue property of the XPathResult class. The node returned is the first occurring one in the document.

❑ XPathResult.NUMBER_TYPE, which returns a number value.

❑ XPathResult.ORDERED_NODE_ITERATOR_TYPE, which returns a document-ordered node set that can be iterated through using the iterateNext() method; therefore, you can easily access each individual node in the set.

❑ XPathResult.ORDERED_NODE_SNAPSHOT_TYPE, which returns a document-ordered node set that is a snapshot of the result set. Any modifications made to the nodes in the document do not affect the retrieved results.

❑ XPathResult.STRING_TYPE, which returns a string value.

❑ XPathResult.UNORDERED_NODE_ITERATOR_TYPE, which returns a node set that can be iterated through; however, the results may or may not be in the same order as they appear in the document.

❑ XPathResult.UNORDERED_NODE_SNAPSHOT_TYPE, which returns an unordered snapshot node set. Any modifications made to the nodes in the document do not affect the result set.

The most common result type is `XPathResult.ORDERED_NODE_ITERATOR_TYPE`:

```
var sXPath = "book/author";
var oResult = oXmlDom.evaluate(sXPath, document, null,
        XPathResult.ORDERED_NODE_ITERATOR_TYPE, null);

var aNodes = new Array;

if (oResult != null) {
    var oElement;
    while (oElement = oResult.iterateNext()) {
        aNodes.push(oElement);
    }
}
```

This code uses the `evaluate()` method of a DOM object to evaluate the XPath expression `book/author` in the context of the document's root element. Because the result type is `ORDERED_NODE_ITERATOR_TYPE`, the evaluation returns a node set that you can iterate through using the `iterateNext()`.

The `iterateNext()` method resembles the `nextSibling` property of a DOM node in that it selects the next node in the result set and returns `null` when the end of the result set is reached. This function enables you to use it in a `while` loop as in the previous example; as long as `oElement` is not `null`, it is added to the `aNodes` array through the `push()` method. Populating an array gives you IE-like functionality; therefore, you can use it in a `for` loop or access separate array elements easily.

Working with a Namespace Resolver

A *namespace resolver* translates an element's namespace prefix in an XPath expression into the namespace URI associated with that prefix. The W3C specification states that an `XPathNSResolver` object can be used as a resolver, but it also states that you can define a function to handle the translation. This particular function can have any name.

Writing a namespace resolver is simple. The function must accept a string value as an argument, and it must return a string. The string argument is a namespace prefix, for which the function must return a namespace URI. The following namespace resolver function uses the values from the IE example:

```
function nsResolver(sPrefix) {
    switch (sPrefix) {
        case "na":
            return "http://site1.com";
            break;
        case "pub":
            return "http://site2.com";
            break;
        default:
            return null;
            break;
    }
}
```

With the resolver written, you can use the following XPath expression on the modified `books.xml` document from the IE namespace example:

```
var sXPath = "na:book/pub:name";

var oResult = oXmlDom.evaluate(sXPath,oXmlDom.documentElement,nsResolver,
        XPathResult.ORDERED_NODE_ITERATOR_TYPE, null);

var aNodes = new Array;

if (oResult != null) {
    var oElement;
    while (oElement = oResult.iterateNext()) {
        aNodes.push(oElement);
    }
}
```

This example resembles the last evaluation code. However, notice the addition to the `evaluate()` method: the pointer to the `nsResolver()` function, written earlier, is passed in to handle the namespaces in the XPath expression. The resulting `NodeList` is converted to an array by using the `iterateNext()` method of the `XPathResult` class to iterate through the result.

As you can see, the W3C XPath implementation is quite different from the Microsoft approach; so it is helpful to use a cross-browser library that enables you to perform XPath evaluations easily.

Cross-Browser XPath

The zXml library provides cross-browser XPath functionality through a common interface. The object responsible for providing XPath functionality is `zXPath`, which has two methods.

The first method is `selectSingleNode()`. This method, like the IE method of the same name, returns the first node that matches a pattern. Unlike the IE implementation, this method accepts three arguments: the context node, the XPath expression string, and a hashtable with the prefix as keys and the namespace URIs as values. Following are a couple of examples of how these hashtables can look:

```
//Assigning each key a value
var oXmlNs = {};
oXmlNs["na"]    = "http://site1.com";
oXmlNs["pub"]   = "http://site2.com";
oXmlNs["ns"]    = "http://site3.com";

//Using object literal notation to create a hashtable
var oXmlNs = {
    na    : "http://site1.com",
    pub   : "http://site2.com",
    ns    : "http://site3.com"
};
```

If you are not working with namespaces, then the first two arguments of `selectSingleNode()` are the only required arguments.

The returned result of `selectSingleNode()` is the selected XML node, or `null` if a match cannot be found. If the browser does not support XPath, an error is thrown stating that the browser does not have an XPath engine installed. The following example evaluates an XPath expression against the document element:

```
var oRoot = oXmlDom.documentElement;
var oNode = zXPath.selectSingleNode(oRoot, "book/author", null);

if (oNode) {
    alert(oNode.xml || oNode.getXml());
}
```

This example searches for the first `<author/>` element contained in a `<book/>` element in the context of the document root. If found, the serialized form of the XML data is displayed to the user in an alert box.

The second method of `zXPath` is `selectNodes()`, which returns a node set much like the IE `selectNodes()` method. The syntax closely resembles that of the `selectSingleNode()` method above, and the arguments are exactly the same, and the same namespace rules apply. Also as with `selectSingleNode()`, an error is thrown in the event that the browser does not have an XPath engine installed. The next example demonstrates the `selectNodes()` method:

```
var oNamespaces = {
    na    : "http://site1.com",
    pub   : "http://site2.com"
};

var oRoot = oXmlDom.documentElement;
var sXPath = "na:book/pub:name";
var oNodes = zXPath.selectNodes(oRoot, sXPath, oNamespaces);

if (oNodes.length > 0) {
    alert(oNodes.length);
}
```

This example, much like the `selectSingleNode()` example, searches for all author elements of a document that incorporates namespaces. If the result set has a length greater than 0, the length of the result is displayed to the user.

XPath is a powerful tool to navigate through and select certain nodes in an XML document, although it was never intended to be used as a standalone tool. Instead, it was created for use in XSL Transformations.

XSL Transformation Support in Browsers

eXtensible Stylesheet Language (XSL) is a family of languages that are designed to transform XML data. XSL refers to three main languages: XSL Transformations (XSLT), which is a language that transforms XML documents into other XML documents; XPath, which was discussed in the previous section; and XSL Formatting Objects (XSL-FO), which describes how the transformed data should be rendered when presented. Since no browser currently supports XSL-FO, all transformations must be accomplished through the use of XSLT.

Introduction to XSLT

XSLT is an XML-based language designed to transform an XML document into another data form. This definition may make XSLT to be a not-so-useful technology, but the truth is far from the matter. The most popular use of XSLT is to transform XML documents into HTML documents, which is precisely what this introduction covers.

XSLT documents are nothing more than specialized XML documents, so they must conform to the same rules as all XML documents: they must contain an XML declaration, they must have a single root element, and they must be well formed.

As an example, consider `books.xml`. The information contained in this file can be transformed into HTML using XSLT, without the need to build the DOM structure manually. For starters, you need an XSLT document, `books.xsl`, which begins with an XML declaration and a root element:

```
<?xml version="1.0" encoding="UTF-8" ?>

<xsl:stylesheet version="1.0" xmlns:xsl="http://www.w3.org/1999/XSL/Transform">
<xsl:output method="html" omit-xml-declaration="yes" indent="yes" />

</xsl:stylesheet>
```

The document element of an XSLT document is `<xsl:stylesheet/>`. In this element, the XSL version is specified and the `xsl` namespace is declared. This required information determines the behavior of the XSLT processor; without it, an error will be thrown. The `xsl` prefix is also important, as this allows all XSL directives to be visibly and logically separate from other code in the document.

The `<xsl:output/>` element defines the format of the resulting output. In this example, the resulting transformation results in HTML data, with the XML declaration omitted and the elements indented. You can specify the format to be plain text, XML, or HTML data.

Just like any application, a transformation must have an entry point. XSLT is a template-based language, and the processor works on an XML document by matching template rules. In this example, the first element to match is the root of the XML document. This is done by using the `<xsl:template/>` directive. *Directives* tell the processor to execute a specific function. The `<xsl:template/>` directive creates a template that is used when the pattern in the `match` attribute is matched:

```
<?xml version="1.0" encoding="UTF-8" ?>

<xsl:stylesheet version="1.0" xmlns:xsl="http://www.w3.org/1999/XSL/Transform">
<xsl:output method="html" omit-xml-declaration="yes" indent="yes" />

<xsl:template match="/">

<html>
    <head>
        <link rel="stylesheet" type="text/css" href="books.css" />
        <title>XSL Transformations</title>
    </head>
```

```
        <body>
            <xsl:apply-templates />
        </body>
    </html>

</xsl:template>

</xsl:stylesheet>
```

The `match` attribute takes an XPath expression to select the proper XML node. In this case, it is the root element of `books.xml` (the XPath expression `/` always selects the root node of the document). Inside of the template, you'll notice HTML elements. These elements are a part of the transformation's output. Inside of the `<body/>` element, another XSL directive is found. The `<xsl:apply-templates />` element tells the processor to start parsing all templates within the context of the document element, which brings the next template into play:

```
<?xml version="1.0" encoding="UTF-8" ?>
<xsl:stylesheet version="1.0" xmlns:xsl="http://www.w3.org/1999/XSL/Transform">
<xsl:output method="html" omit-xml-declaration="yes" indent="yes" />

<xsl:template match="/">

<html>
    <head>
        <link rel="stylesheet" type="text/css" href="books.css" />
        <title>XSL Transformations</title>
    </head>
    <body>
        <xsl:apply-templates />
    </body>
</html>

</xsl:template>

<xsl:template match="book">
    <div class="bookContainer">
        <xsl:variable name="varIsbn" select="@isbn" />
        <xsl:variable name="varTitle" select="title" />
        <img class="bookCover" alt="{$varTitle}" src="images/{$varIsbn}.png" />
        <div class="bookContent">
            <h3><xsl:value-of select="$varTitle" /></h3>
            Written by: <xsl:value-of select="author" /><br />
            ISBN #<xsl:value-of select="$varIsbn" />
            <div class="bookPublisher"><xsl:value-of select="publisher" /></div>
        </div>
    </div>
</xsl:template>

</xsl:stylesheet>
```

This new template matches all `<book/>` elements, so when the processor reaches each `<book/>` in the XML document, this template is used. The first two XSL directives in this template are `<xsl:variable/>`, which define variables.

Variables in XSL are primarily used in XPath expressions or attributes (where elements cannot be used without breaking XML syntax). The `<xsl:variable/>` element has two attributes: `name` and `select`. As you may have guessed, the `name` attribute sets the name of the variable. The `select` attribute specifies an XPath expression and stores the matching value(s) in the variable. After the initial declaration, variables are referenced to with the `$` sign (so, the variable defined as `varIsbn` is later referenced as `$varIsbn`).

The first variable, `$varIsbn`, is assigned the value of the `<book/>` element's `isbn` attribute. The second, `$varTitle`, is assigned the value of the `<title/>` element. These two pieces of information are used in the attributes of the HTML `<img/>` element. To output variables in attributes, you surround the variable name in braces:

```
<img class="bookCover" alt="{$title}" src="images/{$isbn}.png" />
```

Without the braces, the output would use the string literals `"$varTitle"` and `"$varIsbn"` instead.

> **Using variables in attributes of XSL directives, such as the** `select` **and** `name` **attributes to name a few, is the exception to this rule. Using curly braces in these types of attributes will cause an error, and the document transformation will fail.**

The remainder of XSL directives in this example are `<xsl:value-of/>` elements. These elements retrieve the value of the matched variable or node according to the `select` attribute. The `select` attribute behaves in the same way as the `select` attributes of `<xsl:variable/>` do: they take an XPath expression and select the node or variable that matches that expression. The first instance of `<xsl:value-of/>` in this template references the `$varTitle` variable (notice the lack of braces), so the value of the variable is used. Next, the value of the `<author/>` element is used; the same with `$varTitle` and `<publisher/>`.

In order for an XML document to transform in the browser, it must have a stylesheet specified. In `books.xml`, add the following line immediately after the XML declaration:

```
<?xml-stylesheet type="text/xsl" href="books.xsl"?>
```

This tells the XML processor to apply the stylesheet `books.xsl` to this document. Viewing this modified XML document in a web browser will no longer show the XML structure, but it will show the resulting transformation to HTML. However, using this directive won't work through JavaScript. For that, you'll need to use some special objects.

XSLT in IE

There are two ways to transform an XML document in IE, both of which require the use of MSXML. Starting with version 3.0, MSXML has full support for XSLT 1.0. If you don't have Windows XP or IE 6, it is time to upgrade. You can find the latest MSXML downloads at http://msdn.microsoft.com/XML/XMLDownloads/.

The first and easiest method loads both the XML and XSLT documents into separate XML DOM objects:

```
var oXmlDom = zXmlDom.createDocument();
var oXslDom = zXmlDom.createDocument();

oXmlDom.async = false;
oXslDom.async = false;

oXmlDom.load("books.xml");
oXslDom.load("books.xsl");
```

When both documents are loaded, you call the `transformNode()` method to start the transformation:

```
var sResults = oXmlDom.transformNode(oXslDom);
```

The `transformNode()` method takes an XML DOM object as an argument (in this case, the XSL document) and returns the transformed data as a string. But you don't have to call `transformNode()` at the document level; it can be called from any element in the XML document:

```
var sResults = oXmlDom.documentElement.firstChild.transformNode(oXslDom);
```

The `transformNode()` method will transform only the element it was called from and its children. In this example, the first `<book/>` element is transformed, as shown in Figure 6-3.

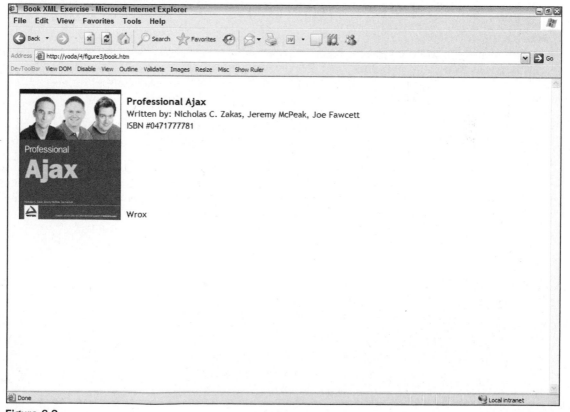

Figure 6-3

The second method of transformations in IE is a bit more involved, but it also gives you more control and features. This process involves creating multiple objects in the MSXML library. The first step in this somewhat lengthy process is to create a thread-safe XML DOM object, which the XSL stylesheet is loaded into:

```
var oXmlDom = zXmlDom.createDocument();
oXmlDom.async = false;
oXmlDom.load("books.xml");
```

```
var oXslDom = new ActiveXObject("Msxml2.FreeThreadedDOMDocument.3.0");
oXslDom.async = false;
oXslDom.load("books.xsl");
```

The `FreeThreadedDOMDocument` class is yet another ActiveX class and a part of the MSXML library. You must use the `FreeThreadedDomDocument` class to create `XSLTemplate` objects, which this example does (the next example shows the creation of a `XSLTemplate` object). In early versions of MSXML, every call to the `transformNode()` method forced a recompile of the XSL stylesheet slowing the transformation process considerably. With a `FreeThreadedDOMDocument`, the compiled stylesheet is cached and ready to use until it's removed from memory.

After the XML DOM object creation, you must create another ActiveX object, an XSL template:

```
var oXslTemplate = new ActiveXObject("Msxml2.XSLTemplate.3.0");
oXslTemplate.stylesheet = oXslDom;
```

The `XSLTemplate` class is used to cache XSL stylesheets and create an `XSLProcessor`; so, after the template is created, the XSL document is assigned to the `XSLTemplate` class's `stylesheet` property, which caches and loads the XSL stylesheet.

The next step in this process is to create an `XSLProcessor`, which is created by calling the `createProcessor()` method of the `XSLTemplate` class:

```
var oXslProcessor = oXslTemplate.createProcessor();
oXslProcessor.input = oXmlDom;
```

After creation of the processor, its `input` property is assigned `oXmlDom`, the XML DOM object containing the XML document to transform. At this point, everything the processor requires is in place, so all that remains is the actual transformation and the retrieval of the output:

```
oXslProcessor.transform();
document.body.innerHTML = oXslProcessor.output;
```

Unlike `transformNodes()`, the `transform()` method does not return the resulting output as a string. To retrieve the output of the transformation, use the `output` property of the `XSLProcessor` object. This entire process requires much more coding than the `transformNode()` method and yields the same result. So, why use this process?

MSXML provides a few extra methods that can be used in these transformations. The first is `addObject()`. This method adds a JavaScript object to the stylesheet, and can even call methods and output property values in the transformed document. Consider the following object:

```
var oBook = {
    propertyOne : "My Current Books",
    methodOne   : function () {
        alert("Welcome to my Book List");
        return "";
    }
};
```

What if you wanted to use this information in the transformation? Using the addObject() method, you can pass this information into the XSLT stylesheet, passing in two arguments: the oBook object and a namespace URI to identify it. So, to add this object with a namespace URI of "http://my-object", you could do the following:

```
var oXmlDom = zXmlDom.createDocument();
oXmlDom.async = false;
oXmlDom.load("books.xml");

var oXslDom = new ActiveXObject("Msxml2.FreeThreadedDOMDocument.3.0");
oXslDom.async = false;
oXslDom.load("books.xsl");

var oXslTemplate = new ActiveXObject("Msxml2.XSLTemplate.3.0");
oXslTemplate.stylesheet = oXslDom;

var oXslProcessor = oXslTemplate.createProcessor();
oXslProcessor.input = oXmlDom;

oXslProcessor.addObject(oBook, "http://my-object");

oXslProcessor.transform();
document.body.innerHTML = oXslProcessor.output;
```

The oBook object is now passed to the XSLProcessor, meaning that the XSLT stylesheet can use it. Now, the XSL document must be changed to look for this object and use its information. The first requirement is to add a new namespace to the root element, <xsl:stylesheet/>. This namespace will match the one used in addObject():

```
<xsl:stylesheet version="1.0" xmlns:xsl="http://www.w3.org/1999/XSL/Transform"
    xmlns:bookObj="http://my-object">
```

The prefix bookObj will be used to access this information. Now that the namespace and prefix are ready to go, some <xsl:value-of/> elements should be added to the document to retrieve the object's members:

```
<xsl:template match="/">

<html>
    <head>
        <link rel="stylesheet" type="text/css" href="books.css" />
    </head>
    <body>
```

```
            <xsl:value-of select="bookObj:methodOne()" />
            <div align="center">
                <b><xsl:value-of select="bookObj:get-propertyOne()" /></b>
            </div>
            <xsl:apply-templates />
        </body>
    </html>

    </xsl:template>
```

Remember that the <xsl:value-of/> XSL directive retrieves the value of an element, or in this case, an object. The first <xsl:value-of/> directive retrieves (or calls) methodOne(), which sends an alert welcoming the user to the page. The second <xsl:value-of/> directive is similar to the first, except that it retrieves the value of the propertyOne property of the oBook object. When the transformed output is displayed in the browser, the user will see the phrase My Current Books at the top of the page.

> When using an object in transformations, all properties and methods must return a value that the XSLProcessor can understand. String, number, and Boolean values all work as expected; returning any other value that cannot be coerced into an XSL data type will throw a JavaScript error when the transformation executes.

The next useful feature of the XSLProcessor is the addParameter() method. Unlike sending an object into a transformation, parameters are a standard part of XSLT. Parameters are passed to the XSL stylesheet and used as variables. To specify a parameter, pass the name and its value, like this:

```
var oXslProcessor = oXslTemplate.createProcessor();
oXslProcessor.input = oXmlDom;
oXslProcessor.addParameter("message", "My Book List");
```

This code adds the "message" parameter to the XSLProcessor. When the XSL transformation executes, the processor uses the value of the parameter, "My Book List", and places it in the according location. Parameters in XSL use the <xsl:param/> directive:

```
<xsl:param name="message" />
```

Notice that the name attribute matches the name passed in addParameter(). This parameter receives the value "My Book List" which is retrieved using the variable syntax you learned earlier:

```
<xsl:value-of select="$message" />
```

In this example, the <xsl:value-of/> directive retrieves the parameters value. The updated XSL stylesheet would look like this:

```
<xsl:stylesheet version="1.0" xmlns:xsl="http://www.w3.org/1999/XSL/Transform">

<xsl:param name="message" />

<xsl:template match="/">
```

```html
<html>
    <head>
        <link rel="stylesheet" type="text/css" href="books.css" />
    </head>
    <body>
        <xsl:value-of select="$message" />
        <xsl:apply-templates />
    </body>
</html>

</xsl:template>
```

The updated stylesheet adds two new lines of code. The first is the addition of the `<xsl:param/>` directive, and the second is the `<xsl:value-of/>` directive that retrieves the value of the parameter. Parameter declarations can exist anywhere in the XSL document. This code shows the parameter declaration at the top of the document, but you are not limited to this location.

One final feature of using an `XSLProcessor` is its speed; it compiles the XSL stylesheet, so subsequent transformations using the same stylesheet result in faster transformations (compared to using `transformNode()`). To do this, use the `reset()` method of the `XSLProcessor` object. This method clears the `input` and `output` properties but not the `stylesheet` property. This readies the processor for the next transformation with the same stylesheet.

XSLT in Other Browsers

Like XML and XPath, the implementation of XSLT transformations in non-IE browsers varies from the IE implementation. These browsers do implement an `XSLTProcessor` class to perform transformations, but the similarities end there.

> **Like XPath, Safari currently doesn't support XSLT transformations.**

The first step in performing a transformation is to load the XML and XSL documents into a DOM object:

```javascript
var oXmlDom = zXmlDom.createDocument();
var oXslDom = zXmlDom.createDocument();

oXmlDom.async = false;
oXslDom.async = false;

oXmlDom.load("books.xml");
oXslDom.load("books.xsl");
```

The `XSLTProcessor` class exposes the `importStylesheet()` method, which takes an XML DOM object containing the XSLT document as an argument:

```javascript
var oXsltProcessor = new XSLTProcessor();
oXsltProcessor.importStylesheet(oXslDom);
```

Last, the transformation methods are called. There are two of these methods: `transformToDocument()` and `transformToFragment()`. The `transformToDocument()` method takes an XML DOM object as an argument and returns a new XML DOM document containing the transformation. Normally, this is the method you want to use:

```
var oNewDom = oXsltProcessor.transformToDocument(oXmlDom);
```

The resulting DOM object can be used like any other XML DOM object. You can select certain nodes with XPath, traverse the node structure with properties and methods, or even use it in another transformation.

The `transformToFragment()` method returns a document fragment, as its name suggests, to append to another DOM document. This method takes two arguments: the first is the XML DOM object you want to transform, and the second is the DOM object you intend to append the result to:

```
var oFragment = oXsltProcessor.transformToFragment(oXmlDom, document);
document.body.appendChild(oFragment);
```

In this example, the resulting document fragment is appended to the body of the `document` object. Note that you can append the resulting fragment to any node within the DOM object passed to the `transformToFragment()` method.

But what if you wanted a string returned as the result of transformation like the `transformNode()` method implemented by Microsoft? You could use the `XMLSerializer` class you learned of earlier. Just pass the transformation result to the `serializeToString()` method:

```
var oSerializer = new XMLSerializer();
var str = oSerializer.serializeToString(oNewDom);
```

When using the zXml library, this is simplified by using the `xml` property:

```
var str = oFragment.xml;
```

The `XSLTProcessor` class also enables you to set parameters to pass to the XSL stylesheet. The `setParameter()` method facilitates this functionality; it accepts three arguments: the namespace URI, the parameter name, and the value to assign the parameter. For example:

```
oXsltProcessor.importStylesheet(oXslDom);
```

```
oXsltProcessor.setParameter(null, "message", "My Book List");
var oNewDom = oXsltProcessor.transformToDocument(oXmlDom);
```

In this example, the parameter message is assigned the value `"My Book List"`. The value of `null` is passed for the namespace URI, which allows the parameter to be used without having to specify a prefix and corresponding namespace URI in the stylesheet:

```
<xsl:param name="message" />
```

The `setParameter()` method must be called before the calling of `transformToDocument()` or `transformToFragment()`, or else the parameter value will not be used in the transformation.

Cross-Browser XSLT

In the previous sections, you've seen how the zXml library makes handling XML data across both main platforms easier. Now you will use the library to perform XSLT transformations. There is only one method for XSLT in the library: `transformToText()`. This method, which returns text from a transformation, takes two arguments: the XML document to transform and the XSL document:

```
var sResult = zXslt.transformToText(oXmlDom, oXslDom);
```

As the name of the method suggests, the returned result is a string. You can then add the result of the transformation (`sResult`) to an HTML document:

```
var oDiv = document.getElementById("transformedData");
oDiv.innerHTML = sResult;
```

This is perhaps the simplest object in the zXml library.

Best Picks Revisited

Imagine once again that you run an online bookstore. Your visitors like the Best Picks feature you implemented, but you start to receive feedback that they want the picks of the previous week as well. You decide to roll with an Ajax solution.

Using XHR, the browser retrieves the book list and the request's `responseText` is loaded into an XML DOM object. The stylesheet also is loaded into its own XML DOM object, and the XML data from the book list is transformed into HTML, which is then written to the page. To provide some usability, you provide a link in the upper-right corner to change from one list to another.

The first step in this solution is to retrieve the XML file with XHR. This is the beginning of the code and the entry point for the mini-application, so you'll encapsulate the code in a function called `init()`:

```
function init(sFilename) {
    var oReq = zXmlHttp.createRequest();
    oReq.onreadystatechange = function () {
        if (oReq.readyState == 4) {
            // only if "OK"
            if (oReq.status == 200) {
                transformXml(oReq.responseText);
            }
        }
    };
    oReq.open("GET", sFilename, true);
    oReq.send();
}
```

The `init()` function accepts one argument: the file name of the XML file to load. For cross-browser compatibility (not to mention easier coding for you), you create an XHR object using the zXml library. This is an asynchronous request, so the `readyState` property must be checked using the `onreadystatechange` event handler. When the request returns as OK, the `responseText` is sent to the `transformXml()` function:

```
function transformXml(sResponseText) {
    var oXmlDom = zXmlDom.createDocument();
    oXmlDom.async = false;
    oXmlDom.loadXML(sResponseText);

    var oXslDom = zXmlDom.createDocument();
    oXslDom.async = false;
    oXslDom.load("books.xsl");

    var str = zXslt.transformToText(oXmlDom,oXslDom);
    document.getElementById("divBookList").innerHTML = str;
}
```

Calling transformXml() loads the passed response text into an XML DOM object using the loadXML() method. The XSL stylesheet is also loaded, and both objects are passed to the transformToText() method in the zXml library. The transformation's result, a string, is then added to an element in the document via the innerHTML property. As a result of this function, this week's book list is visible to the user.

A good portion of the code is written, but you still lack the list-changing feature. To facilitate this ability, another function needs writing, but first, the application needs to know what list to load as the user clicks the link. This is easily handled by Boolean variable called bIsThisWeek. When this week's book list is loaded, bIsThisWeek becomes true; otherwise, it's false. Since this week's list is already loaded, bIsThisWeek is set to true:

```
var bIsThisWeek = true;
```

The link that the user clicks to change the list uses the onclick event, so the next function will handle that event:

```
function changeList() {
    var aChanger = document.getElementById("aChanger");

    if (bIsThisWeek) {
        aChanger.innerHTML = "This Week's Picks";
        init("lastweekbooks.xml");
        bIsThisWeek = false;
    } else {
        aChanger.innerHTML = "Last Week's Picks";
        init("thisweekbooks.xml");
        bIsThisWeek = true;
    }
    return false;
}
```

In this code, the link (aChanger) is retrieved with the getElementById() method. The variable bIsThisWeek is checked. According to its value, the proper list is loaded by sending the file name to the init() function. This retrieves the new list, transforms the data, and writes it to the page. Also, note that the link text changes to cue users of what happens the next time they click the link. The bIsThisWeek variable also changes so that the correct list is loaded the next time the user clicks the link. Last, the function returns false. Since this function is an event handler for a link, returning any other value would cause the link to behave as a link and could take the user away from the application.

Finally, you can complete the mini application with the HTML, and here is the entire document:

```
<!DOCTYPE html PUBLIC "-//W3C//DTD XHTML 1.1//EN"
          "http://www.w3.org/TR/xhtml11/DTD/xhtml11.dtd">
<html xmlns="http://www.w3.org/1999/xhtml" >
<head>
    <title>Book XML Exercise</title>
    <link rel="stylesheet" type="text/css" href="books.css" />
    <script type="text/javascript" src="zxml.js"></script>
    <script type="text/javascript">
        function init(sFilename) {
            var oReq = zXmlHttp.createRequest();
            oReq.onreadystatechange = function () {
                if (oReq.readyState == 4) {
                    // only if "OK"
                    if (oReq.status == 200) {
                        transformXml(oReq.responseText);
                    }
                }
            };
            oReq.open("GET", sFilename, true);
            oReq.send();
        }

        function transformXml(sResponseText) {
            var oXmlDom = zXmlDom.createDocument();
            oXmlDom.async = false;
            oXmlDom.loadXML(sResponseText);

            var oXslDom = zXmlDom.createDocument();
            oXslDom.async = false;
            oXslDom.load("books.xsl");

            var str = zXslt.transformToText(oXmlDom,oXslDom);
            document.getElementById("divBookList").innerHTML = str;
        }

        var bIsThisWeek = true;

        function changeList() {
            var aChanger = document.getElementById("aChanger");
            if (bIsThisWeek) {
                aChanger.innerHTML = "This Week's Picks";
                init("lastweekbooks.xml");
                bIsThisWeek = false;
            } else {
                aChanger.innerHTML = "Last Week's Picks";
                init("thisweekbooks.xml");
                bIsThisWeek = true;
            }
            return false;
        }
    </script>
</head>
```

```
<body onload="init('thisweekbooks.xml')">
    <a id="aChanger" href="#" onclick="changeList();">Last Week's Picks</a>
    <div id="divBookList"></div>
</body>
</html>
```

To run this mini-application, you must run it from a web server because XHR is used. Any web server software will work fine. Just place this HTML file, the zXml library, and the CSS file into a directory called `booklists` on your web server. Then fire up your browser and point it to `http://localhost/booklists/book.htm`.

Summary

In this chapter, you learned how to create and traverse the XML DOM objects in the major browsers of today, as well as the differences between IE and non-IE implementations. You once again used the cross-browser XML library zXml, which enables you to create, traverse, and manipulate XML DOM objects easily using a single interface. You also learned how to load XML data using JavaScript and output it to the page.

In the second section, a brief introduction to XPath showed you the power the language offers for XML documents. You learned how IE and the other browsers implement XPath and namespace support and how they differ from each other. To ease this difficulty, the zXPath object of the zXml library was introduced, again providing one interface to select desired nodes easily for both browsers.

Finally, you learned about XSLT transformations and how to perform them using MSXML and the `XSLTProcessor` class. Although the two interfaces have a few things in common, another cross-browser object of the zXml library was introduced to smooth out the wrinkles: the zXslt object, which allows XSLT transformations to be performed on both platforms with one method call.

7

Syndication with RSS and Atom

The introduction of XML ushered in a new era of information sharing. Previously, data sharing was difficult at best as companies used proprietary transmission protocols and data formats that were unavailable to the public. The idea of transmitting information on a web site using anything other than HTML was a strange, if not unheard of, idea. But this changed in 1998 when Microsoft introduced Internet Explorer 4.0 with a new feature called Active Channels. Built upon the Microsoft-developed Channel Definition Format (CDF), Active Channels allowed web site content to be transmitted (or *syndicated*) to users' desktops using the bundled Active Desktop. The problem with Active Channels, however, was its poor support for the everyday user. Anyone could make a channel from scratch, but the industry lacked tools to create and manage CDF files easily. The primary users of Active Channels, big media companies, pushed users away with excessive ads that increased the amount of bandwidth the channels used. Additionally, there was little demand for or perceived value in using Active Channels. The whole concept of syndication seemed to have died with Active Channels and the failure of CDF to reach recommendation status from the World Wide Web Consortium. Then came RSS.

RSS

In March of 1999, Netscape launched the My Netscape portal, a single place for users to visit for all of their news. The idea was simple: to pull information from any number of news sources and display it on My Netscape. To facilitate this idea, Dan Libby of Netscape Communications developed an XML data format based on the Resource Description Framework (RDF) called RDF Site Summary (RSS). This format would later become known as RSS 0.9.

Shortly after the introduction of RSS 0.9, Dave Winer of Userland Software contacted Libby regarding the RSS 0.9 format. Winer had developed an XML format to use with his site, ScriptingNews, and believed that it and RSS 0.9 could be combined with it and simplified to make a better, more usable, format. In July of 1999, Libby released a prototype of the new Rich Site Summary (also abbreviated as RSS), which became RSS 0.91. My Netscape then began using RSS 0.91 and continued to do so until 2001, when support for external RSS feeds was dropped. Netscape soon lost interest in RSS and left it without an owner. What would follow splintered the RSS format into two different versions.

A mailing list of developers and other interested parties formed in order to continue the development of RSS. This group, called RSS-DEV (http://groups.yahoo.com/group/rss-dev), produced a specification called RSS 1.0, in December 2000. RSS 1.0 was based on the original RDF Site Summary (RSS 0.9) and sought to extend it by modularizing the original 0.9 version. These modules are namespaces that can be created by anyone, allowing new functionality to be added without changing the specification. It's important to note that RSS 1.0 is a descendant of RSS 0.9 but not related to RSS 0.91.

At the same time, Winer declared himself the owner of RSS and continued to develop his own version, releasing what he deemed RSS 2.0 (Really Simple Syndication). This new RSS format was based on RSS 0.91, the version that Winer and Libby developed together. The emphasis for RSS 2.0 was the simplicity of the format. When Winer ended up working at Harvard, he assigned ownership of RSS 2.0 to Harvard's Berkman Center for the Internet & Society, which now manages and publishes the specification at http://blogs.law.harvard.edu/tech/rss. RSS 2.0 is the most widely used RSS format today.

Today, the term RSS encompasses three different versions of the RSS format: RSS 0.91, RSS 1.0, and RSS 2.0.

RSS 0.91

RSS 0.91 is based upon Document Type Declarations (DTDs) and was possibly the most popular RSS version until the release of RSS 2.0. Some statistics show RSS 0.91 capturing 52 percent of the syndication market in 2001, with a steady increase until the introduction of 2.0. Only a handful of 0.91 feeds were in use as of 2006, but RSS 2.0 owes much of its current success to RSS 0.91.

RSS 0.91's DTD lists 24 elements (14 more than RSS 0.9); it is easily read by humans and machines alike. Here's a simple 0.91 example:

```
<?xml version="1.0" encoding="UTF-8" ?>

<!DOCTYPE rss PUBLIC "-//Netscape Communications//DTD RSS 0.91//EN"
    "http://my.netscape.com/publish/formats/rss-0.91.dtd">

<rss version="0.91">
    <channel>
        <title>My Revenge</title>
        <link>http://sithboys.com</link>
        <description>Dedicated to having our revenge</description>
        <item>
            <title>At last!</title>
            <link>http://sithboys.com/atlast.htm</link>
            <description>
                At last we will reveal ourselves to the Jedi. At last we
                will have our revenge.
            </description>
        </item>
    </channel>
</rss>
```

Like Microsoft's CDF, RSS 0.91 (and 2.0, for that matter) feeds are channel-based; a defining feature of the two RSS formats is the inclusion of all data inside the `<channel/>` element. All site information, (the `<title/>`, `<link/>`, `<description/>`, and so forth elements), as well as the `<item/>` elements, are contained by `<channel/>`. This is in stark contrast to RSS 1.0.

RSS 1.0

RSS 1.0 is a departure from the 0.91 standard and follows the RDF format of 0.9. RSS 1.0 is far more verbose than other versions but is also more extensible. This extensibility makes it an attractive format for developers of RDF-based applications.

Although it maintains some resemblance to RSS 0.91, RSS 1.0 is structurally different:

```
<?xml version="1.0"?>

<rdf:RDF xmlns:rdf="http://www.w3.org/1999/02/22-rdf-syntax-ns#"
    xmlns="http://purl.org/rss/1.0/">

    <channel rdf:about="http:// sithboys.com/about.htm">
        <title>My Revenge</title>
        <link> http://sithboys.com</link>
        <description>
            Dedicated to having our revenge
        </description>
        <image rdf:resource="http://sithboys.com/logo.jpg" />
        <items>
            <rdf:Seq>
                <rdf:li resource="http://sithboys.com/atlast.htm" />
            </rdf:Seq>
        </items>
        <textinput rdf:resource="http://sithboys.com/search/" />
    </channel>

    <image rdf:about="http://sithboys.com/logo.jpg">
        <title>The Logo of the Sith</title>
        <link>http://sithboys.com/</link>
        <url>http://sithboys.com/logo.jpg</url>
    </image>

    <item rdf:about="http://sithboys.com/atlast.htm">
        <title>At last!</title>
        <link>http://sithboys.com/atlast.htm</link>
        <description>
            At last we will reveal ourselves to the Jedi. At last we will have
            our revenge.
        </description>
    </item>
</rdf:RDF>
```

The `<item/>` elements outside of `<channel/>` contain the data of each entry; on the other hand, the `<items/>` element inside of `<channel/>` contains a list of values (the `<rdf:Seq/>` element) that reference the `<item/>` elements outside of `<channel/>`. As you can see, it is far more complex than RSS 0.91, and although RSS 1.0 has gained a following, it does not have the popularity that the other formats enjoy.

RSS 1.0 is not DTD-based like version 0.91, so it is not necessary to have one in the document.

RSS 2.0

RSS 2.0 almost exactly mirrors RSS 0.91 but introduces some new elements, such as `<author/>`, while allowing modularized extensions like RSS 1.0. To further simplify things, RSS 2.0 also does away with the required DTD. Given the simplicity it has inherited from RSS 0.91, and the extensibility similar to RSS 1.0, it is no wonder that RSS 2.0 is the most-used RSS format at the time of this writing.

The following is an example of a basic RSS 2.0 document:

```xml
<?xml version="1.0" encoding="UTF-8" ?>

<rss version="2.0">
    <channel>
        <title>My Revenge</title>
        <description>Dedicated to having our revenge</description>
        <link>http://sithboys.com</link>
        <item>
            <title>At last!</title>
            <link>http://sithboys.com/atlast.htm</link>
            <author>DarthMaul@sithboys.com</author>
            <description>
                At last we will reveal ourselves to the Jedi. At last we will have
                our revenge.
            </description>
        </item>
    </channel>
</rss>
```

Atom

Atom is the newest entry on the syndication scene. Since its inception in mid-2003, Atom has received quite a bit of coverage and usage. Atom, unlike RSS, is a strict specification. One of the problems of the RSS specification is the lack of information on how a developer handles HTML markup in its elements. Atom's specification addresses this issue and gives developers strict rules they must follow, as well as a host of new features, enabling developers to choose the content type of an element and specify attributes that designate how a specific element should be handled. With such features, it is no wonder powerhouses like Google and Movable Type are getting behind Atom.

Atom resembles RSS in the sense that they both have the same data constructs. Most of Atom's element names differ from RSS, and the document structure is slightly different:

```xml
<?xml version="1.0" encoding="iso-8859-1"?>

<feed version="1.0" xmlns="http://www.w3.org/2005/Atom" xml:lang="en">
    <title>My Revenge</title>
    <link rel="alternate" type="text/html" href="http://sithboys.com" />
    <modified>2006-06-30T15:51:21-06:00</modified>
```

```
        <tagline>Dedicated to having our revenge</tagline>
        <id>tag:sithboys.com</id>
        <copyright>Copyright (c) 2006</copyright>
        <entry>
            <title>At last!</title>
            <link rel="alternate" type="text/html" href="
                http://sithboys.com/atlast.htm" />
            <modified>2005-06-30T15:51:21-06:00</modified>
            <issued>2005-06-30T15:51:21-06:00</issued>
            <id>tag:sithboys.com/atlast</id>
            <author>
                <name>Darth Maul</name>
            </author>
            <content type="text/html" xml:lang="en"
              xml:base="http://sithboys.com">
                At last we will reveal ourselves to the Jedi. At last we will
                have our revenge.
            </content>
        </entry>
    </feed>
```

According to the Atom specification, all elements in the Atom format must reside in the `http://www.w3`
`.org/2005/Atom` namespace, or else many parsers will not parse the feed. All site-defining elements
exist as direct children to the document element. An Atom feed can also contain many `<entry/>`
elements, resembling the `<item/>` elements of an RSS feed.

XParser

News aggregation sites using syndication formats are gaining popularity as the formats become more
widely used. Many sites use server-side logic to parse RSS and Atom feeds, displaying them in some
sort of user-friendly format. However, it may be necessary to perform the same functions on the client-
side using JavaScript. This is where `XParser` comes in.

`XParser` is a JavaScript library that parses RSS and Atom feeds into JavaScript objects, making the feed's
data easy to access in web applications. Its primary goal is to provide an interface for JavaScript developers to quickly access a feed's most important elements. The code is object–oriented, broken into
abstract classes that the Atom- and RSS-specific classes inherit from. Such a design allows the different
feed types to be parsed according to their specific differences while leaving room for extensions. This
section explains how the `XParser` code is designed and implemented.

The xparser Namespace

XParser begins with the `xparser` namespace. A namespace contains the library's code in one simple
package and protects the contained code from external naming conflicts. Of course, JavaScript does not
implement an official namespace construct; however, you can simulate the behavior of a namespace
quite easily with a simple object.

```
var xparser = {};
```

This code defines the xparser object using object literal notation. It is this object that holds data, methods, and classes for XParser.

Because the script deals with different types of feeds, it needs some way to identify the feed it is parsing. This is easily accomplished with the feedType object:

```
xparser.feedType = {
    rss     : 1,
    atom    : 2
};
```

The feedType object contains two properties (rss and atom), which are assigned numeric values. These numeric constants allow assignment and comparison of a feed's format.

Retrieving the Data

To retrieve data from a specific XML node, the XParser library depends upon the FeedNode class. As its name implies, it represents a DOM node contained in the feed and is responsible for accessing and retrieving the node's value. The class accepts one argument, the XML node:

```
xparser.FeezdNode = function (oNode) {
    this.value = (oNode && (oNode.text || oNode.getText())) || null;
};
```

FeedNode exposes one property called value, which either contains the node's text or a null value.

The text property does not exist in Firefox's DOM, and getText() doesn't exist in Opera. To gain this functionality, XParser uses the zXml library introduced in Chapter 2, which extends Firefox's and Opera's DOM.

The Abstract Classes

As stated earlier, XParser is responsible for parsing two types of feeds, RSS and Atom. While there are many ways to accomplish this, the best is to have one class responsible for parsing each of the two different feed types. Despite their differences, the feed types share some similarities, and finding that common ground can save time and code. To facilitate this design, XParser contains two abstract classes: BaseFeed and BaseItem.

The BaseFeed Class

The BaseFeed class represents the feed as a whole, defining several properties that each feed uses to describe itself. The constructor accepts three arguments: the feed type (1 or 2, as defined in the FeedType object), a function pointer to call when parsing is complete, and the scope in which the call back function should execute. Here's the code for the BaseFeed class:

```
xparser.BaseFeed = function (iFeedType, fpCallBack, oCallBackScope ) {
    this.type           = iFeedType || null;
    this.title          = null;
    this.link           = null;
    this.description    = null;
```

```
        this.copyright      = null;
        this.generator      = null;
        this.modified       = null;
        this.author         = null;
        this.items          = [];

        this.callBack       =
            (typeof fpCallBack == "function") ? fpCallBack : function () {};
        this.callBackScope  =
            (typeof oCallBackScope == "object") ? oCallBackScope : this;
};
```

The first line assigns the feed type, which defaults to `null` if no argument is passed to the constructor. This ensures that no errors are thrown when prototype chaining subclasses (discussed later).

The `title`, `link`, `description`, `copyright`, `generator`, `modified`, and `author` properties are generalized properties that both Atom and RSS feeds contain. These properties, at some point, will hold `FeedNode` objects. The `items` array represents the feed's `<rss:item/>` or `<atom:entry/>` elements. The final four lines of the `BaseFeed` constructor assign the default values for the `callback` and `callBackScope` properties. The former defaults to an empty function, while the latter defaults to the `BaseFeed` instance.

This class exposes a method called `parse()`, which accepts a context node, an associative array (object) of property and element names as keys and values, respectively, and an associate array of namespace prefixes and namespace URIs as arguments:

```
xparser.BaseFeed.prototype = {
    parse : function (oContextNode, oElements, oNamespaces) {

    }
};
```

With the information provided, it's possible to evaluate XPath expressions to extract the desired data. To do this, loop through `oElements` and use the `zXPath` class to perform the XPath evaluation:

```
xparser.BaseFeed.prototype = {
    parse : function (oContextNode, oElements, oNamespaces  ) {
        //Loop through the keys
        for (var sProperty in oElements) {
            if (oElement.hasOwnProperty(sProperty)) {
                //Create FeedNode objects with the node
                //returned from the XPath evaluation
                this[sProperty] = new xparser.FeedNode(
                    zXPath.selectSingleNode(
                        oContextNode,
                        oElements[sProperty],
                        oNamespaces
                    )
                );
            }
        }
    }
};
```

The associative array passed to the oElements parameter contains "title", "link", "description", "copyright", "generator", "modified", and "author" as the keys. These keys correspond directly to the properties of the BaseFeed class. This provides a quick and easy way to assign values to these properties.

> **It's important to note that BaseFeed is an abstract class and as such should not be instantiated directly. These types of classes are designed to be inherited from; therefore, only the child classes need to worry about providing the information in the correct format.**

The BaseItem Class

The BaseItem class follows the same pattern. Like the BaseFeed class, BaseItem's constructor initializes its properties as null:

```
xparser.BaseItem = function () {
    this.title          = null;
    this.author         = null;
    this.link           = null;
    this.description     = null;
    this.date           = null;
};
```

These properties are a generalized equivalent to the feed's item (or entry) elements. Also, like the BaseFeed class, this class exposes a parse() method, which is implemented similarly:

```
xparser.BaseItem.prototype = {
    parse : function (oContextNode, oElements, oNamespaces  ) {
        //Loop through the keys
        for (var sProperty in oElements) {
            if (oElements.hasOwnProperty(sProperty)) {
                //Create FeedNode objects with the node
                //returned from the XPath evaluation
                this[sProperty] = new xparser.FeedNode(
                    zXPath.selectSingleNode(
                        oContextNode,
                        oElements[sProperty],
                        oNamespaces
                    )
                );
            }
        }
    }
};
```

These two classes provide a basis that the RSS and Atom classes can inherit from. Also, this design future-proofs the library, allowing easy addition of new feed types (provided any new feed type uses a compatible format).

Parsing RSS Feeds

The RSSFeed class is in charge of parsing RSS feeds. The constructor accepts three arguments: the root element of the XML document, the callback function, and the scope in which the callback function should run:

```
xparser.RssFeed = function (oRootNode, fpCallBack, oCallBackScope) {
    xparser.BaseFeed.apply(this,
        [xparser.feedType.rss, fpCallBack, oCallBackScope]
    );
};

xparser.RssFeed.prototype = new xparser.BaseFeed();
```

Two things are taking place in this code. First, the BaseFeed constructor is called using the apply() method and passing in the appropriate arguments (including xparser.feedType.rss as the feed type). This is a common way of inheriting properties from a superclass in JavaScript; it ensures that all inherited properties are instantiated with the appropriate values. Second, the RssFeed prototype is set to a new instance of BaseFeed, which inherits all methods from BaseFeed.

> *For more information on inheritance and object-oriented design in JavaScript, see Professional JavaScript for Web Developers (Wiley Publishing, Inc., 2005).*

The next step is to parse the XML data supplied by the oRootNode argument. This is a simple matter of creating an associative array of class properties as keys and the corresponding XML element name as values.

```
xparser.RssFeed = function (oRootNode, fpCallBack, oCallBackScope) {
    xparser.BaseFeed.apply(this,
        [xparser.feedType.rss, fpCallBack, oCallBackScope]
    );

    var oChannelNode = zXPath.selectSingleNode(oRootNode, "channel");

    var oElements = {
        title        : "title",
        link         : "link",
        description  : "description",
        copyright    : "copyright",
        generator    : "generator",
        modified     : "lastbuilddate",
        author       : "managingeditor"
    };

    this.parse(oChannelNode, oElements, []);
};
```

This new code first retrieves the <rss:channel/> element. Remember, the <rss:channel/> element serves as a container for the entire feed. Next, create the oElements associative array by supplying the values of the XML element names. This information is passed to the parse() method, which retrieves the desired elements, creates FeedNode objects with the elements, and assigns them to the class properties.

Next, populate the items array:

```
xparser.RssFeed = function (oRootNode, fpCallBack, oCallBackScope) {
    xparser.BaseFeed.apply(this,
        [xparser.feedType.rss, fpCallBack, oCallBackScope]);

    var oChannelNode = zXPath.selectSingleNode(oRootNode, "channel");

    var oElements = {
        title        : "title",
        link         : "link",
        description  : "description",
        copyright    : "copyright",
        generator    : "generator",
        modified     : "lastbuilddate",
        author       : "managingeditor"
    };


    this.parse(oChannelNode, oElements, []);

    var cItems = zXPath.selectNodes(oChannelNode, "item");

    for (var i = 0, oItem; oItem = cItems[i]; i++) {
        this.items.push(new xparser.RssItem(oItem));
    }

    this.callBack.call(this.callBackScope, this);
};
```

The first new line uses XPath to retrieve the <rss:item/> nodes. Next, the code loops through the selected XML nodes and creates an RssItem object with the element. The new object is added to the items array using the push() method. After the items array is fully populated, the feed is completely parsed; thus, the final line executes the callback function in the specified scope. Also, the RssFeed object is passed to the callback function. This allows easy access to the feed object in case those using the library need easy access to the information the object houses.

Just as a RssFeed extends BaseFeed, an RssItem class extends BaseItem. This item class is quite simple; the RssItem constructor accepts one parameter, the <rss:item/> node:

```
xparser.RssItem = function (oItemNode) {
    xparser.BaseItem.apply(this);

    var oElements = {
        title       : "title",
        link        : "link",
        description : "description",
        date        : "pubdate",
        author      : "author"
    };

    this.parse(oItemNode, oElements, {});
};

xparser.RssItem.prototype = new xparser.BaseItem();
```

This code resembles that of `RssFeed`. The first line calls the parent class constructor to initialize properties. Next, the `oElements` associative array is created and passed, along with the XML node, to the `parse()` method. Since the RSS specification does not specify a namespace, an empty object is passed as the namespace parameter of the `parse()` method.

Parsing Atom

The code for parsing Atom feeds is very similar to the RSS-parsing code. There are just a few key differences to take into account.

The first difference is the use of namespaces. According to the Atom specification, all elements in the feed must reside in the `http://www.w3.org/2005/Atom` namespace. `XParser` may also come across an Atom feed that uses a previous version, in which case, the aforementioned namespace will not work. You can work around this issue, however, by retrieving the namespace URI of the root element:

```
xparser.AtomFeed = function (oRootNode, fpCallBack, oCallBackScope) {
    xparser.BaseFeed.apply(this,
        [xparser.feedType.atom, fpCallBack, oCallBackScope]
    );

    var oNamespaces = {
        atom : oRootNode.namespaceURI
    };
};
```

The first few lines are very similar to the code in the `RssFeed` constructor, the only difference being the `feedType` passed to the `BaseFeed` constructor. The next block of code creates an associative array called `oNamespaces`, which is responsible for holding key/value pairs consisting of the element prefix and the associated namespace URI. In this case, the `atom` key corresponds to the `namespaceURI` of the root element. This ensures that an attempt to parse the Atom feed, regardless of version, takes place.

The next key difference is, of course, the elements to retrieve. As a result of `XParser`'s design, however, this obstacle is easily overcome:

```
xparser.AtomFeed = function (oRootNode, fpCallBack, oCallBackScope) {
    xparser.BaseFeed.apply(this,
        [xparser.feedType.atom, fpCallBack, oCallBackScope]
    );

    var oNamespaces = {
        atom : oRootNode.namespaceURI
    };

    var oElements = {
        title           : "atom:title",
        link            : "atom:link/@href",
        description     : "atom:tagline",
        copyright       : "atom:copyright",
        generator       : "atom:generator",
        modified        : "atom:modified",
        author          : "atom:author"
    };

    this.parse(oRootNode, oElements, oNamespaces);
};
```

The first new block of code creates the `oElements` associative array with the Atom element names. The element's prefix, `atom`, matches the prefix contained in `oNamespaces`. The combined information is then passed to the `parse()` method to assign the properties their proper value.

Next, populate the `items` array:

```
xparser.AtomFeed = function (oRootNode, fpCallBack, oCallBackScope) {
    xparser.BaseFeed.apply(this,
        [xparser.feedType.atom, fpCallBack, oCallBackScope]
    );

    var oNamespaces = {
        atom : oRootNode.namespaceURI
    };

    var oElements = {
        title           : "atom:title",
        link            : "atom:link/@href",
        description     : "atom:tagline",
        copyright       : "atom:copyright",
        generator       : "atom:generator",
        modified        : "atom:modified",
        author          : "atom:author"
    };

    this.parse(oRootNode, oElements, oNamespaces);

    var cEntries = zXPath.selectNodes(oRootNode, "atom:entry", oNamespaces);

    for (var i = 0, oEntry; oEntry = cEntries[i]; i++) {
        this.items.push(new xparser.AtomItem(oEntry, oNamespaces));
    }

    this.callBack.apply(this.callBackScope, [this]);
};
```

The new code selects the `<atom:entry/>` elements and assigns the collection to `cEntries`. Next, the code loops through the collection and adds new `AtomItem` objects to the `items` array. When the parsing is complete, the callback function is executed in the specified scope.

Also, like the `RssFeed` class, the `AtomFeed` class's prototype is set to a new instance of `BaseFeed` to inherit methods:

```
xparser.AtomFeed.prototype = new xparser.BaseFeed();
```

Naturally, the code for `AtomItem` resembles that of `RssItem`. In fact, the only difference between the two is the XML element names contained in `oElements`:

```
xparser.AtomItem = function (oEntryNode, oNamespaces) {
    xparser.BaseItem.apply(this, []);

    var oElements = {
        title       : "atom:title",
```

```
        link         : "atom:link/@href",
        description : "atom:content",
        date         : "atom:issued",
        author       : "atom:author"
    };

    this.parse(oEntryNode, oElements, oNamespaces);
};
```

And of course, you need to assign this new class's prototype as well:

```
xparser.AtomItem.prototype = new xparser.BaseItem();
```

This last line of code completes the parsing aspect of XParser. Of course, this approach is helpful only if you know what type of feed to parse. The library needs some way of creating a feed object, regardless of the feed's type.

Putting It Together

To address this issue, XParser contains a factory method called getFeed(), whose purpose is to retrieve the feed, determine if the feed is usable, and create the feed object. The method relies upon an XHR object to retrieve the feed. In order to do this, the zXml library is used once again, as the zXmlHttp .createRequest() factory method is called to create the XHR object in a cross-browser fashion.

The getFeed() method accepts three arguments: the feed's URL, the callback function pointer, and the callback function's scope.

```
xparser.getFeed = function (sUrl, fpCallBack, oCallBackScope) {
    var oReq = zXmlHttp.createRequest();
    oReq.onreadystatechange = function () {
        if (oReq.readyState == 4) {
            if (oReq.status == 200 || oReq.status == 304) {
                //more code here
            }
        }
    };

    oReq.open("GET", sUrl, true);
    oReq.send(null);
};
```

This code for creating and handle the XHR object is similar to other examples in this book, as the readystatechange handler checks for status codes of both 200 and 304.The next step is to determine the requested feed's type. In order to do this, you need to load the XHR's responseText into an XML DOM:

```
xparser.getFeed = function (sUrl, fpCallBack, oCallBackScope) {
    var oReq = zXmlHttp.createRequest();
    oReq.onreadystatechange = function () {
        if (oReq.readyState == 4) {
            if (oReq.status == 200 || oReq.status == 304) {
```

```
                        var oFeed = null;

                        var oXmlDom = zXmlDom.createDocument();
                        oXmlDom.loadXML(oReq.responseText);

                        if (oXmlDom.parseError.errorCode != 0) {
                            throw new Error("XParser Error: The requested feed is not " +
                                "valid XML and could not be parsed.");
                        } else {
                            var oRootNode = oXmlDom.documentElement;

                            //more code here
                        }
                    }
                }
            };

            oReq.open("GET", sUrl, true);
            oReq.send(null);
        };
```

In this new code, an XML DOM is created and loaded with data. The XML document's
`documentElement` is assigned to a variable for easy access to the node. Also, the variable `oFeed` is
initialized as null; this variable eventually assumes the value of a feed object.

A simple way to determine the feed's format is to check the `documentElement`'s `nodeName` property, since
Atom uses `<feed/>` as its root element and RSS uses `<rss/>`. You also need to take into consideration that
the Atom feed may or may not use a default namespace. This concern is easily addressed by checking
whether or not the root element uses a prefix:

```
xparser.getFeed = function (sUrl, fpCallBack, oCallBackScope) {
    var oReq = zXmlHttp.createRequest();
    oReq.onreadystatechange = function () {
        if (oReq.readyState == 4) {
            if (oReq.status == 200 || oReq.status == 304) {
                var oFeed = null;

                var oXmlDom = zXmlDom.createDocument();
                oXmlDom.loadXML(oReq.responseText);

                if (oXmlDom.parseError.errorCode != 0) {
                    throw new Error("XParser Error: The requested feed is not " +
                        "valid XML and could not be parsed.");
                } else {
                    var oRootNode = oXmlDom.documentElement;

                    //Get the name of the document element.
                    var sRootName;
                    if (oRootNode.nodeName.indexOf(":") > -1)  //a prefix exists
                        sRootName = oRootNode.nodeName.split(":")[1];
                    else
                        sRootName = oRootNode.nodeName;

                    switch (sRootName.toLowerCase()) {
                        case "feed": //It's Atom.
```

```
                            //more code here
                            break;
                        case "rss": //It's RSS
                            //more code here
                            break;
                        default: //The feed isn't supported.
                            //more code here
                            break;
                    }
                }
            }
        }
    };

    oReq.open("GET", sUrl, true);
    oReq.send(null);
};
```

In the newly added code, the root element's name is checked to see if it contains a colon (:). If it does, this means that the element name contains a prefix, so it's split into two parts: the prefix and the tag name. The tag name is assigned to the sRootName variable. If no prefix exists, then sRootName takes on the value of the element's name.

Once the element's name is known, it can be handled accordingly. The switch block determines the next step based on the root element's name. Using this code, the desired AtomFeed or RssFeed object is created:

```
xparser.getFeed = function (sUrl, fpCallBack, oCallBackScope) {
    var oReq = zXmlHttp.createRequest();
    oReq.onreadystatechange = function () {
        if (oReq.readyState == 4) {
            if (oReq.status == 200 || oReq.status == 304) {
                var oFeed = null;

                var oXmlDom = zXmlDom.createDocument();
                oXmlDom.loadXML(oReq.responseText);

                if (oXmlDom.parseError.errorCode != 0) {
                    throw new Error("XParser Error: The requested feed is not " +
                        "valid XML and could not be parsed.");
                } else {
                    var oRootNode = oXmlDom.documentElement;

                    //Get the name of the document element.
                    var sRootName;
                    if (oRootNode.nodeName.indexOf(":") > -1)
                        sRootName = oRootNode.nodeName.split(":")[1];
                    else
                        sRootName = oRootNode.nodeName;

                    switch (sRootName.toLowerCase()) {
                        case "feed": //It's Atom.
                            oFeed = new xparser.AtomFeed(
                                oRootNode,
                                fpCallBack,
```

```
                            oCallBackScope
                        );
                        break;
                case "rss": //It's RSS
                    //Check the version.
                    if (parseInt(oRootNode.getAttribute("version")) < 2)
                        throw new Error("XParser Error! RSS feed " +
                            "version is not supported"
                        );

                    oFeed = new xparser.RssFeed(
                        oRootNode,
                        fpCallBack,
                        oCallBackScope
                    );
                    break;
                default: //The feed isn't supported.
                    throw new Error("XParser Error: The supplied feed " +
                        "is currently not supported."
                    );
                    break;
                }
            }
        }
    }
    };

    oReq.open("GET", sUrl, true);
    oReq.send(null);
};
```

The newly added code creates an `AtomFeed` object and passes it the required arguments. Creating an RSS feed, however, requires a few more steps. First, the RSS version is checked (by checking the `version` attribute in the root element). If the version is less than 2, the code throws an error stating the RSS version isn't supported. If the feed is the correct version, however, an `RssFeed` object is created. Last, if the document's root could not be matched, the feed isn't supported, so an error is thrown. Throwing errors allows a developer using the library to anticipate these types of errors and handle them accordingly.

While we're on the subject of errors, the `getFeed()` method needs one more in case the XHR request fails:

```
xparser.getFeed = function (sUrl, fpCallBack, oCallBackScope) {
    var oReq = zXmlHttp.createRequest();
    oReq.onreadystatechange = function () {
        if (oReq.readyState == 4) {
            if (oReq.status == 200 || oReq.status == 304) {
                var oFeed = null;

                var oXmlDom = zXmlDom.createDocument();
                oXmlDom.loadXML(oReq.responseText);
                if (oXmlDom.parseError.errorCode != 0) {
                    throw new Error("XParser Error: The requested feed is not " +
                        "valid XML and could not be parsed.");
                } else {
```

```
                    var oRootNode = oXmlDom.documentElement;

                    //Get the name of the document element.
                    var sRootName;
                    if (oRootNode.nodeName.indexOf(":") > -1)
                        sRootName = oRootNode.nodeName.split(":")[1];
                    else
                        sRootName = oRootNode.nodeName;

                    switch (sRootName.toLowerCase()) {
                        case "feed": //It's Atom. Create the object.
                            oFeed = new xparser.AtomFeed(
                                oRootNode,
                                fpCallBack,
                                oCallBackScope
                            );
                            break;
                        case "rss": //It's RSS
                            //Check the version.
                            if (parseInt(oRootNode.getAttribute("version")) < 2)
                                throw new Error("XParser Error! RSS feed " +
                                    "version is not supported"
                                );

                            oFeed = new xparser.RssFeed(
                                oRootNode,
                                fpCallBack,
                                oCallBackScope
                            );
                            break;
                        default: //The feed isn't supported.
                            throw new Error("XParser Error: The supplied feed " +
                                "is currently not supported."
                            );
                            break;
                    }
                }
            } else { //The HTTP Status code isn't what we wanted; throw an error.
                throw new Error("XParser Error: XHR failed. " +
                    "HTTP Status: " + oReq.status
                );
            }
        }
    };

    oReq.open("GET", sUrl, true);
    oReq.send(null);
};
```

This new code throws an error if the HTTP status is anything other than 200 or 304, making it easier to debug and realize that the request failed for some reason. Also, notice that the errors are prepended with the string "XParser Error" to clearly indicate that the error occurred within the library.

With these final lines of code, the XParser library can now be used in any web application. The remainder of this chapter walks you through the creation of two components that utilize the XParser library.

Creating a News Ticker

Popular on both television news networks and web sites, a news ticker displays information in a scrolling format. Unlike the static nature of television, the Web enables users to interact with these tickers. If something catches their eye, they can click the news item and it takes them to their desired information. Because of this interactivity, news tickers are quite popular on web sites, and as it turns out, easy to implement using Ajax (see Figure 7-1).

Like any other Ajax-enabled application, a web-based news ticker comes in two parts: a server application and a client application. Since RSS feeds can exist on any server, a PHP server-side proxy is used to retrieve requested feeds for the client. The client application is, of course, a mix of HTML and JavaScript.

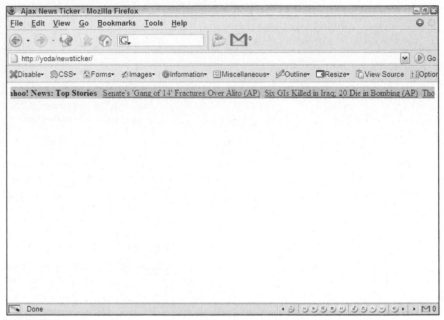

Figure 7-1

The Server-Side Component

The PHP server application is extremely simple. Its only function is to retrieve data from a URL and return it back to the client. To do so, the page expects a `url` variable in the query string to indicate which data to retrieve. For instance:

```
newsticker.php?url=http://rss.news.yahoo.com/rss/topstories
```

This URL tells `newsticker.php`, the server-side component, to retrieve data from the Yahoo! News Top Stories RSS feed.

Because the server's only job is to retrieve remote information, the code is only a few lines long:

```php
<?php
header("Content-Type: text/xml");
header("Cache-Control: no-cache");

if ( isset( $_GET["url"] ) ) {
    $remoteUrl = $_GET["url"];

    $xml = file_get_contents($remoteUrl);

    echo $xml;
} else {
    header("HTTP/1.1 400 Bad Request");
}

?>
```

The first two lines set the `Content-Type` and `Cache-Control` headers, respectively. It is important to set the MIME content type to `text/xml`; otherwise, Mozilla Firefox doesn't recognize the data as XML and won't automatically parse it into an XML DOM document. It also is important to set the `Cache-Control` header to `no-cache` because Internet Explorer caches all data retrieved via XHR unless explicitly told not to.

In the next line of code, the query string is checked for the `url` parameter. To do this, use the `isset()` function, which returns a Boolean value based on whether a variable, function, or object exists. If a value has been passed in, the value of `url` is assigned to the `$remoteUrl` variable and passed to `file_get_contents()`. This function opens a file (local or remote), reads the file, and returns its contents as a string. The last step is to write the file's contents, stored in the `$xml` variable, to the page. This concludes the server-side code.

If the `url` parameter cannot be found in the query string, PHP returns an HTTP status of 400, which signifies a bad request. Because XParser is responsible for making requests to the server, it will handle this HTTP status and throw an error specifying that XHR failed to retrieve the data.

The Client-Side Component

Before delving into the code, consider the client's required functionality. The client:

1. Builds the HTML to display the news feeds.
2. Requests data from the server application. When the server responds with the requested data, the client parses the data with XParser.
3. Places the parsed data into the HTML.
4. Uses JavaScript to animate the ticker.
5. Polls for updated data every 1.5 minutes.

In addition, a few user interface criteria must be met:

❑ The data in the ticker, news article titles, should be links that take the user to the specified news article.

❑ The ticker should stop scrolling when the user's mouse enters the ticker and should resume scrolling when the user mouses out.

To implement this functionality, the client-side code consists of two classes: the NewsTicker class, which builds the ticker in HTML format, animates the ticker, and provides the ability to add news feeds into the ticker, and the NewsTickerFeed class, which requests the feed, parses it, places it in the HTML, and polls for new data.

The NewsTicker Class

The NewsTicker class is the main class of the client-side code. The constructor accepts one argument, which is the HTMLElement to append the news ticker:

```
function NewsTicker(oAppendTo) {
    var oThis = this;
    this.timer = null;
    this.feeds = [];

    //more code to come
}
```

These first few lines of code initialize the properties of the NewsTicker class. First, a pointer to the object is created by assigning the variable oThis. The timer property, initially set to null, will control the scrolling animation (setTimeout() returns a unique timer identifier). The feeds property is an array that will contain NewsTickerFeeds objects.

Next, elements are created for the primary user interface of the news ticker:

```
function NewsTicker(oAppendTo) {
    var oThis = this;
    this.timer = null;
    this.feeds = [];
    this.tickerContainer = document.createElement("div");
    this.ticker = document.createElement("div");
    this.tickerContainer.className = "newsTickerContainer";
    this.ticker.className = "newsTicker";

    //more code to come
}
```

These properties, tickerContainer and ticker, reference newly created <div/> elements. The tickerContainer element does what its name implies: it contains all elements of the widget, whereas the ticker element scrolls the news feeds contained in it. The HTML code output by this constructor is:

```
<div class="newsTickerContainer">
    <div class="newsTicker"></div>
</div>
```

As a part of the user interface, remember that the scrolling animation stops when users move their mouse over the news ticker. To facilitate this functionality, event handlers are assigned for the onmouseover and onmouseout events of tickerContainer:

```javascript
function NewsTicker(oAppendTo) {
    var oThis = this;
    this.timer = null;
    this.feeds = [];
    this.tickerContainer = document.createElement("div");
    this.ticker = document.createElement("div");
    this.tickerContainer.className = "newsTickerContainer";
    this.ticker.className = "newsTicker";

    this.tickerContainer.onmouseover = function () {
        oThis.stopTick();
    };

    this.tickerContainer.onmouseout = function () {
        oThis.tick();
    };
}
```

In the onmouseover event handler, the stopTick() method clears the timer property, which stops the animation. Notice the use of the oThis pointer, since the scope changes inside the event handler. The onmouseout event handler causes the animation to begin again by calling the tick() method, which performs the animation.

The next step is to append the ticker element to tickerContainer and to append the widget's HTML to its parent HTMLElement:

```javascript
function NewsTicker(oAppendTo) {
    var oThis = this;
    this.timer = null;
    this.feeds = [];
    this.tickerContainer = document.createElement("div");
    this.ticker = document.createElement("div");

    this.tickerContainer.className = "newsTickerContainer";
    this.ticker.className = "newsTicker";

    this.tickerContainer.onmouseover = function () {
        clearTimeout(oThis.timer);
    };

    this.tickerContainer.onmouseout = function () {
        oThis.tick();
    };

    this.tickerContainer.appendChild(this.ticker);

    var oToAppend = (oAppendTo)?oAppendTo:document.body;
    oToAppend.appendChild(this.tickerContainer);

    //more code to come
}
```

The first line of this code appends `ticker` to `tickerContainer`, which completes the HTML layout. The next line offers a convenience for developers: if `oAppendTo` exists, then the widget is appended to the value of `oAppendTo`. If it doesn't, the HTML is appended to `document.body`. This gives the argument a default value; to append the widget directly to the document, the argument can be omitted.

The final lines of the constructor initialize the ticker:

```
function NewsTicker(oAppendTo) {
    var oThis = this;
    this.timer = null;
    this.feeds = [];
    this.tickerContainer = document.createElement("div");
    this.ticker = document.createElement("div");

    this.tickerContainer.className = "newsTickerContainer";
    this.ticker.className = "newsTicker";

    this.tickerContainer.onmouseover = function () {
        clearTimeout(oThis.timer);
    };

    this.tickerContainer.onmouseout = function () {
        oThis.tick();
    };

    this.tickerContainer.appendChild(this.ticker);

    var oToAppend = (oAppendTo)?oAppendTo:document.body;
    oToAppend.appendChild(this.tickerContainer);

    this.ticker.style.left = this.tickerContainer.offsetWidth + "px";
    this.tick();
}
```

This code positions the ticker at the farthest right edge of `tickerContainer` (the animation scrolls from right to left) and calls `tick()` to start the animation.

Internet Explorer and Firefox have different modes in which they render markup differently according to the doctype specified in the HTML page. Under what is known as standards mode, you must add `"px"` *to any pixel measurement or the browser will not position the element.*

Animating the Ticker

The basic logic of any animation is to move an element by a set amount of pixels repeatedly and at set intervals until the element reaches a specific location. The scrolling animation used in this widget is probably the simplest type of animation you can perform: a linear, right-to-left movement until the ticker's right edge reaches the container's left edge. The leftmost limit of the animation can be expressed by `this.ticker.offsetWidth`, which gives the element's width in pixels and then negates it to ensure that the entire element is not visible. When the ticker reaches this position in the page, the animation restarts. The `tick()` method begins by gathering this information:

```
NewsTicker.prototype.tick = function () {
    var iTickerLength = this.ticker.offsetWidth;
```

```
        var oThis = this;

        //more code to come
};
```

The `iTickerWidth` variable contains the ending point of the animation: the negative `offsetWidth` of the ticker. Once again, a pointer to the `NewsTicker` object is assigned to `oThis` for later event handler assignments.

The first step in the animation is to decide whether the ticker contains any data, because there's no use in scrolling an empty `<div/>` element:

```
NewsTicker.prototype.tick = function () {
    var iTickerLength = this.ticker.offsetWidth;
    var oThis = this;

    if (this.ticker.innerHTML) {
        if (this.ticker.offsetLeft > -iTickerLength) {
            var iNewLeft = this.ticker.offsetLeft - 1;
            this.ticker.style.left = iNewLeft + "px";
        } else {
            this.ticker.style.left = this.tickerContainer.offsetWidth + "px";
        }
    }

    //more code to come
};
```

This code checks the element's `innerHTML` property; any HTML present in the ticker means that data exists and the animation should begin. The location of the ticker (`offsetLeft`) is checked against the animation's boundary (`iTickerLength`). If the location is greater than the limit, the animation continues. The next line gets the new left position of the ticker: one pixel to the left. The last line of this code block sets the left position to reflect the value contained in `iNewLeft`. This, however, is only one part of the animation. The ticker continues to move until it reaches the boundary; therefore, the ticker must be reset to its original location.

The last step is to perform an animation. Animations are implemented in JavaScript using a timeout that repeatedly calls a function in charge of moving an element. In the case of this animation, that function is the `tick()` method itself, so a wrapper function must be created and passed into the `setTimeout()` function:

```
NewsTicker.prototype.tick = function () {
    var iTickerLength = this.ticker.offsetWidth;
    var oThis = this;

    if (this.ticker.innerHTML) {
        if (this.ticker.offsetLeft > -iTickerLength) {
            var iNewLeft = this.ticker.offsetLeft - 1;
            this.ticker.style.left = iNewLeft + "px";
        } else {
            this.ticker.style.left = this.tickerContainer.offsetWidth + "px";
```

```
        }
    }

    var doSetTimeout = function() {
        oThis.tick();
    };
    this.timer = setTimeout(doSetTimeout,1);
};
```

This last bit of code sets a timeout for the `doSetTimeout()` function, which simply calls `tick()` again. Doing so causes `tick()` to run every millisecond, so the animation continues until it is stopped by clearing the timeout (when the user mouses over the container).

Stopping the Animation

Anything that is started must, at some point, be stopped; so it is with the news ticker animation: the animation stops when the user moves their mouse pointer over the ticker. The `mouseover` event handler calls the `stopTick()` method:

```
NewsTicker.prototype.stopTick = function () {
    clearTimeout(this.timer);
    this.timer = null;
};
```

The `timer` property is passed to the `clearTimeout()` function, canceling the next code execution. Even though the timeout is cleared at that point, the `timer` property still holds the numeric value of that timeout; therefore, assign the property the value of `null`.

Adding Feeds

Now that the animation and HTML layout are complete, the only step left is to add feeds to the ticker. To facilitate this action, the `NewsTicker` class needs an `add()` method. This method accepts a single argument, which is the URL of a remote feed:

```
NewsTicker.prototype.add = function (sUrl) {
    this.feeds.push(new NewsTickerFeed(this, sUrl));
};
```

When this code executes, it creates a new `NewsTickerFeed` object and adds the object to the `feeds` array. This array is only used to initially load the feed data when the news ticker is created.

Removing the News Ticker

The final method of the `NewsTicker` class is the `dispose()` method. This method's job is to remove the ticker from the Web page and clean up the associated memory:

```
NewsTicker.prototype.dispose = function () {
    for (var i = 0; i < this.feeds.length; i++) {
        this.feeds[i].dispose();
    }

    //more code to come
};
```

The first step in this process is the removal of all feeds associated with this ticker, as this code demonstrates by looping through the feeds array and calling the dispose() method of the individual NewsTickerFeed objects. Next, the animation must be stopped by calling the stopTick() method, and the references to the various DOM elements must be deleted:

```
NewsTicker.prototype.dispose = function () {
    for (var i = 0; i < this.feeds.length; i++) {
        this.feeds[i].dispose();
    }

    this.stopTick();

    this.tickerContainer.parentNode.removeChild(this.tickerContainer);
    this.ticker = null;
    this.tickerContainer = null;
};
```

This code stops the animation and removes the HTML elements from the page, setting the ticker and tickerContainer properties to null (doing so prepares the object for the garbage collector).

The NewsTickerFeed Class

A news ticker isn't very useful without content to display. The NewsTickerFeed class pulls the required feeds, parses them with XParser, and assembles the HTML for the ticker. The constructor accepts two arguments: a reference to its the NewsTicker object (this allows access to the NewsTicker properties and methods when needed) and the URL of the feed to download:

```
function NewsTickerFeed(oParent, sUrl) {
    this.parent = oParent;
    this.url = sUrl;
    this.timer = null;
    this.container = null;

    this.poll();
}
```

Compared to the NewsTicker class's constructor, the NewsTickerFeed constructor is relatively simple. This class has four properties: parent (a reference to the parent NewsTicker object); url (the URL of the feed); timer (the reference used in the timeout for updating the feed); and container (the <span/> element containing the feed's information in the ticker). The last step in the constructor is to call the poll() method, which makes a request to the server to retrieve the feed.

Polling for New Information

The poll() method automatically checks for feed updates every minute and a half (this can be configured based on your needs):

```
NewsTickerFeed.prototype.poll = function () {
    var oThis = this;
    var sFullUrl = "newsticker.php?url=" + encodeURIComponent(this.url);
    xparser.getFeed(sFullUrl, this.populateTicker, this);
}
```

This code uses XParser to retrieve the XML feed. Before calling xparser.getFeed(), the URL is built, with the feed URL string being encoded by the encodeURIComponent() JavaScript function. It is important to encode the URL, because this ensures that any characters such as white space, ampersands, quotation marks, and so on are converted to their corresponding escape sequence for proper transmission. The code uses populateTicker as the callback for the request and asks it to be fired within the NewsTickerFeed object's scope.

One final addition to poll() is the automatic updating. To facilitate this, use an approach similar to the tick() method of the NewsTicker class:

```javascript
NewsTickerFeed.prototype.poll = function () {
    var oThis = this;
    var sFullUrl = "newsticker.php?url=" + encodeURIComponent(this.url);
    xparser.getFeed(sFullUrl, this.populateTicker, this);

    var doSetTimeout = function () {
        oThis.poll();
    };

    this.timer = setTimeout(doSetTimeout, 90000);
}
```

This new code creates a function called doSetTimeout() to pass to the setTimeout() method. Because this version of doSetTimeout() exists only in the scope of the poll() method, it will not interfere with the previous function of the same name in tick(). The poll() method is now set to run every 1.5 minutes (every 90,000 milliseconds) and will update the feed.

Stop Automatic Polling

There may be instances where you want to stop a feed from updating. Doing so is as simple as the calling stopPolling():

```javascript
NewsTickerFeed.prototype.stopPolling = function () {
    clearTimeout(this.timer);
    this.timer = null;
};
```

This method simply clears the timeout used for polling and assigns the value of null to the timer property.

Adding Content

When XParser finishes parsing the remote feed, it calls the populateTicker() method and passes itself as an argument. With the supplied XParser object, you can start to create the HTML:

```javascript
NewsTickerFeed.prototype.populateTicker = function (oParser) {
    var spanTickerLinks = document.createElement("span");

    var aFeedTitle = document.createElement("a");
    aFeedTitle.className = "newsTicker-feedTitle";
    aFeedTitle.href = oParser.link.value;
    aFeedTitle.target = "_new";
```

```
        aFeedTitle.innerHTML = oParser.title.value;

        spanTickerLinks.appendChild(aFeedTitle);

        //more code to come
    }
```

The first step is to create an element to encapsulate all the links. This element serves the purpose of convenience: when the feed is updated, it is easier to remove one element with several children than it is to remove several elements one at a time. Also, don't confuse this container with the `container` property. The latter contains `spanTickerLinks`.

To separate the different feeds in the ticker, the feed's title is used. This is also a link, so if the user clicks on the title, a new window pops up taking him or her to the feed's web site. This link is given a CSS class of `newsTicker-feedTitle` and is appended to `spanTickerLinks`.

Next, create the link items by iterating through the `items` array of the `XParser` object:

```
NewsTickerFeed.prototype.populateTicker = function (oParser) {
    var spanTickerLinks = document.createElement("span");

    var aFeedTitle = document.createElement("a");
    aFeedTitle.className = "newsTicker-feedTitle";
    aFeedTitle.href = oParser.link.value;
    aFeedTitle.target = "_new";
    aFeedTitle.innerHTML = oParser.title.value;

    spanTickerLinks.appendChild(aFeedTitle);

    for (var i = 0; i < oParser.items.length; i++) {
        var item = oParser.items[i];

        var aFeedLink = document.createElement("a");
        aFeedLink.href = item.link.value;
        aFeedLink.target = "_blank";
        aFeedLink.className = "newsTicker-feedItem";
        aFeedLink.innerHTML = item.title.value;

        spanLinkContainer.appendChild(aFeedLink);
    }
}
```

Each link opens a new window when clicked and has a CSS class of `newsTicker-feedItem`. When the link is completed, it is appended to `spanLinkContainer`, which is then added to the ticker:

```
NewsTickerFeed.prototype.populateTicker = function (oParser) {
    var spanLinkContainer = document.createElement("span");

    var aFeedTitle = document.createElement("a");
    aFeedTitle.className = "newsTicker-feedTitle";
    aFeedTitle.href = oParser.link.value;
    aFeedTitle.target = "_new";
```

```
        aFeedTitle.innerHTML = oParser.title.value;

        spanLinkContainer.appendChild(aFeedTitle);

        for (var i = 0, itemsLength = oParser.items.length; i < itemsLength; i++) {
            var item = oParser.items[i];

            var aFeedLink = document.createElement("a");
            aFeedLink.href = item.link.value;
            aFeedLink.target = "_new";
            aFeedLink.className = "newsTicker-feedItem";
            aFeedLink.innerHTML = item.title.value;

            spanLinkContainer.appendChild(aFeedLink);
        }
        if (!this.container) {
            this.container = document.createElement("span");
            this.container.className = "newsTicker-feedContainer";
            this.parent.ticker.appendChild(this.container);
        } else {
            this.container.removeChild(this.container.firstChild);
        }

        this.container.appendChild(spanLinkContainer);
    }
```

When a `NewsTickerFeed` class is first created, the `container` property is declared but given a `null` value. This is done for a couple of reasons. First, the ticker's animation does not begin until it contains HTML. To keep the animation from running prematurely, the element referenced by `container` should not be added until the feed's data is retrieved, parsed, and assembled into HTML. This means that appending the `container` to the ticker should occur in `populateTicker()`.

Second, because this operation takes place in `populateTicker()`, it is important not to add the same `container` to the ticker over and over again). Therefore, when the previous code executes, it checks if `container` has been initialized. If not, the `<span/>` element is created and appended to the ticker; otherwise, the link container is removed from `container`, and the newly created link container is added to the widget.

Removing Data

There may be a case where a feed needs to be removed from the ticker, either to be replaced or just simply to free up space. In that case, it's important to free up any memory used by the `NewsTickerFeed` object. This is where the `dispose()` method takes over.

Like the `NewsTicker` method of the same name, the `NewsTickerFeed`'s `dispose()` method performs the removal of the feed from the ticker:

```
NewsTickerFeed.prototype.dispose = function () {
    if (this.timer) this.stopPolling();
    if (this.container) {
        this.parent.ticker.removeChild(this.container);
```

```
        this.container = null;
    }

    this.parent = null;
};
```

The first line checks to see if the feed still automatically updates itself (remember, the `timer` property is assigned the value of `null` when `stopPolling()` is called). If so, then it is stopped from doing so. It then checks for, and removes, the HTML elements used by the `NewsTickerFeed` object. And last, it removes the reference to the `NewsTicker` object that contained the feed.

Styling the News

Since no two sites are the same visually, the ability to style the news ticker is very important. Before looking at the CSS, however, it is important to review the HTML structure of the news ticker:

```html
<div class="newsTickerContainer">
    <div class="newsTicker">
        <span class="newsTicker-feedContainer">
            <span>
                <a />
                <a />
            </span>
        </span>
        <span class="newsTicker-feedContainer">
            <span>
                <a />
                <a />
            </span>
        </span>
    </div>
</div>
```

The outermost `<div/>` element is important for two reasons. First, it encapsulates every part of the widget. Second, it is the viewing box for the news items. Because it contains every element in the widget, it must be an extremely wide box, but you don't want to all the data seen until it enters the visible area. Therefore, the CSS `overflow` property must be set to "hidden":

```css
.newsTickerContainer {
    overflow: hidden;
    position: relative;
    background-color: silver;
    height: 20px;
    width: 100%;
    padding-top: 2px;
}
```

Setting the `overflow` property to "hidden" hides any content that is not positioned within the specified area. Next, the `position` property is set to "relative." Other CSS properties can be customized depending on where the news ticker is being used; in this example code, `height`, `width`, `padding`, and `background-color` are assigned.

The next element contains all the feed links. This `<div/>` element is absolutely positioned so that it can be moved with JavaScript:

```
.newsTicker {
    white-space: nowrap;
    position: absolute;
    height: 25px;
}
```

Note also that the `white-space` property is set to `nowrap`, which disallows line breaks in the text. This is important because, otherwise, the text could end up on multiple lines instead of a single line.

The last two elements exposing CSS classes are the links: `newsTicker-feedTitle` and `newsTicker-feedItem`. The first is the link to the news site. Although none of the following properties is required, they set the feed's title apart from the remaining links:

```
.newsTicker-feedTitle {
    margin: 0px 6px 0px 6px;
    font-weight: bold;
    color: black;
    text-decoration: none;
}
```

There are six pixels of space on the left and right sides, giving distance between the feed items. The text is bold, is black, and has no underline, thus causing more separation in likeness between this link and the others.

The only formatting the feed items have are four pixels of space on each side, giving the links a defined look while still maintaining what the user expects:

```
.newsTicker-feedItem {
    padding: 4px;
}
```

The beauty of CSS is its ability to change the look and feel of any page or widget, regardless of markup (in most circumstances). Feel free to experiment with different CSS properties to format the news ticker to your specifications.

Using the News Ticker Widget

Since the back-end code is PHP, setting up this widget is as simple as uploading files and referencing them in your HTML. To add the JavaScript and CSS into your page, simply add the `<script/>` and `<link/>` tags:

```
<!DOCTYPE html PUBLIC "-//W3C//DTD XHTML 1.1//EN"
        "http://www.w3.org/TR/xhtml11/DTD/xhtml11.dtd">

<html xmlns="http://www.w3.org/1999/xhtml" >
<head>
    <title>Ajax News Ticker</title>
```

```
        <link rel="stylesheet" type="text/css" href="css/newsticker.css" />
        <script type="text/javascript" src="js/zxml.js"></script>
        <script type="text/javascript" src="js/xparser.js"></script>
        <script type="text/javascript" src="js/newsticker.js"></script>
</head>
<body>


</body>
</html>
```

You'll also need to instantiate a new instance of `NewsTicker`. Remember, `NewsTicker` adds itself to an `HTMLElement`, so it's best to create the object when the page loads with the `onload` event:

```
<!DOCTYPE html PUBLIC "-//W3C//DTD XHTML 1.1//EN"
            "http://www.w3.org/TR/xhtml11/DTD/xhtml11.dtd">

<html xmlns="http://www.w3.org/1999/xhtml" >
<head>
    <title>Ajax News Ticker</title>
    <link rel="stylesheet" type="text/css" href="css/newsticker.css" />
    <script type="text/javascript" src="js/zxml.js"></script>
    <script type="text/javascript" src="js/xparser.js"></script>
    <script type="text/javascript" src="js/newsticker.js"></script>
    <script type="text/javascript">
    window.onload = function() {
        var newsTicker = new NewsTicker();
        newsTicker.add("http://rss.news.yahoo.com/rss/topstories");
    }

    </script>
</head>
<body>


</body>
</html>
```

Because this widget uses `XParser` to parse the news feeds, any RSS 2.0 and Atom feed can be used with this widget. (The preceding example pulls the Yahoo! Top Stories feed.) The news ticker elements will be created inside the document's `<body/>` element because no container object was passed in to the `NewsTicker` constructor.

Web Search with RSS

With the ever-expanding technology of the Web, conventional search engines are opening the doors to more unconventional means to get you to the content you desire. The first to jump onto the scene was Yahoo! with their Y!Q service (`http://yq.search.yahoo.com/publisher/index.html`). This new service enables developers to embed search functionality into any web page. Y!Q provides search results related to the content of the page, giving readers more information without leaving the page.

The Y!Q service is a great idea, but it hasn't surfaced without criticism. The main argument? It requires the use of Yahoo!'s JavaScript, and you have to add a `<form/>` element meeting the Yahoo! requirements to perform a search. For many web site authors, it takes too much effort to use the service. And after all the work, the search results are presented in the Yahoo! style, breaking the look and feel of the web site.

Thankfully, Yahoo! isn't the only search engine breaking into this type of service. MSN Search (`http://search.msn.com`) provides a similar service, but it also enables the web developer to control the look, feel, and implementation. This ability comes from MSN Search providing RSS versions of its search results, making it possible to subscribe to a particular search or add the results to your page using Ajax methods.

In mid-2006, Google also jumped into competition for "search from your site" functionality, releasing Google BlogSearch (`http://blogsearch.google.com`), which provides results returned in either RSS or Atom formats.

The Server-Side Component

To run a search and get the results back in RSS format, a request can be made in the following format:

```
http://search.msn.com/results.aspx?q=[SEARCHTERM]&format=rss
```

With this knowledge, it's possible to write server-side code to retrieve the remote feed. Once again, it's necessary to create a server-side proxy to access this information, since it exists on a different server. The URL to request information from the server application looks like this:

```
websearch.php?search=[SEARCHTERM]
```

There's only one variable in the query string: `search`. Therefore, the application should look for this query item:

```php
<?php
header("Content-Type: text/xml");
header("Cache-Control: no-cache");

if ( isset($_GET["search"]) ) {

    $searchTerm = urlencode( stripslashes($_GET["search"]) );

    $url = "http://search.msn.com/results.aspx?q=$searchTerm&format=rss";

    $xml = file_get_contents($url);

    echo $xml;
} else {
    header("HTTP/1.1 400 Bad Request");
}
?>
```

As you know, the first two lines set the required headers so that the browser will handle the data correctly. The next line of code uses the `isset()` function to determine whether the search key is present in the query string.

The search term must go through a variety of functions in order to send a proper request to the remote host. First, it is passed to the `stripslashes()` function. If magic quotes are enabled in the PHP configuration (which is the default), any quote that reaches the PHP engine is automatically escaped with a slash: `\"search query\"`. The `stripslashes()` function removes these escape sequence, leaving only `"search query"`. After the slashes' removal, it then goes to the `urlencode()` function, which properly encodes characters to be used in a query string. Spaces, quotes, ampersands, and other characters are all encoded.

> If the search term is not encoded like this, the MSN server will return a code `400:`
> `Bad Request`.

When the search term is ready for transmission, it is included into the URL and stored in the `$url` variable. Finally, the `file_get_contents()` function opens the remote file, reads the contents, and returns it as a string to the `$xml` variable, which is printed to the page using the `echo` command.

The Client-Side Component

The client-side code departs from the classes created earlier in this chapter. Instead of creating a class and using instances of that class, this widget consists of a static object called `msnWebSearch`:

```
var msnWebSearch = {};
```

This object is created using object literal notation and exposes several methods to get the search results and to draw and position the HTML that contains the data. The first method is `drawResultBox()`, which draws the HTML for search results in the following format:

```
<div class="ajaxWebSearchBox">
    <div class="ajaxWebSearchHeading">MSN Search Results
        <a class="ajaxWebSearchCloseLink" href="#">X</a>
    </div>

    <div class="ajaxWebSearchResults">
        <a class="ajaxWebSearchLink" target="_blank" />
        <a class="ajaxWebSearchLink" target="_blank" />
    </div>
</div>
```

The result box is divided into two parts: a heading and a results pane (see Figure 7-2). The heading tells the user that this new box contains results from an MSN search. It also contains an X, which will close the box. The results pane contains block-style links, which opens a new window when clicked.

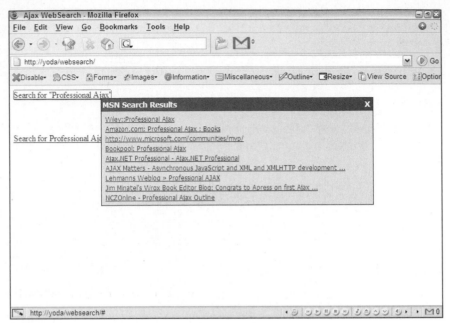

Figure 7-2

Positioning the Search Results

The `position()` method, as you may have guessed, positions the search box. It accepts two arguments: an `event` object and the `HTMLElement` object referencing the result box:

```
msnWebSearch.position = function (e, divSearchBox) {
    var x = e.clientX + document.documentElement.scrollLeft;
    var y = e.clientY + document.documentElement.scrollTop;

    divSearchBox.style.left = x + "px";
    divSearchBox.style.top = y + "px";
};
```

The first two lines get the left and top positions to place the search results box. Two pieces of information are required to perform this operation. First is the x and y coordinates of the mouse. This information is stored in the `clientX` and `clientY` properties.

These coordinates, however, are insufficient to properly position the results box because the `clientX` and `clientY` properties return the mouse position in relation to the client area in the browser window, not the actual coordinates in the page. To account for this, use the `scrollLeft` and `scrollTop` properties of the document element. With the final coordinates calculated, you can finally position the box where the user clicked the mouse.

> **Using** documentElement **to retrieve the** scrollLeft **and** scrollTop **properties only works in the browser's standards mode. In "quirks mode,"** document.body .scrollLeft **and** document.body.scrollTop **must be used.**

Drawing the Results User Interface

The code to generate this HTML is rather lengthy because the elements are generated using DOM methods. The drawResultBox() method accepts one argument, an event object:

```
msnWebSearch.drawResultBox = function (e) {
    var divSearchBox= document.createElement("div");
    var divHeading = document.createElement("div");
    var divResultsPane = document.createElement("div");
    var aCloseLink = document.createElement("a");

    //more code to come
};
```

These first lines create the HTML elements via the createElement() method. After the elements have been created, their properties can be assigned. The first two elements to finalize are a CloseLink and divHeading:

```
msnWebSearch.drawResultBox = function (e) {
    var divSearchBox= document.createElement("div");
    var divHeading = document.createElement("div");
    var divResultsPane = document.createElement("div");
    var aCloseLink = document.createElement("a");

    aCloseLink.href = "#";
    aCloseLink.className = "ajaxWebSearchCloseLink";
    aCloseLink.onclick = this.close;
    aCloseLink.appendChild(document.createTextNode("X"));

    divHeading.className = "ajaxWebSearchHeading";
    divHeading.appendChild(document.createTextNode("MSN Search Results"));
    divHeading.appendChild(aCloseLink);

    //more code to come
};
```

A method, close(), becomes the handler for the close link's onclick event. The next group of lines populate the heading <div/> with text and the closing link.

When this result box is drawn into the page, a response from the server application has not yet been received. To show the user that something is happening, a loading message is displayed (see Figure 7-3).

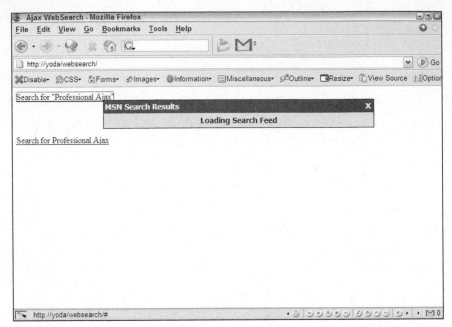

Figure 7-3

To create this loading message, create another element and append it to the `divResultsPane` element:

```
msnWebSearch.drawResultBox = function (e) {
    var divSearchBox= document.createElement("div");
    var divHeading = document.createElement("div");
    var divResultsPane = document.createElement("div");
    var aCloseLink = document.createElement("a");

    aCloseLink.href = "#";
    aCloseLink.className = "ajaxWebSearchCloseLink";
    aCloseLink.onclick = this.close;
    aCloseLink.appendChild(document.createTextNode("X"));

    divHeading.className = "ajaxWebSearchHeading";
    divHeading.appendChild(document.createTextNode("MSN Search Results"));
    divHeading.appendChild(aCloseLink);

    var divLoading = document.createElement("div");
    divLoading.appendChild(document.createTextNode("Loading Search Feed"));

    divResultsPane.className = "ajaxWebSearchResults";
    divResultsPane.appendChild(divLoading);

    //more code to come
};
```

This code creates the loading message and appends it to `divResultsPane`, while also assigning a CSS class name to `divResultsPane`.

With these elements completed, all that remains is to add them to the `divSearchBox` element:

```
msnWebSearch.drawResultBox = function (e) {
    var divSearchBox= document.createElement("div");
    var divHeading = document.createElement("div");
    var divResultsPane = document.createElement("div");
    var aCloseLink = document.createElement("a");

    aCloseLink.href = "#";
    aCloseLink.className = "ajaxWebSearchCloseLink";
    aCloseLink.onclick = this.close;
    aCloseLink.appendChild(document.createTextNode("X"));

    divHeading.className = "ajaxWebSearchHeading";
    divHeading.appendChild(document.createTextNode("MSN Search Results"));
    divHeading.appendChild(aCloseLink);

    var divLoading = document.createElement("div");
    divLoading.appendChild(document.createTextNode("Loading Search Feed"));

    divResultsPane.className = "ajaxWebSearchResults";
    divResultsPane.appendChild(divLoading);

    divSearchBox.className = "ajaxWebSearchBox";
    divSearchBox.appendChild(divHeading);
    divSearchBox.appendChild(divResultsPane);

    document.body.appendChild(divSearchBox);

    //more code to come
};
```

This code appends the `divHeading` and `divResultsPane` elements to the search box and appends the search box to the page.

The final step in `drawResultBox()` is to position the newly drawn box and return `divSearchBox` to its caller:

```
msnWebSearch.drawResultBox = function (e) {
    var divSearchBox= document.createElement("div");
    var divHeading = document.createElement("div");
    var divResultsPane = document.createElement("div");
    var aCloseLink = document.createElement("a");

    aCloseLink.href = "#";
    aCloseLink.className = "ajaxWebSearchCloseLink";
    aCloseLink.onclick = this.close;
    aCloseLink.appendChild(document.createTextNode("X"));

    divHeading.className = "ajaxWebSearchHeading";
```

```
divHeading.appendChild(document.createTextNode("MSN Search Results"));
divHeading.appendChild(aCloseLink);

var divLoading = document.createElement("div");
divLoading.appendChild(document.createTextNode("Loading Search Feed"));

divResultsPane.className = "ajaxWebSearchResults";
divResultsPane.appendChild(divLoading);

divSearchBox.className = "ajaxWebSearchBox";
divSearchBox.appendChild(divHeading);
divSearchBox.appendChild(divResultsPane);

document.body.appendChild(divSearchBox);

    this.position(e, divSearchBox);

    return divSearchBox;
};
```

The way the msnWebSearch object is set up, divSearchBox must be returned to its caller for other operations.

Displaying the Results

The populateResults() method populates the result pane with the search results. It accepts two arguments: the element to contain the results and an XParser object.

```
msnWebSearch.populateResults = function (divResultsPane,oParser) {
    var oFragment = document.createDocumentFragment();

    divResultsPane.removeChild(divResultsPane.firstChild);

    //more code to come
}
```

This method generates <a/> elements programmatically with DOM methods; these elements are appended to a document fragment created in the first line. The next line removes the loading <div/> element appended in drawResultBox().The next step is to create the links:

```
msnWebSearch.populateResults = function (divResultsPane,oParser) {
    var oFragment = document.createDocumentFragment();

    divResultsPane.removeChild(divResultsPane.firstChild);

    for (var i = 0; i < oParser.items.length; i++) {
        var oItem = oParser.items[i];

        var aResultLink = document.createElement("a");
        aResultLink.href = oItem.link.value;
        aResultLink.className = "ajaxWebSearchLink";
        aResultLink.target = "_new";
```

```
        aResultLink.appendChild(document.createTextNode(oItem.title.value));

        oFragment.appendChild(aResultLink);
    }

    divResultsPane.appendChild(oFragment);
}
```

This code cycles through the items of the feed, generates links from the data, and appends the <a/> element to the document fragment. When the loop exits, the document fragment is appended to divResultsPane to display the search results.

Closing the Results Box

To close the search results box, the msnWebSearch object provides the close() method:

```
msnWebSearch.close = function () {
    var divSearchBox = this.parentNode.parentNode;
    document.body.removeChild(divSearchBox);

    return false;
};
```

The search box isn't really closed; in fact, it is removed from the document. To do this, retrieve the divSearchBox element. The first line does this by retrieving the parent node of this element's parent. Because close() handles the onclick event, this references the link. The next line removes the divSearchBox element from the document. The last line, return false, forces the browser not to follow the default behavior of a link (going to the location noted in the href attribute).

Building the Search Interface

The last method of the msnWebSearch object is search(), which provides the interface to perform a search. You can call search() with the onclick event of an element. It accepts two methods, an event object and the search term:

```
msnWebSearch.search = function (e,sSearchTerm) {
    var divSearchBox = this.drawResultBox(e);
    var url = "websearch.php?search=" + encodeURIComponent(sSearchTerm);

    function parserCallback(oParser) {
        msnWebSearch.populateResults(divSearchBox.childNodes[1],oParser);
    }

    xparser.getFeed(url, parserCallback, this);
};
```

The first line calls the drawResultBox() method and passes the event, e, to it. The next line encodes the URL for proper transmission. The enclosed parserCallback() function is the callback function for XParser, and it will call the populateResult() method when the search feed is finished loading to populate the search box with results. The last line uses the xparser.getFeed() method to retrieve the search feed.

Of course, one of the reasons for building this widget is to make it fit the look of your own site.

Customizing the Web Search Widget

Thanks to CSS, you can easily customize the widget for your existing site and any redesign you may have later down the road.

The first CSS class is `ajaxWebSearchBox`, the class for the search box. Because the box is positioned to where the mouse was clicked, it must have a `position` of "absolute":

```
.ajaxWebSearchBox
{
    position: absolute;
    background-color: #0d1e4a;
    width: 500px;
    padding: 1px;
}
```

The absolute position is the only requirement. All other properties are optional according to your needs. In this example, the box has a dark-blue background, a width of 500 pixels, and 1 pixel of padding on all four sides. This padding will give the box a 1-pixel border around the box's contents.

The next class is `ajaxWebSearchHeading`, which contains the box's heading text and the closing link.

```
.ajaxWebSearchHeading
{
    position: relative;
    background-color: #1162cc;
    font: bold 14px tahoma;
    height: 21px;
    color: white;
    padding: 3px 0px 0px 2px;
}
```

Once again, the only required property is `position`. The remaining properties help to give the element a heading-like look. The background color is a lighter blue with white, bold text 14 pixels high and in the Tahoma font. The element's height is 21 pixels, and it is padded on the top and left edges.

The closing link is absolutely positioned in order to place it in the top-right corner:

```
a.ajaxWebSearchCloseLink
{
    position: absolute;
    right: 5px;
    top: 3px;
    text-decoration: none;
    color: white;
}

a.ajaxWebSearchCloseLink:hover
{
    color: red;
}
```

The element is positioned 5 pixels from the right and 3 pixels from the top, placing the element in the top-right corner. This link does not have any text decoration and is colored white. When the user hovers over the link, the text color turns red.

> Note that no `visited` or `active` **pseudo-classes are used. This is because the window always ignores the** `href` **attribute of this link (it has** `return false` **in its event handler). Therefore, the link is never truly active or visited.**

Next, the `ajaxWebSearchResults` class styles the results pane:

```
.ajaxWebSearchResults
{
    background-color: #d3e5fa;
    padding: 5px;
}
```

There are no required CSS properties for this element. The existing properties are merely to define the results pane and make it relatively easy to read. The background color is a light blue, and 5 pixels of padding surround the edges. You can also style the loading message:

```
.ajaxWebSearchResults div
{
    text-align: center;
    font: bold 14px tahoma;
    color: #0a246a;
}
```

This element does not have a class name, but you can still style it by using the `parent child` notation shown in the preceding example. This example places the text in the center of the `<div/>` element and gives it a bold, blue font 14 pixels high.

The last elements you need to style are the result links. These have a class name of `ajaxWebSearchLink`:

```
a.ajaxWebSearchLink
{
    font: 12px tahoma;
    padding: 2px;
    display: block;
    color: #0a246a;
}

a.ajaxWebSearchLink:hover
{
    color: white;
    background-color: #316ac5;
}

a.ajaxWebSearchLink:visited
{
    color: purple;
}
```

The only required property is `display`, which is set to `block`. This gives every link its own line. The padding, two pixels worth, gives a bit of separation between the links, making them easier to read. The font-face is Tahoma and is 12 pixels high. Their color is a dark blue, giving a nice contrast to the light blue background of `ajaxWebSearchResults`. When the user hovers over these links, the background color is set to blue, whereas the text color changes to white.

The `visited` pseudo-class is set, in the last rule in the previous code. This is to provide users with user interface cues they are already used to. By having the `visited` pseudo-class set to display a color of purple, users know they've already visited that link, which can save them time by not visiting a page they may not want to.

Using the Web Search Widget

Using this widget is simple. First, upload the `websearch.php` file to your web server. Next, you need an HTML document to reference all the components. The `msnWebSearch` object relies on the `XParser` class, which in turn depends on the zXml library. You must reference these files:

```html
<!DOCTYPE html PUBLIC "-//W3C//DTD XHTML 1.0 Transitional//EN"
        "http://www.w3.org/TR/xhtml1/DTD/xhtml1-transitional.dtd">
<html xml:lang="en" lang="en"  xmlns="http://www.w3.org/1999/xhtml">
<head>
    <meta http-equiv="Content-Type" content="text/html; charset=utf-8" />
    <title>Ajax WebSearch</title>
    <link rel="stylesheet" type="text/css" href="css/websearch.css" />
    <script type="text/javascript" src="js/zxml.js"></script>
    <script type="text/javascript" src="js/xparser.js"></script>
    <script type="text/javascript" src="js/websearch.js"></script>
</head>

<body>


</body>
</html>
```

To perform a search, set the `msnWebSearch.search()` method as the element's `onclick` handler:

```html
<!DOCTYPE html PUBLIC "-//W3C//DTD XHTML 1.0 Transitional//EN"
        "http://www.w3.org/TR/xhtml1/DTD/xhtml1-transitional.dtd">
<html xml:lang="en" lang="en"  xmlns="http://www.w3.org/1999/xhtml">
<head>
    <meta http-equiv="Content-Type" content="text/html; charset=utf-8" />
    <title>Ajax WebSearch</title>
    <link rel="stylesheet" type="text/css" href="css/websearch.css" />
    <script type="text/javascript" src="js/zxml.js"></script>
    <script type="text/javascript" src="js/xparser.js"></script>
    <script type="text/javascript" src="js/websearch.js"></script>
```

```
  </head>

  <body>
```

```
        <a href="#" onclick='msnWebSearch.search(event,"\"Professional Ajax\"");
            return false;'>Search for "Professional Ajax"</a>

        <br /><br /><br /><br />

        <a href="#" onclick='msnWebSearch.search(event,"Professional Ajax");
            return false;'>Search for Professional Ajax</a>
```

```
  </body>
  </html>
```

The first new link performs a search for the exact phrase Professional Ajax, whereas the second searches for all the words. Also note the `return false` in the `onclick` event. Once again, this forces the browser to ignore the `href` attribute and is required. Clicking these links will draw the search box at the mouse's cursor, and you'll have the search results just pixels away.

Summary

In this chapter, you learned a brief history of online syndication, including the rise of RSS and Atom as the two dominant XML formats for syndication. Next, you learned how to create `XParser`, a JavaScript RSS/Atom parser that provides an easy-to-use interface for developers of web applications based on RSS and Atom. Using this library, you built two widgets that can easily be used in any Web application.

You first learned how to create a news ticker built upon PHP, DHTML, and Ajax to display news feeds in a scrolling format. You also enabled this widget to auto-update, making sure that the latest information is available for your readers.

The second widget implemented an Ajax search, using MSN's search capabilities to display the search results. Through PHP, this widget retrieved the search result RSS feed, and a static JavaScript object displayed the results to the user.

8

JSON

With the popularity of web services around 2004, XML practically became the de facto standard for data transmission. However, XML is not without its detractors. Some consider it to be overly verbose for data transmission purposes, necessitating the sending of many more bytes across the Internet to accomplish what could have been done in a much smaller form. Because of this consideration, new forms of XML compression and even entirely new XML formats, such as Binary XML, have been developed. All these solutions work on extending or adding on to XML, making backward compatibility an issue. Douglas Crockford, a long-time software engineer, proposed a new data format built on JavaScript, called *JavaScript Object Notation* (JSON).

What Is JSON?

JSON is a very lightweight data format based on a subset of the JavaScript syntax, namely array and object literals. Because it uses JavaScript syntax, JSON definitions can be included within JavaScript files and accessed without the extra parsing that comes with XML-based languages. But before you can use JSON, it's important to understand the specific JavaScript syntax for array and object literals.

Array Literals

Array literals are specified by using square brackets ([and]) to enclose a comma-delimited list of JavaScript values (meaning a string, number, Boolean, or null value), such as:

```
var aNames = ["Benjamin", "Michael", "Scott"];
```

This is functionally equivalent to the following, more traditional form:

```
var aNames = new Array("Benjamin", "Michael", "Scott");
```

Regardless of how the array is defined, the result is the same. Values are accessed in the array by using the array name and bracket notation:

```
alert(aNames[0]);     //outputs "Benjamin"
alert(aNames[1]);     //outputs "Michael"
alert(aNames[2]);     //outputs "Scott"
```

Note that the first position in the array is 0, and the value in that position is "Benjamin".

Because arrays in JavaScript are not typed, they can be used to store any number of different datatypes:

```
var aValues = ["string", 24, true, null];
```

This array contains a string, followed by a number, followed by a Boolean, followed by a null value. This is completely legal and perfectly fine JavaScript (though not recommended for maintainability purposes).

> It's important to note that both methods of creating arrays are acceptable when writing JavaScript, but only array literals are valid in JSON.

Object Literals

Object literals are used to store information in name-value pairs, ultimately creating an object. An object literal is defined by two curly braces ({ and }). Inside of these can be placed any number of name-value pairs, defined with a string, a colon, and the value. Each name-value pair must be followed with a comma, except for the last one (making this more like defining an associative array in Perl). For example:

```
var oCar = {
    "color" : "red",
    "doors" : 4,
    "paidFor" : true
};
```

This code creates an object with three properties named color, doors, and paidFor, each containing different values. These properties are accessed by using the object name and dot notation, such as:

```
alert(oCar.color);      //outputs "red"
alert(oCar.doors);      //outputs "4"
alert(oCar.paidFor);    //outputs "true"
```

Bracket notation can also be used by passing in the name of the property as a string value (similar to the way it was defined using object literal notation):

```
alert(oCar["color"]);     //outputs "red"
alert(oCar["doors"]);     //outputs "4"
alert(oCar["paidFor"]);   //outputs "true"
```

The same object could be created using the JavaScript `Object` constructor, like this:

```
var oCar = new Object();
oCar.color = "red";
oCar.doors = 4;
oCar.paidFor = true;
```

As you can see, the object literal notation requires much less code than using the `Object` constructor.

> **Once again, although either approach is valid in JavaScript, only object literal notation is valid in JSON.**

Mixing Literals

It's possible to mix object and array literals, creating an array of objects or an object containing an array. Suppose that you wanted to create an array of car objects similar to the one created in the last section:

```
var aCars = [
    {
        "color" : "red",
        "doors" : 2,
        "paidFor" : true
    },
    {
        "color" : "blue",
        "doors" : 4,
        "paidFor" : true
    },
    {
        "color" : "white",
        "doors" : 2,
        "paidFor" : false
    }
];
```

This code defines an array, `aCars`, which has three objects in it. The three objects each have properties named `color`, `doors`, and `paidFor`. (Each object represents a car, of course.) The information in the array is accessible by using a combination of bracket and dot notation. For example, the following line will get the number of doors on the second car in the array:

```
alert(aCars[1].doors);    //outputs "4"
```

In this example, you are first getting the value in the second position of the array (position 1) and then getting the property named `doors`.

You can also define the array to be inside of object literals, such as:

```
var oCarInfo = {
    "availableColors" : [ "red", "white", "blue" ],
    "availableDoors" : [ 2, 4 ]
};
```

This code defines an object called `oCarInfo` that has two properties, `availableColors` and `availableDoors`. Both of these properties are arrays, containing strings and numbers, respectively. To access a value here, just reverse the order of the bracket and dot notation. So, to get to the second available color, do this:

```
alert(oCarInfo.availableColors[1]);
```

In this example, you are first returning the property named `availableColors` and then getting the value in the second position (position 1). But what does all this have to do with JSON?

JSON Syntax

JSON syntax is really nothing more than the mixture of object and array literals to store data. The only difference from the examples in the last section is that JSON doesn't have variables. Remember, JSON represents only data; it has no concept of variables, assignments, or equality. Therefore, the JSON code for the last example is simply:

```
{
    "availableColors" : [ "red", "white", "blue" ],
    "availableDoors" : [ 2, 4 ]
}
```

Note that the variable `oCarInfo` has been removed, as has the semicolon following the closing curly brace. If this data were transmitted via HTTP to a browser, it would be fairly quick because of the small number of characters. Suppose that this data was retrieved by using XHR (or some other form of client-server communication) and stored in a variable named `sJSON`. You now have a string of information, not an object, and certainly not an object with two arrays. To transform it into an object, simply use the JavaScript `eval()` function:

```
var oCarInfo = eval("(" + sJSON + ")");
```

This example surrounds the JSON text with parentheses and then passes that string into the `eval()` function, which acts like a JavaScript interpreter. The result of this operation is a JavaScript object identical to the `oCarInfo` object defined in the last section. Information in this object can be accessed in the exact same way:

```
alert(oCarInfo.availableColors[0]);    //outputs "red"
alert(oCarInfo.availableDoors[1]);     //ouputs "4"
```

> It's very important to include the extra parentheses around any JSON string before passing it into `eval()`. Remember, curly braces also represent statements in JavaScript (such as used with the `if` statement). The only way the interpreter knows that the curly braces represent an object and not a statement is by looking for an equals sign before it or to look for parentheses around it (which indicates that the code is an expression to be evaluated instead of a statement to be run).

There are obvious benefits to using JSON as a data format for JavaScript communication: it takes the evaluation of the data out of your hands and, therefore, grants you faster access to the information contained within.

JSON Encoding/Decoding

To aid JavaScript developers with JSON usage, Crockford has written a JavaScript library that adds several methods for translating data between JSON and JavaScript. This library is available at www.json.org/json.js. Unlike other JavaScript libraries, this one takes advantage of JavaScript's extensibility, adding methods to `Object`, `Array`, and `String`.

The first method is `parseJSON()`, which is accessible on any string. For instance, if you have a string `sJSON` that contains JSON code, it can be translated into a JavaScript object like this:

```
var oObject = sJSON.parseJSON();
```

This method provides safer evaluation of JSON code than `eval()`, which evaluates all JavaScript code and could potentially allow the execution of arbitrary code. The `parseJSON()` method ensures that the JSON code contains only data and will not result in code being executed.

The library also adds the `toJSONString()` method to all objects, including `Array`. This method recursively serializes any object into a JSON string. Consider the following example:

```
var oCar = new Object();
oCar.doors = 4;
oCar.color = "blue";
oCar.year = 1995;
oCar.drivers = new Array("Penny", "Dan", "Kris");

document.write( oCar.toJSONString());
```

This code outputs the following JSON string:

```
{"doors":4,"color":"blue","year":1995,"drivers":["Penny","Dan","Kris"]}
```

The ability to encode and decode between JavaScript and JSON is an important ability and one that Crockford's library provides in a secure manner. With this tool, you're now ready to use JSON in an enterprise-level web application.

JSON versus XML

As mentioned previously, one of the advantages of JSON over XML is that it's more compact. XML is considered by some to be overly verbose for its purpose. But what does this mean exactly? Consider the following XML data:

```
<classinfo>
    <students>
        <student>
            <name>Michael Smith</name>
            <average>99.5</average>
            <age>17</age>
            <graduating>true</graduating>
        </student>
        <student>
            <name>Steve Johnson</name>
            <average>34.87</average>
            <age>17</age>
            <graduating>false</graduating>
        </student>
        <student>
            <name>Rebecca Young</name>
            <average>89.6</average>
            <age>18</age>
            <graduating>true</graduating>
        </student>
    </students>
</classinfo>
```

This example contains information about three students in a class. Right away, there is some XML information that isn't entirely necessary: the `<classinfo>` and `<students/>` elements. These elements help to define the overall structure and meaning of the information, but the actual information you're interested in is the students and their information. Plus, for each piece of information about the students, the name of the information is repeated twice, although the actual data appears only once (for example, `"name"` appears both in `<name>` and `</name>`. Consider the same information formatted as JSON:

```
{ "classinfo" :
    {
        "students" : [
            {
                "name" : "Michael Smith",
                "average" : 99.5,
                "age" : 17,
                "graduating" : true
            },
            {
                "name" : "Steve Johnson",
                "average" : 34.87,
                "age" : 17,
                "graduating" : false
            },
            {
```

```
                "name" : "Rebecca Young",
                "average" : 89.6,
                "age" : 18,
                "graduating" : true
            }
        ]
    }
}
```

A lot of the superfluous information isn't present in this JSON form. Since closing tags aren't necessary to match opening tags, this greatly reduces the number of bytes needed to transmit the same information. Not including spaces, the JSON data is 224 bytes, whereas the comparable XML data is 365 bytes, saving more than 100 bytes. (This is why Crockford, JSON's creator, calls it the "fat-free alternative to XML.")

The disadvantage to JSON-formatted data as compared to XML is that it's far less readable to the naked eye. Because XML is verbose, it's fairly easy to understand what data is being represented with a simple glance. JSON, with its shorthand notation, can be difficult to decipher without other software tools. Of course, an argument can be made that data exchange formats should never be viewed with the naked eye. Thus, it makes sense that server-side JSON tools are necessary to create the data being sent to the client.

Server-Side JSON Tools

When Crockford first proposed JSON, he was the only one creating tools for encoding and decoding. As the popularity of JSON grew, others started to step up and create client- and server-side libraries to facilitate its use. Although it is beyond the scope of this book to discuss every one of these tools, it is useful to take a look at one and then develop a solution using it.

JSON-PHP

JSON-PHP is a PHP library for encoding and decoding JSON information. This utility, written by Michal Migurski, is available for free at http://mike.teczno.com/json.html. To use this library, simply include the JSON.php file and create an instance of the Services_JSON object:

```php
<?php
    require_once("JSON.php");
    $oJSON = new Services_JSON();
?>
```

The first line includes the JSON.php file that contains the Services_JSON object definition. The second line simply instantiates the object and stores it in the variable $oJSON. Now, you're ready to start encoding and decoding JSON in your PHP page.

The encode() Method

To encode a PHP object into a JSON string, use the encode() method, which accepts a single argument: an object to encode, which can be an array or a full-fledged object. It doesn't matter how the object or array was created, by using a class definition or not; all objects can be encoded using this method. Consider the following class definition:

```php
<?php
    class Person {

        var $age;
        var $hairColor;
        var $name;
        var $siblingNames;

        function Person($name, $age, $hairColor) {
            $this->name = $name;
            $this->age = $age;
            $this->hairColor = $hairColor;
            $this->siblingNames = array();
        }
    }
?>
```

This PHP code defines a class called `Person` that stores some personal information. The class would be used as follows:

```php
<?php
    $oPerson = new Person("Mike", 26, "brown");
    $oPerson->siblingNames[0] = "Matt";
    $oPerson->siblingNames[1] = "Tammy";
?>
```

To encode the `$oPerson` object, simply pass it into the `encode()` method, like this:

```php
<?php
    $sJSONText = $oJSON->encode($oPerson);
?>
```

This creates a JSON string of:

```
{"age":26,"hairColor":"brown","name":"Mike","siblingNames":["Matt","Tammy"]}
```

The `$oPerson` object is now ready to be transferred to JavaScript or any other language that can support JSON-encoded information.

The decode() Method

The `decode()` method is used to perform the opposite function, taking a JSON string and parsing it into an object. Suppose that you have the JSON string displayed previously and want to create a PHP object from it. Just pass the string into the `decode()` method:

```php
<?php
    $oPerson = $oJSON->decode($sJSONText);
?>
```

Now, the $oPerson variable can be used just like the one in the previous example, as if it were created using the Person class:

```php
<?php
    print("<h3>Person Information</h3>");
    print("<p>Name: ".$oPerson->name."<br />");
    print("Age: ".$oPerson->age."<br />");
    print("Hair Color: ".$oPerson->hairColor."<br />");
    print("Sibling Names:</p><ul>");

    for ($i=0; $i < count($oPerson->siblingNames); $i++) {
        print("<li>".$oPerson->siblingNames[$i]."</li>");
    }

    print("</ul>");

?>
```

This code prints out the information contained in the $oPerson object, proving that the object has been constructed appropriately. JSON-PHP is in several projects throughout this book because it is quite simply the easiest way to deal with JSON in a server-side language.

Other Tools

As of 2006, there are JSON libraries for use with every popular server-side language. Depending on your environment, you may find these resources useful:

- ❑ **C#/.NET:** The Json.NET library is a free JSON parser/serializer that mimics the built-in XML functionality of .NET. Json.NET is available at www.newtonsoft.com/products/json.

- ❑ **ColdFusion:** The CFJSON library, written by Jehiah Czebotar, is available at http://jehiah.com/projects/cfjson.

- ❑ **Java/JSP:** The JSON in Java utilities, written by Douglas Crockford, are available at www.json.org/java/.

- ❑ **Perl:** The JSON library, written by Makamaka Hannyaharamitu, is available at http://search.cpan.org/dist/JSON/.

- ❑ **PHP:** In addition to JSON-PHP, there is also php-json, a C extension for PHP written by Omar Kilani and available at www.aurore.net/projects/php-json/. You must be comfortable with compiling PHP with extensions.

- ❑ **Python:** The json-py library, written by Patrick D. Logan, is available at https://sourceforge.net/projects/json-py/.

Douglas Crockford also maintains a fairly comprehensive list of JSON utilities at www.json.org. It's a good idea to check there for other language needs.

Creating an Autosuggest Textbox

The best way to learn about any new programming concept is to put it into a practical example. Google Suggest (located at `www.google.com/webhp?complete=1`) is a very simple Ajax application that many programmers have spent time dissecting, analyzing, and re-creating. If you haven't yet taken a look at the live application, please do so now; it will greatly aid in your understanding of the following example.

Functionality such as this, suggesting to the user values to type in, has been around in desktop applications for some time now. Google Suggest brought the idea to the Web and generated a lot of excitement while doing it. As mentioned earlier in the book, Google Suggest was one of the very early Ajax applications that got developers excited about the concept. It seems fitting to attempt to emulate the behavior of Google Suggest to help others understand Ajax.

The example built in this section aids in the selection of states or provinces in a personal information form. For sites that deal with international customers, it is often vital to include the state or province along with the country. However, it's not optimal to load every state and province in the entire world into a drop-down box for the user to select from. It's much easier to let the user start typing and then retrieve only those results that would make the most sense. Autosuggest functionality is perfect for this use case.

Functionality Overview

Before building anything, it's always helpful to understand exactly what you're building. Anyone can say they are going to emulate the functionality of Google Suggest, but what does that mean? The example you will build in this section has the following functionality:

❑   **Typeahead:** As the user is typing, the rest of the textbox fills in with the best suggestion at the time. As the user continues to type, the textbox automatically adjusts its suggestion. The suggested text always appears selected (highlighted). This should work no matter how fast the user types.

❑   **Suggestions list:** Also as the user is typing, a drop-down list of other suggestions is displayed. These suggestions are generated automatically while the user types so that there is no discernible delay.

❑   **Keyboard controls:** When the suggestions are displayed, the user is able to scroll up and down the list by using the up and down arrows on the keyboard and select a suggestion. Pressing Enter places the value into the textbox and hides the suggestion list. The Esc key can also be used to hide the suggestions.

❑   **Hide suggestions:** The drop-down suggestion list is smart enough to hide itself whenever the textbox is not used or when the browser window is hidden.

As with many applications, it may be shocking how much is actually going on behind the scenes. This is the key with Ajax: you don't stop and think about what's going on, because it works in an intuitive way.

The HTML

The first step in any client-side component is to build the HTML to use. For the autosuggest textbox, this includes the textbox itself as well as the drop-down list of suggestions. You're probably familiar with the HTML textbox:

```
<input type="text" name="txtAutosuggest" value="" />
```

In most cases, this line would be enough to use a textbox. The problem is that some browsers (notably Internet Explorer on Windows and Mozilla Firefox on all operating systems) provide autocomplete functionality that drops down a list of suggestions based on values you've entered before. Since this would compete directly with the suggestions you'll be providing, this has to be turned off. To do so, set the autocomplete attribute to off:

```
<input type="text" name="txtAutosuggest" value="" autocomplete="off" />
```

Now, you can be assured that there will be no interference from the autocomplete browser behavior. The only other user interface component to design is the drop-down list of suggestions.

The suggestion drop-down list is nothing more than an absolutely positioned <div/> element that is positioned below the textbox so as to give the illusion of being a drop-down list (see Figure 8-1).

Figure 8-1

Inside of this <div/> element are several other <div/> elements, one for each suggestion. By changing the style of these elements, it's possible to achieve the look of highlighting a given suggestion. The HTML to create the list displayed in Figure 8-1 is as follows:

```
<div class="suggestions">
    <div class="current">Maine</div>
    <div>Maryland</div>
    <div>Massachusetts</div>
    <div>Michigan</div>
    <div>Minnesota</div>
    <div>Mississippi</div>
    <div>Missouri</div>
    <div>Montana</div>
</div>
```

This HTML isn't coded directly into the main HTML file; instead, it is created dynamically by JavaScript code. However, you need to know the general format of the HTML in order to create it appropriately.

Of course, some CSS is needed to make the drop-down list function properly. The outermost <div/> has a class of suggestions, which is defined as:

```
div.suggestions {
    -moz-box-sizing: border-box;
    box-sizing: border-box;
    background-color: white;
    border: 1px solid black;
    position: absolute;
}
```

The first two lines of this CSS class are for browsers that support two forms of box sizing: content box and border box (for more information, read www.quirksmode.org/css/box.html). In quirks mode, Internet Explorer defaults to border box; in standards mode, Internet Explorer defaults to content box. Most other DOM-compliant browsers (Mozilla, Opera, and Safari) default to content box, meaning that there is a difference in how the <div/> element will be rendered among browsers. To provide for this, the first two lines of the CSS class set rendering to border box. The first line, -moz-box-sizing, is Mozilla-specific and used for older Mozilla browsers; the second line is for browsers that support the official CSS3 box-sizing property. Assuming that you use quirks mode in your page, this class will work just fine. (If you use standards mode, simply remove these first two lines.)

The remaining styles simply add a border and specify that the <div/> element be absolutely positioned.

Next, a little bit of formatting is needed for the drop-down list items:

```
div.suggestions div {
    cursor: default;
    padding: 0px 3px;
}
```

The first line specifies the default cursor (the arrow) to be displayed when the mouse is over an item in the drop-down list. Without this, the cursor would display as the caret, which is the normal cursor for textboxes and web pages in general. The user needs to believe that the drop-down item is not a part of the regular page flow, but an attachment to the textbox, and changing the cursor helps. The second line simply applies some padding to the item (which you can modify as you wish).

Last, some CSS is needed to format the currently selected item in the drop-down list. When an item is selected, the background will be changed to blue and the text color will be changed to white. This provides a basic highlight that is typically used in drop-down menus:

```
div.suggestions div.current {
    background-color: #3366cc;
    color: white;
}
```

All of these styles are to be contained in an external CSS file named autosuggest.css.

The Database Table

In order to easily query the states and provinces that match a particular text snippet, it is necessary to use a database table. The database table can be very simple for this example, although you may need more information to make it practical for your needs. To get this to work, you really need only a single column to store the state and province names. However, it's always best to define a primary key, so this table will include a second column containing an auto-incremented ID number for each state or province. The following SQL statement creates a table named StatesAndProvinces with two columns, Id and Name:

```
CREATE TABLE StatesAndProvinces (
    Id INT NOT NULL AUTO_INCREMENT,
    Name VARCHAR(255) NOT NULL,
    PRIMARY KEY (Id)
) COMMENT = 'States and Provinces';
```

Of course, the time-consuming part is to fill in state and province names from various countries around the world. The code download for this example, available at www.wrox.com, includes a SQL file that populates the table with all U.S. states as well as one that will insert all Canadian provinces and territories.

Setting up this information in a database table enables you to quickly get a list of suggestions for text the user has typed in. If the user has typed the letter *M*, for example, you can run the following query to get the first five suggestions:

```
SELECT *
FROM StatesAndProvinces
WHERE Name LIKE 'M%'
ORDER BY Name ASC
LIMIT 0, 5
```

This statement returns a maximum of five suggestions, in alphabetical order, for all names starting with *M*. Later, this will be used in the PHP code that returns the suggestions.

The Architecture

In Chapter 1, you saw the basic architecture of an Ajax solution involving the user interface and Ajax engine on the client. The autosuggest architecture follows this general format, where the user interface is the autosuggest control and the Ajax engine is a suggestion provider (see Figure 8-2).

In this architecture, the autosuggest control has no idea where the suggestions are coming from; they could be coming from the client or the server. All the autosuggest control knows is how to call the suggestion provider to get suggestions for the text contained within the textbox. The suggestion provider handles all the server communication and notifies the autosuggest control when the suggestions are available. To accomplish this, both the autosuggest control and the suggestion provider need to implement specific interfaces so that each knows what method to call on the other.

Autosuggest Control Architecture

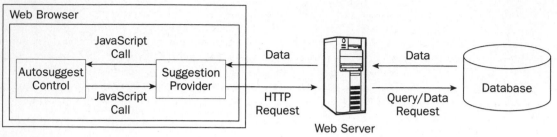

Figure 8-2

The Classes

Two classes are necessary to represent the two client-side components of the autosuggest functionality, appropriately called `AutoSuggestControl` and `SuggestionProvider`. The `AutoSuggestControl` is assigned a `SuggestionProvider` when it is created so that all requests go through it. The `SuggestionProvider` has only one method, `requestSuggestions()`, which is called by the `AutoSuggestControl` whenever suggestions are needed. This method takes two arguments: the `AutoSuggestControl` itself and a Boolean value indicating whether the control should type ahead when the suggestions are returned.

When the suggestions have been retrieved, the `SuggestionProvider` calls the `autosuggest()` method of the `AutoSuggestControl`, passing in the array of suggestions as well as the typeahead flag that was passed into it. This allows for a delay between the request for suggestions and the response, making it possible to use asynchronous requests. This approach sounds more complicated than it is; Figure 8-3 represents the interaction between these two objects in a clearer manner.

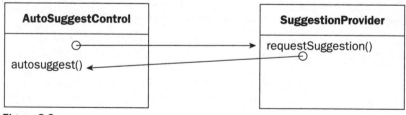

Figure 8-3

With the architecture designed, it's time to start coding.

The AutoSuggest Control

The `AutoSuggestControl` class is the wrapper for all autosuggest functionality. To work properly, the control needs to know which textbox to work on and the suggestion provider to use. This makes for a relatively simple constructor:

```
function AutoSuggestControl(oTextbox, oProvider) {
    this.provider = oProvider;
    this.textbox = oTextbox;
}
```

It's upon this simple base that the complex functionality of an autosuggest textbox is built.

Since the `AutoSuggestControl` class is quite complicated, it's much simpler to break up its explanation into specific types of functionality. The following sections build on each other, and the complete code can be downloaded from www.wrox.com.

Implementing Typeahead

Typeahead textboxes look at what the user has typed and then make a suggestion, highlighting only the part that was added automatically. For example, if you were to type *Ma* into a textbox, the suggestion may be *Maine*, but only *ine* would be highlighted. Doing this allows the user to continue typing without interruption because any new characters simply replace the highlighted section.

Originally, the only type of highlighting possible using JavaScript was to highlight all the text in the textbox using the `select()` method, as follows:

```
var oTextbox = document.getElementById("txtState");
oTextbox.select();
```

This code gets a reference to a textbox with the ID of `txtState` and then selects all the text contained within it. Although this functionality is fine for many everyday uses, it's not very helpful for implementing typeahead. Thankfully, both Internet Explorer and Firefox have ways of selecting parts of the text instead of the entire item (for other browsers, this feature is not available). But as usual, the two biggest combatants in the browser world do things in two completely different ways.

The Internet Explorer solution is to use a text range. Not to be confused with DOM ranges, an Internet Explorer text range is an invisible selection of text on the page, beginning on a single character and ending on a single character. When a text range is filled out, you can highlight just the text contained within it, which is perfect for typeahead. To create a text range for a specific textbox, you use the `createTextRange()` method that Internet Explorer provides on every textbox.

Once you have a text range, its methods enable you to select certain parts of the text. Although there are many text range methods, the only ones of interest for this example are `moveStart()` and `moveEnd()`, both of which accept two arguments: a unit and a number. The unit can be `character`, `word`, `sentence`, or `textedit`, whereas the number indicates the number of units to move from the start or end of the text (this should be a positive number for `moveStart()` and a negative for `moveEnd()`). When the endpoints of the text range are set, you can call its `select()` method to highlight just those characters. For example, to select just the first three characters in a textbox, you could do this:

```
var oRange = oTextbox.createTextRange();
oRange.moveStart("character", 0);
oRange.moveEnd("character", 3 - oTextbox.value.length);
oRange.select();
oTextbox.focus();
```

Note that to get the appropriate value for moveEnd(), it's necessary to subtract the length of the text in the textbox from the number of characters to select (3). The last step is to set the focus to the textbox so that the selection is visible. (Text can be selected only when the textbox has focus.) The process is a bit involved in Internet Explorer, but pretty easy to script. Firefox, on the other hand, is very straightforward.

Textboxes in Firefox have a nonstandard method called setSelectionRange(), which accepts two arguments: the index of the character to start with and the index of character after the last character to select. So, to select the first three characters in a textbox using Mozilla, you need only two lines of code:

```
oTextbox.setSelectionRange(0,3);
oTextbox.focus();
```

The first method you'll need in the AutoSuggestControl class is a method to select a range of characters in a browser-specific way. This method, called selectRange(), handles all the dirty work for you:

```
AutoSuggestControl.prototype.selectRange = function (iStart, iEnd) {
    if (this.textbox.createTextRange) {
        var oRange = this.textbox.createTextRange();
        oRange.moveStart("character", iStart);
        oRange.moveEnd("character", iEnd- this.textbox.value.length);
        oRange.select();
    } else if (this.textbox.setSelectionRange) {
        this.textbox.setSelectionRange(iStart, iEnd);
    }

    this.textbox.focus();
};
```

This method uses feature detection, the process of detecting certain browser features, to determine how to select the characters. It tests for the existence of the createTextRange() method to determine whether the Internet Explorer text ranges should be used, and tests for the setSelectionRange() method to determine whether the Firefox method should be used. The arguments are the first character to select and the number of characters to select. These values are then passed to the browser-specific methods of text selection.

The typeAhead() Method

Now that you can select specific parts of the textbox, it's time to implement the typeahead functionality. To do this, a typeAhead() method is defined that accepts a single argument: the suggestion to display in the textbox. The suggestion being passed in is assumed to be appropriate (and assumed to have at least one character). This method then does three things:

1. Gets the length of the text already in the textbox.
2. Places the suggestion into the textbox.
3. Selects only the portion of the text that the user didn't type using the information from step 1.

Additionally, since typeahead can be supported only in Internet Explorer and Firefox, you should check to make sure that one of those browsers is being used. If the browser doesn't support text selection, then none of the steps should be executed so as not to interrupt the user's typing. Once again, testing for the `createTextRange()` and `setSelectionRange()` methods of the textbox is the way to go:

```
AutoSuggestControl.prototype.typeAhead = function (sSuggestion) {
    if (this.textbox.createTextRange || this.textbox.setSelectionRange) {
        var iLen = this.textbox.value.length;
        this.textbox.value = sSuggestion;
        this.selectRange(iLen, sSuggestion.length);
    }
};
```

With this method complete, you now need another method to call it and pass in the suggestion.

The autosuggest() Method

Perhaps the most important method in the control is `autosuggest()`. This single method is responsible for receiving an array of suggestions for the textbox and then deciding what to do with them. Eventually, this method will be used to implement the full autosuggest functionality (including drop-down suggestions), but for now, it's used to implement typeahead only.

Because `autosuggest()` will be passed an array of suggestions, you have your pick as to which one to use for the typeahead value. It's recommended that you always use the first value in the array to keep things simple. The problem is that there may not always be suggestions for a value, in which case an empty array will be passed. The `typeAhead()` method shouldn't be called if there are no suggestions, so it's important to check the length of the array first:

```
AutoSuggestControl.prototype.autosuggest = function (aSuggestions) {
    if (aSuggestions.length > 0) {
        this.typeAhead(aSuggestions[0]);
    }
};
```

But where do the suggestions come from? It's actually the job of the suggestion provider to call this method and pass in the suggestions. Implementation of this feature is discussed later in the chapter.

Handling Key Events

Of course, the autosuggest functionality has to be tied to the textbox using events. There are three events that deal with keys: `keydown`, `keypress`, and `keyup`. The `keydown` event fires whenever the user presses a key on the keyboard but before any changes occur to the textbox. This obviously won't help with auto-suggest because you need to know the full text of the textbox; using this event would mean being one keystroke behind. For the same reason, the `keypress` event can't be used. It is similar to `keydown` but fires only when a character key is pressed. The `keyup` event, however, fires after changes have been made to the textbox, which is exactly when autosuggest should begin working.

Setting up an event handler for the textbox involves two steps: defining a function and assigning it as an event handler. The function is actually a method of the autosuggest control, called `handleKeyUp()`. This method expects the `event` object to be passed in as an argument (how to accomplish this is discussed later) so that it can tell whether the key being pressed should enact the autosuggest functionality. Since `keyup` fires for all keys, not just character keys, you'll receive events when someone uses a cursor key, the Tab key, and any other key on the keyboard. To avoid interfering with how a textbox works, suggestions should be made only when a character key is pressed. This is where the event object's `keyCode` property enters the picture.

The `keyCode` property is supported by most modern browsers (including Internet Explorer on Windows and Macintosh, Firefox, Opera, and Safari) and returns a numeric code representing the key that was pressed. Using this property, it's possible to set up behaviors for specific keys. Since the autosuggest functionality should happen only when character keys are pressed, you need to check this property for an appropriate value before proceeding. Believe it or not, the easiest way to do this is actually to detect the keys that you want to ignore. This approach is more efficient because there are more character keys than non-character keys. The following table displays the key codes for all keys that should be ignored.

Key	Code	Key	Code
Backspace	8	Print Screen	44
Tab	9	Delete	46
Enter	13	F1	112
Shift	16	F2	113
Ctrl	17	F3	114
Alt	18	F4	115
Pause/Break	19	F5	116
Caps Lock	20	F6	117
Esc	27	F7	118
Page Up	33	F8	119
Page Down	34	F9	120
End	35	F10	121
Home	36	F11	122
Left Arrow	37	F12	123
Up Arrow	38		
Right Arrow	39		
Down Arrow	40		

You may notice a pattern among the key codes. It looks like all keys with a code less than or equal to 46 should be ignored, and all keys with codes between 112 and 123 should be ignored. This is generally true, but there is an exception. The space bar has a key code of 32, so you actually need to check to see if the code is less than 32 (but not 16, which is the Shift key), between 33 and 46, or between 112 and 123. If it's not in any one of these groups, then you know it's a character key.

Here's what the handleKeyUp() method looks like:

```
AutoSuggestControl.prototype.handleKeyUp = function (oEvent) {
    var iKeyCode = oEvent.keyCode;

    if ((iKeyCode != 16 && iKeyCode < 32) || (iKeyCode >= 33 && iKeyCode <= 46)
        || (iKeyCode >= 112 && iKeyCode <= 123)) {

        //ignore
    } else {
        this.provider.requestSuggestions(this);
    }
};
```

When a user presses a character key, the autosuggest functionality begins by calling the suggestion provider's requestSuggestions() method and passing a pointer to the autosuggest control as an argument. Remember, it's the suggestion provider that will call the autosuggest() method defined earlier. The requestSuggestions() method begins the process of retrieving suggestions for usage.

With this method defined, it must be assigned as the event handler for the textbox. It's best to create a separate method to handle initializations for the control such as this (there will be more in the future). The init() method serves this purpose:

```
AutoSuggestControl.prototype.init = function () {
    var oThis = this;
    this.textbox.onkeyup = function (oEvent) {
        if (!oEvent) {
            oEvent = window.event;
        }
        oThis.handleKeyUp(oEvent);
    };
};
```

The init() method starts by creating a pointer to the this object so that it may be used later. An anonymous function is defined for the textbox's onkeyup event handler. Inside of this function, the handleKeyUp() method is called using the oThis pointer. (Using this here would refer to the textbox instead of the autosuggest control.)

Since this method requires the event object to be passed in, it's necessary to check for both DOM and Internet Explorer event objects. The DOM event object is passed in as an argument to the event handler, whereas the Internet Explorer event object is a property of window. Instead of doing a browser detect, you can check to see if the oEvent object is passed into the event handler. If not, then assign window.event into the oEvent variable. The oEvent variable can then be passed directly into the handleKeyUp() event handler.

The `init()` method should be called from within the `AutoSuggestControl` constructor:

```
function AutoSuggestControl(oTextbox, oProvider) {
    this.provider = oProvider;
    this.textbox = oTextbox;
    this.init();
}
```

That's all it takes to implement the typeahead functionality of the autosuggest control. At this point, you are displaying a single suggestion to the user as he or she types. The goal is, of course, to provide multiple suggestions using a drop-down list.

Showing Multiple Suggestions

Earlier in the chapter, you took a look at the HTML and CSS used for the drop-down list of suggestions. Now, the task is to create the HTML programmatically and apply the CSS to create the actual functionality; this is a multistep process. First, a property is needed to store the `<div/>` element because various methods of the `AutoSuggestControl` need access to it. This property is called `layer` and is initially set to `null`:

```
function AutoSuggestControl(oTextbox, oProvider) {
    this.layer = null;
    this.provider = oProvider;
    this.textbox = oTextbox;
    this.init();
}
```

The drop-down list will be created after you define a few simple methods to help control its behavior. The simplest method is `hideSuggestions()`, which hides the drop-down list after it has been shown:

```
AutoSuggestControl.prototype.hideSuggestions = function () {
    this.layer.style.visibility = "hidden";
};
```

Next, a method is needed for highlighting the current suggestion in the drop-down list. The `highlightSuggestion()` method accepts a single argument, which is the `<div/>` element containing the current suggestion. The purpose of this method is to set the `<div/>` element's `class` attribute to `current` on the current suggestion and clear the `class` attribute on all others in the list. Doing so provides a highlighting effect on the drop-down list similar to the regular form controls. The algorithm is quite simple: iterate through the child nodes of the layer. If the child node is equal to the node that was passed in, set the `class` to `current`; otherwise, clear the `class` attribute by setting it to an empty string:

```
AutoSuggestControl.prototype.highlightSuggestion = function (oSuggestionNode) {

    for (var i=0; i < this.layer.childNodes.length; i++) {
        var oNode = this.layer.childNodes[i];
        if (oNode == oSuggestionNode) {
            oNode.className = "current"
        } else if (oNode.className == "current") {
            oNode.className = "";
        }
    }
};
```

With these two methods defined, it's time to create the drop-down list <div/>. The createDropDown() method creates the outermost <div/> element and defines the event handlers for the drop-down list. To create the <div/> element, use the createElement() method and then assign the various styling properties:

```
AutoSuggestControl.prototype.createDropDown = function () {

    this.layer = document.createElement("div");
    this.layer.className = "suggestions";
    this.layer.style.visibility = "hidden";
    this.layer.style.width = this.textbox.offsetWidth;
    document.body.appendChild(this.layer);

    //more code to come
};
```

This code first creates the <div/> element and assigns it to the layer property. From there, the className (equivalent to the class attribute) is set to suggestions, as is needed for the CSS to work properly. The next line hides the layer, since it should be invisible initially. Then, the width of the layer is set equal to the width of the textbox by using the textbox's offsetWidth property (this is optional depending on your individual needs). The very last line adds the layer to the document. With the layer created, it's time to assign the event handlers to control it.

At this point, the only concern is making sure that the drop-down list is functional if the user uses the mouse. That is, when the drop-down list is visible, moving the mouse over a suggestion should highlight it. Likewise, when a suggestion is clicked on, it should be placed in the textbox and the drop-down list should be hidden. To make this happen, you need to assign three event handlers: onmouseover, onmousedown, and onmouseup.

The onmouseover event handler is used simply to highlight the current suggestion; onmousedown is used to select the given suggestion (place the suggestion in the textbox and hide the drop-down list), and onmouseup is used to set the focus back to the textbox after a selection has been made. Because all these events are fired by the drop-down list itself, it's best just to use a single function for all of them, as follows:

```
AutoSuggestControl.prototype.createDropDown = function () {

    this.layer = document.createElement("div");
    this.layer.className = "suggestions";
    this.layer.style.visibility = "hidden";
    this.layer.style.width = this.textbox.offsetWidth;
    document.body.appendChild(this.layer);

    var oThis = this;

    this.layer.onmousedown = this.layer.onmouseup =
    this.layer.onmouseover = function (oEvent) {
        oEvent = oEvent || window.event;
        oTarget = oEvent.target || oEvent.srcElement;

        if (oEvent.type == "mousedown") {
            oThis.textbox.value = oTarget.firstChild.nodeValue;
            oThis.hideSuggestions();
```

```
            } else if (oEvent.type == "mouseover") {
                oThis.highlightSuggestion(oTarget);
            } else {
                oThis.textbox.focus();
            }
        };

    };
```

The first part of this section is the assignment that makes oThis equal to the this object. This is necessary so that a reference to the AutoSuggestControl object is accessible from within the event handler. Next, a compound assignment occurs, assigning the same function as an event handler for onmousedown, onmouseup, and onmouseover. Inside of the function, the first two lines are used to account for the different event models (DOM and IE), using a logical OR (||) to assign the values for oEvent and oTarget. (The target will always be a <div/> element containing a suggestion.)

If the event being handled is mousedown, then set the value of the textbox equal to the text inside of the event target. The text inside of the <div/> element is contained in a text node, which is the first child node. The actual text string is contained in the text node's nodeValue property. After the suggestion is placed into the textbox, the drop-down list is hidden.

When the event being handled is mouseover, the event target is passed into the highlightSuggestion() method to provide the hover effect; when the event is mouseup, the focus is set back to the textbox (this fires immediately after mousedown).

Positioning the Drop-Down List

To get the full effect of the drop-down list, it's imperative that it appear directly below the textbox. If the textbox were absolutely positioned, this wouldn't be much of an issue. In actual practice, textboxes are rarely absolutely positioned and more often are placed inline, which presents a problem in aligning the drop-down list. To calculate the position where the drop-down list should appear, you can use the textbox's offsetLeft, offsetTop, and offsetParent properties.

The offsetLeft and offsetTop properties tell you how many pixels away from the left and top of the offsetParent an element is placed. The offsetParent is usually, but not always, the parent node of the element, so to get the left position of the textbox, you need to add up the offsetLeft properties of the textbox and all of its ancestor elements (stopping at <body/>), as shown here:

```
AutoSuggestControl.prototype.getLeft = function () {

    var oNode = this.textbox;
    var iLeft = 0;

    while(oNode != document.body) {
        iLeft += oNode.offsetLeft;
        oNode = oNode.offsetParent;
    }

    return iLeft;
};
```

The `getLeft()` method begins by pointing `oNode` at the textbox and defining `iLeft` with an initial value of 0. The `while` loop will continue to add `oNode.offsetLeft` to `iLeft` as it traverses up the DOM structure to the `<body/>` element.

The same algorithm can be used to get the top of the textbox:

```
AutoSuggestControl.prototype.getTop = function () {

    var oNode = this.textbox;
    var iTop = 0;

    while(oNode != document.body) {
        iTop += oNode.offsetTop;
        oNode = oNode.offsetParent;
    }

    return iTop;
};
```

These two methods will be used to place the drop-down list in the correct location.

Adding and Displaying Suggestions

The next step in the process is to create a method that adds the suggestions into the drop-down list and then displays it. The `showSuggestions()` method accepts an array of suggestions as an argument and then builds up the necessary DOM elements to display them. From there, the method positions the drop-down list underneath the textbox and displays it to the user:

```
AutoSuggestControl.prototype.showSuggestions = function (aSuggestions) {

    var oDiv = null;
    this.layer.innerHTML = "";

    for (var i=0; i < aSuggestions.length; i++) {
        oDiv = document.createElement("div");
        oDiv.appendChild(document.createTextNode(aSuggestions[i]));
        this.layer.appendChild(oDiv);
    }

    this.layer.style.left = this.getLeft() + "px";
    this.layer.style.top = (this.getTop()+this.textbox.offsetHeight) + "px";
    this.layer.style.visibility = "visible";
};
```

The first line simply defines the variable `oDiv` for later use. The second line clears the contents of the drop-down list by setting the `innerHTML` property to an empty string. Then, the `for` loop creates a `<div/>` element and a text node for each suggestion before adding it to the drop-down list layer.

The next section of code starts by setting the left position of the layer using the `getLeft()` method. To set the top position, you need to add the value from `getTop()` to the height of the textbox (retrieved by using the `offsetHeight` property). Without doing this, the drop-down list would appear directly over the textbox. (Remember, `getTop()` retrieves the top of the textbox, not the top of the drop-down list layer.) Last, the layer's `visibility` property is set to `visible` to show it.

Updating the Functionality

In order to show the drop-down list of suggestions, you'll need to make several changes to the functionality defined previously.

The first update is the addition of a second argument to the `autosuggest()` method, which indicates whether the typeahead functionality should be used (the reason why will be explained shortly). Naturally, the `typeAhead()` method should be called only if this argument is `true`. If there's at least one suggestion, typeahead should be used and the drop-down list of suggestions should be displayed by calling `showSuggestions()`; if there are no suggestions, the drop-down list should be hidden by calling `hideSuggestions()`:

```
AutoSuggestControl.prototype.autosuggest = function (aSuggestions, bTypeAhead) {
    if (aSuggestions.length > 0) {
        if (bTypeAhead) {
            this.typeAhead(aSuggestions[0]);
        }
        this.showSuggestions(aSuggestions);
    } else {
        this.hideSuggestions();
    }
};
```

It's also necessary to update the `handleKeyUp()` method for a couple of different reasons. The first reason is to add the `bTypeAhead` argument to the `requestSuggestions()` call. When called from here, this argument will always be `true`:

```
AutoSuggestControl.prototype.handleKeyUp = function (oEvent) {

    var iKeyCode = oEvent.keyCode;

    if ((iKeyCode != 16 && iKeyCode < 32) || (iKeyCode >= 33 && iKeyCode <= 46)
        || (iKeyCode >= 112 && iKeyCode <= 123)) {
        //ignore
    } else {
        this.provider.requestSuggestions(this, true);
    }
};
```

Remember, the `requestSuggestions()` method is defined on the suggestion provider, which is described later in this chapter.

This functionality now works exactly as it did previously, but there are a couple of other keys that require special attention: Backspace and Delete. When either of these keys is pressed, you don't want to activate the typeahead functionality because it will disrupt the process of removing characters from the textbox. However, there's no reason not to show the drop-down list of suggestions. For the Backspace (key code of 8) and Delete (key code of 46) keys, you can call `requestSuggestions()`, but this time, pass in `false` to indicate that typeahead should not occur:

```
AutoSuggestControl.prototype.handleKeyUp = function (oEvent) {

    var iKeyCode = oEvent.keyCode;
```

```
    if (iKeyCode == 8 || iKeyCode == 46) {
        this.provider.requestSuggestions(this, false);

    } else if (((iKeyCode != 16 && iKeyCode < 32) || (iKeyCode >= 33 && iKeyCode <=
46)
                || (iKeyCode >= 112 && iKeyCode <= 123)) {
        //ignore
    } else {
        this.provider.requestSuggestions(this, true);
    }
};
```

Now when the user is removing characters, suggestions will still be displayed and the user can click one of them to select the value for the textbox. This is acceptable, but to really be usable, the autosuggest control needs to respond to keyboard controls.

Adding Keyboard Support

The desired keyboard functionality revolves around four keys: the up arrow, the down arrow, Esc, and Enter (or Return). When the drop-down suggestion list is displayed, the user should be able to press the down arrow to highlight the first suggestion, then press it again to move to the second, and so on. The up arrow should then be used to move back up the list of suggestions. As each suggestion is highlighted, the value must be placed in the textbox. If the user presses Esc, the suggestions should be hidden and the suggestion removed from the textbox. When the Enter key is pressed, the suggestions should also be hidden, but the last suggestion should remain highlighted in the textbox.

In order for the user to use the up and down arrow keys, you'll need to keep track of the currently selected item in the suggestions list. To do this, you must add two properties to the AutoSuggestControl definition, as follows:

```
function AutoSuggestControl(oTextbox, oProvider) {
    this.cur = -1;
    this.layer = null;
    this.provider = oProvider;
    this.textbox = oTextbox;
    this.userText = oTextbox.value;
    this.init();
}
```

The cur property stores the index of the current suggestion in the suggestions array. By default, this value is set to –1 because there are no suggestions initially. When the arrow keys are pressed, cur will change to point to the current suggestion. The second added property, userText, holds the current value of the textbox and changes to reflect what the user actually typed.

As cur changes, the highlighted suggestion changes as well. To encapsulate this functionality, a method called goToSuggestion() is used. This method accepts only one argument, a number whose sign indicates which direction to move in. For instance, any number greater than 0 moves the selection to the next suggestion; any number less than or equal to 0 moves the selection to the previous suggestion. Here's the code:

```
AutoSuggestControl.prototype.goToSuggestion = function (iDiff) {
    var cSuggestionNodes = this.layer.childNodes;

    if (cSuggestionNodes.length > 0) {
        var oNode = null;

        if (iDiff > 0) {
            if (this.cur < cSuggestionNodes.length-1) {
                oNode = cSuggestionNodes[++this.cur];
            }
        } else {
            if (this.cur > 0) {
                oNode = cSuggestionNodes[--this.cur];
            }
        }

        if (oNode) {
            this.highlightSuggestion(oNode);
            this.textbox.value = oNode.firstChild.nodeValue;
        }
    }
};
```

This method begins by obtaining the collection of child nodes in the drop-down layer. Since only
<div/> elements containing suggestions are child nodes of the layer, the number of child nodes accu-
rately matches the number of suggestions. This number can be used to determine if there are any suggestions (in which case it will be greater than zero). If there are no suggestions, the method need not do
anything.

When there are suggestions, a variable named oNode is created to store a reference to the suggestion
node to highlight, and the method checks to see which direction to go in. If iDiff is greater than 0, it
tries to go to the next suggestion. In doing so, the method first checks to ensure that cur isn't greater
than the number of suggestions minus 1 (because the index of the last element in a collection with
n elements is $n-1$). Assuming that there is a next suggestion, cur is prefix incremented (meaning it
assumes its new value before the line it's on executes) to retrieve the node for the next suggestion.

If iDiff is less than or equal to zero, then that means the previous suggestion needs to be highlighted.
In that case, you must first check to ensure cur is greater than 0 (if cur isn't at least 1, then there isn't a
previous suggestion to go to). Passing that test, cur is then prefix decremented to get a reference to the
correct suggestion node.

The last step in the method is to ensure that oNode isn't null. If it's not, then the node is passed to
highlightSuggestion() and the suggestion text is placed into the textbox; if it is null, then no action
is taken.

Another part of keeping track of the selected suggestion is to be sure that cur is reset at the correct
point; otherwise, you can get some very odd behavior. The correct place to reset cur to –1 is in the
autosuggest() method, just before the drop-down list is displayed:

```
AutoSuggestControl.prototype.autosuggest = function (aSuggestions, bTypeAhead){

    this.cur = -1;

    if (aSuggestions.length > 0) {
        if (bTypeAhead) {
            this.typeAhead(aSuggestions[0]);
        }

        this.showSuggestions(aSuggestions);
    } else {
        this.hideSuggestions();
    }
};
```

Along the same lines, it's important to set userText to the correct value. This should be done in the handleKeyUp() method:

```
AutoSuggestControl.prototype.handleKeyUp = function (oEvent) {

    var iKeyCode = oEvent.keyCode;
    this.userText = this.textbox.value;

    if (iKeyCode == 8 || iKeyCode == 46) {
        this.provider.requestSuggestions(this, false);

    } else if (((iKeyCode != 16 && iKeyCode < 32) || (iKeyCode >= 33 && iKeyCode <=
46)
                || (iKeyCode >= 112 && iKeyCode <= 123)) {
        //ignore
    } else {
        this.provider.requestSuggestions(this, true);
    }
};
```

This small addition saves what the user typed before asking for suggestions. This will be very useful when dealing with the Esc key. With these two methods updates, all that's left is to make sure that goToSuggestion() gets called at the right time.

To handle the up arrow, down arrow, Esc, and Enter keys, a handleKeyDown() method is necessary. Similar to handleKeyUp(), this method also requires the event object to be passed in. And once again, you'll need to rely on the key code to tell which key was pressed. The key codes for the up arrow, down arrow, Esc, and Enter keys are 38, 40, 27, and 13, respectively. The handleKeyDown() method is defined as follows:

```
AutoSuggestControl.prototype.handleKeyDown = function (oEvent) {
    switch(oEvent.keyCode) {
        case 38: //up arrow
            this.goToSuggestion(-1);
            break;
        case 40: //down arrow
            this.goToSuggestion(1);
            break;
```

```
        case 27: //esc
            this.textbox.value = this.userText;
            this.selectRange(this.userText.length, 0);
            /* falls through */
        case 13: //enter
            this.hideSuggestions();
            oEvent.returnValue = false;
            if (oEvent.preventDefault) {
                oEvent.preventDefault();
            }
            break;
    }
};
```

When the up arrow is pressed (key code 38), the `goToSuggestion()` method is called with an argument of –1, indicating that the previous selection should be selected. Likewise, when the down arrow is pressed (key code 40), `goToSuggestion()` is called with 1 as an argument to highlight the next suggestion. If Esc is pressed (key code 27), there are a couple of things to do.

First, you need to set the textbox value back to the original text that the user typed. Second, you need to set the selection in the textbox to be located after what the user typed so that he or she can continue typing. This is done by setting the selection range to the length of the text with a selection length of zero. Then, this case falls through to the Enter key's case (key code 13), which hides the suggestions list. This way, the code contains only one call to `hideSuggestions()` instead of two. Remember, when the user presses the up or down arrows, the suggestion is automatically placed into the textbox. This means that when the Enter key is pressed, you need only hide the drop-down list of suggestions.

For both Esc and Enter, you also must block the default behavior for the key press. This is important to prevent unintended behavior, such as the Enter key submitting the form when the user really just wanted to select the current suggestion. The default behavior is blocked first by setting `event.returnValue` equal to `false` (for IE) and then calling `preventDefault()` (if it's available, for DOM-compliant browsers).

Updating init()

Now that all this new functionality has been added, it must be initialized. Previously, the `init()` method was used to set up the `onkeyup` event handler; now it must be extended to also set up the `onkeydown` and `onblur` event handlers, as well as to create the drop-down suggestion list. The `onkeydown` event handler is set up in a manner similar to `onkeyup`:

```
AutoSuggestControl.prototype.init = function () {

    var oThis = this;

    this.textbox.onkeyup = function (oEvent) {
        if (!oEvent) {
            oEvent = window.event;
        }

        oThis.handleKeyUp(oEvent);
    };
```

```
        this.textbox.onkeydown = function (oEvent) {

            if (!oEvent) {
                oEvent = window.event;
            }

            oThis.handleKeyDown(oEvent);
        };

    //more code to come
};
```

As you can see, the same algorithm is used with the onkeydown event handler: first, determine the location of the event object, and then pass it into the handleKeyDown() method.

Up to this point, the only time the drop-down list is hidden is when the user presses the Enter key. But what if the user clicks elsewhere on the screen or uses the Tab key to switch to a new form field? To prepare for this event, you must set up an onblur event handler, which hides the suggestions whenever the textbox loses focus:

```
AutoSuggestControl.prototype.init = function () {

    var oThis = this;

    this.textbox.onkeyup = function (oEvent) {
        if (!oEvent) {
            oEvent = window.event;
        }

        oThis.handleKeyUp(oEvent);
    };

    this.textbox.onkeydown = function (oEvent) {

        if (!oEvent) {
            oEvent = window.event;
        }

        oThis.handleKeyDown(oEvent);
    };

    this.textbox.onblur = function () {
        oThis.hideSuggestions();
    };

    this.createDropDown();
};
```

You'll also notice that the createDropDown() method is called to create the initial drop-down list structure. This completes the keyboard support for the autosuggest control, but there is one more thing to take into account.

Fast-Type Support

Because the `handleKeyUp()` method requests suggestions whenever a key is pressed, you may be wondering if it can keep up when someone is typing quickly. The answer is no. You may be surprised to know that it is possible to type too fast for the event handling to keep up. In this case, you get suggestions that are too late (including letters you never typed) and a very choppy user experience (with long pauses as you type). So, how can you make sure that fast typists aren't left out of this functionality?

Quite simply, you should wait a short amount of time before requesting suggestions from the server. This can be done using the `setTimeout()` method, which delays the calling of a function for a set time interval. The new functionality works like this: a timeout ID is saved in the `AutoSuggestControl` object. If another key is pressed before the timeout has been activated, the existing timeout is cleared and a new one is put in its place. So basically, when a user presses a key, the control waits a certain amount of time before requesting suggestions. If another key is pressed before the request is made, the control cancels the original request (by clearing the timeout) and asks for a new request to be made after the same amount of time. In this way, you can be sure that the request for suggestions goes out only when the user has paused during typing.

To implement this functionality, the first thing you need is a property to hold the timeout ID. You can add the `timeoutId` property directly to the `AutoSuggestControl` class, as follows:

```
function AutoSuggestControl(oTextbox, oProvider) {
    this.cur = -1;
    this.layer = null;
    this.provider = oProvider;
    this.textbox = oTextbox;
    this.timeoutId = null;
    this.userText = oTextbox.value;
    this.init();
}
```

Next, update the `handleKeyUp()` method to make use of this new property:

```
AutoSuggestControl.prototype.handleKeyUp = function (oEvent /*:Event*/) {

    var iKeyCode = oEvent.keyCode;
    var oThis = this;

    this.userText = this.textbox.value;

    clearTimeout(this.timeoutId);

    if (iKeyCode == 8 || iKeyCode == 46) {

        this.timeoutId = setTimeout( function () {
            oThis.provider.requestSuggestions(oThis, false);
        }, 250);

    } else if (((iKeyCode != 16 && iKeyCode < 32) || (iKeyCode >= 33 && iKeyCode < 46)
            || (iKeyCode >= 112 && iKeyCode <= 123)) {
        //ignore
    } else {
```

```
        this.timeoutId = setTimeout( function () {
            oThis.provider.requestSuggestions(oThis, true);
        }, 250);
    }
};
```

The first new line in this method stores a reference to the `this` object, which is important when using the `setTimeout()` method. The second new line of code clears any timeout that may have already been started; this cancels any suggestion request that may have been initiated. The other two sections of new code change the call to the `requestSuggestions()` to occur after 250 milliseconds (which is plenty of time for this purpose). Each call is wrapped in an anonymous function that is passed in to `setTimeout()`. The result of `setTimeout()`, the timeout ID is stored in the new property for later usage. All in all, this ensures that no requests will be made unless the user has stopped typing for at least 250 milliseconds.

This completes the code for the `AutoSuggestControl` class. All of the functionality has been implemented, and all that's left is to create a suggestion provider to call.

The Suggestion Provider

The `SuggestionProvider` class is relatively simple compared to the `AutoSuggestControl`, since it has only one purpose: to request suggestions from the server and forward them to the control. To do so, `SuggestionProvider` needs an instance of XHR. Instead of using a new object for each request, the same object will be used over and over, to avoid the overhead of creating and destroying objects in rapid succession. This single instance is created using the zXML library's `zXmlHttp` factory and is stored in a property called `xhr`:

```
function SuggestionProvider() {
    this.xhr = zXmlHttp.createRequest();
}
```

The lone method of the suggestion provider is `requestSuggestions()`, which you may remember from the architecture discussion. This method accepts two arguments: the `AutoSuggestControl` to work on and a flag indicating whether typeahead should be used. The complete code is as follows:

```
SuggestionProvider.prototype.requestSuggestions = function (oAutoSuggestControl,
                                                            bTypeAhead) {

    var oXHR = this.xhr;

    //cancel any active requests
    if (oXHR.readyState != 0) {
        oXHR.abort();
    }

    //define the data
    var oData = {
        requesting: "StatesAndProvinces",
        text: oAutoSuggestControl.userText,
        limit: 5
    };
```

```
        //open connection to server
    oXHR.open("post", "suggestions.php", true);
    oXHR.setRequestHeader("Content-type", "text/html");
    oXHR.onreadystatechange = function () {
        if (oXHR.readyState == 4) {
            if (oXHR.status == 200 || oXHRo.status == 304) {
                //evaluate the returned text JavaScript (an array)
                var aSuggestions = oXHR.responseText.parseJSON();

                //provide suggestions to the control
                oAutoSuggestControl.autosuggest(aSuggestions, bTypeAhead);
            }
        }
    };

    //send the request
    oXHR.send( oData.toJSONString());

};
```

The first line inside the method sets oXHR equal to the stored XHR object. This is done simply for convenience and to keep the code clean. Next, you check to make sure that there isn't already a request waiting for a response. If the XHR object is ready to be used cleanly, its readyState will be 0; otherwise, you must cancel the existing request (by calling abort()) before making another request.

Because the data being sent to the server is to be JSON-encoded, you first need to create an object (oData) to hold the information. There are three pieces of information being sent: the table to get the data out of, the current value in the textbox, and the maximum number of suggestions to retrieve (5). The maximum number of suggestions is important because it prevents long database queries from being executed repeatedly.

Next, a request is opened to suggestions.php, the server-side component of the control. This request is asynchronous (last argument of open() is set to true), so it's necessary to provide an onreadystatechange event handler. The event handler first checks to ensure that the readyState is 4, and then parses the returned text as a JSON array of values. This array, along with the original type-ahead flag, is then passed back to the AutoSuggestControl via the autosuggest() method.

The last step in this method is, of course, to send the request. Note that since the request is doing a POST, the data has to be passed into the send() method. The oData object is first encoded into JSON before being sent.

With that, the SuggestionProvider class is complete. The only thing left to do is to write the suggestions.php file that uses the data that is sent.

The Server-Side Component

In many ways, the server-side component for the autosuggest control is the most straightforward: it's just a single thread being executed from top to bottom, with no functions or methods to be concerned about. Note that because this is a PHP page, all the code discussed in this section must be contained within a PHP code block (<?php . . . ?>).

The first part of the page is to set the content type to `text/plain`, indicating that this is a plain text file and shouldn't be handled as anything else. You can optionally specify a character set, but make sure that it is Unicode-compatible, such as UTF-8, since all Unicode characters are valid in JavaScript. Here's the line that assigns the content type:

```
header("Content-Type: text/plain; charset=UTF-8");
```

Next, include the JSON-PHP library and create a new instance of the JSON object:

```
require_once("JSON.php");
$oJSON = new Services_JSON();
```

Normally when data is sent to a PHP page, you can use `$_GET`, `$_POST`, or `$_REQUEST` to retrieve it. In this case, however, the data isn't being sent in traditional name-value pairs; instead, it's being sent as a JSON string, and there is no built-in support for this specific type of data. Instead, you need to get the body of the request and decode it manually. The body of any request is available in PHP through `$HTTP_RAW_POST_DATA`, which contains the original, encoded content that was sent. Because the JSON string wasn't URL-encoded, however, you can just pass this directly into the `decode()` method to reconstitute the `oData` object:

```
$oData = $oJSON->decode($HTTP_RAW_POST_DATA);
```

You'll also need an array to store the suggestions in:

```
$aSuggestions = array();
```

If there are no suggestions, no values will be added to the array and an empty array (`[]`) will be returned to the client.

Before tapping the database for suggestions, make sure that there is actually text in the textbox. Suggestions are requested when the user hits Delete or Backspace, so there's a possibility that the textbox could be empty. You should check for this first by seeing if the length of the text is greater than 0; if so, you can continue on to query the database.

The query string itself is built up from the data submitting from the client. The name of the table, the `LIKE` statement, and the number of results to return are all incorporated into the SQL query. The following code creates a connection to the database, executes the query, and then adds the results of the query to the `$aSuggestions` array:

```
if (strlen($oData->text) > 0) {

    //create the SQL query string
    $sQuery = "Select Name from ".$oData->requesting." where Name like '".
            $oData->text."%' order by Name ASC limit 0,".$oData->limit;

    //make the database connection
    $oLink = mysql_connect($sDBServer,$sDBUsername,$sDBPassword);
    @mysql_select_db($sDBName) or die("Unable to open database");
```

```
        if($oResult = mysql_query($sQuery)) {
            while ($aValues = mysql_fetch_array($oResult,MYSQL_ASSOC)) {
                array_push($aSuggestions, $aValues['Name']);
            }
        }

        mysql_free_result($oResult);
        mysql_close($oLink);
}
```

This code should be fairly familiar to you as it is the same basic algorithm used throughout the book to access a MySQL database using PHP. (You must fill in the appropriate values for $sDBServer, $sDBUsername, and $sDBPassword to reflect your database settings.) The only unique part is that the results are being stored in an array, which facilitates the conversion into a JSON string to be sent back to the client.

The actual encoding is the very last step of the page. In one step, you can encode the array and output it to the page:

```
echo($oJSON->encode($aSuggestions));
```

Now, it's up to the client to parse the JSON code correctly.

The Client-Side Component

So far, you've built the HTML, CSS, JavaScript, and PHP to be used by the autosuggest control. The only thing left to do is to assemble it all into a page that you can use. The most important thing to remember is to include of all necessary JavaScript files. In this case, you need to include json.js, zxml.js, and autosuggest.js. Also important is the inclusion of the stylesheet file, autosuggest.css.

It's also necessary to instantiate the AutoSuggestControl after the page has completely loaded, using the onload event handler. The complete code for the example page is:

```
<html>
    <head>
        <title>Autosuggest Example</title>
        <script type="text/javascript" src="json.js"></script>
        <script type="text/javascript" src="zxml.js"></script>
        <script type="text/javascript" src="autosuggest.js"></script>
        <link rel="stylesheet" type="text/css" href="autosuggest.css" />
        <script type="text/javascript">
            window.onload = function () {
                var oTextbox = new
AutoSuggestControl(document.getElementById("txtState"), new SuggestionProvider());
            }
        </script>
    </head>
    <body>
        <form method="post" action="your_action.php">
            <table border="0">
                <tr>
```

```
            <td>Name:</td>
            <td><input type="text" name="txtName" id="txtName" /></td>
        </tr>
        <tr>
            <td>Address 1:</td>
            <td><input type="text" name="txtAddress1"
                    id="txtAddress1" /></td>
        </tr>
        <tr>
            <td>Address 2:</td>
            <td><input type="text" name="txtAddress2"
                    id="txtAddress2" /></td>
        </tr>
        <tr>
            <td>City:</td>
            <td><input type="text" name="txtCity" id="txtCity" /></td>
        </tr>
        <tr>
            <td>State/Province:</td>
            <td><input type="text" name="txtState" id="txtState"
                    autocomplete="off" /></td>
        </tr>
        <tr>
            <td>Zip Code:</td>
            <td><input type="text" name="txtZip" id="txtZip" /></td>
        </tr>
        <tr>
            <td>Country:</td>
            <td><input type="text" name="txtCountry"
                    id="txtCountry" /></td>
        </tr>
    </table>
    <input type="submit" value="Save Information" />
  </form>
 </body>
</html>
```

Note that once the necessary files are included, you need to place only one line of JavaScript in the `window.onload` event handler to set up the functionality:

```
var oTextbox = new AutoSuggestControl(document.getElementById("txtState"),
                                new SuggestionProvider());
```

This line creates a new `AutoSuggestControl` object, passing a reference to the textbox with the ID of `txtState` and a new `SuggestionProvider()` class. It's important that this line be executed in the `onload` event handler because `document.getElementById()` isn't 100 percent accurate until the entire page has been loaded.

The example itself is done in a way in which this control may be used: filling in personal information. This could be a page where customers can update their information or it could be a shipping form. Whichever way you choose to use this functionality, it is sure to improve the usability of your form. An autosuggest control, although not as flashy as some Ajax solutions, is a good example of how Ajax can be used in a noninterfering way.

Summary

In this chapter, you learned all about JavaScript Object Notation (JSON) as an alternative data transmission format to XML. You learned that JSON has several advantages over XML for data transmission needs, including a smaller amount of code to represent the same data and a logical object-and-array structure that most programming languages can understand and use.

You also learned that while JavaScript can understand and interpret JSON natively, there are several server-side libraries that provide the same functionality. You learned about a JavaScript utility for parsing and encoding JSON data, as well as the JSON-PHP library that can be used to do the same for PHP.

The chapter went on to describe how to make an Ajax-assisted autosuggest control that enables you to display suggestions based on what the user has typed. This control works similarly to the way that Google Suggest does and takes into account user interaction with the mouse and keyboard as well as providing for fast typists. This control helped to illustrate the power of simple Ajax solutions.

The next chapter will expand on what you've learned here to create reusable Ajax widgets for your web site. These widgets can use a variety of data transmission formats, including JSON.

9

Comet

Earlier in the book we discussed how Ajax changed the nature of the Web by freeing users from the traditional click-and-wait paradigm. Although it improves the user experience, Ajax still uses the standard HTTP model: the client sends a request for resources to the server, which is answered by a response from the server with the requested resources (or an error message if they are not available). This is called a *pull* method of communication.

In the pull architecture, the client is in control. Communication begins when the client makes a request and ends when the client receives the response. The pull architecture is how the Web has always worked, but as it continues to evolve and user expectations rise, this communication method is increasingly becoming a burdensome hurdle.

Consider a typical chat client such as Yahoo! Messenger. This type of client uses a *push* architecture, allowing the server to push information out to the client whenever necessary. The result is fast communication because data is being sent as soon as it is available. If chat clients used a pull architecture, their performance would suffer, and there would be significantly more network traffic as the client repeatedly polled to see if new data was available. Since the nature of chat is such that new data may be available several times a second, the push architecture is much more suitable for this purpose.

Given the speed and usability advantages of push architectures, web developers have begun investigating means by which the same functionality can be realized on the Web. Ajax was just the beginning; the next step is going beyond traditional HTTP to implement push-based web systems using one or more of several new techniques. Alex Russell coined the term *Comet* to describe the evolving push architecture of the web (Comet is a tongue-in-cheek jab at Ajax, since both are also household cleaners).

HTTP Streaming

In the time before broadband Internet access was available to the masses, browser developers looked for ways to speed up the perceived rendering time of web pages. One such method is called *progressive rendering*; in this method rendering of the page begins as soon as the <body> tag is received, ensuring that the site display begins as soon as possible. This is the effect seen on long web pages when the vertical scrollbar continues to grow as the page is being loaded. In this circumstance, the browser is completing the displaying of the page as new information is received, creating a longer and longer page with each passing second. This same effect can be observed when connecting to servers that are experiencing very heavy traffic as the server struggles to keep up with the requests.

Consider what's happening when a page is being rendered progressively. The opening <body> tag is read, and then some more data is received. Some time passes. Some more data is received. This pattern is repeated until the entire page has been downloaded and is being displayed to the user. But how does the browser know how long to wait for new data? Further, how does it know how much more data is coming? The answer to both questions is that the browser has no idea. This is the essence of HTTP streaming.

> **HTTP streaming is frequently mislabeled as Persistent HTTP, which has nothing to do with this technique. Persistent HTTP is simply a way of keeping a connection open so that numerous HTTP requests can be sent without opening and closing connections for each request.**

Request Delays

Instead of relying on network latency and server response time to determine the waiting time between data bursts, it's possible to artificially create this delay. The following example comes from the PHP manual for the sleep() method (www.php.net/sleep) and illustrates this technique:

```php
<?php

    // current time
    echo date('h:i:s') . "\n";

    // sleep for 10 seconds
    sleep(10);

    // wake up !
    echo date('h:i:s') . "\n";

?>
```

When loaded into the browser, this page outputs the current time, waits 10 seconds, and then outputs the time again. Granted, this isn't a very useful page, but it does illustrate how to force the server to wait before sending the next piece of data. In practice, you should add calls to ob_flush() and flush() immediately after the calls to echo() to force data to be sent to the client:

```php
<?php

    // current time
    echo date('h:i:s') . "\n";
    ob_flush();
    flush();

    // sleep for 10 seconds
    sleep(10);

    // wake up !
    echo date('h:i:s') . "\n";
    ob_flush();
    flush();
?>
```

Adding these two function calls ensures that the output buffer is completely flushed, forcing the data to be sent to the client.

> This feature of PHP, sending chunks of data periodically to the browser, may not be enabled on all servers. For more information, see www.php.net/flush.

Suppose that the same technique were used to output HTML and JavaScript instead of plain text:

```
<!DOCTYPE html PUBLIC "-//W3C//DTD XHTML 1.0 Transitional//EN"
    "http://www.w3.org/TR/xhtml1/DTD/xhtml1-transitional.dtd">
<html xmlns="http://www.w3.org/1999/xhtml">
    <head>
        <title>HTTP Streaming Example 2</title>
    </head>
    <body>
        <script type="text/javascript">
        //<![CDATA[
            document.title = "First message";
        //]]>
        </script>
<?php
    ob_flush();
    flush();

    // sleep for 10 seconds
    sleep(10);
?>
        <script type="text/javascript">
        //<![CDATA[
            document.title = "Second message";
        //]]>
        </script>
    </body>
</html>
```

The JavaScript in this example simply sets the title of the window two different times. Without the call to `sleep()`, it would happen so fast that you would only see the title change to "Second message." However, with the delay, it is easy to see that both commands are executed as soon as the client receives the data. This proof-of-concept works but doesn't do anything very interesting. What if some sort of command were coupled with the call to `sleep()`?

File Modification Example

Suppose that there's a file whose modification time is of interest. Perhaps data is being written into it that should be picked up as soon as it is available. In any event, it's important to know as soon as the file has been modified. The following PHP code implements this solution:

```
<!DOCTYPE html PUBLIC "-//W3C//DTD XHTML 1.0 Transitional//EN"
    "http://www.w3.org/TR/xhtml1/DTD/xhtml1-transitional.dtd">
<html xmlns="http://www.w3.org/1999/xhtml">
    <head>
        <title>HTTP streaming Example 3</title>
    </head>
    <body>
<?php
    //get the file modification time
    $modified = filemtime('details.txt');
    $lastModified = $modified;

    //clear file statistics
    clearstatcache();

    //check every so often to see if it has changed
    while (true) {

        // sleep for 1 second
        sleep(1);

        //check the modification time
        $lastModified = filemtime('details.txt');

        //clear file statistics
        clearstatcache();

        //check it against the previous time
        if ($modified != $lastModified) {

            $output = date('h:i:s', $lastModified);
?>
            <script type="text/javascript">
            //<![CDATA[
                document.title = "File was modified at <?php echo $output ?>";
            //]]>
            </script>
<?php
            ob_flush();
            flush();
```

```
            $modified = $lastModified;

            // sleep for 1 second
            sleep(1);

        }
    }
?>

    </body>
</html>
```

The PHP code in this example first checks to see when the file in question, details.txt, has been modified. This value is stored in two variables: $modified and $lastModified. Two variables are used so that there will be a point of comparison later on: $modified holds the modification time from the last change (or when the page was first loaded), while $lastModified holds the most recent modification time. It's then possible to compare $lastModified with $modified to see if they're the same; if they're not, that means the file has changed.

After calling filemtime() to retrieve the modification time of the file, clearstatcache() is called. This is a PHP-only necessity, since PHP caches the results of many file operations for faster execution. Then, a while loop begins. This loop will never exit because the control condition is hard-coded to true. In this way, the page will continue to check and report on the modification time of the file indefinitely.

Inside of the loop, sleep() is called to create an artificial delay and free up CPU cycles for other operations. Then, filemtime() is called again, and the value is compared to the previously stored value in $modified. If the modification time is different, a JavaScript call is made to change the document's title. After the JavaScript code is output, calls to ob_flush() and flush() ensure that the data in the buffer is sent across the HTTP stream (instead of being buffered for later transmission). Then, $modified is updated with the new modification time and the thread pauses for another second to prevent sending too much data at one time.

To test this functionality, try uploading details.txt periodically and watch the title bar of the browser. No changes to details.txt are necessary because the process of uploading the file changes the modification time.

Keep in mind that this is a simplified example. The point to take away is that any JavaScript code can be executed in place of the code in this example. Most likely, the code to execute would be a call to some function that specifically keeps track of this data.

Using Iframes

It may seem strange that the previous example continues to execute indefinitely because this is not the way developers learn to create web applications. However, HTTP streaming is a completely different paradigm, just as Ajax is a completely different paradigm from traditional web applications. To make the most of this technique, a change in thought process is necessary. Part of that thought process questions how long an indefinite loop can run on a server, since computers deal only with finites.

Eventually, the infinite loop in the previous example will stop running because servers have a built-in timeout mechanism that prevents long-running scripts from continuing to run and eat up CPU cycles. This is a stopgap system designed to ensure that a single page on a site cannot bring the entire site down. The exact timeout setting is specific to the server being used and can be changed by the server administrators, so there isn't a hard number that can be depended upon. Basically, there's no way to tell when the script will stop running and at what point during its execution that stop will occur. For this reason, it's important not to execute too much code using HTTP streaming. It's also for this reason that a heartbeat is absolutely necessary.

A *heartbeat* is essentially a small piece of code executed periodically to inform some other code that the process is still running. In terms of HTTP streaming, the heartbeat indicates that the request is still being processed, and code execution on the server continues. When a heartbeat fails to be registered, the client must recognize this and restart the server process.

Setting up this sort of system requires two pages. The first page is the main client, the one in which most of the JavaScript code exists. Inside of that page is an iframe that contains the second page, which is the HTTP streaming connection to the server. The inner page is responsible for calling functions on the outer page to display information as well as register heartbeats. The outer page, in turn, must keep track of the heartbeats being sent and know when to reset the server connection. Here's what the outer page looks like:

```
<!DOCTYPE html PUBLIC "-//W3C//DTD XHTML 1.0 Transitional//EN"
    "http://www.w3.org/TR/xhtml1/DTD/xhtml1-transitional.dtd">
<html xmlns="http://www.w3.org/1999/xhtml">
    <head>
        <title>HTTP streaming Example 4</title>
         <script type="text/javascript">
        //<![CDATA[

        var iTimeoutId = null;

        function heartbeat() {
            clearTimeout(iTimeoutId);
            iTimeoutId = setTimeout(resetConnection, 10000);
        }

        function resetConnection() {
            frames["connection"].location.replace(
              "ProgressiveHTTPExample4Connection.php?t=" + (new Date()).getTime());
            heartbeat();
        }

        function modifiedAt(sDateTime) {
            document.getElementById("divStatus").innerHTML =
                                                "Modified at " + sDateTime;
        }

        window.onload = resetConnection;

        //]]>
        </script>
    </head>
```

```
    <body>
        <div id="divStatus">Waiting for first message...</div>
        <iframe src="about:blank" name="connection"></iframe>
    </body>
</html>
```

Most of this page is JavaScript code; the only HTML necessary in the `<body/>` is a `<div/>` to display status information and the `<iframe/>` to contain the connection page.

This example's JavaScript code consists of one variable and three functions.

❑   The `iTimeoutId` variable holds a reference to the timeout instance in charge of checking for dead connections.

❑   The `heartbeat()` function is the one to be called by the connection page periodically, letting it know that the connection is still alive. You find only two lines inside of this function: one to cancel the current timeout and one to start a new one. While the connection is alive, the timeout should never fire (it's set to 10 seconds, and since the `heartbeat()` function should be called roughly once every second, there shouldn't be an overlap). The timeout is set to call the `resetConnection()` function if and when the timeout executes.

❑   The `resetConnection()` function is also quite simple. It resets the iframe's URL to the connection page and appends a timestamp to the end (the timestamp is necessary to avoid getting a cached version of the page). Then, there's a single call to `heartbeat()`, which resets the timeout. The connection page should then begin sending heartbeat signals, and the process will continue.

❑   The last JavaScript function is `modifiedAt()`, which is a function that is called when the file has been modified. The data is passed in and displayed in `divStatus`, so the connection page isn't responsible for displaying this data itself.

As a final step, the window's `onload` event handler is set to call `resetConnection()`, ensuring that a connection will begin as soon as the page loads.

The other part of this example, the connection page, looks very similar to the previous example (the differences are highlighted):

```
<!DOCTYPE html PUBLIC "-//W3C//DTD XHTML 1.0 Transitional//EN"
    "http://www.w3.org/TR/xhtml1/DTD/xhtml1-transitional.dtd">
<html xmlns="http://www.w3.org/1999/xhtml">
    <head>
        <title>HTTP streaming Example 4 Connection</title>
    </head>
    <body>
<?php
    //get the file modification time
    $modified = filemtime('details.txt');
    $lastModified = $modified;

    //clear file statistics
    clearstatcache();

    //check every so often to see if it has changed
    while (true) {
```

```
?>
        <script type="text/javascript">
//<![CDATA[
parent.heartbeat();
//]]>
</script>
<?php
        ob_flush();
        flush();

        // sleep for 1 second
        sleep(1);

        //check the modification time
        $lastModified = filemtime('details.txt');

        //clear file statistics
        clearstatcache();

        //check it against the previous time
        if ($modified != $lastModified) {
            $output = date('h:i:s', $lastModified);
?>
            <script type="text/javascript">
//<![CDATA[
                parent.modifiedAt("<?php echo $output ?>");
//]]>
</script>
<?php
            ob_flush();
            flush();
            $modified = $lastModified;

            // sleep for 1 second
            sleep(1);

        }
    }
?>

    </body>
</html>
```

In this page, a call is made to the heartbeat() function every time the while loop executes. This call uses the parent object to access heartbeat() because it is contained in an iframe and the function exists in its parent page. When the file is modified, another call is made to the parent frame, this time to modifiedAt(), which is passed the timestamp.

> It's very important that each code block be contained within its own <script/> tag. Code execution will not begin in most browsers until the closing </script> tag is read. Even though it seems redundant, you must provide a complete <script/> tag for every function call or logical group of function calls.

Dynamically Created Iframes

In the previous examples, an iframe was already present in the page. It is possible to accomplish the same functionality using dynamically created iframes that aren't visible on the page. To do so, you need to create an iframe using the DOM createElement() method, set the display property to none, and then set the src property:

```
<!DOCTYPE html PUBLIC "-//W3C//DTD XHTML 1.0 Transitional//EN"
    "http://www.w3.org/TR/xhtml1/DTD/xhtml1-transitional.dtd">
<html xmlns="http://www.w3.org/1999/xhtml">
    <head>
        <title>HTTP streaming Example 5</title>
         <script type="text/javascript">
        //<![CDATA[

        var iTimeoutId = null;
        var oFrame = null;

        function heartbeat() {
            clearTimeout(iTimeoutId);
            iTimeoutId = setTimeout(resetConnection, 10000);
        }

        function resetConnection() {
            oFrame.src =
                "ProgressiveHTTPExample4Connection.php?t=" + (new Date()).getTime();
            heartbeat();
        }

        function modifiedAt(sDateTime) {
            document.getElementById("divStatus").innerHTML =
                                            "Modified at " + sDateTime;
        }

        window.onload = function () {
            oFrame = document.createElement("iframe");
            oFrame.style.display = "none";
            document.body.appendChild(oFrame);
            resetConnection();
        };

        //]]>
        </script>
    </head>
    <body>
        <div id="divStatus">Waiting for first message...</div>
    </body>
</html>
```

The first step is to define a global variable called oFrame that holds a reference to the dynamically created iframe. In the window's onload event handler, the iframe is created and stored in oFrame. Then, it is hidden from view by setting display to "none". The iframe is then added to the body of the document (which is required for the iframe to work). Finally, the resetConnection() function is called, which in turn sets the src attribute of the iframe.

Usability Issues

Although using iframes to implement a web-based push architecture can yield some interesting results, it has a major usability flaw. While the connection is open, the browser indicates that it is busy:

❑ In Internet Explorer, the throbber (the animated icon in the upper-right corner) continues to move and the progress bar shows up at the bottom of the screen.

❑ In Firefox, the cursor changes to display an arrow and an hourglass and a message is displayed in the status bar indicating that the browser is waiting for more information.

❑ In Safari, the progress bar continues to expand and the message "Loading" appears in the title bar.

❑ In Opera, the cursor changes to display an arrow and an hourglass.

Although these may seem like minor annoyances, such obvious indications of browser activity can easily confuse inexperienced users. There are, however, other ways of achieving push functionality.

Browser-Specific Approaches

HTTP streaming is still a fairly new concept, and as such, there is no consistency in browser implementation. For some browsers, HTTP streaming is nothing more than a hack using existing technology (such as using iframes in the previous examples); in others, it's a planned feature being implemented in one of many ways. Depending on your individual requirements for browser support, you may need to use combinations of these techniques.

Internet Explorer HTTP Streaming

HTTP streaming support in Internet Explorer was not an intentional design decision but rather was achieved by some enterprising engineers at Google using existing and less documented browser features.

When Google added chat capabilities to its Gmail web client, developers immediately began to dissect what was happening behind the scenes. It was Alex Russell who first posted a message (http://alex.dojotoolkit.org/?p=538) on his blog about the inner workings of the Gmail chat client. He discovered the use of a little-known, safe-for-the-web ActiveX control called HTMLFile.

The HTMLFile ActiveX object is exactly what it sounds like: an implementation of an HTML document that mimics the functionality of the document object in an external form. Because this object exists outside of the normal page flow, it has no ties to the browser window and, thus, can be used to perform all kinds of operations without disturbing the browser's user interface. The Google engineers used this to their advantage, inserting an iframe into this object that could be used to achieve HTTP streaming without involving the browser window. The basic technique involves creating an HTMLFile object with an iframe in it and using that iframe to create a streaming HTTP connection, such as:

```
var oPage = new ActiveXObject("htmlfile");
oPage.open();
oPage.write("<html><body></body></html>");
oPage.close();

oPage.body.innerHTML = "<iframe src=\"connection.php\"></iframe>";
```

This sample code illustrates creating an HTMLFile object and initializing it for Comet communication. After creating the object, it behaves just like document, so you're able to use open(), write(), and close() to set the HTML of the page. Then, the body's innerHTML is set to an iframe containing the connection. This connection will remain open and receive information without influencing the browser window or indicating to the user that something is going on. The only thing left is to use the connection to call JavaScript. This is where a problem occurs.

Because the page containing the iframe is technically not part of the browser hierarchy, there is no way to access the JavaScript in the main page from the iframe. Using parent or top simply returns the HTMLFile object. To access the main page, you need to assign a new property to the HTMLFile object:

```
oPage.parentWindow._parent = self;
```

This one line assigns a reference to the current window into the _parent property of the HTMLFile object's parentWindow. The connection page can now access anything in the main page by using code like this:

```
parent._parent.heartbeat();
```

Thus, the connection file must be modified slightly:

```
<!DOCTYPE html PUBLIC "-//W3C//DTD XHTML 1.0 Transitional//EN"
    "http://www.w3.org/TR/xhtml1/DTD/xhtml1-transitional.dtd">
<html xmlns="http://www.w3.org/1999/xhtml">
    <head>
        <title>IE HTTP Streaming Example Connection</title>
    </head>
    <body>
<?php
    //get the file modification time
    $modified = filemtime('details.txt');
    $lastModified = $modified;

    //clear file statistics
    clearstatcache();

    //check every so often to see if it has changed
    while (true) {
?>
        <script type="text/javascript">
        //<![CDATA[
        parent._parent.heartbeat();
        //]]>
        </script>
<?php
        ob_flush();
        flush();

        // sleep for 1 second
        sleep(1);

        //check the modification time
```

```
        $lastModified = filemtime('details.txt');

        //clear file statistics
        clearstatcache();

        //check it against the previous time
        if ($modified != $lastModified) {
            $output = date('h:i:s', $lastModified);
?>
         <script type="text/javascript">
         //<![CDATA[
             parent._parent.modifiedAt("<?php echo $output ?>");
         //]]>
         </script>
<?php

        ob_flush();
        flush();

        // sleep for 1 second
        sleep(1);

        $modified = $lastModified;
    }
  }
?>

    </body>
</html>
```

The client-side code also must be modified to use the HTMLFile object:

```
<!DOCTYPE html PUBLIC "-//W3C//DTD XHTML 1.0 Transitional//EN"
    "http://www.w3.org/TR/xhtml1/DTD/xhtml1-transitional.dtd">
<html xmlns="http://www.w3.org/1999/xhtml">
    <head>
        <title>IE HTTP Streaming Example 1</title>
         <script type="text/javascript">
         //<![CDATA[

        var iTimeoutId = null;
        var oPage = null;

        function heartbeat() {
            clearTimeout(iTimeoutId);
            iTimeoutId = setTimeout(resetConnection, 10000);
        }

        function resetConnection() {
            oPage.body.innerHTML = "<iframe src=\"IEExampleConnection.php?t="
                                    + (new Date()).getTime() + "\"></iframe>";
            heartbeat();
        }

        function modifiedAt(sDateTime) {
```

```
                    document.getElementById("divStatus").innerHTML =
                                            "Modified at " + sDateTime;
                }

        window.onload = function () {
            oPage = new ActiveXObject("htmlfile");
            oPage.open();
            oPage.write("<html><body></body></html>");
            oPage.close();
            oPage.parentWindow._parent = self;
            resetConnection();
        };

        //]]>
        </script>
    </head>
    <body>
        <div id="divStatus">Waiting for first message...</div>
    </body>
</html>
```

This example now works the same way as the previous one but without involving the browser window.

> **PHP uses chunk encoding by default, which means that it may buffer the output and send it in chunks. This can cause Comet that uses the HTMLFile object not to behave as expected (script execution can be delayed). If using PHP, try disabling chunk encoding for the connection file.**

Firefox HTTP Streaming

Firefox supports HTTP streaming in a clean, though not terribly obvious, way. It is possible to open an HTTP stream using XHR and monitor the readyState property to determine when new data has arrived. Unlike other browsers, the readystatechange event fires every time the browser receives data from the server. While the actual readyState property remains set at 3, the event fires repeatedly, indicating that there is new data ready to be accessed. Consider the following:

```
var oXHR = new XMLHttpRequest();
oXHR.open("get", "connection.php", true);
oXHR.onreadystatechange = function () {
    switch (oXHR.readyState) {
        case 3:
            alert(oXHR.responseText);
            break;

        case 4:
            alert("Done");
    }
};
oXHR.send(null);
```

Whenever the `readystatechange` event fires and the `readyState` is 3, an alert displays the returned text. If the page is streaming content, the alert would show an ever-growing amount of text each time through. This can be problematic since, chances are, you are only interested in the most recently received text. For this reason, the output must be delimited to allow easy access to the most recent data. In the case of JavaScript code, it makes sense to delimit each call with a semicolon (;), so that the returned data looks something like this:

```
;heartbeat();heartbeat();heartbeat();modifiedAt("10:34:56");heartbeat()
```

With this data, it's possible to use an array to quickly get the most recent command:

```
var aCommands = oXHR.responseText.split(";");
var sCommand = aCommands.pop();
```

After this code has run, `sCommand` contains the most recent command from the server (`pop()` always returns the last item in an array). Assuming that semicolon delimitation is used in the commands, the file modification example can be rewritten to use Firefox's HTTP streaming support. First, the client:

```
<!DOCTYPE html PUBLIC "-//W3C//DTD XHTML 1.0 Transitional//EN"
    "http://www.w3.org/TR/xhtml1/DTD/xhtml1-transitional.dtd">
<html xmlns="http://www.w3.org/1999/xhtml">
    <head>
        <title>Firefox HTTP Streaming Example</title>
        <script type="text/javascript">
//<![CDATA[

        var iTimeoutId = null;
        var oXHR = null;

        function heartbeat() {
            clearTimeout(iTimeoutId);
            iTimeoutId = setTimeout(resetConnection, 10000);
        }

        function resetConnection() {
            oXHR.abort();
            oXHR.open("get",
                "FirefoxExampleConnection.php?t=" + (new Date()).getTime(), true);
            oXHR.onreadystatechange = function () {
                switch(oXHR.readyState) {
                    case 3:
                        var aCommands = oXHR.responseText.split(";");
                        var sCommand = aCommands.pop();
                        eval(sCommand);
                        break;
                    case 4:
                        resetConnection();
                        break;
                }
            };
            oXHR.send(null);
            heartbeat();
        }
```

```
        function modifiedAt(sDateTime) {
            document.getElementById("divStatus").innerHTML =
                                            "Modified at " + sDateTime;
        }

        window.onload = function () {
            oXHR = new XMLHttpRequest();
            resetConnection();
        };

        //]]>
        </script>
    </head>
    <body>
        <div id="divStatus">Waiting for first message...</div>
    </body>
</html>
```

The major changes in this version of the example are the creation of an XHR object in the `onload` event handler and the parsing of the returned data/evaluation of the command using `eval()`. Whenever the `readyState` of the XHR object is 3, an array is created containing all commands received to that point. The most recent command must be passed into `eval()` to be interpreted as a JavaScript call.

If `readyState` ever reaches 4, it means that the connection timed out and the connection must be reset. Note that the first line of code inside of `resetConnection()` is a call to the `abort()` method, which effectively resets the XHR object to make it ready for another connection.

Next, take a look at the new server portion of the example:

```
<?php
    header("Content-type: text/javascript");

    //get the file modification time
    $modified = filemtime('details.txt');
    $lastModified = $modified;

    //clear file statistics
    clearstatcache();

    //check every so often to see if it has changed
    while (true) {

        echo(";heartbeat()");
        ob_flush();
        flush();

        // sleep for 1 second
        sleep(1);

        //check the modification time
        $lastModified = filemtime('details.txt');

        //clear file statistics
```

```
        clearstatcache();

        //check it against the previous time
        if ($modified != $lastModified) {
            $output = date('h:i:s', $lastModified);

            echo(";modifiedAt(\"$output\")");
            ob_flush();
            flush();

            $modified = $lastModified;

            // sleep for 1 second
            sleep(1);
        }

    }
?>
```

The changes in this example are subtle: all HTML has been removed. Since each command must be manually interpreted using eval(), there is no need for the HTML tags anymore. The content type of the page has been set to "text/javascript" to indicate the type of data being returned. Further, a semicolon precedes each text output so that it will always be the last item in the commands array on the client.

When you run this example, you will notice that no user interface changes as the page continues to load and send information to the client.

> Some servers put limits on the amount of time that a server process can run, which can cause errors to occur during the execution of this example as well as other Comet processes. Often times when this happens, the server returns an HTML string describing the problem, which can cause an error when passed into eval(). Always check your server's settings to determine the best way to implement Comet solutions.

LiveConnect HTTP Streaming

LiveConnect is a little-known and underutilized technology supported by Firefox, Safari, and Opera, allowing Java objects to be used from within JavaScript. To use LiveConnect, the client machine must have a Java Runtime Environment (JRE) installed, and Java must be enabled in the browser. Most of the objects in the java package and its subpackages are available for use from within JavaScript using LiveConnect, enabling functionality that may not be possible using native JavaScript objects. For a cross-browser, cross-platform method of HTTP streaming, LiveConnect can be used very effectively, thanks to the availability of the java.net package.

The key to using LiveConnect for HTTP streaming is to open a stream over HTTP. This is done by creating a new java.net.URL object and then calling openStream(). Doing so returns an instance of java.io.InputStream, which can then be passed into a java.io.InputStreamReader object. Then, this reader must be passed into a java.io.BufferedReader object for easy access. After that, the reader must be checked periodically to determine when new data is available. Here's the rewritten file modification page:

```
<!DOCTYPE html PUBLIC "-//W3C//DTD XHTML 1.0 Transitional//EN"
    "http://www.w3.org/TR/xhtml1/DTD/xhtml1-transitional.dtd">
<html xmlns="http://www.w3.org/1999/xhtml">
    <head>
        <title>Live Connect Example</title>
        <script type="text/javascript">
        //<![CDATA[

        var iTimeoutId = null;
        var oReader = null;

        function resetConnection() {
            var oURL = new java.net.URL(
                        "http://localhost/LiveConnectExampleConnection.php");
            var oStream = oURL.openStream();
            if (oReader != null) {
                oReader.close();
            }
            oReader = new java.io.BufferedReader(
                                    new java.io.InputStreamReader(oStream));

            checkInput();
        }

        function checkInput() {
            try {
                var sLine = oReader.readLine();
                if (sLine != null) {
                    eval(sLine + "");
                }
                setTimeout(checkInput, 500);
            } catch (oEx) {
                resetConnection();
            }
        }

        function heartbeat() {
            clearTimeout(iTimeoutId);
            iTimeoutId = setTimeout(resetConnection, 10000);
        }

        function modifiedAt(sDateTime) {
            document.getElementById("divStatus").innerHTML =
                                            "Modified at " + sDateTime;
        }

        window.onload = resetConnection;

        //]]>
        </script>
    </head>
    <body>
        <div id="divStatus">Waiting for first message...</div>
    </body>
</html>
```

The key to this example is the global oReader object, which contains a reference to a
java.io.BufferedReader. When resetConnection() is called, a new java.net.URL object is created with the URL to send the request to. Note that this must be an absolute path to the page, since these
Java objects don't know the context of the page in which the JavaScript code is running.

When the openStream() method is called, it returns a reference to an input stream for the URL. Before
continuing on, any existing instance of oReader must be closed (by calling close()) to free any remaining memory. Once it's a sure thing that there are no other readers still in memory, a new
java.io.BufferedReader is created and stored in oReader. Then, checkInput() is called to see if
there's any data.

The checkInput() function does the important part of the process: checking for data and executing
JavaScript commands based on that data. Each time this function is called, readLine() returns
any available data. If any data is available, it is stored in sLine, which is then passed into eval() to
call the JavaScript command returned from the server. Since sLine is returned from a Java method,
it's actually not a JavaScript string but rather an instance of java.lang.String. To convert it into a
JavaScript, an empty string is appended. After that, a timeout is created to call checkInput() in
another 500 milliseconds.

All of the logic inside of checkInput() is wrapped in a try block. At some point, the connection will
time out, and the call to readLine() will throw an error. The try block will catch this error and call
resetConnection() to ensure that the stream is reopened.

The server-side component to this LiveConnect example is very similar to the Firefox equivalent:

```php
<?php
    header("Content-type: text/javascript");

    //get the file modification time
    $modified = filemtime('details.txt');
    $lastModified = $modified;

    //clear file statistics
    clearstatcache();

    //check every so often to see if it has changed
    while (true) {

        echo("heartbeat()\n");
        ob_flush();
        flush();

        // sleep for 1 second
        sleep(1);

        //check the modification time
        $lastModified = filemtime('details.txt');

        //clear file statistics
        clearstatcache();

        //check it against the previous time
```

```
        if ($modified != $lastModified) {
            $output = date('h:i:s', $lastModified);

            echo("modifiedAt(\"$output\")\n");
            ob_flush();
            flush();

            $modified = $lastModified;

            // sleep for 1 second
            sleep(1);
        }

    }
?>
```

The important difference in this page is that each JavaScript call is followed by a new line character (\n). Since the reader on the client side reads in data one line at a time, it's very important that this character be appended to each line of output so that it is read in a timely manner.

Server-Sent DOM Events

The Web Hypertext Application Technology Working Group (known as WHATWG) is a group of developers, companies, and others, interested in pushing browser development toward a platform more suitable for applications. WHATWG publishes a specification called Web Applications 1.0, which is a working draft as of October 2006. While Web Applications 1.0 introduces some very interesting concepts, one of the most interesting is called server-sent DOM events.

Server-sent DOM events allow a server to stream data to the client, which fires events in response to that data, allowing developers easy access to server information. Essentially, the browser opens a persistent connection to a particular page on the server and listens for new data coming in. The data for server-side DOM events comes in the form of event information, such as:

```
Event: MyEvent
Name1: value1
name2: value2

Event: MyEvent
data: See you later!
```

Each time the server sends data it must have an event name (specified by Event:) and some data in name-value pairs. Each part of this data is then made available to the client through JavaScript. There must be one blank line in between events so that the client recognizes an event as being fully received. Also, the content type of the data stream must be "application/x-dom-event-stream".

To receive events from the server, an <event-source/> element is necessary. This is a new element introduced in Web Applications 1.0 and can be accessed using all of the usual DOM methods. The src attribute should be set to the URL providing the streamed data, such as:

```
<event-source src="connection.php" id="source" />
```

Once the element is included in a page, you can use the addEventListener() method to assign event handlers for specific events. For example, to respond to an event called "MyEvent", the code would be:

```
var oSource = document.getElementById("source");
oSource.addEventListener("MyEvent", function (oEvent) {
    alert(oEvent.type);
}, false);
```

When the event is fired and the event handler called, an event object is passed in as the only argument. This event object is exactly the same as any other DOM event object in terms of the properties and methods, so type is the name of the event that was fired and target points to the <event-source/> element. However, there is some extra information provided on the event object in the form of the name-value pairs received in the data stream. If there is a named value called data in the stream, a property named data is accessible on the event object to retrieve that information.

> Note that in the case of custom events, the third argument in addEventListener() has no meaning but is typically set to false.

Firing UI Events

The true power of server-sent DOM events isn't simply in firing custom events; it's in firing UI events on the client from the server. So at any time, the server can decide that a click event should be fired, or mouseover or keydown . . . any event named in the DOM Level 3 Events specification can be fired through server-side DOM events. The complete list of events is:

❑ abort (Event)

❑ blur (UIEvent)

❑ click (MouseEvent)

❑ change (Event)

❑ DOMActivate (UIEvent)

❑ DOMAttrModified (MutationEvent)

❑ DOMAttributeNameChanged (MutationNameEvent)

❑ DOMCharacterDataModified (MutationEvent)

❑ DOMElementNameChanged (MutationNameEvent)

❑ DOMFocusIn (UIEvent)

❑ DOMFocusOut (UIEvent)

❑ DOMNodeInserted (MutationEvent)

❑ DOMNodeInsertedIntoDocument (MutationEvent)

❑ DOMNodeRemoved (MutationEvent)

- ❏ DOMNodeRemovedFromDocument (MutationEvent)
- ❏ DOMSubtreeModified (MutationEvent)
- ❏ error (Event)
- ❏ focus (UIEvent)
- ❏ keydown (KeyboardEvent)
- ❏ keyup (KeyboardEvent)
- ❏ load (Event)
- ❏ mousedown (MouseEvent)
- ❏ mousemove (MouseEvent)
- ❏ mouseover (MouseEvent)
- ❏ mouseout (MouseEvent)
- ❏ mouseup (MouseEvent)
- ❏ reset (Event)
- ❏ resize (UIEvent)
- ❏ scroll (UIEvent)
- ❏ select (Event)
- ❏ submit (Event)
- ❏ textInput (TextEvent)
- ❏ unload (Event)

To fire one of these events, specify its exact name (including case) as the Event value:

```
Event: click
```

Of course, firing a click event isn't very useful without firing it on a particular element. So, in addition to specifying the event, you must also specify a target using the Target attribute:

```
Event: click
Target: #target
```

Since the server doesn't have any DOM references, it needs to send the ID of the element upon which to fire the event. The format is the same as using an ID in CSS: precede the ID with the pound sign (#). It's also possible to fire an event on the document itself by specifying Document as the target:

```
Event: click
Target: Document
```

Depending on the event, you can also specify additional information to be sent:

```
Event: click
Target: #target
button : 2
screenX : 0
screenY : 0
```

In this example, the `button`, `screenX`, and `screenY` properties are filled with specified values. As long as the names of these name-value pairs match properties on the `event` object, they will be assigned appropriately. Any names that don't match will be ignored.

> **When sending UI events to the browser, it is unnecessary to assign event handlers to the `<event-source/>` element. Each of the events is transported automatically to the targeted element and is handled by the event handlers on that element.**

Browser Support

As of October 2006, the only browser supporting server-sent DOM events is Opera 9.01. It was actually an Opera engineer, Ian Hickson, who wrote the original specification back in 2004 (that specification was later incorporated into Web Applications 1.0). While the Opera implementation takes most things into account, there are some limitations to be aware of:

1. The `<event-source/>` element must be in the main markup of the page; creating it using `document.createElement()` doesn't work.

2. You can only use values named `data:` for custom events. All other names are ignored.

It should be noted that these limitations are minor and do not interfere significantly with the ability to make use of this extremely powerful feature. The following example runs on Opera 9.01 and later, and presumably will work with other browsers that implement server-sent DOM events in the future.

> **Server-sent DOM events are also on the Mozilla roadmap, though it is unclear what version of Firefox will be the first to implement it.**

Example

The file modification example becomes extremely simple when using server-sent DOM events. Consider the simplification of the client:

```
<!DOCTYPE html PUBLIC "-//W3C//DTD XHTML 1.0 Transitional//EN"
    "http://www.w3.org/TR/xhtml1/DTD/xhtml1-transitional.dtd">
<html xmlns="http://www.w3.org/1999/xhtml">
    <head>
        <title>Server-Sent DOM Events Example 1</title>
         <script type="text/javascript">
        //<![CDATA[
```

```
        function modifiedAt(sDateTime) {
            document.getElementById("divStatus").innerHTML =
                                        "Modified at " + sDateTime;
        }

        window.onload = function () {
            var oSource = document.getElementById("source");

            oSource.addEventListener("modified", function (oEvent) {
                modifiedAt(oEvent.data);
            }, false);

        };

        //]]>
        </script>
    </head>
    <body>
        <div id="divStatus">Waiting for first message...</div>
        <event-source id="source" src="ServerSentDOMEventsConnection.php" />
    </body>
</html>
```

Here, an <event-source/> element is added in the page with an id of "source" and its src attribute
set to ServerSentDOMEventsConnection.php. This is enough to start the information stream from the
server to the client; however, an event handler must be added to access the data as it comes in. So, in the
onload event handler, a reference to the <event-source/> element is retrieved by using
getElementById(). Then, an event handler is added using addEventListener() and passing in the
name of the custom event "modified". This handler simply retrieves information from the data value
and then passes it to modifiedAt() (which is the same as in previous examples).

On the server, the basic functionality is the same as in previous examples, just with a different format:

```
<?php
    header("Content-type: application/x-dom-event-stream");

    //get the file modification time
    $modified = filemtime('details.txt');
    $lastModified = $modified;

    //clear file statistics
    clearstatcache();

    //check every so often to see if it has changed
    while (true) {

        // sleep for 1 second
        sleep(1);

        //check the modification time
        $lastModified = filemtime('details.txt');

        //clear file statistics
```

```
        clearstatcache();

        //check it against the previous time
        if ($modified != $lastModified) {
            $output = date('h:i:s', $lastModified);
            echo("Event: modified\n");
            echo("data: $output\n\n");
            ob_flush();
            flush();
            $modified = $lastModified;

            // sleep for 1 second
            sleep(1);
        }

    }
?>
```

The major changes here are the different content type for the page (`"application/x-dom-event-stream"`, which is required by the specification) and the output. As opposed to previous examples, this page outputs plain text in the proper format for interpretation:

```
Event: modified
data: 5:23:06
```

That's all it takes to make this example work the same way as the previous ones. The differences are that the browser handles resetting the connection if it dies and access to incoming server data is much easier than using iframes or XHR.

Connection Management

A server implementing HTTP 1.1 allows a maximum of two simultaneous connections to a given client at the same time. Part of the reason for this is to ensure that no one client can overwhelm a server with so many requests that other clients don't get responses. Web browsers following this standard will also only allow two connections to a given domain, which is why pages with lots of external resources (JavaScript files, stylesheets, images, etc.) take longer to finish loading.

If you're going to be implementing a Comet connection, keep in mind that this will be using up one of the two available connections to the server. This can significantly slow down interactivity when an Ajax application requires the use of both traditional Ajax techniques and a Comet connection. With only one free connection available, all Ajax traffic must wait for it to become free before sending a request and receiving a response. Particularly problematic is when one Ajax response takes a long time to be sent, backing up all of the Ajax traffic for the application.

The best solution to this problem is to use a specific subdomain for the Comet connection. For instance, if your web application runs off of www.mywebapplication.com, use comet.mywebapplication.com for your Comet connection. This ensures that both connections are still available to the web application from the main domain (subdomain connections don't count against the two-connection limit) while the Comet connection remains open.

> Remember, JavaScript can't access external domains, so a subdomain is your only choice to work within the HTTP 1.1 limit.

Server-Side Support

Although the concept of HTTP streaming brings a lot of exciting possibilities to web applications, there are some concerns. Normal web browser traffic opens a connection, gets the data it needs, and then closes the connection. If every user is connected to a streaming HTTP web application at the same time, that means one connection must be kept alive for every user. On web applications with a large amount of traffic, this means significant server overhead. Plus, leaving infinite loops running on the server necessitates better memory management than typical web application servers provide. Fortunately, there are several server-side solutions designed to enable web servers to handle Comet-style communication.

❑ **Twisted** (`http://twistedmatrix.com/trac/`): An open source server-side event-publishing framework designed for optimal network usage. Twisted is written in Python and works over a large number of network protocols (not just HTTP). It's worth noting that Twisted wasn't designed specifically for Comet, but its server event paradigm works exceptionally well for the management of HTTP streaming.

❑ **Pushlets** (`http://www.pushlets.com`): An open source approach to HTTP streaming for JSP application servers. Pushlets use an event-publishing/subscribing model similar to server-sent DOM events to enable client-server communication. The framework comes with both server- and client-side libraries.

❑ **DivMod: Nevow** (`http://divmod.org/trac/wiki/DivmodNevow`): An open source web application framework built in Python with Comet support through a feature called Athena. Athena includes both server-side classes and a client-side library to implement Comet communication.

As with the emergence of Ajax solutions, server-side Comet solutions are being released more and more frequently. Be sure to investigate appropriate solutions for your server architecture before implementing Comet for your web application.

> You should not implement Comet-style interactions on any web application without first talking to the people in charge of your server system. Make sure that they understand what you are trying to accomplish so that an accurate assessment can be made for server needs.

Summary

In this chapter, you learned about Comet, a push architecture for web applications. Instead of using Ajax techniques such as polling to get updated data, the information is pushed out to the client via HTTP streaming — a continuous connection with the server that pushes out data periodically. You learned how to implement HTTP streaming solutions using Internet Explorer, Firefox, and LiveConnect.

Next, you learned about server-sent DOM events, part of the Web Applications 1.0 specification published by the Web Hypertext Application Technology Working Group (WHATWG). This technology allows the server to fire DOM events, such as click, mouseover, and keydown, as well as custom events that developers can subscribe to using the <event-source/> element. You learned how to use this technology in Opera.

You then were introduced to some basic concepts of connection management. The two-connection limit of HTTP 1.1 was discussed in relation to Ajax and Comet, and you learned that using a subdomain for a Comet connection is preferable because it still leaves two connections available to the main domain for other Ajax requests.

Last, you learned about several server-side solutions for implementing Comet. Since Comet puts more stress on traditional web application servers, it's preferable to use a system designed specifically for HTTP streaming.

10

Maps and Mashups

In the beginning, there was MapQuest (www.mapquest.com), a site that allowed users to find maps and get driving directions in the United States. Debuting during the dot-com era, MapQuest grew incredibly popular and even went public, being listed on the NASDAQ exchange. All of the hype caught the eye of America Online, which acquired the company in 2000. Competitive mapping sites were developed by others, most notably Yahoo! and Microsoft, but MapQuest remained the most popular site for mapping and driving directions. Mapping web sites went through iterative changes over the next few years, but for the most part, things stayed still.

When Google Maps (maps.google.com, later local.google.com) came online in 2004, it offered a revolutionary interface for the traditional web-based mapping systems. Instead of the traditional click-and-wait interaction that MapQuest and others used to pan and zoom maps, Google Maps used Ajax communication to download additional mapping info or maps at different zoom levels without reloading the page. Additionally, the ability to drag the map around instead of relying on the ubiquitous compass interface provided a truly unique user experience in the world of online mapping.

The development of Google Maps reignited interest in online mapping and the possibilities that Ajax opened for this particular usage. Yahoo!, Microsoft, and even MapQuest rushed to update their map offerings to be more competitive with Google Maps, using Ajax and other, more responsive user interface paradigms.

As with many new developments in technology, developers were immediately drawn to the new interfaces used by Google Maps and other Ajax-enabled applications. Savvy web developers reverse-engineered Google Maps, embedding its interface in their own pages as a proof of concept. Though not harmful, this occurrence opened the eyes of Google, and soon they released the Google Maps API to the public. As before, Yahoo!, Microsoft, and MapQuest each followed suit with their own Ajax-enabled mapping APIs, flooding the technology world with numerous options for embedding maps into web pages.

The Rise of Mashups

Closely related to the various mapping APIs is the concept of a mashup. *Mashups* are web applications that combine information from a number of sources to provide a new user experience. This information isn't located at a single source; rather, it comes from numerous sources that publish information publicly through web services, RSS feeds, or other means. Traditionally, mashups involve combining such information with a map.

Chicago Crime (`www.chicagocrime.org`) is widely considered to be the first mashup, combining crime information for Chicago with a map generated by the Google Maps API. This site is credited with the rise of mashups as its developers integrated Google Maps long before the API was available. Over time, and through the use of the evolving Google Maps API, Chicago Crime has grown into a mashup covering nearly all aspects of crime in the Chicago area, with breakdowns by crime type, street, district, ward, and more.

Another popular first-mover in the realm of mashups was Housing Maps (`www.housingmaps.com`), which combines housing listings from Craig's List (`www.craigslist.org`) with a map generated by Google Maps. The map is used to show locations where there are listings as well as the addresses and photos of available properties.

To create a map-enabled mashup such as these, you must have access to location-based information. Most such information is represented by physical street addresses, such as those used to get directions. However, these addresses must be mapped to specific locations on the map using a technique called geocoding.

Geocoding

Geocoding is the process by which information is associated with particular geographic points in the world. These points are identified by degrees in latitude and longitude, which you may remember from grade school as the north-south and east-west measurements, respectively. It may surprise you to know that most mapping APIs don't actually know the location of addresses; they know the location of points given in latitude and longitude. All addresses must be converted to a set of points before being located on a map.

All of the mapping APIs require the use of degree decimals for both latitude and longitude. This is different from what you probably learned about in school, where latitude and longitude are identified by degrees, minutes, and seconds. If you have a location in this format, you'll need to use a converter to get the degree decimal values. And of course, if you have an address, you'll need to convert that to latitude and longitude into degree decimals as well.

Geocoding Web Sites

Most countries provided geocoded information about the terrain through census records. In the United States, for instance, the U.S. Census Bureau geocodes nearly every highway and surface street in the country. Further, this data is in the public domain and can be accessed via the Topologically Integrated Geographic Encoding and Referencing system (Tiger, `www.census.gov/geo/www/tiger`). Plowing through all of this information is an arduous process since there's more than 20 GB of data for the United States alone. With the new interest in mapping and mashups, a number of services have arisen to allow easier access to geocoded information.

❑ **geocoder.us** (`www.geocoder.us`): This web site can return the latitude and longitude of any address in the United States. Simply go to the web site and enter in an address. The information returned includes both the degrees/minutes/seconds and degree decimal formats of the location, as well as an up-close map.

❑ **Travel GIS** (`www.travelgis.com/geocode`): This site offers geocoded information for 24 countries in a very simple interface. Addresses are returned in decimal format only.

❑ **worldKit GeoCoder** (`http://brainoff.com/geocoder`): This is a simple web site where you can enter in an address and it returns the latitude/longitude coordinates in decimal format along with some additional information. It gives you a map of the world and pinpoints each location you enter on that map with a red dot. You can zoom in and out on the map as well as click on it to get the latitude and longitude of any point in the world.

Geocoding Services

Even though web sites providing geocode information are useful, they are only minimally so when creating a mashup. Most mashups require a dynamic lookup of geocoded information as the user interacts with the application. To aid in this case, there are several geocoding web services offering address lookup in real time:

❑ **Yahoo! Maps Geocoding Service** (`http://developer.yahoo.com/maps/rest/V1/geocode.html`): This RESTful service returns XML containing the latitude, longitude, street address, city, state, and zip code of the entered address. As this is purely for noncommercial purposes, you are limited to 5,000 lookups per day, and you must sign up for a Yahoo! Application ID at `http://api.search.yahoo.com/webservices/register_application`.

❑ **Google Maps Geocoding Service** (`www.google.com/apis/maps/documentation/#Geocoding_Examples`): This lightweight API can be formatted to return data in XML, KML (Google's Keyhole Markup Language), CSV, or JSON and returns all of the information about a given address, including its coordinates and full address information (country, zip code, etc.). As with the Yahoo! version, this is for noncommercial use only; there is also a limit of 50,000 lookups per day. Before using the Google Maps Geocoding Service, you must sign up for an API key at `www.google.com/apis/maps/signup.html`. The Google Maps API also has JavaScript access to geocoding information.

Google Maps API

When Google Maps first debuted, it was the victim of numerous hackers. People were enthralled with this next-generation Ajax application that did things no one had ever seen done before. Developers from around the world wanted to know how it worked and how they could use it to their advantage. Though not damaging in any way, these early Google Maps hackers opened the eyes of the folks in Mountain View, California, and soon the Google Maps API was released to the public.

How Does It Work?

The Google Maps API is one of the most interesting uses of Ajax in that it doesn't necessarily need to use XHR or iframes to accomplish its functionality. Instead, the API uses the dynamic nature of images to fetch new information from the server on demand. Although it doesn't use the Ajax image technique discussed in Chapter 2, the same basic idea is at work: images can have their sources changed at any time. The Google Maps API uses this functionality to create the illusion of panning over one large image when, in reality, it loads only small pieces of the overall image to give the perception of a much larger one.

The initial view of the map is split into several images that are placed next to each other, giving the appearance of one large image. When a map is first loaded, the API determines how many of these images are necessary to completely fill the map container. The images are arranged in a grid that overlaps the ends of the map container. If the map is zoomed, each of the tiled images is set to a different URL, loading a new image into the <img/> element. This gives the illusion of an asynchronous zoom when, in reality, it's just a new take on the old image-swapping technique that has been around since the late 1990s.

When the map is panned or dragged by the user, it appears as if the map is neverending image thanks to some interesting JavaScript. The images are, indeed, moved as the user drags the mouse, but once the images disappear out of the map's viewable area, they are removed and placed at the other end of the map. For instance, images that disappear off the right side of the map are placed just out of view on the left, and images that disappear off the bottom of the map are placed just out of view on the top. It's this constant repositioning of image tiles that gives the illusion that the user is panning over a single large image. Joel Webber, one of the first developers to dissect how Google Maps works, likened the technique to building a railroad track by taking a piece from the end and placing it at the front: images are neither created nor destroyed, just moved around.

Behind the scenes, there's also some XML and XSLT performing extra functions on the map, but the majority of the work is handled by images.

Getting Started

To begin, you need to have a Google account (such as to access Gmail). If you don't have a Google account yet, go to www.google.com/accounts for information on how to sign up. The next step is to go to www.google.com/apis/maps/signup.html to sign up for an API key. To do so, you must provide a URL indicating the location at which the API will be used. This location is a specific directory on your server; so www.mydomain.com/maps1 and www.mydomain.com/maps2 would each require separate keys.

The Google Maps API does have some important limitations you should be aware of:

❑   The API is for noncommercial use only. To obtain a commercial license, you'll need to contact Google directly.

❑   The page using the Google Maps API has no page view limits; however, if you anticipate more than 500,000 page views per day, you'll need to contact Google about getting a commercial license.

❑   You are prohibited from obscuring attributions or ads that appear within the map viewport.

❑   You must keep your site up to date with the most current version of the API. Google generally gives users a month to upgrade to a newly released version.

There is only one JavaScript file necessary for you to begin using the Google Maps API. Unlike other APIs, you can't download the files locally. Instead, you'll need to access the file located on the Google Maps server. This file must include the version and your key in this format:

```
http://maps.google.com/maps?file=api&v={version}&key={your key}
```

For instance, if the most recent version is version 2, the following code should be included:

```
<script type="text/javascript"
        src="http://maps.google.com/maps?file=api&v=2&key={your key}"></script>
```

Once the file is included, you can begin writing your application.

Google Maps Basics

The main object in the Google Maps API is called GMap2. The constructor accepts a single argument, which is the element that should contain the map. It is recommended that this container element be a `<div/>` for best compatibility and extensibility. This `<div/>` element can be styled as normal, minimally specifying the width and height. The GMap2 object is smart enough to work within the styles provided for the container `<div/>`, so the page's overall layout will never be compromised due to the inclusion of a map. To create a map using a `<div/>` element with an ID of `"divMap"`, use the following:

```
var oMap = new GMap2(document.getElementById("divMap"));
```

Once the map object is created, you must initialize the view to a specific area. This is done by calling the `setCenter()` method of the map, which accepts two arguments: a point given in latitude/longitude and a zoom level. The first argument must be a GLatLng object (creating by passing in a latitude and a longitude in decimal format); the second argument is a zoom level where 0 is completely zoomed out and any number greater than 0 reveals more detail in the map. For example, the following code centers a map on the United States so that the entire country is in view:

```
var oMap = new GMap2(document.getElementById("divMap"));
oMap.setCenter(new GLatLng(32, -92), 3);
```

There are some browsers that may not support the Google Maps API, so it's best to check ahead of time before creating a new GMap2 object, by using the `GBrowserIsCompatible()` function:

```
if (GBrowserIsCompatible()) {
    var oMap = new GMap2(document.getElementById("divMap"));
    oMap.setCenter(new GLatLng(32, -92), 3);
}
```

These four lines of code are all that it takes to get a simple map instantiated on a page (see Figure 10-1).

The map display with this code is very basic and fairly limited. While the map of the United States is plainly visible, there is little user interaction. It's possible to move the viewport of the map by dragging the image, but other than that, there's no zooming or view switching. The easiest way to enable this functionality is to include one or more controls.

Figure 10-1

Controls

The official Google Maps interface at http://maps.google.com has a number of different ways the user can manipulate the map. Each of these manipulations is handled by a different control. The Google Maps API provides a number of default controls that can be used to implement the full Google Maps interface or just the parts necessary for your purposes:

❑ GLargeMapControl: The typical pan/zoom control displayed on http://maps.google.com.

❑ GSmallMapControl: A smaller version of the previous control, with only plus/minus and directional controls (but no zoom slider).

❑ GSmallZoomControl: The zoom slider control without any directional controls.

❑ GScaleControl: A scale indicating units in miles and kilometers.

❑ GOverviewMapControl: A zoomed-out view of the map with the current viewport area highlighted.

❑ GMapTypeControl: The Map/Satellite/Hybrid control.

One or more of these controls can be added to the map via the addControl() method. Each of the controls can be created without any parameters and passed into the method:

```
oMap.addControl(new GSmallMapControl());
```

Though this is most often done just after creating a GMap2 object, controls can be added at any time. Additionally, controls can be removed using the removeControl() method if you have a reference to the control:

```
var oControl = new GSmallMapControl();
oMap.addControl(oControl);

//do some other stuff

oMap.removeControl(oControl);
```

The first three controls, GLargeMapControl, GSmallMapControl, and GSmallZoomControl should not be used together, since they all occupy the same location on the map (upper-left corner). The GMapTypeControl can safely be used with any of the others, since it occupies the upper-right corner.

If you want your map to have controls right from the onset, you should add them immediately after creating the GMap2 object but before you call setCenter(), such as:

```
if (GBrowserIsCompatible()) {
    var oMap = new GMap2(document.getElementById("divMap"));
    oMap.addControl(new GSmallMapControl());
    oMap.addControl(new GMapTypeControl());
    oMap.setCenter(new GLatLng(32, -92), 3);
}
```

Adding these controls yields the map in Figure 10-2.

Figure 10-2

Moving the Map

It's possible to dynamically control the view of the map once it's been loaded by using several methods of the `GMap2` object. Although the user can access various controls on the map to zoom and move the map view, it may be necessary to control the map separately. All of the navigation that can be performed using the controls can also be accomplished by directly calling the JavaScript methods for the specific behavior.

The `setCenter()` method was used earlier to initialize the map display, but it can also be used at any time to recenter the map on a specific point. This recentering is immediate and has no animation associated with it. For a smoother transition to a new point on the map, there are several methods available:

- ❑ `panBy(distance)`: Specifies the distance (as a `GSize`) that the map should be moved by.

- ❑ `panDirection(x, y)`: Specifies the direction that the map should be panned to. The x argument should be -1 to move left, 0 to not move, or 1 to move right; the y argument should be -1 to move up, 0 to not move, or 1 to move down.

- ❑ `panTo(center)`: Specifies a `GLatLng` object that should be the new center of the map. The map that animates moving to that position (same as `setCenter()`, except with animation).

These methods can be used as any time to move the map to a new position, for example:

```
oMap.panBy(new GSize(20,20));        //Pans the maps by 20 pixels in each direction
oMap.panDirection(1, 0);             //Pans the maps to the right
oMap.panTo(new GLatLng(50, -80));    //Pans map to the specified location
```

Info Windows

Info windows provide additional information about a point on the map. On the Google Maps web site, info windows are used to provide address information about a point on the map, although they can be used for many more purposes. Visually, info windows look like dialogue bubbles from a comic strip: a round, white bubble anchored by a white triangle pointing to a specific location on the map (see Figure 10-3).

Figure 10-3

Basic Info Windows

An info window can be opened at any time by using the `openInfoWindow()` method of the `GMap2` object. This method accepts three arguments: a `GLatLng` object specifying where the info window should be anchored, a DOM node providing the contents of the info window, and an optional configuration object.

To open a very simple info window at the center of the map, the following code can be used:

```
oMap.openInfoWindow(oMap.getCenter(),
                    document.createTextNode("Center of the map!"));
```

The `getCenter()` method of the `GMap2` object returns a `GLatLng` object for the center of the map, ensuring that the info window points to the exact center. Even though this info window displays only text, it's still necessary to pass in a DOM node for the second argument, so a text node is created with the message to display.

There is a second method, `openInfoWindowHtml()`, that allows an HTML string to be passed in as the body of the info window instead of a DOM node. This method accepts the same three arguments (a point to anchor to, the contents of the window, and an optional configuration object) and is called like this:

```
oMap.openInfoWindowHtml(oMap.getCenter(), "<em>Center of the map!</em>");
```

This example opens an info window with stylized text (italics, assuming that there are no styles overriding the default display of `<em/>`). In this way, it's possible to create rich text on the fly and display it in an info window without the need to create DOM objects.

Configuration Options

The third argument to both of the previously mentioned methods is a configuration object for the info window. This object can contain one more of the following properties:

❑   `maxWidth`: The maximum allowable width of the info window in pixels

❑   `onCloseFn`: A function to call once the info window has been closed

❑   `onOpenFn`: A function to call once the info window has been opened

This configuration object can be included as an object literal, such as:

```
oMap.openInfoWindowHtml(oMap.getCenter(), "<em>Center of the map!</em>",
                        { onCloseFn: function() { alert("Closed") } });
```

When you run this code, an alert is displayed after the user clicks the close button on the info window. Generally speaking, the `onCloseFn` option is the most useful of the available options, since it provides a hook to an otherwise untraceable event. `maxWidth` can otherwise be set using CSS and `onOpenFn` can easily be mimicked by calling a function right after the call to `openInfoWindow()` or `openInfoWindowHtml()`, since both are synchronous operations.

Tabbed Info Windows

A new addition to version 2 of the Google Maps API is the tabbed info window. Tabbed info windows can be used to present more information about a particular point on the map without taking up extra horizontal and vertical space (see Figure 10-4).

307

Figure 10-4

As with nontabbed info windows, the tabbed version can be created with two methods: `openInfoWindowTabs()` and `openInfoWindowTabsHtml()`. Both methods accept three arguments: a `GLatLng` object indicating where on the map to point to, an array of `GInfoWindowTab` objects representing the tabs, and an optional configuration object. The difference between the two methods has to do with the data available within each `GInfoWindowTab` object. When you use `openInfoWindowTabs()`, each `GInfoWindowTab` object must be created using a string for the tab title and a DOM node for the tab contents; `openInfoWindowTabsHtml()` expects each `GInfoWindowTab` to have been created using a string for the tab title and a string for the contents (which can contain HTML). The following code creates an info window with two tabs:

```
var aTabs = [
    new GInfoWindowTab("First tab", document.createTextNode("First tab text")),
    new GInfoWindowTab("Second tab", document.createTextNode("Second tab text"))
];
oMap.openInfoWindowTabs(oMap.getCenter(), aTabs);
```

The first part of this code creates an array containing two `GInfoWindowTab` objects whose contents are text nodes. This array is then passed in as the second argument of `openInfoWindowTabs()` to display the info window. To display formatted HTML text instead of plain text, use `openInfoWindowTabs()` and assign the tab contents as a string:

```
var aTabs = [
    new GInfoWindowTab("First tab", "<em>First</em> tab text"),
    new GInfoWindowTab("Second tab", "<em>Second</em> tab text")
];
oMap.openInfoWindowTabsHtml(oMap.getCenter(), aTabs);
```

This code produces the result seen previously in Figure 10-4. Note that only three lines have changed: the two lines defining the `GInfoWindowTab` objects and the method call.

The configuration object can contain the same options as those used with non-tabbed info windows, as well as an additional property called `selectedTab`. This value is an integer indicating the number of the tab that should be selected when the info window is initially displayed; the default value is 0, which selects the first tab. To select the second tab by default, the following code passes in a configuration object with `selectedTab` set to 1:

```
var aTabs = [
    new GInfoWindowTab("First tab", "<em>First</em> tab text"),
    new GInfoWindowTab("Second tab", "<em>Second</em> tab text")
];
oMap.openInfoWindowTabsHtml(oMap.getCenter(), aTabs, { selectedTab: 1 });
```

Map Blowups

A *map blowup* is a special type of info window that shows a zoomed-in view of a particular point on the map. The contents of this info window are a smaller version of the main map, complete with buttons for changing the map type and a zoom control (see Figure 10-5).

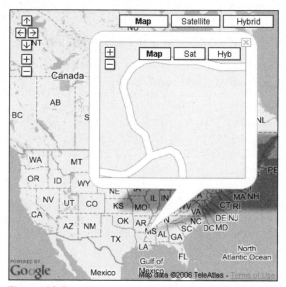

Figure 10-5

The `showMapBlowup()` method is used to open a map blowup info window. This method accepts two arguments: a `GLatLng` object indicating the point to both anchor on and blow up and an optional configuration object. For example, to show a blowup of the center of the map, use the following code:

```
oMap.showMapBlowup(oMap.getCenter());
```

When the second argument is specified, the configuration object has two additional properties to interact with map blowups. The first is `zoomLevel`, which indicates the zoom factor of the map shown in the info window. The second is `mapType`, which indicates what type of map should be displayed (one of

G_NORMAL_MAP, G_SATELLITE_MAP, G_HYBRID_MAP or any custom map type). To display a blowup of the center of the map at a zoom level of 5 showing a satellite map, the following code can be used:

```
oMap.showMapBlowup(oMap.getCenter(), {zoomLevel: 5, mapType: G_SATELLITE_MAP});
```

Aside from these two properties, the same three basic configuration options are available (maxWidth, onOpenFn, and onCloseFn).

Manipulating Info Windows

Once an info window is opened, a reference to the GInfoWindow object can be retrieved by calling the getInfoWindow() method. The GInfoWindow object can be helpful when it's necessary to interact with the info window outside of user action. For instance, an info window may need to be hidden after a certain amount of time. This can be accomplished by using a timeout and calling the hide() method, like this:

```
setTimeout(function () {
    var oInfoWindow = oMap.getInfoWindow();
    oInfoWindow.hide();
}, 5000);
```

It's also possible to redisplay an info window after it's been hidden using the show() method:

```
setTimeout(function () {
    var oInfoWindow = oMap.getInfoWindow();
    oInfoWindow.hide();

    setTimeout(function () {
        oInfoWindow.show();
    }, 5000);

}, 5000);
```

Since the contents of the info window aren't overwritten until either openInfoWindow() or openInfoWindowHtml() is called, the original contents are redisplayed when show() is called. Each time hide() or show() is called, an internal flag is set indicating the info window's state. This flag is accessed using the isHidden() method:

```
setTimeout(function () {
    var oInfoWindow = oMap.getInfoWindow();
    oInfoWindow.hide();
    alert("Hidden? " + oInfoWindow.isHidden());

    setTimeout(function () {
        oInfoWindow.show();
        alert("Hidden? " + oInfoWindow.isHidden());
    }, 5000);

}, 5000);
```

This code outputs the returned value of isHidden() after the call to hide() and after the call to show(), indicating the status of the internal flag.

The info window also remembers which point it was set up to be anchored to; this value can be retrieved using the getPoint() method, which returns the GLatLng object that was originally used to create the info window. Similarly, it's possible to determine how far away the tip of the info window arrow is to that point by using the getPixelOffset() method, which returns a GSize object indicating how far away the info window is:

```
var oInfoWindow = oMap.getInfoWindow();
var oPoint = oInfoWindow.getPoint();
var oOffset = oInfoWindow.getPixelOffset();

alert("Info window points to (" + oPoint.lat() + "," + oPoint.lng()
      + ") and the arrow tip is " + oOffset.height + " y pixels and "
      + oOffset.width + " x pixels from that point.");
```

Tabbed info windows have several other methods designed to interact with the tabs. The selectTab() method can be called at any time to change the selected tab in the info window. As with the selectedTab property of the configuration object, pass in the index of the tab that should be selected (where 0 is for the first tab, 1 is for the second, etc.):

```
setTimeout(function () {
    var oInfoWindow = oMap.getInfoWindow();
    oInfoWindow.selectTab(1);
}, 5000);
```

The index of the currently selected tab can be determined by using getSelectedTab():

```
setTimeout(function () {
    var oInfoWindow = oMap.getInfoWindow();
    alert("Selected tab: " + oInfoWindow.getSelectedTab());
    oInfoWindow.selectTab(1);
    alert("Selected tab: " + oInfoWindow.getSelectedTab());
}, 5000);
```

In this example, the index of the selected tab is output before and after the call to selectTab() in order to show that the tab has changed.

There are also a couple of other methods that can be used to retrieve other information about the tabbed info window:

❑   getContentContainers(): Returns an array of DOM nodes corresponding to the contents of each tab.

❑   getTabs(): Returns the array of GInfoWindowTab objects that was originally passed in to create the tabbed info window.

Events

Most objects in the Google Maps API support custom events. To access these events, there is a GEvent object with a couple of methods. The first, addListener(), is used to assign a function as an event handler for a particular event. This method accepts three arguments: the object to observe, the name of the event, and a function to call when the event occurs. For example, to listen to the `load` event of a `GMap2` object, the following code can be used:

```
GEvent.addListener(oMap, "load", function () {
    alert("Map is loaded.");
});
```

This code displays an alert when the map has finished loading and is ready to be interacted with.

The other method of `GEvent` is called `bind()`, and its purpose is to add an event handler that is a method of an object. It takes four arguments: the object to observe, the name of the event, the object on which the method exists, and the method to call. Consider the following example:

```
var oCustom = new Object();
oCustom.message = "Complete";
oCustom.handleMapLoad = function () {
    alert(this.message);
};

GEvent.bind(oMap, "load", oCustom, oCustom.handleMapLoad);
```

This example creates a custom object called `oCustom` that contains a method to call when the map has finished loaded (called `handleMapLoad`). The `GEvent.bind()` method specifies `oCustom` and `oCustom.handleMapLoad` as the third and fourth arguments. This ensures that the `handleMapLoad()` method is called when the map is fully loaded.

The `GMap2` object supports the following events:

❑ `addmaptype`: Fires when a map type is added to the map; supplies a `maptype` argument to the event handler.

❑ `addoverlay`: Fires when an overlay is added; the overlay is passed in as an argument to the event handler.

❑ `click`: Fires when the map is clicked; supplies a point (`GPoint` object) as an argument to the event handler. If the click occurred on an overlay (discussed later), then the overlay is also passed in as an argument.

❑ `clearoverlays`: Fires when the `clearOverlays()` method is called.

❑ `drag`: Fires repeatedly while the user is dragging the map.

❑ `dragend`: Fires when the user stops dragging the map.

❑ `dragstart`: Fires when the user starts to drag the map.

❑ `infowindowclose`: Fires when an info window closes.

❑ `infowindowopen`: Fires when an info window opens.

❑ `load`: Fires when the map is completely loaded.

❑ `maptypechanged`: Fires when the map type changes (for example, from Map to Satellite).

❏   mousemove: Fires when the cursor moves across the map; a GLatLng object indicating the last position of the mouse inside the map is passed in as an argument to the event handler.

❏   mouseout: Fires when the cursor moves from the map to the outside of the map; a GLatLng object indicating the last position inside of the map is passed in as an argument to the event handler.

❏   mouseover: Fires when the cursor moves onto the map from outside of the map; a GLatLng object indicating the mouse position on the map is passed in as an argument to the event handler.

❏   move: Fires repeatedly as the map is moving.

❏   moveend: Fires when the map stops moving.

❏   movestart: Fires when the map begins to move.

❏   removemaptype: Fires when a map type is removed from the map; supplies a maptype argument to the event handler.

❏   removeoverlay: Fires when an overlay is removed; the overlay is passed in as an argument to the event handler.

❏   zoomend: Fires when the map has stopped zooming; old zoom level and new zoom level are provided as arguments to the event handler.

These events can be used to monitor the user's interaction with the map at any particular time. Keep in mind that most objects on the map also support their own events.

Map Overlays

A *map overlay* is any graphical marker placed onto a map to indicate some geographic location. When using the Google Maps site, areas of interest are often indicated by an icon or some other marker placed directly on the map; these are examples of overlays.

There are three methods on the GMap2 object relating directly to overlays. The first is addOverlay(), which adds the specified overlay object to the map control. To add an overlay stored in a variable called oOverlay, the following code can be used:

```
oMap.addOverlay(oOverlay);
```

Of course, anything that can be added can also be removed, so the second method is removeOverlay(), which removes a specified overlay from the map. In order to remove a specific overlay, you need a reference to it (not unlike the way event handlers are removed). Once you have a reference, the method can be called like this:

```
oMap.removeOverlay(oOverlay);
```

It may not be practical to keep track of all the overlays used on a map, so it's also possible to remove all of the overlays using the third method, clearOverlays(). This method is called without any arguments:

```
oMap.clearOverlays();
```

This method removes all overlays added since the map was created. The Google Maps API provides several types of overlays that can be used with just a little configuration.

Markers

The simplest of the provided overlays are markers. Markers are the most commonly used indicator on the Google Maps web site: a red pushpin-like image that is based at a point of interest. A marker can be created by instantiating a `GMarker` object. The constructor of the `GMarker` accepts two arguments: a `GLatLng` object indicating where the marker should be set, and a configuration object containing additional information for the marker (this second argument is optional). Creating a simple marker can be done like this:

```
var oMarker =  new GMarker(new GLatLng(32, -92));
```

This code creates a marker that can be added to the map at any time. The optional second argument specifies additional information for the marker and can be specified as an object literal with one or more of the following properties:

❑ `title`: Text that should be displayed when the cursor is moved over the marker.

❑ `icon`: An icon that should be used for the overlay instead of the default icon.

❑ `clickable`: If false, disables click events for the marker; the default value is true.

❑ `draggable`: When set to true, allows the marker to be dragged and repositioned by the user; the default value is false.

❑ `dragCrossMove`: Set to true to force dragged markers to appear under the cursor instead of floating above; the default value is false. This setting only applies if draggable is true.

❑ `bouncy`: Determines if a dragged marker should bounce when it's dropped; the default value is false.

❑ `bounceGravity`: A number indicating the acceleration of the bounce when a marker is dropped. Only used when `bouncy` is set to `true`.

To create a marker whose tooltip text is `"My marker"`, the code is as follows:

```
var oMarker =  new GMarker(new GLatLng(32, -92), { title: "My marker" });
```

This essentially sets the `title` attribute of the element used to represent the marker; it uses the default behavior to enable this functionality. It's also possible to change the icon displayed for the marker by using the `icon` option in the configuration object. This property's value must be a `GIcon` object.

Specifying an Icon

The `GIcon` object is used to specify icons that can be used in Google Maps. Though there are a number of properties, only three are required.

❑ The first property is `image`, which specifies the URL of the image to display:

```
var oIcon = new GIcon();
oIcon.image = "flag.gif";
```

❑ Next, the `iconSize` property must be provided. This value must be a `GSize()` object indicating the width and height of the image specified in the `image` property. The `GSize()` object constructor accepts two arguments, the width and height of the image in pixels. So, if the image is 26 pixels wide by 33 pixels high, the size is specified like this:

```
var oIcon = new GIcon();
oIcon.image = "flag.gif";
oIcon.iconSize = new GSize(26, 33);
```

❑ The final required property is `iconAnchor`, which indicates what point on the image should be centered on the `GLatLng` location. This value is a `GPoint` object, which specifies an x and y coordinate of the image. To have the lower-left corner of the image appear at the coordinate on the map, the following code can be used:

```
var oIcon = new GIcon();
oIcon.image = "flag.gif";
oIcon.iconSize = new GSize(26, 33);
oIcon.iconAnchor = new GPoint(0, 33);
```

This code specifies the anchor to be at the point (0, 33) on the image, which is the lower-left corner. After adding this property, the `GIcon` object can be specified as part of a marker:

```
var oIcon = new GIcon();
oIcon.image = "flag.gif";
oIcon.iconSize = new GSize(26, 33);
oIcon.iconAnchor = new GPoint(0, 33);

var oMarker =  new GMarker(new GLatLng(32, -92), {title:"My marker", icon: oIcon});
oMap.addOverlay(oMarker);
```

There are other properties on a `GIcon` object that can be set, depending on your needs:

❑ `shadow`: The URL for an image to use as the shadow of the marker. According to Google's documentation, this shadow should be at 45 degrees to stylistically agree with default shadows provided by the API.

❑ `shadowSize`: A `GSize` object indicating the size of the shadow image.

❑ `infoWindowAnchor`: A `GPoint` object indicating where info windows should be anchored within the icon. When you are opening an info window from a marker with an icon, this property must be specified. Info windows are discussed later in this chapter.

❑ `printImage`: The URL of an image to use for the print version of the map. This image must be the same size as the one specified by `image`.

❑ `mozPrintImage`: The URL of an image to use for the print version of the map in Mozilla-based browsers such as Firefox. This image must be the same size of the one specified by `image`.

❑ `printShadow`: The URL of a shadow image to use for printed maps. This image must be the same size of the one specified by `shadow`.

❑ `transparent`: The URL of a 24-bit PNG image with 1 percent opacity that has the same size and shape as the image specified by `image`. This is used by Internet Explorer to specify the clickable area of the marker.

Manipulating Markers

There are several methods available on marker objects that allow the manipulation of position and functionality as well as providing information about the marker. For instance, the GIcon object used for the marker can be returned via the getIcon() method, and the GLatLng object used to anchor the marker can be retrieved using getPoint():

```
var oIcon = oMarker.getIcon();
var oAnchor = oMarker.getPoint();
```

If the marker needs to be moved once it has been placed on the map, this can be done using the setPoint() method. This method accepts a GLatLng object that the marker should be moved to. For example:

```
oMarker.setPoint(new GLatLng(33, -91));
```

A call to setPoint() moves the marker immediately. There is no animation; the marker simply disappears from the first point and reappears at the second.

There are also several methods relating to draggable markers. The draggable() method returns true or false to indicate if the marker is draggable by the user. If it is, you can enable or disable dragging using enableDragging() and disableDragging(), respectively. When using these methods, the draggingEnabled() method returns true or false to indicate if the marker is enabled for dragging:

```
function toggleDraggable(oMarker) {
    if (oMarker.draggable()) {
        if (oMarker.draggingEnabled()) {
            oMarker.disableDragging();
        } else {
            oMarker.enableDragging();
        }
    }
}
```

This function toggles the draggability of a marker and illustrates the use of these methods. If the marker is capable of being dragged, then draggable() returns true, even if dragging is disabled. Then, draggingEnabled() indicates if the marker can currently be dragged. If it can, the dragging is disabled using disableDragging(); otherwise, it's enabled using enableDragging(). Note that for enableDragging() and disableDragging() to work, the marker must have been created using the draggable option.

Marker Info Windows

If an info window should be pointing to a specific marker on the map, the marker can open an info window itself by using its own versions of openInfoWindow(), openInfoWindowHtml(), openInfoWindowTabs(), openInfoWindowTabsHtml(), and showMapBlowup(). The difference is that these methods don't need to be passed a GLatLng object to indicate where the info window should be anchored; the marker itself is used as the anchor.

Each of these methods accepts one less argument than its GMap2 counterpart, meaning that openInfoWindow() and openInfoWindowHtml() accept two arguments: the content (either a DOM node or HTML string, respectively) and an optional configuration object (only the maxWidth property is valid when using these methods). The `openInfoWindowTabs()` and `openInfoWindowTabsHtml()` methods also only accept two arguments: an array of `GInfoWindowTab` objects and an optional configuration object (only the `maxWidth` and `selectedTab` properties are valid when using this method). The `showMapBlowup()` method accepts only an optional configuration object (only `zoomLevel` and `mapType` are valid properties when using this method). Some basic examples:

```
oMarker.openInfoWindow(document.createTextNode("Marker info window"));

oMarker.openInfoWindowHtml("<em>Marker info window</em>", { maxWidth: 500 });

oMarker.showMapBlowup({ zoomLevel: 5, mapType: G_HYBRID_MAP });

oMarker.openInfoWindowTabsHtml([new GInfoWindowTab("Tab 1", "Tab 1 Content")]);

oMarker.openInfoWindowTabs(
    [new GInfoWindowTab("Tab 1", document.createTextNode("Tab 1 Content")),
     new GInfoWindowTab("Tab 2", document.createTextNode("Tab 2 Content"))],
    { selectedTab: 1});
```

Marker Events

As mentioned previously, most of the objects in the Google Maps API support events. Markers support a number of events that can be handled by custom event handlers:

- ❑ click: Fires when the marker is clicked. This event bubbles to the containing GMap2 object.
- ❑ dblclick: Fires when the marker is double-clicked. This event bubbles to the containing GMap2 object.
- ❑ dragstart: Fires when the marker starts being dragged (only if the marker has draggable set to true).
- ❑ drag: Fires when the marker is being dragged (only if the marker has draggable set to true).
- ❑ dragend: Fires when the marker stops being dragged (only if the marker has draggable set to true).
- ❑ infowindowopen: Fires when an info window is opened from the marker.
- ❑ infowindowclose: Fires when the info window opened from the marker is closed.
- ❑ mousedown: Fires when a mouse button is pressed down over the marker.
- ❑ mouseup: Fires when a mouse button is released over the marker.
- ❑ mouseout: Fires when the mouse is moved from over the marker to outside of the marker.
- ❑ mouseover: Fires when the mouse is first moved over the marker.
- ❑ remove: Fires when the marker is removed through removeOverlay() or clearOverlays().

To open an example when a marker is clicked, the following code can be used:

```
GEvent.addListener(oMarker, "click", function () {
    oMarker.openInfoWindowHtml("This is my marker.");
});
```

317

When the user clicks on this marker, an info window is displayed pointing right to the marker (an `infowindowopen` event is also fired). The map will scroll appropriately so that the entire info window can be displayed to the user. When this info window is closed, the `infowindowclose` event is fired, which can also be listened to:

```
GEvent.addListener(oMarker, "infowindowclose", function () {
    alert("Info window was closed.");
});
```

Note that the `onOpenFn` and `onCloseFn` properties of the configuration object cannot be used with info windows created from markers, so the `infowindowopen` and `infowindowclose` events must be used instead.

Using a Marker Manager

If a map contains a large number of markers, it's not always optimal to display every marker all the time. For instance, it would not make sense to show the weather for each individual city when the map of the entire United States is visible; it's just too much information to show at that level. To aid in this type of case, the Google Maps API provides the `GMarkerManager` object.

Generally speaking, a `GMarkerManager` object is used to determine which markers to display under what circumstances. Instead of adding markers to the `GMap2` object, markers are added to a `GMarkerManager` object, which informs the `GMap2` object when markers need to be displayed. To accomplish this, the `GMarkerManager` watches the zoom level and center of the map, checking for markers that need to be visible within the viewport.

To create a `GMarkerManager`, pass in a reference to the `GMap2` object it should be working with. There is also a second optional argument, which is an object with one or more of the following properties:

❑ `borderPadding`: The number of pixels outside of the viewable area that the manager should observe. This is a buffer area around the outside of the map within which markers are displayed so that there is no delay in their appearance when the map is panned.

❑ `maxZoom`: The maximum zoom level (where 0 is the smallest value) monitored by the manager. If not specified, the manager monitors all zoom levels.

❑ `trackMarkers`: Determines if the manager should keep track of markers that are moved either by users or by using the `setPoint()` method. The default value is `false`.

For example, the following code creates a marker manager that monitors 20 pixels outside of the viewport in each direction and all zoom levels up to 10:

```
var oManager = new GMarkerManager(oMap, { borderPadding: 20, maxZoom: 10 });
```

Once the object is instantiated, markers can be added by using `addMarker()`, which accepts three arguments: the marker, a minimum zoom level that must be met before the marker is displayed, and an optional maximum zoom level beyond which the marker won't be displayed. If the last two arguments are omitted, it's assumed that the marker should be displayed at all zoom levels; if only the last argument is omitted, it's assumed that the marker should be shown for all zoom levels past the minimum. For example:

```
oManager.addMarker(new GMarker(new GLatLng(32, -92)), 3);
oManager.addMarker(new GMarker(new GLatLng(33, -91)), 5, 10);
```

This code specifies two markers on the map. The first marker is displayed only at zoom levels of 3 or greater, while the second is displayed only between zoom levels of 5 and 10. Typically, a range is specified for markers that represent regions. For instance, the weather going on in the northern part of a state should be shown only until the zoom level is such that individual cities can have their own weather markers (which would be more specific than the weather for the region).

There is also an `addMarkers()` method, which allows the addition of multiple markers using the same zoom level requirements. The `addMarkers()` method also accepts three arguments: the first is an array of markers as opposed to a single marker; the other arguments are the same as in `addMarker()` (the minimum zoom level and an optional maximum zoom level). For example:

```
oManager.addMarkers([
    new GMarker(new GLatLng(31, -93)),
    new GMarker(new GLatLng(33, -93))
], 7, 13);
```

Here, two markers are added that are displayed when the zoom level is between 7 and 13. If there are a number of markers that should be displayed using the same criteria, it is more efficient to use `addMarkers()` rather than individual calls to `addMarker()`.

The final step after adding markers to the manager is to call the `refresh()` method. This method sets up the initial display of the map and sets up the necessary hooks to monitor the viewport. After calling `refresh()`, the manager handles all other viewport updates automatically. Make sure that this method is called after adding all of the markers:

```
oManager.addMarker(new GMarker(new GLatLng(32, -92)), 3);
oManager.addMarker(new GMarker(new GLatLng(33, -91)), 5, 10);
oManager.addMarkers([
    new GMarker(new GLatLng(31, -93)),
    new GMarker(new GLatLng(33, -93))
], 7, 13);
oManager.refresh();
```

Marker managers are best used for maps that show regional information with possible drilldowns into more local information. As previously discussed, a weather map is a good candidate for using a marker manager.

Polylines

A *polyline* is a line that overlays the map, connecting two or more geographic points. On the Google Maps site, polylines are frequently used to show the route between two locations. Polylines, however, need not be created strictly along roadways; in fact, polylines can be placed anywhere on the map.

Polylines are implemented differently depending on the capabilities of the browser being used, so before using them, it's necessary to ensure that all of the necessary information is present in the page. In Internet Explorer, Vector Markup Language (VML) is used to draw polylines, and this requires inclusion of the Microsoft VML namespace and the definition of a VML CSS rule:

```
<!DOCTYPE html PUBLIC "-//W3C//DTD XHTML 1.0 Transitional//EN"
    "http://www.w3.org/TR/xhtml1/DTD/xhtml1-transitional.dtd">
<html xmlns="http://www.w3.org/1999/xhtml" xmlns:v="urn:schemas-microsoft-com:vml">
  <head>
     <style type="text/css">
```

```
            v\:* {
                behavior:url(#default#VML);
            }
        </style>
    </head>
    <body>
        <!-- page body -->
    </body>
</html>
```

Including these sections of code ensures that polylines will work appropriately in Internet Explorer; this code is safely ignored in other browsers.

Polylines can be added to the map by creating GPolyline objects and adding them to the map via the addOverlay() method. The GPolyline constructor accepts four arguments: an array of GLatLng objects indicating two or more vertices for the polyline, an optional string indicating the color of the line, an optional number indicating the weight of the line (how many pixels wide it is), and an optional floating point number (decimal between 0 and 1) indicating the opacity of the line. Here's a simple example:

```
var oPolyline = new GPolyline([
    new GLatLng(40.758224, -73.917404),
    new GLatLng(34.101509, -118.32691)
], "#f00", 10);

oMap.addOverlay(oPolyline);
```

The first point in this example corresponds to the corner of 42nd Street and Broadway in New York while the second is the corner of Hollywood and Vine in Los Angeles. The line created is red ("#f00" is the hexadecimal shorthand code for red) and 10 pixels wide. Effectively, this code creates a diagonal line across the United States (see Figure 10-6).

Figure 10-6

The more points provided for the polyline, the more turns the line takes. When there are more than two points, the order in which they are presented is important, since the line is drawn from the first point to the second, from the second to the third, and so on.

Once a polyline is created, you can get information about it via two methods: `getVertexCount()` and `getVertex()`. The `getVertexCount()` method returns the number of vertices in the polyline (the number of points provided). The `getVertex()` method accepts a single argument, which is the index of the vertex to retrieve (0 for the first vertex, 1 for the second, etc.), and returns a `GLatLng` object with the vertex information. For example:

```
alert("Number of vertices: " + oPolyline.getVertexCount());
alert("First vertex: " + oPolyline.getVertex(0));
```

This simple example outputs the number of vertices and the first vertex in the polyline. Essentially, these two methods are used to retrieve the information that was first passed in when the polyline was created.

As with markers, polylines can be removed from the map at any time using the `removeOverlay()` or `clearOverlays()` methods.

Additional Information

The Google Maps API is actually quite extensive, and it is beyond the scope of this book to point out all the details. However, you should be aware that the API contains many more objects and features than are discussed in this book; the information presented here is intended to be a jumping-off point only. Google maintains documentation for the API online at `http://www.google.com/apis/maps/documentation/`. The documentation includes a complete class reference for all of the API's objects as well as detailed examples for various features. Additionally, the Wrox book *Google Maps Mashups* (Wiley 2007) contains extensive examples and information on building mashups using the Google Maps API.

Yahoo! Maps API

The Yahoo! Maps API debuted around the same time as the Google Maps API, but with less fanfare. The folks at Yahoo! decided to take an interesting approach to their new mapping product, developing both Ajax and Flash APIs. The Ajax API (covered here) is composed of JavaScript objects used to implement maps on any web site. The Flash API, on the other hand, can be embedded within Flash movies or Flex applications as well as embedded in web sites. Both the Ajax and Flash APIs use the same data and image sources, so visually there is very little difference between the two.

Getting Started

To use the Yahoo! Maps API, you must have a Yahoo! ID. If you don't have one, go to `http://edit.yahoo.com` and click on the "Sign Up" link. After signing up, go to `http://api.search.yahoo.com/webservices/register_application` to request an application ID. This application ID can be used not only for the Yahoo! Maps API but also for the other public Yahoo! APIs.

There are some limitations on using the Yahoo! Maps API:

❑ The API is for noncommercial use only. You can contact Yahoo! directly to inquire about a commercial license.

❑ The attribution inside of the map must not be obscured.

❑ You are limited to 50,000 requests per day. If you anticipate needing more than that, you'll need to discuss your needs with Yahoo! directly.

Once you have agreed to the terms of use and received an application ID, you'll need to include the Yahoo! Maps API JavaScript file in your page. This file resides on Yahoo! servers and must be accessed directly from there by providing the API version number and your application ID in the following format:

```
http://api.maps.yahoo.com/ajaxymap?v={api version}&appid={your application ID}
```

At the time of writing, the most recent version is 3.4, so the code can be included using a `<script/>` tag like this:

```
<script type="text/javascript"
        src="http://api.maps.yahoo.com/ajaxymap?v=3.4&appid={app ID}"></script>
```

This is the only file necessary to begin using Yahoo! Maps on your site.

Yahoo! Maps Basics

The map object in the Yahoo! Maps API is `YMap`. The constructor for a `YMap` object can accepts three arguments: the container element in which to create the map, an optional map type indicating which type of map to display (map, satellite, or hybrid), and an optional `YSize` object indicating the dimensions of the map container. Generally, the third argument isn't needed as long as the width and height of the container element are specified.

To create a map using a `<div/>` element with an ID of `"divMap"`, use the following:

```
var oMap = new YMap(document.getElementById("divMap"));
```

This code initializes the map container element as a Yahoo! map control, but the map itself hasn't been drawn yet. To display the map, the `drawZoomAndCenter()` method must be called, passing in the coordinate on which to center and the zoom level. Map coordinates are represented by `YGeoPoint` objects in the Yahoo! Maps API, which store the decimal format latitude and longitude of a location. The zoom level is a number between 1 and 16, where 1 is zoomed all the way in and 16 is zoomed all the way out. To display a map that shows the entire United States, use the following code:

```
var oMap = new YMap(document.getElementById("divMap"));
oMap.drawZoomAndCenter(new YGeoPoint(32, -92), 14);
```

These two lines of code produce a basic map with a distance legend (see Figure 10-7).

Figure 10-7

It's possible to specify a different map type for the initial view of the map. The possible values are YAHOO_MAP_REG (the regular map), YAHOO_MAP_SAT (satellite photos), and YAHOO_MAP_HYB (hybrid combination of map and photos). One of these values can be passed in to the YMap constructor to set the initial map type:

```
var oMap = new YMap(document.getElementById("divMap"), YAHOO_MAP_SAT);
oMap.drawZoomAndCenter(new YGeoPoint(32, -92), 14);
```

This code creates the same basic view of the map but with satellite imagery. There's also a setMapType() method that can be used to change the map type at any time:

```
var oMap = new YMap(document.getElementById("divMap"));
oMap.drawZoomAndCenter(new YGeoPoint(32, -92), 14);
oMap.setMapType(YAHOO_MAP_SAT);
```

Since every map has a map type set either by default or by the developer, the map type can be retrieved using the getCurrentMapType() method, which returns one of the three constants used in the setMapType() method:

```
switch(oMap.getCurrentMapType()) {
    case YAHOO_MAP_REG:
        alert("Regular map");
        break;
    case YAHOO_MAP_SAT:
        alert("Satellite map");
        break;
    case YAHOO_MAP_HYB:
        alert("Hybrid map");
        break;
}
```

Although it's possible to set the map type programmatically, it's also helpful to allow the user to decide how to display the map. To allow more fine-grained user control of the map, you'll need to use controls.

Controls

Controls allow users to manipulate the view of the map directly. The Yahoo! Maps API provides several built-in controls that can be added to the map individually depending on your specific needs. These built-in controls are added using one of the following methods on the YMap object:

❑ addPanControl(): Adds a pan control containing arrows pointing north, south, east, and west; clicking on any of these buttons pans the map in the specified direction. This control is placed in the upper-right corner of the map. The control can be removed by using removePanControl().

❑ addTypeControl(): Adds a map type control containing buttons for each of the three map types. Clicking on a button changes the map's view to that of the specified map type. This control is placed in the upper-left corner of the map. The control can be removed by using removeTypeControl().

❑ addZoomLong(): Adds a large zoom control to the map made up of plus and minus buttons, as well as a zoom scale. This control is placed in the upper-right corner of the map. The control can be removed by using removeZoomControl().

❑ addZoomScale(): Adds a zoom scale control to the map indicating the measurements being used in the current map view. This control is added by default and is placed in the lower-left corner of the map. The control can be removed by using removeZoomScale().

❑ addZoomShort(): Adds a small zoom control to the map made up of only a plus and minus button. This control is placed in the upper-right corner of the map. The control can be removed using removeZoomControl().

To create a map with a pan control, map type control, and long zoom control, use the following code:

```
var oMap = new YMap(document.getElementById("divMap"));
oMap.addPanControl();
oMap.addTypeControl();
oMap.addZoomLong();
oMap.drawZoomAndCenter(new YGeoPoint(32, -92), 14);
```

This code creates the map displayed in Figure 10-8.

Note that the zoom scale control is in the lower-left corner by default, since removeZoomScale() wasn't called. It's best to call these methods before the call to drawZoomAndCenter().

Figure 10-8

Moving the Map

By default, a map created using the Yahoo! Maps API can be dragged by the user to pan the view. Adding a pan control to the map gives users another way to scroll the viewport of the map. The view can also be panned programmatically using a couple of methods available on the YMap object.

The first method, `panToLatLon()`, pans the map to a specific location given by latitude and longitude. This method accepts a single argument, which is a YGeoPoint, indicating where the map should be panned to. When the map is panned, this method uses animation to move the map to that position, providing a smooth scrolling effect that is similar to the panning animation used in the Google Maps API. Panning via latitude/longitude can be accomplished like this:

```
oMap.panToLatLon(new YGeoPoint(50, -80));
```

This method pans the map to a specific location, meaning that subsequent calls using the same data won't move the map at all. It is possible to move the map relative to the current view, by pixels, using the `panToXY()` method. This method accepts a single argument, a YCoordPoint object, which represents the x and y coordinates in pixels. The map is panned so that the center is the location that was represented at those coordinates. To pan the map to the location 20 pixels from the top and left of the map,use the following code:

```
oMap.panToXY(new YCoordPoint(20, 20));
```

Because the information is relative to the current view of the map, this line of code can be executed repeatedly and will cause the map to move each time until the end of the map is reached.

Smart Windows

To display information about a location the map, Yahoo! Maps uses a smart window. *Smart windows* are small, white bubbles that point to a specific location with a small triangle and display text or some other HTML code. All smart windows are also created with a close button, a small "X" in the upper-right corner (see Figure 10-9).

Figure 10-9

Smart windows are opened using the showSmartWindow() method of the YMap object. This method accepts two arguments: a YGeoPoint to anchor to and the content for the smart window. The content can be an HTML string or a DOM text node. The following code opens a smart window at the center of the map with a simple message:

```
oMap.showSmartWindow(oMap.getCenterLatLon(), "Hello world!");
```

This code uses the getCenterLatLon() method to retrieve a YGeoPoint object for the center of the map so that the smart window can be opened in the exact location. The second argument is plain text, though it could just as easily have contained HTML:

```
oMap.showSmartWindow(oMap.getCenterLatLon(), "<strong>Hello</strong> world!");
```

If you need output characters that are part of HTML syntax, such as less than (<), then creating a text node is the way to go:

```
oMap.showSmartWindow(oMap.getCenterLatLon(), document.createTextNode("5 < 10"));
```

Events

Most of the objects in the Yahoo! Maps API support events that can be handled to provide an increased level of interaction. The YEvent object publishes a single method called Capture() that is used to assign event handlers. The Capture() method accepts four arguments: the target object, the name of the event, a function to call when the event occurs, and an optional scope object (used if the function to call is a method of another object). All supported Yahoo! Maps events are contained in the EventsList object, which has properties corresponding to specific events that can be managed. For the YMap object, the following events are supported:

❑ EventsList.changeZoom: Occurs when the zoom level changes.

❑ EventsList.endAutoPan: Occurs when an "auto" pan occurs (pan to a specific point as opposed to the map being dragged around arbitrarily).

❑ EventsList.endMapDraw: Occurs when the drawing of the map is finished.

❑ EventsList.endPan: Occurs when the panning of the map stops.

❑ EventsList.KeyDown: Occurs when a key is pressed.

❑ EventsList.KeyUp: Occurs when a key is released.

❑ EventsList.MouseClick: Occurs when the mouse is clicked on the map.

❑ EventsList.MouseDown: Occurs when the mouse button is pressed down when the cursor is on the map.

❑ EventsList.MouseDoubleClick: Occurs when the mouse is double-clicked on the map.

❑ EventsList.MouseOut: Occurs when the mouse leaves the map area.

❑ EventsList.MouseOver: Occurs when the mouse first enters the map area.

❑ EventsList.MouseUp: Occurs when a mouse button is released when the cursor is over the map.

❑ EventsList.onPan: Occurs repeatedly as the map is panned.

❑ EventsList.onEndGeoCode: Occurs when a geocode request returns.

❑ EventsList.onEndLocalSearch: Occurs when a local search request returns.

❑ EventsList.onEndTrafficSearch: Occurs when a traffic search request returns.

❑ EventsList.polylineAdded: Occurs when a polyline has been added to the map.

❑ EventsList.polylineRemoved: Occurs when a polyline has been removed from the map.

❑ EventsList.startAutoPan: Occurs when an auto-pan is started.

❑ EventsList.startPan: Occurs when a pan is started.

To handle the EventsList.changeZoom event, for example, the following code can be used:

```
YEvent.Capture(oMap, EventsList.changeZoom, function () {
    alert("Zoom level changed.");
});
```

Or, if the event handler function is a method of an object, the code can be changed to this:

```
var oCustom = {
    handleZoom : function () {
        alert("Zoom level changed.");
    }
};

YEvent.Capture(oMap, EventsList.changeZoom, oCustom.handleZoom, oCustom);
```

Here, the object oCustom has a method called handleZoom() that should be called when the map's zoom level has changed. The third argument is a pointer to the handleZoom() method on the oCustom object, and the fourth argument passes in the oCustom object itself, which tells the event handler that the function is actually a method of this object.

Map Overlays

To add an overlay to a Yahoo! map, use the addOverlay() method. All available overlays can be added using this method, including markers, customer markers, and polylines. Unlike the Google Maps API, overlays in Yahoo! Maps can be created relative to a geographic location (YGeoPoint) or a point on the map container (YCoordPoint). The latter makes it possible place an overlay on the map that remains in the same spot no matter how the map is panned or zoomed.

Markers

The simplest type of overlay is a marker. A *marker* on a Yahoo! Map looks almost like a small smart window without any text that points to a specific location. There are two ways to add a marker to the map. The first is to use the addMarker() method, which accepts a YGeoPoint and an ID string as arguments (the ID can be used later to retrieve information about the marker if necessary). For example, to add a marker at the center of the map, the following code can be used:

```
oMap.addMarker(oMap.getCenterLatLon(), "marker1");
```

This is the fastest way to add a marker to the map when there's no additional information necessary. A more verbose way is to create a YMarker object and add it to the map using the addOverlay() method. A YMarker object is created by simply passing in a YGeoPoint object indicating where the marker should be placed:

```
var oMarker = new YMarker(oMap.getCenterLatLon());
oMap.addOverlay(oMarker);
```

A YMarker object can be retrieved for markers added via addMarker() using the getMarkerObject() method and passing in the ID:

```
var oMarker = oMap.getMarkerObject("marker1");
```

In either case, a YMarker object can be further augmented to customize the marker.

Working with Labels

Markers can display small labels on top of the image. These labels are best left to one or two characters due to the limited amount of space available on the marker. A label is added to a marker using the `addLabel()` method, which accepts an HTML string as an argument. This method can be called anytime after a marker has been created:

```
var oMarker = new YMarker(oMap.getCenterLatLon());
oMarker.addLabel("1");
oMap.addOverlay(oMarker);
```

This code adds a label of `"1"` to the given marker before adding it to the map. This produces a marker such as the one displayed in Figure 10-10.

It's important to note that `addLabel()` can be called only once per marker. After that point, the label can be changed by calling `reLabel()`:

```
var oMarker = new YMarker(oMap.getCenterLatLon());
oMarker.addLabel("1");
oMap.addOverlay(oMarker);

//other code

oMarker.reLabel("2");
```

Calls to `reLabel()` erase any previous label and replace it with the specified HTML string.

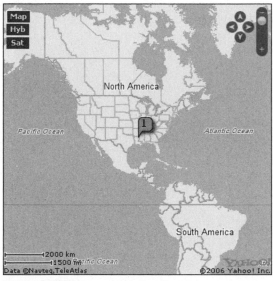

Figure 10-10

Auto-Expand Windows

Closely related to the concept of labels are auto-expand windows. *Auto-expand windows* appear automatically when the mouse cursor is moved over a marker, and they disappear when the cursor moves away from the marker. The purpose of auto-expand windows is to show small additional amounts of information about a particular location. Visually, auto-expand windows look like smaller versions of smart windows without a close button (see Figure 10-11).

Figure 10-11

To define an auto-expand window, use the `addAutoExpand()` method, which accepts an HTML string as its only argument:

```
var oMarker = new YMarker(oMap.getCenterLatLon());
oMarker.addLabel("1");
oMarker.addAutoExpand("The first marker.");
oMap.addOverlay(oMarker);
```

The call to `addAutoExpand()` automatically assigns all of the relevant event-handling code for the marker. It is also possible to open and close the auto-expand window programmatically instead of waiting for a user action using `openAutoExpand()` and `closeAutoExpand()`. Calls to these methods don't interfere with the event handling assigned to the marker, so auto-expand windows opened using `openAutoExpand()` will still close if the cursor is moved over the marker and then away from it.

Specifying a Custom Image

There may be a case when a marker should have a custom image (instead of the default marker image). An image can be specified when a `YMarker` object is created as the second argument in the constructor. This argument is a `YImage` object whose constructor accepts four arguments: the source URL for the image to use, an optional `YSize` object indicating the width and height to use instead of the default values, a optional `YCoordPoint` giving the offset for a smart window from the image, and an optional `YCoordPoint` specifying where the image should be placed relative to the lower-left corner of the image. In most cases, only the first argument is necessary:

```
var oImage = new YImage("flag.gif");
var oMarker = new YMarker(oMap.getCenterLatLon(), oImage);
oMap.addOverlay(oMarker);
```

Because the flag icon used in this example has its flagpole on the left of the image, the flag is anchored exactly at the specific coordinates on the map. Suppose that you wanted to use a smiley face image with a width and height of 29 pixels that had its center at an exact coordinate on the map; you would need to specify the fourth argument of the `YImage` constructor:

```
var oImage = new YImage("smiley.gif", null, null, new YCoordPoint(-15, 15));
var oMarker = new YMarker(oMap.getCenterLatLon(), oImage);
oMap.addOverlay(oMarker);
```

The fourth argument to the `YImage` constructor is a `YCoordPoint` specifying how the image should be offset when it's placed. Since the center of the image is 15 pixels from the top and 15 pixels from the left, the `YCoordPoint` is created with -15 as an x-offset (moving the image 15 pixels to the left) and 15 as a y-offset (moving the image 15 pixels down).

Marker Smart Windows

Smart windows can be opened directly from marker objects, ensuring that the smart window is anchored at the same location as the marker. The `openSmartWindow()` method accepts only one argument, which is the content to display in the smart window. As with the `YMap` method of the same name, the content can be an HTML string or a DOM text node. Typically, marker smart windows are assigned to appear when a marker is clicked, such as:

```
YEvent.Capture(oMarker, EventsList.MouseClick, function () {
    oMarker.openSmartWindow("Information about the marker.");
});
```

This code displays a smart window over the marker when it is clicked by using the Yahoo! Maps API event-handling capabilities. Once a smart window is open, its contents can be changed by using the `updateSmartWindow()` method:

```
oMarker.updateSmartWindow("Updated information about the marker.");
```

It's also possible to close the marker's smart window programmatically using the `closeSmartWindow()` method:

```
oMarker.closeSmartWindow();
```

Both the `openSmartWindow()` and `closeSmartWindow()` methods fire events of the same name. For example, to listen for a marker smart window to be closed, use the following code:

```
YEvent.Capture(oMarker, EventsList.closeSmartWindow, function () {
    alert("Closed smart window.");
});
```

The `EventsList.closeSmartWindow` event fires both when the user clicks the close button on the smart window and when the `closeSmartWindow()` method is called.

Polylines

Polylines in the Yahoo! Maps API are implemented the same way regardless of the browser being used, so unlike with the Google Maps API, there is no need to include extra namespaces or CSS code to use this feature. All that is necessary is to create a `YPolyline` object and add it to the map using `addOverlay()`. The constructor for `YPolyline` accepts four arguments: an array of `YGeoPoint` objects indicating where the vertices are, an optional color string indicating the color of the polyline, an optional width (integer) specifying how thick the polyline should be, and an optional alpha setting (floating point value between 0 and 1). For example:

```
var oPolyline = new YPolyline([
    new YGeoPoint(40.758224, -73.917404),
    new YGeoPoint(34.101509, -118.32691)
], "#f00", 10);

oMap.addOverlay(oPolyline);
```

This recreation of the Google Maps example creates a red line that is 10 pixels wide spanning from New York to Los Angeles.

A polyline can be removed by using the `removeOverlay()` method and passing in the `YPolyline` object:

```
oMap.removeOverlay(oPolyline);
```

Both adding and removing polylines cause events to fire on the `YMap` object. To listen to both events, use the `EventsList.polylineAdded` and `EventsList.polylineRemoved` events:

```
YEvent.Capture(oMap, EventsList.polylineAdded, function () {
    alert("Polyline added.");
});

YEvent.Capture(oMap, EventsList.polylineRemoved, function () {
    alert("Polyline removed.");
});
```

These events can come in handy if your application creates and removes polylines based on user data.

Custom Overlays

Yahoo! Maps makes it easy to add custom overlays to a map using the `YCustomOverlay` object. The constructor for `YCustomOverlay` accepts two arguments: a point to place the overlay at and a DOM node to place at that point. The first argument can be either a `YGeoPoint`, to create a location-specific overlay, or a `YCoordPoint`, to create an overlay that remains at the same position on the map no matter the zoom level or movement of the underlying map.

As an example, consider placing a small blue box at the center of the map. This can be accomplished by creating a <div/> element, sizing it appropriately, setting its background color to blue, and then passing it into the YCustomOverlay constructor:

```
var oDiv = document.createElement("div");
oDiv.style.width = "16px";
oDiv.style.height = "16px";
oDiv.style.backgroundColor = "blue";

oMap.addOverlay(new YCustomOverlay(oMap.getCenterLatLon(), oDiv));
```

The blue <div/> created in this example moves as the map moves so that it's upper-left corner is located at the geographic point specified in the YCustomOverlay constructor. To create the same small blue square at a specific position within the map container, just replace the first argument with a YCoordPoint:

```
var oDiv = document.createElement("div");
oDiv.style.width = "16px";
oDiv.style.height = "16px";
oDiv.style.backgroundColor = "blue";

oMap.addOverlay(new YCustomOverlay(new YCoordPoint(200, 20), oDiv));
```

This code places the blue square 200 pixels from the left and 20 pixels from the top of the map container. It will remain in that exact location regardless of zooming and panning. This type of custom overlay is helpful when making custom controls for the map.

GeoRSS Support

GeoRSS is an XML-based language designed to describe geographic information. The Yahoo! Maps API can make use of GeoRSS information for various purposes. For example, if you have set up a number of markers or other overlay information on a map that you want to save and be able to call up at any time, you can export the map data to GeoRSS code using YMap object's exportFormat() method:

```
var sGeoRSS = oMap.exportFormat("GEORSS");
```

This code returns a GeoRSS string that representing all of the data contained in the map. The argument "GEORSS" is required even though the exportFormat() method doesn't currently support any other data formats.

GeoRSS text can also be stored in external files and loaded into a map using the YGeoRSS object, which is another type of map overlay. A YGeoRSS object is created by passing in a URL to a file containing GeoRSS information. This information is then read by the API and transformed into a series of markers, overlays, etc., representing the data contained in the file. The Yahoo! Maps developer site offers a sample GeoRSS file at http://developer.yahoo.com/maps/sample.xml. To load this file, use the following JavaScript code:

```
oMap.addOverlay(new YGeoRSS("http://developer.yahoo.com/maps/sample.xml"));
```

This creates markers for various locations around the Sunnyvale, California, area, complete with smart windows containing more information when each marker is clicked.

Using GeoRSS files can significantly reduce the amount of coding necessary to add a large amount of markers to a map. It's worth noting that the Yahoo! Maps API adds some of its own custom elements to the standard GeoRSS format to support features like smart windows.

Address Lookup

The Yahoo! Maps API supports address lookup, meaning that it can locate a plain-text address on the map. For example, suppose that you wanted to center the map on your favorite zip code; just pass the zip code into the drawZoomAndCenter() method:

```
oMap.drawZoomAndCenter("90210", 12);
```

This code centers the map on Beverly Hills, California, at a zoom level of 12. Address determination can deal with full addresses as well, so it's possible to center on a specific address, such as:

```
oMap.drawZoomAndCenter("701 First Avenue, Sunnyvale, CA", 12);
```

Of course, centering on a specific address has limited usefulness, which is why it's possible to place markers at specific addresses as well:

```
oMap.addMarker("701 First Avenue, Sunnyvale, CA");
```

This code adds a marker at the address specified. Behind the scenes of each of these calls is a geocoding request that takes the address and returns the geographic location as a YGeoPoint. However, that detail is abstracted away, making the API even more powerful due to its simplicity.

> **Note that address lookup does require an extra request to the server for the geocode information, so it may slow down the redrawing/placing of markers on the map compared to using latitude and longitude coordinates.**

Additional Information

As with many APIs, the Yahoo! Maps API is quite large, and it's beyond the scope of this book to cover every feature in depth. There are, however, some excellent resources available online at http://developer.yahoo.com/maps/ajax/, including numerous examples exploring custom functionality. The complete class reference is located at http://developer.yahoo.com/maps/ajax/V3.4/reference.html (the URL changes for each new version of the API, so make sure to check the version you are using).

There is also another Wrox book, *Yahoo! Maps Mashups* (Wiley 2007), that contains examples that mash up data from multiple locations, including Flickr and Upcoming.org. Additionally, this book explores uses of the Yahoo! Maps Flash API along with the Ajax API.

Other Mapping APIs

Though the Google and Yahoo! mappings APIs are the popularly used, there are two other major competitors in the arena of Ajax maps. The first is MapQuest (`www.mapquest.com`), which has upgraded its mapping service to use Ajax, producing a user experience very similar to that of Google and Yahoo!. To learn more about the MapQuest Open API, visit `www.mapquest.com/openapi`. The MapQuest Open API has similar limitations to the Google and Yahoo! APIs in terms of commercial use and rate limits.

The other mapping API option is the Virtual Earth API from Microsoft. Virtual Earth is used to power Microsoft's Live Local Search (`http://local.live.com`). Virtual Earth has some interesting features, such as "bird's eye view" that shows a non-flat view of certain areas, as well as an interesting zoom animation. Where the Virtual Earth API falls short is in its documentation, which consists mostly of developer blog posts and sample applications. To get started with the Virtual Earth API, visit `http://dev.live.com/virtualearth/`.

Summary

In this chapter, you learned about the emerging Ajax mapping trend. Before delving into a discussion on mapping APIs, the topic of geocoding was discussed. Geocoding is a technique for assigning information to a particular location in the world. You learned that geocoded information must be in decimal format for latitude and longitude to be used by mapping APIs, and you were presented with various options for obtaining such information.

Next, you learned about the Google Maps API and how it works. You learned about creating a map and about using overlaying markers and polylines in order to indicate information about a spot on the map. Various ways to manipulate the map, including zooming and panning, were discussed, including how to add the built-in Google Maps controls to your custom map. You also learned about the different types of info windows available, including map blowups and tabbed info windows.

After that, the Yahoo! Maps API was introduced. You learned how to accomplish similar tasks including the use of markers and polylines as well as the use of GeoRSS data for adding information to maps. Using built-in Yahoo! Maps controls was discussed, as well as ways to programmatically add controls to the map view. You learned how to create custom overlays using DOM elements and how to place overlays relative to the map container's size instead of relative to geographic locations.

To round out the chapter, you learned about two other mapping APIs that are available: the MapQuest Open API and the Microsoft Virtual Earth API.

Ultimately, the mapping API that you use will be more of a matter of personal preference than anything else. All of the mapping APIs are fairly robust and provide very similar feature sets. Make sure that you understand your requirements for customization and interaction when evaluating each of these APIs because they offer slightly different user experiences.

11

Ajax Debugging Tools

One of the most important parts of the software development cycle is testing. In most companies, the developers who write the software are at least partially responsible for testing their code. The responsibilities vary from writing case studies for quality assurance personnel to creating and running unit tests themselves. In any case, software bugs will occur, and that is when debugging software becomes an invaluable tool.

Debuggers have come a long way since their humble beginnings. What used to be an arduous journey at a text-based console has given way to today's graphic debuggers, complete with color-coded information to make rapid application development more, well, rapid.

For Ajax applications, debugging has historically been difficult. The mixture of JavaScript and client-server communication proved to be a unique challenge for programmers trying to bullet-proof their code. More recently, however, new techniques and technologies have arisen that make debugging Ajax applications much easier.

The Problem

Debugging JavaScript code has traditionally been very difficult. For a long time, browsers had little or no support for JavaScript developers. Early editions of Safari had no JavaScript console and Opera only added a console after version 8. Firefox included a JavaScript console in version 1.0 but had no built-in support for anything other than outputting JavaScript messages. Internet Explorer, as of version 7.0, still has no JavaScript console, relying solely on pop-up error messages when something goes wrong.

With these tools, or lack thereof, most developers resorted to an age-old way of debugging: calling `alert()` at various spots in the code. This was useful for determining if code execution reached a certain block of code or to figure out the value of a particular variable. Of course, this is not an optimal solution since it interrupts the flow of code. Given the loosely typed nature of JavaScript, the lack of debugging tools stymied the growth of JavaScript solutions. It wasn't until true JavaScript debuggers arose that developers were able to build more extensive applications.

Microsoft introduced the Microsoft Script Debugger, which was a free add-on utility for Internet Explorer. It was a simple program that could intercept JavaScript errors and open up the offending code in a text viewer. Script Debugger also displayed the call stack, but beyond that, had little more to offer. Microsoft did follow this up by allowing Visual Studio to interact with Internet Explorer as a JavaScript debugger along with introducing the Microsoft Script Editor (packaged with Microsoft Office 2003 or later). These two tools had much more useful JavaScript debugging mechanisms, including support for watches and a command line interface to the JavaScript being executed.

An extension called Venkman brought powerful debugging capabilities to Mozilla, and later, to Firefox. Venkman (available at www.mozilla.org/projects/venkman/) began the evolution of standalone JavaScript debuggers for Firefox, supporting many features typically seen in expensive IDEs. Though a bit sluggish, Venkman works seamlessly with Firefox and includes watches and a command line interface.

For these two browsers, JavaScript debugging was much easier, allowing you to step through code line by line. This worked great until Ajax became a popular form of programming. Stepping through code couldn't solve the majority of problems you encounter in Ajax because of the asynchronous nature of the code. Further, code execution can fork based on information received from the server.

Suddenly, the JavaScript debuggers that web developers depended on were no longer useful. Errors occurred because the server returned unexpected information, and with no tools to help, it was back to using alert() statements for Ajax debugging. Traditionally, JavaScript debuggers cared only about what was happening on the client. Now, they had to know two more important pieces of information: the data being sent to the server and the data being received from the server. Ajax development was slowed significantly until a new crop of tools emerged.

FireBug

Mozilla's Firefox has long inspired creative add-ons due to its open and fairly straightforward add-on capabilities. In 2006, Firefox contributor Joe Hewitt introduced FireBug as a new tool to help developers create and debug web sites and web applications. Built into FireBug are tools that allow DOM inspection of the page that is currently loaded, style information about particular elements, and the part most interesting to Ajax developers, monitoring of all traffic from the XHR object.

Installation and Setup

FireBug is available for free from www.getfirebug.com. FireBug is downloaded as an XPI, meaning that Firefox knows how to install it. Once you have clicked on the download link, you'll be prompted to allow the package to be installed. Clicking OK on this dialog installs FireBug (though you'll need to restart the browser to use it).

FireBug augments the Firefox window in two ways.

❑ First, it adds a small panel on the right of the status bar to display error information for the page (green if there are no errors, red if there are errors).

❑   Second, a main panel displaying information about the currently loaded page is displayed at the bottom of the window. This panel can be visible or hidden by default and can be quickly toggled by clicking on the status panel.

The Interface

The basic FireBug 1.0 interface has three tabs in the main panel.

❑   The first tab is called **Console**, and it contains a basic command line JavaScript interface. It is on this tab that JavaScript error messages are logged, but it's also possible to interact with the page by typing in JavaScript commands (see Figure 11-1).

Figure 11-1

❑   The second tab is called **HTML**, and it contains a basic DOM inspector. From this tab, you can view the entire page as a hierarchy of DOM nodes, including style, event, and property information.

❑   The third tab is called **CSS**, and it contains a CSS inspector, allowing you to view all of the loaded style sheets and modify the styles dynamically.

❑ The fourth tab is called **Script**, and it contains a basic JavaScript debugger. You can select from the currently loaded script files and set breakpoints. While not as powerful as Venkman, this FireBug's debugger is suitable for basic debugging tasks.

❑ The fifth tab is called **DOM**, which is a bit of a misnomer since it displays a hierarchical list of all objects that exist in the window scope. You can then drill down on each object to get more information about its properties.

❑ The last tab is called **Net** and contains a graph indicating the resources that were loaded by the page at specific points in time. This can be useful to see the order in which resources are being loaded as well as how long each request takes.

FireBug tries to be a one-stop shop for web debugging by providing all of these tools. However, it has one feature that other Firefox extensions don't: XHR logging.

XHR Logging

Though there are many ways of establishing Ajax communication, the most common is still the XHR object. It follows, then, that many problems with such communication are most likely related to XHR usage. FireBug aims to assist in debugging these types of problems by logging all requests made via XHR.

Every time an XHR object is used to make an HTTP request, that information is logged onto the Console tab as a line item. The line contains the method of request (typically GET or POST) as well as the URL used for the request followed by the amount of time (in milliseconds) it took for the response to be fully received. This line can be expanded (by clicking on the triangle next to the request) to display more tabs (see Figure 11-2).

If a GET request was sent, there are three tabs: Params, Headers, and Response.

❑ The **Params tab** enumerates the name-value pairs of query string arguments. It displays the arguments unencoded so you can easily see what data the server is receiving.

❑ The **Headers tab** contains the HTTP response headers sent along with the data as well as the headers sent with the request. This tab can contain helpful information such as cookie data, content type, and the timestamp of the response.

❑ The **Response tab** contains the raw text sent back from the server to the client. This is the exact, unformatted server response, so it may be necessary to copy this text and paste it into an editor to view it in a more human-readable manner.

If a POST request was sent, there are four tabs. Added to the Params, Headers, and Response tabs that are also present for GET requests, a Post tab displays the data sent to the server. Since data for POST requests are sent as the request body, the URL alone doesn't provide enough information about what the server received.

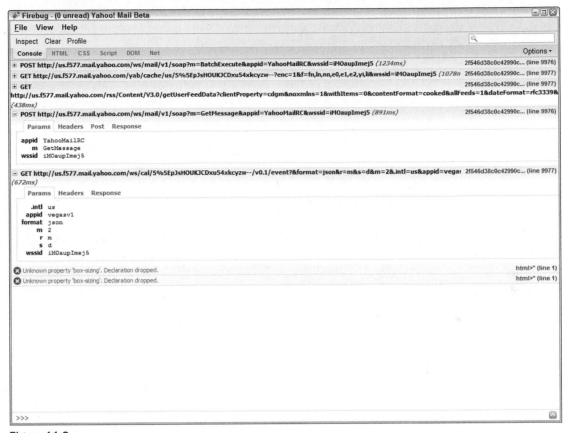

Figure 11-2

Ajax Debugging with FireBug

Here's a short list of things you want to be on the lookout for when debugging your Ajax application using FireBug:

❑ **Is the outgoing data correct?** For GET requests, always double-check to ensure that the query string is properly encoded and that all of the expected data is included. For POST requests, ensure that the data being posted is in the correct format (plain text, JSON, XML, etc.) and contains the information that is necessary. An error in any of these indicates there is a problem with the JavaScript that is creating and sending the request.

❑ **Is the incoming data correct?** Both GET and POST requests can receive information from the server in any number of formats. Make sure that the format is correct and the data is what you are expecting. Double-check the data that is being sent to the server to ensure that it is correct. If you are sending the correct data, then this type of error indicates a problem with the server-side code.

❑ **Are the headers correct?** Always make sure that the correct HTTP headers are being sent back to the client. For instance, if the server is returning XML data, make sure that the `Content-Type` header is set to "text/xml" so that the `responseXML` object can be used.

Remember, FireBug is simply outputting data relating to the Ajax requests going back and forth, but it has no control over the data being sent or received. Further, you can't set breakpoints in the requests or responses; all you get is the information after the response has been received.

FireBug Limitations

As discussed earlier in the book, Ajax communication is not limited to the use of XHR. While FireBug does a great job dissecting requests made using the XHR object, it doesn't address any of the other Ajax communication techniques. So, if you are using hidden frames or any of the other techniques discussed in Chapter 2, FireBug won't be of any help.

Another limitation is that FireBug doesn't log information until a response is received from the server. This means that you may have outstanding requests in transit that have not yet received a response and therefore won't have been logged to the console. A good understanding of when your application makes these requests is key to debugging using FireBug.

Microsoft Fiddler

Since the core of Ajax relies on requests going to servers (and responses being received from them), it makes sense that debugging Ajax applications relies heavily on understanding what is being sent to and received from the server. FireBug for Firefox inspects the requests and responses sent through XHR objects, but this is only a very small percentage compared to all of the requests and responses used during a typical user session. And, as discussed in the previous section, many requests may be sent without using XHR at all. The way to solve these problems is to use an HTTP proxy.

An HTTP proxy is a small program running on the client computer that intercepts all HTTP requests and responses. In normal HTTP communication, the browser initiates and sends a request over the Internet to a server. The server then sends a response back to the browser, which then acts upon the data it received. When an HTTP proxy is used, all requests are first sent through the proxy; it's the proxy's job to send that request to the server. The response is sent back to the proxy as well, and the proxy then forwards it to the browser (see Figure 11-3).

However, the true value of the HTTP proxy isn't the simple interception of requests and responses but rather the ability to log the details of this communication. By being able to see the entirety of each request or response, including headers, debugging Ajax communication is made much simpler. This is where Microsoft Fiddler comes in.

> **Even though this section focuses on using Fiddler for debugging Ajax applications, it's worth pointing out that it has many uses. Since Fiddler intercepts all HTTP traffic coming to and leaving from the client, it's possible to monitor traffic caused by desktop applications.**

Normal Browser Communication

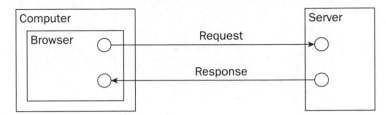

HTTP Proxy Communication

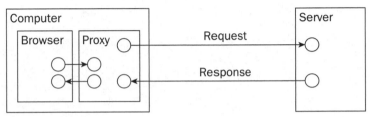

Figure 11-3

Installation and Setup

One of the most useful and easiest to use HTTP proxies available is Microsoft Fiddler. This free tool (available from www.fiddlertool.com) installs itself as an HTTP proxy for WinInet, which is the Internet communication library used by many desktop applications, including Internet Explorer. Once installed, Fiddler automatically begins intercepting HTTP traffic to and from your computer.

To intercept HTTP traffic from Internet Explorer or Opera, no further setup is required. Since both use WinInet, Fiddler automatically sets itself up to intercept requests and responses for them. To intercept HTTP traffic for Firefox, you'll need to modify some settings in the browser:

1. Under the Tools menu, select Options.

2. Click on the General tab if it's not already selected.

3. Click on the Connection Settings button.

4. In the Connection Settings window, select Manual proxy configuration.

5. For HTTP Proxy, enter 127.0.0.1. For Port, enter 8888 (see Figure 11-4).

6. Click OK on the Connection Settings window, and then Click OK on the Options window.

After this point, all HTTP traffic for Firefox goes through Fiddler along with any other traffic coming from other browsers on your machine.

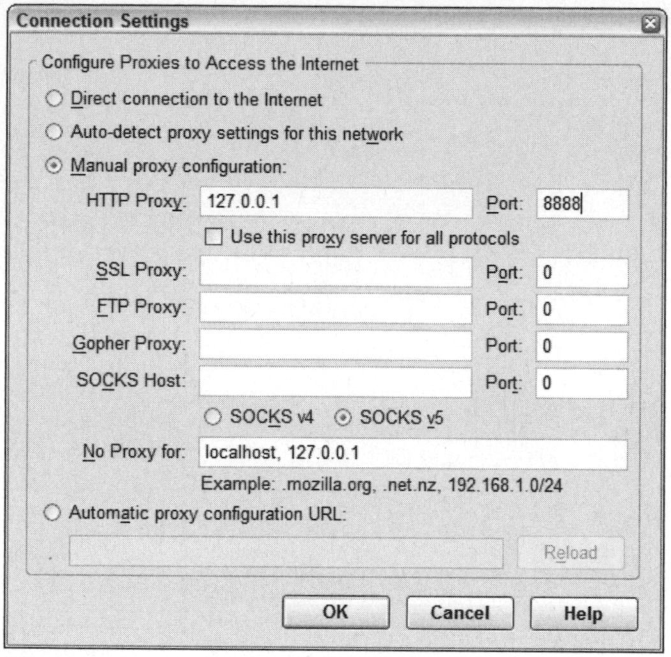

Connection Settings

Configure Proxies to Access the Internet

○ _D_irect connection to the Internet

○ _A_uto-detect proxy settings for this net_w_ork

⦿ _M_anual proxy configuration:

HTTP Pro_x_y: `127.0.0.1`   _P_ort: `8888`

☐ Use this pro_x_y server for all protocols

_S_SL Proxy: P_o_rt: `0`

_F_TP Proxy: Po_r_t: `0`

_G_opher Proxy: Port: `0`

SO_C_KS Host: Por_t_: `0`

○ SO_C_KS v4   ⦿ SOCKS v_5_

_N_o Proxy for: `localhost, 127.0.0.1`

Example: .mozilla.org, .net.nz, 192.168.1.0/24

○ Auto_m_atic proxy configuration URL:

` `   Re_l_oad

OK   Cancel   Help

Figure 11-4

The Interface

The Fiddler window is fairly unrefined and simple. There are two main regions: the left side and the right side. The left side of the window contains a list of HTTP requests sent from the machine. Each request takes a single line and is accompanied by an icon that indicates the type of data returned from that request. The line includes the response status, the protocol used (usually HTTP), the host name, the URL, the caching type, the length of the response, and the content type (see Figure 11-5).

There is a context menu for each request; right-clicking on a single request or a group of selected requests brings up several options: a Copy menu allows copying specific parts of a request to the clipboard, and a Save menu allows saving request data to text files.

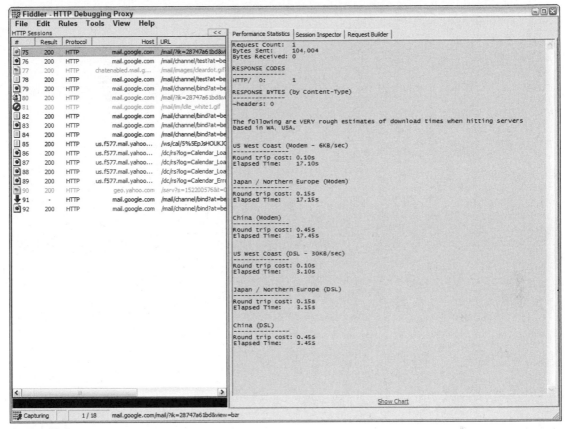

Figure 11-5

On the right side of the window are three tabs. The first tab (pictured in Figure 11-5) is Performance Statistics. This tab displays information relating to data transmission rates, including the number of bytes sent and received as well as the types of data received. It also gives estimated roundtrip times from various locations in the world using different connection methods (modem, DSL, etc.).

The second tab on the right is the Session Inspector. This tab provides specific information about each request and accompanying response. It is separated into two sections: the top contains information about the request and the bottom contains information about the response (see Figure 11-6).

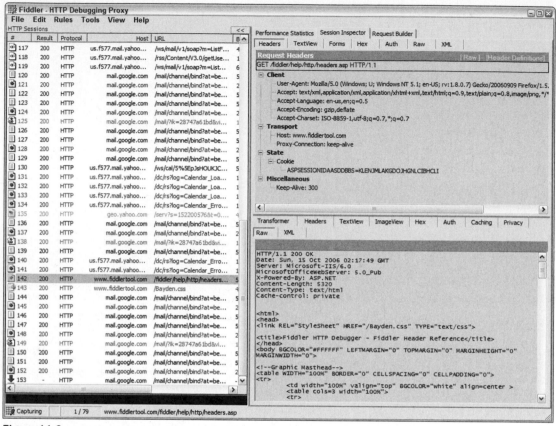

Figure 11-6

In the request section, you can choose from any number of data views:

- **Headers:** Displays the HTTP request headers that were sent to the server from the client. This data is represented in a hierarchical view and typically contains information about the web browser along with basic request information.

- **TextView:** Displays the body of the request (for POST requests only).

- **Forms:** Displays information that appears on the query string and in the body of the request, provided that the body is formatted with a content type of "application/x-www-form-urlen-coded."

- **Hex:** Displays the hexadecimal representation of the request.

- **Auth:** Displays information from `Proxy-Authorization` and `Authorization` headers.

- **Raw:** Displays the entire request as simple text.

- **XML:** Displays the body as a hierarchical XML tree if the body of the request is an XML document.

The response section of the Session Inspector tab has similar options for viewing information about the response:

❑ **Transformer:** Displays encoding information about the response.

❑ **Headers:** Displays a hierarchical tree of response headers.

❑ **TextView:** Displays the plain text of the response body.

❑ **ImageView:** Displays an image if the response retrieved one.

❑ **Hex:** Displays the hexadecimal representation of the response.

❑ **Auth:** Displays information from `Proxy-Authenticate` and `WWW-Authenticate` headers.

❑ **Caching:** Displays caching information about the response.

❑ **Privacy:** Displays privacy (P3P) information about the response

❑ **Raw:** Displays the raw text of the response.

❑ **XML:** Displays the response body as an XML hierarchy if the response is an XML document.

The third tab is the Request Builder, which allows you to manually construct an HTTP request (including all headers and the request body) and inspect the response. This can be very helpful when testing the server-side portion of an Ajax solution. It's also possible to clone a request that has already been made by dragging the request from the left side of the window onto the Request Builder tab. This prefills the Request Builder fields with information from that request.

HTTP Breakpoints

One of the most interesting and powerful options in Fiddler is the ability to set breakpoints for HTTP requests and responses. Under the Rules menu, select Automatic Breakpoints, and you'll see options for Before Requests, After Responses, Disabled, and Ignore Images. By selecting Before Requests, Fiddler intercepts outgoing requests (it will ignore any image requests if Ignore Images is checked) and holds them in the window (see Figure 11-7).

When a request breakpoint is set, a special icon is shown on the request in the list of requests. Selecting the request fills the Session Inspector tab with all of the information about the request. It's then possible to edit all of the request information before it's sent on to the server. After that, there are two options displayed in the window: Break on Response or Run to Completion. Clicking Break on Response sends the request and then sets a breakpoint for the response before it is returned to the browser (the same as selecting After Responses on the Automatic Breakpoints submenu); clicking Run to Completion sends the request and doesn't interfere with the response.

A response breakpoint is very similar to a request breakpoint: it holds the response and allows you to edit the details before the browser receives the data. Once again, using the Session Inspector, you can edit the headers and response body. After editing the information, the only option is Run to Completion, which sends the modified response to the browser.

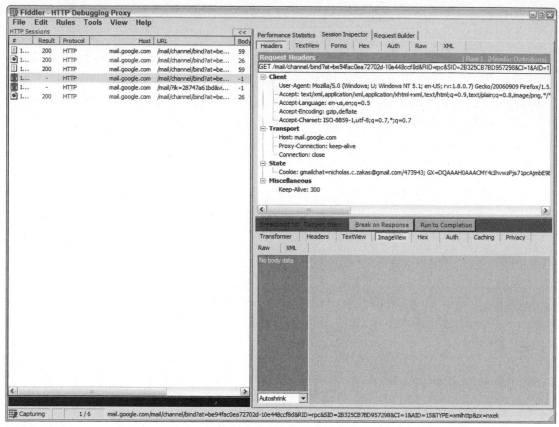

Figure 11-7

Ajax Debugging with Fiddler

With all of these powerful features, Fiddler is an ideal environment for Ajax debugging. Here are some things you can use Fiddler for:

❑ **Is the outgoing data correct?** As with FireBug, ensure that the data being sent to the server is in the correct format and contains the correct data. Errors here indicate a problem with the JavaScript constructing the request.

❑ **Is the incoming data correct?** Also as with FireBug, check that the incoming data is in the correct format and contains appropriate data. A problem here indicates an error on the server.

❑ **Confirm your assumptions.** If you think there's an error in a request or response, set a breakpoint and try running the request/response again. This is especially helpful if you don't own the server-side code that may be the problem.

Since Fiddler monitors all HTTP traffic, these techniques can be using not just for Ajax communication initiated through XHR but also through hidden frames and any other Ajax technique discussed in Chapter 2.

Summary

Ajax debugging has traditionally been very difficult because of the asynchronous nature of the code combined with the data exchange between client and server. In this chapter, you learned about two tools that can aid in the debugging of Ajax applications.

First, you learned about FireBug, an extension for Firefox. This extension installs into the Firefox window as a panel containing information about the current page. One of FireBug's features is the ability to log all communication initiated using the XHR. Every time a request is made and a response received, an entry is made in the FireBug console containing the URL, the headers, and the response, and any data that was sent to the server in a POST request.

Next, you learned about the Microsoft Fiddler HTTP proxy tool. This tool intercepts all of the HTTP requests and responses sent from and received by your computer. Using Fiddler, it's possible to look at all of the information being sent between client and server, including headers, body, and more. What's more, Fiddler allows you to set breakpoints for requests and responses, which allows you to modify requests before they are sent to the server and modify responses before they are received in the browser.

As the importance of Ajax debugging becomes more evident, more tools are likely to arise. For the time being, though, FireBug and Microsoft Fiddler provide excellent Ajax debugging for free.

12

Web Site Widgets

Both on the desktop and on the Web, widgets have become a highly sought-after commodity. A *widget* is a small, self-contained application that performs a specific function. Programs like the Yahoo! Widget Engine (`http://widgets.yahoo.com/`) offers users a platform to run widgets on their computers. Ranging from newsreaders to eBay feedback monitors, these widgets provide useful information to people that want them. They are applications that require little to no setup and perform only their allotted function.

On the Web, most widgets are DHTML-based and designed to emulate operating system controls such as menus, structure trees, and toolbars. While these widgets have provided a means to emulate traditional applications, they don't offer much more than that. With the introduction of Ajax, web widgets are changing to incorporate data manipulation and retrieval, creating rich widgets that have traditionally been found only on the desktop.

Creating a Weather Widget

Weather information is popular to display both on the desktop and on the Web. Many applications and widgets are solely devoted to retrieving and displaying this information. Since weather changes constantly, Ajax is well suited to this type of widget.

The Weather.com SDK

The first step in creating this widget is to locate a source of weather information. Probably the most popular is the Weather.com XML weather service. The use of the Weather.com XML service hinges upon following their guidelines. To use their XML feeds, you must first register for a license at `http://registration.weather.com/registration/xmloap/step1`. After you register, Weather.com sends an e-mail with a link to the XML feed SDK and provides you with a license key and partner ID.

For web-based applications, like this widget, you must limit how often you retrieve information from the service. As specified in the SDK documentation, the refresh rate for the Current Conditions information is 30 minutes; therefore, the server application must cache the retrieved weather information and only refresh the information every 30 minutes. There are two ways to accomplish this:

1. Create a smart thread that runs independently of the web application and pulls the feed every 30 minutes. The application then solely uses the cached feed and never worries about the time span between information pulls.

2. With every page request, the application can keep track of the last time the feed was retrieved and allow refreshing of the data only after 30 minutes have passed.

Although the first option is ideal, limiting the amount of file system operations to once per half-hour, it is difficult to implement due to timeout restrictions. For instance, an ASP.NET application times out after 20 minutes of inactivity. The second option is simpler to implement and doesn't require any configuration changes on the server. The weather widget uses this option.

The Server-Side Component

At the heart of the server application lie two classes created within the `Wrox.ProfessionalAjax.Weather` namespace. These classes can be compiled into a class library (a `.dll` file) or used natively within an application. For the purposes of this example, the classes are used directly in the application, so no reference to an external library is needed.

The Settings Class

The `Settings` class is a static class that contains all of the information required to pull weather information from Weather.com. Static classes are used to create data and functions that can be accessed without creating objects of the class. Only three pieces of information are required to retrieve this data: your license key, your partner ID, and the location ID.

This information could be considered sensitive data, because you do not want anyone abusing the Weather.com's service with your information. Therefore, it's recommended that you use the `Web.config` file to store the license information by adding settings to the `<appSettings/>` element.

```
<appSettings>
    <add key="license" value="[license key]" />
    <add key="partner" value="[partner id]" />
    <add key="location" value="[location id]" />
</appSettings>
```

With this information added to the application settings, not only is it secure, but it is also easily accessible by your application.

Note that you need to replace the bracketed items with your own information.

The Settings class exposes three public properties to access this information.

By using the `System.Configuration.ConfigurationManager` class, you can extract the settings in the `<appSettings/>` elements in `Web.config`. Just pass the value used in the `key` attribute:

```
public static class Settings
{
    public static string LicenseKey
    {
        get
        {
            return ConfigurationManager.AppSettings["license"];
        }
    }

    public static string PartnerId
    {
        get
        {
            return ConfigurationManager.AppSettings["partner"];
        }
    }

    public static string LocationId
    {
        get
        {
            return ConfigurationManager.AppSettings["location"];
        }
    }
}
```

These properties provide read-only access to the application settings because there is no need for them to change.

> *Don't forget to add* System.Configuration *to the* using *statements before attempting to use* ConfigurationManager *without* System.Configuration *in front of it.*

The WeatherInfo Class

The WeatherInfo class provides methods to retrieve the information from the Weather.com XML service; its constructor accepts one argument that contains the path to the application:

```
public class WeatherInfo
{
    private string _path;  //Path of the application
    private string _cachedFile; //Path of the cached file.

    public WeatherInfo(string path)
    {
        _path = path;
        _cachedFile = String.Format("{0}/weather_cache.xml",_path);
    }

    //more code here
}
```

This class has two private fields, path and cachedFile. The former is assigned the path argument, and the latter contains the path to the cached weather feed.

Reading Cached Weather Data

When the client requests data, and the 30 minutes have not yet passed from the last Weather.com request, then it should be read from the cached file. The _getCachedWeather() method retrieves data from the cached file and return its contents as a string.

```
private string _getCachedWeather()
{
    string str = String.Empty;

    //Open and read the cached weather feed.
    using (StreamReader reader = new StreamReader(_cachedFile))
    {
        str = reader.ReadToEnd();
    }

    //Return the contents
    return str;
}
```

First, the variable str is created and initialized as an empty string; this variable will contain the contents of the cached file when it is read. Next, a StreamReader object is created to open the cached weather feed; the contents are read via the ReadToEnd() method and stored in str. Finally, _getCachedWeather() exits and returns the data.

Getting Weather Data from the Web

When the cached data is too old, the server should retrieve new weather information from Weather.com. The _getWebWeather() method performs this operation.

```
private string _getWebWeather()
{
    //more code here
}
```

According to the SDK, the URL to retrieve the weather feed looks like the following:

```
http://xoap.weather.com/weather/local/[locID]?cc=*&prod=xoap&par=[partID]&key=[lic]
```

The information contained in brackets is the location ID, partner ID, and license key. Using the String.Format() method, you can format the URL to contain your own settings information:

```
private string _getWebWeather()
{
    //Get the base url for using the service.
    string baseUrl =
        "http://xoap.weather.com/weather/local/{0}?cc=*&prod=xoap&par={1}&key={2}";

    //Now format the url with the needed information
    string url = String.Format(baseUrl, Settings.LocationId, Settings.PartnerId,
        Settings.LicenseKey);

    //more code here
}
```

This is primarily where the `Settings` class is used. The resulting string returned from `String.Format()` is complete with the required information that the Weather.com guidelines dictate.

The next operation makes a request to the remote host and retrieves the weather feed:

```
private string _getWebWeather()
{
    //Get the base url for using the service.
    string baseUrl =
        "http://xoap.weather.com/weather/local/{0}?cc=*&prod=xoap&par={1}&key={2}";

    //Now format the url with the needed information
    string url = String.Format(baseUrl, Settings.LocationId, Settings.PartnerId,
        Settings.LicenseKey);

    //Use a web client. It's less coding than an HttpWebRequest.
    using (WebClient client = new WebClient())
    {
        //Read the results
        try
        {
            //Create an XmlReader to read the response
            XmlTextReader xml = new XmlTextReader(client.OpenRead(url));
        }
        catch (WebException exception)
        {
            //more code here
        }
    }
}
```

At the beginning of this new code, a `WebClient` object is created to connect to Weather.com's service. The server's response is read using the `OpenRead()` method, which returns a `Stream` object that can be read with an `XmlTextReader` object, which is used in an XSL Transformation.

Transforming the data on the server is advantageous for several reasons. For one, it greatly simplifies the client-side code. The data sent to the client is already in HTML, so it is easily added to the page. A server-side transformation also makes the client work less. The data is complete when it reaches the client; no other data manipulation, other than placing in the page, is required.

XSL transformations in .NET closely resemble the transformations provided by MSXML covered in Chapter 6. The first step in a transformation is to create the objects involved. Transformations in .NET 2.0 require an `XslCompiledTransform` object, an `XmlReader` object (`XmlTextReader` in this case), and a `Stream` object (a `StreamWriter`), which contains the resulting transformed data:

```
private string _getWebWeather()
{
    //String that the weather feed will be written to
    string xmlStr = String.Empty;

    //Get the base url for using the service.
    string baseUrl =
```

```
               "http://xoap.weather.com/weather/local/{0}?cc=*&prod=xoap&par={1}&key={2}";

        //Now format the url with the needed information
        string url = String.Format(baseUrl, Settings.LocationId, Settings.PartnerId,
            Settings.LicenseKey);

        //Use a web client. It's less coding than an HttpWebRequest.
        using (WebClient client = new WebClient())
        {
            //Read the results
            try
            {
                //Create an XmlReader to read the response
                XmlTextReader xml = new XmlTextReader(client.OpenRead(url));

                //Get the XSLT object ready
                XslCompiledTransform xslt = new XslCompiledTransform();
                xslt.Load(_path + "/weather.xslt");

                //Write the resulting XSLT to the cache file
                using (StreamWriter writer = new StreamWriter(_cachedFile))
                {
                    xslt.Transform(xml, null, writer);
                }

                //return the cached copy
                return _getCachedWeather();
            }
            catch (WebException exception)
            {
                //more code here
            }
        }
    }
}
```

The first step in this process is to load the XSL document into the XslCompiledTransform object. Next, create a StreamWriter object to create or overwrite the cache file. This StreamWriter object, along with the XML data, is then passed to the Transform() method. The StreamWriter object serves as the transformation's output, so as the XslCompiledTransform object transforms the XML data, the transformed data is being written to the cache file. When the transformation is complete, the cached copy is returned to the caller by returning _getCachedWeather().

Handling Web-Related Errors

If for some reason this operation fails (most likely as a result of not finding the remote host), code execution drops the catch block where the error is handled. Since the weather data begins as XML and is transformed into HTML, having the error information follow the same pattern seems fitting. Therefore, the following code creates a simple XML document:

```
private string _getWebWeather()
{
    //String that the weather feed will be written to
    string xmlStr = String.Empty;

    //Get the base url for using the service.
    string baseUrl =
        "http://xoap.weather.com/weather/local/{0}?cc=*&prod=xoap&par={1}&key={2}";

    //Now format the url with the needed information
    string url = String.Format(baseUrl, Settings.LocationId, Settings.PartnerId,
        Settings.LicenseKey);

    //Use a web client. It's less coding than an HttpWebRequest.
    using (WebClient client = new WebClient())
    {
        //Read the results
        try
        {
            //Create an XmlReader to read the response
            XmlTextReader xml = new XmlTextReader(client.OpenRead(url));

            //Get the XSLT object ready
            XslCompiledTransform xslt = new XslCompiledTransform();
            xslt.Load(_path + "/weather.xslt");

            //Write the resulting XSLT to the cache file
            using (StreamWriter writer = new StreamWriter(_cachedFile))
            {
                xslt.Transform(xml, null, writer);
            }

            //return the cached copy
            return _getCachedWeather();
        }
        catch (WebException exception)
        {
            //Write up the XML, and put in the exception info
            string xmlStr = "<errorDoc>";
            xmlStr += "<alert>An Error Occurred!</alert>";
            xmlStr += String.Format("<message>{0}</message>", exception.Message);
            xmlStr += "</errorDoc>";

            //Load it into an XmlDocument
            XmlDocument doc = new XmlDocument();
            doc.LoadXml(xmlStr);

            //more code here
        }
    }
}
```

The next step is to perform the transformation on this XML document. This XSL Transformation is similar to that of the weather data, except that instead of the output being written to the file, the output is returned as a string to the caller.

```
private string _getWebWeather()
{
    //String that the weather feed will be written to
    string xmlStr = String.Empty;

    //Get the base url for using the service.
    string baseUrl =
        "http://xoap.weather.com/weather/local/{0}?cc=*&prod=xoap&par={1}&key={2}";

    //Now format the url with the needed information
    string url = String.Format(baseUrl, Settings.LocationId, Settings.PartnerId,
        Settings.LicenseKey);

    //Use a web client. It's less coding than an HttpWebRequest.
    using (WebClient client = new WebClient())
    {
        //Read the results
        try
        {
            //Create an XmlReader to read the response
            XmlTextReader xml = new XmlTextReader(client.OpenRead(url));

            //Get the XSLT object ready
            XslCompiledTransform xslt = new XslCompiledTransform();
            xslt.Load(_path + "/weather.xslt");

            //Write the resulting XSLT to the cache file
            using (StreamWriter writer = new StreamWriter(_cachedFile))
            {
                xslt.Transform(xml, null, writer);
            }

            //return the cached copy
            return _getCachedWeather();
        }
        catch (WebException exception)
        {
            //Write up the XML, and put in the exception info
            string xmlStr = "<errorDoc>";
            xmlStr += "<alert>An Error Occurred!</alert>";
            xmlStr += String.Format("<message>{0}</message>", exception.Message);
            xmlStr += "</errorDoc>";

            //Load it into an XmlDocument
            XmlDocument doc = new XmlDocument();
            doc.LoadXml(xmlStr);
```

```
                    //And put it into an XmlReader
                    XmlNodeReader reader = new XmlNodeReader(doc);

                    //XSLT
                    XslCompiledTransform xslt = new XslCompiledTransform();
                    xslt.Load(_path + "/weather.xslt");

                    //Load the XmlWriter data into the result document
                    XmlDocument resultDocument = new XmlDocument();
                    using (XmlWriter writer =
                            resultDocument.CreateNavigator().AppendChild())
                    {
                        xslt.Transform(reader, null, writer);
                    }

                    //Output the serialized XML
                    return resultDocument.OuterXml;
            }
        }
    }
```

Because of the XslCompiledTransform class's architecture, it does not support transforming XML data into an XmlReader. This XSL class is new in .NET 2.0, and it provides better performance than the XslTransform class in earlier .NET versions. Instead, the solution is to use an XPathNavigator object to load an XML tree into an XmlDocument from an XmlWriter object. By using the OuterXml property of the resulting XmlDocument object, the serialized HTML can be returned.

In order for the application to update the contents of weather_cache.xml, *ASP.NET must have the proper modify permissions for the file.*

Deciding Which Version to Use

The _getWebWeather() and _getCachedWeather() methods are the primary workhorses of the application. All that's left is to determine which method to call when weather information is required. This determination is made by a public method, GetWeather(), which decides whether to pull the feed from the Web or from the cache based on the time that the cached file was last modified. A public read-only property called LastModified provides easy access to this information:

```
public DateTime LastModified
{
    get
    {
        if ((File.Exists(_cachedFile)))
        {
            return File.GetLastWriteTime(_cachedFile);
        }
        else
        {
            return new DateTime(1,1,1);
        }
    }
}
```

This property gets the date and time that the cached file was last written to. Before checking the file modification time, you must be certain that the file exists by using `File.Exists()`. If it exists, the `GetLastWriteTime()` method returns the date and time of the last modification; if the file does not exist, a `DateTime` instance is created using the earliest possible values by passing the value of 1 for the year, month, and day. This ensures that the application will always pull a new feed if the cached file does not exist.

The `GetWeather()` method uses this information to decide whether to pull a newer feed:

```
public string GetWeather()
{
    DateTime timeLimit = LastModified.AddMinutes(30);

    //more code here
}
```

Using the `AddMinutes()` method, 30 minutes are added to the time `LastModified` returns. This new `DateTime` instance, `timeLimit`, must be compared to the current time by using the `CompareTo()` method:

```
public string GetWeather()
{
    DateTime timeLimit = LastModified.AddMinutes(30);

    if (DateTime.Now.CompareTo(timeLimit) > -1)
    {
        return _getWebWeather();
    }
    else
    {
        return _getCachedWeather();
    }
}
```

The `CompareTo()` method returns an integer value that's either greater than zero, equal to zero, or less than zero. If the current time (specified by `DateTime.Now`) is greater than `timeLimit`, the returned integer is greater than zero. If the two times are equal, the method returns zero. If the current time is less than `timeLimit`, then a negative integer is returned. The retrieval of a newer feed occurs only when at least 30 minutes have passed (`CompareTo()` returns zero or a number greater than zero); otherwise, the cached version is retrieved.

Using the WeatherInfo Class

The ASP.NET file `weather.aspx` serves as a proxy between the client and the Weather.com XML service. It is in this page that the `WeatherInfo` class is used. The first step in implementing the `weather.aspx` page is to create an instance of `WeatherInfo`. This should be done in the `Page_Load` event handler:

```
protected void Page_Load(object sender, EventArgs e)
{
    WeatherInfo weather = new WeatherInfo(Server.MapPath(String.Empty));
    string weatherData = weather.GetWeather();

    //more code here
}
```

In this code, an instance of the `WeatherInfo` class is created by passing the path to the application with `Server.MapPath(String.Empty)`. The weather information is then retrieved using the `GetWeather()` method. The next, and final, step is to set the headers and to output the weather data:

```
protected void Page_Load(object sender, EventArgs e)
{
    WeatherInfo weather = new WeatherInfo(Server.MapPath(String.Empty));
    string weatherData = weather.GetWeather();

    Response.ContentType = "text/xml";
    Response.CacheControl = "no-cache";

    Response.Write(weatherData);
}
```

This completes the server portion of the weather widget. The next step is to create a client to consume the information.

The Client-Side Component

The client code for this widget is very simple due to all of the work performed by the server. It's the job of the `AjaxWeatherWidget` class to manage the widget on the client side. This class has one property and one method. The property is `element`, which is the element to attach weather information to. The `getWeather()` method is responsible for retrieving the data from the server and updating the display.

The `AjaxWeatherWidget` constructor is:

```
function AjaxWeatherWidget(oElement) {
    this.element = (oElement)?oElement:document.body;

    this.getWeather();
}
```

The `AjaxWeatherWidget` constructor accepts one argument: the `HTMLElement` on which to append the data, which is assigned to the `element` property. In the event that no argument is supplied, `element` becomes `document.body`. The constructor calls `getWeather()` to retrieve data from the server as soon as the object is created.

Getting Data from the Server

The `getWeather()` method contacts the server application and retrieves the weather information with XHR.

```
AjaxWeatherWidget.prototype.getWeather = function () {
    var oThis = this;

    var oReq = zXmlHttp.createRequest();

    //more code here

    oReq.open("GET", "weather.aspx", true);
    oReq.send(null);
};
```

The method starts by creating a pointer to the object and storing it in oThis. Then an XHR object is created, primed, and sent to the server. Next, handle the readystatechange event.

```
AjaxWeatherWidget.prototype.getWeather = function () {
    var oThis = this;

    var oReq = zXmlHttp.createRequest();

    oReq.onreadystatechange = function () {
        if (oReq.readyState == 4) {
            if (oReq.status == 200 || oReq.status == 304) {
                oThis.element.innerHTML = oReq.responseText;
            }
        }
    };

    oReq.open("GET", "weather.aspx", true);
    oReq.send(null);
};
```

When the request is successful, the server's response is added to the page with the HTMLElement's innerHTML property. Because the server does all the work, this is all that is required of the client code.

Customizing the Weather Widget

Out of the box, this widget fits nicely into a sidebar, providing visitors with the weather information you dictate. The look of the widget relies upon custom images as well as the weather images provided in the SDK (see Figure 12-1).

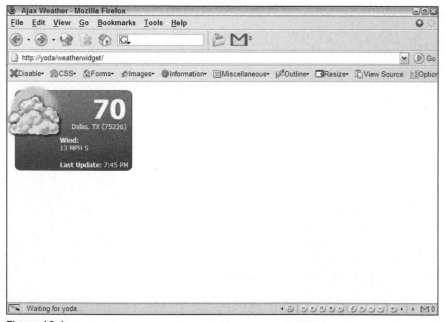

Figure 12-1

Giving the widget the look and feel in the example files relies heavily upon CSS positioning; nearly every element is absolutely positioned, so the HTML structure isn't extremely important. All you need is valid (X)HTML:

```
<div id="weatherContainer">
    <div id="weatherIcon"><img src="img/weather/32.png" /></div>
    <div id="weatherTemp">70</div>
    <div id="weatherLocation">Dallas, TX (75226)</div>
    <div id="weatherWind">Wind:
        <div>13 MPH S</div>
    </div>
    <div id="weatherTime">Last Update:
        <span>7:45 PM</span>
    </div>
</div>
```

This XHTML is a result of an XSL transformation. When going over each piece of information in this section, the XPath expression to the location of the information in the XML feed is given.

To achieve this look, it is important to note that the containing `<div/>` element, `weatherContainer`, does not have a default (inherit) position; otherwise, the contained, absolutely positioned elements will position themselves based on the document and not `weatherContainer`:

```
#weatherContainer {
    position: relative;
    background: url(../img/background.gif);
    width: 220px;
    height: 149px;
}
```

A relative position doesn't interfere with the page flow unless you provide top and left coordinates. The background of this `<div/>` element is a custom-made GIF file the same size as the `<div/>`: 220 pixels wide and 149 pixels high.

The SDK includes Weather.com's own images to provide a visual display of the current weather conditions. These image files are PNG images and are named xx.png, where xx is a number. This number, found in the XML feed, resides at `weather/cc/icon` (cc stands for current conditions). To achieve the look of the example, give this element an absolute position, which enables you to place it anywhere in its container and removes it from the document flow.

```
#weatherIcon {
    position: absolute;
    top: -25px;
    left: -25px;
}
```

This code places the image 25 pixels to the left and top from the top-left corner of the container. Because the images provided by Weather.com are PNGs, additional coding is required for Internet Explorer 6 because the browser ignores the transparency information.

Internet Explorer 7 correctly displays PNGs using their transparency channel.

Microsoft exposes a DirectX filter called `AlphaImageLoader`, which makes PNGs correctly display transparency. However, the use of this filter is limiting, because it must be applied with CSS. To resolve this issue, you can download the PNG Behavior at WebFX (`http://webfx.eae.net/dhtml/pngbehavior/pngbehavior.html`). It is an excellent tool, and is perfect in this situation. To use it, simply add the following rule to your CSS:

```
#weatherIcon img {
    width: 128px;
    height: 128px;
    behavior: url(css/pngbehavior.htc);
}
```

In Internet Explorer, this rule applies the PNG Behavior to every `<img/>` element in the widget, but it only applies the `AlphaImageLoader` filter for PNG files. All other `<img/>` tags with `.gif`, `.jpg`, or any other extension are left alone. The filter property is Internet Explorer–specific; therefore, all other browsers ignore the property and its value.

> **You must set the** `height` **and** `width` **properties when using** `AlphaImageLoader`.

The next item in the widget is the temperature, contained in a `<div/>` element with an `id` of `weatherTemp` and located in the XML at `weather/cc/temp`. The styling of this information is:

```
#weatherTemp {
    position: absolute;
    color: white;
    font: bold 48px Tahoma;
    right: 12px;
    top: 5px;
}
```

Positioning this element as absolute enables you to place it anywhere in the container you want. In this situation, its location resides in the top-right corner. The text contained in this element is colored white and is 48 pixels tall.

Below the temperature is the weather location information. From the XML feed, this information is located in `weather/loc/dnam`. This text is colored white and uses a smaller font:

```
#weatherLocation {
    font: 12px Tahoma;
    color: white;
    position: absolute;
    right: 12px;
    top: 60px;
}
```

Once again, this element is absolutely positioned. The right edge is 12 pixels from the right edge of `weatherContainer` and is 60 pixels from its top. The font is 12 pixels tall and in the Tahoma typeface.

The wind is another important piece of information to display. In the XML document, the information is located in `weather/cc/wind`:

```
#weatherWind {
    position: absolute;
    font: bold 12px Tahoma;
    color: white;
    left: 85px;
    top: 85px;
}

#weatherWind div {
    font-weight: normal;
}
```

If you remember from the HTML structure discussed earlier in this section, `weatherWind` contains another `<div/>` element. This inner `<div/>` contains the actual wind information, whereas its parent merely serves as a label and positions the information. Unlike the previous elements, `weatherWind` is positioned using the `left` property, instead of `right`, to position the element horizontally, and the element is positioned 85 pixels from the top. The label text is bolded, whereas the wind information is not.

The final piece of information this widget displays is the time it was last updated. This information also exists in the XML data. Its location: `weather/loc/tm`. Like the wind information previously discussed, the HTML structure for the time information consists of a parent element (`weatherTime`) and a child element (`<span/>`). The outer element positions the information and serves as a label; the inner element contains the actual time information:

```
#weatherTime {
    position: absolute;
    font: bold 12px Tahoma;
    color: white;
    left: 85px;
    bottom: 5px;
}

#weatherTime span {
    font-weight: normal;
}
```

The premise behind the time is the same as the wind, except with a `<span/>` the data is displayed inline instead of on a new line.

In the event of an error, the HTML structure returned to the client looks like this:

```
<div id="weatherContainer">
    <div id="weatherIcon"><img src="img/error.png" /></div>
    <div id="weatherErrorAlert">An Error Occurred!</div>
    <div id="weatherErrorMessage">Error Description</div>
</div>
```

The `weatherIcon` `<div/>` element remains, and the `<img/>` element inside it contains an image called `error.png`. The next `<div/>` element, `weatherErrorAlert`, contains the text that tells the user an error occurred.

```
#weatherErrorAlert
{
    color: white;
    font: bold 14px Tahoma;
    position: absolute;
    right: 7px;
    top: 10px;
}
```

The text in this element keeps with the current theme. The color is white and bolded in Tahoma font. It is positioned absolutely 7 pixels from the right and 10 pixels from the top of the container `<div/>`. This puts the text to the right of the error icon.

The error message that contains the description of the error is in the `weatherErrorMessage` `<div/>` element.

```
#weatherErrorMessage
{
    font: 12px Tahoma;
    color: white;
    position: absolute;
    right: 15px;
    top: 85px;
}
```

This rule styles the text white in color. It's positioned 85 pixels from the top, placing it well into the "body" of the container, making it easily readable by the reader.

Because this widget depends on the XSL stylesheet, total customization essentially rests in your hands; you have the ability to completely change the markup, structure, and style of the data. In this section, the path to the information was given for each element. These few elements are by no means a full list of the available elements in the XML feed. The SDK does not cover these elements; however, this information resides within the Weather.com DTD, located at `www.weather.com/documentation/xml/weather.dtd`.

Setting Up the Weather Widget as an Application

Setting up ASP.NET web applications requires a few extra steps compared to other web applications.

The first requirement is to make sure that Internet Information Services (IIS) is installed on the machine. IIS is Microsoft's web server and is available only for owners of Windows 2000 Professional, Windows 2000 Server, Windows XP Professional, and Windows Server 2003. Installing IIS requires the Windows CD and can be done in the Add/Remove Windows Components section of the Add/Remove Programs Control Panel applet (see Figure 12-2).

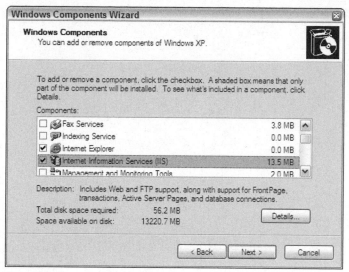

Figure 12-2

Next, you also must install the .NET Framework version 2.0 or better. It is freely available at http://msdn2.microsoft.com/en-us/netframework/aa731542.aspx for users of Windows 2000 and later versions.

When IIS and the .NET Framework are installed, create a folder called WeatherWidget in the IIS wwwroot directory, located at c:\Inetpub\, and move all the widget's files and folders to the newly created WeatherWidget folder. After the files have been placed in the WeatherWidget directory, you need to register the application in IIS, which you can do in the IIS Management Console (see Figure 12-3). In the computer's Control Panel (Start⇨Control Panel), double-click Administrative Tools, and then double-click the Internet Information Services icon.

In the console, you will see a list of files and folders. These items are contained in the IIS root folder. In the left-hand pane, locate the WeatherWidget folder. Right-click the folder and choose Properties from the context menu. You are now looking at the web properties of the WeatherWidget folder (see Figure 12-4).

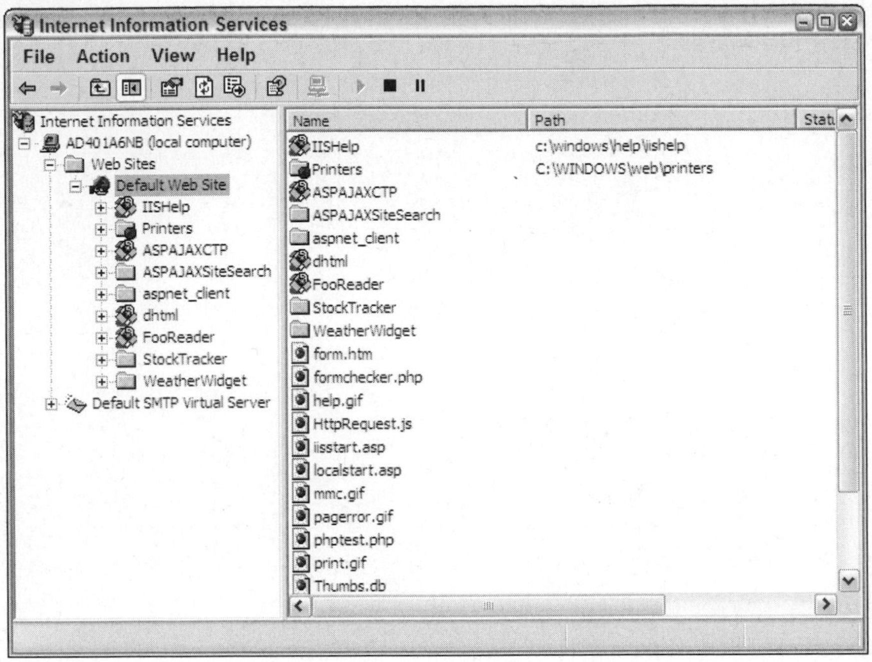

Figure 12-3

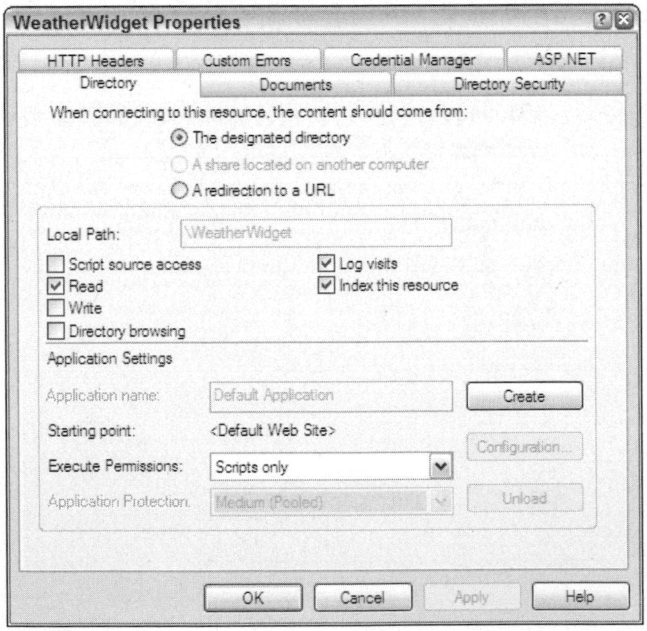

Figure 12-4

On the Directory tab, you see an Application Settings section in the bottom part of the window. Click the Create button, and the Properties window is displayed (see Figure 12-5).

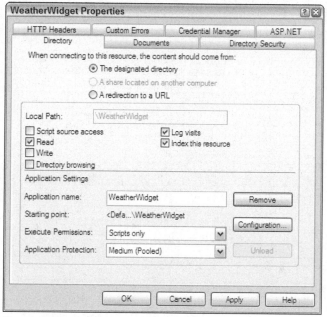

Figure 12-5

Now click on the ASP.NET tab. You should see a drop down box that allows you to change the ASP.NET version. Make sure that 2.0.xxxx is selected (Figure 12-6).

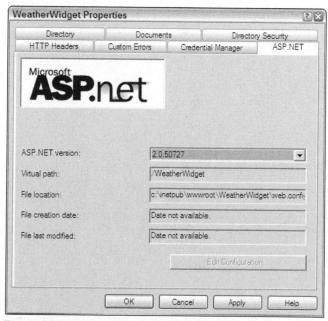

Figure 12-6

Click OK. IIS now knows to treat the contents of the `WeatherWidget` folder as an application, and will run it as one. The Weather widget is now installed.

Adding the Weather Widget to the Web Page

Because the back-end code consists mainly of a C# class, your options of implementation are twofold:

1. You can add the class to an already existing ASP.NET-enabled web site. Doing so would require a recompilation of your code. If you take this route, you will need to modify the `weather.aspx` page to fit your namespace.

2. You can use the code contained in the downloadable examples as its own freestanding mini-application (the steps outlined in the previous section).

The choice is ultimately yours, but the remainder of the section assumes that you chose the latter option. To implement the `AjaxWeatherWidget` class, you should reference the proper CSS and JavaScript files in your HTML:

```
<!DOCTYPE html PUBLIC "-//W3C//DTD XHTML 1.1//EN"
        "http://www.w3.org/TR/xhtml11/DTD/xhtml11.dtd">

<html xmlns="http://www.w3.org/1999/xhtml" >
<head>
    <title>Ajax Weather</title>
    <link rel="stylesheet" type="text/css" href="css/weatherwidget.css"/>
    <script type="text/javascript" src="js/zxml.js"></script>
    <script type="text/javascript" src="js/weatherwidget.js"></script>
</head>
<body>
</body>
</html>
```

The Weather widget's only outside dependency is the zXml library, which you also should reference in your HTML.

All that remains is to create an `AjaxWeatherWidget` object and append it to an HTML element:

```
<!DOCTYPE html PUBLIC "-//W3C//DTD XHTML 1.1//EN"
        "http://www.w3.org/TR/xhtml11/DTD/xhtml11.dtd">

<html xmlns="http://www.w3.org/1999/xhtml" >
<head>
    <title>Ajax Weather</title>
    <link rel="stylesheet" type="text/css" href="css/weatherwidget.css"/>
    <script type="text/javascript" src="js/zxml.js"></script>
    <script type="text/javascript" src="js/weatherwidget.js"></script>
    <script type="text/javascript">
    function init() {
        var divMyWeather = document.getElementById("myWeather");
        var oWeather = new AjaxWeatherWidget(divMyWeather);
    }

    onload = init;
    </script>
```

```
    </head>
    <body>
        <div id="myWeather"></div>
    </body>
    </html>
```

This new code adds another `<script/>` element containing a function called `init()`. Inside this function, retrieve a reference to the `<div/>` element with `myWeather` as its ID. This `<div/>` element will serve as the weather widget container. Also, it is important to run `init()` during the `onload` event, because the browser will not find the `myWeather` `<div/>` element and will not append the widget to it.

The Weather widget is a simple widget, especially in the client-side component; the ASP.NET classes do all the work. Compare this with the next widget, the Stock Watcher, where both the client and server side are more complex, yet they're easily implemented to retrieve stock information.

Watching Stocks

Nothing changed the stock market quite like the Web. What used to be the domain of financial experts has become something that the everyman can now take part in. Online trading companies like E*Trade have changed the face of stock trading forever. Regardless of this change, the Web is first, and foremost, a vast repository of information, and stock price information is no exception.

Getting Yahoo! Finance Information

While not as feature filled as some Yahoo! premium services, basic stock reporting with Yahoo! Finance can easily be used in any Web application. The 15-minute delay certainly isn't desirable for anyone wanting up-to-the-second information, but this free service could satisfy anyone who wants to casually watch certain stocks during the day.

Yahoo! Finance stock information comes in comma-separated value (CSV) format, and you use the following URL to download information on any stock:

```
http://finance.yahoo.com/d/quotes.csv?s=stock_symbols&f=special_tags
```

Stock symbols should be separated by a plus sign (+). There's a host of information available for each individual stock, and you can specify what pieces of information you want with special tags. For example, the URL to get the day's opening price and the last trade's price for Microsoft's and GE's stock would look like this:

```
http://finance.yahoo.com/d/quotes.csv?s=MSFT+GE&f=ol1
```

For a complete list of available tags, visit www.gummy-stuff.org/Yahoo-data.htm.

The widget built in this section retrieves the stock symbol (tag: s), the company's name (tag: n), the last trade price (tag: l1), and the change since opening (tag: c1).

The Stock Quote Proxy

You'll use PHP to retrieve the stock quotes in CSV format and create a JSON structure (to send to the browser), which looks like this:

```
{
    "error"     : true || false,
    "stocks"    :
    [
        {
            "symbol"        : "stock symbol",
            "companyName"   : "company's name",
            "lastTrade"     : "23.54",
            "change"        : "0.03"
        }
    ]
}
```

The first property in the object is `error`, which will hold a Boolean value (`false` means no error occurred). Next is `stocks`, an array of objects containing the requested data for each stock.

Organizing Stock Data

The structure of the stock objects comes from a PHP class called `Stock`, contained in the `stock.class.php` file.

```
class Stock {
    var $symbol;
    var $companyName;
    var $lastTrade;
    var $change;

    //More code to come.
}
```

The `Stock` class has four properties: `symbol`, `companyName`, `lastTrade`, and `change`. The constructor accepts one argument, `$stock_data`, which is a string containing the stock quote data.

```
class Stock {
    var $symbol;
    var $companyName;
    var $lastTrade;
    var $change;

    function Stock($stock_data) {
        //Split the data by commas.
        $split_data = explode(",", $stock_data);

        //Add the data to the properties
        $this->symbol       = $split_data[0];
        $this->companyName   = $split_data[1];
        $this->lastTrade     = $split_data[2];
        $this->change        = $split_data[3];
    }
}
```

`$stock_data` is in CSV format, so use the `explode()` function to split the string into an array and assign the class's properties their corresponding values. You can rely upon this order of assignment, as the data received from Yahoo! is in `symbol, companyName, lastTrade, change` format.

Retrieving the Stock Quotes

Aside from the JSON PHP class introduced in Chapter 8, the remainder of PHP code is contained in `stockproxy.php`, which is primarily responsible for retrieving data from Yahoo! Finance. Because JSON is used in this widget, the first two lines of this file set the required headers:

```
header("Content-Type: text/plain; charset=UTF-8");
header("Cache-Control: no-cache");

//more to come
```

The first line sets the `Content-Type` header to `text/plain` with a UTF-8 character set, and the second line sets the `Cache-Control` header, forcing browsers to not cache the information. Next, include the needed PHP files.

```
header("Content-Type: text/plain; charset=UTF-8");
header("Cache-Control: no-cache");

require_once("inc/stock.class.php");
require_once("inc/JSON.php");

class JSONObject {}

$SYMBOLS = array(
    "MSFT",
    "GE"
);

//more to come
```

Also, a generic class called `JSONObject` is defined; an instance of this class holds data in a structured format until it is time to serialize it into a JSON string. And `$SYMBOLS` is an array that contains stock symbols. These symbols are used to retrieve quotes from Yahoo! Finance.

The workhorse of this PHP application is the `get_stock_quotes()` function. This function attempts to retrieve information from `http://finance.yahoo.com`, and if successful, structures the data for JSON serialization.

```
//Header, required files, and JSONObject

$SYMBOLS = array(
    "MSFT",
    "GE"
);

function get_stock_quotes() {
    global $SYMBOLS;

    //Get the symbols in the format we need.
```

```
    $symbol_string = implode("+", $SYMBOLS);

    //Build the URL
    $url = "http://finance.yahoo.com/d/quotes.csv?s=". $symbol_string ."&f=snl1c1";

    //Get the data.
    $data = file_get_contents($url);

    //Create the JSON object.
    $json = new Services_JSON ();

    //Create the JSONObject
    $object_to_serialize = new JSONObject();

    //more to come
}
```

The first step of this function is to transform the $SYMBOLS array into the format that you need
(SYMBOL1+SYMBOL2+SYMBOL3, etc). The implode() function does this and returns the string to
$symbol_string. Next, build the URL with $symbol_string, and use file_get_contents() to
retrieve the data from Yahoo!. The last lines of this code create a Services_JSON object called $json,
and a JSONObject object called $object_to_serialize.

If file_get_contents() failed to retrieve data from Yahoo!'s server, the $data variable will be false.
So first, check to see if the request was successful:

```
function get_stock_quotes() {
    //Code cut for space......

    //Create the JSON object.
    $json = new Services_JSON ();

    //Create the JSONObject
    $object_to_serialize = new JSONObject();

    if (!$data) {
        $object_to_serialize->error = true;
    } else {
        //more to come
    }

    //more to come
}
```

If not, then add a property to $object_to_serialize called error, and set it to true. This informa-
tion is utilized by the client, allowing the user to know that an error occurred. If the request was successful, then the data needs to be parsed.

The data received looks something like this:

```
"MSFT","MICROSOFT CP",27.87,-0.05
"GE","GEN ELECTRIC CO",36.14,-0.15
```

Each quote is followed by "\r\n", and string data is contained within double quotation marks. The code needs to take these factors into account.

```php
if (!$data) {
    $object_to_serialize->error = true;
} else {
    //Start to populate our JSON object.
    $object_to_serialize->error = false;
    $object_to_serialize->stocks = array();

    //Remove the quotes that we get from Yahoo!
    $data = preg_replace('/"/', "", $data);

    //Create an array.
    $split_data = explode("\r\n", $data);

    //The last element is just \r\n. Pop it off.
    array_pop($split_data);

    foreach($split_data as $stock_data)
        $object_to_serialize->stocks[] = new Stock($stock_data);

    //more code here
}
```

The first step is to add `error` and `stocks` properties to `$object_to_serialize`. The `error` property is set to `false`, and `stocks` is an array. Next, use the `preg_replace()` function to remove the double quotation marks from the string values.

The next goal is to remove the carriage returns and separate the quotes from each other. To do this, use the `explode()` function. The result is an array with each element containing one quote. The last quote in the CSV, however, has a carriage return at the end of the line, which gives `$split_data` an extra array element in the last position of the array. By using `array_pop()`, you can remove the last element in the array, leaving nothing but stock quote data contained in `$split_data`.

Last, parse the data by looping through the `$split_data` array and adding `Stock` instances to the `$object_to_serialize->stock` property.

The final step of `get_stock_quotes()`, and the `stockproxy.php` file, is to output the serialized `$object_to_serialize` object and call the `get_stock_quotes()` function:

```php
header("Content-Type: text/plain; charset=UTF-8");
header("Cache-Control: no-cache");

require_once("inc/stock.class.php");
require_once("inc/JSON.php");

class JSONObject {}

$SYMBOLS = array(
    "MSFT",
    "GE"
```

```
    );

    function get_stock_quotes() {
        global $SYMBOLS;

        //Get the symbols in a format we can use.
        $symbol_string = implode("+", $SYMBOLS);

        //Build the URL
        $url = "http://finance.yahoo.com/d/quotes.csv?s=". $symbol_string ."&f=snl1c1";

        //Get the data.
        $data = file_get_contents($url);

        //Create the JSON object.
        $json = new Services_JSON ();

        //Create the JSONObject
        $object_to_serialize = new JSONObject();

        if (!$data) {
            $object_to_serialize->error = true;
        } else {
            //Remove the quotes that we get from Yahoo!
            $data = preg_replace('/"/',"",$data);

            //Start to populate our JSON object.
            $object_to_serialize->error = false;
            $object_to_serialize->stocks = array();

            //Create an array.
            $split_data = explode("\r\n", $data);

            //The last element is just \r\n. Pop it off.
            array_pop($split_data);

            foreach($split_data as $stock_data)
                $object_to_serialize->stocks[] = new Stock($stock_data);
        }

        //Echo the serialized data, yo!
        echo $json->encode($object_to_serialize);
    }

    get_stock_quotes();
```

Client Component: The AjaxStockWatcher Class

The client portion of this widget isn't overly complex; it is a class designed to poll data from the server, build an HTML table, populate it with data, and update it every so often. Before digging into the JavaScript, take a look at the HTML structure the script creates.

The User Interface

The table is a three-column table; the first cell contains the company name, followed by the last trade price, and finishing off with the change.

```html
<table class="ajaxStockWatcher-Table">
  <tr>
    <td class="ajaxStockWatcher-stockName">
      <a href="http://finance.yahoo.com/q?s=[STOCK_SYMBOL]>Company Name</a>
    </td>
    <td class="ajaxStockWatcher-lastTrade">10.00</td>
    <td class="ajaxStockWatcher-change ajaxStockWatcher-change-up">+1.00</td>
  </tr>
  <tr>
    <td class="ajaxStockWatcher-stockName">
      <a href="http://finance.yahoo.com/q?s=[STOCK_SYMBOL2]>Company Name2</a>
    </td>
    <td class="ajaxStockWatcher-lastTrade">8.00</td>
    <td class="ajaxStockWatcher-change ajaxStockWatcher-change-down">-2.00</td>
  </tr>
</table>
```

Each quote exists in its own table row, and the company's name is used in a hyperlink to take the user to Yahoo! Finance report on the stock. Notice that the third cell in each row uses two CSS classes. This allows anyone who applies this widget to their web site greater flexibility when writing the CSS rules. For example, they could use the ajaxStockWatcher-change class to apply styling to the cell, and use the ajaxStockWatcher-change-up and -down classes to color the text green or red, depending upon if the stock's change is up or down.

The Class Constructor

The AjaxStockWatcher class constructor accepts one optional argument: the HTMLElement you append the HTML built by the widget to:

```javascript
function AjaxStockWatcher(oElement) {
    //Get the element we'll append to.
    //If one's not specified, use the document's <body/>
    this.toAppend = (oElement) ? oElement : document.body;

    //Create the table that'll house our data
    this.table = document.createElement("table");

    //Assign its CSS class
    this.table.className = "ajaxStockWatcher-table";

    //and append it to toAppend
    this.toAppend.appendChild(this.table);

    //more code here
}
```

The first line of code defines the toAppend property. This property's value points to the HTMLElement specified in the oElement argument. If no value is passed to the constructor, then toAppend assumes the value of document.body. The next few lines of code create the <table/> element, assign its CSS class to ajaxStockWatcher-table, and append it toAppend.

The class preparation is nearly complete. All that remains is to set up the automatic polling with this next code:

```
function AjaxStockWatcher(oElement) {
    //Get the element we'll append to.
    //If one's not specified, use the document's <body/>
    this.toAppend = (oElement) ? oElement : document.body;

    //Create the table that'll house our data
    this.table = document.createElement("table");

    //Assign its CSS class
    this.table.className = "ajaxStockWatcher-table";

    //and append it to toAppend
    this.toAppend.appendChild(this.table);

    //For the timeout
    this.timer = null;

    //Begin polling.
    this.poll();
}
```

The first new line of code initializes the timer property to null. The AjaxStockWatcher class uses this property to keep track of the timeouts used for automatic polling. The last line of the constructor calls the poll() method, which starts the polling cycle.

Polling for Data

The poll() method is responsible for requesting and receiving stock information from the server component with an XHR object.

```
AjaxStockWatcher.prototype.poll = function() {
    //Pointer to the current object.
    var oThis = this;

    //Create the XHR object and handle the o.r.s.c. event
    var oReq = zXmlHttp.createRequest();
    oReq.onreadystatechange = function () {
        if (oReq.readyState == 4) {
            if (oReq.status == 200 || oReq.status == 304) {
                oThis.handleResponse(oReq.responseText);
            }
        }
    };

    //Send the request
    oReq.open("GET", "stockproxy.php", true);
    oReq.send(null);
};
```

The method first begins with creating a variable called oThis, a pointer to the current object. Next, an XHR object is created, and the onreadystatechange event handler is assigned. On a successful request, the XHR object's responseText is passed to the handleResponse() method, and finally, the request is sent to stockproxy.php.

Handling the Server's Response

On a successful request, the AjaxStockWatcher object needs to take the received data and populate the table. This job is delegated to the handleResponse() method. This method accepts one argument called sJson, the serialized data from the server component.

```
AjaxStockWatcher.prototype.handleResponse = function (sJson) {
    //Parse the JSON string
    var oResult = sJson.parseJSON();

    //more code here
}
```

The first line takes the serialized data and parses it into a JavaScript object by using the JSON library. Next, the contents of the table are cleared by looping through the rows collection and removing each row from the table. Then, the method determines if a server-side error occurred. This is accomplished by checking the error property of the oResult object:

```
AjaxStockWatcher.prototype.handleResponse = function (sJson) {
    //Parse the JSON string
    var oResult = sJson.parseJSON();

    //Delete the existing stocks shown.
    while (this.table.rows.length > 0)
        this.table.deleteRow(0);

    if (!oResult.error) {
        //No error. Display the information.
        for (var i = 0; i < oResult.stocks.length; i++) {
            var oStock = oResult.stocks[i];

            //Insert a new row
            var oRow = this.table.insertRow(i);

            //more code here

        }
    }
}
```

If the server component had no errors, then handleResponse() loops through the stocks array and create the table row for the current stock with the insertRow() method.

Adding the Data Cells and Data

Next, you add in the data cells as follows:

```
AjaxStockWatcher.prototype.handleResponse = function (sJson) {
    //Parse the JSON string
    var oResult = sJson.parseJSON();

    //Delete the existing stocks shown.
    while (this.table.rows.length > 0)
        this.table.deleteRow(0);

    if (!oResult.error) {
        //No error. Display the information.
        for (var i = 0; i < oResult.stocks.length; i++) {
            var oStock = oResult.stocks[i];

            //Insert a new row
            var oRow = this.table.insertRow(i);

            //Add a cell for the stock's name
            var tdName = oRow.insertCell(0);
            tdName.className = "ajaxStockWatcher-stockName";

            //And the last trade amount.
            var tdLastTrade = oRow.insertCell(1);
            tdLastTrade.className = "ajaxStockWatcher-lastTrade";

            //And the change
            var tdChange = oRow.insertCell(2);
            tdChange.className = "ajaxStockWatcher-change";
            tdChange.className += (parseFloat(oStock.change) > 0) ?
                " ajaxStockWatcher-change-up" : " ajaxStockWatcher-change-down";

            //more code here
        }
    }
}
```

By using the `insertCell()` method, you can easily add cells to an existing `<tr/>` elements, as this code illustrates. This code is straightforward, except for perhaps the `className` assignment for the `tdChange` element. The first assignment statement sets the cell's CSS class to `ajaxStockWatcher-change`. Then, the `className` is appended according to `oStock.change`'s value. If it is a positive value, the "up" class is used; otherwise, the "down" class is added to the `className` property.

With the cells added to the table, you can now add data to them.

```
AjaxStockWatcher.prototype.handleResponse = function (sJson) {
    //Parse the JSON string
    var oResult = sJson.parseJSON();

    //When we should call poll() again.
```

```
        //30 seconds is the default.
        var iTimeForNextPoll = 30;

        //Delete the existing stocks shown.
        while (this.table.rows.length > 0)
            this.table.deleteRow(0);

        if (!oResult.error) {
            //No error. Display the information.
            for (var i = 0; i < oResult.stocks.length; i++) {
                var oStock = oResult.stocks[i];

                //Insert a new row
                var oRow = this.table.insertRow(i);

                //Add a cell for the stock's name
                var tdName = oRow.insertCell(0);
                tdName.className = "ajaxStockWatcher-stockName";

                //And the last trade amount.
                var tdLastTrade = oRow.insertCell(1);
                tdLastTrade.className = "ajaxStockWatcher-lastTrade";

                //And the change
                var tdChange = oRow.insertCell(2);
                tdChange.className = "ajaxStockWatcher-change";
                tdChange.className += (parseFloat(oStock.change) > 0) ?
                    " ajaxStockWatcher-change-up" : " ajaxStockWatcher-change-down";

                //Create the link used as
                var aLinkToYahoo = document.createElement("a");
                aLinkToYahoo.appendChild(document.createTextNode(oStock.companyName));
                aLinkToYahoo.href = "http://finance.yahoo.com/q?s=" + oStock.symbol;


                //Append the data to the <td/>s
                tdName.appendChild(aLinkToYahoo);
                tdLastTrade.appendChild(document.createTextNode(oStock.lastTrade));
                tdChange.appendChild(document.createTextNode(oStock.change));
            }
        }
        //more code here
    }
```

This new code first creates the hyperlink that takes the user to Yahoo! Finance's web page for this particular stock. Then, the link and remaining stock data (the last trade and price change) are appended to their corresponding cells in the table row.

Handling Errors

If the server component returns an error, for whatever reason, the user should know why stock data is not displayed. This is easily accomplished with the following code:

```
AjaxStockWatcher.prototype.handleResponse = function (sJson) {
    //Parse the JSON string
    var oResult = sJson.parseJSON();

    //When we should call poll() again.
    //30 seconds is the default.
    var iTimeForNextPoll = 30;

    //Delete the existing stocks shown.
    while (this.table.rows.length > 0)
        this.table.deleteRow(0);

    if (!oResult.error) {
        //No error. Display the information.
        for (var i = 0; i < oResult.stocks.length; i++) {
            var oStock = oResult.stocks[i];

            //Insert a new row
            var oRow = this.table.insertRow(i);

            //Add a cell for the stock's name
            var tdName = oRow.insertCell(0);
            tdName.className = "ajaxStockWatcher-stockName";

            //And the last trade amount.
            var tdLastTrade = oRow.insertCell(1);
            tdLastTrade.className = "ajaxStockWatcher-lastTrade";

            //And the change
            var tdChange = oRow.insertCell(2);
            tdChange.className = "ajaxStockWatcher-change";
            tdChange.className += (parseFloat(oStock.change) > 0) ?
                " ajaxStockWatcher-change-up" : " ajaxStockWatcher-change-down";

            var aLinkToYahoo = document.createElement("a");
            aLinkToYahoo.appendChild(document.createTextNode(oStock.companyName));
            aLinkToYahoo.href = "http://finance.yahoo.com/q?s=" + oStock.symbol;


            //Append the data to the <td/>s
            tdName.appendChild(aLinkToYahoo);
            tdLastTrade.appendChild(document.createTextNode(oStock.lastTrade));
            tdChange.appendChild(document.createTextNode(oStock.change));
        }

    } else { //An error occurred. Probably network related.
        //Insert a new row
        var oRow = this.table.insertRow(0);

        //Add a cell, and text to tell the user
        //an error occurred
        var tdError = oRow.insertCell(0)
        tdError.colSpan = 3;
        tdError.appendChild(
```

```
                        document.createTextNode(
                            "An error occurred. Attempting to reconnect..."
                        )
                );
            }

        //more code here
    }
```

This code creates a new row in the table (if an error occurred, it'll be the only row in the table). Then a data cell is created, and a text node is appended to it stating that an error occurred and that the widget is attempting to retrieve the information again. This approach allows you to keep the user informed in a graceful way (as opposed to using an alert box every 30 seconds).

Retrieving Updated Information

The `handleResponse()` method should do one more thing: call `poll()` again in 30 seconds to retrieve updated information, and this is easily accomplished with the following code.

```
AjaxStockWatcher.prototype.handleResponse = function (sJson) {
    //Parse the JSON string
    var oResult = sJson.parseJSON();

    //When we should call poll() again.
    //30 seconds is the default.
    var iTimeForNextPoll = 30;

    //Delete the existing stocks shown.
    while (this.table.rows.length > 0)
        this.table.deleteRow(0);


    if (!oResult.error) {
        //No error. Display the information.
        for (var i = 0; i < oResult.stocks.length; i++) {
            var oStock = oResult.stocks[i];

            //Insert a new row
            var oRow = this.table.insertRow(i);

            //Add a cell for the stock's name
            var tdName = oRow.insertCell(0);
            tdName.className = "ajaxStockWatcher-stockName";

            //And the last trade amount.
            var tdLastTrade = oRow.insertCell(1);
            tdLastTrade.className = "ajaxStockWatcher-lastTrade";

            //And the change
            var tdChange = oRow.insertCell(2);
            tdChange.className = "ajaxStockWatcher-change";
            tdChange.className += (parseFloat(oStock.change) > 0) ?
                " ajaxStockWatcher-change-up" : " ajaxStockWatcher-change-down";

            var aLinkToYahoo = document.createElement("a");
```

```
aLinkToYahoo.appendChild(document.createTextNode(oStock.companyName));
aLinkToYahoo.href = "http://finance.yahoo.com/q?s=" + oStock.symbol;


        //Append the data to the <td/>s
        tdName.appendChild(aLinkToYahoo);
        tdLastTrade.appendChild(document.createTextNode(oStock.lastTrade));
        tdChange.appendChild(document.createTextNode(oStock.change));
    }

} else { //An error occurred. Probably network related.
    //Insert a new row
    var oRow = this.table.insertRow(0);

    //Add a cell, and text to tell the user
    //an error occurred
    var tdError = oRow.insertCell(0)
    tdError.colSpan = 3;
    tdError.appendChild(
        document.createTextNode(
            "An error occurred. Attempting to reconnect..."
        )
    );
}
```

```
    //Pointer to the current object.
    var oThis = this;

    //For the timeout
    var doSetTimeout = function () {
        oThis.poll();
    };

    //Run doSetTimeout() in 30 seconds.
    this.timer = setTimeout(doSetTimeout, 30000);
}
```

This new code assigns a pointer to the current object to the oThis variable. Next, a function called doSetTimeout() is created to call the poll() method. Then, by using setTimeout(), the enclosed method is set to be called in 30 seconds, thus facilitating the automatic update feature.

Stop Automatic Updates

Of course, there are times when it's desirable to stop a script from automatically updating itself; therefore, the widget needs a mechanism to do just that. The last method of the AjaxStockWatcher class, and the simplest one, is the stopPoll() method.

```
AjaxStockWatcher.prototype.stopPoll = function () {
    //Stop the polling
    clearTimeout(this.timer);
};
```

The one line of code in this method uses the clearTimeout() method to stop the timeout created in handleResponse().

Customizing the Stock Quotes

The style sheet provided in the code download styles this widget to fit into a sidebar (see Figure 12-7).

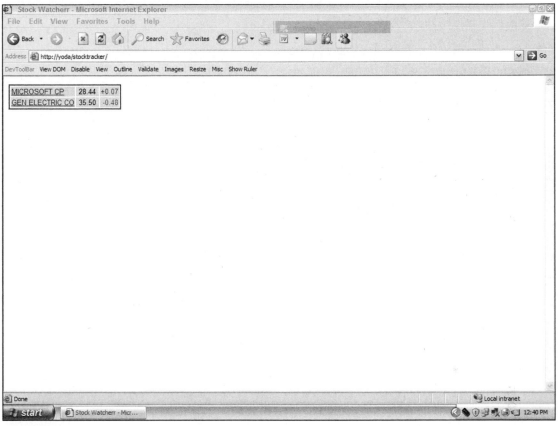

Figure 12-7

Giving the HTML this look and feel relies upon a simple CSS style sheet. Only the `<table/>` and `<td/>` elements have associated CSS classes, but you can easily style other HTML elements used in the widget.

```
/* The stock watcher table */
.ajaxStockWatcher-table
{
    font: 13px Arial;
    border: 2px solid #0066CC;
}

/* The table rows */
.ajaxStockWatcher-table tr
{
    background-color: #D4E2F7;
}
```

The first rule of the style sheet is the `ajaxStockWatcher-table` class. The text inside the table is 13 pixels in height and uses the Arial font face. A blue border, two pixels in width, also surrounds the table. Next, the `<tr/>` elements within the table are styled to have a light-blue background. This makes the information easier to read.

The next step is to style the data cells.

```css
/* <td/> with the stock company's name */
.ajaxStockWatcher-stockName {}

/* <td/> with the last trade price */
.ajaxStockWatcher-lastTrade
{
    padding-left: 5px;
    padding-right: 5px;
    text-align: right;
}

/* <td/> with the change amount */
.ajaxStockWatcher-change
{
    text-align: right;
}
```

The first rule in this code is `ajaxStockWatcher-stockName`. It currently has no CSS properties, but you can easily style it, the hyperlink, and the text if you so desire. Following the stock name is the `ajaxStockWatcher-lastTrade` class. The left and right portions of this cell are padded with 5 pixels, and the right alignment of the text is how currency is typical displayed. The next rule, the `ajaxStockWatcher-change` class, aligns the text to the right for the same reasons for the `-lastTrade` class.

Two classes remain in the style sheet, and they are the `ajaxStockWatcher-change-up` and `-down` classes. These classes merely change the color of the text:

```css
/* Used when the stock is up */
.ajaxStockWatcher-change-up
{
    color: green;
}

/* Used when the stock is down */
.ajaxStockWatcher-change-down
{
    color: red;
}
```

When the stock change is positive, the text color is green. When the stock's down, the color is red. This visual effect allows the viewer to easily correlate up and down stocks quickly, because one can identify color quicker than one can read plain text.

Using the Stock Watcher Widget

To add the widget to a web page, you must reference the required files. The widget relies upon the zXml and JSON libraries, so make sure they're added.

```
<!DOCTYPE html PUBLIC "-//W3C//DTD XHTML 1.0 Transitional//EN"
    "http://www.w3.org/TR/xhtml1/DTD/xhtml1-transitional.dtd">

<html xmlns="http://www.w3.org/1999/xhtml" >
    <head>
        <title>Stock Watcher</title>
        <link rel="stylesheet" type="text/css" href="css/ajaxstocktracker.css" />
        <script type="text/javascript" src="js/zxml.js"></script>
        <script type="text/javascript" src="js/json.js"></script>
        <script type="text/javascript" src="js/ajaxStockTracker.js"></script>
    </head>
    <body>
    </body>
</html>
```

Also required are the `ajaxStockTracker.css` and `ajaxStockTracker.js` files. Next, create an instance of the `AjaxStockWatcher` class:

```
<!DOCTYPE html PUBLIC "-//W3C//DTD XHTML 1.0 Transitional//EN"
    "http://www.w3.org/TR/xhtml1/DTD/xhtml1-transitional.dtd">

<html xmlns="http://www.w3.org/1999/xhtml" >
    <head>
        <title>Stock Watcher</title>
        <link rel="stylesheet" type="text/css" href="css/ajaxstocktracker.css" />
        <script type="text/javascript" src="js/zxml.js"></script>
        <script type="text/javascript" src="js/json.js"></script>
        <script type="text/javascript" src="js/ajaxStockTracker.js"></script>
        <script type="text/javascript">
            var stockWatcher;
            onload = function() {
                stockWatcher = new AjaxStockWatcher();
            };
        </script>
    </head>
    <body>
    </body>
</html>
```

This code appends the table to the document's body. If you wanted to add it to a preexisting element, your code might look like this:

```
<!DOCTYPE html PUBLIC "-//W3C//DTD XHTML 1.0 Transitional//EN"
    "http://www.w3.org/TR/xhtml1/DTD/xhtml1-transitional.dtd">

<html xmlns="http://www.w3.org/1999/xhtml" >
    <head>
        <title>Stock Watcher</title>
        <link rel="stylesheet" type="text/css" href="css/ajaxstocktracker.css" />
```

```
        <script type="text/javascript" src="js/zxml.js"></script>
        <script type="text/javascript" src="js/json.js"></script>
        <script type="text/javascript" src="js/ajaxStockTracker.js"></script>
        <script type="text/javascript">
            var stockWatcher;
            onload = function() {
                var divStocks = document.getElementById("divStocks");
                stockWatcher = new AjaxStockWatcher(divStocks);
            };
        </script>
    </head>
    <body>
        <div id="divStocks"></div>
    </body>
</html>
```

This approach allows you to easily add the widget into a predesigned location.

The Stock Watcher widget in this section varies from the Weather widget discussed earlier in the chapter. Both the client- and server-side components have a level of complexity; the server retrieved the information, parsed it, and formatted it into JSON. The client code took the JSON, parsed it, and dynamically created the HTML to display the information.

The next widget follows along the same lines as the Stock Watcher: the server retrieves information and returns it as JSON, and the client displays that information. The major difference is the following widget, the Site Search widget, uses the .NET Framework.

Creating a Site Search Widget

Search functionality is an integral part of any web site; it enables your viewers to find the data they desire quickly and easily. However, conventional search mechanisms suffer from the same problems as the rest of the Web: they require a page refresh and may lose data when the search is performed.

Within the past year, many Ajax solutions have cropped up, with one standing out from the rest: LiveSearch. LiveSearch (http://blog.bitflux.ch/wiki/LiveSearch), developed by the people at BitFlux (www.bitflux.ch), is a search-as-you-type solution that emulates the Apple Spotlight feature in OSX Tiger.

LiveSearch presents a new take on web site searches, but it also has its critics. For one thing, it offers a different approach to achieving the desired results. The average user is used to entering his or her search criteria and pressing a Search button. LiveSearch, on the other hand, uses the onkeypress DOM event and returns the results as you type. This method may be more efficient in terms of getting your results, but it is unexpected by the user, which can cause confusion.

This next widget is an Ajax solution for searching a site that uses a SQL database as a data store. It will feature a user interface that users are already accustomed to: a search box, a submit button, and a <div/> element that displays the search results (see Figure 12-8).

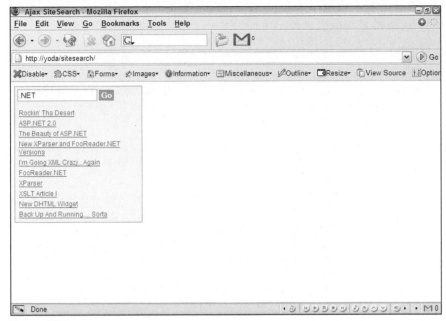

Figure 12-8

The Server-Side Component

You will use the .NET Framework and C# language to interface with an MSSQL database to perform the search query. The returned results will be in JSON, thanks to the Json.NET library mentioned in Chapter 8 (http://www.newtonsoft.com/products/json/). The code in the following sections will use a SQL query to search a database containing the posts on a web log (blog).

The Database Information

The database table for this specific blog is relatively simple. It contains four columns: id, title, date, and posting. The following SQL statement creates this table, called BlogPosts:

```
CREATE TABLE BlogPosts (
    BlogId int IDENTITY (1, 1) NOT NULL,
    Title text NOT NULL,
    Post text NOT NULL,
    Date datetime NOT NULL
)
```

When this query runs, it creates the table, but it is empty. The code download for this example, located at www.wrox.com, contains a SQL file that will add records to the table.

There are primarily two pieces of desired information needed for the search results: id (used in the URL to the blog post) and title. With this knowledge, you can create the search query:

```
SELECT TOP 10
BlogId, title
FROM BlogPosts
WHERE Post LIKE '%SEARCHSTRING%' OR
Title LIKE '%SEARCHSTRING%'
ORDER BY Date DESC
```

This query selects the id and title columns from the BlogPosts table where the contents of posting and title contain an instance of the search string. The results returned are ordered by descending date, and only 10 records are returned.

The Database Connection String

There are a variety of ways you can store the database connection string in the application. The best practice, however, is to store it in the Web.config file, an ASP.NET configuration file that contains settings readily available and accessible within the application. This file's purpose is twofold:

1. It provides a central location for all application settings.

2. It provides a secure means of storing settings that contain sensitive data (such as database information), as the web server will not serve .config files.

.NET 2.0 Web.config files have a special section called <connectionStrings/> where you can add multiple database connection strings and give them unique names. To add a new connection string, use the <add/> element.

```
<connectionStrings>
    <add
        name="SiteSearch"
        connectionString="Data Source=localhost;
            Initial Catalog=BlogDatabase;User ID=sa;Password=pwd"
        providerName="System.Data.SqlClient"
    />
</connectionStrings>
```

The name attribute defines a key to access the connection string within the application code. The string "SiteSearch" is used to distinguish what this connection string is used for. The connectionString attribute defines the connection string value, and the providerName attribute is the name of the ADO.NET provider to use to access the database.

In order to access this connection string within the application, use the ConfigurationManager.ConnectionStrings collection.

```
string conString =
    ConfigurationManager.ConnectionStrings["SiteSearch"].ConnectionString;
```

This retrieves the database connection string associated with the string "SiteSearch".

The connection string is now kept in a secure location. Before delving into the code, however, the returned data structure needs discussing.

The Returned Data Structure

The only two pieces of information retrieved are the blog post ID and its title, and a result of a search could contain more than one blog post. At this point, you need a result set of objects that each contains `title` and `id` properties:

```
[
    {
        "title" : "Title 1",
        "id"    : "1"
    },

    {
        "title" : "Title 2",
        "id"    : "2"
    },

    {
        "title" : "Title 3",
        "id"    : "3"
    }
]
```

This code illustrates what the data returned from the server looks like. The structure is an array containing several objects, each with `title` and `id` properties.

The SearchResults Class

The object portions of the JSON structure are provided by a class called `SearchResults`, which takes information from the database and organizes each returned row as an object. This is a simple class. It has two public properties called `id` and `title`. The class definition is as follows:

```csharp
public class SearchResult
{
    public string id;
    public string title;

    public SearchResult(string id, string title)
    {
        this.id = id;
        this.title = title;
    }
}
```

The names of the properties are intentionally lowercase. While this does go against .NET naming conventions (the first letter of public members' names are supposed to be uppercase), it ensures the serialized form of `SearchResult` objects follow the conventional JavaScript camel-case naming conventions.

The AjaxSiteSearch Class

This widget uses a simple static class called `AjaxSiteSearch` to connect to the database, perform the search query, and return the results as a JSON string.

```
public static class AjaxSiteSearch
{
    //more code here
}
```

This class contains one static method called `Search()`, and as you've probably already guessed, this method searches the database for a particular search string. This method accepts one argument, the search string, which is used in the `String.Format()` method to format the search query:

```
public static class AjaxSiteSearch
{
    public static string Search (string searchString)
    {
        //Get the connection string.
        string conString =
            ConfigurationManager.ConnectionStrings["SiteSearch"].ConnectionString;

        //Get our connection string.
        string query = String.Format("SELECT TOP 10 BlogId, Title FROM BlogPosts
            WHERE Post LIKE '%{0}%' OR Title LIKE '%{0}%' ORDER BY Date DESC",
            searchString);

        //more code here
    }
}
```

The variable `query` now holds the completed query string used later in the method.

The Json.NET library provides methods to serialize .NET objects into JSON strings without having to cast objects to a different type. Referring to the returned data structure, remember that the client code expects an array of objects. Therefore, the next step is to instantiate an `ArrayList` object.

```
public static class AjaxSiteSearch
{
    public static string Search (string searchString)
    {
        //Get the connection string.
        string conString =
            ConfigurationManager.ConnectionStrings["SiteSearch"].ConnectionString;

        //Get our connection string.
        string query = String.Format("SELECT TOP 10 BlogId, Title FROM BlogPosts
            WHERE Post LIKE '%{0}%' OR Title LIKE '%{0}%' ORDER BY Date DESC",
            searchString);

        //Initialize the JSON Array
        ArrayList searchResults = new ArrayList();

        //more code here
    }
}
```

Next, create a database connection and a `SqlCommand`:

```
public static class AjaxSiteSearch
{
    public static string Search (string searchString)
    {
        //Get the connection string.
        string conString =
            ConfigurationManager.ConnectionStrings["SiteSearch"].ConnectionString;

        //Get our connection string.
        string query = String.Format("SELECT TOP 10 BlogId, Title FROM BlogPosts
            WHERE Post LIKE '%{0}%' OR Title LIKE '%{0}%' ORDER BY Date DESC",
            searchString);

        //Initialize the JSON Array
        ArrayList searchResults = new ArrayList();

        //Setup the database connection
        using (SqlConnection conn = new SqlConnection(conString))
        {
            //And get the command ready
            SqlCommand command = new SqlCommand(query, conn);
            //Open the connection
            conn.Open();

            //Perform the query.
            using (SqlDataReader reader = command.ExecuteReader())
            {
                //more code here
            }
        }
    }
}
```

This code creates the database connection using the connection string stored in `conString`. Next, create a new `SqlCommand` using the search query and database connection. Doing this prepares the query to run against the database, which the second `using` block in the previous code does by creating a `SqlDataReader` returned by the `ExecuteReader()` method. This data reader provides the ability to read the result from the executed database query.

Before any data is retrieved from the data reader, first check if the result contains any rows by using the `HasRows` property:

```
public static class AjaxSiteSearch
{
    public static string Search (string searchString)
    {
        //Get the connection string.
        string conString =
            ConfigurationManager.ConnectionStrings["SiteSearch"].ConnectionString;

        //Get our connection string.
```

```
string query = String.Format("SELECT TOP 10 BlogId, Title FROM BlogPosts
    WHERE Post LIKE '%{0}%' OR Title LIKE '%{0}%' ORDER BY Date DESC",
    searchString);

//Initialize the JSON Array
ArrayList searchResults = new ArrayList();

//Setup the database connection
using (SqlConnection conn = new SqlConnection(conString))
{
    //And get the command ready
    SqlCommand command = new SqlCommand(query, conn);
    //Open the connection
    conn.Open();

    //Perform the query.
    using (SqlDataReader reader = command.ExecuteReader())
    {
        try
        {
            //If we got results...
            if (reader.HasRows)
            {
                //Add the info to the JSON Array
                while (reader.Read())
                {
                    //more code here
                }
            }
        }
        catch { }
    }
}
```

This code uses the HasRows property to determine if the data reader contains any rows. If so, the processing of the contained data can begin.

The while loop is used to read the result set through the Read() method of the SqlDataReader class. The Read() method returns a Boolean value; when the end of the result set is reached, Read() returns false and the loop exits.

Inside the loop, create a SearchResult object by passing the appropriate column information to the constructor. To access the database column's value, pass the column name as the index to reader:

```
public static class AjaxSiteSearch
{
    public static string Search (string searchString)
    {
        //Get the connection string.
        string conString =
            ConfigurationManager.ConnectionStrings["SiteSearch"].ConnectionString;

        //Get our connection string.
```

```
string query = String.Format("SELECT TOP 10 BlogId, Title FROM BlogPosts
    WHERE Post LIKE '%{0}%' OR Title LIKE '%{0}%' ORDER BY Date DESC",
    searchString);

//Initialize the JSON Array
ArrayList searchResults = new ArrayList();

//Setup the database connection
using (SqlConnection conn = new SqlConnection(conString))
{
    //And get the command ready
    SqlCommand command = new SqlCommand(query, conn);
    //Open the connection
    conn.Open();

    //Perform the query.
    using (SqlDataReader reader = command.ExecuteReader())
    {
        try
        {
            //If we got results...
            if (reader.HasRows)
            {
                //Add the info to the JSON Array
                while (reader.Read())
                {
                    searchResults.Add(
                        new SearchResult(
                            reader["BlogId"].ToString(),
                            reader["Title"].ToString()
                        )
                    );
                }
            }
        }
        catch { }
    }
    //more code here
}
}
```

This code not only creates the `SearchResult` object, but it also adds it to the `ArrayList` by using the `Add()` method.

When the loop exits, the `ArrayList` is completed and ready to return to the caller. But what if the query returned no results? The client-side code handles this functionality. In the event that no rows are found from the query, an empty array is returned. The client-side code will check the length of the result set and perform the necessary operation.

At this point, the objects involved with the JSON string construction are complete. The final step is to serialize the `ArrayList` by using the `JavaScriptConvert.SerializeObject()` method.

```csharp
public static class AjaxSiteSearch
{
    public static string Search (string searchString)
    {
        //Get the connection string.
        string conString =
            ConfigurationManager.ConnectionStrings["SiteSearch"].ConnectionString;

        //Get our connection string.
        string query = String.Format("SELECT TOP 10 BlogId, Title FROM BlogPosts
            WHERE Post LIKE '%{0}%' OR Title LIKE '%{0}%' ORDER BY Date DESC",
            searchString);

        //Initialize the JSON Array
        ArrayList searchResults = new ArrayList();

        //Setup the database connection
        using (SqlConnection conn = new SqlConnection(conString))
        {
            //And get the command ready
            SqlCommand command = new SqlCommand(query, conn);
            //Open the connection
            conn.Open();

            //Perform the query.
            using (SqlDataReader reader = command.ExecuteReader())
            {
                try
                {
                    //If we got results...
                    if (reader.HasRows)
                    {
                        //Add the info to the JSON Array
                        int i = 0;
                        while (reader.Read())
                        {
                            searchResults.Add(
                                new SearchResult(
                                    reader["BlogId"].ToString(),
                                    reader["Title"].ToString()
                                )
                            );
                        }
                    }
                }
                catch { }
            }
        }

        //Return the JSON data.
        return JavaScriptConvert.SerializeObject(searchResults);
    }
}
```

This last line returns the JSON string to be written into the page.

Building the Search Page

With the `AjaxSiteSearch` class completed, all that remains on the server-side is the search page. This page will accept an argument in the query string called `search`, which contains the search term. An example query string could look like the following:

```
http://yoursite.com/search.aspx?search=ajax
```

To provide this functionality, check for the existence of this parameter by using the `Response.QueryString` collection:

```
Response.CacheControl = "no-cache";
Response.ContentType = "text/plain; charset=UTF-8";

if (Request.QueryString["search"] != null)
{
    //more code here
}
```

The first two lines should be familiar to you by now. The first line sets the `CacheControl` header to `no-cache` so that the browser will not cache the data, while the second sets the MIME `ContentType` to `text/plain` with UTF-8 encoding.

As you learned in Chapter 8, plain text with Unicode encoding is the desired content type for JSON strings.

After the headers are set, check the existence of the `search` parameter in the query string. Next, perform the search:

```
Response.CacheControl = "no-cache";
Response.ContentType = "text/plain; charset=UTF-8";

if (Request.QueryString["search"] != null)
{
    string searchTerm = Request.QueryString["search"];

    string json = AjaxSiteSearch.Search(searchTerm);
    Response.Write(json);
}
```

The first new line creates the `searchTerm` variable, a string storing the value of the `search` parameter in the query string, followed by the database connection string. Next, pass the `searchTerm` variable to the `AjaxSiteSearch.Search()` method to perform the search. The resulting JSON string is returned and stored in the `json` variable, which is then written to the page via the `Response.Write()` method.

You could add an `else` block to handle the case when the search parameter in the query string does not exist; however, the client-side code will handle form validation making it unnecessary to do so.

The Client-Side Component

Client functionality is overly important, especially for a widget such as this. Before using the search capabilities of your site, the user already made the assumption of how it works. Therefore, it is important to follow a couple of guidelines:

❑ **The user will enter text to search and press either Enter or the Submit button.** The search-as-you-type feature of LiveSearch is revolutionary, but it goes against what the user is already accustomed to. Near instantaneous results without a page refresh is enough new functionality.

❑ **The user expects to be told when no results are found.** If you remember from the `SiteSearch` class, an empty JSON array is returned when no results are found; therefore, this responsibility is passed to the client code.

These guidelines may seem like a no-brainer, but it is important to consider the user's experience. What's hip and cool isn't necessarily always the right thing to do.

The User Interface

The first step in any client-side component is to build the user interface with HTML. For this widget, you will use four elements contained within a `<div/>` element:

```
<div class="ajaxSiteSearchContainer">
    <form class="ajaxSiteSearchForm">
        <input class="ajaxSiteSearchTextBox" />
        <input type="submit" value="Go" class="ajaxSiteSearchButton" />
    </form>
    <div class="ajaxSiteSearchResultPane">
        <a class="ajaxSiteSearchLink" href="http://yoursite.com">Result Text</a>
    </div>
</div>
```

Every element contains a `class` attribute. This ensures that the widget is easily customizable with CSS, and you can tailor it to fit in almost every web site.

Of course, you will not add this HTML directly into the HTML code of your web site; JavaScript dynamically creates the HTML and appends it to the desired HTML element.

The AjaxSiteSearch Class

The `AjaxSiteSearch` class encapsulates everything needed to display the user interface, make requests to the server, and display the server's response, aside from the CSS information and other dependencies. The class's constructor accepts one argument, an HTML element to append the search user interface:

```
function AjaxSiteSearch(oElement) {
    //more code here
}
```

The first step is to write the HTML elements that make up the user interface. This is done, naturally, with DOM methods:

```
function AjaxSiteSearch(oElement) {
    var oThis = this;
    this.result = null;

    this.widgetContainer = document.createElement("div");
    this.form = document.createElement("form");
    this.textBox = document.createElement("input");
    this.submitButton = document.createElement("input");
    this.resultPane = document.createElement("div");

    this.widgetContainer.className = "ajaxSiteSearchContainer";
    this.form.className = "ajaxSiteSearchForm";
    this.textBox.className = "ajaxSiteSearchTextBox";
    this.submitButton.className = "ajaxSiteSearchButton";
    this.resultPane.className = "ajaxSiteSearchResultPane";

    this.submitButton.type = "submit";
    this.submitButton.value = "Go";

    //more code here
}
```

The first line of this code creates the oThis variable, a pointer to the object. This comes in handy later in the constructor. The following lines create the needed HTML elements and assign their class names, and the Submit button's type and value attributes are set to submit and Go, respectively.

When the user clicks the Submit button or presses the Enter key when the form has focus, the form's onsubmit event fires. The following event handler will start the search process:

```
function AjaxSiteSearch(oElement) {
    var oThis = this;
    this.result = null;

    this.widgetContainer = document.createElement("div");
    this.form = document.createElement("form");
    this.textBox = document.createElement("input");
    this.submitButton = document.createElement("input");
    this.resultPane = document.createElement("div");

    this.widgetContainer.className = "ajaxSiteSearchContainer";
    this.form.className = "ajaxSiteSearchForm";
    this.textBox.className = "ajaxSiteSearchTextBox";
    this.submitButton.className = "ajaxSiteSearchButton";
    this.resultPane.className = "ajaxSiteSearchResultPane";

    this.submitButton.type = "submit";
    this.submitButton.value = "Go";

    this.form.onsubmit = function () {
        oThis.clearResults();

        //more code here

        return false;
    };
}
```

This is where the object pointer's use is required. Inside the onsubmit event handler, the scope changes; so, this references the <form/> element instead of the AjaxSiteSearch object. Because the event handler makes calls to the AjaxSiteSearch object, an external variable referencing the object is required, and that is what oThis does.

The first line of the onsubmit event handler calls the object's clearResults() method. This method, covered later, removes any links in the results list from a prior search. This ensures that only the results from the current search request are displayed. In the last line, the value of false is returned. This overrides the form's default behavior, which is to submit the form.

Also during the onsubmit event, the form is validated. If the textbox does not contain any text, the user is notified that no text is entered:

```
function AjaxSiteSearch(oElement) {
    var oThis = this;
    this.result = null;

    this.widgetContainer = document.createElement("div");
    this.form = document.createElement("form");
    this.textBox = document.createElement("input");
    this.submitButton = document.createElement("input");
    this.resultPane = document.createElement("div");

    this.widgetContainer.className = "ajaxSiteSearchContainer";
    this.form.className = "ajaxSiteSearchForm";
    this.textBox.className = "ajaxSiteSearchTextBox";
    this.submitButton.className = "ajaxSiteSearchButton";
    this.resultPane.className = "ajaxSiteSearchResultPane";

    this.submitButton.type = "submit";
    this.submitButton.value = "Go";

    this.form.onsubmit = function () {
        oThis.clearResults();

        if (oThis.textBox.value != "") {
            oThis.search();
        } else {
            alert("Please enter a search term");
        }

        return false;
    };

    //more code here
}
```

If text is entered, however, the object's search() method is called. This method, also covered shortly, is responsible for retrieving the search term and making the XHR request to the server.

With the elements created and the onsubmit event handler written, all that remains in the constructor is appending the elements to the document:

```
function AjaxSiteSearch(oElement) {
    var oThis = this;
    this.result = null;

    this.widgetContainer = document.createElement("div");
    this.form = document.createElement("form");
    this.textBox = document.createElement("input");
    this.submitButton = document.createElement("input");
    this.resultPane = document.createElement("div");

    this.widgetContainer.className = "ajaxSiteSearchContainer";
    this.form.className = "ajaxSiteSearchForm";
    this.textBox.className = "ajaxSiteSearchTextBox";
    this.submitButton.className = "ajaxSiteSearchButton";
    this.resultPane.className = "ajaxSiteSearchResultPane";

    this.submitButton.type = "submit";
    this.submitButton.value = "Go";

    this.form.onsubmit = function () {
        oThis.clearResults();

        if (oThis.textBox.value != "") {
            oThis.search();
        } else {
            alert("Please enter a search term");
        }

        return false;
    };

    this.form.appendChild(this.textBox);
    this.form.appendChild(this.submitButton);
    this.widgetContainer.appendChild(this.form);
    this.widgetContainer.appendChild(this.resultPane);

    var oToAppend = (oElement)?oElement:document.body;
    oToAppend.appendChild(this.widgetContainer);
}
```

Because this widget appends itself to the given HTML element, it is a good idea to create an `AjaxSiteSearch` object during the page's `onload` event. Otherwise, the desired destination element could not exist, thus throwing an error.

Clearing the Results

The `clearResults()` method is a simple method to remove all child nodes in the results `<div/>` element:

```
AjaxSiteSearch.prototype.clearResults = function () {
    while (this.resultPane.hasChildNodes()) {
        this.resultPane.removeChild(this.resultPane.firstChild);
    }
};
```

This method utilizes the `hasChildNodes()` method, a method exposed by a node in the DOM. As long as the results `<div/>` contains children, the first child is removed. It is a simple method, but it gets the job done.

Making the XHR Request

As stated before, the `search()` method makes the request to the server to perform the search:

```
AjaxSiteSearch.prototype.search = function () {
    var oThis = this;
    var sUrl = encodeURI("search.aspx?search=" + this.textBox.value);

    var oReq = zXmlHttp.createRequest();
    oReq.onreadystatechange = function () {
        if (oReq.readyState == 4) {
            if (oReq.status == 200 || oReq.status == 304) {
                oThis.handleResponse(oReq.responseText);
            }
        }
    };

    oReq.open("GET", sUrl, true);
    oReq.send();
};
```

The familiar first line creates a pointer to the object used inside of the XHR object's `onreadystatechange` event handler. The second line encodes the search URL and search term with the `encodeURI()` function. Doing this replaces certain characters with their appropriate escape sequence (for example: white space is turned into `%20`).

The remainder of the code performs the XHR request. On a successful request, the `responseText` is passed to the `handleResponse()` method.

Processing the Information

The `handleResponse()` method takes the server's response (the JSON string), decodes it, and displays the results as links in the results `<div/>` element. This method accepts one argument, a JSON string:

```
AjaxSiteSearch.prototype.handleResponse = function (sJson) {
    this.result = sJson.parseJSON();

    //more code here
};
```

This code takes the `sJson` argument and passes it to the `JSON.parse()` method to convert the string into JavaScript.

Now that the information can be used programmatically, the code begins to go through a decision-making process. Remember, the result from the server is an array of objects; therefore, you can use the `length` property to determine if the search returned any results:

```
AjaxSiteSearch.prototype.handleResponse = function (sJson) {
    this.result = JSON.parse(sJson);

    if (this.result.length > 0) {
        //more code here
    } else {
        alert("Your search returned no results.");
    }
};
```

Naturally, if any results are present, you want to display that information. If not, the user is notified through an alert box that no results were found from the search.

Displaying the results is as simple as creating <a/> elements:

```
AjaxSiteSearch.prototype.handleResponse = function (sJson) {
    this.result = sJson.parseJSON();

    if (this.result.length > 0) {
        var oFragment = document.createDocumentFragment();
        for (var i = 0; i < this.result.length; i++) {
            var linkResult = document.createElement("a");
            linkResult.href = "http://yoursite.com/?postid=" + this.result[i].id;
            linkResult.innerHTML = this.result[i].title;
            linkResult.className = "ajaxSiteSearchLink";

            oFragment.appendChild(linkResult);
        }

        this.resultPane.appendChild(oFragment);
    } else {
        alert("Your search returned no results.");
    }
};
```

The first new line of code creates a document fragment to append the <a/> elements to. The next block of code, a for loop, generates the links. Notice the assignment of the href property of the link. In order for this to work on your site, you must change the href value to reflect your own web site.

When the link creation is complete, it is added to the document fragment, which is appended to the results <div/> element. These links remain visible until a new search is performed, which will clear the results pane and populate it with new results.

Customizing the Site Search Widget

To make the Site Search widget conform to your page's look and feel, it was designed to be fully customizable. Every element in the widget has a corresponding CSS classification, making customization a snap.

The outermost <div/> element, the widget's container, has the CSS class ajaxSiteSearchContainer. You can give your search widget its overall look with this element; you can also set a global style, since all elements will inherit many of its style properties:

```
div.ajaxSiteSearchContainer
{
    background-color: #fdfed4;
    border: 1px solid #7F9DB9;
    font: 12px arial;
    padding: 5px;
    width: 225px;
}
```

The first two lines set the background color of the element and its border, respectively. These two properties give the visual idea that everything within the border and background color belongs to the widget. This can be helpful to the user, especially when text seems to appear from the ether. The next line sets the font size and family for the widget. This setting is inherited by the results <div/> element and the links it contains. The 5-pixel padding is mainly for visual purposes; otherwise, everything could look scrunched together. Last, the width is applied to the widget. This confines the widget into a specified space, and text will wrap accordingly.

The <form/> element also possesses the ability for styling. The given class name for this element is ajaxSiteSearchForm:

```
form.ajaxSiteSearchForm {}
```

This example does not apply any style to the element, but the ability exists to do so. By applying padding or a border (or any other style for that matter), you can give the visual impression of separating the form from the results.

The <form/> contains two child elements, the textbox and the Submit button, both of which are <input/> elements:

```
input.ajaxSiteSearchTextBox
{
    border: 1px solid #7F9DB9;
    padding: 2px;
}

input.ajaxSiteSearchButton
{
    background-color: #7F9DB9;
    border: 0px;
    color: white;
    font-weight: bold;
    margin-left: 3px;
    padding: 1px;
}
```

The textbox's CSS (class ajaxSiteSearchTextBox) gives the box a solid, colored border 1 pixel in width and pads the contents by 2 pixels. The button, whose class name is ajaxSiteSearchButton, has a background color and no border but is padded on all sides by one pixel. The text inside the button is white and bold. It is scooted 3 pixels to the right by setting its left margin to 3 pixels.

The results `<div/>` in this example does not have any styling. Instead, it inherits the font size and family from its parent:

```
div.ajaxSiteSearchResultPane {}
```

The final elements in this widget are the links:

```
a.ajaxSiteSearchLink
{
    color: #316ac5;
    display: block;
    padding: 2px;
}

a:hover.ajaxSiteSearchLink
{
    color: #9b1a1a;
}
```

In the example CSS, only two states are styled: a normal link and a link when the mouse hovers over it. In the former (default) state, the links are treated as block-level elements, meaning that each link starts on its own line. They have a bluish color and contain two pixels of padding. When the user mouses over a link, the hover state is activated. The only style change made is the color, which turns the text color from bluish to reddish.

These style properties are for example only; the real fun with widgets is making them your own and fitting them into your own page. Feel free to bend these elements to your will.

Adding the Site Search Widget to a Page

Much as with the weather widget, your options for implementation are twofold:

1. You can add the class to an already existing ASP.NET-enabled web site. Doing so, however, would require you to recompile your code and modify the search.aspx page to fit your namespace.

2. You can use the code contained in the downloadable examples as its own freestanding mini-application. You can follow the steps outlined earlier in the chapter.

Just as with the weather widget, the choice of implementation is yours; however, the remainder of the code assumes that you chose the latter option. On the client page, you need to reference all files needed to use this widget. The AjaxSiteSearch class depends on the zXml and JSON libraries to function properly:

```
<!DOCTYPE html PUBLIC "-//W3C//DTD XHTML 1.1//EN"
        "http://www.w3.org/TR/xhtml11/DTD/xhtml11.dtd">
<html xmlns="http://www.w3.org/1999/xhtml" >
<head>
    <title>Ajax SiteSearch</title>
    <link rel="stylesheet" type="text/css" href="css/ajaxsitesearch.css" />
    <script type="text/javascript" src="js/json.js"></script>
```

```
    <script type="text/javascript" src="js/zxml.js"></script>
    <script type="text/javascript" src="js/ajaxsitesearch.js"></script>
</head>
<body>

</body>
</html>
```

To instantiate an `AjaxSiteSearch` object, use the `new` keyword:

```
<!DOCTYPE html PUBLIC "-//W3C//DTD XHTML 1.1//EN"
        "http://www.w3.org/TR/xhtml11/DTD/xhtml11.dtd">
<html xmlns="http://www.w3.org/1999/xhtml" >
<head>
    <title>Ajax SiteSearch</title>
    <link rel="stylesheet" type="text/css" href="css/ajaxsitesearch.css" />
    <script type="text/javascript" src="js/json.js"></script>
    <script type="text/javascript" src="js/zxml.js"></script>
    <script type="text/javascript" src="js/ajaxsitesearch.js"></script>
    <script type="text/javascript">
    function init() {
        var oSiteSearch = new AjaxSiteSearch();
    }

    onload = init;
    </script>
</head>
<body>

</body>
</html>
```

When creating the `AjaxSiteSearch` object, pass the desired element you want the widget to be appended to. If no `HTMLElement` is passed to the constructor, it is appended to the `document.body`. Creating an object automatically generates the required HTML elements, so there is nothing left to do to implement the widget.

Summary

In this chapter, you took the skills you have learned thus far and applied them to building your own Web-based widgets. This chapter showed you many practical widgets that Ajax makes possible.

First, you learned how to build a widget to consume the Weather.com XML service, transform the XML, and display the data to the user. Next, you learned how to use Yahoo! Finance's stock quote CSV services to create a stock watcher widget. The chapter went on to describe how to create a widget to search a blog's database using MSSQL. Using the Json.NET library, you learned how to build JSON strings and output them to the client.

13

Ajax Frameworks

Up to this point, the examples and discussions in the book have focused on writing every piece of functionality for both client and server. You may have noticed that there can be a fair amount of repetition between examples, code being duplicated and altered only slightly to produce a different result. It is undoubtedly innefficient for numerous developers to be writing the same code over and over again. The identifyication of these common threads in Ajax solutions has given rise to several frameworks that aim to allow rapid development of Ajax applications by freeing the developer from programming low-level communication between client and server.

The frameworks covered in this chapter are known as *remote invocation frameworks*, meaning that the framework is responsible for generating client-side JavaScript that abstracts out the XMLHttp communication, parameter passing, and response handling. Fortunately, there are frameworks available for each of the three major application server technologies: PHP, JSP, and ASP.NET.

JPSpan

JPSpan is an open source Ajax framework for PHP (available for download at www.sourceforge. net/projects/jpspan) that creates JavaScript wrappers for PHP objects and methods. It accomplishes this task by using reflection to inspect the composition of an object. *Reflection* is a common feature of object-oriented languages, allowing developers to determine information about the makeup of an object at runtime. By using reflection, JPSpan is able to create appropriate JavaScript wrappers for each method of the object. These JavaScript functions handle the cross-browser creation of XHR objects as well as the instantiation of objects on the server and data type conversion of arguments and results.

What's more, since JPSpan is simply a series of PHP pages and JavaScript files, there is no real installation to speak of. Simply download the files from the previously mentioned web site and copy the JPSpan folder to the PHP web server.

Using JPSpan

Most of the coding for a JPSpan Ajax solution takes place on the server using a `PostOffice` object. The `PostOffice` object is responsible for two things: generating the JavaScript for the client and handling Ajax requests on the server. Generally speaking, the same PHP file handles both activities, depending on the query string of the request. The standard way of doing this using JPSpan is to have the query string equal to "client" when the JavaScript wrappers should be generated (for example, `myserver.php?client`) and to omit the word "client" when server requests are being handled. The latter is actually handled by the JavaScript wrappers directly, so developers never have to worry about the correct format for handling requests.

The basic format for a JPSpan server page is as follows:

```php
<?php
    //include the necessary files
    require_once '../JPSpan/JPSpan.php';
    require_once JPSPAN . 'Server/PostOffice.php';

    //create the PostOffice object
    $server = & new JPSpan_Server_PostOffice();

    //add a handler for your class
    $server->addHandler(new MyCustomObject());

    //check the query string
    if (isset($_SERVER['QUERY_STRING'])
        && strcasecmp($_SERVER['QUERY_STRING'], 'client') == 0){

        //turn off JavaScript compression
        define('JPSPAN_INCLUDE_COMPRESS', false);

        //output the JavaScript wrappers
        $server->displayClient();
    } else {

        //include the error handler
        require_once JPSPAN . 'ErrorHandler.php';

        //handle incoming requests
        $server->serve();
    }
?>
```

The first two lines of code include the main JPSpan library (which defines a global constant called `JPSPAN` containing the directory in which the framework was installed) and the `PostOffice` class that is used for generating the client-side code for the solution. After that, an instance of `JPSpan_Server_PostOffice` is created and stored in `$server`; this is the object that contains all of the Ajax logic.

Next, the `PostOffice` is assigned an object to handle using the `addHandler()` method. This method accepts a single argument, which is an object (not a class) that should be available to the client and whose functionality should be handled by the server. Any number of objects can be handled by a single `PostOffice`.

After the objects have been added to the PostOffice, it's time to determine whether the request should return the JavaScript wrappers or handle a request. The if statement checks to see if the query string is exactly equal to "client", indicating that the JavaScript wrappers should be emitted to the client. This is done using the displayClient() method, which outputs the JavaScript for all of the handled objects (defining JSPAN_INCLUDE_COMPRESS as false turns off server-side code compression that's intended to remove white space due to performance issues). If the query string is not "client", then the server begins listening for requests. The first step is to include ErrorHandler.php, which handles any errors caused by the request. Then, the serve() method is called to handle the request.

To include the JavaScript in a page, include the file in a <script/> tag, such as:

```
<script type="text/javascript" src="/myserver.php?client"></script>
```

This single line includes all of the generated JavaScript for each object handled by the PostOffice. For each of the handled objects, a JavaScript constructor is defined. This constructor is the name of the PHP class in all lowercase (due to a quirk in PHP's implementation of reflection) and accepts a single object containing callback functions for each PHP method. For example, consider the following PHP class:

```
class MyCustomObject {
    function MyCustomObject() {
        if (!isset($_SESSION['message'])) {
            $_SESSION['message'] = 'Hello world!';
        }
    }

    function getMessage() {
        return $_SESSION['message'];
    }

    function setMessage($message) {
        $_SESSION['message'] = $message;
        return true;
    }
}
```

In this class there is a constructor and two methods. The constructor simply stores a message in the session so that the other methods have data to work with. The getMessage() method returns the value stored in the session, while the setMessage() method changes that value to something else. It's important to note that this value must be stored in the session because this object doesn't persist from request to request. Each request sent back to the server creates a new instance of MyCustomObject, thus disallowing access to property values stored in a previous instance.

The generated JavaScript contains a constructor named mycustomobject (all lowercase due to a quirk in the PHP implementation of reflection). When instantiated, this object contains methods called getmessage() and setmessage() (again, both in all lowercase) that are used to invoke the methods of the same name on the server.

When creating an instance of mycustomobject, you must pass in a single argument. This argument is an object containing methods called getmessage() and setmessage() as well. The difference is that these methods are actually callback functions that receive the result of the server request as their only argument. For instance:

```
var oHandlers = {
    getmessage : function (oResult) {
        alert("Got: " + oResult);
    },

    setmessage : function (oResult) {
        if (oResult) {
            alert("Message set.");
        } else {
            alert("An error occurred while setting the message.");
        }
    }
};

var oObject = new mycustomobject(oHandlers);

oObject.setmessage("Welcome");

//other logic here

oObject.getmessage();   //outputs "Got: Welcome"
```

In this example, oHandlers is an object containing callback functions for getmessage() and setmessage(). Whenever either one of these methods is called, the result is automatically passed into the corresponding callback function. This object is passed into the mycustomobject constructor to create a new object. After that, each of the two methods is called. The oResult value for the setmessage() callback should be a Boolean value of true; if it's not, that means that something went wrong on the server. For the getmessage() callback, oResult is just the string value that was stored, so it is displayed in an alert.

As you can see, there is no XHR programming required to make JPSpan code work. Using reflection, all of the necessary hooks are accounted for, making it possible to focus on the server-side portion of the code without worrying about the client-server communication.

Type Translation

Anytime data is being sent from the server to the client or vice versa, data must be provided in a way that both can understand. If this isn't possible, then the data must be translated. JPSpan includes three PHP files responsible for this data translation: Serializer.php, Types.php, and Unserializer.php.

Serializer.php contains the mappings for translation from PHP to JavaScript in an array called _JPSPAN_SERIALIZER_MAP. This array contains an element for each PHP type that can be represented in JavaScript:

```
$GLOBALS['_JPSPAN_SERIALIZER_MAP'] = array(
    'string'=>array(
        'class'=>'JPSpan_SerializedString',
        'file'=>NULL
        ),
```

```
    'integer'=>array(
        'class'=>'JPSpan_SerializedInteger',
        'file'=>NULL
        ),
    'boolean'=>array(
        'class'=>'JPSpan_SerializedBoolean',
        'file'=>NULL
        ),
    'double'=>array(
        'class'=>'JPSpan_SerializedFloat',
        'file'=>NULL
        ),
    'null'=>array(
        'class'=>'JPSpan_SerializedNull',
        'file'=>NULL
        ),
    'array'=>array(
        'class'=>'JPSpan_SerializedArray',
        'file'=>NULL
        ),
    'object'=>array(
        'class'=>'JPSpan_SerializedObject',
        'file'=>NULL
        ),
    'jpspan_error'=>array(
        'class'=>'JPSpan_SerializedError',
        'file'=>NULL
        ),
);
```

Each item in the array is an associative array containing two properties: `class`, which indicates the serializer class to use for translating this type of data, and `file`, which indicates the file in which the specified class exists. In this example, `file` is `NULL` for all items because these are default mappings contained within the same file. If you were to override the default mapping, you would need to provide the location for the custom class.

The files `Unserializer.php` and `Types.php` are used for conversion from JavaScript to PHP. `Types.php` contains definitions for two base types: `JPSpan_Object` and `JPSpan_Error`; all JavaScript values are converted into one of these two types. The `JPSpan_Object` class is simply an empty class that serves as a base for more specific implementations; `JPSpan_Error` has the properties `code`, `name`, and `message`.

The `Unserializer.php` file uses two classes for deserialization, both of which are found in the unserializer folder: `JPSpan_Unserializer_XML` in `XML.php` and `JPSpan_Unserializer_PHP` in `PHP.php`. By default, JPSpan uses XML to contain all of the information about a remote method call. For example, the data being sent to the server for a call to `setMessage()` with a string of "Welcome" as the only argument looks like this:

```
<r><a><e k="0"><s>Welcome</s></e></a></r>
```

Note that there is no mention of the actual method name being called. The `<r/>` element is simply the root of the XML document while the `<a/>` element represents an array of values (the arguments). Inside of the array is any number of elements, each represented by an `<e/>` element containing a property called k, which indicates the key value for associative arrays or the index for sequential arrays (in this case it's an index). Within each <e/> element is an element representing the type of value being passed. In the case of setMessage(), the argument is a string, so the <s/> element is used to surround the actual string value. There are also other elements used for other types of values, such as <b/> for Boolean values and <i/> for integer values.

This information is useful if you need to augment JPSpan for custom data types. Otherwise, you never need to touch these files. The default JPSpan settings should be good enough for most needs.

Error Handling

Errors can occur with any application, especially when communicating between client and server. JPSpan has a means of trapping nonfatal errors that occur when processing the request and having them appear as standard client-side exceptions. The ErrorHandler.php file is a generic handler that propagates nonfatal errors to the client. It can handle general PHP errors as well as those caused specifically by JPSpan components. There are two basic configuration settings for error handling.

❑   The first setting is JPSPAN_ERROR_MESSAGES, which is a Boolean value that determines how much information to send to the client when a generic PHP error occurs. When defined as TRUE, detailed error messages are returned only for JPSpan-specific exceptions; PHP errors simply return an error that says, "Server unable to respond." If defined as FALSE, verbose error information is returned for all types of errors. This setting is defined such as:

```
if (!defined('JPSPAN_ERROR_MESSAGES')){
    define ('JPSPAN_ERROR_MESSAGES', TRUE);
}
```

❑   The second setting is JPSPAN_ERROR_DEBUG, which allows even more information to be sent to the client. When this setting is set to TRUE, two additional pieces of information are returned with error messages: the filename in which the error occurred and the line number that caused the error. Since this information is sensitive, it is set to FALSE by default. You can change the setting by doing the following:

```
if (!defined('JPSPAN_ERROR_DEBUG') )
{
    define ('JPSPAN_ERROR_DEBUG', TRUE);
}
```

    This setting should be set to TRUE only while debugging; production code should have this setting as FALSE.

Should you decide to modify either of these settings, this code should occur before inclusion of ErrorHandler.php in the server page.

JPSpan Example

In order to truly understand how to use JPSpan, it's helpful to look at a familiar example. Here, you will be rebuilding the example from Chapter 2, retrieving data about a customer when given a customer ID. The same database table, Customers, will be used, as will the same sample data.

The CustomerInfo Class

The most important part of this example is the `CustomerInfo` class, which contains the logic used to communicate with the database. For simplicity, this class has only one method: `getCustomerInfo()`. This method accepts a single argument, the customer ID, and returns a string of information about the customer:

```php
<?php

class CustomerInfo {

    function getCustomerInfo($sId) {

        if (is_numeric($sId)) {

            //variable to hold customer info
            $sInfo = "";

            //database information
            $sDBServer = "your.databaser.server";
            $sDBName = "your_db_name";
            $sDBUsername = "your_db_username";
            $sDBPassword = "your_db_password";

            //create the SQL query string
            $sQuery = "Select * from Customers where CustomerId=".$sId;

            //make the database connection
            $oLink = mysql_connect($sDBServer,$sDBUsername,$sDBPassword);
            @mysql_select_db($sDBName) or $sInfo = "Unable to open database";

            if ($sInfo == "") {
                if($oResult = mysql_query($sQuery)
                        and mysql_num_rows($oResult) > 0) {
                    $aValues = mysql_fetch_array($oResult,MYSQL_ASSOC);
                    $sInfo = $aValues['Name']."<br />".$aValues['Address']."<br />".
                            $aValues['City']."<br />".$aValues['State']."<br />".
                            $aValues['Zip']."<br /><br />Phone: ".
                            $aValues['Phone']."<br />".
                            "<a href=\"mailto:".$aValues['Email']."\">".
                            $aValues['Email']."</a>";
                    mysql_free_result($oResult);
                } else {
                    $sInfo = "Customer with ID $sId doesn't exist.";
                }
            }
            mysql_close($oLink);
        } else {
            $sInfo = "Invalid customer ID.";
        }

        return $sInfo;

    }

}

?>
```

413

The getCustomerInfo() method is fairly straightforward. It does a database lookup based on the customer ID that is passed in as an argument. The logic is the same as that in the examples in Chapter 2.

This class is stored in a file named CustomerInfo.php so that it can be included in the JPSpan server page.

Creating the Server Page

The server page is very similar to the sample page shown earlier in this section. In fact, there are only two changes to the overall code:

```php
<?php
    //include the necessary files
    require_once '../JPSpan/JPSpan.php';
    require_once JPSPAN . 'Server/PostOffice.php';

    //include the CustomerInfo class
    require_once 'CustomerInfo.php';

    //create the PostOffice object
    $server = & new JPSpan_Server_PostOffice();

    //add a handler for your class
    $server->addHandler(new CustomerInfo());

    //check the query string
    if (isset($_SERVER['QUERY_STRING'])
        && strcasecmp($_SERVER['QUERY_STRING'], 'client') == 0){

        //turn off JavaScript compression
        define('JPSPAN_INCLUDE_COMPRESS', false);

        //output the JavaScript wrappers
        $server->displayClient();
    } else {

        //include the error handler
        require_once JPSPAN . 'ErrorHandler.php';

        //handle incoming requests
        $server->serve();
    }
?>
```

The highlighted lines are necessary to include the CustomerInfo class and add handling for a Customer object, respectively. This file is saved as CustomerInfoServer.php.

Creating the Client Page

Now that the CustomerInfo class is incorporated into the server page, it's time to construct the client page. Once again, this code is very similar to that of Chapter 2:

```
<!DOCTYPE html PUBLIC "-//W3C//DTD XHTML 1.0 Transitional//EN"
"http://www.w3.org/TR/xhtml1/DTD/xhtml1-transitional.dtd">
```

```
<html xmlns="http://www.w3.org/1999/xhtml">
<head>
    <title>JPSpan Example</title>
    <script type="text/javascript"src="CustomerInfoServer.php?client"></script>
    <script type="text/javascript"src="JPSpanExample.js"></script>
</head>
<body>
    <p>Enter customer ID number to retrieve information:</p>
    <p>Customer ID: <input type="text" id="txtCustomerId" value="" /></p>
    <p><input type="button" value="Get Customer Info"
            onclick="requestCustomerInfo()" /></p>
    <div id="divCustomerInfo"></div>
</body>
</html>
```

The first highlighted line includes the JavaScript necessary to call the JPSpan server. Note that this example assumes `CustomerInfoServer.php` to be in the same directory as the client page. The second line includes the JavaScript file necessary to use the JPSpan wrappers. This file contains the following code:

```
var oHandlers = {
    getcustomerinfo : function (sInfo) {
        displayCustomerInfo(sInfo);
    }
};

var oInfo = new customerinfo(oHandlers);

function requestCustomerInfo() {
    var sId = document.getElementById("txtCustomerId").value;
    oInfo.getcustomerinfo(sId);
}

function displayCustomerInfo(sText) {
    var divCustomerInfo = document.getElementById("divCustomerInfo");
    divCustomerInfo.innerHTML = sText;
}
```

The differences in this code versus the examples in Chapter 2 are the use of the JPSpan methods. First, an object called `oHandlers` is created to contain the callback function for `getcustomerinfo()`. Within this callback function, the `displayCustomerInfo()` function is called (which is unchanged from Chapter 2). The information returned from the server is in HTML format, so it can be passed directly. Next, an instance of `customerinfo` is created and stored in `oInfo` so that it can be used to retrieve the data.

As you can see from the small amount of JavaScript code necessary to make this example work, JPSpan eliminates much of the client-side development. In addition, it allows work on the server to focus purely on the logic necessary to perform the task in question rather than worrying about data type formatting and how the client should be communicating with the server.

Summary of JPSpan

JPSpan is easy to use and integrates well with PHP. It can cope with classes that use the built-in types and more complex ones if they themselves are built from these. If JPSpan has one main failing, it is that

415

the online documentation is somewhat sparse. Although PHP is covered extensively by numerous sites, if you need to customize JPSpan itself, you will need to dig into the source files and examples included in the basic installation.

DWR

Direct Web Remoting (DWR) is an Ajax framework for Java/JSP available for download at `http://getahead.ltd.uk/dwr`. DWR works similarly to JPSpan in that it uses Java's version of reflection to examine Java bean classes and then create JavaScript wrappers to call the various methods. Also like JPSpan, DWR includes its own JavaScript library for cross-browser Ajax communication, freeing the developer from worrying about browser incompatibilities. DWR assumes the use of Apache Tomcat (`http://tomcat.apache.org`).

> DWR expects that the classes you use will be Java beans, meaning that they can be created without passing any information to the constructor. This is important because the server-side objects don't persist from request to request and need to be created from scratch each time.

Using DWR

Setting up DWR in your web application is very simple. The first step is to place the `dwr.jar` file into the `WEB-INF/lib` directory. The next step is to edit the `web.xml` file contained in `WEB-INF`. There are two sections that need to be added.

❏   The first section describes the DWR invoker servlet:

```
<servlet>
  <servlet-name>dwr-invoker</servlet-name>
  <display-name>DWR Servlet</display-name>
  <servlet-class>uk.ltd.getahead.dwr.DWRServlet</servlet-class>
  <init-param>
    <param-name>debug</param-name>
    <param-value>true</param-value>
  </init-param>
</servlet>
```

This code needs to go with the other `<servlet/>` tags inside of `web.xml`.

❏   The second section that needs to be added is as follows:

```
<servlet-mapping>
  <servlet-name>dwr-invoker</servlet-name>
  <url-pattern>/dwr/*</url-pattern>
</servlet-mapping>
```

This information provides the URL that can be used to call the DWR invoker and must be located alongside any other `<servlet-mapping/>` tags in the file.

The final step is to create a file called `dwr.xml` in the `WEB-INF` directory. This file specifies the Java classes that should be wrapped by DWR for use on the client:

```xml
<!DOCTYPE dwr PUBLIC
    "-//GetAhead Limited//DTD Direct Web Remoting 1.0//EN"
    "http://www.getahead.ltd.uk/dwr/dwr10.dtd">
<dwr>
  <allow>
    <create creator="new" javascript="JDate">
      <param name="class" value="java.util.Date"/>
    </create>
    <create creator="new" javascript="Demo">
      <param name="class" value="your.java.Bean"/>
    </create>
  </allow>
</dwr>
```

This is the example file suggested on DWR's web site. The root element, `<dwr/>`, contains an `<allow/>` element. Each of the `<create/>` elements contained within specify objects that are allowed to be created by JavaScript. In each `<create/>` element, the `javascript` attribute specifies the name that must be used in JavaScript to invoke the Java bean. Since there is already a `Date` object in JavaScript, this example specifies the constructor name `JDate` for using the Java `Date` object. The `<param/>` element specifies the complete class name for the bean to use. You can add any number of `<create/>` elements to allow JavaScript wrappers for your custom beans.

After making these changes, you can go to the following URL to test the installation:

```
http://hostname/webappName/dwr/
```

In this URL, `hostname` should be your machine name and `webappName` should be the name of your web application (the folder name in which the files are contained). This redirects you to a test suite page that displays all of the Java beans that are available for remote invocation. Clicking on one of these class names brings up a test suite page that allows direct invocation of certain methods (see Figure 13-1).

Figure 13-1 displays the test page for the Java `Date` object. It displays helpful information such as what JavaScript URLs to include if you want to use the object, as well as warnings about using overloaded methods.

If you see an error message when going to the test page that seems to originate from one of the Java XML classes, it's possible that you have two copies of the XML API on your system. To remedy this situation, go to the installation folder for Tomcat, which is normally named `jakarta-tomcat-5.x.x`, *and open the folder* `common\endorsed`. *Rename the file* `xml-apis.jar` *to* `xml-apis.jar.bak`. *If this doesn't fix the problem, try restarting Tomcat.*

To use a Java bean from JavaScript, you need to include at least two files. The first needs to be a URL that tells DWR what bean you want to use. That URL is in the following format:

```html
<script type="text/javascript" src="/webappName/dwr/interface/bean.js"></script>
```

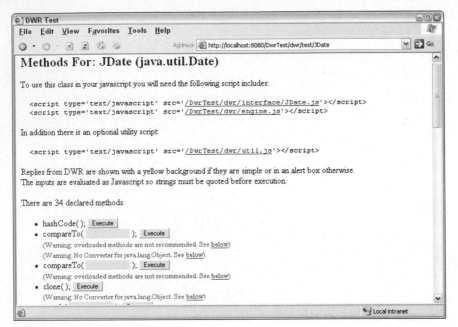

Figure 13-1

In this example, webappName is once again the directory in which your web application resides and bean is the name used in the javascript attribute of the <create/> element relating to the specific bean you want to use. For example, to use the Java Date object from the example dwr.xml file, include this in your page:

```
<script type="text/javascript" src="/webappName/dwr/interface/JDate.js"></script>
```

There should be one of these <script/> elements for each Java bean that is to be used on the client. After that, you need to include the DWR JavaScript engine:

```
<script type="text/javascript" src="/webappName/dwr/engine.js"></script>
```

It's this file that's responsible for handling the cross-browser communication between client and server.

On the client side, each bean is encapsulated in an object with methods identical to those that exist on the server. For example, the Java Date object is represented through a JavaScript object called JDate, which has all of the methods of the Java Date object. Unlike using JPSpan, DWR doesn't require you to create a new object for each call; every method is treated as static on the client. Additionally, each method accepts one extra argument: a callback function that accepts the return value from the method call. To call the Date object's toGMTString() method, for instance, the code looks like this:

```
function handleGMTStringResponse(sResponse) {
    alert(sResponse);
}

JDate.toGMTString(handleGMTStringResponse);
```

Note again that no objects need to be created; the toGMTString() method is called directly off of the JDate object. Since toGMTString() doesn't accept any arguments, the only argument passed in is the callback function, handleGMTStringResponse(). If the method did accept arguments, then the callback function would be the last argument.

DWR Example

Since DWR works in a similar fashion as JPSpan, it makes sense to recreate the same example. Once again, you'll be pulling information out of the database about a specific customer. In order to access a MySQL database from a Java, you'll need to download MySQL Connector/J from www.mysql.com/products/connector/j. Install the most recent version using the instructions provided with the download.

Next, create a new directory under webapps called DwrExample. Under that directory, create a WEB-INF directory with two subdirectories: classes and lib. Copy the web.xml file from another application or create one using the code in the previous section and place it in the WEB-INF directory. Also copy the dwr.xml file from the previous section into this directory.

> *All of this code is available for downloading at* www.wrox.com. *You may download this example and simply copy it into your* webapps *directory.*

The CustomerInfo Class

As with the previous example, the CustomerInfo class handles most of the work:

```
package wrox;
import java.sql.*;

public class CustomerInfo {

    public String getCustomerInfo(int id) {

        //more code here
    }
}
```

In order to use databases, the java.sql package is included in this file. These objects will be used in the getCustomerInfo() method to retrieve the information from the database. The very first step in that method is to attempt to create the MySQL driver for database access:

```
package wrox;
import java.sql.*;

public class CustomerInfo {

    public String getCustomerInfo(int id) {
        try {

            Class.forName("com.mysql.jdbc.Driver").newInstance();

            //more code here

        } catch (Exception e){
```

```
            return "An error occurred while trying to get customer info.";
        }
    }
}
```

This is the standard way of creating database drivers in Java, passing in the fully qualified class name to `Class.forName()`. Calling `newInstance()` is necessary due to some quirkiness in Java implementations. This effectively loads the database driver (or causes an error, which is caught and an error message is returned).

Next, a connection must be made to the database server. This is done using a URL in the following format:

```
jdbc:mysql://dbservername/dbname?user=your_user_name&password=your_password
```

The `dbservername` may be localhost but may also be a full domain name for the database server; the `dbname` should be the name of the database being accessed. Of course, you need to provide the appropriate username and password for that database as well. This all comes together as an argument to `getConnection()` method for `DriverManager`:

```
package wrox;
import java.sql.*;

public class CustomerInfo {

    public String getCustomerInfo(int id) {
        try {

            Class.forName("com.mysql.jdbc.Driver").newInstance();

            String dbservername = "localhost";
            String dbname = "your_db_name";
            String username = "your_user_name";
            String password = "your_password";
            String url = "jdbc:mysql://" + dbservername + "/" + dbname + "?user="
                            + username + "&password=" + password;

            Connection conn = DriverManager.getConnection(url);

            //more code here

        } catch (Exception e){
            return "An error occurred while trying to get customer info.";
        }
    }
}
```

This new section of code creates a connection to the database and stores it in the variable `conn`, which now can be used to run queries:

```
package wrox;
import java.sql.*;

public class CustomerInfo {
```

```
        public String getCustomerInfo(int id) {
            try {

                Class.forName("com.mysql.jdbc.Driver").newInstance();

                String dbservername = "localhost";
                String dbname = "your_db_name";
                String username = "your_user_name";
                String password = "your_password";
                String url = "jdbc:mysql://" + dbservername + "/" + dbname + "?user="
                            + username + "&password=" + password;

                Connection conn = DriverManager.getConnection(url);

                String sql = "Select * from Customers where CustomerId=" + id;
                Statement stmt = conn.createStatement();
                ResultSet rs = stmt.executeQuery(sql);
                boolean found = rs.next();

                //more code here

            } catch (Exception e){
                return "An error occurred while trying to get customer info.";
            }
        }
    }
```

Here, a `Statement` object is created using the `createStatement()` method. This object can then be used to execute the query by passing the SQL query into `executeQuery()`, which returns a `ResultSet` object. The `next()` method on a `ResultSet` object returns `false` if there are no matching records or `true` if there's at least one (in this case, there should be only one). So if `found` is `true`, that means the data is available and can be used. All that's left is to return the data formatted appropriately:

```
package wrox;
import java.sql.*;

public class CustomerInfo {

    public String getCustomerInfo(int id) {
        try {

            Class.forName("com.mysql.jdbc.Driver").newInstance();

            String dbservername = "localhost";
            String dbname = "your_db_name";
            String username = "your_user_name";
            String password = "your_password";
            String url = "jdbc:mysql://" + dbservername + "/" + dbname + "?user="
                        + username + "&password=" + password;

            Connection conn = DriverManager.getConnection(url);

            String sql = "Select * from Customers where CustomerId=" + id;
            Statement stmt = conn.createStatement();
```

```
        ResultSet rs = stmt.executeQuery(sql);
        boolean found = rs.next();

        StringBuffer message = new StringBuffer();

        if (found) {
            message.append(rs.getString("Name"));
            message.append("<br />");
            message.append(rs.getString("Address"));
            message.append("<br />");
            message.append(rs.getString("City"));
            message.append("<br />");
            message.append(rs.getString("State"));
            message.append("<br />");
            message.append(rs.getString("Zip"));
            message.append("<br /><br />");
            message.append("Phone: " + rs.getString("Phone"));
            message.append("<br /><a href=\"mailto:");
            message.append(rs.getString("Email"));
            message.append("\">");
            message.append(rs.getString("Email"));
            message.append("</a>");
        } else {
            message.append("Customer with ID ");
            message.append(id);
            message.append(" could not be found.");
        }

        rs.close();
        conn.close();

        return message.toString();
    } catch (Exception e){
        return "An error occurred while trying to get customer info.";
    }
  }
}
```

In this final section of the code, a `StringBuffer` object is created to hold the response that will be sent back to the client. If a record is found, then a block of text with HTML formatting is returned, which is done by using the `getString()` method of the `RecordSet`, passing in the name of each column. If a record is not found, an error message is built up in the `message` object. Then, the `RecordSet` and `Connection` are both closed and the message is returned by calling `toString()`.

Save this class in `CustomerInfo.java`. You'll need to compile the class and place it into the `WEB-INF/classes/wrox` directory to be accessible to DWR.

Updating dwr.xml

In order for DWR to know that you need this class on the client, some additions to `dwr.xml` are necessary. The following code must be added inside of the `<allow/>` element:

```
<create creator="new" javascript="CustomerInfo">
  <param name="class" value="wrox.CustomerInfo" />
</create>
```

After making this change, restart Tomcat to ensure that the new settings have been picked up. Now, you can go to `http://localhost/DwrExample/dwr` to verify that the `CustomerInfo` class is being handled properly. If it is, you should see it listed on the test page and be able to call `getCustomerInfo()`.

Creating the Client Page

The client page is the same as the JPSpan example, with the obvious difference being the inclusion of the DWR files:

```html
<!DOCTYPE html PUBLIC "-//W3C//DTD XHTML 1.0 Transitional//EN"
"http://www.w3.org/TR/xhtml1/DTD/xhtml1-transitional.dtd">
<html xmlns="http://www.w3.org/1999/xhtml">
<head>
    <title>JPSpan Example</title>
    <script type="text/javascript"
            src="/DwrExample/dwr/interface/CustomerInfo.js"></script>
    <script type="text/javascript"src="/DwrExample/dwr/engine.js"></script>
    <script type="text/javascript"src="DwrExample.js"></script>
</head>
<body>
    <p>Enter customer ID number to retrieve information:</p>
    <p>Customer ID: <input type="text" id="txtCustomerId" value="" /></p>
    <p><input type="button" value="Get Customer Info"
                onclick="requestCustomerInfo()" /></p>
    <div id="divCustomerInfo"></div>
</body>
</html>
```

There are three JavaScript files included in this page. The first is the JavaScript wrapper for the `CustomerInfo` class, the second is the DWR JavaScript engine, and the third is the code to tie it all together:

```javascript
function handleGetCustomerInfoResponse(sInfo) {
    displayCustomerInfo(sInfo);
}

function requestCustomerInfo() {
    var sId = document.getElementById("txtCustomerId").value;
    CustomerInfo.getCustomerInfo(parseInt(sId), handleGetCustomerInfoResponse);
}

function displayCustomerInfo(sText) {
    var divCustomerInfo = document.getElementById("divCustomerInfo");
    divCustomerInfo.innerHTML = sText;
}
```

As with the JPSpan example, you can see the advantage of using DWR for Ajax communication: the code becomes much simpler. By using only a callback function and the generated `CustomerInfo` object, all of the client-server communication is hidden from the developer.

More about dwr.xml

The dwr.xml file used in the previous example was fairly simple, including a element for the CustomerInfo object with basic settings:

```
<create creator="new" javascript="CustomerInfo">
  <param name="class" value="wrox.CustomerInfo" />
</create>
```

This code tells DWR to create a CustomerInfo object using the Java new operator and allow the client to call any of the methods on that object. Calling getCustomerInfo() from the client performs the following on the server:

```
CustomerInfo info = new CustomerInfo();
String result = info.getCustomerInfo(id);
```

For many cases, this approach is all that is needed. However, DWR provides several customization options for more complicated use cases.

Excluding Methods

Suppose that there are methods on a Java bean that should not be called by the client. This is possible when a bean is used both for client-side and server-side execution. You can exclude a method from the JavaScript wrapper by creating an <exclude/> element inside of the <create/> element. For example, the following excludes the toGMTString() method from being called on the Date class:

```
<create creator="new" javascript="JDate">
  <param name="class" value="java.util.Date"/>
  <exclude method="toGMTString"/>
</create>
```

If an attempt is made to call this method on the client, a JavaScript runtime error will occur.

The Script Creator

As mentioned previously, DWR creates beans by using the Java new operator by default. However, there are some objects that cannot be created by simply using a constructor; they may be accessible only via the methods on another class or from a call to a static getInstance() method. An example of this is the EmailValidator class from the org.apache.commons.validator package, which does not have a public constructor. In order to create an instance of EmailValidator, it's necessary to use the static method getInstance(). To provide for this, DWR allows you to create a small script section for the creation of an object.

Using BeanShell, one of the Bean Scripted Framework (BSF) languages, you can provide code to create the instance of the class. To do so, the creator attribute of the <create/> element must be set to "script". The <param/> element that previously indicated the Java class to instantiate now must specify the scripting language as BeanShell. Then, a second <param/> element is necessary, with its name attribute set to "script". Inside of this element is where the BeanShell code must import the necessary Java packages and return the object instance. For example, to create an instance of EmailValidator, use the following version of the <create> element:

```
<create creator="script" javascript="EmailValidator">
  <param name="language" value="beanshell"/>
  <param name="script">
    import org.apache.commons.validator.EmailValidator;
    return EmailValidator.getInstance();
  </param>
</create>
```

Note that there is no mention of a Java class outside of the BeanShell code. Any class of object may be created and returned through the script.

> You can read more on BeanShell at www.beanshell.org/ and see other languages supported by BSF at http://jakarta.apache.org/bsf/index.html.

The Spring Creator

The Spring framework (www.springframework.org) is designed to bring together a number of different Java technologies as well as enable practical code reuse and sophisticated management of Java beans. It is a lightweight replacement for parts of the Java 2 Enterprise Edition (J2EE), which is used to create highly scalable applications where high numbers of users are expected to use the system simultaneously. In these situations, resources such as memory need to be carefully managed. DWR provides hooks to allow usage of the Spring framework.

To access an enterprise bean from the client, you need to specify the creator attribute as "spring". Then, provide <param/> elements specifying the name of the bean and the location of the Spring configuration file, such as:

```
<create creator="spring" javascript="MyBean">
  <param name="beanName" value="MyBean"/>
  <param name="location" value="beans.xml"/>
</create>
```

It is beyond the scope of this book to discuss the full extent of the Spring framework. For more information on the Spring framework, visit www.springframework.org; for more information on the Spring integration in DWR, visit http://getahead.ltd.uk/dwr/server/spring.

The scope Attribute

The <create/> element can also accept an attribute named scope, which defines the scope in which the object should be created and stored. This value can be any one of standard Java bean scopes:

❑   request: The object is created at the time of a request and destroyed after a response has been sent. This is the default if not otherwise specified.

❑   page: For the purposes of DWR, essentially the same as request.

❑   session: The object is created and then stored and reused for all requests during the session. In this way, you can set object values and access them in later requests.

❑   application: The object is created and used by every session connecting to the web application.

If you want to use the `CustomerInfo` class across a session, for example, the syntax would be as follows:

```
<create creator="new" javascript="Customer" scope="session">
  <param name="class" value="wrox.Customer"/>
</create>
```

The `scope` attribute is particularly useful when data needs to be stored throughout the context of a session, allowing the client to set and get information off of a Java bean.

Converters

Generally speaking, DWR is very good at converting Java data types to JavaScript data types and vice versa. Strings in Java get mapped to strings to JavaScript, integers and floats in Java get mapped to number in JavaScript, and hashtables in Java get mapped to objects in JavaScript. To provide these mappings, DWR uses converters.

Converters simply convert data types between Java and JavaScript. There are a number of predefined converters that ship with DWR, such as the `DateConverter`, which works between the `java.util.Date` and the JavaScript `Date` object, the `ArrayConverter`, and the `StringConverter`. There is also the `BeanConverter`, which works between beans and JavaScript objects. This particular converter is disabled by default for security reasons. You can allow it by including a single line of code within the `<allow/>` element in `dwr.xml`:

```
<dwr>
  <allow>
    <convert converter="bean" match="your.full.package.BeanName"/>
  <!-- other allowed converters and creators -->
  </allow>
</dwr>
```

The `match` attribute specifies which bean to allow. You can allow an entire package by using an asterisk as a wildcard:

```
<convert converter="bean" match="your.full.package.*"/>
```

Also, it's possible to exclude certain properties from being converted by adding a `<param/>` element like this:

```
<convert converter="bean" match="your.full.package.BeanName">
  <param name="exclude" value="property1, property2"/>
</convert>
```

The properties and methods you want to exclude should be separated by a comma and a space. Alternatively, and more safely, you can specify which properties can be converted (all others are ignored):

```
<convert converter="bean" match="your.full.package.BeanName">
  <param name="include" value="property1, property2"/>
</convert>
```

> For more information on which converters are available and which need to be enabled before they can be used in your code, see http://getahead.ltd.uk/dwr/server/dwrxml/converters.

Summary of DWR

DWR is an excellent way to harness the power of Java for use in web applications. Joe Walker, the primary developer of DWR, constantly is updates the framework with new functionality designed to make web applications more responsive. Since DWR works with the literally hundreds of available Java packages, chances are that there's something already available that can perform the operations necessary for your application. There is also the advantage that there is no shortage of information, tutorials, and experts willing to share their knowledge about the Java platform.

Ajax.NET Professional

Ajax.NET Professional (available at www.ajaxpro.info) is an Ajax framework designed for use with the .NET framework, specifically ASP.NET. As with JPSpan and DWR, Ajax.NET allows developers to create classes on the server that can be accessed via the client. This is done by once again abstracting out the communication between client and server, providing cross-browser communication behind the scenes.

This framework uses the .NET version of reflection to inspect the classes and create a JavaScript interface. Ajax.NET Professional also takes advantage of a .NET feature called *attributes*, which are used to mark specific methods that should be available to the client. This allows developers to concentrate on the true object-oriented design without worrying about exposing sensitive methods to the client.

Using Ajax.NET Professional

To use Ajax.NET Professional, you need to be running IIS version 5 or greater and have the .NET Framework installed. Download the package of DLLs from the web site. There are two sets of DLLs, one for use with .NET 1.1 and one for .NET 2.0. If you already have an ASP.NET project (Visual Studio .NET) or a web site (Visual Studio Web Developer Express or Visual Studio 2005), you can use it with Ajax.NET Professional by referencing the appropriate DLLs. If you are using .NET 1.1, add a reference to AjaxPro.dll to your project; for .NET 2.0, add a reference to AjaxPro.2.dll. This should be done for every project/web site that needs to reference Ajax.NET Professional.

Next, open up web.config and add the following inside of the <system.web/> element:

```
<?xml version="1.0" encoding="utf-8" ?>
<configuration>
  <system.web>
    <httpHandlers>
      <add verb="POST,GET" path="ajaxpro/*.ashx"
          type="AjaxPro.AjaxHandlerFactory, AjaxPro.2"/>
    </httpHandlers>
    <!-- more code here -->
  </system.web>
</configuration>
```

These lines create a new HTTP handler for the web application. For all POST and GET requests to the server that come through the path ajaxpro and end with an extension of .ashx, the AjaxPro.AjaxHandlerFactory will be used instead of the default handler (this has no effect on other requests coming into the server).

Marking Methods

Ajax.NET Professional expects the developer to mark any methods that should be available on the client with the AjaxPro.AjaxMethod attribute. This should be placed just before the method definition in the source code. For example, consider this simple C# class:

```
namespace AjaxNET.Example {
    public class ExampleClass {

        [AjaxPro.AjaxMethod]
        public String GetMessage() {
            return "Hello world!";
        }
    }
}
```

The highlighted line is the attribute necessary for publishing the GetMessage() method for client-side use. There is one additional step necessary for generating the JavaScript wrappers.

When the page that needs to use this class is instantiated, it must indicate which classes should be available to the client. This is done by calling AjaxPro.Utility.RegisterTypeForAjax() and passing in the type of class to marshal, such as:

```
AjaxPro.Utility.RegisterTypeForAjax(typeof(AjaxNET.Example.ExampleClass));
```

This call should take place in the Page_Load method of an ASP.NET page to ensure that the class will be available when called and also includes all of the necessary JavaScript resources.

> **Make sure you have at least one** < form runat=" server" > **element in your page, as Ajax.NET Professional uses this to insert the JavaScript files.**

Using the JavaScript Wrappers

The JavaScript wrappers generated for .NET classes function similarly to those created by DWR; each method of an object becomes a static method of a corresponding JavaScript. Arguments are passed in as if it was a normal JavaScript function, and the last argument is a callback function to handle the server response.

Callback functions in Ajax.NET Professional receive a response object as their only argument. This object contains three properties: error, which is set to true if there was a communication error; request, which contains the XMLHttp object used to make the request; and value, which is the return value of the method call. For example, the GetMessage() method in the previous example can be called like this:

```
function handleResponse(oResponse) {
    if (!oResponse.error) {
        alert(oResponse.value);
    }
}
AjaxNET.Example.ExampleClass.GetMessage(handleResponse);
```

In most cases, it will be necessary to look only at the response object's `error` and `value` properties, as in this example. This creates an asynchronous request to the server, ultimately executing the appropriate method. However, Ajax.NET Professional also offers the ability to make a call synchronously.

To create a synchronous call to the server, you need only omit the callback function when calling the method. If the last argument isn't a function, Ajax.NET Professional assumes that the call should be made synchronously and instead of using a callback function it returns the response object as the function value:

```
var oResponse = AjaxNET.Example.ExampleClass.GetMessage();
if (!oResponse.error) {
    alert(oResponse.value);
}
```

The response object returned from a synchronous call is the exact same object that would have been returned from an asynchronous call. Once again, it's best to check for errors before using the value that was returned.

> As mentioned throughout the book, synchronous calls should be used sparingly if at all. Every synchronous requests locks the user interface while waiting for a response, so it could drastically effect the experience of users should a call take longer than usual to return.

Type Conversion

By default, Ajax.NET Professional handles the seamless conversion of JavaScript data types and objects to .NET and back. Additionally, there is some built-in support for common .NET complex types, such as an ADO.NET `DataSet`. Ajax.NET Professional creates appropriate JavaScript object definitions. When it provides such an interface, the same properties and methods are available on the client as there on the server, the only difference being that it is completely read-only.

It's also possible to return a custom class to JavaScript. To do so, it must be marked with the `Serializable` attribute so that Ajax.NET Professional can convert it into a JSON format. For example, consider a class that represents a web site user:

```
[Serializable()]
public class User
{
    private string _userName = "";
    private string _userEmail = "";

    public string UserName
```

```
    {
      get
      {
        return _userName;
      }
    }

    public string UserEmail
    {
      get
      {
        return _userEmail;
      }
    }
    public User(string Name, string Email)
    {
      _userName = Name;
      _userEmail = Email;
    }
}
```

Assuming that a `User` object was returned by a method named `GetUserFromId()`, the properties would be available in JavaScript, such as:

```
MyClass.GetUserFromId(6, callback);

function callback(oResponse)
{
  var oUser = oResponse.value;
  alert(oUser.UserName + "\n" + oUser.UserEmail);
}
```

Session Access

`Ajax.NET` Professional can also allow access to objects in the session scope. This is accomplished by passing a parameter to the `AjaxPro.AjaxMethod()` attribute specifying the level of access that is needed. The access level is specified by an enumeration called `HttpSessionStateRequirement`, which has three values: `Read`, `Write`, and `ReadWrite`. This type of access is established like this:

```
[AjaxPro.AjaxMethod(HttpSessionStateRequirement.Read)]
public string MyMethod()
{
    //code here
}
```

This code specifies that `MyMethod()` should have read access to variables that are in the session scope when called from the client. Without specifying this argument to the `AjaxPro.AjaxMethod()` attribute, the method would be unable to access `HttpContext.Current.Session` when called using JavaScript.

> When specifying access to session-level variables, it's best to go with the lowest permission level necessary to complete the task. For instance, don't specify `ReadWrite` if you only need `Read`.

Ajax.NET Professional Example

Once again, this example focuses on retrieving customer information from the server. However, since .NET applications typically use SQL Server, this example assumes that the same `Customers` table used in the previous examples exists in a SQL Server database.

> *A SQL script for creating the Customers table in SQL Server is included in the code example download at* www.wrox.com.

This example requires a web site (.NET 2.0); you can either create a new web site or add on to an existing one. Either way, your first step is to modify the `web.config` file as specified earlier in this section. The next step after that is to begin coding the `CustomerInfo` class.

The CustomerInfo Class

The `CustomerInfo` class in .NET is very similar to the one used for DWR and Java. The basic makeup of the class is once again an object with a single method called `GetCustomerInfo()` that accepts an integer ID and returns a string of HTML formatted code:

```
using System.Data.SqlClient;

namespace Wrox {

    public class CustomerInfo {

        [AjaxPro.AjaxMethod()]
        public string GetCustomerInfo(int id) {
            //more code here
        }

    }
}
```

This class must include the `System.Data.SqlClient` namespace, which contains the objects necessary for connecting to a database. Before initiating a database connection, however, several variables must be defined containing information about the database to connect to:

```
using System.Data.SqlClient;

namespace Wrox {

    public class CustomerInfo {

        [AjaxPro.AjaxMethod()]
        public string GetCustomerInfo(int id) {

            string info = "";
            string dataSourceName = @"localhost\SQLEXPRESS";
            string catalogName = "ProAjax";
            string connectString = String.Format(
                "Data Source={0};Integrated Security=SSPI;Initial Catalog={1}",
                dataSourceName, catalogName);
```

```
        string query = String.Format(
                "Select * from Customers where CustomerId={0}", id);

        SqlConnection conn = null;
        SqlCommand command = null;

        //more code here

        return info;
    }

  }

}
```

The very first variable defined, info, is the string that holds either the customer information string or an error message to return to the client. The next few string variables define the information necessary for connecting to a SQL Server. These variables have default values here that assume you have a version of SQL Server Express running on the same server as IIS; these settings should be changed to appropriate values for your server configuration. The last two variables are conn, which is a database connection, and command, which is the method by which SQL commands are executed. Next, the database connection must be created, and the query must be run:

```
using System.Data.SqlClient;

namespace Wrox {

    public class CustomerInfo {

        [AjaxPro.AjaxMethod()]
        public string GetCustomerInfo(int id) {

            string info = "";
            string dataSourceName = @"localhost\SQLEXPRESS";
            string catalogName = "ProAjax";
            string connectString = String.Format(
                    "Data Source={0};Integrated Security=SSPI;Initial Catalog={1}",
                    dataSourceName, catalogName);
            string query = String.Format(
                    "Select * from Customers where CustomerId={0}", id);

            SqlConnection conn = null;
            SqlCommand command = null;

            try
            {
                conn = new SqlConnection(connectString);
                command = new SqlCommand(query, conn);

                conn.Open();
                SqlDataReader reader = command.ExecuteReader();

            //more code here
```

```
                    conn.Close();
                }
                catch (Exception ex)
                {
                    info = "Error occurred while trying to connect to database: "
                            + ex.Message;
                }

            return info;
        }

    }
}
```

As it is with Java, it's important to wrap database operations inside of a `try...catch` block because there are numerous places where an error may occur. The first new step here is to create an instance of `SqlConnection` by passing in the previously defined connection string. Then, a new `SqlCommand` object is created by using `query` and the newly created connection; this is the interface by which the query can be executed. With the objects defined, it's time to open the connection using the `Open()` method. Now the query can be run by using the `command` variable, and more specifically, the `ExecuteReader()` method, which creates and returns a `SqlDataReader` object. If an error occurs at any time during this code, it is caught and the `info` variable is filled with an error message returned to the client.

The last step is to add in the code that reads from the database and formats an HTML string:

```
using System.Data.SqlClient;

namespace Wrox {

    public class CustomerInfo {

        [AjaxPro.AjaxMethod()]
        public string GetCustomerInfo(int id) {

            string info = "";
            string dataSourceName = @"localhost\SQLEXPRESS";
            string catalogName = "ProAjax";
            string connectString = String.Format(
                    "Data Source={0};Integrated Security=SSPI;Initial Catalog={1}",
                    dataSourceName, catalogName);
            string query = String.Format(
                    "Select * from Customers where CustomerId={0}", id);

            SqlConnection conn = null;
            SqlCommand command = null;

            try
            {
                conn = new SqlConnection(connectString);
                command = new SqlCommand(query, conn);

                conn.Open();
                SqlDataReader reader = command.ExecuteReader();
```

```
                    if (reader.HasRows)
                    {
                        reader.Read();
                        info = String.Format("{0}<br />{1}<br />{2}<br />{3}<br
/>{4}<br /><br />Phone: {5}<br /><a href=\"mailto:{6}\">{6}</a>",
                            reader.GetString(reader.GetOrdinal("Name")),
                            reader.GetString(reader.GetOrdinal("Address")),
                            reader.GetString(reader.GetOrdinal("City")),
                            reader.GetString(reader.GetOrdinal("State")),
                            reader.GetString(reader.GetOrdinal("Zip")),
                            reader.GetString(reader.GetOrdinal("Phone")),
                            reader.GetString(reader.GetOrdinal("Email"))
                        );
                    }
                    else
                    {
                        info = String.Format("Customer with ID {0} doesn't exist.",
                                        id);
                    }
```

```
                conn.Close();
            }
            catch (Exception ex)
            {
                info = "Error occurred while trying to connect to database: "
                        + ex.Message;
            }

            return info;
        }

    }
}
```

After the query has been executed, calling reader.hasRows() determines if there are any results. If so, then reader.Read() moves the reader to the first (and in this case, only) matching row. Then, the string is constructed getting using String.Format() to insert information into the correct location. If, on the other hand, there is no matching row, info gets filled with a message indicating that the customer doesn't exist. Then you're ready to move to the next step, creating the client page.

> **If you are using .NET 2.0, this class file should be contained within the special** App_Code **directory of the web site.**

Creating the Client Page

The client page is a new ASPX file with a codebehind file. This example assumes C# as the server-side language, but it's also possible to create the same functionality using any other .NET language. The ASPX file is fairly simple:

```
<%@ Page Language="C#" AutoEventWireup="true" CodeFile="AjaxNETExample.aspx.cs"
    Inherits="AjaxNETExample" %>
<!DOCTYPE html PUBLIC "-//W3C//DTD XHTML 1.0 Transitional//EN"
"http://www.w3.org/TR/xhtml1/DTD/xhtml1-transitional.dtd">
<html xmlns="http://www.w3.org/1999/xhtml">
<head>
    <title>Ajax.NET Professional Example</title>
    <script type="text/javascript"src="AjaxNETExample.js"></script>
</head>
<body>
    <form runat="server"></form>
    <p>Enter customer ID number to retrieve information:</p>
    <p>Customer ID: <input type="text" id="txtCustomerId" value="" /></p>
    <p><input type="button" value="Get Customer Info"
               onclick="requestCustomerInfo()" /></p>
    <div id="divCustomerInfo"></div>
</body>
</html>
```

The highlighted lines of code in this example are the only changes from the previous iteration of this example. The codebehind file has most of the important code:

```csharp
using System;
using System.Data;
using System.Configuration;
using System.Collections;
using System.Web;
using System.Web.Security;
using System.Web.UI;
using System.Web.UI.WebControls;
using System.Web.UI.WebControls.WebParts;
using System.Web.UI.HtmlControls;

public partial class AjaxNETExample : System.Web.UI.Page
{
    protected void Page_Load(object sender, EventArgs e)
    {
        AjaxPro.Utility.RegisterTypeForAjax(typeof(Wrox.CustomerInfo), this);
    }
}
```

The most important line in the codebehind is the call to `AjaxPro.Utility.RegisterTypeForAjax()`, which signals that JavaScript wrappers should be created for the `Wrox.CustomerInfo` class. That's all that is necessary to generate the client-side code. To use the generated JavaScript wrappers, the front end code looks very similar to that of the DWR example:

```javascript
function handleGetCustomerInfoResponse(oResponse) {
    if (!oResponse.error) {
        displayCustomerInfo(oResponse.value);
    } else {
        alert("An error occurred.");
    }
}
```

```
function requestCustomerInfo() {
    var sId = document.getElementById("txtCustomerId").value;
    Wrox.CustomerInfo.GetCustomerInfo(parseInt(sId),
        handleGetCustomerInfoResponse);
}

function displayCustomerInfo(sText) {
    var divCustomerInfo = document.getElementById("divCustomerInfo");
    divCustomerInfo.innerHTML = sText;
}
```

And that's all it takes to recreate this example using Ajax.NET Professional. Note that the `GetCustomerInfo()` method is specified in .NET-style Pascal case. This is something to be careful of when using C# objects in JavaScript. Also note that the full namespace of the class is used on the client side (`Wrox.CustomerInfo` instead of just `CustomerInfo`).

Summary of Ajax.NET Professional

If you are using ASP.NET to run a web site or web application, Ajax.NET Professional provides very powerful remote scripting capabilities with very little setup. The author, Michael Schwarz, seems to have taken into account most of the needs of Ajax applications in creating this framework. The data type conversion for Ajax.NET Professional is very strong, and it can handle almost any type of custom class, not to mention enumerations. As far as downsides go, Ajax.NET Professional is lacking in documentation, so it can be a bit challenging to work through its quirks in the beginning. There is, however, an active e-mail support list available at `http://groups.google.com/group/ajaxpro`. Also, Ajax.NET Professional has been tested only on Internet Explorer and Firefox, so developers looking for Safari or Opera support may have to do a bit of testing on their own.

Summary

This chapter introduced you to the concept of Ajax frameworks. Where Ajax libraries are primarily client-side objects designed to ease Ajax communication, frameworks provide support for both the client and server sides of Ajax communication. The libraries covered in this chapter all provide developers with an automated way of creating JavaScript wrappers for corresponding server objects. These wrappers include cross-browser Ajax communication that is completely abstracted away from the developer's view.

Next, you were introduced to open source Ajax frameworks for each of the three major web application servers. The first framework covered was JPSpan, an Ajax framework for PHP. Next, Direct Web Remoting (DWR) was introduced as an Ajax framework for JSP. Last, Ajax.NET Professional was discussed as an Ajax framework for ASP.NET.

The same example was used for each of these frameworks so that you could see the similarities and differences among the three. Each framework uses reflection to inspect server-side objects and create appropriate JavaScript wrappers for those objects. As with most open source projects, these frameworks may very well change in the future or be discontinued, so choose your framework carefully.

14

ASP.NET AJAX
Extensions (Atlas)

As Microsoft readied the release of .NET 2.0, the software giant announced that it had begun work on project known as "Atlas," an Ajax framework built to interface seamlessly with ASP.NET 2.0. Microsoft's original goal for Atlas was ambitious: a cross-browser framework for building Ajax-enabled applications with rich UI and connectivity to web services and/or an ASP.NET 2.0 application. Over one year later, Microsoft came close to the mark with the newly renamed ASP.NET AJAX Extensions (note that the official name of the framework has the word "AJAX" in all capital letters, as opposed to the way it is used throughout this book).

While ASP.NET AJAX Extensions contains "ASP.NET" in its name and is released to work with ASP.NET, the framework contains tools that any JavaScript developer can use. The core libraries and the Community Technology Preview (CTP) releases contain a variety of JavaScript functionality, such as an Ajax library, namespace and interface constructs, and classes that wrap DOM elements (Microsoft calls these "controls"), providing a development environment similar to what Windows developers are accustomed to.

But don't assume that ASP.NET AJAX Extensions are strictly client side. The framework contains a variety of new .NET classes and server controls, providing developers with a simple, and seamless, interface for developing Ajax-enabled applications.

Whether you're an ASP.NET developer or someone looking for a set of tools to aid your Ajax development, ASP.NET AJAX Extensions could be for you.

> Note that the December 2006 CTP of ASP.NET AJAX Extensions RC 1 is used for examples in this chapter. Make sure to check the current release when you try to make use of it in your own code.

Requirements and Setup

In order to run the ASP.NET AJAX Extensions, you must be running Windows 2000 or later and have the .NET Framework 2.0 installed (which is freely available at `http://msdn2.microsoft.com/en-us/netframework/`) on any machine used to develop or run an application using this framework.

Although not necessary, you should consider installing a version of Visual Studio 2005 before installing the AJAX Extensions. Microsoft provides a wide array of Visual Studio versions, including the free Microsoft Visual Web Developer 2005 Express Edition (`http://msdn.microsoft.com/vstudio/express/vwd/`). When installed, the AJAX Extensions, as well as the CTP, install files for Visual Studio, adding new project types that aid in the rapid development of Ajax applications. Although a version of Visual Studio is not required, this chapter assumes that Microsoft Visual Web Developer 2005 Express Edition (called Visual Studio for short) is installed.

Next, you'll need to download the AJAX Extensions. Before Atlas was renamed ASP.NET AJAX, Microsoft released the package as a single CTP every few months. When the framework entered beta, Microsoft changed the distribution format. ASP.NET AJAX Extensions now consists of two downloads:

❑ **ASP.NET AJAX 1.0** provides the core ASP.NET AJAX Extensions for client- and server-side development. The components in this download are feature complete.

❑ **ASP.NET 2.0 AJAX Futures CTP** contains features that extend the core framework with additional functionality. The components in this download continue to be in development.

The second package is optional; however, it is recommended to download it in order to take advantage of extra features. Both packages can be found at `http://ajax.asp.net`. Make sure to install ASP.NET AJAX 1.0 before the Futures CTP.

The AJAX Client Library

While the server components of the AJAX Extensions are limited to use with ASP.NET, a good portion of the client components can be used with any web site regardless of the application server. With this having been said, ASP.NET developers have easier access to the client tools via Visual Studio.

Accessing the Client Tools with ASP.NET

Ironically, the simplest way to access the client tools with ASP.NET is to use the new server controls that come with the Extensions. To begin, you'll need an Ajax-enabled ASP.NET web site.

Open Visual Web Dev, and pull up the New Web Site dialog (see Figure 14-1) by going to the File menu and choosing New Web Site.

The AJAX Extensions CTP installs two new templates: ASP.NET AJAX-Enabled Web Site and ASP.NET AJAX CTP-Enabled Web Site; choose the second option and press OK. When Visual Studio creates and opens the project, the source code for the `Default.aspx` file is opened. It consists of the `Page` declaration at the top of the file, followed by the HTML's doctype, head, and body.

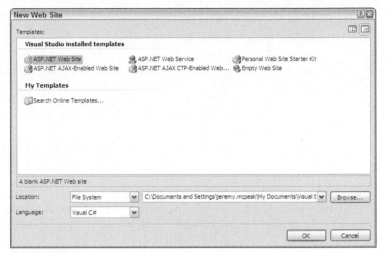

Figure 14-1

Inside the page's body is a server control:

```
<asp:ScriptManager ID="ScriptManager1" runat="server" />
```

The `ScriptManager` control manages the JavaScript components, partial-page rendering, and HTTP requests/responses for ASP.NET Ajax pages. In short, this control adds the core JavaScript files to the web page. This enables the use of components like the `WebRequest` class and the namespace constructs. It doesn't, however, add the JavaScript files from the CTP. For this, add a `ScriptReference` control.

```
<asp:ScriptManager ID="ScriptManager1" runat="server">
    <Scripts>
        <asp:ScriptReference Assembly="Microsoft.Web.Preview"
            Name="PreviewScript.js" />
    </Scripts>
</asp:ScriptManager>
```

The `ScriptReference` control registers a JavaScript file for use within the web page. This control can register a standalone JavaScript file or a script file that is embedded within an assembly. This example registers the `PreviewScript.js` file within the `Microsoft.Web.Preview` assembly, which contains UI controls (wrappers for DOM elements), among other components, and DOM extensions for Gecko-based browsers.

By use of the `ScriptManager` and `ScriptReference` server controls, the appropriate JavaScript files are added to the web page when the server processes this page. Of course, using these controls isn't the only way to add ASP.NET AJAX JavaScript files to the page.

Accessing the Client Tools without ASP.NET

When the Extensions are installed, it places the .NET binaries and the JavaScript files onto your hard drive at `%Program Files%\Microsoft ASP.NET\ASP.NET 2.0 AJAX Extensions\v1.0.61025` (your version number may be different). In the `ScriptLibrary` directory, you'll find the `Debug` and `Release` subdirectories containing JavaScript files. The `Debug` folder contains the original JavaScript files, while the scripts in the `Release` folder have had all white space removed.

These JavaScript files can be copied to other locations and referenced with a normal `<script/>` tag. The two files used in this section are `MicrosoftAjax.js` and `PreviewScript.js`.

You can use either the debug or release versions of the code for development purposes; however, the release files are smaller.

Using Classes

Before digging into the classes available, it is important to know how they are written. Like any other class, the ones included with the AJAX Library have constructors and methods. The real difference, however, comes with what are called *properties*. In traditional JavaScript, a property is a construct that gets or sets class data.

```
//Traditional property usage
element.style.top = "10px"; //Use the top property to set the top position
alert(element.style.top);   //Display the element's top position.
```

Properties in ASP.NET AJAX classes are actually methods, prefixed with either `get_` (to get the value of a property) or `set_` (to set the value of a property), that provide access to JavaScript properties within the class. Therefore, "properties" are accessed like this:

```
object.set_propertyName(newValue);
var value = object.get_propertyName();
```

Keep this in mind when using classes of the ASP.NET AJAX library, because they follow this pattern.

Writing Code with the ASP.NET AJAX Library

The ASP.NET AJAX library extends JavaScript with object-oriented programming constructs, such as namespaces, enumerations, and interfaces, as well as extending existing constructs such as classes and subclasses. Microsoft does this by introducing a new datatyping system much like the one that exists within the .NET Framework Class Library.

At the heart of this new typing system is the `Type` class, which exposes a number of static methods to aid in the creation of datatypes.

Registering Namespaces

JavaScript technically does not have a namespace construct. However, developers have emulated namespaces by using objects. Consider the following code:

```
//create the ProAjax namespace
var ProAjax = {
    //create the Ch12 namespace
    Ch12    : {
        //create the Person class
```

```
        Person   : function () {
            //constructor logic
        }
    }
}
```

This code creates an object called `ProAjax`, where another object, `Ch12`, is defined within it. This essentially emulates two levels of a namespace. Inside `Ch12` is the `Person` class; so to access this class, you must go through the two levels:

```
var oPerson = new ProAjax.Ch12.Person();
```

This works fine. However, it lacks any sense of a type: `ProAjax` and `ProAjax.Ch12` are both considered objects, not namespaces.

Microsoft addresses this issue by creating its own namespace construct. Of course, these namespaces are just JavaScript objects, but the AJAX Extensions expose methods that allow the marking of an object as a namespace and the testing of an object to determine if it is a namespace.

To create a namespace, use the `Type.registerNamespace()` method:

```
Type.registerNamespace("ProAjax");
```

This code creates the `ProAjax` namespace. Once a namespace is created, another namespace, a class, an interface, or an enumeration can be declared to reside in that namespace. To recreate the namespace made in the previous example, the following code can be used:

```
Type.registerNamespace("ProAjax.Ch12");
```

This code actually does two things. First, it extracts "`ProAjax`" and tests to see if a namespace already exists with that name. If not, it creates the `ProAjax` namespace. Then, it goes on to perform the same process on "`Ch12`"; it creates the namespace only if it doesn't already exist.

To determine if an object is a namespace, use the `Type.isNamespace()` method like this:

```
Type.isNamespace(ProAjax.Ch12); //returns true
```

This method returns `true` if the object is a namespace, and `false` if not.

Registering Classes

Classes are another concept that JavaScript does not technically support. It does, however, provide the logical equivalent: constructors and the ability to create objects with these constructors. JavaScript also provides developers with the means to check if objects are an instance of a certain class, with the `instanceof` operator (which also allows you to check for inheritance relationships). But generally, JavaScript sees classes as functions, not proper class definitions.

Microsoft addresses these issues by emulating classes. Registering a class consists of three steps:

1. Create the class as you normally would. If the class is to be in a namespace, declare the class within the namespace.

2. Initialize the class with the `initializeBase()` method if you plan on using inheritance.

3. Register the class with the `registerClass()` method.

To declare a class called `ProAjax.Ch12.Person`, the following code is used:

```
ProAjax.Ch12.Person = function() {
    //more code here
};
```

This creates the `Person` class within the `ProAjax.Ch12` namespace. Next, initialize the class for inheritance:

```
ProAjax.Ch12.Person = function() {
    ProAjax.Ch12.Person.initializeBase(this);
};
```

```
//more code here
```

The `initializeBase()` method initializes the base class and its members within the context of a given instance. This method accepts two arguments, in fact, the same two arguments used with the `Function.apply()` method. The first is the object to initialize, and the second is an array of arguments to pass to the base constructor (which may be `null`).

The final step in this process is to register the class.

```
ProAjax.Ch12.Person = function() {
    ProAjax.Ch12.Person.initializeBase(this);
};
```

```
ProAjax.Ch12.Person.registerClass("ProAjax.Ch12.Person");
```

The `registerClass()` method is invoked directly from the class, as demonstrated in this code. This method accepts multiple arguments. The first argument is required and is a string representing the fully qualified name of the class. The second argument is an optional base class to inherit from. Any argument passed after the second is considered an interface that the class implements.

Deriving a class from another class follows the same pattern. First create the class, then initialize it with `initializeBase()`, and register the class. However, the call to `registerClass()` must include the superclass to inherit from. For example, if a class `ProAjax.Ch12.Author` is to extend `ProAjax.Ch12.Person`, the following code is used:

```
ProAjax.Ch12.Person = function() {
    ProAjax.Ch12.Person.initializeBase(this);
};
```

```
ProAjax.Ch12.Person.registerClass("ProAjax.Ch12.Person");
```

```
ProAjax.Ch12.Author = function() {
    ProAjax.Ch12.Author.initializeBase(this);
};

ProAjax.Ch12.Author.registerClass("ProAjax.Ch12.Author", ProAjax.Ch12.Person);
```

This code ensures that the `ProAjax.Ch12.Author` class inherits all properties and methods of `ProAjax.Ch12.Person`.

In the event you need to determine if a specific type or function is a class, simply use the `Type.isClass()` method:

```
Type.isClass(ProAjax.Ch12.Person);   //returns true
```

It's also possible to determine if one class inherits from another by using the `inheritsFrom()` method. This method is called directly from the subclass, such as:

```
ProAjax.Ch12.Author.inheritsFrom(ProAjax.Ch12.Person); //returns true
```

There are also two methods to deal directly with the type of class, `getType()` and `getTypeName()`. The `getType()` method returns the constructor used to create a particular object, whereas `getTypeName()` returns the fully qualified class name of the object (including the namespace). For example:

```
var oAuthor = new ProAjax.Ch12.Author();
var fnConstructor = Object.getType(oAuthor);

var bInherits = fnConstructor.inheritsFrom(ProAjax.Ch12.Person); //returns true
alert(Object.getTypeName(oAuthor)); //alerts "ProAjax.Ch12.Author"
```

Registering Enumerations

ASP.NET AJAX also allows the registration of enumeration (enum) types, because they are a concept not formally supported in JavaScript.

The registration of enums is a multistep process as well:

1. Create the type.
2. Add the name-value pairs to the `prototype`..
3. Register the type as an enum.

Creating an enum type is essentially the same as creating a class, except that the constructor is empty. To create an enum called `ProAjax.Ch12.Color`, the first step is to define the constructor:

```
ProAjax.Ch12.Color = function() {};
```

This code creates the `Color` type. This will become an enum with `red`, `green`, and `blue` as its named constants:

```
ProAjax.Ch12.Color = function() {};
ProAjax.Ch12.Color.prototype = {
    red   : 0xFF0000,
    blue  : 0x0000FF,
    green: 0x00FF00
};
//more code here
```

The last step is to register the type as an enum using the `registerEnum()` method:

```
ProAjax.Ch12.Color = function() {};
ProAjax.Ch12.Color.prototype = {
    red   : 0xFF0000,
    blue  : 0x0000FF,
    green: 0x00FF00
};
```

```
ProAjax.Ch12.Color.registerEnum("ProAjax.Ch12.Color");
```

The `registerEnum()` method is called directly from the constructor. Like the previous registration methods, `registerEnum()` accepts a string argument that contains the fully qualified name of the enum. There is an optional second argument, a Boolean value, which indicates if the enum is a bit field (a field containing only binary values).

Registering Interfaces

An *interface*, in object-oriented programming, is a contract for a class. Traditional interfaces define a set of methods and properties that a class must implement. A class that implements an interface must implement all of the properties and methods of that interface.

Interface definitions using the AJAX Extensions closely resemble class and enum definitions:

```
//IAuthor interface
ProAjax.Ch12.IAuthor = function() {
    //more code here
};

ProAjax.Ch12.IAuthor.prototype = {
    get_books : function () {
        //more code here
    }
};

//more code here
```

In traditional JavaScript, this code creates a class called `IAuthor` and assigns the class' `prototype` to contain a method called `get_books()`. To make this an AJAX Extensions interface, you must make a few changes.

1. First, the constructor must throw an error, since interfaces cannot be instantiated.

2. Then, since interface methods don't contain the implementation details, each method must also throw an error.

3. The last step is to call `registerInterface()`:

```
ProAjax.Ch12.IAuthor = function() {
    throw Error.notImplemented();
};

ProAjax.Ch12.IAuthor.prototype = {
    get_books : function () {
        var sTypeName = Object.getTypeName(this);
        throw Error.notImplemented(sTypeName + " does not " +
            "fully implement this interface.");
    }
};
```

```
ProAjax.Ch12.IAuthor.registerInterface("ProAjax.Ch12.IAuthor");
```

The `Error.notImplemented()` method creates an Error object that is thrown to stop code execution. When a class implements this interface but does not implement the `get_books()` method, an error is thrown when the method is called. This error states that the class (retrieved via `Object.getTypeName()`) does not fully implement the interface. The last line calls `registerInterface()` on the interface constructor and passes in the fully qualified name of the interface.

Interfaces are applied to a class when the class is registered via the `registerClass()` method. The following code changes the previous registration of the `Author` class to implement the `ProAjax.Ch12.IAuthor` interface:

```
ProAjax.Ch12.Author = function() {
    ProAjax.Ch12.Author.initializeBase(this);
};
```

```
ProAjax.Ch12.Author.prototype = {
    get_books    : function () {
        alert("We're in get_books()!");
    }
};
```

```
ProAjax.Ch12.Author.registerClass("ProAjax.Ch12.Author", ProAjax.Ch12.Person,
    ProAjax.Ch12.IAuthor);
```

Since `Author` now implements the `IAuthor` interface, it must implement all of the properties and methods of `IAuthor`. This new code defines the `Author`'s prototype, which contains the `get_books()` method (the only method defined on `IAuthor`). There is no limit to the amount of interfaces a class can inherit from; simply pass the extra interfaces to the `registerClass()` method.

There may be times when it's necessary to determine if a particular object or class implements an interface. To do this, use the `implementsInterface()` method on the class in question:

```
var author = new ProAjax.Ch12.Author();

if (ProAjax.Ch12.Author.implementsInterface(ProAjax.Ch12.IAuthor)) {
    //It's safe to execute the following line
    author.get_books();
}
```

In this code, the `ProAjax.Ch12.Author` class is checked to see if it implements `ProAjax.Ch12.IAuthor`. If so, it is then safe to assume that an object of type `ProAjax.Ch12.Author` has the method `get_books()`. Though this is helpful, it's much more useful to check a specific object before it's used. To do so, pass the object in question to `Object.getType()` and then call `implementsInterface()` on the result (which is the class constructor):

```
var author = new ProAjax.Ch12.Author();

if (Object.getType(author).implementsInterface(ProAjax.Ch12.IAuthor)) {
    //It's safe to execute the following line
    author.get_books();
}
```

Here, the class constructor of author is returned and checked to see if it implements the specified interface. If the result is `true`, then it is safe to call `get_books()`. An alternate approach is to use the `isImplementedBy()` method that is present on the interface itself. This method accepts a single argument, which is the object to check. So, this example can be rewritten as:

```
var author = new ProAjax.Ch12.Author();

if (ProAjax.Ch12.IAuthor.isImplementedBy(author)) {
    //It's safe to execute the following line
    author.get_books();
}
```

All of these approaches are valid; use whichever approach fits your situation.

> **It's been debated whether or not JavaScript needs interfaces. The main argument against interfaces is that it's easy enough to discover if a particular object implements some method or property with the `typeof` operator. With that said, ASP.NET AJAX brings the functionality to JavaScript, so it's up to developers whether or not to use the feature.**

Using Controls

In Windows development terminology, *controls* are UI elements that the user interacts with; text boxes, images, drop-down boxes, and menus are all examples of controls. The more basic controls are mostly used in forms, allowing the user to input data and labeling form fields so that the user knows where to input data. The controls present in ASP.NET AJAX are similar in these aspects, because they are essentially wrappers for common HTML elements and offer alternate ways of accessing data (as opposed to DOM properties and methods).

The controls discussed in this section are not yet a part of the core library; they are features of the Futures CTP. All of the controls reside in the `PreviewScript.js` file and in the `Sys.Preview.UI` namespace. Each control constructor accepts an `HTMLElement` as an argument. Once an element is associated with the control, that association cannot be changed. To retrieve the `HTMLElement`, you can either use the `document.getElementById()` method or the AJAX Extensions-provided `$get()` function, which behaves in the same manner.

The TextBox Control

The `Sys.Preview.UI.TextBox` control corresponds directly to `<input/>` elements whose `type` attribute is set to `"text"` and `<textarea/>` elements. The constructor accepts either an `HTMLInputElement` or an `HTMLTextAreaElement` as an argument. To begin, assume that the following `<input/>` element is in the document's body.

```
<input id="inputUsername" type="text" />
```

Because the creation of this control depends upon the `HTMLInputElement`, the following code must execute after the element is loaded into the document (during the `window`'s `load` event, for example):

```
var oUsername = new Sys.Preview.UI.TextBox($get("inputUsername"));
```

This code creates a `TextBox` control by calling the `Sys.Preview.UI.Textbox` constructor and supplying it an element with the `id` of "inputUsername".

The `TextBox` control exposes one property: `text`, which can get and set the value in the text box:

```
oUsername.set_text("Enter Your Username."); //set the text

var sUsername = oUsername.get_text(); //gets the text in the TextBox
```

Using the `TextBox` control can be beneficial when you are dealing with forms. Once the control is created, retrieving the box's value is as simple as calling `get_text()` (and setting it is it just as easy). Of course, some state that the `get_text()` and `set_text()` methods are not necessary, as once you've found the element in the DOM, using the `value` property to get and set the text box's value is actually easier (and involves less typing) than using the `TextBox` properties. However, if you're using other controls, using the `TextBox` control keeps your code unified, as opposed to a mix of controls and DOM scripting. Ultimately, it boils down to personal preference.

The Button Control

The `Sys.Preview.UI.Button` control is used for elements that can exhibit button-like behavior; in other words, anything that can receive a `click` event can most likely be a `Button`. This is in stark contrast to the `TextBox` control, where only two types of elements can be used. For instance, a Button can be a simple `<div/>` element, such as:

```
<div id="divButton">A DIV Button</div>
```

To create a `Button` control using this `<div/>` element, use the `Sys.Preview.UI.Button` constructor and pass in a reference to the element:

```
var oDivButton = new Sys.Preview.UI.Button($get("divButton"));
```

This code retrieves the `<div/>` element and passes it to the `Button` constructor. The next step is to initialize the control by calling `initialize()` (a step that wasn't necessary with the `Textbox` control). This must be done before event handlers can be added to the control:

```
var oDivButton = new Sys.Preview.UI.Button($get("divButton"));

oDivButton.initialize();
```

The final step is to add event handlers to the `Button`. This control exposes only one event: `click`. To add event handlers for the `click` event, use the `add_click()` method:

```
var oDivButton = new Sys.Preview.UI.Button($get("divButton"));

oDivButton.initialize();

function divButton_click(oButton, oEventArgs) {
    alert("You clicked a <div/> button!");
}

oDivButton.add_click(divButton_click);
```

The `add_click()` method emulates the behavior of the `attachEvent()` method in IE and the `addEventListener()` method in standards-based browsers; any number of handlers can be added to handle the `click` event.

Event handlers in the ASP.NET AJAX Library have two arguments passed to them. The first is the object that raised the event; the second is any event arguments that may be passed to event handler. In this case, the `Button` control is passed as the first argument, and an empty object is passed in the second.

To remove a `click` event handler, use the `remove_click()` method and pass in the same function pointer that was used with `add_click()`:

```
oDivButton.remove_click(divButton_click);
```

Unlike the `TextBox` control, the `Button` control is a bit more diverse in its usage, since anything that can receive a `click` event can be a button, and the fact that the ASP.NET AJAX Library handles event handling in its own cross-browser way saves time when building applications for multiple browsers.

The Selector Control

The `Sys.Preview.UI.Selector` control is a wrapper for the `<select/>` element, such as:

```
<select id="selectBooks">
    <option value="9780470109496">Professional Ajax</option>
    <option value="0764579088">Professional JavaScript for Web Developers</option>
    <option value="0470051515">Beginning JavaScript, 3rd Ed</option>
</select>
```

There are three options in this drop-down box. The words displayed in the options are titles of books, and their values are the corresponding ISBN numbers.

To create a `Selector` control using this element, pass it to the `Sys.Preview.UI.Selector` constructor and then call the `initialize()` method:

```
var oSelectBooks = new Sys.Preview.UI.Selector($get("selectBooks"));

oSelectBooks.initialize();
```

Now that the control has been initialized, you are free to use the control's properties and assign event handlers. The most common event to handle is the `selectionChanged` event. To add a handler for this event, use the `add_selectionChanged()` method:

```
var oSelectBooks = new Sys.Preview.UI.Selector($get("selectBooks"));

oSelectBooks.initialize();

function selectBooks_selectionChanged(oSelect, oEventArgs) {
    //more code here
}

oSelectBooks.add_selectionChanged(selectBooks_selectionChanged);
```

This code creates the `selectBooks_selectionChanged()` function to handle the `selectionChanged` event. The event handler accepts two arguments: the `Selector` control and an event arguments object.

The `Selector` control also exposes a property called `selectedValue`, which gets or sets the value of the selected item:

```
var oSelectBooks = new Sys.Preview.UI.Selector($get("selectBooks"));

oSelectBooks.initialize();

function selectBooks_selectionChanged(oSelect, oEventArgs) {
    alert("Value: " + oSelect.get_selectedValue());
}

oSelectBooks.add_selectionChanged(selectBooks_selectionChanged);
```

This code gets the `selectedValue` and displays it to the user when the selection changes. Setting this property changes the selected item in the drop-down box to the option with the corresponding value. The following code changes the selected item to "Beginning JavaScript, 3rd Ed":

```
oSelectBooks.set_selectedValue("0470051515");
```

If the value passed to the property does not exist in any of the `<option/>` elements, no change is made and no error is thrown. Also, setting the `selectedValue` property does not raise the `selectionChanged` event.

The Label Control

In Windows programming, a `Label` control contains only text, and it usually is used to label form fields. In the AJAX Extensions, the `Sys.Preview.UI.Label` control wraps almost any `HTMLElement` that can contain text or markup, with the most common being `<span/>` or `<div/>` elements, such as:

```
<div id="divTextLabel"></div>
<div id="divHtmlLabel"></div>
```

To create a `Label` control, use the `Sys.Preview.UI.Label` class constructor and pass in a reference to an element:

```
var oDivTextLabel = new Sys.Preview.UI.Label($get("divTextLabel"));
var oDivHtmlLabel = new Sys.Preview.UI.Label($get("divHtmlLabel"));
```

This code creates two `Label` controls using the two `<div/>` elements. The `Label` class exposes two properties.

❑   The first, text, gets or sets the content of the `Label`; it can be either plain text or HTML markup.

❑   The second property, `htmlEncode`, is a Boolean value specifying how the content should be displayed: `true` for plain text or `false` for HTML (the default).

The following uses both properties to set the content for the `oDivTextLabel` to plain text:

```
var oDivTextLabel = new Sys.Preview.UI.Label($get("divTextLabel"));
var oDivHtmlLabel = new Sys.Preview.UI.Label($get("divHtmlLabel"));
```

```
oDivTextLabel.set_htmlEncode(true);
oDivTextLabel.set_text("<b>Plain text label.</b>");
```

As a result of setting `htmlEncode` to `true`, the `Label` displays any content set by the `text` property as plain text, so any HTML tags passed to the `text` property are encoded using appropriate HTML entities. The `oDivTextLabel` element, therefore, displays the following:

```
&lt;b&gt;Plain text label&lt;/b&gt;
```

Compare this to setting up a label for HTML content:

```
var oDivTextLabel = new Sys.Preview.UI.Label($get("divTextLabel"));
var oDivHtmlLabel = new Sys.Preview.UI.Label($get("divHtmlLabel"));

oDivTextLabel.set_htmlEncode(true);
oDivTextLabel.set_text("<b>Plain text label.</b>");
```

```
oDivHtmlLabel.set_text("<b>HTML label.</b>");
```

The default for `htmlEncode` is `false`, so the text in `oDivHtmlLabel` is displayed as bold text (because the `<b/>` element is taken literally).

> It is important to note that when set to `true`, the `htmlEncode` property only encodes HTML tags passed to the `text` property; any HTML set by other means is still rendered as HTML.

Making HTTP Requests

The ASP.NET AJAX Extensions wouldn't be much of an Ajax framework without providing its own API for asynchronous HTTP communication. The framework provides the `WebRequest` class in the `Sys.Net` namespace to perform GET or POST HTTP requests.

Making GET Requests

To create an instance of this class, use the `WebRequest` constructor:

```
var oRequest = new Sys.Net.WebRequest();

//more code here
```

The next step is to assign the `url` property with a URL to send the request to. The URL can be set to a fully qualified URL, an absolute URL, or a relative URL.

```
var oRequest = new Sys.Net.WebRequest();

oRequest.set_url("textfile.txt");

//more code here
```

This code assigns the property a relative URL value of `textfile.txt`.

Before the request is sent, however, the `WebRequest` object needs some way of dealing with the data it receives from the server. When using the zXml library, you had to code every step of the request and had to take several things into consideration (handling the `readyStateChange` event and checking the `readyState` property, for example). ASP.NET AJAX does all this for you; all you need to do is handle the `completed` event. To assign a handler, use the `add_completed()` method:

```
var oRequest = new Sys.Net.WebRequest();

oRequest.set_url("textfile.txt");
oRequest.add_completed(request_completed);

//more code here

function request_completed(oExecutor, oEventArgs) {
    //more code here
}
```

Like the `click` event of the `Button` control and the `selectionChanged` event of the `Selector` control, the handler for the `completed` event accepts two arguments. The first is an `XMLHttpExecutor` object, and the second is an event arguments object (which most of the time is empty). The `XMLHttpExecutor` class makes an asynchronous network request to the provided URL using the browser's XHR component. From this object it's possible to retrieve the server's response.

The first step in doing this is to make sure that a response was received from the server. This is done with the responseAvailable property.

```
var oRequest = new Sys.Net.WebRequest();

oRequest.set_url("textfile.txt");
oRequest.add_completed(request_completed);

//more code here

function request_completed(oExecutor, oEventArgs) {
    var sStatusCode = oExecutor.get_statusCode();

    //If data is available, fill the page with information
    if (oExecutor.get_responseAvailable() &&
        (sStatusCode == "200" ||
        sStatusCode == "304")) {
            //more code here
    }
    //otherwise something went wrong
    else {
        //more code here
    }
}
```

This code checks to see if a response is available and then checks the statusCode property for the HTTP response status. When it has been determined that the request was successful, the response body can be retrieved from the responseData property. If a response wasn't received, the XMLHttpExecutor object can provide some insight as to the reason by using the timedOut and aborted properties:

```
var oRequest = new Sys.Net.WebRequest();

oRequest.set_url("textfile.txt");
oRequest.add_completed(request_completed);

//more code here

function request_completed(oExecutor, oEventArgs) {
    var sStatusCode = oExecutor.get_statusCode();

    //If data is available, fill the page with information
    if (oExecutor.get_responseAvailable() &&
        (sStatusCode == "200" ||
        sStatusCode == "304")) {
            alert(oExecutor.get_responseData());
    }
    //otherwise something went wrong
    else {
```

```
        //Check to see if the request timed out
        if (oExecutor.get_timedOut()) {
            alert("Request Timed Out");
        }
        //if not, check to see if it was aborted
        else if (oExecutor.get_aborted()) {
            alert("Request Aborted");
        }

        else if (sStatusCode != 200 || sStatusCode != 304) {
            alert("HTTP Error! Status: " + sStatusCode);
        }
    }
}
```

The changes to the code handle the possible errors that might have occurred if the request failed. It uses the timedOut, aborted, and statusCode properties to generate an alert with an appropriate message for the cause of the failure.

The final step of the request process is to send the request to the server. This is done with the invoke() method:

```
var oRequest = new Sys.Net.WebRequest();

oRequest.set_url("textfile.txt");
oRequest.add_completed(request_completed);

oRequest.invoke();

function request_completed(oExecutor, oEventArgs) {
    var sStatusCode = oExecutor.get_statusCode();

    //If data is available, fill the page with information
    if (oExecutor.get_responseAvailable() &&
       (sStatusCode == "200" ||
        sStatusCode == "304")) {
            alert(oExecutor.get_responseData());
    }
    //otherwise something went wrong
    else {
        //Check to see if the request timed out
        if (oExecutor.get_timedOut()) {
            alert("Request Timed Out");
        }
        //if not, check to see if it was aborted
        else if (oExecutor.get_aborted()) {
            alert("Request Aborted");
        }

        else if (sStatusCode != 200 || sStatusCode != 304) {
            alert("HTTP Error! Status: " + sStatusCode);
        }
    }
}
```

It's possible to access the WebRequest object inside the completed event handler by using the webRequest property of the executor. Also, if your requested data is XML, you can use the executor's xml property, which attempts to load the response data into an XML DOM.

Making POST Requests

POST requests follow the same pattern as GET requests; the only difference is that POST requests incorporate the use of the body property. The following code makes two changes to the previous code:

```
var oRequest = new Sys.Net.WebRequest();

oRequest.set_url("posttest.aspx");
oRequest.set_body("name=Jeremy");
oRequest.add_completed(request_completed);

oRequest.invoke();

function request_completed(oExecutor, oEventArgs) {
    var sStatusCode = oExecutor.get_statusCode();

    //If data is available, fill the page with information
    if (oExecutor.get_responseAvailable() &&
        (sStatusCode == "200" ||
        sStatusCode == "304")) {
            alert(oExecutor.get_responseData());
    }
    //otherwise something went wrong
    else {
        //Check to see if the request timed out
        if (oExecutor.get_timedOut()) {
            alert("Request Timed Out");
        }
        //if not, check to see if it was aborted
        else if (oExecutor.get_aborted()) {
            alert("Request Aborted");
        }

        else if (sStatusCode != 200 || sStatusCode != 304) {
            alert("HTTP Error! Status: " + sStatusCode);
        }
    }
}
```

The highlighted portion of the code changes the url property to posttest.aspx. It also sets the body property to "name=Jeremy".

The posttest.aspx ASP.NET file simply gets the value of the name argument and concats that value with the string "Hello, [name]". Its code is:

```
protected void Page_Load(object sender, EventArgs e)
{
    Response.ContentType = "text/plain";
    Response.CacheControl = "No-cache";

    if (Request.Form["name"] != null)
```

```
    {
        string name = Request.Form["name"].ToString();
        Response.Write("Hello, " + name + "!");
    }
    else
    {
        Response.Write("I'm sorry, but no name could be found");
    }
}
```

When the request is made, and a response received, an alert box shows "Hello, Jeremy!" as in Figure 14-2.

Figure 14-2

The key to POST requests is the `body` property. If the value of `get_body()` is non-null, then the `WebRequest` object performs a POST request. If `get_body()` is `null`, then a GET request executes.

The UpdatePanel Control

The `UpdatePanel` control, in conjunction with the `ScriptManager`, defines areas within the web page to be partially updated without refreshing the entire page. These areas can be updated independently of one another and are usually triggered to update the content contained in them. An `UpdatePanel` can be added to the page declaratively with tags or programmatically.

Adding the UpdatePanel to the Page

Adding an `UpdatePanel` is a simple process. The first step is to add a `ScriptManager` control to the page.

```
<asp:ScriptManager ID="ScriptManager1" runat="server" />
```

The next step is to decide how the `UpdatePanel` behaves. The `UpdatePanel` class inherits the `System.Web.UI.Control` class, so all the attributes exposed by the parent are exposed by the child class. The most important attributes, however, are specific to the `UpdatePanel` class. They are:

❑ `ChildrenAsTriggers`: A Boolean value that indicates whether or not the `UpdatePanel` should be updated when immediate child controls cause a postback. A *postback* is the process of sending and receiving data from the server. The default value for this attribute is `true`. Note that children of a nested `UpdatePanel` do not cause an update of the parent `UpdatePanel`.

❑ `RenderMode`: Indicates how the panel is rendered. If set to "`Block`" (the default), the ASP.NET engine renders the `UpdatePanel` as a `<div/>` element. If "`Inline`", the panel is rendered as a `<span/>` element.

❑ UpdateMode: Determines how the panel's contents are updated. If set to "Always", the default value, the panel updates with every postback that originates from the page, including asynchronous postbacks (updates from other panels). The second value, "Conditional", updates the panels when the following conditions are met:

> ❑ The Update() method of the UpdatePanel instance is explicitly called.
>
> ❑ The postback is caused by a control that is defined as a trigger (more on triggers later). The triggering control can be either inside or outside the UpdatePanel control.
>
> ❑ The ChildrenAsTriggers attribute is set to true, and a child control causes a postback.

Keeping these conditions in mind, an UpdatePanel that continually updates itself is added to the page like this:

```
<asp:ScriptManager ID="ScriptManager1" runat="server" />

<asp:UpdatePanel ID="UpdatePanel1" UpdateMode="Conditional" runat="server">

    <%-- More Code Here --%>

</asp:UpdatePanel>
```

Adding Content to the UpdatePanel

The whole purpose of an UpdatePanel is to update content, and the content of an UpdatePanel control is housed inside a <ContentTemplate/> element. The ContentTemplate is actually a property of the UpdatePanel class, but the element allows you to add content to the panel declaratively.

```
<asp:ScriptManager ID="ScriptManager1" runat="server" />

<asp:UpdatePanel ID="UpdatePanel1" UpdateMode="Conditional" runat="server">
    <ContentTemplate>
        <%-- More Code Here --%>
    </ContentTemplate>

    <%-- More Code Here --%>
</asp:UpdatePanel>
```

The content contained within <ContentTemplate/> can be a mix of HTML and ASP.NET controls. The following code adds a TextBox server control to the <ContentTemplate/>:

```
<asp:ScriptManager ID="ScriptManager1" runat="server" />

<asp:UpdatePanel ID="UpdatePanel1" UpdateMode="Conditional" runat="server">
    <ContentTemplate>
        <asp:TextBox ID="TextBox1" Text="0" runat="server" />
    </ContentTemplate>

    <%-- More Code Here --%>
</asp:UpdatePanel>
```

The TextBox control, like that of the client library, is for text input from the user. This particular code places a normal text box into the page and initializes its text as the number zero (0).

Triggering an Update

The UpdatePanel has been added to the page and has content ready to update. However, there's nothing (yet) to cause the TextBox to be updated with new data. Since the UpdatePanel in this example is set for Conditional UpdateMode, the update must be triggered according to the criteria listed in the previous section.

Probably the most common way to trigger an update is to assign triggers. *Triggers* are events from other controls that cause an UpdatePanel to refresh, and they can be added declaratively to the UpdatePanel control with the <Triggers/> element.

```
<asp:ScriptManager ID="ScriptManager1" runat="server" />

<asp:UpdatePanel ID="UpdatePanel1" UpdateMode="Conditional" runat="server">
    <ContentTemplate>
        <asp:TextBox ID="TextBox1" Text="0" runat="server" />
    </ContentTemplate>
    <Triggers>
        <%-- More Code Here --%>
    </Triggers>
</asp:UpdatePanel>

<asp:Button ID="Button1" Text="Add More" runat="server" />
```

Triggers are bound to other ASP.NET controls, which can be either inside or outside of the UpdatePanel. This code declares a Button control, which will be bound to a trigger. But first, there are two types of triggers that can be used.

❑ The first, PostBackTrigger, causes a normal postback (the whole page is refreshed). This trigger type can be useful when performing functions like uploading a file, because files cannot be uploaded asynchronously. The PostBackTrigger element allows for only one attribute: ControlID, which corresponds to another control's ID property.

❑ The second trigger type, AsyncPostBackTrigger, causes an asynchronous postback. The element that declares this trigger has two possible attributes: ControlID and EventName. The ControlID attribute is the same as it is with PostBackTrigger. The new attribute, EventName, is optional, but it can be set to a specific event of the bound control to trigger the update (otherwise, any event will trigger the update). For example, if EventName is set to "Click", the UpdatePanel will be updated only when the trigger control is clicked.

Of these two trigger types, only one fits the goals of this example: the AsyncPostBackTrigger. The following code binds the Button1 control to a trigger:

```
<asp:ScriptManager ID="ScriptManager1" runat="server" />

<asp:UpdatePanel ID="UpdatePanel1" UpdateMode="Conditional" runat="server">
    <ContentTemplate>
        <asp:TextBox ID="TextBox1" Text="0" runat="server" />
    </ContentTemplate>
    <Triggers>
        <asp:AsyncPostBackTrigger ControlID="Button1" EventName="Click" />
```

```
        </Triggers>
</asp:UpdatePanel>

<asp:Button ID="Button1" Text="Add More" runat="server" />
```

This new code binds the Button control to the trigger, and it triggers an update only when the Button is clicked. In its current state, however, nothing will happen, because the Click event is not handled.

Don't confuse the Click event of a Button control with the click event in the browser's DOM. The former is a server event that executes server-side code, whereas the latter executes code within the browser. They both serve a similar purpose, but one does not call the other.

Finishing Up

The meat of the application is complete; however, nothing happens when the Button control is clicked. The purpose of this application is to take whatever number is in the TextBox control and increment it when the Button is clicked. This is a simple algorithm to code in C#:

```
protected void Button1_Click(object sender, EventArgs e)
{
    long oldNumber = System.Convert.ToInt64(TextBox1.Text);
    long newNumber = ++oldNumber;
    TextBox1.Text = newNumber.ToString();
}

protected void ScriptManager1_AsyncPostBackError(object sender,
                                        AsyncPostBackErrorEventArgs e)
{
    ScriptManager1.AsyncPostBackErrorMessage = e.Exception.Message;
}
```

The first function handles the Button's Click event. When executed, this method retrieves the string value from the TextBox control and converts it to a long integer. The next line increments the value contained in oldNumber and assigns it to the newNumber variable. The final line converts the number to a string and sets the TextBox so that it contains that new value.

If a non-number is entered into the TextBox, the application throws a FormatException error. When this happens, the ScriptManager's AsyncPostBackError event fires. The second function in this code handles this event, and it sets the ScriptManager object's AsyncPostBackErrorMessage property to the exception's message. This information is then sent back to the client, which displays the message in an alert box. Figure 14-3 shows what happens when *Ajax* is typed into the text box instead of a numeric value.

Figure 14-3

The last step in this process is to assign the function to handle the two events:

```
<asp:ScriptManager ID="ScriptManager1" runat="server"
    OnAsyncPostBackError="ScriptManager1_AsyncPostBackError" />
```

```
<asp:UpdatePanel ID="UpdatePanel1" UpdateMode="Conditional" runat="server">
    <ContentTemplate>
        <asp:TextBox ID="TextBox1" Text="0" runat="server" />
    </ContentTemplate>
    <Triggers>
        <asp:AsyncPostBackTrigger ControlID="Button1" EventName="Click" />
    </Triggers>
</asp:UpdatePanel>
```

```
<asp:Button ID="Button1" Text="Add More" OnClick="Button1_Click" runat="server" />
```

This new code adds the `OnClick` event handler to the `Button` control declaration. Now when the user clicks the button, it will trigger the `UpdatePanel` to asynchronously update itself. To prove it works, add a JavaScript `onload` event handler to alert you when the page refreshes.

SiteSearch Revisited

Earlier in the book, the creation of an Ajax Site Search widget was discussed. That widget demonstrated a typical Ajax application that retrieves data from the server and displays that data with dynamically created HTML. In this section, this widget is revisited using the AJAX Extensions. This change alters many aspects of the original AjaxSiteSearch; the HTML structure changes to accommodate the inclusion of server controls, and a few adjustments to the C# code are required. Also, you won't write one line of JavaScript code.

The User Interface

The UI is still important, so the new UI doesn't change much from the original AjaxSiteSearch widget. The HTML structure, however, does change slightly due to the server controls. Also, this new version includes a new button to clear the search results. The resulting HTML looks like this:

```
<div class="ajaxSiteSearchContainer">
 <form class="ajaxSiteSearchForm">
   <span id="upTextBoxUpdate">
     <input type="text" id="txtSearchTerm" class="ajaxSiteSearchTextBox" />
   </span>
   <input type="submit" value="Go" id="btnSearch" class="ajaxSiteSearchButton" />
   <input type="submit" value="Clear" id="btnClear" class="ajaxSiteSearchButton" />
     <div class="ajaxSiteSearchResultPane">
       <div id="upResultsUpdate">
          <div id="plhResults">
             <a class="ajaxSiteSearchLink">Result Text</a>
          </div>
       </div>
     </div>
 </form>
</div>
```

Aside from the extra button, the three key changes are the `<span/>` and `<div/>` elements with the IDs of `"upTextBoxUpdate"`, `"upResultsUpdate"`, and the `"plhResults"`. The `<span/>` and the first `<div/>` elements are added by the `UpdatePanel` controls. The second `<div/>` element (`"plhResults"`) is added by another control called `PlaceHolder`; these controls reserve a location in the page, allowing the addition of future controls at runtime.

Getting Started

Open up Visual Studio and create a new ASP.NET AJAX–enabled web site. Set the language to Visual C#, and name the project `ASPAjaxSiteSearch`. Make sure that you save this web site in your web server's wwwroot directory. When Visual Studio creates and opens the project, you should be greeted with the default project. `Default.aspx` should be open, and you should have `Default.aspx` and `Web.config` in the Solution Explorer panel.

The Database Connection String

The first order of business is to edit the `Web.config` file so that it contains the database connection string. This version of the widget uses the same data as the original AjaxSiteSearch widget; therefore, the connection string will remain the same. Add the following `<add/>` element to the `<connectionStrings/>` element:

```
<add
    name="SiteSearch"
    connectionString="Data Source=localhost;
        Initial Catalog=BlogDatabase;User ID=sa;Password=pwd"
    providerName="System.Data.SqlClient"
/>
```

Don't forget to input your own credentials into this connection string.

Adding the Style Sheet

Next, right-click on the project's name in the Solution Explorer and create a new folder called `css`. Right-click on this folder and choose the "Add Existing Item..." option. Locate the `ajaxsitesearch.css` file created for the original widget and add it to the project. Although the HTML structure changes, the style sheet will not need any editing.

Declaring the Form

With `Default.aspx` open, switch over to Source view mode (the button is in the lower-left corner of the viewable area). Remove everything within the page's body and add the following HTML:

```
<div class="ajaxSiteSearchContainer">
    <form id="form1" class="ajaxSiteSearchForm" runat="server">

        <%-- More Code Here --%>

        <div class="ajaxSiteSearchResultPane">
            <%-- More Code Here --%>
        </div>
    </form>
</div>
```

Note that the opening `<form/>` tag has an attribute called `runat`. When set to "server," this attribute tells the ASP.NET engine that it needs to parse the element and its children.

The next step is to add the Go and Clear buttons. These are `Button` controls.

```
<div class="ajaxSiteSearchContainer">
    <form id="form1" class="ajaxSiteSearchForm" runat="server">

        <%-- More Code Here --%>

        <asp:Button CssClass="ajaxSiteSearchButton" ID="btnSearch" Text="Go"
            runat="server"  />
        <asp:Button CssClass="ajaxSiteSearchButton" ID="btnClear" Text="Clear"
            runat="server"  />

        <div class="ajaxSiteSearchResultPane">
            <%-- More Code Here --%>
        </div>
    </form>
</div>
```

`Button` controls have a variety of attributes available to use. In this code, the `CssClass` attribute is set to `"ajaxSiteSearchButton"`. When the ASP.NET engine parses these controls, it transforms the `CssClass` attribute to the HTML `class` attribute. The next attribute, `ID`, serves two purposes. First, this attribute is used as the resulting `<input/>` element's id attribute, and second, it serves as an identifier when writing C# code. The `Text` attribute sets the button's text that is displayed to the user.

Now it's time to add the `ScriptManager` and `UpdatePanel` controls. This application uses two `UpdatePanel` controls. The first panel is for the `TextBox` control, and it is updated when the Clear button is clicked:

```
<div class="ajaxSiteSearchContainer">
    <form id="form1" class="ajaxSiteSearchForm" runat="server">
        <asp:ScriptManager ID="ScriptManager1" runat="server" />
        <asp:UpdatePanel ID="upTextBoxUpdate" RenderMode="Inline" runat="server">
            <ContentTemplate>
                <asp:Textbox CssClass="ajaxSiteSearchTextBox"
                        ID="txtSearchTerm" runat="server" />
            </ContentTemplate>
        </asp:UpdatePanel>

        <asp:Button CssClass="ajaxSiteSearchButton" ID="btnSearch" Text="Go"
            runat="server"  />
        <asp:Button CssClass="ajaxSiteSearchButton" ID="btnClear" Text="Clear"
            runat="server"  />

        <div class="ajaxSiteSearchResultPane">
            <%-- More Code Here --%>
        </div>
    </form>
</div>
```

The content of the first panel is the `txtSearchTerm` `TextBox` control; this is where users type in their search query. This `UpdatePanel` is set to update the `TextBox` control on every postback (remember, the `UpdateMode` attribute is optional and defaults to "Always").

461

The second `UpdatePanel` updates the search results. In the original AjaxSiteSearch widget, the results were appended to the `<div/>` element with a CSS class of `"ajaxSiteSearchResultPane"`. This element still exists in this new version; however, the results are appended to a `<div/>` element inside of the original. This is due to the use of a `PlaceHolder` control:

```
<div class="ajaxSiteSearchContainer">
    <form id="form1" class="ajaxSiteSearchForm" runat="server">
        <asp:ScriptManager ID="ScriptManager1" runat="server" />
        <asp:UpdatePanel ID="upTextBoxUpdate" RenderMode="Inline" runat="server">
            <ContentTemplate>
                <asp:Textbox CssClass="ajaxSiteSearchTextBox"
                            ID="txtSearchTerm" runat="server" />
            </ContentTemplate>
        </asp:UpdatePanel>

        <asp:Button CssClass="ajaxSiteSearchButton" ID="btnSearch" Text="Go"
            runat="server"  />
        <asp:Button CssClass="ajaxSiteSearchButton" ID="btnClear" Text="Clear"
            runat="server"  />

        <div class="ajaxSiteSearchResultPane">
            <asp:UpdatePanel UpdateMode="Conditional" ID="upResultsUpdate"
                runat="server">
            <ContentTemplate>
                <asp:PlaceHolder ID="plhResults" runat="server" />
            </ContentTemplate>
            <Triggers>
                <asp:AsyncPostBackTrigger ControlID="btnSearch"
                    EventName="Click" />
                <asp:AsyncPostBackTrigger ControlID="btnClear" EventName="Click" />
            </Triggers>
            </asp:UpdatePanel>
        </div>
    </form>
</div>
```

As mentioned earlier, `PlaceHolder` controls reserve space in the web page; this application uses this space by adding (and clearing) the search results. This control resides in the `ContentTemplate` of this `UpdatePanel`, which is updated when the Go and Clear `Button` controls' `Click` event fires. Clicking the `btnSearch` button fills the `PlaceHolder` with data, and the `btnClear` button clears that data.

Performing the Search

The search should execute when the Go button is clicked. The `Click` event handler, called `btnSearch_Click()`, resembles that of the `AjaxSiteSearch.Search()` method in the original widget. In fact, a good portion of that code is reused. The main changes result from adapting the code to use ASP.NET controls.

The `btnSearch_click()` event handler accepts two arguments. The first, `sender`, is the object that received the event. The second, `e`, is the event arguments that describe the event.

```
protected void btnSearch_Click(object sender, EventArgs e)
{
    //Get the search string
    string searchString = txtSearchTerm.Text;

    //more code here
}
```

The first step is to get the search string. Since ASP.NET controls can be used to get this information, it's not necessary to rely on fetching arguments out of the query string. To get the search term, use the Text property of the txtSearchTerm TextBox control. Then compare that value to an empty string. Doing so allows you to tell the user that he or she needs to enter text into the TextBox:

```
protected void btnSearch_Click(object sender, EventArgs e)
{
    //Get the search string
    string searchString = txtSearchTerm.Text;

    //Check to see if anything was entered.
    //If not, tell the user to enter text.
    if (searchString == String.Empty)
    {
        throw new Exception("Please enter a search term.");
    }
    //more code here
}
```

This code compares the searchString variable to an empty string. If it is true, this code throws a generic exception, which in turns fires the ScriptManager's AsyncPostBackError event (the handler will be written shortly).

If the user did enter text, a search should be performed with that text. This is where the code becomes familiar:

```
protected void btnSearch_Click(object sender, EventArgs e)
{
    //Get the search string
    string searchString = txtSearchTerm.Text;

    //Check to see if anything was entered.
    //If not, tell the user to enter text.
    if (searchString == String.Empty)
    {
        throw new Exception("Please enter a search term.");
    }
    else
    {
        //Get our connection string.
        string connectionString =
ConfigurationManager.ConnectionStrings["SiteSearch"].ConnectionString;
        //Build the query.
        string query = String.Format("SELECT TOP 10 BlogId, " +
            "Title FROM BlogPosts WHERE Post LIKE '%{0}%' " +
```

```
                  "OR Title LIKE '%{0}%' ORDER BY Date DESC", searchString);

            //Set up the database connection
            using (SqlConnection conn = new SqlConnection(connectionString))
            {
                //And get the command ready
                SqlCommand command = new SqlCommand(query, conn);
                //Open the connection.
                conn.Open();

                //Perform the query.
                using (SqlDataReader reader = command.ExecuteReader())
                {
                    //If we got results...
                    if (reader.HasRows)
                    {
                        //Loop through them
                        while (reader.Read())
                        {
                            //more code here
                        }
                    }
                    else //No results found
                    {
                        //more code here
                    }
                }
            }
        }
    }
}
```

This code is exactly like that from `AjaxSiteSearch.Search()`. The database connection string is obtained from the application's configuration, the query is built, a connection to the database is opened, and the query is executed against the database.

The difference this time around is in the data sent back to the client. The `AjaxSiteSearch.Search()` method returned a JSON string, which the client-side code used to create hyperlinks dynamically. In `btnSearch_Click()`, `HyperLink` controls will be added to the `PlaceHolder`. The end result is the same (links added to an HTML element), but this saves you from writing any JavaScript.

```
protected void btnSearch_Click(object sender, EventArgs e)
{
    //Get the search string
    string searchString = txtSearchTerm.Text;

    //Check to see if anything was entered.
    //If not, tell the user to enter text.
    if (searchString == String.Empty)
    {
        throw new Exception("Please enter a search term.");
    }
    else
```

```
        {
            //Get our connection string.
            string connectionString =
    ConfigurationManager.ConnectionStrings["SiteSearch"].ConnectionString;
            //Build the query.
            string query = String.Format("SELECT TOP 10 BlogId, " +
                "Title FROM BlogPosts WHERE Post LIKE '%{0}%' " +
                "OR Title LIKE '%{0}%' ORDER BY Date DESC", searchString);

            //Set up the database connection
            using (SqlConnection conn = new SqlConnection(connectionString))
            {
                //And get the command ready
                SqlCommand command = new SqlCommand(query, conn);
                //Open the connection.
                conn.Open();

                //Perform the query.
                using (SqlDataReader reader = command.ExecuteReader())
                {
                    //If we got results...
                    if (reader.HasRows)
                    {
                        //Loop through them
                        while (reader.Read())
                        {
                            //Create a link
                            HyperLink link = new HyperLink();

                            link.Text = reader["Title"].ToString();
                            link.NavigateUrl = "http://www.yoursite.com/" +
                                reader["BlogId"].ToString();
                            link.CssClass = "ajaxSiteSearchLink";

                            //Add it to the PlaceHolder
                            plhResults.Controls.Add(link);
                        }
                    }
                    else //No results found
                    {
                        //more code here
                    }
                }
            }
        }
    }
```

The HyperLink control represents a normal hyperlink. It contains data and has a URL to navigate to when clicked. This code creates a HyperLink control programmatically by creating an instance of the HyperLink class. The value of the Title database column is assigned to the Text, the NavigateUrl property is set to the URL to navigate to, and the CssClass property assumes the value of "ajaxSiteSearchLink". After building the HyperLink, it is then added to plhResults.

The final step in `btnSearch_Click()` is to tell the user when a search did not find a match; throwing a simple exception works just fine for this purpose due to the AJAX Extensions' handling of server-side errors:

```
protected void btnSearch_Click(object sender, EventArgs e)
{
    //Get the search string
    string searchString = txtSearchTerm.Text;

    //Check to see if anything was entered.
    //If not, tell the user to enter text.
    if (searchString == String.Empty)
    {
        throw new Exception("Please enter a search term.");
    }
    else
    {
        //Get our connection string.
        string connectionString =
ConfigurationManager.ConnectionStrings["SiteSearch"].ConnectionString;
        //Build the query.
        string query = String.Format("SELECT TOP 10 BlogId, " +
            "Title FROM BlogPosts WHERE Post LIKE '%{0}%' " +
            "OR Title LIKE '%{0}%' ORDER BY Date DESC", searchString);

        //Set up the database connection
        using (SqlConnection conn = new SqlConnection(connectionString))
        {
            //And get the command ready
            SqlCommand command = new SqlCommand(query, conn);
            //Open the connection.
            conn.Open();

            //Perform the query.
            using (SqlDataReader reader = command.ExecuteReader())
            {
                //If we got results...
                if (reader.HasRows)
                {
                    //Loop through them
                    while (reader.Read())
                    {
                        //Create a link
                        HyperLink link = new HyperLink();

                        link.Text = reader["Title"].ToString();
                        link.NavigateUrl = "http://www.yoursite.com/" +
                            reader["BlogId"].ToString();
                        link.CssClass = "ajaxSiteSearchLink";

                        //Add it to the PlaceHolder
                        plhResults.Controls.Add(link);
                    }
                }
```

```
                else //No results found
                {
                    //Let the user know.
                    throw new Exception("No match could be found.");
                }
            }
        }
    }
}
```

This final line in this event handler throws a new generic exception, telling the user that no match could be found.

Clearing the Results

The results are cleared when the Clear button is clicked:

```
protected void btnClear_Click(object sender, EventArgs e)
{
    foreach (Control control in plhResults.Controls)
        plhResults.Controls.Remove(control);

    txtSearchTerm.Text = String.Empty;
}
```

Clearing the form involves two operations. The first removes the PlaceHolder's child controls (HyperLink controls). By using a foreach loop to loop through the PlaceHolder's controls, this code removes each control with the Controls.Remove() method. Once empty, the Text property of the txtSearchTerm TextBox is set to an empty string, clearing any search term that the user entered.

The TextBox's UpdatePanel *is set to always update. If it were set to update conditionally, this code would not clear the text within the box.*

Handling Errors

The btnSearch_Click() event handler throws two errors, so the AsyncPostBackError event for the ScriptManager must be handled.

```
protected void ScriptManager1_AsyncPostBackError(object sender,
                                        AsyncPostBackErrorEventArgs e)
{
    ScriptManager1.AsyncPostBackErrorMessage = e.Exception.Message;
}
```

This code simply sets the AsyncPostBackErrorMessage property so that the user gets informational error messages.

Hooking Up the Events

The final step in this rewrite is hooking up the event handlers to the Button controls. For this example, the event handlers are added through the markup:

```
<div class="ajaxSiteSearchContainer">
    <form id="form1" class="ajaxSiteSearchForm" runat="server">
        <asp:ScriptManager ID="ScriptManager1" runat="server"
            OnAsyncPostBackError="ScriptManager1_AsyncPostBackError" />
        <asp:UpdatePanel ID="upTextBoxUpdate" RenderMode="Inline" runat="server">
            <ContentTemplate>
                <asp:Textbox CssClass="ajaxSiteSearchTextBox"
                            ID="txtSearchTerm" runat="server" />
            </ContentTemplate>
        </asp:UpdatePanel>

        <asp:Button CssClass="ajaxSiteSearchButton" ID="btnSearch" Text="Go"
            OnClick="btnSearch_Click" runat="server"   />
        <asp:Button CssClass="ajaxSiteSearchButton" ID="btnClear" Text="Clear"
            OnClick="btnClear_Click" runat="server"   />

        <div class="ajaxSiteSearchResultPane">
            <asp:UpdatePanel UpdateMode="Conditional" ID="upResultsUpdate"
                runat="server">
                <ContentTemplate>
                    <asp:PlaceHolder ID="plhResults" runat="server" />
                </ContentTemplate>
                <Triggers>
                    <asp:AsyncPostBackTrigger ControlID="btnSearch"
                        EventName="Click" />
                    <asp:AsyncPostBackTrigger ControlID="btnClear" EventName="Click"
/>
                </Triggers>
            </asp:UpdatePanel>
        </div>
    </form>
</div>
```

This new code simply adds the OnClick event handler to the Button controls. Now when they're clicked, the events will execute the correct code.

With this addition, the rewrite is complete. Open your web browser and point it to http://yourserver/ASPAjaxSiteSearch. You'll see Figure 14-4.

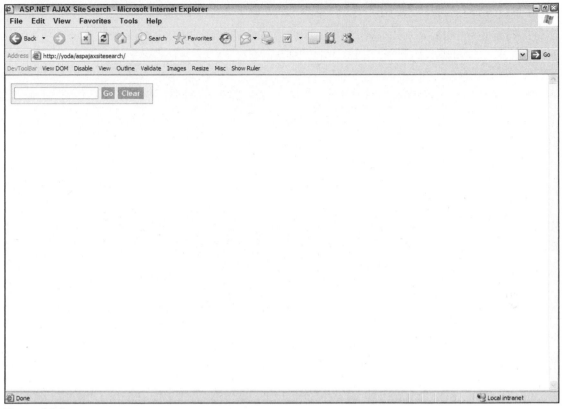

Figure 14-4

Now type "lo" in the search box and click the Go button. Figure 14-5 shows what you should see.

That's it! You've duplicated the AjaxSiteSearch widget from Chapter 12, and even expanded on it, while writing less code and without writing any JavaScript!

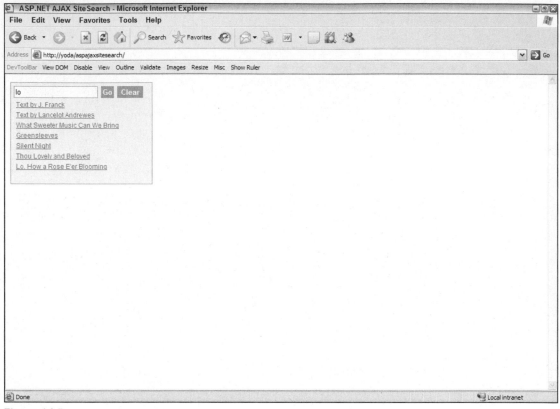

Figure 14-5

Summary

This chapter covered the new ASP.NET AJAX Extensions, which consists of client-side JavaScript code and server extensions.

The chapter began by walking you through many aspects of the ASP.NET AJAX client library, showing you how it expands JavaScript to include a typed system. You learned how to create namespaces, classes, enumerations, and interfaces.

Next, you learned how to utilize some of the client-side controls, wrappers for normal HTMLElements that provide an easy to use API. You learned about the TextBox, Button, Selector, and Label controls.

After covering many aspects of the client library, the chapter moved into the server-side of the AJAX Extensions, and introduced the UpdatePanel. You built a simple example of the UpdatePanel's use by updating contents in a TextBox.

Finally, you rewrote the AjaxSiteSearch widget from Chapter 12 and refactored the code to utilize the ASP.NET AJAX Extensions. By doing so, you saw how you can write Ajax-enabled applications with writing little to no JavaScript.

Case Study: FooReader.NET

15

Chapter 7 covered syndication with RSS and Atom and how easy it is to share information. In order to view information from several different sources, an application called an *aggregator* is used to combine the different feeds in one location. An aggregator makes it easier and faster to stay up to date with information collected from around the Web (much easier than visiting several web sites each day).

FooReader.NET is a web-based, .NET RSS/Atom aggregator ported from ForgetFoo's ColdFusion-based FooReader (`http://reader.forgetfoo.com/`). With many conventional applications filling the aggregator void, including popular e-mail and browser applications, why build a web-based RSS/Atom aggregator? Consider the following reasons:

❑ **The Web is cross-platform.** Building a web-based aggregator ensures that anyone with Internet Explorer 6+, Firefox, or Opera can access it.

❑ **The Web is centrally located.** One of the problems with conventional aggregators that are installed on the computer is the upkeep of data in many locations. If you like to read syndicated feeds at work and at home, you must install an aggregator on each computer and load it with the appropriate feeds. A web-based aggregator eliminates this problem because any change made to the feed list is seen regardless of the user's location.

This chapter explains how FooReader.NET is built using Ajax, and as with any web application, there are two main components: the client side and the server side.

If you installed a version of Visual Studio, open it and create a new web site called FooReader. Make sure that the language is C#.

The Client Components

The client-side components of an Ajax solution are in charge of communicating with the server and displaying the received data to the user. For FooReader.NET, several client-side components are necessary to manage the overall user experience.

❑ **The user interface:** The UI ties the user to his or her data. Because the UI is essentially a web page, the usual suspects of web browser technologies are used. The design is marked up in HTML, and CSS (and a little bit of JavaScript) styles it for the desired look and feel.

❑ **XParser:** The JavaScript library responsible for requesting and parsing feeds.

❑ **The JavaScript code:** Drives the UI, taking the information XParser received and displaying it to the user. This is contained in the `fooreader.js` file.

The User Interface

The key to any successful application is the design of the user interface. If the user cannot use the application, there is no reason for the application to exist. FooReader.NET was designed for ease of use. In fact, it borrows heavily from the Microsoft Outlook 2003 (and later) user interface. It has a three-pane interface. The first two panes are fixed width, while the third pane is fluid. (See Figure 15-1.)

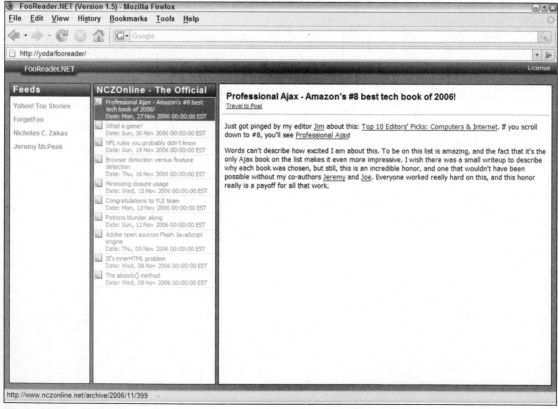

Figure 15-1

The interface is contained in `default.htm`, and its layout is as follows:

```html
<!DOCTYPE html PUBLIC "-//W3C//DTD XHTML 1.0 Transitional//EN"
    "http://www.w3.org/TR/xhtml1/DTD/xhtml1-transitional.dtd">

<html xml:lang="en" lang="en"  xmlns="http://www.w3.org/1999/xhtml">
<head>
    <title>FooReader.NET (Version 1.5)</title>
    <link rel="stylesheet" type="text/css" href="css/FooReader.css" />
    <script type="text/javascript" src="js/zxml.src.js"></script>
    <script type="text/javascript" src="js/XParser.js"></script>
    <script type="text/javascript" src="js/FooReader.js"></script>
</head>
<body>
    <div id="divLoading">
        <img src="img/progress.gif" alt="Loading" />
    </div>

    <div id="divTopBar">
        <img src="img/top_logo.gif" alt="FooReader.NET" />
        <div id="divLicense">
            <a href="http://creativecommons.org/licenses/by-nc-sa/2.5/"
                title="Some Rights Reserved" target="_blank">License</a>
        </div>
    </div>

    <div id="divPaneContainer">
        <div id="divFeedsPane">
            <div class="paneheader">Feeds</div>
            <div id="divFeedList"></div>
        </div>

        <div id="divItemsPane">
            <div id="divViewingItem" class="paneheader">Items</div>
            <div id="divItemList"></div>
        </div>

        <div id="divReadingPane">
            <div id="divMessageContainer">
                <div id="divMessageHeader">
                    <div id="divMessageTitle"></div>
                    <a href="" id="aMessageLink" title="Click to goto posting."
                        target="_new">Travel to Post</a>
                </div>
                <div id="divMessageBody"></div>
            </div>
        </div>
    </div>
</body>
</html>
```

The first two direct children of the document's body are the `divLoading` and `divTopBar` elements. The former provides a UI cue, telling the user that the application is loading a feed. It appears when a request is made to the server application and hides when the server's response is received and processed. The `divTopBar` element primarily serves as a title bar in conventional applications; it tells the user that the application they're using is FooReader.NET, and it provides a link to the Creative Commons license that it is released under.

Next is the `divPaneContainer` element. As its name suggests, the three panes reside in this element. This element allows certain styles to easily be applied to the group of panes, as opposed to applying them to each pane separately.

The first pane, called the *feeds pane*, displays the different feeds as links that the user can click on. A `<div/>` element with an `id` of `divFeedList` in the feeds pane allows the feeds list to be dynamically written to the document. Feeds are block level `<a/>` elements with a CSS class of `"feedlink"`. The following is the HTML of these links.

```
<a href="[url of feed]" class="feedlink" title="Load [feed title]">Feed title</a>
```

When the user clicks on a feed, the feed's items are loaded into the second pane: the *items pane*. This pane has two elements that are used to display information.

❑   The first is a `<div/>` element with an `id` of `divViewingItem` (it is also the pane's header). This element displays which feed is currently loaded into the application.

❑   The second element is another `<div/>` element, whose `id` attribute is set to `divItemList`. This element will contain a list of `<item/>` RSS elements or `<entry/>` Atom elements, and they are dynamically added to `divItemList`.

The HTML structure for these items is as follows.

```
<a class="itemlink" href="[item url]" frfeeditem="[item number]" id="item[number]">
    <div class="itemheadline">[Headline]</div>
    <div class="itemdate">[Date]</div>
</a>
```

This HTML is fairly standard, except for the `frfeeditem` attribute in the `<a/>` element. When a feed is loaded and the items are added to the page, each item is assigned a number by which to identify itself.

When the user clicks an item, it loads the item into the last pane: the *reading pane*. This pane has three elements that display the item's information. The first, whose `id` is `divMessageTitle`, is where the `<title/>` element of RSS and Atom feeds is displayed. The second element has an `id` of `aMessageLink` whose `href` attribute is changed dynamically. Finally, the last element is `divMessageBody`, where the contents of the `<rss:description/>` and `<atom:content/>` elements are displayed.

This page requires one style sheet, `FooReader.css`, along with three JavaScript files: the zXml library, XParser, and `FooReader.js`, which contains all the client functionality.

> *Since FooReader.NET uses XParser, the application will not work in Safari. It does, however, work in IE 6+, Firefox 1+, and Opera 9+.*

The finished UI is achieved by a combination of CSS and JavaScript; the CSS sets the size of the document's body (a necessity for Opera), the three panes, and styles the other elements. JavaScript sizes the elements inside the panes.

Styling the Interface

The only style sheet used in FooReader.NET is `FooReader.css`, and it exists in the `css` directory. One of the keys to making this interface work is the size of the browser's viewport. The page is explicitly set to use all available vertical space in the browser's window.

```css
html, body {
    height: 100%;
    margin: 0px;
    overflow: hidden;
    background-color: gray;
    font: 11px verdana, arial, helvetica, sans-serif;
}
```

The `height` property is set to `100%`. This property is necessary for Opera; otherwise, the JavaScript portion of styling the elements would have to branch code to accommodate the differing Browser Object Models. The `overflow` is set to `hidden`, because some of the elements in the page will cause scrollbars to appear in the browser's window. The goal of the UI is to make FooReader.NET feel like a normal application, and scrollbars at the document level inhibit that feeling (the individual panes will scroll, if necessary).

The Topbar

The next rules are for `divTopBar`, and the elements contained in it:

```css
/* The Topbar */
#divTopBar {
    background: gray url("../img/top_bg.gif") repeat-x;
    height: 31px;
    padding-left: 25px;
    position: relative;
}
```

The top bar has a background color of gray (to match the gray background of the page) and a background image of `top_bg.gif`. Its left side is padded by 25 pixels. This pushes the `<img/>` element to the right. Its relative position allows for any child elements to be positioned within the confines of the element, like the following `divLicense` element:

```css
#divLicense {
    position: absolute;
    right: 10px;
    top: 3px;
}

#divLicense a {
    color: white;
    padding: 1px 4px 2px 4px;
}

#divLicense a:hover {
    background: blue url("../img/toolbar_back.gif") repeat-x;
    border: 1px solid #000080;
    color: #000080;
    padding: 0px 3px 1px 3px;
}
```

This element contains one link: the license. It is absolutely positioned 10 pixels from the right edge and 3 pixels from the top of divTopBar. The link inside divLicense has a text color of white. When the user moves their mouse pointer over the link, it gains a background image that repeats horizontally, a blue border 1 pixel in width, the text color changes to a dark blue, and the padding is adjusted to be 1 pixel less on all sides. This change in padding occurs because a border is added to the element. If no adjustment was made to the padding, the link would actually grow 1 pixel on each side.

The Loading Cue

In the HTML structure, the divLoading element contains an image. This image shows an animated progress bar; it's about 5 to 10 pixels high and a little under 300 pixels in length.

The image's parent element, the <div/> element, is absolutely positioned, and its display property is set to none, removing it completely from the document flow.

```
/* The loading <div/> */
#divLoading {
    position: absolute;
    display: none;
    top: 20%;
    left: 35%;
    width: 302px;
    z-index: 5;
    background: transparent url("../img/loading.gif") no-repeat;
    padding: 30px 10px;
}
```

Probably the most important style declaration is z-index. Since the element is first in the HTML document, it is hidden by the other elements in the page. Specifying a z-index greater than 0 causes the loading <div/> element to be placed in front of the other elements, making it visible to the user (see Figure 15-2).

The Panes

The three panes are contained within the aptly named divPaneContainer element. This element positions the panes in their desired location: away from the browser's left edge and the top bar:

```
#divPaneContainer {
    position: relative;
    top: 10px;
    left: 10px;
}
```

Positioning this element allows freedom from the tedium of positioning all the panes individually.

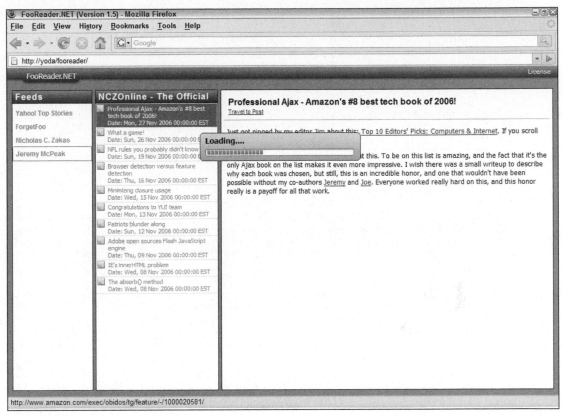

Figure 15-2

The feeds and items pane also have a header at the top of each pane. This header lets the user know what type of data the two panes contain. They are 20 pixels in height and have bold, white text. Here is its style rule:

```
.paneheader {
    height: 20px;
    background-image: url("../img/header_background.gif");
    font: bold 16px arial;
    color: white;
    padding: 2px 0px 2px 5px;
    letter-spacing: 1px;
    overflow: hidden;
}
```

The Feeds Pane

The first pane is the feed pane. The `divFeedsPane` element itself is simple, as the following rule shows:

```
#divFeedsPane {
    float: left;
    width: 148px;
    border: 1px solid navy;
    background-color: white;
    overflow: hidden;
}
```

The element is set to float left and is 148 pixels wide. Floating an element shifts the element to the right or left. In this case, `divFeedsPane` is shifted to the left. This makes the items pane flow along its right side, even though they are both block-level elements. To ensure that the pane always maintains it size, its overflow property is set to `hidden`. This hides any content that extends beyond the pane's boundaries. It is desirable, however, for the pane's contents to scroll. That is part of `divFeedList`'s job, and here is its CSS rule:

```
#divFeedList {
    padding: 5px 1px 5px 1px;
    overflow: auto;
}
```

This element contains the feed links. Its `overflow` property is set to `auto`. This allows `divFeedList` to scroll if its contents make the element larger than `divFeedsPane`. The scrollbars will appear inside `divFeedsPane`, making the contents scrollable, while keeping the pane itself the same (see Figure 15-3).

Figure 15-3

The links in this pane are styled as block-level elements. They have padding to give them visual separation from each other.

```
a.feedlink {
    display: block;
    padding: 5px;
    font: bold 12px arial;
    text-decoration: none;
    color: #5583d3;
}

a.feedlink:hover {
    color: #3768B9;
    text-decoration: underline;
}
```

The Items Pane

The items pane's CSS rule closely resembles that of the feed's pane:

```css
#divItemsPane {
    float: left;
    width: 225px;
    border: 1px solid navy;
    background-color: white;
    margin-left: 5px;
    margin-right: 5px !important;
    margin-right: 2px;
    overflow: hidden;
}
```

It, too, floats left and hides its overflow. The right and left margins add space between this pane and the other two panes; however, IE6 and the other browsers render margins differently. In order for every browser to render the UI the same, the !important declarative must be used. The first margin-right uses this. So IE7, Firefox, and Opera will use that specific value regardless of what margin-right is assigned in the next declaration. The second assignment is for IE6. It adds an extra line to the CSS, but it makes the UI look uniform in all four browsers.

The items in this pane also have their own styling. If you refer back to the item HTML structure mentioned earlier, you see that they are simply `<a/>` elements with a CSS class of itemlink. These items have two states. The first is their normal state; how they look when the user hasn't clicked one. When a user clicks an item, it the JavaScript code changes the CSS class to itemlink-selected. Both states share many similar style declarations.

```css
a.itemlink, a.itemlink-selected {
    border-bottom: 1px solid #EAE9E1;
    background-image: url("../img/item_icon.gif");
    background-repeat: no-repeat;
    cursor: pointer;
    text-decoration: none;
    display: block;
    padding: 2px;
    font: 11px tahoma;
}
```

The remaining rules for the items are to differentiate the two states from each other, as well as define the :hover pseudo-classes for the normal state:

```css
a.itemlink {
    background-color: white;
    color: #808080;
}

a.itemlink:hover {
    background-color: #D3E5FA;
}

a.itemlink:hover .itemheadline {
    color: black;
```

```
    }

    .itemheadline,.itemdate {
        margin-left: 20px;
    }

    a.itemlink-selected {
        background-color: #316AC5;
        color: white;
    }
```

The Reading Pane

The third pane is different from the other panes in that it has no defined width, as the following CSS shows:

```
#divReadingPane {
    margin: 0px 20px 0px 0px;
    border: 1px solid black;
    background-color: white;
    height: 100%;
    overflow: hidden;
}
```

Instead, the browser automatically sizes the element's width to fill the remainder of divPaneContainer, and the margin declaration in this CSS rule brings the right edge in by 20 pixels. Like the two previous panes, the reading pane's overflow is set to hidden. Unlike the other panes, however, the height is specified to 100%. This makes the pane's height that of the pane container.

The direct child of divReadingPane is divMessageContainer, which contains the message elements. Other than serving this purpose, it pads the message area by 5 pixels on all sides:

```
#divMessageContainer {
    padding: 5px;
}
```

The first part of a message is the header, which contains the article's title and a link to take the user to the article. Its CSS follows:

```
#divMessageHeader {
    height: 34px;
    background-color: white;
    border-bottom: 1px solid #ACA899;
    padding: 8px;
}

#divMessageTitle {
    font: bold 16px arial;
}

#aMessageLink {
    font: 11px arial;
}
```

The `divMessageBody` element is where the feed item's content is displayed, and the following CSS rule applies to this element.

```css
#divMessageBody {
    background-color: white;
    padding: 0px 0px 0px 5px;
    font: 13px tahoma;
    overflow: auto;
}
```

This portion of the reading pane scrolls if the contents exceed the height of the reading pane. Its height is not specified.

The height of the elements that contain content (`divFeedList`, `divItemList`, and `divMessageBody`) are not styled through CSS. Instead, that is handled by JavaScript.

Driving the UI

The JavaScript contained in `fooreader.js` controls all aspects of the UI. It retrieves the feed list, parses it, and populates the feeds pane. It creates XParser objects to request, receive, and parse RSS and Atom feeds, and uses that information to populate the items and reading panes. It sizes many elements of the UI and resizes them when the window's size changes. In short, it's the backbone of the client-side components.

The Helper Functions

The majority of code is contained inside the `fooReader` object, but two functions stand alone to aid in the element's resizing. The first function is called `getStyle()`, and it is a cross-browser approach to getting the value of a specific style property. It accepts two arguments, the element and the CSS property name.

```javascript
function getStyle(oElement, sProperty) {
    var sStyle;

    if (typeof window.getComputedStyle == "undefined") {
        sStyle = oElement.currentStyle[sProperty];
    } else {
        sStyle = getComputedStyle(oElement, "")[sProperty];
    }

    return sStyle;
}
```

This code uses IE's `currentStyle` property and the W3C DOM `getComputedStyle()` method to retrieve the value of a specific property.

The second function, `getStyleNumber()`, performs a similar activity, except that it returns an integer instead of a string:

```javascript
function getStyleNumber(oElement, sProperty) {
    return parseInt(getStyle(oElement, sProperty));
}
```

The fooReader Object

As mentioned earlier, the `fooReader` object contains most of the JavaScript code, making it the main part of the application. It contains various properties and methods necessary to run the UI. It is the only object of its kind in the application. Therefore, it is defined in object literal notation:

```
var fooReader = {
    parser   : null,
    feeds    : [],

    //HTML elements
    divFeedList      : null,
    divViewingItem   : null,
    divItemList      : null,
    divMessageTitle  : null,
    aMessageLink     : null,
    divMessageBody   : null,
    divLoading       : null,

    selectedItem     : null,

    //more code here
}

//more code here
```

The properties that comprise this definition are as follows:

❑ The first property, `parser`, contains an XParser feed object.

❑ Next is an array called `feeds`, and this contains a list of feeds retrieved from the feeds list.

❑ The next seven properties reference `HTMLElement` objects. These elements are constantly used throughout the application's session, so it makes good sense to cache them.

❑ The last property, `selectedItem`, is a pointer to the item (`<a/>` element) last clicked by the user.

These properties are initialized as `null` to prevent any errors from occurring.

Initializing the UI

Before the user can interact with the UI, the `HTMLElement` properties need to be initialized. The method for this is called `init()`, and aside from assigning the properties for the elements, it sizes the UI elements that need dynamic sizes. This method is called only on the `load` and `resize` events of the window. Therefore, the function exists as a method of the `fooReader` object, but its definition lies outside of the main object definition. This doesn't really do anything except present the visual differentiation between this method and the other members of `fooReader`.

```
var fooReader = {
    parser   : null,
    feeds    : [],

    //HTML elements
```

```
        divFeedList     : null,
        divViewingItem  : null,
        divItemList     : null,
        divMessageTitle : null,
        aMessageLink    : null,
        divMessageBody  : null,
        divLoading      : null,

        selectedItem    : null,

        //more code here
}
```

```
fooReader.init = function (evt) {
    evt = evt || window.event;

    if (evt.type == "load") { //Things to initialize only on the load event
        fooReader.divFeedList      = document.getElementById("divFeedList");
        fooReader.divViewingItem   = document.getElementById("divViewingItem");
        fooReader.divItemList      = document.getElementById("divItemList");
        fooReader.divMessageTitle  = document.getElementById("divMessageTitle");
        fooReader.aMessageLink     = document.getElementById("aMessageLink");
        fooReader.divMessageBody   = document.getElementById("divMessageBody");
        fooReader.divLoading       = document.getElementById("divLoading");

        //more code here
    }

    var divPaneContainer = document.getElementById("divPaneContainer");
    var divReadingPane = document.getElementById("divReadingPane");
    var divMessageContainer = document.getElementById("divMessageContainer");
    var divMessageHeader = document.getElementById("divMessageHeader");

    //more code here

};

window.onload   = fooReader.init;
window.onresize = fooReader.init;
```

Since developers still have to cope with differing event models, the first line of the method retrieves the correct event object. Next, the event's type is checked to determine whether it was the load event that fired. If this is true, the various HTMLElement properties are assigned with the document.getElementById() method.

Outside the if block, other HTMLElements are retrieved and assigned to variables. These variables are used in the sizing operations that follow:

```
//fooReader object code here

fooReader.init = function (evt) {
    evt = evt || window.event;

    if (evt.type == "load") { //Things to initialize only on the load event
        fooReader.divFeedList      = document.getElementById("divFeedList");
```

483

```
fooReader.divViewingItem    = document.getElementById("divViewingItem");
fooReader.divItemList       = document.getElementById("divItemList");
fooReader.divMessageTitle   = document.getElementById("divMessageTitle");
fooReader.aMessageLink      = document.getElementById("aMessageLink");
fooReader.divMessageBody    = document.getElementById("divMessageBody");
fooReader.divLoading        = document.getElementById("divLoading");

    //more code here
}

var divPaneContainer = document.getElementById("divPaneContainer");
var divReadingPane = document.getElementById("divReadingPane");
var divMessageContainer = document.getElementById("divMessageContainer");
var divMessageHeader = document.getElementById("divMessageHeader");

var iDocHeight = document.documentElement.clientHeight;
divPaneContainer.style.height = iDocHeight -
                            divPaneContainer.offsetTop - 12 + "px";

var iFeedsListHeight = divPaneContainer.offsetHeight -
                    fooReader.divViewingItem.offsetHeight -
                    getStyleNumber(fooReader.divFeedList, "paddingTop") -
                    getStyleNumber(fooReader.divFeedList, "paddingBottom");


fooReader.divFeedList.style.height = iFeedsListHeight +  "px";

//more code here
};

window.onload   = fooReader.init;
window.onresize = fooReader.init;
```

This new code begins by getting the height of the viewport with `document.documentElement`
`.clientHeight`. That value is then used in conjunction with `divPaneContainer`'s `offsetTop` to set
`divPaneContainer`'s height. The numeric constant, 12, is for visual purposes only, because it provides
12 pixels of space between the bottom of the container and the bottom of the window.

Next is the assignment of the `iFeedsListHeight` variable, which is used to set the height of
`divFeedList`. This element's height is set to fill all available space in the pane. So, the calculation takes
the size of the pane container's height, subtracts the size of the pane header by using the
`divViewingItem`'s `offsetHeight` property, and finally subtracts the `paddingTop` and
`paddingBottom` style values from `divFeedList` itself. The two latter values both contribute to
`divFeedList`'s height. Therefore, they need to be included in the calculation. This size in combination
with `overflow: auto` in the CSS makes the contents of this pane scroll if it exceeds the size of the pane.

Next, use the same process for the items pane, except substitute `fooReader.divFeedList` for
`fooReader.divItemList`, like this:

```
//fooReader object code here

fooReader.init = function (evt) {
    evt = evt || window.event;
```

```
if (evt.type == "load") { //Things to initialize only on the load event
    fooReader.divFeedList      = document.getElementById("divFeedList");
    fooReader.divViewingItem   = document.getElementById("divViewingItem");
    fooReader.divItemList      = document.getElementById("divItemList");
    fooReader.divMessageTitle  = document.getElementById("divMessageTitle");
    fooReader.aMessageLink     = document.getElementById("aMessageLink");
    fooReader.divMessageBody   = document.getElementById("divMessageBody");
    fooReader.divLoading       = document.getElementById("divLoading");

    //more code here
}

var divPaneContainer = document.getElementById("divPaneContainer");
var divReadingPane = document.getElementById("divReadingPane");
var divMessageContainer = document.getElementById("divMessageContainer");
var divMessageHeader = document.getElementById("divMessageHeader");

var iDocHeight = document.documentElement.clientHeight;
divPaneContainer.style.height = iDocHeight -
                        divPaneContainer.offsetTop - 12 + "px";

var iFeedsListHeight = divPaneContainer.offsetHeight -
                    fooReader.divViewingItem.offsetHeight -
                    getStyleNumber(fooReader.divFeedList, "paddingTop") -
                    getStyleNumber(fooReader.divFeedList, "paddingBottom");


fooReader.divFeedList.style.height = iFeedsListHeight +  "px";


var iItemListHeight = divPaneContainer.offsetHeight -
                    fooReader.divViewingItem.offsetHeight -
                    getStyleNumber(fooReader.divItemList, "paddingTop") -
                    getStyleNumber(fooReader.divItemList, "paddingBottom");

fooReader.divItemList.style.height = iItemListHeight  + "px";


var iMessageBodyHeight = divReadingPane.offsetHeight -
                    divMessageHeader.offsetHeight -
                    getStyleNumber(divMessageContainer, "paddingTop") -
                    getStyleNumber(divMessageContainer, "paddingTop");

fooReader.divMessageBody.style.height = iMessageBodyHeight + "px";
};

window.onload   = fooReader.init;
window.onresize = fooReader.init;
```

Setting the height of divMessageBody follows somewhat the same pattern you've just seen. It uses the reading pane's and the message header's height instead of the pane container and header. It also gets the vertical padding values from the divMessageContainer element as opposed of the divMessageBody. The end result is the same, however. When the message body's height is set, the content will scroll if necessary.

Showing and Hiding Loading Cues

The `fooReader` object exposes two methods for showing and hiding the loading cue:
`showLoadingDiv()` and `hideLoadingDiv()`.

```
hideLoadingDiv : function () {
        this.divLoading.style.display = "none";
},

showLoadingDiv : function () {
    this.divLoading.style.display = "block";
},
```

These methods simply change the `display` property to `"none"` or `"block"` to hide and show the element.

Setting the Reading Pane's Content

There is one method that sets the content in the reading pane, and it is called `setMessage()`. This
method adds content to the `divMessageTitle`, `aMessageLink`, and `divMessageBody` elements. It
accepts three arguments, the message title, the link associated with the message, and the message's body,
and it uses the values accordingly.

```
setMessage : function (sTitle, sHref, sMessageBody) {
    this.divMessageTitle.innerHTML = sTitle;
    this.aMessageLink.href = sHref;
    this.divMessageBody.innerHTML = sMessageBody;
},
```

Item Methods

There are four methods associated with the items pane, and they are responsible for populating the
item pane with items, changing the item pane header, clearing the item pane, and selecting an item
programmatically.

Adding Items

The first method, `addItem()`, dynamically creates an item's HTML and appends it to the item pane. It
accepts two arguments: an XParser item object and the number associated with the item.

```
addItem : function (oItem, iNum) {
    var aItem = document.createElement("A");
    aItem.className = "itemlink";
    aItem.href = oItem.link.value;

    aItem.setAttribute("frFeedItem",iNum);
    aItem.id = "item" + iNum;

    var divHeadline = document.createElement("DIV");
    divHeadline.className = "itemheadline";
    divHeadline.innerHTML = oItem.title.value;

    var divDate = document.createElement("DIV");
    divDate.className = "itemdate";
```

```
            divDate.appendChild(document.createTextNode("Date: " + oItem.date.value));
            aItem.appendChild(divHeadline);
            aItem.appendChild(divDate);

            //more code here

            this.divItemList.appendChild(aItem);
    },
```

This code uses the information contained in the XParser item object to create the item's HTML. Notice that an attribute called "frFeedItem" is created for the aItem element. This attribute is used to contain the number associated with this item and is used later to add content to the reading pane.

At this point, clicking the item does nothing for the application. In fact, it takes the user to the URL specified in aItem's href property. This is not the desired functionality, so the click event must be handled. Clicking the item should do two things.

❑ First, the currently selected item should return to its normal state, and the newly clicked item should become selected.

❑ Second, the reading pane should be populated with content.

The onclick event handler executes in the scope of the <a/> element. Therefore, the code needs to use fooReader's API to access parts of the UI.

```
    addItem : function (oItem, iNum) {
        var aItem = document.createElement("A");
        aItem.className = "itemlink";
        aItem.href = oItem.link.value;

        aItem.onclick = function () {
            var oSelectedItem = fooReader.selectedItem;

            if (oSelectedItem != this) {
                if (oSelectedItem) {
                    oSelectedItem.className = "itemlink";
                }

                fooReader.selectedItem = this;
                this.className = "itemlink-selected";
            }

            var iItemNum = this.getAttribute("frFeedItem");

            var oItem = fooReader.parser.items[iItemNum];
            fooReader.setMessage(oItem.title.value,
                                 oItem.link.value,
                                 oItem.description.value);
            return false;
        };

        //more code here
```

```
        aItem.setAttribute("frFeedItem",iNum);
        aItem.id = "item" + iNum;

        var divHeadline = document.createElement("DIV");
        divHeadline.className = "itemheadline";
        divHeadline.innerHTML = oItem.title.value;

        var divDate = document.createElement("DIV");
        divDate.className = "itemdate";
        divDate.appendChild(document.createTextNode("Date: " + oItem.date.value));
        aItem.appendChild(divHeadline);
        aItem.appendChild(divDate);

        this.divItemList.appendChild(aItem);
    },
```

The first few lines of this code retrieve `fooReader.selectedItem` and determine whether or not this is a new item being clicked. If it is, then the old selected item's `className` property is set to `"itemlink"` to return it to the normal state. Then `fooReader.selectedItem` stores the new selected item and changes its `className` to `"itemlink-selected"`.

Next, the value contained in the link's `frFeedItem` attribute is retrieved and used in the `fooReader.parser.items` collection to retrieve the correct item, and its information is sent to the `setMessage()` method. Finally, the event handler returns `false`, forcing the browser not to navigate to the URL specified by the `href` property.

The items now populate the items pane and perform the desired function when clicked. However, it would add a nice touch to do something when the item is double-clicked. In Outlook 2003+, double-clicking an item pulls up the e-mail message in a new window. FooReader.NET can essentially do the same thing; it can open a new window and navigate to the article's URL.

```
addItem : function (oItem, iNum) {
    var aItem = document.createElement("A");
    aItem.className = "itemlink";
    aItem.href = oItem.link.value;

    aItem.onclick = function () {
        var oSelectedItem = fooReader.selectedItem;

        if (oSelectedItem != this) {
            if (oSelectedItem) {
                oSelectedItem.className = "itemlink";
            }

            fooReader.selectedItem = this;
            this.className = "itemlink-selected";
        }

        var iItemNum = this.getAttribute("frFeedItem");

        var oItem = fooReader.parser.items[iItemNum];
        fooReader.setMessage(oItem.title.value,
                             oItem.link.value,
                             oItem.description.value);
```

```
        return false;
    };

    aItem.ondblclick = function () {
        window.open(this.href);
    };

    aItem.setAttribute("frFeedItem",iNum);
    aItem.id = "item" + iNum;

    var divHeadline = document.createElement("DIV");
    divHeadline.className = "itemheadline";
    divHeadline.innerHTML = oItem.title.value;

    var divDate = document.createElement("DIV");
    divDate.className = "itemdate";
    divDate.appendChild(document.createTextNode("Date: " + oItem.date.value));
    aItem.appendChild(divHeadline);
    aItem.appendChild(divDate);

    this.divItemList.appendChild(aItem);
},
```

This code defines the `ondbclick` event handler, and like the `onclick` event handler, `ondbclick` executes within the context of the `<a/>` element. So, the `this` keyword references the `HTMLAnchorElement`. The body of the handler is simple: the `window.open()` method is called and the value of the `href` property is passed to it. The result is a new window opening to the new URL.

Changing the Heading Information

Letting the user know what feed is currently loaded is important, so a method called `setViewingItem()` is responsible for changing the item pane's heading to that of the feed's title. It accepts one argument, a string value containing the text to change to.

```
setViewingItem : function (sViewingItem) {
    this.divViewingItem.innerHTML = sViewingItem;
},
```

The `divViewingItem` element's CSS hides the element's overflow, so if the text is larger than the element's specified dimensions, it will not resize the element.

Clearing Items

Before loading a new feed into the application, the old feed's items must be removed from the items pane. The `clearItems()` method does this and accepts no arguments. It simply loops through and removes the child nodes of the `divItemList` element.

```
clearItems : function () {
    while (this.divItemList.hasChildNodes()) {
        this.divItemList.removeChild(this.divItemList.lastChild);
    }
},
```

When the loop exists, all items are removed from the pane, and it is ready to be populated again.

Selecting Items

There are times when selecting a specific item programmatically is necessary. For example, when a feed loads into the application, the first item is selected automatically. The `selectItem()` method does this, and the action simulates the effect of clicking an item. It accepts an integer argument, the number of the item to select.

```
selectItem     : function (iItemNum) {
    if (iItemNum > -1 && iItemNum < fooReader.parser.items.length) {
        var oItem = document.getElementById("item" + iItemNum);

        oItem.onclick.call(oItem);
    } else {
        throw new Error("FooReader Error: Supplied index is out of range.");
    }
},
```

This method first checks to see if `iItemNum` is within the range of 0 and the length of the `fooReader` `.parser.items` array. If so, then the code retrieves the item with `document.getElementById()`. Next, the item's `onclick` method is invoked in the scope of the item with the `call()` method. This doesn't actually raise the click event, but it simulates the action performed by a click in this application. Ideally, the DOM 2 `dispatchEvent()` method would be called, but IE does not support the method.

If the value of `iItemNum` is outside the specified bounds, then an error is thrown, stating that the value is out of range.

Feed Methods

There are a variety of methods involved with the feeds pane, and they load specific feeds, add feeds to the pane, and parse and retrieve the feed list.

Loading Specific Feeds

Loading a specific feed to be displayed into the UI involves the `loadFeed()` method. This method accepts one argument: the URL of the feed to retrieve. Its job is to show the loading cue and request the feed from the server by using XParser.

```
loadFeed : function (sUrl) {
    this.showLoadingDiv();

    var sUrl = "xmlproxy.aspx?feed=" + encodeURIComponent(sUrl);

    xparser.getFeed(sUrl, this.loadFeed_callBack, this);
},
```

The URL provided to the `loadFeed()` function is passed to the `encodeURIComponent()` JavaScript function to ensure proper transmission. Then by using XParser, the request is made to the server to retrieve the feed. When the request is completed, the `loadFeed_callBack()` method is called.

The callback method's purpose is to take the information from the XParser feed object, populate the items pane, and hide the loading cue.

```
loadFeed_callBack : function (oFeed) {
    this.parser = oFeed;

    this.clearItems();

    this.setViewingItem(this.parser.title.value);

    for (var i = 0, item; item = this.parser.items[i]; i++) {
        this.addItem(item, i);
    }

    this.hideLoadingDiv();

    this.selectItem(0);
},
```

The final step is selecting the first item in the items pane, which in turns loads data into the reading pane.

Adding Feeds

Adding feeds to the feeds pane is similar to adding items to the items pane. The method responsible for this is addFeed(), and it accepts two arguments: the feed's title and its URL.

```
addFeed : function (sTitle, sUrl) {
    var aFeedLink = document.createElement("a");
    aFeedLink.appendChild(document.createTextNode(sTitle));
    aFeedLink.href = sUrl;
    aFeedLink.className = "feedlink";
    aFeedLink.title = "Load " + sTitle;

    aFeedLink.onclick = function () {
        fooReader.loadFeed(this.href);
        return false;
    };

    this.divFeedList.appendChild(aFeedLink);
},
```

When the feed is clicked, the onclick event handler loads the selected feed with the loadFeed() method, which in turn populates the items pane and loads the first item into the reading pane.

The Feeds List

The list of feeds used by FooReader.NET is contained in the feeds.xml file. The XML in this file is in the Outline Processor Markup Language (OPML). OPML is an XML format developed by Dave Winer (who also developed RSS) for marking up outlines. It now has become the standard exchange format for feed lists in RSS and Atom aggregators.

OPML's structure is simple, and it looks like the following (and this is the list provided in the code download).

```
<opml version="1.0">
  <head>
    <title>FooReader Feed List</title>
  </head>
  <body>
    <outline text="Yahoo! Top Stories" title="Yahoo! Top Stories"
       type="rss" xmlUrl="http://rss.news.yahoo.com/rss/topstories"></outline>

    <outline text="Nicholas C. Zakas" title="Nicholas C. Zakas"
       type="rss" xmlUrl="http://www.nczonline.net/rss/"></outline>

    <outline text="Jeremy McPeak" title="Jeremy McPeak"
       type="rss" xmlUrl="http://www.wdonline.com/rss/"></outline>
  </body>
</opml>
```

The root element is `<opml/>`, and it must contain a `version` attribute. As of this writing, version 1.0 is the only version available. The root element contains two child elements: `<head/>` and `<body/>`.

The `<head/>` element is reminiscent of HTML's `<head/>` element in that it contains metadata. The previous example shows the `<title/>` element, and it represents the title of the document. Other elements valid in the `<head/>` are `dateCreated`, `dateModified`, `ownerName`, `ownerEmail`, `expansionState`, `vertScrollState`, `windowTop`, `windowLeft`, `windowBottom`, `windowRight`. The `expansionState` element contains a comma-separated list of line numbers that the aggregator should expand when displayed. The window elements define the position and size of the display window. An OPML processor may disregard any of these elements, but the most commonly used are `title`, `dateCreated`, and `dateModified`. The `<body/>` element contains the outline data, and it must contain at least one `<outline/>` element.

The `<outline/>` element represents one line of the outline. You can nest `<outline/>` elements with other `<outline/>` elements to create a hierarchical outline structure. The `<outline/>` element has a variety of attributes, but the most common are `text`, `title`, `type`, and `xmlUrl`.

❑   The `text` and `title` attributes are used interchangeably, although it is recommended to use both and assign them the same value.

❑   The `type` attribute contains the type of feed this line represents.

❑   The `xmlUrl` attribute contains the link to the external feed.

While it is perfectly legal to nest `<outline/>` elements in the body, FooReader.NET recognizes only `<outline/>` elements that are direct children of `<body/>`.

Parsing the Feeds List

The `fooReader` object exposes a method and a class to parse the feeds list and organize the individual feeds.

The OpmlFileFeed class is a representation of a feed contained in feeds.xml. The constructor accepts one argument, the <outline/> node:

```
OpmlFileFeed : function (oFeedNode) {
    this.title = oFeedNode.getAttribute("title");
    this.url = oFeedNode.getAttribute("xmlUrl");
},
```

The class has two properties: title and url, which map to the title and xmlUrl attributes respectively. It is a simple class, and the instances of this class are assigned as elements of the fooReader.feeds[] array.

The function that reads feeds.xml is called readOpmlFile(). It accepts one argument: serialized XML data.

```
readOpmlFile : function (sXmlText) {
    var oXmlDom = zXmlDom.createDocument();
    oXmlDom.loadXML(sXmlText);

    var nlFeeds = zXPath.selectNodes(oXmlDom.documentElement, "body/outline");

    for (var i = 0, oFeed; oFeed = nlFeeds[i]; i++) {
        this.feeds.push( new this.OpmlFileFeed(oFeed) );
    }
},
```

This code creates an XML DOM and loads the XML data into it. Next, it uses an XPath evaluation to retrieve a NodeList of <outline/> elements and loops through them to populate the feeds[] array with OpmlFileFeed objects.

Retrieving the Feeds List

The last method of the application, and also the second to execute (after fooReader.init), is getFeedList(). This method creates an XHR request and requests the feeds.xml file from the server.

```
getFeedList : function () {
    var oHttp = zXmlHttp.createRequest();

    oHttp.onreadystatechange = function () {
        if (oHttp.readyState == 4) {
            if (oHttp.status == 200 || oHttp.status == 304) {
                //more code here
            }
        }
    };

    var date = (new Date()).getTime();
    oHttp.open("GET", "feeds.xml?time=" + date, true);
    oHttp.send(null);
}
```

It is important to note that the `feeds.xml` file is static. It is not dynamically created by the server application, and thus it is cached the first time it is requested. To get around this issue, an argument called `time` is added to the query string, and its value is set to the time of when `getFeedList()` executes. This ensures a unique request every time this method executes, foiling the caching attempts made by the browser.

Once the XHR receives the full response from the server, the application can begin to initialize.

```
getFeedList : function () {
    var oHttp = zXmlHttp.createRequest();

    oHttp.onreadystatechange = function () {
        if (oHttp.readyState == 4) {
            if (oHttp.status == 200 || oHttp.status == 304) {
                fooReader.readOpmlFile(oHttp.responseText);

                for (var i = 0, feed; feed = fooReader.feeds[i]; i++) {
                    fooReader.addFeed(feed.title, feed.url);
                }

                fooReader.loadFeed(fooReader.feeds[0].url);
            }
        }
    };

    var date = (new Date()).getTime();
    oHttp.open("GET", "feeds.xml?time=" + date, true);
    oHttp.send(null);
}
```

The first step is to parse the feeds list with the `readOpmlFile()` method. Once the `feeds[]` array is populated, the code then loops through that array and populates the feeds pane with `addFeed()`. The last new line uses the `loadFeed()` method to load the first feed in the list.

Finishing Up

All the code is in place and ready to execute, but nowhere in the code is `getFeedsList()` called. This is actually called in the `init()` method.

```
fooReader.init = function (evt) {
    evt = evt || window.event;

    if (evt.type == "load") { //Things to initialize only on the load event
        fooReader.divFeedList      = document.getElementById("divFeedList");
        fooReader.divViewingItem   = document.getElementById("divViewingItem");
        fooReader.divItemList      = document.getElementById("divItemList");
        fooReader.divMessageTitle  = document.getElementById("divMessageTitle");
        fooReader.aMessageLink     = document.getElementById("aMessageLink");
        fooReader.divMessageBody   = document.getElementById("divMessageBody");
        fooReader.divLoading       = document.getElementById("divLoading");

        fooReader.getFeedList();
    }

    var divPaneContainer = document.getElementById("divPaneContainer");
    var divReadingPane = document.getElementById("divReadingPane");
```

```
        var divMessageContainer = document.getElementById("divMessageContainer");
        var divMessageHeader = document.getElementById("divMessageHeader");

        var iDocHeight = document.documentElement.clientHeight;
        divPaneContainer.style.height = iDocHeight -
                                divPaneContainer.offsetTop - 12 + "px";

        var iFeedsListHeight = divPaneContainer.offsetHeight -
                        fooReader.divViewingItem.offsetHeight -
                        getStyleNumber(fooReader.divFeedList, "paddingTop") -
                        getStyleNumber(fooReader.divFeedList, "paddingBottom");


        fooReader.divFeedList.style.height = iFeedsListHeight +  "px";


        var iItemListHeight = divPaneContainer.offsetHeight -
                        fooReader.divViewingItem.offsetHeight -
                        getStyleNumber(fooReader.divItemList, "paddingTop") -
                        getStyleNumber(fooReader.divItemList, "paddingBottom");

        fooReader.divItemList.style.height = iItemListHeight  + "px";


        var iMessageBodyHeight = divReadingPane.offsetHeight -
                        divMessageHeader.offsetHeight -
                        getStyleNumber(divMessageContainer, "paddingTop") -
                        getStyleNumber(divMessageContainer, "paddingTop");

        fooReader.divMessageBody.style.height = iMessageBodyHeight + "px";
    };
```

The getFeedsList() method is called only when the load event fires in the browser. Otherwise, it would execute each time the browser's window resizes, and it would interrupt the user's reading.

The code execution of the client-side application is a chain reaction. One method calls another method until the reading pane displays content. When the user clicks a feed or an item, the reaction begins from that point and continues until the reading pane's contents are updated.

The server-side application is different in that its sole purpose is to retrieve data from a remote server.

The Server Application

In a perfect world, an application such as FooReader.NET would be strictly client-side. JavaScript would be able to retrieve XML feeds across domains with XHR, and there would be no need to make any calls to a server component. Because of JavaScript's security restrictions, however, it is not possible to retrieve data from a different domain; thus, a server-side component is required.

Possible Paradigms

The server's job in FooReader.NET is to retrieve the remote XML feeds for the client to use. Following this model, there are two possible design paths for the server; both have their pros and cons.

The first method is a cached feed architecture. The server program would act as a service, fetching a list of feeds at a certain time interval, caching them, and serving the cached feeds to the client when requested. This option potentially saves bandwidth, but it also risks the reader not having up-to-date feeds. More user action would be required to display the current, up-to-date feeds, which goes against the Ajax ideology.

The second method is a delivery on demand architecture, where the server would retrieve any given feed when the user requests it. This may use more bandwidth, but it ensures the reader will have up-to-date information; moreover, this design is inline with the Ajax concepts and is what the user would expect.

Implementation

The solution implemented in FooReader.NET uses a hybrid approach. The requested feeds are retrieved with the delivery-on-demand model, but the application caches a feed when it is fetched. The cached version is used only in the event that the remote host cannot be contacted, and an up-to-date feed cannot be retrieved. This ensures that the user has something to read, even though it is older data.

Because the server is only responsible for pulling and caching remote feeds, it makes sense to have one ASP.NET page responsible for these operations. This page, called `xmlproxy.aspx`, will have a code-behind file where the ASP.NET code is contained.

> *Codebehind is a method for authoring web pages for the ASP.NET platform. Unlike inline programming models, where the server-side code is interspersed with HTML markup (like PHP and ASP), codebehind enables you to remove all logic from the HTML code and place it in a separate class file. This results in a clean separation of HTML and your .NET programming language of choice.*

The language of choice for this project is C#, which is the language created specifically for the .NET Framework.

Providing Errors

The problem with the approach of providing XML data to the client is handling errors. The client-side component expects all data to be XML data in either RSS or Atom format. While this does present a problem, its solution is rather simple: provide the error message in one of the two formats.

> *If you're following along with Visual Studio, create a new class file and call it* `FooReaderError.cs`. *Visual Studio will ask you if you want to place the file in the* `App_Code` *folder. Choose yes.*

The `FooReaderError` class is a static class, and it builds a simple RSS document with data from an `Exception` instance. It exposes one static method called `WriteErrorDocument()` that accepts an `Exception` object as a parameter. The following is the code for the `FooReaderError` class:

```
public static class FooReaderError
{
    public static string WriteErrorDocument(Exception exception)
    {
        string xml = "<?xml version=\"1.0\" encoding=\"utf-8\" ?>";
        xml += "<rss version=\"2.0\">";
        xml += "<channel>";
        xml += "<title>FooReader Error</title>";
```

```
                xml += "<description>FooReader Error</description> ";
                xml += "<link>javascript:void(0);</link>";
                xml += "<item>";
                xml += "<pubDate>Just Now</pubDate>";
                xml += String.Format("<title>FooReader Error: {0}</title>",
                                     exception.GetType().ToString());

                xml += "<description>";
                xml += "<![CDATA[";
                xml += "<p>An error occurred.</p>";
                xml += String.Format("<p style='color: red'>{0}</p>", exception.Message);
                xml += "]]>";
                xml += "</description>";
                xml += "<link>javascript:void(0);</link>";
                xml += "</item>";
                xml += "</channel> ";
                xml += "</rss>";

                return xml;
        }
}
```

This code builds an RSS document to inform the user of two things.

❑   The first gives the error's type by using `exception.GetType().ToString()`. This information is placed into the `<item/>` element's `<title/>`.

❑   The second piece of information is the error message itself, which is displayed as red text.

The resulting XML file looks like this:

```
<?xml version="1.0" encoding="utf-8" ?>

<rss version="2.0">
    <channel>
        <title>FooReader Error</title>
        <description>FooReader Error</description>
        <link>javascript: void(0);</link>

        <item>
            <pubDate>Just Now</pubDate>
            <title>FooReader Error: [Error Type]</title>
            <description>
                <![CDATA[
                    <p>An error occurred.</p>
                    <p style='color: red'>[Error Message]</p>
                ]]>
            </description>
            <link>javascript: void(0);</link>
        </item>
    </channel>
</rss>
```

With the error strategy in place, the proxy code can handle and display errors when needed.

Building the Proxy

ASP.NET pages are classes that inherit from the `System.Web.UI.Page` class, and as such, they have formal class definitions and can have any number of properties and methods. The `xmlproxy` class, named after the file name, has one private method, aside from the usual protected `Page_Load` event handler.

If you're following along in Visual Studio, don't forget to add the proper `using` statement at the top of the class file. They are `System.IO` and `System.Net`.

```
public partial class xmlproxy : System.Web.UI.Page
{
    protected void Page_Load(object sender, EventArgs e)
    {
        //more code here
    }

    private string getLocalFile(string path)
    {
        string contents = String.Empty;
        using (StreamReader file = File.OpenText(path))
        {
            contents = file.ReadToEnd();
        }
        return contents;
    }
}
```

The `getLocalFile()` method is a private method for retrieving files located in the server's file system. This method is called to retrieve a cached feed. It uses a `System.IO.StreamReader` object to open the file and extract and return the file's contents.

Setting the Headers

The entry point for the server side is the `Page_Load` event handler, and all code, with the exception of the `getLocalFile()` method and the `FooReaderError` class, is contained in the event handler. The first step is to set two headers. Settings headers in ASP.NET is a simple task:

```
Response.ContentType = "text/xml";
Response.CacheControl = "No-cache";

//more code here
```

Headers are set with the `Response` object, which encapsulates HTTP response information. Setting the MIME content type is imperative to the operation of the application. Mozilla-based browsers will not load an XML file as XML unless the MIME specifies an XML document, and "`text/xml`" is one of many types that do this.

It is also important to make sure that the XML data retrieved with XHR is not cached. Today's browsers cache all data retrieved with XHR unless explicitly told not to with the `CacheControl` header. If this header is not set, the browser will use the cached data until the browser's cache is dumped.

Getting the Remote Feed

FooReader.NET's server component works as a simple proxy server. The client asks for a specific URL, and the application essentially forwards that request to the remote server. To determine the feed to retrieve, the server relies upon the query string. When requesting a feed, the client component sends a request in the following format:

```
xmlproxy.aspx?feed=[feed_url]
```

In ASP.NET, the `Request` object contains a `NameValueCollection` called `QueryString`. Using this collection, you can extract the value of the feed variable like this:

```
Response.ContentType = "text/xml";
Response.CacheControl = "No-cache";

if (Request.QueryString["feed"] != null)
{
    Uri url = null;

    try
    {
        url = new Uri(Request.QueryString["feed"]);
    }
    catch (UriFormatException exception)
    {
        Response.Write(FooReaderError.WriteErrorDocument(exception));

        Response.End();
    }

    string fileName = String.Format(@"{0}\xml\{1}.xml",
        Server.MapPath(String.Empty),
        HttpUtility.UrlEncode(url.AbsoluteUri)
    );

    //more code here
}
else
{
    try
    {
        throw new Exception("No feed specified for retrieval.");
    }
    catch (Exception exception)
    {
        Response.Write(FooReaderError.WriteErrorDocument(exception));
    }
}
```

This new code first checks the existence of the `feed` variable in the query string and attempts to create a `Uri` object with its value. If the value of `feed` is not in the correct format, the ASP.NET runtime throws a `UriFormatException` exception. If this happens, the `UriFormException` instance is passed to `FooReaderError.WriteErrorDocument()`. The resulting XML is written to the page with the

Response.Write() method, and the application is terminated with Response.End(). Otherwise, the code continues, and a string called fileName is created. This variable is used as the file name of the cached feed when it is received.

If the feed argument could not be found in the query string, then a new Exception is thrown and caught to display the appropriate message to the user. This error should not occur through the FooReader.NET application because the client-side code will always include feed and its value in the query string.

> String.Format(), as its name implies, formats strings (duh!). The first argument passed to the method is the string to format. This string most likely contains characters called format items that look like {0}, {1}, {2}, and so on. These format items are replaced with the corresponding arguments passed to the method. In the example above, {0} is replaced with the resulting string that Server.MapPath(String.Empty) returns.

> The @ operator before a string tells the compiler not to process escape strings. The string in the above example could have been written as "{0}\\xml\\{1}.xml" with the same results.

The .NET Framework provides a variety of classes that can retrieve data from a remote server. In fact, the Weather Widget in Chapter 12 used the System.Net.WebClient class to retrieve data from Weather.com's weather service. The WebClient class offers a simple interface; however, its simplicity can also be a drawback. For example, WebClient does not have any way of setting an amount of time to wait before the request times out. It also lacks the ability to let the remote server know what kind of application is requesting the feed. It is for these reasons that FooReader.NET does not use WebClient, but uses System.Net.HttpWebRequest instead.

The HttpWebRequest class derives from the System.Net.WebRequest abstract class and provides HTTP-specific functionality, so it is best suited for this application. To create an HttpWebRequest object, call the Create() method of the WebRequest class and cast it as HttpWebRequest as the following code does:

```
Response.ContentType = "text/xml";
Response.CacheControl = "No-cache";

if (Request.QueryString["feed"] != null)
{
    Uri url = null;

    try
    {
        url = new Uri(Request.QueryString["feed"]);
    }
    catch (UriFormatException exception)
    {
        Response.Write(FooReaderError.WriteErrorDocument(exception));

        Response.End();
    }

    string fileName = String.Format(@"{0}\xml\{1}.xml",
        Server.MapPath(String.Empty),
        HttpUtility.UrlEncode(url.AbsoluteUri)
    );
```

```
        try
        {
            HttpWebRequest request = (HttpWebRequest)WebRequest.Create(url);

            request.UserAgent = "FooReader.NET 1.5 (http://reader.wdonline.com)";
            request.Timeout = 5000;

            //more code here
        }
        catch (WebException exception)
        {
            if (System.IO.File.Exists(fileName))
            {
                Response.Write(getLocalFile(fileName));
            }
            else
            {
                Response.Write(FooReaderError.WriteErrorDocument(exception));
            }
        }
    }
    else
    {
        try
        {
            throw new Exception("No feed specified for retrieval.");
        }
            catch (Exception exception)
        {
            Response.Write(FooReaderError.WriteErrorDocument(exception));
        }
    }
```

After the request object's creation, this code uses the UserAgent property to assign the user-agent HTTP header. It is not necessary to use this property, but it accurately documents what is hitting the remote server. Many conventional aggregators have their own user-agent string; FooReader.NET does, too.

Following the UserAgent line, the Timeout property is set to 5 seconds. If no response is received from the remote server after 5 seconds, the request times out. If this happens, a WebException exception is thrown, in which case control is dropped to the catch block. The first line checks to see if the cached file exists in the file system; if so, it is retrieved with getLocalFile() and written to the page. If not, then the FooReaderError class provides an error document and outputs it to the application's response.

A WebException error can be thrown for any error that is network-related, not just for time outs.

At this point, however, the request has not been sent yet; the code is just ready to handle any web-related errors when it's sent. Sending the request involves invoking the HttpWebRequest object's GetResponse() method, which returns a WebResponse instance. The following new code does this.

```
Response.ContentType = "text/xml";
Response.CacheControl = "No-cache";

if (Request.QueryString["feed"] != null)
```

```
    {
        Uri url = null;

        try
        {
            url = new Uri(Request.QueryString["feed"]);
        }
        catch (UriFormatException exception)
        {
            Response.Write(FooReaderError.WriteErrorDocument(exception));

            Response.End();
        }

        string fileName = String.Format(@"{0}\xml\{1}.xml",
            Server.MapPath(String.Empty),
            HttpUtility.UrlEncode(url.AbsoluteUri)
        );

        try
        {
            HttpWebRequest request = (HttpWebRequest)WebRequest.Create(url);

            request.UserAgent = "FooReader.NET 1.5 (http://reader.wdonline.com)";
            request.Timeout = 5000;

            using (HttpWebResponse response = (HttpWebResponse)request.GetResponse())
            {
                using (StreamReader reader =new
StreamReader(response.GetResponseStream()))
                {
                    string feedXml = reader.ReadToEnd();

                    Response.Write(feedXml);

                    //more code here
                }
            }
        }
        catch (WebException exception)
        {
            if (System.IO.File.Exists(fileName))
            {
                Response.Write(getLocalFile(fileName));
            }
            else
            {
                Response.Write(FooReaderError.WriteErrorDocument(exception));
            }
        }
        //more code here
    }
    else
    {
```

```
    try
    {
        throw new Exception("No feed specified for retrieval.");
    }
        catch (Exception exception)
    {
        Response.Write(FooReaderError.WriteErrorDocument(exception));
    }
}
```

When the request is sent, and the response is received, you can get the contents of the server's response by using the `GetResponseStream()` method, a member of the `HttpWebResponse` class. This method returns a `Stream` object and can be read with a `System.IO.StreamReader` object, which is created in the second `using` block. The contents of the stream are then "read" and stored in the `feedXml` variable. The value contained in `feedXml` is then written to the page with `Response.Write()`. Since the `using` statement is used for the creation of the `HttpWebResponse` and `StreamReader` objects, they will be properly disposed of and do not require closing.

Caching the Feed

Caching the feed is beneficial to the user in case the remote server cannot be reached. FooReader.NET is a newsreader, and it is desirable for the user to have something to read, even if it is an older version. A `System.IO.StreamWriter` object is perfect for this job for its ease of use and its default UTF-8 encoding:

```
Response.ContentType = "text/xml";
Response.CacheControl = "No-cache";

if (Request.QueryString["feed"] != null)
{
    Uri url = null;

    try
    {
        url = new Uri(Request.QueryString["feed"]);
    }
    catch (UriFormatException exception)
    {
        Response.Write(FooReaderError.WriteErrorDocument(exception));

        Response.End();
    }

    string fileName = String.Format(@"{0}\xml\{1}.xml",
        Server.MapPath(String.Empty),
        HttpUtility.UrlEncode(url.AbsoluteUri)
    );

    try
    {
        HttpWebRequest request = (HttpWebRequest)WebRequest.Create(url);

        request.UserAgent = "FooReader.NET 1.5 (http://reader.wdonline.com)";
```

```
                request.Timeout = 5000;

                using (HttpWebResponse response = (HttpWebResponse)request.GetResponse())
                {
                    using (StreamReader reader =new
        StreamReader(response.GetResponseStream()))
                    {
                        string feedXml = reader.ReadToEnd();

                        Response.Write(feedXml);

                        using (StreamWriter writer = new StreamWriter(fileName))
                        {
                            writer.Write(feedXml);
                        }
                    }
                }
            }
            catch (WebException exception)
            {
                if (System.IO.File.Exists(fileName))
                {
                    Response.Write(getLocalFile(fileName));
                }
                else
                {
                    Response.Write(FooReaderError.WriteErrorDocument(exception));
                }
            }
            catch (IOException exception)
            {
                //do nothing here
            }

            //more code here
        }
        else
        {
            try
            {
                throw new Exception("No feed specified for retrieval.");
            }
            catch (Exception exception)
            {
                Response.Write(FooReaderError.WriteErrorDocument(exception));
            }
        }
```

The fileName variable, created earlier, is passed to the StreamWriter class's constructor. This creates the file or overwrites an existing one with the same name. The XML data contained in feedXml is then written to the file using the Write() method. This will cache the file, but any file system operation can increase the chance of an error. Therefore, it's important to handle a System.IO.IOException exception. This error is not critical. If the application got to the point of caching the file, then the request was successful, and data is available to send to the client-side component.

Only two errors are caught in this stage of the application. However, many others could occur, so it's important to catch every error possible. This can be done by catching a generic `Exception` like this:

```
Response.ContentType = "text/xml";
Response.CacheControl = "No-cache";

if (Request.QueryString["feed"] != null)
{
    Uri url = null;

    try
    {
        url = new Uri(Request.QueryString["feed"]);
    }
    catch (UriFormatException exception)
    {
        Response.Write(FooReaderError.WriteErrorDocument(exception));

        Response.End();
    }

    string fileName = String.Format(@"{0}\xml\{1}.xml",
        Server.MapPath(String.Empty),
        HttpUtility.UrlEncode(url.AbsoluteUri)
    );

    try
    {
        HttpWebRequest request = (HttpWebRequest)WebRequest.Create(url);

        request.UserAgent = "FooReader.NET 1.5 (http://reader.wdonline.com)";
        request.Timeout = 5000;

        using (HttpWebResponse response = (HttpWebResponse)request.GetResponse())
        {
            using (StreamReader reader =new
StreamReader(response.GetResponseStream()))
            {
                string feedXml = reader.ReadToEnd();

                Response.Write(feedXml);

                using (StreamWriter writer = new StreamWriter(fileName))
                {
                    writer.Write(feedXml);
                }
            }
        }
    }
    catch (WebException exception)
    {
        if (System.IO.File.Exists(fileName))
        {
            Response.Write(getLocalFile(fileName));
        }
```

```
        else
        {
            Response.Write(FooReaderError.WriteErrorDocument(exception));
        }
    }
    catch (IOException exception)
    {
        //do nothing here
    }
    catch (Exception exception)
    {
        Response.Write(FooReaderError.WriteErrorDocument(exception));
    }
}
else
{
    try
    {
        throw new Exception("No feed specified for retrieval.");
    }
        catch (Exception exception)
    {
        Response.Write(FooReaderError.WriteErrorDocument(exception));
    }
}
```

Doing this allows the application to appear responsive to the user because every action (even if it is an error) causes the application to do something. It also allows them to address any issue that may arise because the error and the cause for the error are displayed for the user to see.

It also ensures that the client receives XML data every time it gets a response from the server. This is important because the client-side components depend on data being in RSS or Atom format.

Now that both the client and server components are completed, it is time to set up FooReader.NET on the web server.

Setup and Testing

Because FooReader.NET is an ASP.NET application, setting it up on the web server requires following the same steps outlined in Chapter 12. Turn to the section of Chapter 12 that discusses setting up the Weather Widget as an application for more information.

Before deploying any web application, it is always a good idea to test the installation. Open your browser and navigate to http://localhost/fooreader/xmlproxy.aspx?feed=http://rss.news.yahoo.com/rss/topstories.

This tests to make sure that the server-side component is able to retrieve an external news feed properly. If everything is working correctly, you should see the XML feed displayed in your browser. Figure 15-4 shows the results in Firefox 2.0.

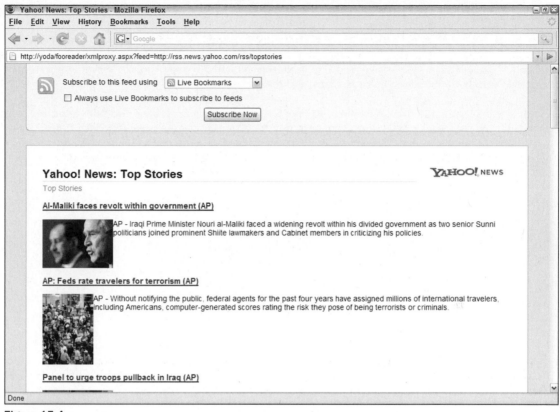

Figure 15-4

If for some reason you see an ASP.NET error, the error message will tell you what you should do. The most common error is an Access Denied error, in which case the proper modify rights should be given to the ASP.NET user account (or NETWORK SERVICE for Windows 2003).

If you do not have access to set permissions for the web server, such as when you rent web space from a provider, you may be able to solve Access Denied errors by turning on impersonation. The impersonation settings are located in the `web.config` file.

The `web.config` file is an XML-based configuration file for a web application. The root element of `web.config` is `<configuration/>`, which is usually followed by the `<system.web/>` element. You can add the following line to the `<system.web/>` element:

```
<identity impersonate="true"/>
```

Bear in mind that this solution is highly situational and depends on the web server's settings. However, it may solve unauthorized access errors you may encounter in a rented-server environment.

Once the application is tested and is confirmed to work, you can edit `feeds.xml` to contain whatever feeds you desire.

Summary

In this chapter, you learned how to build an ASP.NET RSS and Atom aggregator. You built a three-pane HTML page to serve as the UI for the application and styled it with CSS; then you built the client-side application to dynamically resize the UI, to request feeds with XParser from the server application, and to use the data to populate the feeds, items, and reading panes.

You learned that while the client-side components of a web application are a necessity to properly display data to the user, server-side components are needed to retrieve the necessary data. Using C# and the .NET Framework, you learned how to retrieve remote XML feeds, cache them, and output them to a page. You also learned how to set HTTP headers so that browsers will know what to expect, and remote servers will know what is hitting them.

Finally, you learned how to set up the application in IIS and test it to make sure that it was properly installed.

16

Case Study: AjaxMail

One of the most popular Ajax applications is Gmail, a web-based e-mail system that incorporates a lot of Ajax techniques to create a seamless user experience. Gmail loads a single page and then makes changes to reflect user actions, eliminating almost entirely the "click-and-wait" experience of most web applications. There is a lot of back and forth with the server to retrieve information that the user never knows is occurring because of the system's design. Because Gmail is an excellent example of how to build an Ajax-based web application, this chapter focuses on developing a similar application called AjaxMail.

In this chapter, you will use techniques learned throughout the book to bring AjaxMail to life. Both hidden frames and the XHR object will be used for communicating with the server, and you will be reminded when and how to use each technique. Remember, the whole point of using Ajax is to improve the user's experience; this chapter gives you the opportunity to see first-hand how to create an application with the user in mind.

> **AjaxMail is open source. The most recent version of all files are freely available at** `www.sourceforge.net/projects/ajaxmail`.

Requirements

Before building a web application, it's always good to define the requirements and build to them. You may never have considered the requirements for an e-mail application before. You probably use an e-mail application like Outlook, Thunderbird, or Eudora on a daily basis and have never really stopped to think about all the things it must do to provide a good user experience. For simplicity, AjaxMail will support a subset of what these applications do (although it is easy enough to extend the functionality on your own).

The requirements for AjaxMail are:

❑   Support for POP3 to receive mail and SMTP to send mail

❑   Ability to read a list of e-mail messages from the server

❑   Visual indication if a message contains an attachment

❑   Ability to read an individual e-mail with support for plain text messages only

❑   Notification when new mail messages arrive

❑   Ability to send, forward, and reply to messages

To implement these requirements, a variety of Ajax patterns and communication techniques will be used. There is extensive use of XHR, requiring the use of the zXml library, as well as some hidden iframes. In building this application, you will learn how to incorporate and integrate the various techniques you have learned in this book.

Architecture

AjaxMail is built using PHP for the server-side language and MySQL for the database. A database is necessary to keep track of information relating to specific messages, such as what folder they are in and whether they have been read. Both of these can be accomplished by setting specific flags for a message in the database.

There are two folders in AjaxMail: Inbox and Trash. When a message is deleted from the Inbox, it is moved to the Trash. The message is permanently deleted when the Trash is emptied; otherwise, the message remains in the Trash. (It is also possible to restore a message from the Trash and place it back in the Inbox.) Even though this chapter uses only these two folders, you may use as many folders as you wish.

Each time a request is made to the server, AjaxMail checks to see if there are any new messages in the specified POP3 e-mail account. If there are, the messages are downloaded and saved into the MySQL database. The messages are then read out of the database and sent back to the client.

Resources Used

AjaxMail uses several open source software libraries to achieve its functionality:

❑   **zXml Library:** The cross-browser XML JavaScript library used throughout this book. Available at www.nczonline.net/downloads.

❑   **Douglas Crockford's JSON JavaScript Library:** The JavaScript JSON parser. Available at www.json.org.

❑   **PHPMailer:** A PHP SMTP e-mail sending solution. Available at http://phpmailer.source forge.net.

❑   **JSON-PHP:** The PHP JSON library. Available at http://mike.teczno.com/json.html.

❑   **POP3Lib:** A PHP POP3 mail interface written by one of your authors, Jeremy McPeak. Available at www.wdonline.com/php/pop3lib.zip.

Note that all these resources are included in the book's example code downloads, available at www.wrox.com.

The Database Tables

Because AjaxMail will need e-mails to be stored in the database, several tables must be created. If you have sufficient rights to create a new database on the MySQL server, you should create a database named *AjaxMail*. (You may also use any other database that is already set up.) There are three tables to add: AjaxMailFolders, AjaxMailMessages, and AjaxMailAttachments.

The first table, AjaxMailFolders, defines the various folders available in AjaxMail:

```
CREATE TABLE AjaxMailFolders (
  FolderId int(11) NOT NULL auto_increment,
  Name text NOT NULL,
  PRIMARY KEY  (FolderId)
);

INSERT INTO AjaxMailFolders VALUES (1, 'Inbox');
INSERT INTO AjaxMailFolders VALUES (2, 'Trash');
```

Each folder in AjaxMail is assigned a FolderId (an auto-incrementing primary key) and a name. For the purposes of this chapter, there are only two folders: Inbox and Trash. You can feel free to add more to suit your own needs.

The AjaxMailMessages table holds each e-mail's information. It consists of 11 columns: a unique identification number (auto-incremented ,so you don't need to worry about it), the different fields of an e-mail (To, From, Subject, and so on), what folder it exists in (Inbox, Trash, and so on), and whether the user has read the e-mail. You can create the table using the following SQL statement:

```
CREATE TABLE AjaxMailMessages (
    MessageId int(11) NOT NULL auto_increment,
    `To` text NOT NULL,
    CC text NOT NULL,
    BCC text NOT NULL,
    `From` text NOT NULL,
    Subject text NOT NULL,
    Date bigint(20) default NULL,
    Message text NOT NULL,
    HasAttachments tinyint(1) NOT NULL default '0',
    Unread tinyint(1) NOT NULL default '1',
    FolderId int(11) NOT NULL default '0',
    PRIMARY KEY  (MessageId)
);
```

The MessageId field is an auto-incrementing field and provides the e-mail with a unique ID number in the database; it is also the table's primary key. The To, CC, BCC, From, Subject, Date, and Message fields are parts of an e-mail message. (To and From must be enclosed in backtick symbols because they are keywords in SQL.) The HasAttachments and Unread fields are tinyint, which means that they can have values of 0 or 1 (false or true). Finally, the FolderId field contains the ID number of the folder in which the message is stored. This enables you to select messages that exist only in the Inbox or Trash folders.

If an e-mail contains any attachments, they are stored in the AjaxMailAttachments table:

```
CREATE TABLE AjaxMailAttachments (
  AttachmentId int(11) NOT NULL auto_increment,
  MessageId int(11) NOT NULL default '0',
  Filename text NOT NULL,
  ContentType text NOT NULL,
  Size int(11) NOT NULL default '0',
  Data longtext NOT NULL,
  PRIMARY KEY  (AttachmentId)
)
```

Like the AjaxMailMessages table, the AjaxMailAttachments table contains an auto-incrementing field. This filed is called AttachmentId and provides each attachment with a unique ID number. The next field, MessageId, houses the message ID of the e-mail to which it was attached (this number matches the MessageId field in AjaxMailMessages). Next, the Filename and ContentType columns store the attachment's reported file name and content type (both are necessary to enable the user to download the attachment later). Last, the Size and Data fields store the attachment's size (in bytes) and the binary/text data of the file, respectively.

The Configuration File

Much like any application, AjaxMail relies on a configuration file, called config.inc.php, to provide information required to function properly. Because this information is required in many different areas of the application, it's best to store it as constants. In PHP, constants give you the advantage of being available in every scope of the application, meaning that you don't need to define them using the global keyword as you do with other global variables.

To create a constant in PHP, use the define() method, passing in the name of the constant (as a string) and its value. For example:

```
define("MY_CONSTANT", "my value");
```

The first group of constants relates directly to your MySQL database:

```
define("DB_USER", "root");
define("DB_PASSWORD", "password");
define("DB_SERVER", "localhost");
define("DB_NAME", "AjaxMail");
```

These constants are used when connecting to the database and must be replaced to reflect your database settings. Next, some constants are needed to provide information about your POP3 server:

```
define("POP3_USER", "test@domain.com");
define("POP3_PASSWORD", "password");
define("POP3_SERVER", "mail.domain.com");
```

Once again, these constants must be replaced with the information specific to your POP3 server. As you may have guessed, you also must supply some information about the SMTP server:

```
define("SMTP_DO_AUTHORIZATION", true);
define("SMTP_USER", "test@domain.com");
define("SMTP_PASSWORD", "password");
define("SMTP_SERVER", "mail.domain.com");

define("EMAIL_FROM_ADDRESS", "test@domain.com");
define("EMAIL_FROM_NAME", "Joe Somebody");
```

The first four lines set constant variables relating to user authentication for your SMTP server. The first variable sets whether or not your SMTP server requires user authentication to send e-mail. If set to `true`, the SMTP_USER and SMTP_PASSWORD must be set. (`false` means no authentication is required to send mail through the SMTP server.)

The second group of SMTP settings defines the user settings. You should set EMAIL_FROM_ADDRESS to contain your e-mail address, and set EMAIL_FROM_NAME to contain your name. When you send an e-mail, your recipient will see these values as the sender.

The final setting is the MESSAGES_PER_PAGE constant, which defines how many e-mail messages should be displayed per page:

```
define("MESSAGES_PER_PAGE", 10);
```

These constants are used throughout the application: when retrieving e-mail, connecting to the database, sending mail, and even displaying the information.

The AjaxMailbox Class

The code contained in the file called `AjaxMail.inc.php` serves as the workhorse of the server-side application. This file houses the `AjaxMailbox` class, which is the primary interface by which all the mail is handled. A few helper classes, mainly used for JSON encoding, also exist in this file.

The `AjaxMailbox` class, which you will build in this section, begins with an empty class declaration:

```
class AjaxMailbox {

    //more code here
}
```

Database Operations

It's the responsibility of `AjaxMailbox` to handle all the interaction with the database. To facilitate this communication, several methods relate just to the database.

The first method is `connect()`, which, as you may expect, initiates a connection to the database:

```
class AjaxMailbox {

    function connect() {
        $conn = mysql_connect(DB_SERVER, DB_USER, DB_PASSWORD)
            or die("Could not connect : " . mysql_error());
        mysql_select_db(DB_NAME);
        return $conn;
    }

    //more code here
}
```

Using the database constants defined in `config.inc.php`, this method creates a database connection and stores it in the variable `$conn`. Then, the specific database is selected and `$conn` is returned. Of course, you also need to be able to disconnect from the database:

```
class AjaxMailbox {

    function connect() {
        $conn = mysql_connect(DB_SERVER, DB_USER, DB_PASSWORD)
            or die("Could not connect : " . mysql_error());
        mysql_select_db(DB_NAME);
        return $conn;
    }

    function disconnect($conn) {
        mysql_close($conn);
    }

    //more code here
}
```

The `disconnect()` method accepts a connection object (the same one returned from `connect()`) and uses `mysql_close()` to close that connection.

During development of a database application, you may sometimes end up with bad data in your database tables. At such times, it's best just to clear all the data from the tables and start fresh. As a means of database maintenance, `AjaxMailbox` has a method, `clearAll()`, that does just this:

```
class AjaxMailbox {

    //connect and disconnect methods

    function clearAll() {
        $conn = $this->connect();

        $query = "truncate table AjaxMailMessages";
        mysql_query($query,$conn);

        $query = "truncate table AjaxMailAttachments";
```

```
        mysql_query($query,$conn);

        $this->disconnect($conn);
    }

    //more code here

}
```

This method begins by calling `connect()` to create a database connection. Then, two SQL statements are executed, using the `TRUNCATE` command to clear out both `AjaxMailMessages` and `AjaxMailAttachments`. The `TRUNCATE` command is used for two reasons. First, it is generally faster than deleting every row in a table, and second, it clears the `AUTO_INCREMENT` handler, so any fields that automatically increment will start back at 1. The last step is to disconnect from the database by calling `disconnect()`.

Retrieving E-Mail

Retrieving e-mail from a POP3 server is not an easy task, and it is beyond the scope of this book to walk you through the lengthy process. Instead, AjaxMail uses POP3Lib to interface with the POP3 server. This library contains numerous classes that aid in this type of communication. These classes are used in the `checkMail()` method, which is responsible for downloading messages from the POP3 server and inserting them into the database.

The method begins by creating a new instance of the `Pop3` class, which is the POP3Lib main class for communicating with a POP3 server. Its constructor accepts four arguments, three of which are required. The first argument is the POP3 server name, the second is the user name, the third is the password for that user name, and the fourth (optional) argument is the port at which to connect to the POP3 server (default is 110). To create a connection to the POP3 server, use the `login()` method. This method returns a Boolean value indicating the success (`true`) or failure (`false`) of the login attempt:

```
class AjaxMailbox {

    //database methods

    function checkMail() {
        $pop = new Pop3(POP3_SERVER, POP3_USER, POP3_PASSWORD);

        if ($pop->login()) {
            //Email downloading/database manipulation code here.
        }

    }

    //more code here

}
```

The `checkMail()` method begins by creating a `Pop3` object using the constant information defined in `config.inc.php`. Then, the `login()` method is called to try connecting to the server.

With a successful login, the `Pop3` object retrieves the number of messages found on the server and assigns this value to the `mailCount` property. Additionally, the `messages` array is initialized and populated with the header information of all e-mails residing on the server (the header information includes to, from, subject, date, and attachment information). Each item in the messages array at this point is a `Pop3Header` object.

To retrieve the entire e-mail, which includes the headers, message, and attachments, you must call the `getEmails()` method. This method completely repopulates the `messages` array with `Pop3Message` objects that contain all the e-mail information. A `Pop3Message` object has the following properties and methods:

Property/Method	Description
from	The sender's e-mail address.
to	The recipient's e-mail address. This property also contains all recipients if the e-mail was sent with multiple addresses in the To field.
subject	The subject of the e-mail.
cc	The recipient information held in the CC field.
bcc	If you receive an e-mail as a blind carbon copy, your e-mail address is in this property.
date	The date of the e-mail in RFC 2822 format.
unixTimeStamp	The date in a Unix timestamp (number of seconds since midnight on January 1, 1970).
hasAttachments	A Boolean value indicating whether the e-mail contains one or more attachments.
attachments	An array of attachments sent with the e-mail.
getTextMessage()	Retrieves the plain text body of an e-mail.
getHTMLMessage()	Retrieves the HTML body of an e-mail (if any).

These properties and methods are used to extract information about an e-mail and insert it into the database.

After a successful login, the first thing to do is to check for any e-mails on the server. You can do so by using the `mailCount` property. If `mailCount` is greater than zero, `getEmails()` is called to retrieve all the e-mail information and a database connection is made, anticipating the insertion of new e-mails:

```
class AjaxMailbox {

    //database methods

    function checkMail() {
        $pop = new Pop3(POP3_SERVER, POP3_USER, POP3_PASSWORD);

        if ($pop->login()) {
```

```
                    if ($pop->mailCount > 0) {

                        $conn = $this->connect();
                        $pop->getEmails();

                        //more code here

                        $this->disconnect($conn);
                    }

                    $pop->logoff();
            }
    }

    //more code here

}
```

In this code snippet, the `disconnect()` and `logoff()` methods are called in their appropriate locations. The `logoff()` method, as you may have guessed, closes the connection to the POP3 server.

With all the e-mail information now retrieved, you can begin inserting data into the database by iterating over the e-mails in the `messages` array:

```
class AjaxMailbox {

    //database methods

    function checkMail() {
        $pop = new Pop3(POP3_SERVER, POP3_USER, POP3_PASSWORD);

        if ($pop->login()) {

            if ($pop->mailCount > 0) {

                $conn = $this->connect();
                $pop->getEmails();

                foreach ($pop->messages as $message) {
                    $query = "insert into AjaxMailMessages(`To`,CC,BCC,`From`,";
                    $query .=
                        "Subject,`Date`,Message,HasAttachments,FolderId,Unread)";
                    $query .= " values('%s','%s','%s','%s','%s',%s,'%s',"
                            .$message->hasAttachments.",1,1)";
                    $query = sprintf($query,
                                    (addslashes($message->to)),
                                    (addslashes($message->cc)),
                                    (addslashes($message->bcc)),
                                    (addslashes($message->from)),
                                    (addslashes($message->subject)),
                                    $message->unixTimeStamp,
```

```
                                (addslashes($message->getTextMessage()))
                    );

                $result = mysql_query($query, $conn);

                //more code here

            }
            $this->disconnect($conn);
        }

        $pop->logoff();
    }
}

//more code here

}
```

A `foreach` loop is used to iterate over the messages array. For each message, a SQL INSERT statement is created and then executed. Since the SQL statement is so long, `sprintf()` is used to insert the information into the right location. Note that each value, (aside from `unixTimeStamp`) must be encoded using `addslashes()` so that the string will be proper SQL syntax. The statement is executing using `mysql_query()`. The only remaining part is to deal with attachments.

You can determine if a message has attachments by using the `hasAttachments` property of a message. If there are attachments, you first must retrieve the ID of the most recently added e-mail message. (Remember, attachments are tied to the e-mail from which they were attached.) After the ID is determined, SQL INSERT statements are created for each attachment:

```
class AjaxMailbox {

    //database methods

    function checkMail() {
        $pop = new Pop3(POP3_SERVER, POP3_USER, POP3_PASSWORD);

        if ($pop->login()) {

            if ($pop->mailCount > 0) {

                $conn = $this->connect();
                $pop->getEmails();

                foreach ($pop->messages as $message) {
                    $query = "insert into AjaxMailMessages(`To`,CC,BCC,`From`,";
                    $query .=
                            "Subject,`Date`,Message,HasAttachments,FolderId,Unread)";
                    $query .= " values('%s','%s','%s','%s','%s',%s,'%s',"
                            .$message->hasAttachments.",1,1)";
                    $query = sprintf($query,
                                    (addslashes($message->to)),
                                    (addslashes($message->cc)),
```

```
                              (addslashes($message->bcc)),
                              (addslashes($message->from)),
                              (addslashes($message->subject)),
                              $message->unixTimeStamp,
                              (addslashes($message->getTextMessage()))
                    );

        $result = mysql_query($query, $conn);

        if ($message->hasAttachments) {

            $messageId = mysql_insert_id($conn);

            foreach ($message->attachments as $attachment) {
                $query = "insert into AjaxMailAttachments(MessageId,";
                $query .= "Filename, ContentType, Size, Data)";
                $query .= "values($messageId, '%s', '%s', '%s', '%s')";
                $query = sprintf($query,
                                addslashes($attachment->fileName),
                                $attachment->contentType,
                                strlen($attachment->data),
                                addslashes($attachment->data));
                mysql_query($query, $conn);
            }
        }

    }
    $this->disconnect($conn);
}

$pop->logoff();
        }
    }

    //more code here

}
```

The most recently inserted ID can be retrieved using `mysql_insert_id()`. Then, the attachments are iterated over, using a `foreach` loop. Each item in the attachments array is a `Pop3Attachment` object. This class represents attachment data for a particular e-mail and contains three properties: `contentType`, which contains the attachment's MIME content-type, `fileName`, which represents the file name of the attachment, and `data`, which contains the actual attachment file data. Depending on the content-type of the attachment, `data` can be either binary or plain text information.

Once again, the `sprintf()` function is used to format the query string. Notice the use of `strlen()` on the attachment data; this retrieves the size of the data in bytes for easy retrieval later on. After the string has been formatted, the query is run against the database to insert the data into `AjaxMailAttachments`. This concludes the `checkMail()` method.

This method is never called directly; instead, it is called whenever a request to the server is made. In essence, `checkMail()` is piggybacked onto other requests so that the user is always viewing the most recent data.

Getting the E-Mail List

Probably the most common operation of the application is to retrieve a list of e-mails to display to the user. The method responsible for this operation, getFolderPage(), accepts two arguments: the ID number of the folder and the page number to retrieve:

```
class AjaxMailbox {

    //database methods

    //check mail method

    function getFolderPage($folder, $page) {
        $this->checkMail();

        //more code here
    }

}
```

When called, getFolderPage() first calls checkMail() to ensure that the most recent data is available in the database. If there are any new messages, they will be inserted into the database so that any queries run thereafter will be up to date.

The next step is to build a JSON string to send back to the client. To aid in this, a generic class called JSONObject is defined:

```
class JSONObject {
}
```

A JSONObject instance is used merely to hold data until it is time to be serialized into the JSON format. For getFolderPage(), this object contains information about the folder. The JSON data contains many useful bits of information: the total number of messages (messageCount), the current page (page), the total number of pages (pageCount), the folder number (folder), the first message returned (firstMessage), the total number of unread messages (unreadCount), and finally an array of messages in the page (messages). The data structure looks like this:

```
{
    "messageCount":0,
    "page":1,
    "pageCount":1,
    "folder":1,
    "firstMessage":0,
    "unreadCount": 0,
    "messages":[]
}
```

The JSONObject is created and initialized with several properties relating to information in the database:

```
class AjaxMailbox {

    //database methods
```

```
//check mail method

function getFolderPage($folder, $page) {
    $this->checkMail();

    $conn = $this->connect();

    $query = "select count(MessageId) as count from AjaxMailMessages";
    $query .= " where FolderId=$folder";

    $result = mysql_query($query, $conn);
    $row = mysql_fetch_assoc($result);

    $info = new JSONObject();
    $info->messageCount = (int) $row["count"];
    $info->page = $page;
    $info->pageCount = (int) ceil($info->messageCount/MESSAGES_PER_PAGE);
    $info->folder = $folder;

    $firstMessageNum = ($page-1) * MESSAGES_PER_PAGE;
    $info->firstMessage = $firstMessageNum+1;
    $info->messages = array();

    $info->unreadCount = $this->getUnreadCount($conn);

    //more code here
}

}
```

Using the SQL count() function, you can easily retrieve the total number of messages in a given folder. A JSONObject is created and stored in $info, and its messageCount property is set to the value retrieved from the database. Next, the page number is assigned to the page property (this is the same value that was passed into the method). The pageCount property determines how many total pages exist for the current folder. This is done by dividing the messageCount by the MESSAGES_PER_PAGE constant and applying the mathematical ceiling function (essentially, round up to the nearest whole number). Then, the folder ID is assigned to the folder property.

Next, the index of the first message to display on the page is calculated and stored in $firstMessageNum. This number is important because it keeps the database from retrieving too much information. The $info object is assigned a property of firstMessage that is equal to $firstMessageNum plus one. This is done because this value will be displayed to the user, and you never want to show message number zero; the first message should always be message number one. A property called messages is created and initialized to an empty array; this will contain message objects later.

The last step in this section of code is to create a property named unreadCount and assign it the number of unread messages in the database. To do so, use the getUnreadCount() method, defined as follows:

```
class AjaxMailbox {

    //other methods

    function getUnreadCount($conn) {
        $query = "select count(MessageId) as UnreadCount from AjaxMailMessages";
```

```
        $query .= " where FolderId=1 and Unread=1";
        $result = mysql_query($query, $conn);
        $row = mysql_fetch_assoc($result);
        return intval($row["UnreadCount"]);
    }

    //other methods
}
```

After getting this information, it's time to retrieve specific e-mail messages. To do so, execute a query on all messages in a given folder, ordered by the date. This is where the first message number comes into play; by adding a LIMIT statement to the end of the query, you can ensure the exact messages are contained in the result set. The first message number is specified and then the total number of messages, the LIMIT statement retrieves just those messages:

```
class AjaxMailbox {

    //database methods

    //check mail method

    function getFolderPage($folder, $page) {
        $this->checkMail();

        $conn = $this->connect();

        $query = "select count(MessageId) as count from AjaxMailMessages";
        $query .= " where FolderId=$folder";

        $result = mysql_query($query, $conn);
        $row = mysql_fetch_assoc($result);

        $info = new JSONObject();
        $info->messageCount = (int) $row["count"];
        $info->page = $page;
        $info->pageCount = (int) ceil($info->messageCount/MESSAGES_PER_PAGE);
        $info->folder = $folder;

        $firstMessageNum = ($page-1) * MESSAGES_PER_PAGE;
        $info->firstMessage = $firstMessageNum+1;
        $info->messages = array();

        $info->unreadCount = $this->getUnreadCount($conn);

        $query = "select * from AjaxMailMessages where FolderId=$folder";
        $query .= " order by date desc limit $firstMessageNum, ";
        $query .= MESSAGES_PER_PAGE;

        $result = mysql_query($query, $conn);


        //more code here
    }

}
```

The complete SQL statement selects all messages where the value in `FolderId` matches `$folder` and orders the returned rows by date in descending order. It also starts the selection from the value in `$firstMessageNum`, and retrieves only the amount specified by `MESSAGES_PER_PAGE`.

At this point, there are two possible scenarios: either the database returned results or it didn't. In the application, it is important to know when either situation takes place. Thankfully, it is easy to discern when a query is not successful. The `mysql_query()` function returns `false` on an unsuccessful query; therefore, you can check to see if a query failed by checking the `$result` variable. If there is an error, it can be returned in a property of the `$info` object. Otherwise, you'll need to iterate through the rows that were returned, creating a new `JSONObject` for each message and adding it to the `messages` array:

```
class AjaxMailbox {

    //database methods

    //check mail method

    function getFolderPage($folder, $page) {
        $this->checkMail();

        $conn = $this->connect();

        $query = "select count(MessageId) as count from AjaxMailMessages";
        $query .= " where FolderId=$folder";

        $result = mysql_query($query, $conn);
        $row = mysql_fetch_assoc($result);

        $info = new JSONObject();
        $info->messageCount = (int) $row["count"];
        $info->page = $page;
        $info->pageCount = (int) ceil($info->messageCount/MESSAGES_PER_PAGE);
        $info->folder = $folder;

        $firstMessageNum = ($page-1) * MESSAGES_PER_PAGE;
        $info->firstMessage = $firstMessageNum+1;
        $info->messages = array();

        $info->unreadCount = $this->getUnreadCount($conn);

        $query = "select * from AjaxMailMessages where FolderId=$folder";
        $query .= " order by date desc limit $firstMessageNum, ";
        $query .= MESSAGES_PER_PAGE;

        $result = mysql_query($query, $conn);
        if (!$result) {
            $info->error = mysql_error($conn);
        } else {            while ($row = mysql_fetch_assoc($result)) {
                $message = new JSONObject();
                $message->id = $row['MessageId'];
                $message->from = $row['From'];
                $message->subject = $row['Subject'];
                $message->date = date("M j Y", intval($row["Date"]));
```

```
                $message->hasAttachments = ($row['HasAttachments'] == 1);
                $message->unread = ($row['Unread'] == 1);                    $info-
>messages[] = $message;
            }
        }

        $this->disconnect($conn);
        return $info;
    }

}
```

In this code, the $result variable is checked. If the query failed, an error property is added to the $info object and assigned the error message retrieved from mysql_error(). Client-side code can then check this property to determine if an error occurred. If the query executed successfully, a new instance of JSONObject is created to contain the message information; this is stored in $message. This object is populated with all the information from the $row object, paying particular attention to format the message date so that it displays the month, day, and year only. (This eliminates the need for JavaScript to format the date.) Also, since the HasAttachments and Unread fields are bits, they are compared to the number 1 so that the corresponding properties on $message are filled with Boolean values instead of integers. The last line inside of the while loop adds the $message object to the end of the messages array.

After that is completed, you can safely disconnect from the database (using disconnect()) and return the $info object. It is up to the process using getFolderPage() to JSON-encode the object to be sent to the client.

Getting a Specific Message

Retrieving a specific message involves two helper classes, AjaxMailMessage and AjaxMailAttachmentHeader, and a method of the AjaxMailbox class called getMessage(). The two helper classes are used purely to store information that will later be JSON-encoded and sent to the client.

The first helper class, AjaxMailMessage, represents a single e-mail message:

```
class AjaxMailMessage {

    var $to;
    var $from;
    var $cc;
    var $bcc;
    var $subject;
    var $message;
    var $date;
    var $attachments;
    var $unread;
    var $hasAttachments;
    var $id;

    function AjaxMailMessage() {
        $this->attachments = array();
    }
}
```

The properties of this class resemble those of the field names in the database; the sole exception is the `attachments` property, which is an array of attachments associated with this e-mail. The JSON structure of the `AjaxMailMessage` class looks like this:

```
{
    to : "to",
    from : "from",
    cc : "cc",
    bcc : "bcc",
    subject : "subject",
    message : "message",
    date : "date",
    attachments : [],
    unread : false,
    hasAttachments : true,
    id : 1
}
```

The attachments array actually contains instances of `AjaxMailAttachmentHeader`, which provide general information about an attachment without containing the actual binary or text data:

```
class AjaxMailAttachmentHeader {
    var $id;
    var $filename;
    var $size;

    function AjaxMailAttachmentHeader($id, $filename, $size) {
        $this->id = $id;
        $this->filename = $filename;
        $this->size = "" . (round($size/1024*100)/100)." KB";
    }
}
```

The constructor for this class accepts three arguments: the attachment ID (the value of the `AttachmentId` column of the `AjaxMailAttachments` table), the file name, and the size of the attachment in bytes. The size is converted into a string (indicated by the number of kilobytes in the file) by dividing the size by 1024 and then rounding to the nearest hundredth of a kilobyte (so you can get a string such as "0.55 KB"). When JSON-encoded, the `AjaxMailAttachmentHeader` object is added to the previous JSON structure, as follows:

```
{
    "to" : "to",
    "from" : "from",
    "cc" : "cc",
    "bcc" : "bcc",
    "subject" : "subject",
    "message" : "message",
    "date" : "date",
    "attachments" :
    [
        {
            "id" : 1,
            "filename" : "filename",
```

```
                "size" : "1KB"
        }
    ],
    "unread" : false,
    "hasAttachments" : true,
    "id" : 1
}
```

The `getMessage()` method utilizes these two classes when assembling the data for transmission to the client. This method takes one argument, the message ID number that corresponds to the `MessageId` column in the `AjaxMailMessages` table:

```
class AjaxMailbox {

    //other methods

    function getMessage($messageId) {
        $conn = $this->connect();

        //get the information
        $query = "select MessageId, `To`, `From`, CC, BCC, Subject, Date, ";
        $query .= "Message, HasAttachments, Unread from AjaxMailMessages where";
        $query .= " MessageId=$messageId";
        $result = mysql_query($query, $conn);
        $row = mysql_fetch_assoc($result);

        //more code here

    }

    //other methods
}
```

This method begins by making a connection to the database using the `connect()` method. Then, a query to retrieve the various parts of the e-mail is created (stored in `$query`) and executed, with the results ending up in the `$row` object.

The next step is to create an `AjaxMailMessage` object and populate it with all the data from the database:

```
class AjaxMailbox {

    //other methods

    function getMessage($messageId) {
        $conn = $this->connect();

        //get the information
        $query = "select MessageId, `To`, `From`, CC, BCC, Subject, Date, ";
        $query .= "Message, HasAttachments, Unread from AjaxMailMessages where";
        $query .= " MessageId=$messageId";
        $result = mysql_query($query, $conn);
```

```
                      $row = mysql_fetch_assoc($result);

                      $message = new AjaxMailMessage();
                      $message->id = $row["MessageId"];
                      $message->to = $row["To"];
                      $message->cc = $row["CC"];
                      $message->bcc = $row["BCC"];
                      $message->unread = ($row["Unread"]==1);
                      $message->from = $row["From"];
                      $message->subject = $row["Subject"];
                      $message->date = date("M j, Y h:i A", intval($row["Date"]));
                      $message->hasAttachments = ($row["HasAttachments"]==1);
                      $message->unreadCount = $this->getUnreadCount($conn);
                      $message->message = $row["Message"];

                      //more code here
              }

       //other methods
   }
```

As with `getFolderPage()`, the database fields represented as bits are compared to 1 to get a Boolean value. The date is also formatted into a longer string, one that contains both the date and time (formatted as in "Oct 28, 2005 05:17 AM"). You'll also notice that the `unreadCount` property is added to the message. Although this doesn't pertain to the message itself, it helps to keep the user interface updated with the most recent number of unread mails in the database.

The last part of this method is to return information about the attachments (if any).

```
   class AjaxMailbox {

       //other methods

       function getMessage($messageId) {
           $conn = $this->connect();

           //get the information
           $query = "select MessageId, `To`, `From`, CC, BCC, Subject, Date, ";
           $query .= "Message, HasAttachments, Unread from AjaxMailMessages where";
           $query .= " MessageId=$messageId";
           $result = mysql_query($query, $conn);
           $row = mysql_fetch_assoc($result);

           $message = new AjaxMailMessage();
           $message->id = $row["MessageId"];
           $message->to = $row["To"];
           $message->cc = $row["CC"];
           $message->bcc = $row["BCC"];
           $message->unread = ($row["Unread"]==1);
           $message->from = $row["From"];
           $message->subject = $row["Subject"];
           $message->date = date("M j, Y h:i A", intval($row["Date"]));
           $message->hasAttachments = ($row["HasAttachments"]==1);
```

```
        $message->unreadCount = $this->getUnreadCount($conn);
        $message->message = $row["Message"];

        if ($message->hasAttachments) {
            $query = "select AttachmentId,Filename,Size from AjaxMailAttachments";
            $query .= " where MessageId=$messageId";

            $result = mysql_query($query, $conn);

            while ($row = mysql_fetch_assoc($result)) {
                $message->attachments[] = new AjaxMailAttachmentHeader(
                                              $row["AttachmentId"],
                                              $row["Filename"],
                                              (int) $row["Size"]);

            }
        }

        $this->disconnect($conn);
        return $message;
    }

    //other methods
}
```

In this section of code, you begin by verifying whether there are any attachments on the e-mail. If an attachment exists, a query is run to return all the attachments in the database. Note that the actual contents of the attachment aren't returned, just the attachment ID, file name, and size. Using a `while` loop to iterate over the results, a new `AjaxMailAttachmentHeader` is created for each attachment and added to the `$message` object's `attachments` array. After that, you need only disconnect from the database and return the `$message` object. Once again, it is up to the process using this method to JSON-encode the returned object.

Sending an E-Mail

AjaxMail relies on the PHPMailer library (`http://phpmailer.sourceforge.net`) to send e-mails. This full-featured library enables you to send mail either through an SMTP server or the sendmail application (`www.sendmail.org`). As discussed earlier, AjaxMail uses SMTP exclusively.

The method used to send mail is called `sendMail()`. This method accepts four arguments, with only the first three being required. These arguments are `$to` (the string containing the e-mail addresses to send to), `$subject` (the subject of the e-mail), `$message` (the body of the e-mail), and `$cc` (which can optionally specify who to send a carbon copy to).

The first step in this method is to create an instance of the `PHPMailer` class and assign the To and CC fields. You can add these by using the `AddAddress()` and `AddCC()` methods of the `PHPMailer` object, respectively. Each of these accepts two arguments: the e-mail address and the real name of the person. This presents a problem in that the `$to` and `$cc` arguments can contain multiple e-mail addresses separated by semicolons or commas and may consist of *name <e-mail>* pairs. For example, an e-mail sent to two recipients without carbon copying could look like this:

```
Joe Somebody <joe@somebody.com>; Jim Somebody <jim@somebody.com>
```

You must take this into account when sending mail using PHPMailer:

```php
class AjaxMailbox {

    //other methods here

    function sendMail($to, $subject, $message, $cc="") {
        $mailer = new PHPMailer();

        $tos = preg_split ("/;|,/", $to);
        foreach ($tos as $to) {
            preg_match("/(.*?)<?([a-z0-9\._%\-]+@[a-z\d\.\-]+\.[a-z]{2,3})>?/i",
$to, $matches);

            $mailer->AddAddress($matches[2],str_replace('"','',$matches[1]));
        }

        if ($cc != "") {
            $ccs = preg_split ("/;|,/", $cc);

            foreach ($ccs as $cc) {
                preg_match("/(.*?)<?([a-z0-9\._%\-]+@[a-z\d\.\-]+\.[a-z]{2,3})>?/i", $cc, $matches);

                $mailer->AddCC($matches[2],str_replace('"','',$matches[1]));
            }
        }

        //more code here
    }

    //other methods here
}
```

The first line in the method creates an instance of PHPMailer. In the next line, the $to string is split by both semicolons and commas with the preg_split() function, which returns an array of e-mail addresses. Then, iterating through the $tos array, the code checks for a match to *real name <email>* with the preg_match() function. The regular expression used in the preg_match() function returns an array with three matches. The first is the entire string, the second is the real name if it exists, and the third is the e-mail address. You can then add the addresses by using AddAddress() and passing in the second and third matches. Since the real name may be enclosed in quotation marks, str_replace() is used to strip out any quotation marks that may be in the real name part of the string. This same process is repeated for the $cc string, where the AddCC() method is used.

You will always have three elements in the $matches array, even if no name is in the string.

Next, you need to assign the pertinent SMTP information to the $mailer object, along with the subject and message body. Then, you can send the e-mail:

```php
class AjaxMailbox {

    //other methods here

    function sendMail($to, $subject, $message, $cc="") {
```

```
          $mailer = new PHPMailer();

          $tos = preg_split ("/;|,/", $to);
          foreach ($tos as $to) {
              preg_match("/(.*?)<?([a-z0-9\._%\-]+@[a-z\d\.\-]+\.[a-z]{2,3})>?/i",
$to, $matches);

              $mailer->AddAddress($matches[2],str_replace('"','',$matches[1]));
          }

          if ($cc != "") {
              $ccs = preg_split ("/;|,/", $cc);

              foreach ($ccs as $cc) {
                  preg_match("/(.*?)<?([a-z0-9\._%\-]+@[a-z\d\.\-]+\.[a-
z]{2,3})>?/i", $cc, $matches);

                  $mailer->AddCC($matches[2],str_replace('"','',$matches[1]));
              }
          }

          $mailer->Subject = $subject;
          $mailer->Body = $message;
          $mailer->From = EMAIL_FROM_ADDRESS;
          $mailer->FromName = EMAIL_FROM_NAME;
          $mailer->SMTPAuth = SMTP_DO_AUTHORIZATION;
          $mailer->Username = SMTP_USER;
          $mailer->Password = SMTP_PASSWORD;
          $mailer->Host = SMTP_SERVER;
          $mailer->Mailer = "smtp";

          $mailer->Send();
          $mailer->SmtpClose();

          //more code here
      }

      //other methods here
  }
```

For the first two properties, Subject and Body, simply use the values that were passed into the method. You set their values equal to those passed to the method. Next, the From and FromName properties are set to the constant values from config.inc.php; the first represents the sender's e-mail address, and the second contains the sender's real name (which many e-mail clients simply display as the sender).

The properties following those are the SMTP authorization settings. Some SMTP servers require authentication to send e-mail messages and some don't. If SMTPAuth is false, PHPMailer attempts to send e-mails without sending the Username and Password. If true, the class sends those values to the server in an attempt to authorize the sending of the e-mail.

The final two properties before sending an e-mail are the SMTP server and the method of which to send. The Host property is assigned to SMTP_SERVER, and the Mailer property is set to "smtp", indicating the type of mailer being used (as opposed to "sendmail").

After setting those properties, you can invoke the `Send()` method to actually send the e-mail and then call `SmtpClose()` to close the SMTP connection. But the method isn't quite done yet. The client still needs to know if the e-mail message was sent successfully. To provide that information, you'll need to create a response object containing information about the transmission:

```
class AjaxMailbox {

    //other methods here

    function sendMail($to, $subject, $message, $cc="") {
        $mailer = new PHPMailer();

        $tos = preg_split ("/;|,/", $to);
        foreach ($tos as $to) {
            preg_match("/(.*?)<?([a-z0-9\._%\-]+@[a-z\d\.\-]+\.[a-z]{2,3})>?/i",
$to, $matches);

            $mailer->AddAddress($matches[2],str_replace('"','',$matches[1]));
        }

        if ($cc != "") {
            $ccs = preg_split ("/;|,/", $cc);

            foreach ($ccs as $cc) {
                preg_match("/(.*?)<?([a-z0-9\._%\-]+@[a-z\d\.\-]+\.[a-
z]{2,3})>?/i", $cc, $matches);

                $mailer->AddCC($matches[2],str_replace('"','',$matches[1]));
            }
        }

        $mailer->Subject = $subject;
        $mailer->Body = $message;
        $mailer->From = EMAIL_FROM_ADDRESS;
        $mailer->FromName = EMAIL_FROM_NAME;
        $mailer->SMTPAuth = SMTP_DO_AUTHORIZATION;
        $mailer->Username = SMTP_USER;
        $mailer->Password = SMTP_PASSWORD;
        $mailer->Host = SMTP_SERVER;
        $mailer->Mailer = "smtp";

        $mailer->Send();
        $mailer->SmtpClose();

        $response = new JSONObject();

        if ($mailer->IsError()) {
            $response->error = true;
            $response->message = $mailer->ErrorInfo;
        } else {
            $response->error = false;
            $response->message = "Your message has been sent.";
        }

        return $response;
```

531

```
    }

    //other methods here
}
```

A `JSONObject` is instantiated to carry the information back to the client. PHPMailer provides a method called `IsError()`, which returns a Boolean value indicating the success or failure of the sending process. If it returns `true`, that means the e-mail was not sent successfully, so the `$response` object has its `error` property set to `true` and the error message is extracted from the `ErrorInfo` property of `$mailer`. Otherwise, the `error` property is set to `false` and a simple confirmation message is sent. The last step is to return the `$response` object.

Getting Attachment Data

When attachments are stored in the database, you need a way to get them back out. The `getAttachment()` method provides all the information necessary to enable a user to download an attachment. This method takes one argument, the attachment ID, and returns an `AjaxMailAttachment` object. The `AjaxMailAttachment` class is another helper that encapsulates all the information about an attachment:

```
class AjaxMailAttachment {
    var $contentType;
    var $filename;
    var $size;
    var $data;

    function AjaxMailAttachment($contentType, $filename, $size, $data) {
        $this->contentType = $contentType;
        $this->filename = $filename;
        $this->size = $size;
        $this->data = $data;
    }
}
```

The `getAttachment()` method itself is fairly straightforward:

```
class AjaxMailbox {

    //other methods here

    function getAttachment($attachmentId) {
        $conn = $this->connect();

        $query = "select * from AjaxMailAttachments where ";
        $query .= " AttachmentId=$attachmentId";
        $result = mysql_query($query, $conn);
        $row = mysql_fetch_assoc($result);

        $this->disconnect($conn);

        return new AjaxMailAttachment(
            $row["ContentType"],
            $row["Filename"],
```

```
            $row["Size"],
            $row["Data"]
        );
    }

    //other methods here
}
```

This code connects to the database with the `connect()` method and performs the database query. This particular query selects all fields from `AjaxMailAttachments` where `AttachmentId` is equal to the method's argument. After running the query, the database connection is closed and an `AjaxMailAttachment` object is returned containing all the information about the attachment.

Handling the Trash

Four methods in the `AjaxMailbox` class deal with moving messages to and from the Trash. The first method, `deleteMessage()`, doesn't actually delete the e-mail message; instead, it updates the `FolderId` column in the database so that it has a value of 2, meaning that the message now resides in the Trash. This method accepts one argument, the identification number of the message:

```
class AjaxMailbox {

    //other methods here

    function deleteMessage($messageId) {
        $conn = $this->connect();

        $query = "update AjaxMailMessages set FolderId=2 where ";
        $query .= " MessageId=$messageId";
        mysql_query($query,$conn);

        $this->disconnect($conn);
    }

    //other methods here
}
```

This method simply connects to the database, runs the SQL statement to change the `FolderId`, and then disconnects from the database. Of course, you can also restore a message from the Trash once it has been moved there. To do so, simply set the `FolderId` back to 1; this is the job of the `restoreMessage()` method.

The `restoreMessage()` method also accepts one argument, the message ID, and follows the same basic algorithm:

```
class AjaxMailbox {

    //other methods here

    function restoreMessage($messageId) {
        $conn = $this->connect();

        $query = "update AjaxMailMessages set FolderId=1 where ";
```

```
        $query .= " MessageId=$messageId";
        mysql_query($query,$conn);

        $this->disconnect($conn);
    }

    //other methods here
}
```

This method mirrors `deleteMethod()`, with the only difference being the value of `FolderId` to be set.

From time to time, there will be a lot of e-mail messages in the Trash. There may come a time when the user decides that he or she no longer needs them and the Trash should be emptied. The `emptyTrash()` method deletes every message with a `FolderId` value of 2 as well as any attachments those messages may have had.

The `emptyTrash()` method relies on two queries to delete the message and attachment information in the database. The first query deletes the attachments of messages in the Trash, and the second query deletes the messages themselves:

```
class AjaxMailbox {

    //other methods here

    function emptyTrash() {
        $conn = $this->connect();

        $query = "delete from AjaxMailAttachments where MessageId in ";
        $query .= " (select MessageId from AjaxMailMessages where FolderId=2)";

        mysql_query($query, $conn);

        $query = "delete from AjaxMailMessages where FolderId=2";
        mysql_query($query,$conn);

        $this->disconnect($conn);
    }

    //other methods here
}
```

The first query uses a feature called subquerying to select `MessageIds` of messages that are in the Trash. Subqueries are a feature in MySQL 4 and above (if you use MySQL 3.x, you need to upgrade before using this code). The second query is very straightforward, simply deleting all messages with a `FolderId` of 2. The last step, of course, is to disconnect from the database.

Marking Messages as Read

Nearly every e-mail client marks messages as unread when they first arrive. This feature enables users to keep track of the messages they previously read and easily tell which messages are new. The methods responsible for this feature in AjaxMail resemble those of deleting and restoring messages because they simply accept a message ID as an argument and then update a single column in the database.

The first method, `markMessageAsRead()`, marks the message as read after the user opens it:

```
class AjaxMailbox {

    //other methods here

    function markMessageAsRead($messageId) {
        $conn = $this->connect();

        $query = "update AjaxMailMessages set Unread=0 where MessageId=$messageId";
        mysql_query($query,$conn);

        $this->disconnect($conn);
    }

    //other methods here
}
```

This code runs an UPDATE statement that sets the message's Unread column to 0, specifying the message as read.

Similarly, the method to mark a message as unread performs almost the exact same query:

```
class AjaxMailbox {

    //other methods here

    function markMessageAsUnread($messageId) {
        $conn = $this->connect();

        $query = "update AjaxMailMessages set Unread=1 where MessageId=$messageId";
        mysql_query($query,$conn);

        $this->disconnect($conn);
    }

    //other methods here
}
```

The only difference between the `markMessageAsUnread()` method and the `markMessageAsRead()` method is the value the Unread column is assigned when you run the query.

Performing Actions

AjaxMail, like many other PHP applications, relies on an action-based architecture to perform certain operations. In other words, the application queries a separate PHP file that handles certain actions and executes code according to the action. There are several files that perform action requests from the client in different ways.

AjaxMailAction.php

The `AjaxMailAction.php`. file is one of the files used by the client to perform various actions. Your first step in writing this file is to include all the required files. Because this file uses the `AjaxMailbox` class, you need to include quite a few files, including the `config.inc.php` file, the four files in POP3Lib, `AjaxMail.inc.php`, and `JSON.php` for JSON encoding:

```php
require_once("inc/config.inc.php");
require_once("inc/pop3lib/pop3.class.php");
require_once("inc/pop3lib/pop3message.class.php");
require_once("inc/pop3lib/pop3header.class.php");
require_once("inc/pop3lib/pop3attachment.class.php");
require_once("inc/AjaxMail.inc.php");
require_once("inc/JSON.php");
```

You also need to set several headers:

```php
header("Content-Type: text/plain");
header("Cache-Control: No-Cache");
header("Pragma: No-Cache");
```

The first header sets the `Content-Type` to `text/plain`, a requirement because this page returns a JSON-encoded string as opposed to HTML or XML. Because this file will be used repeatedly, you must include the `No-Cache` headers described in Chapter 2 to avoid incorrect data.

When using `AjaxMailAction.php`, at least three pieces of information are sent: the action to perform, the current folder ID, and the page number. An optional fourth piece of information, a message ID, can be sent as well. So, the query string for this file may look something like this:

```
AjaxMailAction.php?action=myAction&page=1&folder=1&id=123
```

Because the message ID is used only in certain circumstances, you don't have to retrieve it until it is needed. In the meantime, you can retrieve the three other arguments as follows:

```php
$folder = $_GET["folder"];
$page = (int) $_GET["page"];
$action = $_GET["action"];
```

This code retrieves the values of the variables in the query string. The page number is cast to an integer value for compatibility with methods in `AjaxMailbox`. Next, create an instance of `AjaxMailbox` and `JSON`, as well as a variable named `$output`, which will be filled with a JSON string:

```php
$mailbox = new AjaxMailbox();

$oJSON = new Services_JSON();

$output = "";
```

The next step is to perform the desired action. Using a `switch` statement on the `$action` enables you to easily determine what should be done. There are two actions that need the message ID argument, `delete` and `restore`:

```
switch($action) {
    case "delete":
        $mailbox->deleteMessage($_GET["id"]);
        break;
    case "restore":
        $mailbox->restoreMessage($_GET["id"]);
        break;
    case "empty":
        $mailbox->emptyTrash();
        break;
    case "getfolder":
        //no extra processing needed
        break;
}
```

This code performs a specific operation based on the $action string. In the case of delete, the deleteMessage() method is called and the message ID parameter is passed in. For restore, the restoreMessage() method is called with the message ID. If empty is the action, the emptyTrash() method is called. Otherwise, if the action is getfolder, no additional operation is required. This is because AjaxMailAction.php always returns JSON-encoded folder information regardless of the action that is performed:

```
$info = $mailbox->getFolderPage($folder, $page);
$output = $oJSON->encode($info);
echo $output;
```

Here, the getFolderPage() method is used to retrieve a list of e-mails to return to the client. Remember, getFolderPage() checks for new messages before returning a list, so you will have the most recent information. The result of getFolderPage() is encoded using $oJSON->encode() and then output to the client using the echo operator.

AjaxMailNavigate.php

AjaxMail uses both XHR and a hidden iframe to make requests back to the server. The AjaxMailNavigate.php file is used inside the hidden iframe and, as such, must contain valid HTML and JavaScript code. This file expects the same query string as AjaxMailAction.php because it uses the same information.

The first part of this file is the PHP code that performs the requested action:

```
<?php
    require_once("inc/config.inc.php");
    require_once("inc/pop3lib/pop3.class.php");
    require_once("inc/pop3lib/pop3message.class.php");
    require_once("inc/pop3lib/pop3header.class.php");
    require_once("inc/pop3lib/pop3attachment.class.php");
    require_once("inc/AjaxMail.inc.php");
    require_once("inc/JSON.php");

    header("Cache-control: No-Cache");
    header("Pragma: No-Cache");

    $folder = $_GET["folder"];
```

537

```
    $page = (int) $_GET["page"];
    $id = "";
    if (isset($_GET["id"])) {
        $id = (int) $_GET["id"];
    }
    $action = $_GET["action"];

    $mailbox = new AjaxMailbox();
    $oJSON = new Services_JSON();

    $output = "";

    switch($action) {
        case "getfolder":
            $info = $mailbox->getFolderPage($folder, $page);
            $output = $oJSON->encode($info);
            break;
        case "getmessage":
            $message = $mailbox->getMessage($id);
            if ($message->unread) {
                $mailbox->markMessageAsRead($id);
            }
            $output = $oJSON->encode($message);
            break;
        default:
            $output = "null";
    }

?>
```

This file requires the same include files as `AjaxMailAction.php`, although it needs only the `no cache` headers because the content being returned is HTML (not `plain/text`). Next, the information is pulled out of the query string and stored in variables. New instances of `AjaxMailbox` and `JSON` are created in anticipation of performing an action.

As with `AjaxMailAction.php`, the `$action` variable is placed into a `switch` statement to determine what to do. The `getfolder` action calls `getFolderPage()` to retrieve the information for the given page in the given folder. The result is JSON-encoded and stored in the `$output` variable.

If the action is `getmessage`, the `getMessage()` method is called. If the message hasn't been read, it is marked as read. The message is then JSON-encoded and assigned to the `$output` variable. If the `$action` is something else, `$output` is assigned a value of `null`.

The next part of the page is the HTML content:

```
<!DOCTYPE html PUBLIC "-//W3C//DTD XHTML 1.0 Transitional//EN"
    "http://www.w3.org/TR/xhtml1/DTD/xhtml1-transitional.dtd">
<html xmlns="http://www.w3.org/1999/xhtml" xml:lang="en" lang="en">
    <head>
        <title>Ajax Mail Navigate</title>
    </head>
    <body>
        <script language="JavaScript" type="text/javascript">
```

```
        //<![CDATA[

            window.onload = function () {
                var oInfo = <?php echo $output ?>;
<?php
    switch($action) {
        case "getfolder":
            echo "parent.oMailbox.displayFolder(oInfo);";
            break;
        case "getmessage":
            echo "parent.oMailbox.displayMessage(oInfo);";
            break;
        case "compose":
            echo "parent.oMailbox.displayCompose();";
            break;
        case "reply":
            echo "parent.oMailbox.displayReply();";
            break;
        case "replyall":
            echo "parent.oMailbox.displayReplyAll();";
            break;
        case "forward":
            echo "parent.oMailbox.displayForward();";
            break;
    }
?>

            };

        //]]>
        </script>
    </body>
</html>
```

In this part of the page, the $output variable is output to the page into the JavaScript variable oInfo. Because $output is either null or a JSON-encoded string, it is valid JavaScript. The variable is assigned in the window.onload event handler. Then, based on the $action, a different JavaScript method is output to the page and called.

AjaxMailSend.php

To handle the sending of e-mail from the client, the AjaxMailSend.php file is used. Its sole purpose is to gather the information from the server and then send the e-mail. It needs to include config.inc.php, JSON.php, and AjaxMail.inc.php, as with the other files. However, it doesn't need to include the POP3Lib files because there will be no interaction with the POP3 server. Instead, the PHPMailer files class.phpmailer.php and class.smtp.php must be included:

```
<?php
    require_once("inc/config.inc.php");
    require_once("inc/phpmailer/class.phpmailer.php");
    require_once("inc/phpmailer/class.smtp.php");
    require_once("inc/JSON.php");
    require_once("inc/AjaxMail.inc.php");

    header("Content-Type: text/plain");
```

```
    header("Cache-control: No-Cache");
    header("Pragma: No-Cache");

    $to = $_POST["txtTo"];
    $cc = $_POST["txtCC"];
    $subject = $_POST["txtSubject"];
    $message = $_POST["txtMessage"];

    $mailbox = new AjaxMailbox();

    $oJSON = new Services_JSON();

    $response = $mailbox->sendMail($to, $subject, $message, $cc);
    $output = $oJSON->encode($response);
    echo $output;
?>
```

You'll note that the same headers are set for this page as they are for `AjaxMailAction.php` because it will also return a JSON-encoded string. The next section gathers the information from the submitted form. Then, new instances of `AjaxMailbox` and `JSON` are created. The information from the form is passed into the `sendMail()` method, and the response is JSON-encoded and then output using `echo`.

AjaxMailAttachment.php

The last file, `AjaxMailAttachment.php`, facilitates the downloading of a specific attachment. This file accepts a single query string parameter: the ID of the attachment to download. To do this, you need to once again include all the POP3Lib files, `config.inc.php`, and `AjaxMail.inc.php`:

```
<?php
    require_once("inc/config.inc.php");
    require_once("inc/pop3lib/pop3.class.php");
    require_once("inc/pop3lib/pop3message.class.php");
    require_once("inc/pop3lib/pop3header.class.php");
    require_once("inc/pop3lib/pop3attachment.class.php");
    require_once("inc/AjaxMail.inc.php");

    $id = $_GET["id"];
    $mailbox = new AjaxMailbox();
    $attachment = $mailbox->getAttachment($id);

    header("Content-Type: $attachment->contentType");
    header("Content-Disposition: attachment; filename=$attachment->filename");

    echo $attachment->data;
?>
```

After including the required files, the attachment ID is retrieved and stored in `$id`. A new `AjaxMailbox` object is created and `getAttachment()` is called to retrieve the specific attachment information. Next, the content-type header is set to the content type of the attachment (retrieved from `$attachment->contentType`) and the content-disposition header is set to `attachment`, passing in the file name of the attachment. This second header does two things. First, it forces the browser to show a dialog box asking if you want to open the file or save it; second, it suggests the file name to use when downloading the file. The last part of the file outputs the attachment data to the page, effectively mimicking a direct file download.

The User Interface

The key to any successful (and useful) web application is the design of the user interface. Because AjaxMail is meant to demonstrate the use of Ajax techniques, the user interface is quite simple and bare-bones. There are three different views of the user interface:

❑ **Folder view:** Displays a folder of messages (either Inbox or Trash)

❑ **Read view:** Displays a received message

❑ **Compose view:** Displays a form so that you can send e-mails

All the views are designed to be very simple, and all are loaded when the main page, index.php, is initially loaded.

The basic layout of index.php is as follows:

```
<!DOCTYPE html PUBLIC "-//W3C//DTD XHTML 1.0 Transitional//EN"
    "http://www.w3.org/TR/xhtml1/DTD/xhtml1-transitional.dtd">
<html xmlns="http://www.w3.org/1999/xhtml" xml:lang="en" lang="en">
    <head>
        <title>Ajax Mail</title>
        <link rel="stylesheet" type="text/css" href="styles/AjaxMail.css" />
        <script type="text/javascript" src="scripts/zxml.js"></script>
        <script type="text/javascript" src="scripts/json.js"></script>
        <script type="text/javascript" src="scripts/AjaxMail.js"></script>
    </head>
    <body>
        <ul id="ulMainMenu">
            <li id="liCompose">
                <span class="link" id="spnCompose">Compose Mail</span></li>
            <li><span class="link" id="spnInbox">Inbox
                <span id="spnUnreadMail"></span></span></li>
            <li><span class="link" id="spnTrash">Trash</span>
                (<span class="link" id="spnEmpty">Empty</span>)</li>
        </ul>
        <div id="divNotice"></div>
        <div id="divFolder">
            <!-- folder view -->
        </div>
        <div id="divReadMail" style="display: none">
            <!-- read mail view -->
        </div>

        <div id="divComposeMail" style="display: none">
            <!-- compose mail view -->
        </div>
        <iframe id="iLoader" src="about:blank"></iframe>
    </body>
</html>
```

The page requires a style sheet, AjaxMail.css, along with three JavaScript files, the zXml library file (zxml.js), the JSON library (json.js), and the JavaScript file containing all the AjaxMail functionality (AjaxMail.js). Within the body is an unordered list containing three links, one each for Compose Mail, the Inbox, and the Trash. The Trash link also has a link for Empty next to it, which can be used to purge any messages in the Trash. Because each of these links is to call a JavaScript function, there is no need to use a regular <a/> tag. Instead, each link is implemented as a <span/> with a CSS class of link, which formats the text to look like a regular link. The first link, Compose Mail, is made bold to call it out from the others. The complete CSS for the main menu (contained in AjaxMail.css) is:

```css
span.link {
    text-decoration: underline;
    color: blue;
    cursor: pointer;
    cursor: hand;
}

#ulMainMenu {
    position: absolute;
    left: 0px;
    top: 0px;
    margin: 0px;
    padding: 10px;
}

#ulMainMenu li {
    display: block;
    padding: 2px 0px 2px 0px;
    margin: 0px;
    font-size: 80%;
}

#ulMainMenu #liCompose {
    font-weight: bold;
    padding: 2px 0px 8px 0px;
}
```

Next in the index.php page is a <div/> element called divNotice. This element is used to display notifications to the user, which is critical in an Ajax application. Because the page itself doesn't reload or change to another page, there is no indication if a particular operation was successful. This area is used to relay such information.

AjaxMail needs two different types of notifications: one for general information and one for error information. General information includes such things as notifying the user when an e-mail is sent or deleted; error information is important when one of these actions is supposed to occur but doesn't. A general information notification appears as a yellow box with a small "i" icon to the left, whereas an error notification appears as a red box with an exclamation point icon to the left (see Figure 16-1).

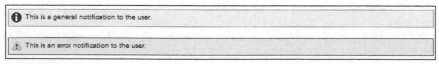

This is a general notification to the user.

This is an error notification to the user.

Figure 16-1

The `divNotice` element is dynamically assigned text as well as an appropriate CSS class, `info` or `error`, to create the desired appearance. The styles are defined as follows:

```
#divNotice {
    -moz-box-sizing: border-box;
    box-sizing: border-box;
    padding: 4px;
    background-repeat: no-repeat;
    background-position: 4px 4px;
    padding-left: 24px;
    font-size: 60%;
    font-family: Arial,Helvetica,Sans-Serif;
    visibility: hidden;
    height: 16px;
    position: absolute;
    top: 5px;
    left: 150px;
    width: 600px;
}

div.info {
    background-color: #F7FFCD;
    background-image: url(../images/icon_info.gif);
    border: 1px solid #A5A54A;
}

div.error {
    background-color: #FFE6E6;
    background-image: url(../images/icon_alert.gif);
    border: 1px solid red;
}
```

By using the `background-image` property to assign the appropriate icon, you are able to completely control the appearance of the notification area by using styles instead of worrying about changing an `<img/>` element when the style is changed. The `background-position` property states where the image should appear, and setting the `background-repeat` property to `no-repeat` ensures that only one copy of the image will be visible.

After the notification element comes a `<div/>` for each of the three AjaxMail views. The `<div/>` element for the folder view, `divFolder`, is first in the page and is always visible by default. The other two `<div/>` elements, `divReadMail` and `divComposeMail`, each have their display property set to `none` so that they are not visible when the page is first loaded. The contents of each `<div/>` element will be discussed later.

The last part of the page is an `<iframe/>` called `iLoader`. This hidden frame is used to navigate back and forth throughout the three views of AjaxMail. Anytime a user interface switch is made, the request goes through the hidden frame to allow the use of the Back and Forward browser buttons.

The Folder View

The folder view is the first thing the user sees after the application is loaded. It consists of the title of the folder (either Inbox or Trash), a pagination control that displays which messages are being displayed and the total number of messages, and a list of e-mail messages (see Figure 16-2). Taking a cue from Gmail, AjaxMail doesn't use table headers for the list of messages because people are accustomed to seeing e-mail listed by the person who sent it, subject, and date.

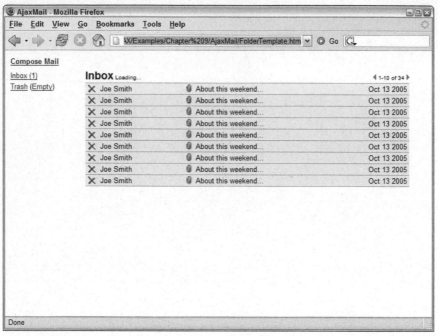

Figure 16-2

You may notice that the traditional check box next to each e-mail is missing. That's because there is only one thing you can do with an e-mail in AjaxMail: delete it. Instead of a check box, there is a red X next to each e-mail that can be clicked to delete it (move it to the Trash). When you switch to the Trash folder, the icons change to green arrows that, when clicked, moves the e-mail back into the Inbox (see Figure 16-3).

Aside from this difference, the folder view is the same regardless of which folder is displayed. Additionally, each e-mail has an optional attachment indicator that appears next to the subject if the e-mail contains an attachment. This icon is displayed only when an attachment is detected on the e-mail; otherwise, it is hidden.

There's also a small "loading" message next to the name of the folder. This is used to indicate when there is an open request to the server and disappears when the request is complete. While a request is processing, no other actions can be taken to prevent overriding of requests.

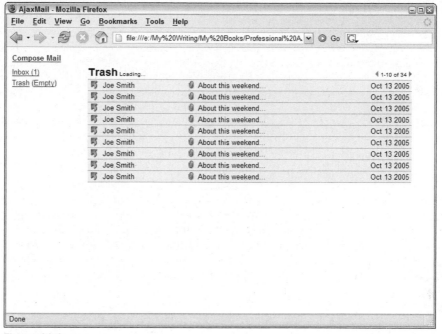

Figure 16-3

The HTML for the folder view is fairly simple because a large amount of the display is created by JavaScript depending on data received from the server:

```html
<div id="divFolder">
    <div id="divFolderHeader" class="header">
        <h1 id="hFolderTitle">Inbox</h1>
        <div id="divFolderStatus" class="status">Loading...</div>
        <div id="divItemCount">
            <img src="images/btn_prev.gif" alt="Previous Page"
                title="Previous Page" id="imgPrev" />
            <span id="spnItems"></span>
            <img src="images/btn_next.gif" alt="Next Page"
                title="Next Page" id="imgNext" />
        </div>
    </div>
    <table border="0" cellpadding="0" cellspacing="0" id="tblMain">
        <thead>
            <tr id="trTemplate">
                <td><img src="images/icon_delete.gif" /></td>
                <td class="from"></td>
                <td class="attachment">
                    <img src="images/icon_attachment.gif" title="Attachment"
/></td>
                <td class="subject"></td>
                <td class="date" nowrap="nowrap"></td>
            </tr>
```

```
            <tr id="trNoMessages">
                <td colspan="5">There are no messages in this folder.</td>
            </tr>
        </thead>
        <tbody>
            <tr style="visibility: hidden">
                <td colspan="5"></td>
            </tr>
        </tbody>
    </table>
</div>
```

The first thing to notice about this code is that nearly every element has an id attribute assigned. Any element that must be accessed via JavaScript needs to have an id attribute so that it can be accessed using the document.getElementById() method directly. For example, hFolderTitle contains the name of the folder, which is assigned by JavaScript after the folder data is retrieved. Because this will happen frequently, the JavaScript needs a reference to this element. Likewise, the divFolderStatus element that contains the loading message needs an id attribute so that it can be shown and hidden when appropriate. The spnItems element will be filled in with information about which messages are being displayed. The trickiest part of the HTML is the table to display the messages.

Within the table is a <thead/> element that contains two rows: one called trTemplate and one called trNoMessages. These rows are used as templates by JavaScript to create rows on the fly. Since rows with these formats will be needed frequently, it is faster and more effective to create the HTML and hide it from the user then to duplicate it and fill in the necessary information. You'll see how this is done later in the chapter. For now, just know that neither of these rows is directly visible to the user.

The <tbody/> element contains a single hidden row. This is done to set the initial browser measurements for the table. Without this, each table row would be displayed incorrectly initially because the browser had no standards from which to base its measurements. Providing this hidden row gives the browser enough information to make sure that any further rows are displayed properly.

Read View

The read view is quite simply designed to display an e-mail message so that the user can read it (see Figure 16-4). It consists of a subject line followed by spaces for the sender's e-mail address, the recipient's e-mail address, and the message date. There are also additional spaces for displaying both CC and BCC information if necessary.

Under the message header information are links for Reply, Reply All, Forward, and View Attachments. The last link appears only if there are attachments on the message. Each of the first three links switches you to the compose view with some prefilled information allowing you to easily send an e-mail.

Below the links is the message body. Because AjaxMail supports only plain text messages, it's easy to format the text using CSS. If there are any attachments, they are listed below the main message text. You can click the name of an attachment to download it.

Figure 16-4

The read view HTML is also very simple for the same reason, because most of the information is added later on by JavaScript.

```html
<div id="divReadMail" style="display: none">
    <div class="header">
        <h1 id="hSubject"></h1>
    </div>
     <div class="message-headers">
        <div id="divMessageFrom"></div>
        <div id="divMessageDate"></div>
     </div>
     <div id="divMessageTo"></div>
     <div id="divMessageCC"></div>
     <div id="divMessageBCC"></div>
     <ul class="message-actions">
        <li><span class="link" id="spnReply">Reply</span></li>
        <li><span class="link" id="spnReplyAll">Reply All</span></li>
        <li><span class="link" id="spnForward">Forward</span></li>
        <li id="liAttachments"><a href="#attachments">View Attachments</a></li>
     </ul>
    <div id="divMessageBody"></div>
    <a name="attachments" id="aAttachments">Attachments</a>
    <div id="divMessageAttachments">
        <ul id="ulAttachments">
        </ul>
    </div>
</div>
```

As with the folder view, nearly every element for the read view has an id attribute. The hSubject element is used to display the subject of the message, whereas the divMessageBody element is used to display the message text. The divMessageFrom, divMessageDate, divMessageTo, divMessageCC, and divMessageBCC elements are used to display each type of header information for the message. Immediately following those elements are the message actions, Reply, Reply All, Forward, and View Attachments. Note that only the View Attachments link uses an <a/> element. This is to take advantage of HTML anchors to move the screen's view down the page to the attachments list. All the other links are implemented using <span/> elements with the link CSS class. The attachments are listed in the ulAttachments element. If there are no attachments, the entire divMessageAttachments element is hidden.

Compose View

The compose view does a lot of work in the user interface for AjaxMail. It is used not only to create new e-mail messages, but also for replying to and forwarding e-mails. To keep things simple for this book, the compose view supports only the To and CC fields (no BCC) and does not enable you to send attachments.

This view consists of a text box for the To, CC, and subject fields, and the message of the e-mail (see Figure 16-5). There are also two links, Send and Cancel. Send begins the process of sending the e-mail, and Cancel places the user back into the previous view (either folder view or read view).

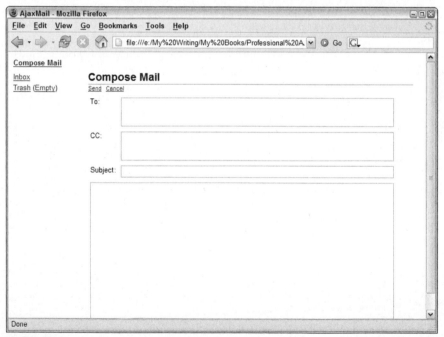

Figure 16-5

The HTML for this view consists mostly of a form with text fields:

```html
<div id="divComposeMail" style="display: none">
    <div class="header">
        <h1 id="hComposeHeader">Compose Mail</h1>
    </div>
    <div id="divComposeMailForm">
        <ul id="ulComposeActions" class="message-actions">
            <li><span class="link" id="spnSend">Send</span></li>
            <li><span class="link" id="spnCancel">Cancel</span></li>
        </ul>
     <div id="divComposeBody">
        <form method="post" name="frmSendMail">
            <table border="0" cellpadding="0" cellspacing="0">
                <tr>
                    <td class="field-label-container">
                            <label for="txtTo" class="field-label">To:</label></td>
                    <td class="field-container">
                            <textarea rows="2" cols="30" id="txtTo" name="txtTo"
                                    class="form-field"></textarea></td>
                </tr>
                <tr>
                    <td class="field-label-container">
                            <label for="txtCC" class="field-label">CC:</label></td>
                    <td class="field-container">
                            <textarea rows="2" cols="30" id="txtCC" name="txtCC"
                                    class="form-field"></textarea></td>
                </tr>
                <tr>
                    <td class="field-label-container">
                        <label for="txtSubject"
                                class="field-label">Subject:</label></td>
                    <td class="field-container">
                        <input type="text" id="txtSubject" name="txtSubject"
                                class="form-field" /></td>
                </tr>
                <tr>
                    <td class="message-container" colspan="2">
                            <textarea id="txtMessage" name="txtMessage" rows="15"
                                    cols="30" class="form-field"></textarea></td>
                </tr>
            </table>
        </form>
    </div>
    </div>
    <div id="divComposeMailStatus" style="display: none">
        <h2>Sending...</h2>
        <img src="images/sendmail.gif" />
    </div>
</div>
```

There are two main parts of this view: divComposeBody, which contains the form, and divComposeMailStatus, which displays a notification that a message is being sent. When Send is clicked, divComposeMailStatus is shown with the Sending . . . message as well as an animated image to indicate that the message is in the process of being sent. If an error occurs during the process, an alert will be displayed to the user and the form will once again be made visible. If, on the other hand, the message goes through without any problems, the user is returned to the previous view (as if he or she clicked Cancel) and a notification is displayed stating that the message was sent successfully.

Layout

To ensure the user interface has a consistent feel, each view must be laid out so that one can easily slide into the place of the others when necessary. To accomplish this, each view is positioned absolutely in the same location:

```
#divFolder,
#divReadMail,
#divComposeMail {
    position: absolute;
    top: 35px;
    left: 150px;
    width: 600px;
    -moz-box-sizing: border-box;
    box-sizing: border-box;
}
```

The last two CSS properties, -moz-box-sizing and box-sizing, are used to ensure that the measurements are the same across all browsers. By default, Internet Explorer renders everything using the border box calculations, whereas others don't. These two lines (the first for Mozilla, the second for others) ensure that the size remains consistent regardless of the browser. The rest of the style information places each view in the same location on the screen and makes each view have the same width (although the height is allowed to grow and shrink, as necessary).

Next, the iframe must be hidden so that it doesn't disrupt the page flow. Because the iframe's id attribute is set, you can refer to it directly:

```
#iLoader {
    display: none;
}
```

Also remember that the <thead/> element needs to be hidden so that it won't display the template rows in the folder view:

```
thead {
    display: none;
}
```

Tying It All Together

Now that you know all about the architecture, database, user interface, and server-side components, it's time to glue it all together using JavaScript. To begin, you need to define some constants. The first constants are simply locations of various resources that need to be used by AjaxMail:

```
var sAjaxMailURL = "AjaxMailAction.php";
var sAjaxMailNavigateURL = "AjaxMailNavigate.php";
var sAjaxMailAttachmentURL = "AjaxMailAttachment.php";
var sAjaxMailSendURL = "AjaxMailSend.php";

var sImagesDir = "images/";
var sRestoreIcon = sImagesDir + "icon_restore.gif";
var sDeleteIcon = sImagesDir + "icon_delete.gif";
var sInfoIcon = sImagesDir + "icon_info.gif";
var sErrorIcon = sImagesDir + "icon_alert.gif";
var aPreloadImages = [sRestoreIcon, sDeleteIcon, sInfoIcon, sErrorIcon];
```

The first parts of this code simply define the URLs used to make requests back to the server. These will be used later to integrate the Ajax interface. The second part of this code identifies images that are necessary for the user interface and then places them into an array called `aPreloadImages`. These images are preloaded so that the user interface responds quickly:

```
for (var i=0; i < aPreloadImages.length; i++) {
    var oImg = new Image();
    oImg.src = aPreloadImages[i];
}
```

This code uses an `Image` object, which is essentially an invisible `<img/>` element. Because not all of these images are necessary when the application is first loaded, most won't be loaded until used for the first time. This could result in a delay that may be confusing to users. Preloading the images prevents this issue from occurring.

Next, there are some messages and strings that need to be displayed to the user. It helps to define these early in the code so that it's easy to change the messages in the future, if necessary:

```
var sEmptyTrashConfirm =
        "You are about to permanently delete everything in the Trash. Continue?";
var sEmptyTrashNotice = "The Trash has been emptied.";
var sDeleteMailNotice = "The message has been moved to the Trash.";
var sRestoreMailNotice = "The message has been moved to your Inbox.";
var sRestore = "Restore";
var sDelete = "Move to the Trash";
var sTo = "To ";
var sCC = "CC ";
var sBCC = "BCC ";
var sFrom = "From ";
```

When one of the notices is displayed, you really want to show it only for a short amount of time so that it doesn't become distracting to the user or blend in with the rest of the screen. The variable `iShowNoticeTime` indicates the duration (in number of milliseconds) for a notice to appear on the screen. By default, this is 5 seconds (5000 milliseconds):

```
var iShowNoticeTime = 5000;
```

The last bit of code to be defined ahead of time is a couple of constants and an array:

```
var INBOX = 1;
var TRASH = 2;
var aFolders = ["","Inbox", "Trash"];
```

In this code, the first two variables are constants defining the numeric identifiers for the Inbox and Trash folders. These coincide with the values they have in the database. The array of strings contains the names for each of the folders, so these don't have to be returned from the database all the time. The first string in the array is empty, since it will never be used. (There is no folder with a numeric ID of zero.)

In an actual implementation, you may choose to have these variables generated by some server-side process that reads the values out of the database and outputs appropriate JavaScript code. For simplicity in this example, these values are defined right in the JavaScript file.

Helper Functions

Before diving into the main part of the code, there are some helper functions that are necessary. *Helper functions* are functions that aren't necessarily specific to a particular application but perform some process that is necessary. AjaxMail has a handful of helper functions.

The first helper function is one that you have seen before. The getRequestBody() function was introduced in Chapter 2 to serialize the data in an HTML form so that it can be passed into an XHR request. This function is necessary once again for AjaxMail. To refresh your memory, here's what the function looks like:

```
function getRequestBody(oForm) {
    var aParams = new Array();

    for (var i=0 ; i < oForm.elements.length; i++) {
        var sParam = encodeURIComponent(oForm.elements[i].name);
        sParam += "=";
        sParam += encodeURIComponent(oForm.elements[i].value);
        aParams.push(sParam);
    }

    return aParams.join("&");
}
```

This code is exactly the same as it was in Chapter 2 and will be used to send e-mail messages.

One problem with e-mail addresses is that they can be specified in any number of formats. For example:

❑   myname@somewhere.com

❑   My Real Name <myname@somewhere.com>

❑   "My Real Name" <myname@somewhere.com>

If you use e-mail frequently, you'll probably recognize these formats as they are used in most major e-mail applications. When displaying an e-mail's sender in the folder view, AjaxMail displays the real name only. If no real name is present, the e-mail address is shown. To handle this, a helper function called `cleanupEmail()` is used:

```
var reNameAndEmail = /(.*?)<(.*?)>/i;

function cleanupEmail(sText) {
    if (reNameAndEmail.test(sText)) {
        return RegExp.$1.replace(/"/g, "");
    } else {
        return sText;
    }
}
```

The most important part of the function is actually the regular expression `reNameAndEmail`, which matches a string containing both a real name and an e-mail address regardless of the use of quotation marks. Inside the function, the text is tested against this regular expression. If `test()` returns `true`, that means the e-mail address contains both pieces of information, and you should extract the real name (which is stored in `RegExp.$1`). However, this name may have quotation marks in it, so the next step is to replace all the quotation marks with an empty string using the `replace()` method. If, on the other hand, the regular expression doesn't match the text that was passed in, this means that it contains just an e-mail address, so it is returned without any changes.

The last helper function is called `htmlEncode()`, and it simply replaces greater-than (>), less-than (<), ampersand (&), and quote (") characters with their appropriate HTML entities. This ensures that no dangerous HTML will be created when reading text from an e-mail:

```
function htmlEncode(sText) {
    if (sText) {
        return sText.replace(/&/g, "&amp;").replace(/</g, "&lt;").replace(/>/g,
                              "&gt;").replace(/"/g, "&quot;")
    } else {
        return "";
    }
}
```

This function also checks to make sure text is passed in. If `sText` is `null`, the function returns an empty string; otherwise, the replacements are done using the `replace()` method.

The Mailbox

The main part of the AjaxMail application is the mailbox. This is a single JavaScript object containing all the properties and methods necessary to run the user interface. Because there should be only one instance of this object, it is defined using object literal notation:

```
var oMailbox = {

    info: new Object(),
    processing: false,
    message: new Object(),
```

```
    nextNotice: null,

    //more code here
}
```

The mailbox object is stored in a variable named `oMailbox` and has four properties. The first property, `info`, is an object that will contain the folder information for the folder view. This object will be returned from the server but is initialized here to a generic object to avoid possible errors. Next is the `processing` property, which is simply a Boolean flag indicating whether the application is processing a request. When set to `true`, no other processes can be initiated. The third property is `message`, which will contain an object describing the message being read in the read view. Once again, this property is initialized to an empty object in order to avoid possible errors. The last property, `nextNotice`, is used by several callback functions to determine which notice should be displayed once a particular process has completed.

Before you can begin interacting with the user interface, it helps to store references to the elements you'll be using the most. You can do this by using `document.getElementById()` repeatedly, but that would require a lot of lines of code for all the elements used in AjaxMail. Instead, it's faster and more efficient to iterate over all the elements in a page and add a reference to each one that has an `id` attribute. This is part of the job of the `init()` method:

```
init: function () {
    var colAllElements = document.getElementsByTagName("*");
    if (colAllElements.length == 0) {
        colAllElements = document.all;
    }

    for (var i=0; i < colAllElements.length; i++) {
        if (colAllElements[i].id.length > 0) {
            this[colAllElements[i].id] = colAllElements[i];
        }
    }

    //more code here
},
```

This method first calls `document.getElementsByTagName()` and passes in an asterisk. In DOM-compliant browsers, this should return a collection of all the elements in the document. However, the Internet Explorer implementation doesn't support this usage, so you'll also need to be prepared for this. If the returned collection has no elements (`length` is not greater than zero), this means that Internet Explorer is in use. To work around this limitation, you can use the `document.all` collection (supported in Internet Explorer only) in place of the collection returned from `getElementsByTagName()`. Once `colAllElements` contains a usable collection, you can then iterate over the collection using a `for` loop. If the element has an `id` property (the `length` of the `id` property is greater than zero), a reference is saved on the mailbox object. So, `divFolderStatus` is saved to the mailbox object as a property named `divFolderStatus` and can be accessed using `this.divFolderStatus` inside of a method or `oMailbox.divFolderStatus` outside of a method.

Data-Loading Methods

The mailbox object uses two types of data: folder information and message information. Folder information is returned as a JSON string from the server and then parsed into an object containing information about the given folder. A typical folder information object looks like this:

```
{
    "messageCount":2,
    "page":1,
    "pageCount":1,
    "folder":1,
    "firstMessage":1,
    "unreadCount": 1,
    "messages":[
        {
            "id":"64",
            "from":"Joe Smith <joe@smith.com>",
            "subject":"Re: How about this weekend?",
            "date":"Oct 29 2005",
            "hasAttachments":false,
            "unread":true
        },
        {
            "id":"63",
            "from":"Joe Smith <joe@smith.com>",
            "subject":"How about this weekend?",
            "date":"Oct 29 2005",
            "hasAttachments":false,
            "unread":false
        }
    ]
}
```

This object is stored in the `info` property of the mailbox so that it can be used by all methods. To assign the data, the `loadInfo()` method is used. Because you may have an object or a JSON string to assign, this method needs to check the type of the argument that is passed in:

```
loadInfo: function (vInfo) {
    if (typeof vInfo == "string") {
        this.info = vInfo.parseJSON();
    } else {
        this.info = vInfo;
    }
},
```

If `vInfo` is a string, it is parsed into an object using the `parseJSON()` method (which is added to the `String` class via `json.js`); otherwise, it's an object, so it can be directly assigned to the `info` property. This object is used whenever a folder page is rendered, but there is also some data needed to display an individual e-mail.

The JSON object representing a single e-mail message is in the following format:

```
{
    "id":"63",
    "to":"you@somewhere.com",
    "from":"Joe Smith <joe@smith.com>",
    "cc":"",
    "subject":"How about this weekend?",
    "bcc":"",
    "date":"Oct 29, 2005 05:15 AM",
    "hasAttachments":false,
    "unread":true,
    "message":"I was thinking this weekend would be good? How about you?<br />Joe",
    "attachments":[],
    "unreadCount":8
}
```

When a message is viewed in AjaxMail, this information is assigned to the `message` property so that it is accessible from all methods. The `loadMessage()` method accepts either an object or a JSON string containing this message information and assigns it to the message property:

```
loadMessage: function (vMessage) {
    if (typeof vMessage == "string") {
        this.message = vMessage.parseJSON();
    } else {
        this.message = vMessage;
    }
},
```

As you can see, this is essentially the same as `loadInfo()`; it just deals with different data. These two methods are critical because they are the primary means of passing data from the server to the client.

User Notification Methods

You will remember the `processing` property from the mailbox object description earlier. To set the value of this property, a special method called `setProcessing()` is used. The sole argument for this method is a Boolean value, set to `true` when the mailbox is processing or `false` when it is not. This method also shows the `divFolderStatus` element whenever the mailbox is processing:

```
setProcessing: function (bProcessing) {
    this.processing = bProcessing;
    this.divFolderStatus.style.display = bProcessing ? "block" : "none";
},
```

If the `bProcessing` argument is true, the `divFolderStatus` element has its `display` property set to `block`, ensuring that it is visible; otherwise, the property is set to `none`, hiding it from view. This method is used throughout the mailbox object to prevent multiple simultaneous requests from occurring.

Another method used throughout is `showNotice()`, which displays a notice to the user regarding the state of a request:

```
showNotice: function (sType, sMessage) {
    var divNotice = this.divNotice;
    divNotice.className = sType;
    divNotice.innerHTML = sMessage;
    divNotice.style.visibility = "visible";
    setTimeout(function () {
        divNotice.style.visibility = "hidden";
    }, iShowNoticeTime);
},
```

This method accepts two arguments: the type of message (either `info` or `error`) and the message to be displayed. The type of message also is the CSS class that will be assigned to `divNotice`, giving it the appropriate format. The message is assigned to the element via the `innerHTML` property, which means you can include HTML code in the message if necessary. After that, the element is made visible to the user by setting the `visibility` property to `visible`. Since the message should be displayed only for a specific amount of time, the `setTimeout()` function is used to determine when the `visibility` property should be set back to `hidden`. The interval is the global variable `iShowNoticeTime` that was defined earlier. Any notice displayed using this method will be shown immediately and then disappear after the designated amount of time.

Communication Methods

There are two different ways that AjaxMail communicates with the server: through XHR and through a hidden iframe. To provide for this, several methods are used to encapsulate most of the communication functionality so that other functions can use them directly.

All XHR GET requests are made through the `request()` method. This method takes three arguments: the action to perform, a callback function to notify when the request is complete, and an optional e-mail message ID. Every request going through this method goes to `AjaxMailAction.php`, passing in the action (the first argument) on the query string. Here's the complete method:

```
request: function (sAction, fnCallback, sId) {
    if (this.processing) return;
    try {
        this.setProcessing(true);
        var oXHR = zXmlHttp.createRequest();
        var sURL = sAjaxMailURL + "?folder=" +this.info.folder + "&page="
                    + this.info.page + "&action=" + sAction;
        if (sId) {
            sURL += "&id=" + sId;
        }

        oXHR.open("get", sURL, true);
        oXHR.onreadystatechange = function (){
            try {
                if (oXHR.readyState == 4) {
                    if (oXHR.status == 200) {
                        fnCallback(oXHR.responseText);
                    } else {
                        throw new Error("An error occurred while attempting to
contact the server. The action (" + sAction + ") did not complete.");
                    }
```

```
                    }
                } catch (oException) {
                    oMailbox.showNotice("error", oException.message);
                }
            };
            oXHR.send(null);
        } catch (oException) {
            this.showNotice("error", oException.message);
        }
    },
```

Note that the very first line checks to see if the mailbox is processing another request. If it is, the function returns without executing the next request. Otherwise, the standard try...catch arrangement involving an XHR object is executed. Before anything is done, setProcessing() is called to indicate that a request has begun. The URL is constructed by adding the current folder ID and page to the query string, followed by the action to perform. If a message ID is specified (sID), that is also added to the query string so that the action can be completed. Next, the XHR object is initialized and the onreadystatechange event handler is assigned. Inside the event handler, the callback function (fnCallback) is called when the request succeeds, passing in the response text. If an error occurs during this process, a custom error is thrown. When the catch statement intervenes, the showNotice() method is used to display details about the message.

The method to send an e-mail is very similar, but uses a POST request instead:

```
sendMail: function () {
    if (this.processing) return;
    this.divComposeMailForm.style.display  = "none";
    this.divComposeMailStatus.style.display = "block";

    try {
        this.setProcessing(true);
        var oXHR = zXmlHttp.createRequest();
        var sData = getRequestBody(document.forms["frmSendMail"]);

        oXHR.open("post", sAjaxMailSendURL, true);
        oXHR.setRequestHeader("Content-Type",
                              "application/x-www-form-urlencoded");

        oXHR.onreadystatechange = function (){
            try {
                if (oXHR.readyState == 4) {
                    if (oXHR.status == 200 || oXHR.status == 304) {
                        sendConfirmation(oXHR.responseText);
                    } else {
                        oMailbox.showNotice("error",
                            "An error occurred while attempting to contact the
server. The mail was not sent.");
                    }
                }
            } catch (oException) {
                oMailbox.showNotice("error", oException.message);
            }
```

```
            };
            oXHR.send(sData);
        } catch (oException) {
            this.showNotice("error", oException.message);
        }
    },
```

As with the `request()` method, the `sendMail()` method begins by checking to see if the mailbox is processing a request. If there are no other requests active, some user interface changes are made. First, the compose mail form is hidden from view by setting its `display` property to `none`. Then, the status area is shown by setting its `display` property to `block`. This effectively shows that the mail is being sent as an animated GIF plays.

Next, the `setProcessing()` method is called to indicate a request has begun and a data string is created by calling `getRequestBody()` on the mail form. After initializing the `oXHR` object, the appropriate request header is set. The `onreadystatechange` event handler is the standard setup, and the response text is passed into the `sendConfirmation()` function (described in the upcoming Callback Functions section).

The last communication method is `navigate()`, which is used whenever the user interface change should be recorded in the browser history (allowing the user to click Back and Forward to navigate through the user interface changes). This method uses the hidden iframe to make requests to the server and receive responses back:

```
navigate: function (sAction, sId) {
    if (this.processing) return;
    try {
        this.setProcessing(true);
        var sURL = sAjaxMailNavigateURL + "?folder=" +this.info.folder
                            + "&page=" + this.info.page + "&action=" + sAction;
        if (sId) {
            sURL += "&id=" + sId;
        }
        this.iLoader.src = sURL;
    } catch (oException) {
        this.showNotice("error", oException.message);
    }
},
```

This method accepts only two arguments: an action to perform and an optional message ID (similar to `request()`). As with the other communication methods, this one begins by checking to see if the mailbox is processing another request and exits the method if that is the case. Otherwise, a standard `try...catch` block surrounds the rest of the code to catch any errors that may occur. Then, the `processing` flag is set to `true` to indicate a new request has begun. The URL is constructed in the same manner as in `request()`, adding the message ID only if it has been supplied. Last, the URL is assigned to the iframe via the `src` property. Now it is up to the page returned in the iframe to notify the mailbox that processing has been completed.

Rendering Methods

The most complex methods of the mailbox object are those relating to the rendering of data onto the screen. There are two methods: `renderFolder()`, which displays a mailbox folder, and `renderMessage()`, which displays a single e-mail message. Both of these use a small method called `updateUnreadCount()` that is responsible for updating the number of unread messages next to the Inbox link:

```
updateUnreadCount: function (iCount) {
    this.spnUnreadMail.innerHTML = iCount > 0 ? " (" + iCount + ")" : "";
}
```

This method expects the number of unread messages to be passed in as an argument. If that number is greater than 0, the `spnUnreadMail` element is updated to display that number; otherwise, the element is assigned an empty string. With this method defined, it's time to take a look at the two more complicated methods.

The `renderFolder()` method uses the `info` property to display the appropriate e-mail messages in the folder view. To begin, this method clears the folder view of all message information so that it can easily build up and insert new information:

```
renderFolder: function () {;
    var tblMain = this.tblMain;

    while (tblMain.tBodies[0].hasChildNodes()) {
        tblMain.tBodies[0].removeChild(tblMain.tBodies[0].firstChild);
    }

    //more code here
},
```

This first part of the method stores a reference to `tblMain` in a local variable and then proceeds to remove all the child nodes from the `<tbody/>` element (referenced as `tblMain.tBodies[0]`). With all of the rows removed, it's now okay to start adding rows.

The next part of the method creates the DOM representation for the messages. Note that for simplicity, only the additions to the method are shown:

```
renderFolder: function () {;

    //remove all existing rows

    var oFragment = document.createDocumentFragment();

    if (this.info.messages.length) {
        for (var i=0; i < this.info.messages.length; i++) {
            var oMessage = this.info.messages[i];
            var oNewTR = this.trTemplate.cloneNode(true);
            oNewTR.id = "tr" + oMessage.id;
            oNewTR.onclick = readMail;

            if (oMessage.unread) {
```

```
                    oNewTR.className = "new";
                }

                var colCells = oNewTR.getElementsByTagName("td");
                var imgAction = colCells[0].childNodes[0];
                imgAction.id = oMessage.id;
                if (this.info.folder == TRASH) {
                    imgAction.onclick = restoreMail;
                    imgAction.src = sRestoreIcon;
                    imgAction.title = sRestore;
                } else {
                    imgAction.onclick = deleteMail;
                    imgAction.src = sDeleteIcon;
                    imgAction.title = sDelete;
                }

                colCells[1].appendChild(
                    document.createTextNode(cleanupEmail(oMessage.from)));
                colCells[2].firstChild.style.visibility = oMessage.hasAttachments ?
                    "visible" : "hidden";
                colCells[3].appendChild(
                    document.createTextNode(htmlEncode(oMessage.subject)));
                colCells[4].appendChild(document.createTextNode(oMessage.date));
                oFragment.appendChild(oNewTR);
            }
        } else {
            var oNewTR = this.trNoMessages.cloneNode(true);
            oFragment.appendChild(oNewTR);
        }

        tblMain.tBodies[0].appendChild(oFragment);

        //more code here
    },
```

In this section of the code, the first step is to create a document fragment upon which the DOM will be built. Next, the number of messages is checked. If there is at least one message, the view must be built accordingly; otherwise, a clone of trNoMessages is created and added to the fragment in place of any other rows. When there are messages, however, the process is a bit more involved.

For each message, the process begins by storing the message in a local variable, oMessage. This is retrieved from the info property in the messages array. Next, a clone of the template row trTemplate is created and stored in oNewTR (passing in true to cloneNode() ensures that all nodes are cloned, not just the <tr/> element itself). Next, the ID of the row is assigned by prepending tr to the message's ID. Then, the onclick event handler is assigned to be readMail(), which is defined later in the "Event Handlers" section. If the message hasn't been read yet, oMessage.unread will be true, so the row will be assigned a CSS class of new. The next step is to assign data into each of the table cells.

To make references to the cells easier, the getElementsByTagName() method is used to extract a collection of just the table cells (colCells). The action icon, either to delete or restore the message, is in the first cell. The actual <img/> element is stored in imgAction for easy reference. Then, the image is assigned an ID equal to the message ID. To determine what the image should do when clicked, the current folder is checked by using info.folder. If the current folder is the Trash, then the image is set up to restore the e-mail by setting the `onclick`, `src`, and `title` properties to restore-specific values; otherwise, the icon is set up to delete e-mail by setting the same properties to delete-specific values. Both `restoreMail()` and `deleteMail()` are global functions used as event handlers. These are discussed in the "Event Handlers" section.

The second cell in each row should display who the e-mail is from, so `oMessage.from` is passed to the helper function `cleanupEmail()`, which was defined earlier in the chapter. The result of this function call is passed into `document.createTextNode()` to create the text for the cell, which is added using `appendChild()`.

For the third cell in the row, you need to decide if the attachments icon should be displayed or not. If `oMessage.hasAttachments` is `true`, then the `visibility` of the icon is set to `visible`; otherwise, it's set to `hidden`. This is done using a compound assignment statement instead of an `if` statement for simplicity.

The fourth table cell contains the e-mail subject, which is passed into `htmlEncode()` to ensure that all characters are displayed correctly. This text is then used to create a text node that is added to the cell in the same way as the first cell. The fifth cell simply displays the message date after it is added to it as a text node. Then, the entire row is added to the document fragment before the loop begins again.

Regardless of the number of messages, the fragment is passed into the `appendChild()` method of the table body to add the rows to the folder view. However, the user interface isn't complete yet; there is still other information that must be updated.

Specifically, the folder title must be displayed, the unread message count must be updated, and the pagination control must be initialized:

```
renderFolder:function () {

    //delete all existing rows

    //create rows for messages

    if (this.hFolderTitle.innerHTML != aFolders[this.info.folder]) {
        this.hFolderTitle.innerHTML = aFolders[this.info.folder];
    }

    this.updateUnreadCount(this.info.unreadCount);

    this.spnItems.style.visibility = this.info.messages.length ?
        "visible" : "hidden";
    this.spnItems.innerHTML = this.info.firstMessage + "-"
        + (this.info.firstMessage + this.info.messages.length - 1) + " of "
        + this.info.messageCount;

    if (this.info.pageCount > 1) {
        this.imgNext.style.visibility = this.info.page < this.info.pageCount ?
            "visible" : "hidden";
        this.imgPrev.style.visibility = this.info.page > 1 ? "visible" : "hidden";
    } else {
        this.imgNext.style.visibility = "hidden";
        this.imgPrev.style.visibility = "hidden";
```

```
        }

        this.divFolder.style.display = "block";
        this.divReadMail.style.display = "none";
        this.divComposeMail.style.display = "none";
    },
```

The first step in this section of code is to set the contents of the hFolderTitle element to the name of the folder, but only if it's different from the one currently being displayed. To do so, use the innerHTML element to both get and set the value (if necessary). Next, the number of unread messages is passed into updateUnreadCount() to update the number of unread messages next to the Inbox link.

If there is at least one message, spnItems must be displayed. This is the element that displays the currently viewed message count, such as "1-10 of 21." If there is at least one message, its visibility property is set to visible; otherwise, it is set to hidden. Then, the contents of the element are created by using various properties of the info object. The firstMessage property returns the number of the first message returned in this page. You can then calculate the number of the last message returned by adding the number of messages to firstMessage and then subtracting one. The total number of messages is returned in the messageCount property.

When there is more than one page of messages to be displayed, the imgNext and imgPrev images should be shown, but not always at the same time. If you are on the first page, for instance, imgPrev should not be shown; likewise for imgNext on the last page. By using the page property to get the current page, you can determine whether the image should be visible and display the appropriate value for the visibility property. Of course, if there is only one page, neither image needs to be displayed.

The very last step is to show the divFolder element and hide both divReadMail and divComposeMail from sight. This initializes the application to the folder view. When the user clicks a message in the list, it brings up the read view, which is rendered by the renderMessage() method.

Just as the renderFolder() method used the info property to determine what to render, the renderMessage() method uses the message property for the same reason. All the information necessary to display a single e-mail is contained within the message property. To begin, you assign the contents of each element in the read view by using values from message:

```
renderMessage: function () {
    this.hSubject.innerHTML = htmlEncode(this.message.subject);
    this.divMessageFrom.innerHTML = sFrom + " " + htmlEncode(this.message.from);
    this.divMessageTo.innerHTML = sTo + " " + htmlEncode(this.message.to);
    this.divMessageCC.innerHTML = this.message.cc.length ?
        sCC + " " + htmlEncode(this.message.cc) : "";
    this.divMessageBCC.innerHTML = this.message.bcc.length ?
        sBCC + " " + htmlEncode(this.message.bcc) : "";
    this.divMessageDate.innerHTML = this.message.date;
    this.divMessageBody.innerHTML = this.message.message;

    //more code here

    this.updateUnreadCount(this.message.unreadCount);
    this.divFolder.style.display = "none";
    this.divReadMail.style.display = "block";
    this.divComposeMail.style.display = "none";
},
```

Each of the elements responsible for displaying the various parts of the e-mail is assigned data from the message object. Of course, most of these values use `htmlEncode()` to ensure that the data is displayed correctly. For the CC and BCC fields, their values are assigned only if they contain data to begin with. If not, the `divMessageCC` and `divMessageBCC` fields are assigned empty strings, which effectively hides them from view.

Then the unread message count is updated. This is being updated here as well because there's no reason to waste a roundtrip to the server and not get such a small piece of information. The last step in the process is to hide `divFolder` and `divComposeMail` while showing `divReadMail`. However, there is some code missing from this method. The previous code doesn't take into account attachments.

Dealing with attachments essentially means outputting a list of all the attachments for a message and linking them so that each can be downloaded with a simple click. The `ulAttachments` element, which is part of the code in `index.php`, should be shown only when there is at least one attachment. Here's how to build this section of the view:

```
renderMessage: function () {
    this.hSubject.innerHTML = htmlEncode(this.message.subject);
    this.divMessageFrom.innerHTML = sFrom + " " + htmlEncode(this.message.from);
    this.divMessageTo.innerHTML = sTo + " " + htmlEncode(this.message.to);
    this.divMessageCC.innerHTML = this.message.cc.length ?
        sCC + " " + htmlEncode(this.message.cc) : "";
    this.divMessageBCC.innerHTML = this.message.bcc.length ?
        sBCC + " " + htmlEncode(this.message.bcc) : "";
    this.divMessageDate.innerHTML = this.message.date;
    this.divMessageBody.innerHTML = htmlEncode(this.message.message);

    if (this.message.hasAttachments) {
        this.ulAttachments.style.display = "";

        var oFragment = document.createDocumentFragment();

        for (var i=0; i < this.message.attachments.length; i++) {
            var oLI = document.createElement("li");
            oLI.className = "attachment";
            oLI.innerHTML = "<a href=\"" + sAjaxMailAttachmentURL + "?id="
                + this.message.attachments[i].id + "\" target=\"_blank\">"
                + this.message.attachments[i].filename + "</a> ("
                + this.message.attachments[i].size + ")";
            oFragment.appendChild(oLI);
        }

        this.ulAttachments.appendChild(oFragment);
        this.liAttachments.style.display = "";
    } else {
        this.ulAttachments.style.display = "none";
        this.liAttachments.style.display = "none";
        this.ulAttachments.innerHTML = "";
    }

    this.updateUnreadCount(this.message.unreadCount);
    this.divFolder.style.display = "none";
```

```
        this.divReadMail.style.display = "block";
        this.divComposeMail.style.display = "none";
    },
```

Naturally, the first step in rendering attachment information is to check if there are any attachments using the hasAttachments property. If there are attachments, the ulAttachments element is displayed and the attachments are iterated over, creating a new <li/> element for each one and assigning additional information using the innerHTML property. Each of these new elements is added to a document fragment for efficiency. When all attachments have had their DOM representation created, the fragment is appended to ulAttachments. Then, the liAttachments element is displayed by setting its display property to an empty string. This element contains the View Attachments link in the message header.

If there are no attachments to the message, ulAttachments and liAttachments are hidden from view by setting their display properties to none. Additionally, ulAttachments is cleared of all its data by setting innerHTML to an empty string. This prevents attachments from showing up on e-mails that they weren't attached to.

Action Methods

With all the Ajax request methods and callback functions in place, you now have all the tools necessary to create the functionality of an e-mail application. For each action, it's important to have a clear idea of how the user interface should respond and what the user would expect.

To begin, consider the task of deleting an e-mail message. When the user clicks on the red X next to a message, the message should be deleted (moved to the Trash). The Back and Forward button are of no use here, because you'd never want to take the user back to a point where the e-mail is still in the list. That means the request() method should be used. Next, should this action cause a user interface change? Yes, the message should disappear from the list. Therefore, you need to use the request() method with the loadAndRender() callback function:

```
deleteMessage: function (sId) {
    this.nextNotice = sDeleteMailNotice;
    this.request("delete", loadAndRender, sId);
},
```

Because you want to delete a specific message, the message ID must be passed into the method. To prepare for the action, the nextNotice property is set to the delete mail notice string. Then, request() is called, passing in the delete string, the loadAndRender() callback function, and the message ID. When the request is completed, the notice is displayed and the user can continue interacting with the application, knowing that the message has been moved to the Trash. To restore the message from the Trash, you can use the same methodology.

When the user is viewing the messages in the Trash, a click on the green arrow restores the message (moves it to the Inbox). This is essentially the same as the delete operation; it simply changes where the message is stored. Not surprising, the method is very similar:

```
restoreMessage: function (sId) {
    this.nextNotice = sRestoreMailNotice;
    this.request("restore", loadAndRender, sId);
},
```

Once again, this function assigns a notice to be displayed when the request completes and uses `request()` to restore the message represented by the message ID (`sID`).

The Trash also has a special action: `empty`. When the Trash is emptied, all the messages in it are permanently deleted and cannot be recovered. This action is interesting in that it behaves differently depending on what the user is looking at. If the Inbox is being viewed, it's still possible to click the Empty link. In this case, you don't want to change the user interface, aside from letting the user know that the Trash has been emptied. If, on the other hand, the user is viewing the message in the Trash, the user interface should be refreshed to show that the Trash is empty. Therefore, the `emptyTrash()` method is a little more involved:

```
emptyTrash: function () {
    if (confirm(sEmptyTrashConfirm)) {
        this.nextNotice = sEmptyTrashNotice;
        if (this.info.folder == TRASH) {
            this.request("empty", loadAndRender);
        } else {
            this.request("empty", execute);
        }
    }
},
```

In this method, the first step is to confirm that the user actually wants to empty the Trash. Using the JavaScript `confirm()` function with `sEmptyTrashConfirm` presents a dialog box to the user with two options: OK or Cancel. If the user clicks OK, `confirm()` returns `true` and the Trash should be emptied. So, the `nextNotice` property is assigned as with the previous methods. Next, the currently displayed folder is checked. If it's the Trash, `request()` is called with the `loadAndRender()` callback function to update the display; if it's not Trash, `request()` is called with `execute()` so that the user interface isn't updated.

Thus far, the methods in this section have dealt with performing an action on e-mail messages. The `getMessages()` method actually is responsible for retrieving the folder information from the server. It accepts the folder ID and the page number to retrieve as arguments and then uses the `navigate()` method to retrieve the desired information:

```
getMessages: function (iFolder, iPage) {
    this.info.folder = iFolder;
    this.info.page = iPage;
    this.navigate("getfolder");
},
```

To retrieve the correct message, the folder and page properties of the `info` object must be set to the appropriate values. Then, when `navigate()` is called, the URL will contain the correct folder and page information. This method is then used in both `nextPage()` and `prevPage()` to move through the different pages of messages in a given folder:

```
nextPage: function () {
    this.getMessages(this.info.folder, this.info.page+1);
},

prevPage: function () {
    this.getMessages(this.info.folder, this.info.page-1);
},
```

Both methods pass in the current folder to `getMessages()`, but the page argument is different. For `nextPage()`, the current page number is incremented by one, whereas `prevPage()` decrements it by one.

There may be times when a user just wants to refresh the information about a folder instead of switching folders. For instance, to check for new mail the user can click the Inbox link while the Inbox is already being displayed. In this case, you don't want to add anything to the browser history because you certainly will never want to go back to an older view of the folder, so you should use `request()` instead of `navigate()`:

```
refreshFolder: function (iFolder) {
    this.info.folder = iFolder;
    this.info.page = 1;
    this.request("getfolder", loadAndRender);
},
```

This method is very similar to `getMessages()` in that the folder ID needs to be passed in and assigned to the `info.folder` property. The `page` is set to `1` because any refresh needs to begin with the first page. And because the action requires the user interface to change, the `loadAndRender()` callback function is passed in when calling `request()`.

A similar method is `switchFolder()`, which retrieves the first page of messages for the given folder:

```
switchFolder: function (iNewFolder) {
    this.getMessages(iNewFolder, 1);
},
```

This method is used for switching to the Inbox from the Trash or vice versa. A simple call to `getMessages()` inside of the method is all that is necessary.

Navigation Methods

Keeping the navigation straight in an Ajax application can be tricky, but thanks to the `navigate()` method defined earlier, things are much more straightforward. Whenever you need to move from one view of AjaxMail to another, you can simply pass a string to the `navigate()` method and wait for the action to be completed. To that end, there are four methods that either directly or indirectly make use of the `navigate()` method to perform their function:

```
cancelReply: function () {
    history.go(-1);
},

compose: function () {
    this.navigate("compose");
},

forward: function () {
    this.navigate("forward");
},

readMessage: function (sId) {
```

```
        this.navigate("getmessage", sId);
    },

    reply: function (blnAll) {
        this.navigate("reply" + (blnAll ? "all" : ""));
    },
```

The first method, cancelReply(), uses the browser's internal history to do its job. When users click Compose Mail, Forward, Reply, or Reply All, the navigate() method is called to put them into compose view. To undo this and move back to the previous view, the history object can be used because the move was recorded in the hidden iframe. Using the go() method with a –1 value moves the browser back to the previous view.

All the other methods in this section simply pass a string value to navigate(), indicating the action that should be taken next. The readMessage() method also accepts the ID of the message to retrieve, and the reply() method accepts a single Boolean argument that indicates whether the action should be reply or replyall; when set to true, it is the latter.

You'll remember from earlier that AjaxMailNavigate.php calls different JavaScript mailbox methods depending on what action has taken place. Each of these methods begins with the word "display," and each has a specific view to initialize.

The displayFolder() method does exactly what it says: it displays a folder of e-mail messages. It accepts a folder info object as its only argument and then renders the folder before setting the processing flag back to false:

```
    displayFolder: function (oInfo) {
        this.loadInfo(oInfo);
        this.renderFolder();
        this.setProcessing(false);
    },
```

A similar method is displayMessage(), which accepts a message information object, loads it, renders the message, and then sets the processing flag to false:

```
    displayMessage: function (oMessage) {
        this.loadMessage(oMessage);
        this.renderMessage();
        this.setProcessing(false);
    },
```

These two methods take care of the Folder view and Read view, respectively. The Compose view is a little bit different because there are so many ways it can be used. It can be used to create a new e-mail, in which case all fields are blank, or it could be used to send a reply, reply all, or forward, in which case different information needs to be prefilled in the form. To facilitate the different requirements of these user actions, a single method is used:

```
    displayComposeMailForm: function (sTo, sCC, sSubject, sMessage) {
        this.txtTo.value = sTo;
        this.txtCC.value = sCC;
        this.txtSubject.value = sSubject;
```

```
        this.txtMessage.value = sMessage;
        this.divReadMail.style.display = "none";
        this.divComposeMail.style.display = "block";
        this.divFolder.style.display = "none";
        this.setProcessing(false);
    },
```

The `displayComposeMailForm()` method accepts all the various information that could be assigned to the compose view and places it into the correct fields. Then, `divReadMail` and `divFolder` are hidden while `divComposeMail` is shown. Last, the `processing` flag is set to `true`. The `displayComposeMailForm()` method is not called by `AjaxMailNavigate.php`, but is instead called by several more specific methods, each catering to a specific action:

```
displayCompose: function () {
    this.displayComposeMailForm("", "", "", "");
},

displayForward: function () {
    this.displayComposeMailForm("", "",
                "Fwd: " + this.message.subject,
                "---------- Forwarded message ----------\n"
                    + this.message.message);
},

displayReply: function () {
    var sTo = this.message.from;
    var sCC = "";

    this.displayComposeMailForm(sTo, sCC, "Re: " + this.message.subject,
        "\n\n\n\n\n" + this.message.from + "said: \n" + this.message.message);

},

displayReplyAll: function () {
    var sTo = this.message.from + "," + this.message.to;
    var sCC = this.message.cc;

    this.displayComposeMailForm(sTo, sCC, "Re: " + this.message.subject,
        "\n\n\n\n\n" + this.message.from + "said: \n" + this.message.message);

},
```

The `displayCompose()` method, which simply displays a blank compose view, passes in an empty string to `displayComposeMailForm()`. The `displayForward()` method prepends "Fwd:" to the front of the message subject and "-----Forwarded Message------" to the front of the message from the e-mail that's currently being viewed. Both `displayReply()` and `displayReplyAll()` prepend "Re:" in front of the message subject and then include a short string before the current e-mail's body text. The only difference between these two methods is what the prefilled values of the To and CC fields are. For `displayReply()`, the To field is simply filled with whoever sent the message initially; for `displayReplyAll()`, the To field also includes everyone else the e-mail was sent to and the CC field contains the same CC recipients as the original message.

Initialization Methods

The last section of methods in the mailbox object initializes the properties and data. Earlier, you saw the beginnings of the `init()` method; the next part involves assigning event handlers to various user interface elements:

```
init: function () {
    var colAllElements = document.getElementsByTagName("*");
    if (!colAllElements.length) {
        colAllElements = document.all;
    }

    for (var i=0; i < colAllElements.length; i++) {
        if (colAllElements[i].id.length > 0) {
            this[colAllElements[i].id] = colAllElements[i];
        }
    }

    this.imgPrev.onclick = function () {
        oMailbox.prevPage();
    };
    this.imgNext.onclick = function () {
        oMailbox.nextPage();
    };
    this.spnCompose.onclick = function () {
        oMailbox.compose();
    };
    this.spnEmpty.onclick = function () {
        oMailbox.emptyTrash();
    };
    this.spnReply.onclick = function () {
        oMailbox.reply(false);
    };
    this.spnReplyAll.onclick = function () {
        oMailbox.reply(true);
    };
    this.spnForward.onclick = function () {
        oMailbox.forward();
    };
    this.spnCancel.onclick = function () {
        oMailbox.cancelReply();
    };
    this.spnSend.onclick = function () {
        oMailbox.sendMail();
    };

    //more code here
},
```

All the event handlers assigned here simply call a mailbox method that was defined earlier in this chapter. You also need to assign the event handlers for the Inbox and Trash links:

```
this.spnInbox.onclick = function () {
    if (oMailbox.info.folder == INBOX) {
        oMailbox.refreshFolder(INBOX);
```

```
        } else {
            oMailbox.switchFolder(INBOX);
        }
    };

    this.spnTrash.onclick = function () {
        if (oMailbox.info.folder == TRASH) {
            oMailbox.refreshFolder(TRASH);
        } else {
            oMailbox.switchFolder(TRASH);
        }
    };
```

These lines occur where the "more code here" comment is in the previous listing but are pulled out here for easier explanation. Each of these two links can perform one of two operations: either switching to the folder view or refreshing it. To determine which of these actions to take, each event handler first checks to see what the currently displayed folder is. For the Inbox link, if the current folder is already Inbox, then it calls refreshFolder(); otherwise, it calls switchFolder(). The same holds true for the Trash link, except that it checks to see if Trash is the folder already being displayed.

The init() method is actually called by another method called load(), defined as:

```
load: function () {
    this.init();
    this.getMessages(INBOX, 1);
},
```

This method first initializes the user interface by calling init() and then makes the initial request for the first page of the Inbox folder using getMessages(). When index.php is loaded, this method must be called (as described later).

Callback Functions

To make use of the request() and sendMail() methods of the mailbox object, several callback functions are necessary. These are functions that take over processing once data has been returned from the server. Each of these functions is standalone; that is, they are not methods of the mailbox object.

When the e-mail messages are first downloaded from the server, the data must be loaded into the info property and then rendered:

```
function loadAndRender(sInfo) {

    oMailbox.loadInfo(sInfo);
    oMailbox.renderFolder();

    if (oMailbox.nextNotice) {
        oMailbox.showNotice("info", oMailbox.nextNotice);
        oMailbox.nextNotice = null;
    }
    oMailbox.setProcessing(false);
}
```

The `loadAndRender()` function expects a JSON string to be passed in as an argument. That data is loaded using the `loadInfo()` method. Once that happens, the `renderFolder()` method is called to begin displaying the new information. After that, the function checks to see if there is a notice that needs to be displayed (stored in `nextNotice`). If so, that notice is displayed and `nextNotice` is set back to `null`. The very last step is to set the `processing` flag to `false`, indicating that the mailbox is free to make other requests.

The simpler case is when a command has to be executed on the server without returning any information. When the request has completed, you simply want to display any notification that may be waiting and then reset the processing flag to `false`. To do so, use the `execute()` callback function:

```
function execute(sInfo) {
    if (oMailbox.nextNotice) {
        oMailbox.showNotice("info", oMailbox.nextNotice);
        oMailbox.nextNotice = null;
    }
    oMailbox.setProcessing(false);
}
```

Using this callback function instead of `loadAndRender()` prevents the user interface from updating when the request completes. The action taken is done purely behind the scenes and is indicated only by the notice (if any) that is displayed. As with `loadAndRender()`, the last step is to set `processing` back to `false`.

The last callback function, `sendConfirmation()`, is used only when sending mail. It expects a simple JSON object to be returned with two properties: `error` and `message`. If `error` is `true`, an error has occurred and the `message` property contains an error message to display to the user; otherwise, the mail was sent successfully and `message` contains a confirmation message to be displayed using `showNotice()`:

```
function sendConfirmation(sData) {
    var oResponse = sData.parseJSON();
    if (oResponse.error) {
        alert("An error occurred:\n" + oResponse.message);
    } else {
        oMailbox.showNotice("info", oResponse.message);
        oMailbox.divComposeMail.style.display = "none";
        oMailbox.divReadMail.style.display = "none";
        oMailbox.divFolder.style.display = "block";
    }
    oMailbox.divComposeMailForm.style.display  = "block";
    oMailbox.divComposeMailStatus.style.display = "none";
    oMailbox.setProcessing(false);
}
```

This function also resets some of the user interface. If the message was sent successfully, it sends the user back to folder view by hiding `divComposeMail` and `divReadMail` and then showing `divFolder`. Regardless of the success, `divComposeMailForm` has its `display` property set back to `block`, whereas `divComposeMailStatus` has its `display` property set to `none`, effectively resetting the compose view.

Event Handlers

The "Action Methods" section described methods of the mailbox object that are used to perform specific actions. To facilitate the assigning of event handlers that use these methods, a handful of small functions are used:

```
function deleteMail() {
    oMailbox.deleteMessage(this.id);
}

function restoreMail() {
    oMailbox.restoreMessage(this.id);
}

function readMail() {
    oMailbox.readMessage(this.id.substring(2));
}
```

Each of these functions simply calls a method of `oMailbox` and passes in some identifier. Because these functions are used as event handlers, the `this` object points to the element upon which the event handler has been assigned. (You could also use `event.srcElement` in Internet Explorer or `event.target` in DOM-compliant browsers.) For `deleteMail()` and `restoreMail()`, the ID of the element is equivalent to a message ID, so it can be passed directly into the `deleteMessage()` and `restoreMessage()` methods, respectively. The `readMail()` function is applied to a table row whose ID is in the format "trID", so the first two character must be stripped off using the `substring()` method before being passed into `readMessage()`.

> By defining these functions globally, you avoid using closures to assign event handlers. Closures are a manner in which it's possible to define a function that makes use of variables defined outside of it. They also happen to be the main cause of memory leaks in many web browsers. Whenever possible, it is preferable to create standalone functions to use as event handlers.

The Last Step

The last step in making AjaxMail functional is to call `oMailbox.load()` when the page has been loaded. To accomplish this, use the window's `onload` event handler:

```
window.onload = function () {
    oMailbox.load();
};
```

Now, when the page has finished loading, the Ajax initialization begins and the application is ready to use.

To test AjaxMail, navigate to `www.yourdomainname.com/AjaxMail`. This loads the initial view and you are ready to go.

Summary

In this chapter, you learned how to create a full-fledged Ajax application called AjaxMail. You began by designing the server-side architecture. Using PHP and MySQL, you designed a back-end system designed to download messages from a POP3 server and store them in a database. You created several database tables to handle the various data associated with an e-mail application. POP3Lib was used for POP3 communication, and PHPMailer was used for SMTP communication.

You then designed a dynamic user interface that doesn't require any page reloads. Communication is accomplished by using a combination of XHR and a hidden iframe. The XHR requests performed actions such as deleting a specific e-mail message, whereas the hidden iframe was used to allow the Back and Forward buttons to function as usual.

Licenses for Libraries and Frameworks

For your convenience the source code download includes the following libraries or frameworks that are discussed and used in the book.

- ❏   Ajax.NET Professional
- ❏   DWR
- ❏   JPSpan
- ❏   jQuery
- ❏   JSON-PHP
- ❏   Prototype
- ❏   YUI library

The following sections reprint the appropriate licensing information for this software.

Ajax.NET Professional

Copyright © 2006, Michael Schwarz

Permission is hereby granted, free of charge, to any person obtaining a copy of this software and associated documentation files (the "Software"), to deal in the Software without restriction, including without limitation the rights to use, copy, modify, merge, publish, distribute, sublicense, and/or sell copies of the Software, and to permit persons to whom the Software is furnished to do so, subject to the following conditions:

The above copyright notice and this permission notice shall be included in all copies or substantial portions of the Software.

THE SOFTWARE IS PROVIDED "AS IS", WITHOUT WARRANTY OF ANY KIND, EXPRESS OR IMPLIED, INCLUDING BUT NOT LIMITED TO THE WARRANTIES OF MERCHANTABILITY, FITNESS FOR A PARTICULAR PURPOSE AND NONINFRINGEMENT. IN NO EVENT SHALL THE AUTHORS OR COPYRIGHT HOLDERS BE LIABLE FOR ANY CLAIM, DAMAGES OR OTHER LIABILITY, WHETHER IN AN ACTION OF CONTRACT, TORT OR OTHERWISE, ARISING FROM, OUT OF OR IN CONNECTION WITH THE SOFTWARE OR THE USE OR OTHER DEALINGS IN THE SOFTWARE.

DWR

Apache License

Version 2.0, January 2004

http://www.apache.org/licenses/

TERMS AND CONDITIONS FOR USE, REPRODUCTION, AND DISTRIBUTION

1. Definitions.

"License" shall mean the terms and conditions for use, reproduction, and distribution as defined by Sections 1 through 9 of this document.

"Licensor" shall mean the copyright owner or entity authorized by the copyright owner that is granting the License.

"Legal Entity" shall mean the union of the acting entity and all other entities that control, are controlled by, or are under common control with that entity. For the purposes of this definition, "control" means (i) the power, direct or indirect, to cause the direction or management of such entity, whether by contract or otherwise, or (ii) ownership of fifty percent (50%) or more of the outstanding shares, or (iii) beneficial ownership of such entity.

"You" (or "Your") shall mean an individual or Legal Entity exercising permissions granted by this License.

"Source" form shall mean the preferred form for making modifications, including but not limited to software source code, documentation source, and configuration files.

"Object" form shall mean any form resulting from mechanical transformation or translation of a Source form, including but not limited to compiled object code, generated documentation, and conversions to other media types.

"Work" shall mean the work of authorship, whether in Source or Object form, made available under the License, as indicated by a copyright notice that is included in or attached to the work (an example is provided in the Appendix below).

"Derivative Works" shall mean any work, whether in Source or Object form, that is based on (or derived from) the Work and for which the editorial revisions, annotations, elaborations, or other modifications represent, as a whole, an original work of authorship. For the purposes of this

License, Derivative Works shall not include works that remain separable from, or merely link (or bind by name) to the interfaces of, the Work and Derivative Works thereof.

"Contribution" shall mean any work of authorship, including the original version of the Work and any modifications or additions to that Work or Derivative Works thereof, that is intentionally submitted to Licensor for inclusion in the Work by the copyright owner or by an individual or Legal Entity authorized to submit on behalf of the copyright owner. For the purposes of this definition, "submitted" means any form of electronic, verbal, or written communication sent to the Licensor or its representatives, including but not limited to communication on electronic mailing lists, source code control systems, and issue tracking systems that are managed by, or on behalf of, the Licensor for the purpose of discussing and improving the Work, but excluding communication that is conspicuously marked or otherwise designated in writing by the copyright owner as "Not a Contribution."

"Contributor" shall mean Licensor and any individual or Legal Entity on behalf of whom a Contribution has been received by Licensor and subsequently incorporated within the Work.

2.   Grant of Copyright License. Subject to the terms and conditions of this License, each Contributor hereby grants to You a perpetual, worldwide, non-exclusive, no-charge, royalty-free, irrevocable copyright license to reproduce, prepare Derivative Works of, publicly display, publicly perform, sublicense, and distribute the Work and such Derivative Works in Source or Object form.

3.   Grant of Patent License. Subject to the terms and conditions of this License, each Contributor hereby grants to You a perpetual, worldwide, non-exclusive, no-charge, royalty-free, irrevocable (except as stated in this section) patent license to make, have made, use, offer to sell, sell, import, and otherwise transfer the Work, where such license applies only to those patent claims licensable by such Contributor that are necessarily infringed by their Contribution(s) alone or by combination of their Contribution(s) with the Work to which such Contribution(s) was submitted. If You institute patent litigation against any entity (including a cross-claim or counterclaim in a lawsuit) alleging that the Work or a Contribution incorporated within the Work constitutes direct or contributory patent infringement, then any patent licenses granted to You under this License for that Work shall terminate as of the date such litigation is filed.

4.   Redistribution. You may reproduce and distribute copies of the Work or Derivative Works thereof in any medium, with or without modifications, and in Source or Object form, provided that You meet the following conditions:

(a)   You must give any other recipients of the Work or Derivative Works a copy of this License; and

(b)   You must cause any modified files to carry prominent notices stating that You changed the files; and

(c)   You must retain, in the Source form of any Derivative Works that You distribute, all copyright, patent, trademark, and attribution notices from the Source form of the Work, excluding those notices that do not pertain to any part of the Derivative Works; and

(d)   If the Work includes a "NOTICE" text file as part of its distribution, then any Derivative Works that You distribute must include a readable copy of the attribution notices contained within such NOTICE file, excluding those notices that do not pertain to any part of the Derivative Works, in at least one of the following places: within a NOTICE text file distributed as part of the Derivative Works; within the Source form or documentation, if provided along with the Derivative Works; or, within a display generated by the

577

Derivative Works, if and wherever such third-party notices normally appear. The contents of the NOTICE file are for informational purposes only and do not modify the License. You may add Your own attribution notices within Derivative Works that You distribute, alongside or as an addendum to the NOTICE text from the Work, provided that such additional attribution notices cannot be construed as modifying the License.

You may add Your own copyright statement to Your modifications and may provide additional or different license terms and conditions for use, reproduction, or distribution of Your modifications, or for any such Derivative Works as a whole, provided Your use, reproduction, and distribution of the Work otherwise complies with the conditions stated in this License.

5. Submission of Contributions. Unless You explicitly state otherwise, any Contribution intentionally submitted for inclusion in the Work by You to the Licensor shall be under the terms and conditions of this License, without any additional terms or conditions. Notwithstanding the above, nothing herein shall supersede or modify the terms of any separate license agreement you may have executed with Licensor regarding such Contributions.

6. Trademarks. This License does not grant permission to use the trade names, trademarks, service marks, or product names of the Licensor, except as required for reasonable and customary use in describing the origin of the Work and reproducing the content of the NOTICE file.

7. Disclaimer of Warranty. Unless required by applicable law or agreed to in writing, Licensor provides the Work (and each Contributor provides its Contributions) on an "AS IS" BASIS, WITHOUT WARRANTIES OR CONDITIONS OF ANY KIND, either express or implied, including, without limitation, any warranties or conditions of TITLE, NON-INFRINGEMENT, MERCHANTABILITY, or FITNESS FOR A PARTICULAR PURPOSE. You are solely responsible for determining the appropriateness of using or redistributing the Work and assume any risks associated with Your exercise of permissions under this License.

8. Limitation of Liability. In no event and under no legal theory, whether in tort (including negligence), contract, or otherwise, unless required by applicable law (such as deliberate and grossly negligent acts) or agreed to in writing, shall any Contributor be liable to You for damages, including any direct, indirect, special, incidental, or consequential damages of any character arising as a result of this License or out of the use or inability to use the Work (including but not limited to damages for loss of goodwill, work stoppage, computer failure or malfunction, or any and all other commercial damages or losses), even if such Contributor has been advised of the possibility of such damages.

9. Accepting Warranty or Additional Liability. While redistributing the Work or Derivative Works thereof, You may choose to offer, and charge a fee for, acceptance of support, warranty, indemnity, or other liability obligations and/or rights consistent with this License. However, in accepting such obligations, You may act only on Your own behalf and on Your sole responsibility, not on behalf of any other Contributor, and only if You agree to indemnify, defend, and hold each Contributor harmless for any liability incurred by, or claims asserted against, such Contributor by reason of your accepting any such warranty or additional liability.

END OF TERMS AND CONDITIONS

APPENDIX: How to apply the Apache License to your work.

To apply the Apache License to your work, attach the following boilerplate notice, with the fields enclosed by brackets "[]" replaced with your own identifying information. (Don't include the brackets!)

The text should be enclosed in the appropriate comment syntax for the file format. We also recommend that a file or class name and description of purpose be included on the same "printed page" as the copyright notice for easier identification within third-party archives.

> Copyright [yyyy] [name of copyright owner]
>
> Licensed under the Apache License, Version 2.0 (the "License"); you may not use this file except in compliance with the License. You may obtain a copy of the License at
>
> http://www.apache.org/licenses/LICENSE-2.0
>
> Unless required by applicable law or agreed to in writing, software distributed under the License is distributed on an "AS IS" BASIS, WITHOUT WARRANTIES OR CONDITIONS OF ANY KIND, either express or implied. See the License for the specific language governing permissions and limitations under the License.

JPSpan

The PHP License, version 3.0

Copyright © 1999 - 2004 The PHP Group. All rights reserved.

Redistribution and use in source and binary forms, with or without modification, is permitted provided that the following conditions are met:

1. Redistributions of source code must retain the above copyright notice, this list of conditions and the following disclaimer.

2. Redistributions in binary form must reproduce the above copyright notice, this list of conditions and the following disclaimer in the documentation and/or other materials provided with the distribution.

3. The name "PHP" must not be used to endorse or promote products derived from this software without prior written permission. For written permission, please contact group@php.net.

4. Products derived from this software may not be called "PHP", nor may "PHP" appear in their name, without prior written permission from group@php.net. You may indicate that your software works in conjunction with PHP by saying "Foo for PHP" instead of calling it "PHP Foo" or "phpfoo"

5. The PHP Group may publish revised and/or new versions of the license from time to time. Each version will be given a distinguishing version number.

   Once covered code has been published under a particular version of the license, you may always continue to use it under the terms of that version. You may also choose to use such covered code under the terms of any subsequent version of the license published by the PHP Group. No one other than the PHP Group has the right to modify the terms applicable to covered code created under this License.

6. Redistributions of any form whatsoever must retain the following acknowledgment:

   "This product includes PHP, freely available from <http://www.php.net/>".

THIS SOFTWARE IS PROVIDED BY THE PHP DEVELOPMENT TEAM "AS IS"' AND ANY EXPRESSED OR IMPLIED WARRANTIES, INCLUDING, BUT NOT LIMITED TO, THE IMPLIED WARRANTIES OF MERCHANTABILITY AND FITNESS FOR A PARTICULAR PURPOSE ARE DISCLAIMED. IN NO EVENT SHALL THE PHP DEVELOPMENT TEAM OR ITS CONTRIBUTORS BE LIABLE FOR ANY DIRECT, INDIRECT, INCIDENTAL, SPECIAL, EXEMPLARY, OR CONSEQUENTIAL DAMAGES (INCLUDING, BUT NOT LIMITED TO, PROCUREMENT OF SUBSTITUTE GOODS OR SERVICES; LOSS OF USE, DATA, OR PROFITS; OR BUSINESS INTERRUPTION) HOWEVER CAUSED AND ON ANY THEORY OF LIABILITY, WHETHER IN CONTRACT, STRICT LIABILITY, OR TORT (INCLUDING NEGLIGENCE OR OTHERWISE) ARISING IN ANY WAY OUT OF THE USE OF THIS SOFTWARE, EVEN IF ADVISED OF THE POSSIBILITY OF SUCH DAMAGE.

jQuery

Copyright © 2006 John Resig, http://jquery.com/

Permission is hereby granted, free of charge, to any person obtaining a copy of this software and associated documentation files (the "Software"), to deal in the Software without restriction, including without limitation the rights to use, copy, modify, merge, publish, distribute, sublicense, and/or sell copies of the Software, and to permit persons to whom the Software is furnished to do so, subject to the following conditions:

The above copyright notice and this permission notice shall be included in all copies or substantial portions of the Software.

THE SOFTWARE IS PROVIDED "AS IS", WITHOUT WARRANTY OF ANY KIND, EXPRESS OR IMPLIED, INCLUDING BUT NOT LIMITED TO THE WARRANTIES OF MERCHANTABILITY, FITNESS FOR A PARTICULAR PURPOSE AND NONINFRINGEMENT. IN NO EVENT SHALL THE AUTHORS OR COPYRIGHT HOLDERS BE LIABLE FOR ANY CLAIM, DAMAGES OR OTHER LIABILITY, WHETHER IN AN ACTION OF CONTRACT, TORT OR OTHERWISE, ARISING FROM, OUT OF OR IN CONNECTION WITH THE SOFTWARE OR THE USE OR OTHER DEALINGS IN THE SOFTWARE.

> **See also the GPL, which appears at the back of the book.**

JSON-PHP

THIS SOFTWARE IS PROVIDED "AS IS" AND ANY EXPRESS OR IMPLIED WARRANTIES, INCLUDING, BUT NOT LIMITED TO, THE IMPLIED WARRANTIES OF MERCHANTABILITY AND FITNESS FOR A PARTICULAR PURPOSE ARE DISCLAIMED. IN NO EVENT SHALL CONTRIBUTORS BE LIABLE FOR ANY DIRECT, INDIRECT, INCIDENTAL, SPECIAL, EXEMPLARY, OR CONSEQUENTIAL DAMAGES (INCLUDING, BUT NOT LIMITED TO, PROCUREMENT OF SUBSTITUTE GOODS OR SERVICES; LOSS OF USE, DATA, OR PROFITS; OR BUSINESS INTERRUPTION) HOWEVER CAUSED AND ON ANY THEORY OF LIABILITY, WHETHER IN CONTRACT, STRICT LIABILITY, OR TORT (INCLUDING NEGLIGENCE OR OTHERWISE) ARISING IN ANY WAY OUT OF THE USE OF THIS SOFTWARE, EVEN IF ADVISED OF THE POSSIBILITY OF SUCH DAMAGE.

Prototype

Copyright © 2005 Sam Stephenson

Permission is hereby granted, free of charge, to any person obtaining a copy of this software and associated documentation files (the "Software"), to deal in the Software without restriction, including without limitation the rights to use, copy, modify, merge, publish, distribute, sublicense, and/or sell copies of the Software, and to permit persons to whom the Software is furnished to do so, subject to the following conditions:

YUI Library

Software License Agreement (BSD License)

Copyright © 2006, Yahoo! Inc.

All rights reserved.

Redistribution and use of this software in source and binary forms, with or without modification, are permitted provided that the following conditions are met:

❏ Redistributions of source code must retain the above copyright notice, this list of conditions and the following disclaimer.

❏ Redistributions in binary form must reproduce the above copyright notice, this list of conditions and the following disclaimer in the documentation and/or other materials provided with the distribution.

❏ Neither the name of Yahoo! Inc. nor the names of its contributors may be used to endorse or promote products derived from this software without specific prior written permission of Yahoo! Inc.

Index

GNU General Public License

Version 2, June 1991

Copyright © 1989, 1991 Free Software Foundation, Inc., 59 Temple Place - Suite 330, Boston, MA 02111-1307, USA

Preamble

The licenses for most software are designed to take away your freedom to share and change it. By contrast, the GNU General Public License is intended to guarantee your freedom to share and change free software--to make sure the software is free for all its users. This General Public License applies to most of the Free Software Foundation's software and to any other program whose authors commit to using it. (Some other Free Software Foundation software is covered by the GNU Library General Public License instead.) You can apply it to your programs, too.

When we speak of free software, we are referring to freedom, not price. Our General Public Licenses are designed to make sure that you have the freedom to distribute copies of free software (and charge for this service if you wish), that you receive source code or can get it if you want it, that you can change the software or use pieces of it in new free programs; and that you know you can do these things.

To protect your rights, we need to make restrictions that forbid anyone to deny you these rights or to ask you to surrender the rights. These restrictions translate to certain responsibilities for you if you distribute copies of the software, or if you modify it.

For example, if you distribute copies of such a program, whether gratis or for a fee, you must give the recipients all the rights that you have. You must make sure that they, too, receive or can get the source code. And you must show them these terms so they know their rights.

We protect your rights with two steps: (1) copyright the software, and (2) offer you this license which gives you legal permission to copy, distribute and/or modify the software.

Also, for each author's protection and ours, we want to make certain that everyone understands that there is no warranty for this free software. If the software is modified by someone else and passed on, we want its recipients to know that what they have is not the original, so that any problems introduced by others will not reflect on the original authors' reputations.

Finally, any free program is threatened constantly by software patents. We wish to avoid the danger that redistributors of a free program will individually obtain patent licenses, in effect making the program proprietary. To prevent this, we have made it clear that any patent must be licensed for everyone's free use or not licensed at all.

The precise terms and conditions for copying, distribution and modification follow.

Terms and Conditions for Copying, Distribution and Modification

0. This License applies to any program or other work which contains a notice placed by the copyright holder saying it may be distributed under the terms of this General Public License. The "Program", below, refers to any such program or work, and a "work based on the Program" means either the Program or any derivative work under copyright law: that is to say, a work containing the Program or a portion of it, either verbatim or with modifications and/or translated into another language. (Hereinafter, translation is included without limitation in the term "modification".) Each licensee is addressed as "you".

   Activities other than copying, distribution and modification are not covered by this License; they are outside its scope. The act of running the Program is not restricted, and the output from the Program is covered only if its contents constitute a work based on the Program (independent of having been made by running the Program). Whether that is true depends on what the Program does.

1. You may copy and distribute verbatim copies of the Program's source code as you receive it, in any medium, provided that you conspicuously and appropriately publish on each copy an appropriate copyright notice and disclaimer of warranty; keep intact all the notices that refer to this License and to the absence of any warranty; and give any other recipients of the Program a copy of this License along with the Program.

   You may charge a fee for the physical act of transferring a copy, and you may at your option offer warranty protection in exchange for a fee.

2. You may modify your copy or copies of the Program or any portion of it, thus forming a work based on the Program, and copy and distribute such modifications or work under the terms of Section 1 above, provided that you also meet all of these conditions:

   a) You must cause the modified files to carry prominent notices stating that you changed the files and the date of any change.

   b) You must cause any work that you distribute or publish, that in whole or in part contains or is derived from the Program or any part thereof, to be licensed as a whole at no charge to all third parties under the terms of this License.

   c) If the modified program normally reads commands interactively when run, you must cause it, when started running for such interactive use in the most ordinary way, to print or display an announcement including an appropriate copyright notice and a notice that there is no warranty (or else, saying that you provide a warranty) and that users may redistribute the program under these conditions, and telling the user how to view a copy of this License. (Exception: if the Program itself is interactive but does not normally print such an announcement, your work based on the Program is not required to print an announcement.)

   These requirements apply to the modified work as a whole. If identifiable sections of that work are not derived from the Program, and can be reasonably considered independent and separate works in themselves, then this License, and its terms, do not apply to those sections when you distribute them as separate works. But when you distribute the same sections as part of a whole which is a work based on the Program, the distribution of the whole must be on the terms of this License, whose permissions for other licensees extend to the entire whole, and thus to each and every part regardless of who wrote it.

Thus, it is not the intent of this section to claim rights or contest your rights to work written entirely by you; rather, the intent is to exercise the right to control the distribution of derivative or collective works based on the Program.

In addition, mere aggregation of another work not based on the Program with the Program (or with a work based on the Program) on a volume of a storage or distribution medium does not bring the other work under the scope of this License.

3. You may copy and distribute the Program (or a work based on it, under Section 2) in object code or executable form under the terms of Sections 1 and 2 above provided that you also do one of the following:

    a) Accompany it with the complete corresponding machine-readable source code, which must be distributed under the terms of Sections 1 and 2 above on a medium customarily used for software interchange; or,

    b) Accompany it with a written offer, valid for at least three years, to give any third party, for a charge no more than your cost of physically performing source distribution, a complete machine-readable copy of the corresponding source code, to be distributed under the terms of Sections 1 and 2 above on a medium customarily used for software interchange; or,

    c) Accompany it with the information you received as to the offer to distribute corresponding source code. (This alternative is allowed only for noncommercial distribution and only if you received the program in object code or executable form with such an offer, in accord with Subsection b above.)

The source code for a work means the preferred form of the work for making modifications to it. For an executable work, complete source code means all the source code for all modules it contains, plus any associated interface definition files, plus the scripts used to control compilation and installation of the executable. However, as a special exception, the source code distributed need not include anything that is normally distributed (in either source or binary form) with the major components (compiler, kernel, and so on) of the operating system on which the executable runs, unless that component itself accompanies the executable.

If distribution of executable or object code is made by offering access to copy from a designated place, then offering equivalent access to copy the source code from the same place counts as distribution of the source code, even though third parties are not compelled to copy the source along with the object code.

4. You may not copy, modify, sublicense, or distribute the Program except as expressly provided under this License. Any attempt otherwise to copy, modify, sublicense or distribute the Program is void, and will automatically terminate your rights under this License. However, parties who have received copies, or rights, from you under this License will not have their licenses terminated so long as such parties remain in full compliance.

5. You are not required to accept this License, since you have not signed it. However, nothing else grants you permission to modify or distribute the Program or its derivative works. These actions are prohibited by law if you do not accept this License. Therefore, by modifying or distributing the Program (or any work based on the Program), you indicate your acceptance of this License to do so, and all its terms and conditions for copying, distributing or modifying the Program or works based on it.